International Film Guide

2009

the definitive annual review of world cinema

edited by Ian Haydn Smith

45th edition

WALLFLOWER PRESS

LONDON & NEW YORK

14-18 October 2009

FRANKFURTER BUCHMESSE

GUEST OF HONOUR >CHINA<

Film Rights Centre

Your market place
for film rights from
14 to 18 October 2009
(Forum, Level 0)

ACCREDITATION AND INFORMATION:
Anna-Katharina Werdnik
werdnik@book-fair.com | www.book-fair.com

60 YEARS
FRANKFURT
BOOK FAIR

Credits

Wallflower Press
6 Market Place
London
W1W 8AF
tel: +44 (0)20 7436 9494
info@wallflowerpress.co.uk
www.wallflowerpress.co.uk

ISBN 978-1-905674-99-2

A catalogue record for this book is
available from the British Library

Printed and bound in Poland;
produced by Polskabook

For information on sales and distribution in all territories worldwide,
please contact Wallflower Press on
info@wallflowerpress.co.uk

Editor
Ian Haydn Smith

Publisher
Yoram Allon, Wallflower Press

Founding Editor
Peter Cowie

Consultant Editor
Daniel Rosenthal

Editorial Assistants
Anne Hudson, Benny Morgan,
Yannick Pucci

Select Contributors
Nadia Attia, Lorenzo Codelli,
Chris Darke, Dan Fainaru, Dina
Iordanova, Michelle Le Blanc, Sandy
Mandelberger, Eleanor McKeown,
Colin Odell, Hannah Patterson,
Liz Rosenthal, Jason Wood

Design
Elsa Mathern

Photo Consultants
The Kobal Collection
www.picture-desk.com

Business Manager
Sara Tyler

International Advertising Manager
Sara Tyler
Europe, film festivals
saraifg@aol.com

International Sales Consultants

Sherif Awad
Egypt, Iran, Turkey
sherif_awad@link.net

Voula Georgakakou
Cyprus, Greece
vgeo@artfree.org

Sheri Jennings
Italy, USA
sheri.ifg@gmail.com

Ksenia Koltsova and Elena Kurilova
Russia
leks_cinema@inbox.ru

Anita Lewton
Republic of Ireland, United Kingdom
anita.lewton@googlemail.com

Michael Marshall
Belgium, France, Spain
marshallmichael@aol.com

Shih Mei-yan
Tawian
scipio.shih@gmail.com

Lisa Ray
Middle East, South East Asia,
South Africa
l.ray@hotmail.co.uk

Ana Villoslada Sánchez
Spanish film festivals
anavillos@yahoo.es

Front Cover
Ari Folman's **Waltz with Bashir**, which premiered at the 2008 Cannes Film Festival and has been nominated
for Best Foreign Film at the 2009 Golden Globes and the 2009 Academy Awards.
Image used by kind permission of the Bridgit Folman Film Gang.

62nd
Film Festival Locarno
5–15 | 8 | 2009

Festival internazionale del film Locarno
Via Ciseri 23, CH-6601 Locarno
t +41 (0)91 756 21 21, f +41 (0)91 756 21 49
info@pardo.ch, www.pardo.ch

Main sponsors:

UBS · æt · MANOR · swisscom

Contents

International Liaison

Afghanistan: Sandra Schäfer
Algeria: Myryam Touzani
Angola: Martin P. Botha
Argentina: Alfredo Friedlander
Armenia: Susanna Harutyunyan
Australia: Peter Thompson
Austria: Gunnar Landsgesell
Bangladesh: Ahmed Muztaba Zamal
Belarus: Andrei Rasinski
Belgium: Erik Martens
Benin: Steve Ayorinde
Bhutan: Ahmed Muztaba Zamal
Bolivia: José Sánchez-H.
Bosnia & Herzegovina: Rada Šešić
Brazil: Nelson Hoineff
Bulgaria: Pavlina Jeleva
Burkina Faso: Honoré Essoh
Burundi: Ogova Ondego
Cambodia: Anne-larue Porée
Cameroon: Honoré Essoh
Canada: Tom McSorely
Chad: Agnes Thomasi
Chile: Hugo Diaz Gutierrez
China: Luna Lin
Colombia: Jaime E. Manrique and
   Pedro Adrián Zuluaga
Costa Rica: Maria Lourdes Cortés
Croatia: Tomislav Kurelec
Cuba: Jorge Yglesias
Cyprus: Nino Feneck-Mikelidis
Czech Republic: Eva Zaoralová
Democratic Republic of Congo:
   Ogova Ondego
Denmark: Christian Monngaard
Ecuador: Gabriela Alemán
Egypt: Fawzi Soliman
El Salvador: Maria Lourdes Cortés
Eritrea: Ogova Ondego
Estonia: Jaan Ruus
Fiji: Lorenzo Codelli
Finland: Antii Selkokari

France: Michel Ciment
Gabon: Agnes Thomasi
Georgia: Nino Ekvtimishvili
Germany: Andrea Dittgen
Ghana: Steve Ayorinde
Greece: Nino Feneck-Mikelidis
Guatemala: Maria Lourdes Cortés
Guinea: Agnes Thomasi
Hong Kong: Tim Youngs
Hungary: John Cunningham
Iceland: Eddie Cockrell
India: Uma Da Cunha
Indonesia: Lisabona Rahman
Iran: Kamyar Mohsenin
Iraq: Ali Jaafar
Ireland: Michael Dwyer
Israel: Dan Fainru
Italy: Lorenzo Codelli
Ivory Coast: Honoré Essoh
Japan: Katsuta Tomomi
Jordan: Ali Jaafar
Kazakhstan: Gulnara Abikeyeva
Kenya: Ogova Ondego
Kyrgyzstan: Gulnara Abikeyeva
Latvia: Andris Rozenbergs
Lebanon: Ali Jafaar
Luxembourg: Boyd van Hoeij
Malaysia: Hassan Abd Muthalib
Mali: Honoré Essoh
Malta: Daniel Rosenthal
Mauritania: Agnes Thomasi
Mexico: Carlos Bonfil
Morocco: Maryam Touzani
Mozambique: Martin P. Botha
Namibia: Martin P. Botha
Nepal: Prabesh Subedi
Netherlands: Leo Bankersen
New Zealand: Peter Calder
Nicaragua: Maria Lourdes Cortés
Niger: Honoré Essoh
Nigeria: Steve Ayorinde
North Korea: James Bell

Norway: Trond Olav Svendsen
Pakistan: Aijaz Gul
Palestine: Ali Jaafar
Panama: Maria Lourdes Cortés
Peru: Isaac Léon Frías
Philippines: Tessa Jazmines
Poland: Barbara Hollander
Portugal: Martin Dale
Puerto Rico: Raúl Ríos-Díaz
Romania: Cristina Corciovescu
Russia: Kirill Razlogov
Rwanda: Ogova Ondego
Senegal: Ogova Ondego
Serbia & Montenegro: Goran Gocić
Singapore: Yvonne Ng
Slovakia: Miro Ulman
Slovenia: Ziva Emersic
South Africa: Martin P. Botha
South Korea: Nikki J.Y. Lee
Spain: Jonathan Holland
Swaziland: Martin P. Botha
Sweden: Gunnar Rehlin
Switzerland: Marcy Goldberg
Taiwan: David Frazier
Tajikistan: Gulnara Abikeyeva
Tanzania: Ogova Ondego
Thailand: Anchalee Chaiworaporn
The Gambia: Agnes Thomasi
Tunisia: Maryam Touzani
Turkey: Atilla Dorsay
Turkmenistan: Gulnara Abikeyeva
Uganda: Ogova Ondego
Ukraine: Volodymyr Voytenko
United Kingdom: Philip Kemp
United States: Shane Danielsen
Uruguay: Jorge Jellinek
Uzbekistan: Gulnara Abikeyeva
Venezuela: Martha Escalona Zerpa
Vietnam: Sylvie Blum-Reid
Zambia: Martin P. Botha
Zimbabwe: Martin P. Botha

Notes from the Editor

Welcome to the 45th edition of the *International Film Guide*. Maintaining the high standard of previous years, this year's IFG has also expanded, covering new areas and developments in film, from conventional cinema and home entertainment to the growth in new platforms for production, distribution and exhibition.

Last year's record coverage of 98 countries has been increased to 123, nearing our goal of reporting on every film-producing country for each year. The new entries span the globe, from Bhutan, Eritrea and Iraq, to Mauritania, Palestine and Vietnam. We also report on North Korea, possibly the only country or state whose leader is a published film theorist!

This year's 'Country Focus' is on Israel, a national cinema whose development over the last decade has been nothing short of miraculous. Following the international success of *Late Marriage*, *Beaufort* and *The Band's Visit*, 2008 saw one of the most remarkable achievements in world cinema with Ari Folman's *Waltz with Bashir*, which defied simple generic categorisation in favour of a complex and riveting mix of animation, documentary and personal memoir. Few films this year represented so well the potential of cinema to challenge, to cross boundaries and to engage with audiences around the world, hence its selection as the cover image for this year's edition.

New platforms are as much an essential part of the IFG project as they are the future of cinema. In 2009, I will be working with Sandy Mandelberger (Web Editor) to bring all 45 years of the publication online. With its mix of archive and news, as well as coverage from festivals around the world, the IFG website will be an essential portal for film industry

Ian Haydn Smith

professionals, scholars and researchers, and anyone with an interest in film (please visit www.internationalfilmguide.com). It is fitting, then, that this edition of the IFG should initiate an annual review of digital and Internet platforms for film. Few people are better placed to discuss this than Liz Rosenthal, Director of Power to the Pixel, whose 'Industry Focus' looks at the potential for distribution and exhibition outside traditional avenues.

Home entertainment is also undergoing a significant technological change. With Blu-Ray chosen as the future replacement of DVD and digital downloads becoming widespread, smaller, niche DVD labels are facing tough decisions in the next few years over how best to move forward. Once again, the market leader is the Criterion Collection, who are gradually re-releasing titles on the new format, but are also offering the ability to download films and DVD extras. At the same time, new labels are appearing, offering audiences an ever-wider availability of films, ranging from fiction and documentary to animation and shorts, as well as cult and experimental titles.

At the Venice Film Festival in September, Agnès Varda announced that her latest film, *The Beaches of Agnès*, would be her last. It is fitting then that she should be one of our 'Directors of the Year'. John Sayles is also featured, although it is amazing that it has taken so long for one of America's most articulate filmmakers to appear here. Perhaps more of a surprise is that Miyazaki Hayao is the first animation director to feature, but with such an inspired body of work, there is little doubt of his position as one of the world's finest – and most popular – filmmakers. Finally, we include two European filmmakers whose body of work has marked them out as important figures within the map of world cinema, Nuri Bilge Ceylan and Paolo Sorrentino.

As the geopolitical map of the world changes, so the impact on a country's film industry can alter dramatically. In this year's 'Special Focus', Dina Iordanova assesses the transition of Eastern and Central European countries that have become members of the European Union over the last few years. Has being part of a regional economic and political block led to more financial and artistic security for each of these countries, or has an element of homogeneity resulted in the dilution of these nations' cinematic culture?

And what of the countries themselves? It is generally agreed that, like so many economies, the film industry around the world stands on the edge of a precipice. The effects of the economic downturn in the second half of 2008 have yet to be fully felt, but there is a sense that, like so many other industries, the film world is bracing itself for harsher times than it has experienced in recent memory. But measures are being taken to counteract the negative impacts of a recession. In the days before this book went to press, the French parliament passed a landmark ruling that introduced a 20% tax break for foreign films shooting locally.

Our expanded focus on Africa, Asia and the Middle East highlights the fact that,

although some countries have in the past experienced better years cinematically, the desire to make films has only increased. Access to digital technology has seen films made in all corners of the globe, with some remarkable results. Ghana's Gollywood is catching up with Nigeria's Nollywood, one of the most industrious film centres in the world. Nicaragua returned to feature filmmaking with the arrival of Florence Jaugey's *La Yuma*, as did Jordan, with Amin Matalqa's *Captain Abu Raed*. Even the occasional Hollywood blockbuster betrayed evidence of a higher intelligence at work. Andrew Stanton's *WALL-E* was a remarkable achievement while, for some, Christopher Nolan's *The Dark Knight* attempted to grapple with terrorism. However, Frank Darabont's stand against religious fundamentalism in *The Mist* was, for me, Hollywood's most impressive and daring political film of the year.

Expanding its role beyond merely recording events throughout the year, the *International Film Guide*, publisher Wallflower Press and the Criterion Collection have teamed up to present the IFG Inspiration Award at selected festivals. Its aim is to acknowledge and promote the most promising filmmakers of the future. The first four winners are featured on pages 381–2.

On a personal note, one of my highlights of the year was the return to cinema of Terence Davies, arguably the UK's greatest living director. His work, like that of so many filmmakers around the world, shows how cinema can engage us emotionally and challenge the way we think. Above all else, it allows us a window into the lives of others, from people living next door to those on the other side of the world.

Films of the year – Editor's choice
Waltz with Bashir (Ari Folman, Israel)
The Headless Woman (Lucrecia Martel, Argentina)
Of Time and the City (Terence Davies, UK)
Sugar (Ana Boden & Ryan Fleck, USA)
The Mist (Frank Darabont, USA)

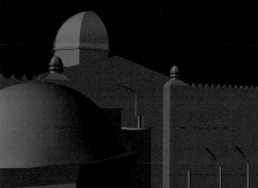

Directors of the Year

Nuri Bilge Ceylan by Jason Wood

C ombining unusually modest working methods with a highly distinctive visual sensibility, the films of Turkish auteur Nuri Bilge Ceylan eloquently speak of the emotional impassivity that is an affliction of twenty-first-century living. Uncompromising in their honesty, and imbued with a personal touch increasingly rare in an industry in thrall to the imperatives of populist entertainment, with just five features and a short Ceylan has established himself as one of the major voices in contemporary world cinema.

Country Life

Born in Istanbul, Nuri Bilge Ceylan graduated with an engineering degree from Bosphorus University. Cultivating a burgeoning interest in cinema and photography, he travelled to London to study film, but found the cost of life in London to be prohibitive and returned

to Istanbul where he enrolled on a four-year cinematography course at Mimar Sinan University. After two years Ceylan dropped out, believing 'the actual process of filmmaking to be more important in terms of gaining an education'.

Initially working as a photographer (he is also an electrical engineer and claims 'an affinity with the technical side of things'), Ceylan's first foray into the moving image was the short, *Cocoon* (*Koza*, 1995). Shot in striking black and white, with Ceylan also acting as the film's producer, co-editor and cinematographer, the wordless film concerns an elderly couple (Fatma Ceylan and Mehmet Emin Ceylan, the director's parents) in their seventies who, due to some painful experiences in their past, now live separately. One day they meet again, but their hope that it will heal the lingering pain and lead to reconciliation does not bring the expected results. The first of many Cannes invitations, *Cocoon* tentatively tilts at the impossibility of companionship, one of the defining thematics of Ceylan's career.

Building upon this interest, Ceylan made his feature debut two years later with the vibrant,

Small Town

poetic and self-funded *Small Town* (*Kasaba*, 1997). Told from the perspective of two children, and in four entwined parts running parallel to the seasons, *Small Town* served notice of Ceylan's gift for wry comedy and of his distinctive approach to framing characters and landscapes. The opening section is set in a primary school and concerns the struggles of an eleven-year-old girl to adapt to her new social surroundings. The second part unfolds during springtime and covers the journey of the girl and her brother to a cornfield where their family awaits. As they pass through the countryside, they encounter the mysteries of nature before, in the third section, being forced to endure and confront the harsh complexities of the adult world. The final segment takes place in the siblings' home and gently probes the intimacies and intimations of life in a remote Aegean village. Based on a semi-autobiographical story by Ceylan's sister, Emine, the film is evocative of Iranian cinema in its touching portrayal of childhood and adolescence. Premiered at the 1998 Berlin Film Festival, it again featured Ceylan in a wide capacity of roles: producer, writer, cinematographer and co-editor alongside the talented Ayhan Ergürsel, one of the key figures in recent Turkish cinema and the editor on all of Ceylan's films.

Cementing Ceylan's clarity of vision and his sensitivity to the delicate nuances of life, *Clouds of May* (*Mayis Sikintisi*, 1999) takes another crisply composed look at the vagaries of country living. Muzaffer (Muzaffer Özdemir) returns to his native town to make a movie. His father, Emin (Mehmet Emin Ceylan), is bent on saving the small forest he cultivates on his property from confiscation by the authorities. Muzaffer's nephew, nine-year-old Ali (Muhammed Zimbaoglu), wants a musical watch. In an attempt to secure it, he must carry an egg in his pocket for forty days without it cracking, according to the terms of an agreement made with his aunt, who has promised to convince Ali's father to buy it for him if he is successful. Meanwhile, Muzaffer's cousin, Saffet (Mehmet Emin Toprak), harbours

dreams of making a success of himself in Istanbul, but his endeavours seem doomed to failure through a combination of bad luck and his own rebellious nature. As Muzaffer sets about recruiting family and friends to work on his film, Ceylan deftly observes people coming together, briefly interacting and then gently drifting apart again. Inscribed with a reverence for the lives of its characters, *Clouds of May* is a tale of warmth and beauty that foretells the director's future exploration of the dichotomy between rural and urban living and the import of seemingly insignificant objects.

Clouds of May

Metropolis

Generally casting non-professional actors, many of whom are family members – his parents frequently feature – and continuing to call upon his increasing stature as a photographer to shoot his own films (examples of Ceylan's photography can be found on his website www.nuribilgeceylan.com), Ceylan brought these elements, and his interest in estrangement and communication to wonderful fruition with the vaguely autobiographical *Distant* (*Uzak*, 2002). Mahmut (Muzaffer Özdemir) is a successful commercial photographer who is nonetheless struggling to come to terms with the growing gap between his artistic ideals and his professional obligations. Clinging to the melancholic and obsessive routines of his solitary life, the photographer's world is thrown into confusion when Yusuf (Mehmet Emin Toprak), a distant relative, arrives from the country in search of employment aboard one of the port's many ships. Despite the odd gesture towards a sense of familiarity, most notably an uneventful assignment in which Mahmut's apathy envelops him and he resists even setting up his camera despite a wonderful photographic opportunity, the two equally taciturn men struggle to form any kind of connection and inevitably part.

Distant

Rendering modern Istanbul as a desolate, if intermittently picturesque, snow-cloaked metropolis, Ceylan draws on Chekhov and Tarkovsky in his analysis of the alienating effects of urban life: 'City-dwellers try to organise their lives in a way that they don't have to count on anyone but themselves, and end up building their own prison cell. We don't ask anything of anyone, nor do we give anything either. Solidarity is a much more rural trait; it is somewhat of a necessity out in the country.' Minimising costs on the film by working with a very small crew and with available lighting, Ceylan also used familiar props and locations, including his own car and house, complete with photography studio. Claiming that he never sets out to be humorous, but just to reflect the way that he sees life, Distant, despite its ability to intelligently probe prescient themes and ideas, is nonetheless incredibly droll, most notably in the moments where Mahmut makes a meal of setting a trap for a resident mouse. There

is also an overt reference to Tarkovsky, who Ceylan admits to admiring whilst citing Ozu as more of a direct influence, when Yusuf walks in on his less-than-benevolent host watching a porn film only for Mahmut to quickly switch over to another channel where a Tarkovsky film is conveniently playing. Another aspect of the film that skilfully blends humour and poignancy is Mahmut's relationship with his ex-wife. He follows her to the airport prior to her departure for a new life and then can't bring himself to actually say 'goodbye', hiding behind various pillars and obstacles to conceal his presence. Ceylan claims that Mahmut has left his wife 'because he thought much more interesting things were going to happen in his life and she began to appear as an obstacle to him; I think many men in Turkey and in the world are like this'. The director's view of men in Distant is generally poor. In future films it would get a lot worse.

Highly acclaimed by the international press at the Cannes Film Festival in 2003, Distant was awarded both the Grand Prix and the Best Actor prize, which was shared between Özdemir and Emin Toprak. The latter award was tinged with sadness as Özdemir, Ceylan's cousin, was killed in a car crash shortly after the film was completed. Going on to collect numerous other prestigious prizes, including Best Film, Best Director and the International Critics' Prize at the 2003 Istanbul Film Festival, the aptly titled Distant firmly placed Ceylan at the forefront of contemporary world directors and helped turn the spotlight on cinema from Turkey, with figures such as Reha Erdem and the veteran Zeki Demirkubuz benefiting from the resultant curiosity.

Distant

The Penetrating Gaze

Ceylan's fourth feature represents his fullest collaboration yet with his talented wife, Ebru. An acclaimed photographer who graduated from the Film and TV Department of Marmara University, Istanbul, Ebru Ceylan also studied film at Mimar Sinan. Her first short film, *On the Edge* (*Kiyida*) was officially selected for Cannes in 1998. A contributor to her husband's films in a variety of guises, *Climates* (*Iklimler*, 2006) sees Ebru and Nuri stepping in front of the camera's penetrating gaze for an intense and unflinching look at a marriage on the brink of collapse. Comparable to Atom Egoyan's *Calendar* (1993) in its wilful blurring of the distinction between on- and off-screen lives, *Climates* makes for frequently uncomfortable viewing but it is also undeniably bold and brilliant, and arguably stands as Ceylan's existentialist masterpiece.

Climates

The Ceylans play a successful Istanbul couple, Bahar and Isa, first seen on a hot and humid summer holiday in Kas. A taut dinner with friends and a tense, startlingly realised motorbike ride imparts that their relationship is on the downward slide and Bahar

Climates

subsequently sets off for home alone. In the rainy autumn – the film's seasonal structure reaches back to *Kasaba* – Isa, an ill-tempered university professor, encounters Serap (Nazan Kesal), a bewitching former flame to whom he is evidently still drawn and with whom, it is suggested, he may have been unfaithful. In an extended, technically perfect take characteristic of Ceylan's work, Isa forces his sexual attentions on Serap at her apartment. Though far from explicit and assiduously avoiding any overtures towards titillation, the sequence is, in it's own way, very difficult to watch. Finally, in the bleak midwinter snow, Isa tracks Bahar to a remote, snowbound province where she is working on a TV programme. A rapprochement appears to be in the air, but it's clear that Isa is not nearly as capable of change as he insists.

It has been commented that Ceylan's stories and his films may be considered relatively small in scale but that their impact is devastating. This is certainly true of *Climates*, which takes the prevailing mood of ennui and disappointment common to Ceylan's universe to courageous new heights. Far from a potentially self-indulgent attempt at therapy, the film reveals Ceylan as a master storyteller who recognises and investigates the great potential for loneliness and self-destruction within us all. A brutally honest dissection of the failings of man – this is unarguably more Isa's story than Bahar's – Ceylan's casting of himself at the film's centre offers what Jonathan Romney describes as one of the most 'merciless self-portraits ever seen in cinema'. Of course, the director has frequently incorporated aspects of his own life and personality into his work (and again his parents cameo as Isa's mother and father) and so one should resist the urge to read *Climates* as purely the cinema of autobiography. The first of the director's films to be shot using high-definition digital video, with Gökhan Tiryaki assuming cinematography duties, the film captures with enhanced clarity and precision the stunning Turkish locations. The physical details of the protagonists are also beautifully rendered; witness the opening scene of Isa and Bahar frolicking, first playfully and then with the aim of causing provocation, on a golden sandy beach. Such moments lend *Climates* a pronounced and profound sense of intimacy.

The World of Secrets

The production notes that accompany Ceylan's films are as lean and economical as the works themselves, but the blurb for *Climates* did reveal Ceylan's belief that 'man was made to be happy for simple reasons and unhappy for even simpler ones – just as he is born for simple reasons and dies for even simpler ones...' This is wholly applicable to *Three Monkeys* (*Üç maymun*, 2008), the director's fifth feature and most recent work at the time of writing. In certain ways an expansion of the central thread in *Climates*, namely the unspoken dynamics in a dysfunctional family, the film differs from Ceylan's previous works in that it more closely corresponds to genre tropes. Exhilaratingly ambitious in scope, the film, which adopts the proverbial 'see no evil, hear no evil, speak no evil' as its moral anchor, is a gripping and tightly wound psychological drama.

Three Monkeys

Servet (Ercan Kesal, who, alongside Ebru, also collaborated on the film's script), a wealthy politician, has caused a hit-and-run accident, and persuades his perennially cash-strapped driver, Eyüp (Yavuz Bingöl), to assume responsibility in return for a considerable financial reward. Convinced that he will endure only a short spell in jail, Eyüp accepts. In his absence, Eyüp's seductive wife Hacer (Hatice Aslan) becomes involved with Servet, and the couple's brooding teenaged son Ismail (Ahmet Rıfat Şungar) must carry the weight of their secret when he visits his father in prison. Eyüp's release functions as a metaphorical unleashing of past indiscretions and various family deceits, desires and anxieties, and all too soon the increasingly fractured family find themselves entangled in an ever more complex web of subterfuge.

Three Monkeys

Weaving a carefully calibrated maelstrom of violence, moral decay and ruined lives, *Three Monkeys* is in many ways the director's darkest and most pessimistic work yet. Though still managing to find the time to accommodate the inspired flashes of ironic humour that frequently punctuate Ceylan's cinematic universe (including a humiliating climb down in a traffic jam when the offending vehicle is revealed to contain three brutish types), the overall feeling here is of a darkly malevolent society slowly suffocating through its own avarice and weakness. The dysfunction at the heart of the film is not confined to a single family struggling through their differences, but rather a wider and seemingly irreparable affliction.

Working again with cinematographer Gökhan Tiryaki, Ceylan continues to act as a pioneer in the use of high-definition images. Largely restricting himself to sombre tones, the director still imbues his urban milieu with an astonishing richness and compositional depth. As a peek into the tortured window of the human soul, *Three Monkeys* is, like *Cocoon*, *Small Town*, *Clouds of May*, *Distant* and *Climates*, a wonder to ponder and behold.

JASON WOOD is a writer and film programmer. His books include *100 American Independent Films* (2004), *The Faber Book of Mexican Cinema* (2005), *Nick Broomfield: Documenting Icons* (2005), *Talking Movies: Contemporary World Filmmakers in Interview* (2006) and *100 Road Movies* (2006).

Nuri Bilge Ceylan filmography

[feature-film directing credits only]

1997
KASABA (Small Town)
Script: Nuri Bilge Ceylan, based on a story by Emine Ceylan. *Photography:* Nuri Bilge Ceylan. *Production Design:* Ebru Ceylan. *Editing:* Ayhan Ergürsel, Nuri Bilge Ceylan. *Players:* Mehmet Emin Toprak (Saffet), *Havva Saglam* (Hulya), *Cihat Butun* (Ali), *Fatma Ceylan* (Grandmother), *Mehmet Emin Ceylan* (Grandfather), *Sercihan Alioglu* (Father), *Semra Yilmaz* (Mother), *Latif Altintas* (Teacher), *Muzaffer Ozdemir* (Mad Ahmet). *Produced by Nuri Bilge Ceylan.* *82 mins*

1999
MAYIS SIKINTISI (Clouds of May)
Script: Nuri Bilge Ceylan. *Photography:* Nuri Bilge Ceylan. *Editing:* Ayhan Ergürsel, Nuri Bilge Ceylan. *Players:* Mehmet Emin Ceylan (Emin), *Muzaffer Özdemir* (Muzaffer), *Fatma Ceylan* (Fatma), *Mehmet Emin Toprak* (Saffet), *Muhammed Zimbaoglu* (Ali), *Sadik Incesu* (Sadik). *Produced by Nuri Bilge Ceylan. 117 mins*

2002
UZAK (Distant)
Script: Nuri Bilge Ceylan. *Photography:* Nuri Bilge Ceylan. *Production Design:* Ebru Ceylan.

Editing: Ayhan Ergürsel, Nuri Bilge Ceylan. *Players:* Muzaffer Özdemir (Mahmut), *Mehmet Emin Toprak* (Yusuf), *Zuhal Gencer Erkaya* (Nazan), *Nazan Kirilmis* (Lover), *Feridun Koc* (Janitor), *Fatma Ceylan* (Mother), *Ebru Ceylan* (Young girl). *Produced by Nuri Bilge Ceylan. 110 mins*

2006
IKLIMLER (Climates)
Script: Nuri Bilge Ceylan. *Photography:* Gökhan Tiryaki. *Editing:* Ayhan Ergürsel, Nuri Bilge Ceylan. *Players:* Ebru Ceylan (Bahar), *Nuri Bilge Ceylan* (Isa), *Nazan Kesal* (Serap), *Mehmet Eryılmaz* (Mehmet), *Arif Aşçı* (Arif), *Can Özbatur* (Güven), *Ufuk Bayraktar* (Taxi driver), *Fatma Ceylan* (Isa's mother), *M. Emin Ceylan* (Isa's father), *Semra Yılmaz* (Semra), *Ceren Olcay* (TV series actress), *Abdullah Demirkubuz*

(TV series actor), *Feridun Koç* (TV series director), *Zafer Saka* (TV series crew member). *Produced by Nuri Bilge Ceylan, Cemal Noyan, Zeynep Özbatur, Fabienne Vonier. 101 mins*

2008
ÜÇ MAYMUN (Three Monkeys)
Script: Ebru Ceylan, Nuri Bilge Ceylan, Ercan Kesal. *Photography:* Gökhan Tiryaki. *Production Design:* Ebru Ceylan. *Editing:* Ayhan Ergürsel, Bora Gökşingöl, Nuri Bilge Ceylan. *Players:* Yavuz Bingöl (Eyüp), *Hatice Aslan* (Hacer), *Ahmet Rıfat Şungar* (İsmail), *Ercan Kesal* (Servet),*Cafer Köse* (Bayram), *Gürkan Aydın* (The child). *Produced by Nuri Bilge Ceylan, Cemal Noyan, Zeynep Özbatur, Valerio De Paolis, Fabienne Vonier. 109 mins*

Miyazaki Hayao by Colin Odell and Michelle Le Blanc

In July 2008, Japan waited in anticipation for the screen event of the year, the release of *Ponyo on the Cliff by the Sea* (*Gake no ue no Ponyo*). Preview information had been decidedly scarce and the film's veil of secrecy was seemingly impenetrable. The main reason behind this strategy was that the film's creator wanted his audience to see it as freshly as possible, with eyes unencumbered by the baggage of preconception. For most studios, this marketing approach would be dangerous. But when the film is from Studio Ghibli and the director is Miyazaki Hayao, it's a whole different ball game. Miyazaki is Japan's most renowned animator; his films are revered for their breathtaking artistry and engaging storylines. Not only huge box office hits worldwide (Studio Ghibli films are amongst the most financially successful non-English-language films of all time) they are also critically acclaimed, and with good reason. Miyazaki is uncompromising when it comes to realising his artistic vision; flights of glorious fantasy mix with a worldview that is childlike in its quest for wonder and discovery but never childish or patronising. His films are popular globally but many are distinctive in the way they blend the environmental aspects of Japan's indigenous Shinto religion into strong narratives.

Early Years

Miyazaki Hayao was born in Tokyo on 5 January 1941, the second of four brothers. He grew up in turbulent and difficult times, during Japan's slow recovery under US occupation, following the end of the Second World War. The young Miyazaki took a great interest in his father's work for Miyazaki Airplane, a company owned by his uncle. The flying machines fascinated the boy and triggered a lifelong passion for aviation, which would fuel the vertiginous flying scenes in his films and also lead him to design his own vehicles for other projects and hobbyist magazines. Miyazaki's mother was an independent-minded intellectual who suffered from a form of spinal tuberculosis that meant the family frequently had to move home to facilitate her treatment. Like many growing up in the post-war years, Miyazaki became interested in manga, Japanese comics that had been popularised by the artist Tezuka Osamu. He gradually began to develop his drawing skills. The manga industry had an associated spin-off, anime, kickstarted in 1958 by *Hakujaden* (*The Tale of the White Serpent*), often credited as Japan's first feature-length colour anime. Studios soon expanded to fulfil a new appetite for animation, particularly on television. The largest of these was, and still is, Tōei (formerly Tōei Dōga). Miyazaki began working for them in 1963, after graduating in political science and economics from Gakushuin University. Tōei ran its animation wing like a factory, and the artists formed a strong, radicalised union. Miyazaki was eager to become involved and it was through union activities that he met fellow animator Takahata Isao. The two would collaborate on many projects before co-founding Studio Ghibli. The most notable early example of these was Takahata's socialist fantasy, *Horusu: Prince of the Sun* (1968) on which Miyazaki worked as a key animator and designer. Eventually Miyazaki and Takahata left Tōei to pursue projects elsewhere, including the TV series *Lupin III* (1971). In 1972 the pair worked on the first of two *Panda Kopanda* films from a script by Miyazaki, a charming fantasy about a girl and her friendship with a panda and his cub. Back on the small screen, a series of productions for World Masterpiece Theater, including versions of *Heidi* and *Anne of Green Gables*, honed their skills to perfection and, through production visits to Europe, informed much of Miyazaki's later work. It was on the series *Future Boy Conan* (1978) that Miyazaki's talent really began to shine. He designed and directed nearly all 26 episodes, revelling in scenes of flying and adventure as young Conan, survivor of a near-apocalyptic war, embarks on an epic quest to save Lana, the potential saviour of his people, from the clutches of an evil military regime.

Miyazaki's big break came when he was asked to direct *Lupin III: The Castle of Cagliostro* (1979), a feature film spin-off from the TV series. Arsène Lupin III, the roguish hero, accompanied by an assortment of hilarious sidekicks, attempts to break into a virtually impregnable castle to locate the source behind forged banknotes. As if the Grand Duke of Cagliostro's deadly guards and booby traps were not enough, Lupin has to shake off Inspector Zenigata of Interpol, who is desperate to see the lovable larcenist behind bars. He also has to rescue the delectable Princess Clarisse, awaiting a forced marriage to the ruthless Duke. The combination of slapstick comedy and fast-paced action is exhilarating; its perfectly exaggerated characterisation matched by an acute attention to detail. The opening car chase is one of cinema's finest and funniest. Although *The Castle of Cagliostro* was a success Miyazaki returned to working

for television, filling the time between projects producing a science fiction manga, *Nausicaä of the Valley of the Wind*, on an ad hoc basis for *Animage* magazine. The comic proved immensely popular and eventually *Animage*'s parent company agreed to finance a feature film based on the incomplete work.

Nausicaä of the Valley of the Wind

Nausicaä of the Valley of the Wind (1984) is set 1,000 years in the future, where humans are struggling to emerge from the devastation of their industrial past. Princess Nausicaä's studies into the toxins that render most of the world uninhabitable without protective equipment are put on hold when the Tolmekians take over her village, kill her father and set about resurrecting a god of destruction to eradicate the giant insects that roam the polluted lands. *Nausicaä* is a sweeping epic about the effect of humankind on its environment, of the conflict between technology and nature, themes that run throughout Miyazaki's work. Central to the film is the battle between the environmentally aware Princess Nausicaä and Princess Kushana's dictator. Miyazaki's eye for action set-pieces elegantly contrasts with the overriding argument about harmony with nature and the need for community. Even without considering the limitations of Miyazaki's resources, *Nausicaä* is an astonishing and complex eco-fable filled with imaginative design.

The Fledgling Studio Ghibli

Nausicaä's success led Miyazaki and Takahata to form an animation company of their own, which could free them from the artistic constraints that other companies had placed on them, and to nurture future animation talent. Studio Ghibli was born.

Laputa: Castle in the Sky (1986) was Ghibli's first feature, an energetic fantasy tangentially informed by Swift's *Gulliver's Travels*. Set in a Welsh mining town at the close of an alternative nineteenth century it is partly informed by reconnaissance trips to Wales around the time of the miners' strikes. 'I admired the way they battled to save their way of life, just as the coal miners in Japan did,' Miyazaki said. Young Pazu's world is changed forever when a girl, Sheeta, literally falls from the sky and floats into his arms. Sheeta holds the key to unlocking the secrets of Laputa – a floating island of immeasurable power. Would-be dictator Colonel Muska abducts Sheeta in order to find Laputa, forcing Pazu to form an uneasy alliance with a clan of sky pirates, led by the feisty Mama Dola.

Laputa: Castle in the Sky

In *Laputa: Castle in the Sky*, there is always room for the redemption of even the most hardened of criminals, provided they have a sense of community. What is perhaps surprising is the way Miyazaki elicits emotional attachment in unlikely areas. When a giant Laputa robot is first reanimated, we witness it administering impressive laser destruction, but later one is shown tending a grave with flowers, quietly servile and serene. It is in these contrasts that Miyazaki creates genuinely touching scenes against the backdrop of a rip-roaring adventure.

Miyazaki followed *Laputa* with *My Neighbour Totoro* (1988), a film for which Studio Ghibli struggled to find financing because the proposal seemed too childish for investors. To obtain funding, it was released alongside Takahata's devastatingly powerful war film *Grave of the Fireflies* (1988). It is hard to imagine a more incongruous double bill. *My Neighbour Totoro* is a delightful, whimsical triumph of imagination. The story is simple – Mei and Satsuki move to a home in the countryside with their father while their mother is convalescing in hospital. There, under the imposing shadow of an ancient camphor tree, they encounter strange woodland spirits, the most commanding of which is Totoro, a huge bellowing furry creature, and his associate, an enormous cat.

My Neighbour Totoro is the perfect example of Miyazaki's inquisitive, unprejudiced and childlike view of the world – a film that is as captivating to five-year-olds as it is to 85-year-olds. It has an honesty devoid of the saccharine cynicism often associated with family films and sees its young heroines respecting their surroundings and interacting with them in a way that is harmonious with Shinto beliefs. They are rewarded for their courtesy with increasingly fanciful encounters with the forest spirits, from totoros of various sizes to the wonderful grinning nekobasu – a many-legged cat with headlights for eyes, who provides a flying bus service. The film was not a success on initial release but subsequently

My Neighbour Totoro

became one of Ghibli's most beloved films, with a bewildering amount of merchandise available. Totoro in his various guises became part of the company's identity and Totoro's profile announces the start of every Ghibli film.

Kiki's Delivery Service

Based upon a popular children's book by Kadono Eiko, *Kiki's Delivery Service* (1989) is a captivating story about growing up. The independent and eternally cheerful Kiki, one of Miyazaki's many plucky young heroines, has left home with her talking cat, Jiji, to embark upon her induction into witchdom. Realising that her potion skills aren't up to much, she plays to her strong card – flying on her broom. Landing at a port town, Kiki and Jiji find lodgings in the attic of a friendly baker and set about earning their keep through Kiki's business, a broom-based parcel delivery service. Naturally, things don't always go smoothly, but the pair endear themselves to the townsfolk, especially to the young Tombo, who is in awe of Kiki's ability to fly.

On the surface, *Kiki's Delivery Service* is Miyazaki's most conventional film, but this belies his elegant narrative skills. For all the action in the film's daring flying sequences, the true art of Miyazaki's direction lies in the details of the narrative: the awkwardness of growing up and becoming socially aware; Jiji losing his voice, which marks our heroine's puberty; and a heart-stopping moment of suspense at the film's climax.

Flying Success

The highest box office earner of its year, *Porco Rosso* (1992) began life as a commissioned in-flight short movie for JAL (Japan Airlines) before Miyazaki's ambitions and enthusiasm for what was a very personal project meant additional funds were required to make it feature length. Captain Marco Pagot is a loner, a free-spirited man who roams the skies in his distinctive red plane. He's also a bipedal pig, unique in a world that's currently on the brink of war. Marco spends his days rescuing schoolchildren from pirates and drowning his sorrows in Gina's Flying Club bar. But that all changes when Curtis, an arrogant American pilot and all-round scallywag, becomes his nemesis, gunning him down and leaving him for dead. With the aid of plucky engineer Fio, Marco repairs his plane and patches himself up, ready to face Curtis and save his secret love, Gina.

Porco Rosso

Porco Rosso is a celebration of aviation. Its multitude of aircraft, all bar one (Curtis's) designed by Miyazaki but completely in keeping with its 1920/1930s aesthetic, are lovingly detailed and exquisitely animated, and the way that Miyazaki plays with an apparently 3D space is liberating and intoxicating. Although the story is slight, there are serious messages about the rise of fascism in Italy and the ultimate lack of humanity possessed by the bulk of humankind. *Porco Rosso* is a spirited blend of Hemingway, *Wings* (1927), *Casablanca* (1942) and *Only Angels Have Wings* (1939). But with a pig.

Scripting as well as directing a short but stunning sequence in the enchanting coming-of-age drama, *Whisper of the Heart* (1995), Miyazaki returned to full-time director duties with *Princess Mononoke* (1997), briefly Japan's biggest box office hit. Ashitaka saves his village from destruction at the tusks of a rampaging boar god, driven insane by poison. But Ashitaka becomes tainted in the process and faces certain death unless he can travel to find the root of the blight that is ravaging the land. His journey takes him through sacred forests overseen by the deer god and he catches glimpses of demi-god Princess Mononoke, a feral girl who runs with the wolves. Mononoke is running a campaign to rid the land of Lady Eboshi, owner of an iron factory fortress that manufactures increasingly deadly weapons, who is eradicating the sacred forests in her insatiable need to smelt metal and obtain further earthly riches.

Princess Mononoke

An epic on a scale comparable to Kurosawa's finest work, *Princess Mononoke* is so much more than an adventure story. It is an eco-fable steeped heavily in the culture and spirituality of Japan; a companion piece to *Nausicaä*, which looks at the origins of industrialism during the transition from feudalism. This is an age where the gods roam among the people, visible and revered. Miyazaki's gods and spirits range from the hordes of tiny white kodomo, eerily clicking their heads around in rapt concentration, to the mountain-sized majesty and dreadful awe of the Nightwalker unleashing his wrath. But among these scenes of wonder and threatened Götterdämmerung, Miyazaki constructs a complex political picture

of the times, which gives the film a sense of existing on a far broader canvas.

Surpassing *Princess Mononoke*'s formidable box office clout and scooping an Academy Award for Best Animated Film, *Spirited Away* (2001) is a whirlwind of imagination and inventiveness. Plucky teenager Chihiro faces an uncertain and dangerous future when her parents are transformed into gorging swine, after they tuck into a cursed feast they happen upon in an apparently disused amusement park. Chihiro is plunged into a chaotic spirit world of menace and dread, overseen by cackling bird-witch Yubaba. Working to survive, our resourceful heroine faces the loss not only of her identity, but also of her life.

In many ways the flip-side to *My Neighbour Totoro*, *Spirited Away* shows the malevolent aspects of the spirit world, a world that has now all but shunned mankind and is brutal to those who dare to stumble into it. Chihiro faces a bleak fate, cleaning out filthy baths or dealing with Yubaba's elephantine-sized mewling offspring. Miyazaki's menagerie of creatures – dragons, masked ghosts, sootbunnies and all manner of grotesque or quirky denizens – vie for space in a dangerous land. Chihiro confronts this adversity with aplomb but the palpable sense of threat is genuine. She represents a vision of hope for the future of Japan, passing the baton from the current generation, who are viewed as selfish, materialistic and shallow, on to a youth who must learn to respect their heritage and environment.

Spirited Away

Howl's Moving Castle

Miyazaki has vowed to retire from directing on a number of occasions, as a result of the pressures inherent in realising his exacting visions, but somehow he has always been persuaded to continue animating. *Howl's Moving Castle* (2004), adapted from the book by Diana Wynne Jones, tells the tale of cheerful but self-deprecating milliner Sophie who, following a brief encounter with Howl, a narcissistic free-roaming shape-shifting wizard, is turned into an old woman by the Witch of the Waste. Howl lives in a ramshackle castle on legs, powered by an irrepressible fire demon that huffs and puffs its way around a world facing a terrible and futile war.

Like *Spirited Away*, *Howl's Moving Castle* is a film about identity and humanity, about what it is to be human and how the choices we make affect our communities. Howl's narcissism and cowardice give way to a nobler self when Sophie comes into his chaotic life amd he realises that beauty is not a matter for the eyes, but for the heart. *Howl's Moving Castle* tempers its pessimism regarding mankind's propensity for war with the redemptive nature of the human spirit.

Miyazaki's latest film, *Ponyo on the Cliff by the Sea* (2008), is aimed squarely at a younger audience, but nevertheless contains many of the themes that pervade his work. A young girl-fish escapes the clutches of her father, submarine-bound experimenter Fujimoto, but he sends sinister aqua fish to find her. Meanwhile, the girl-fish has found herself in the company of perky schoolboy Sōsuke, who keeps her alive in a bucket of water and names

her Ponyo. Ponyo wants to become human, but could her attempts to realise her aim cause a catastrophe? Completely devoid of CGI, *Ponyo on the Cliff by the Sea* delights in a hand-crafted aesthetic that suits its narrative. The opening scenes of sub-aquatic life and Ponyo's uncountable sisters are breathtaking in the number of animated elements expertly rendered, while some of the action sequences are as exhilarating as *The Castle of Cagliostro*. Once again, Miyazaki delivers a fantasy world amidst our own, where strange creatures and demi-gods contrast with the realities of day-to-day living. A feel-good adventure of discovery, *Ponyo on the Cliff by the Sea* is also graced with an infectious end-credit song, dutifully sung with gusto by children enamoured of Ponyo's considerable charms.

Ponyo on the Cliff by the Sea

Miyazaki's films show inherent artistry and honesty, exploring the conflicts between humankind, nature and technology, often within a fantasy context. He is comfortable showing us both fantastical wonders and horrifying consequences in worlds that are truly believable. The dangers are genuine but there is always a chance of redemption. Throughout, his heroes show personal fortitude and a pronounced sense of community. His use of the traditional cell animation technique gives his films an organic quality that is timeless. That his films are so popular, given that his vision as a director is never compromised, demonstrates a rare merging of art and commerce.

COLIN ODELL and **MICHELLE LE BLANC** are authors, broadcasters and film journalists. They have written on David Lynch, Tim Burton, John Carpenter and horror and vampire films, among others. Their latest book, the *Studio Ghibli Kamera Book* (2009), explores the films of Miyazaki and Takahata Isao.

Miyazaki Hayao filmography

[feature-film directing credits only]

1979
RUPAN SANSEI:
KARIOSUTORO NO SHIRO
(The Castle of Cagliostro)
Script: Miyazaki Hayao.
Photography: Takahashi Hirokata.
Art Direction: Shichirō Kobayashi.
Editing: Tsurubuchi Mitsutoshi.
Players: Yamada Yasuo (Lupin),
Kobayashi Kiyoshi (Jigen),
Masuyama Eiko (Fujiko), Naya
Gorō (Zenigata), Shimamoto Sumi
(Clarisse). Produced by Katayama
Tetsuo. 100 mins

1984
KAZE NO TANI NO NAUSHIKA
(Nausicaä of the Valley of the
Wind)
Script: Miyazaki Hayao.
Photography: Kyonen Hideshi.
Art Direction: Nakamura Mitsuki
(Nakamura Mitsuyoshi). Editing:
Kaneko Naoki, Kida Tomoko, Sakai
Shōji. Players: Shimamoto Sumi
(Nausicaä), Naya Gorō (Yupa),
Sakakibara Yoshiko (Kushana).
Produced by Takahata Isao.
116 mins

1986
TENKŪ NO SHIRO RAPYUTA
(Laputa: Castle in the Sky)
Script: Miyazaki Hayao. Art
Direction: Nozaki Toshio, Yamamoto
Nizō. Editing: Kasahara Yoshihiro,
Seyama Takeshi. Players: Tanaka
Mayumi (Pazu), Yokozawa Keiko
(Sheeta), Terada Minori (Muska).

Produced by Takahata Isao.
124 mins

1988
TONARI NO TOTORO
(My Neighbour Totoro)
Script: Miyazaki Hayao.
Photography: Shirai Hisao. Art
Direction: Oga Kazuo. Editing:
Seyama Takeshi. Players: Sakamoto
Chika (Mei), Hidaka Noriko
(Satsuki), Takagi Hitoshi (Totoro),
Itoi Shigesato (Tatsuo). Produced by
Hara Toru. 86 mins

1989
MAJO NO TAKKYŪBIN
(Kiki's Delivery Service)
Script: Miyazaki Hayao.
Photography: Sugimura Shigeo. Art
Direction: Ono Hiroshi. Editing:
Seyama Takeshi. Players: Takayama
Minami (Kiki), Sakuma Rei (Jiji),
Yamaguchi Kappei (Tombo).
Produced by Miyazaki Hayao, Hara
Toru. 102 mins

1992
KURENAI NO BUTA
(Porco Rosso)
Script: Miyazaki Hayao. Art
Direction: Hisamura Katsu. Editing:
Seyama Takeshi. Players: Moriyama
Shūichirō (Marco), Kato Tokiko
(Jina), Okamura Akemi (Fio).
Produced by Suzuki Toshio. 94 mins

1997
MONONOKE HIME
(Princess Mononoke)
Script: Miyazaki Hayao.
Photography: Okui Atsushi. Art

Direction: Kuroda Satoshi, Oga
Kazuo, Takeshige Yōji, Tanaka
Naoya, Yamamoto Nizō. Editing:
Seyama Takeshi. Players: Matsuda
Yōji (Ashitaka), Tanaka Yūko
(Eboshi), Ishida Yuriko (San),
Kobayashi Kaoru (Jiko). Produced
by Suzuki Toshio. 134 mins

2001
SEN TO CHIHIRO NO
KAMIKAKUSHI
(Spirited Away)
Script: Miyazaki Hayao.
Photography: Okui Atsushi. Art
Direction: Takeshige Yōji. Editing:
Seyama Takeshi. Players: Hiiragi
Rumi (Chihiro), Irino Miyu (Haku),
Natsuki Mari (Yubaba). Produced by
Suzuki Toshio. 125 mins

2004
HAURU NO UGOKU SHIRO
(Howl's Moving Castle)
Script: Miyazaki Hayao.
Photography: Okui Atsushi. Art
Direction: Takeshige Yōji, Yoshida
Noboru. Editing: Seyama Takeshi.
Players: Baishō Chieko (Sophie),
Kimura Takuya (Howl). Produced
by Suzuki Toshio. 118 mins

2008
GAKE NO UE NO PONYO
(Ponyo on the Cliff by the Sea)
Script: Miyazaki Hayao.
Photography: Okui Atsushi. Art
Direction: Yoshida Noboru. Editing:
Seyama Takeshi. Players: Nara
Yuria (Ponyo), Doi Hiroki (Sōsuke),
Tokoro Jôji (Fujimoto). Produced by
Suzuki Toshio. 108 mins

John Sayles by Hannah Patterson

I n 2007, John Sayles released his sixteenth film as writer-director. An affectionate and charmingly rendered story of rock 'n' roll coming to small-town 1950s Alabama, with its attendant themes of race, class and identity, *Honeydripper* is a reminder of why Sayles is still such an inspirational, singular filmmaker after thirty years working in the industry. Redolent of his best work, it is considered, thought provoking, touching, entertaining, character led, expertly acted, politically aware and socially engaged. And, like a great many of his projects, self-financed.

Hard to conceive that funding could prove so elusive for America's leading proponent of independent cinema, but for Sayles and his long-time producing (and personal) partner, Maggie Renzi, it was ever thus. 'There seems to be a kind of mutual understanding between Hollywood and me,' Sayles has said: 'Most of what they make I wouldn't be interested in directing, and most of what I make they'd have no idea how to sell.'

True enough, there are no easy hooks with Sayles' films. He isn't showy or hip like

Tarantino, cool like Soderbergh or Jarmusch, or quirky like Hartley and the emergent Mumblecore gang. Despite working across a host of genres, his themes, or more accurately concerns, have, by and large, remained constant. Whether drawing on and subverting the traditions of the melodrama (*Lianna*, 1983; *Passion Fish*, 1992), sci-fi (*The Brother From Another Planet*, 1984), western (*Lone Star*, 1996), thriller (*Limbo*, 1999) and noir (*Silver City*, 2004), much of his work focuses in on communities that function as microcosms of society, ranging every strata, from wealthy to poor, across myriad ethnicities and races. With each film set in a different region, from the bayous of Louisiana to the wilderness of Alaska, his body of work adds up to an extraordinary portrait of American life and culture.

Where Peter Weir, another director with a penchant for working across genres, draws the surface of a world only to reveal alternative, parallel realities, Sayles likes to show the one that's staring you in the face. He gives us the overview that we're incapable of seeing ourselves, a glimpse, or delve into the life of the person living down the street, or in a nearby neighbourhood. It's a world shaped by the forces of history and circumstance, and the past inevitably looms large in his work, often fraught with racial tensions, ancient feuds or painful personal memories. Interesting and complex, yes, but hardly concept driven, or an easy sell at the multiplex.

Consequently, throughout his career Sayles has chosen to sustain this unique brand of intelligent, non-studio filmmaking by keeping one screenwriting foot firmly planted in the mainstream. It's his work as a writer for hire, sometimes credited (*The Lady in Red*, 1979; *The Spiderwick Chonicles*, 2008), often not

(*The Quick and the Dead*, 1995; *Apollo 13*, 1995; *Mimic*, 1997), that has allowed him to make personal projects on his own terms; and when needs must, bankrolling them himself. He's an astonishingly versatile scribe, working across narratives with a studied ease, authenticity and enviable speed. It's as a writer that he really excels; as a writer, too, that he first entered the business.

Born to schoolteachers on 28 September 1950, in Schenectady, New York, Sayles studied at Williams College in Massachusetts, majoring in psychology. He variously worked as a meat packer, construction worker, nursing home orderly, factory worker and stage actor, all jobs that would bring him into contact with a wide and diverse range of people, in particular blue-collar workers whose lives he chronicles so well and often. Starting out with fiction, and the novels *Pride of the Bimbos* (1975) and *Union Dues* (1978), the latter nominated for a National Book Award and National Critics' Circle Award, he subsequently moved to California and penned scripts for Roger Corman's New World Pictures: *The Lady in Red*, *Piranha* (1978) and *Battle Beyond the Stars* (1980). With gigs writing the B-movie *Alligator* (1980) and werewolf shocker *The Howling* (1981) to follow, Sayles was able to make his debut as director-writer-editor with *The Return of the Secaucus Seven* (1980), on his own money and a budget of US$40,000.

A precursor to Sundance, often cited as one of the most influential indie films, the story of *Secaucus*, set in small-town New Hampshire, revolves around the reunion of a group of friends at the house of couple Katie and Mike, who function as a Greek chorus of sorts, commenting on the behaviour of their companions. They play volleyball and charades, swim naked in the creek, drink, argue, have sex and get arrested, leading them to reminiscence over their detainment ten years earlier on their way to a political demonstration. Now hitting their thirties, each is coming to terms with their evolving politics and shifting priorities, disillusionments and unfulfilled dreams.

The warm and affectionate tone throughout hints at several of Sayles' abiding preoccupations: the humanism that would go on to infuse all of his films, his interest in multiple-character narratives (he has cited *Nashville*, 1975, as inspiration), ability to create distinct voices and illicit great performances (Renzi, in particular, puts in a wonderfully droll turn as Katie) and an engagement with political issues of the day. Often mentioned as the antecedent of *The Big Chill* (1983) (though Lawrence Kasdan denies having seen it), it's certainly a lesson in how to go low budget: opt for simple settings, write a smart script and concentrate on character.

This choice of style, however, has – somewhat ironically – dogged Sayles' entire career. Probably the biggest criticism levelled at his work is that it lacks a sense of cinematography; that his films are in essence un-cinematic. There's certainly some truth in the accusation. If it's flamboyant visuals you're after, or obsessive attention to ocular detail, his films aren't for you. 'My main interest is making films about people,' he admits. 'I'm not interested in cinematic art.'

The Return of the Secaucus Seven

Lianna

His abiding interest in the human condition is evidenced in Sayles' subsequent film, *Lianna*, which shares something in common with chamber pieces such as *Ordinary People* (1980) and *Shoot the Moon* (1982), which were beginning to register the disintegration of the family unit. Sayles took it one step further in dramatising the problems for a married mother of two (movingly played by Linda Griffiths) living with an unfaithful husband, film professor Dick (John DeVries), who falls in love with her female tutor (Jane Hallaren) and embraces lesbianism. Released the same year as Robert Towne's lesbian-themed sports picture *Personal Best* (1982), Sayles never sensationalises his story, allowing Griffiths the time to register Lianna's every new emotion: the joy of sexual liberation, frustration with societal convention, the sting of her daughter's fearful rejection, and the pain of an ultimately unrealised love. The writing is naturalistic, the settings and emotions authentic in detail.

Baby It's You (1983), Sayles' first foray into studio filmmaking, though still of the low-budget variety, is a teen movie, but more grown up and philosophical than many of the decade. Based on actor-producer Amy Robinson's experiences of high school in the 1960s, Rosanna Arquette plays blue-collar, actress-hopeful Jill who's persuaded into a relationship with Vincent Spano's Sheik, an opportunist obsessed with his clothes, Frank Sinatra and her. With so much working against them, in particular their class divide, the romance is doomed from the start. Despite

some initial wrangles over the edit, the film is Sayles' final cut, but its attempts to show the realities of high-school life and the changes that come for Jill at college, means that it meanders along the way. Sheik is difficult to get a handle on, and consequently, for much of the film, hard to empathise with. Hampered by song rights issues, its video release was delayed and the film suffered from an almost non-existent marketing campaign.

In 1982, whilst in post-production on *Baby*, Sayles was awarded a McArthur Foundation 'genius grant': US$32,000, tax free, for each of the next five years.

Made with the money he had in the bank at the time, *The Brother from Another Planet* proved a generic departure, falling ostensibly into the sci-fi camp. The story of a mute alien landing in Harlem pursued by bounty hunters from outer space, on closer inspection its concerns are typical of his work. At heart it's a human-interest story. From the moment the alien lands on Ellis Island, his journey as he tries to make sense of this foreign country parallels that of the immigrant experience.

The Brother from Another Planet

Joe Morton is oddly endearing as the wide-eyed naïf wandering the streets, reading people's minds, healing their wounds and fixing their arcade games. Some scenes play straight out of silent cinema and Morton is physically up to the job. Sayles and David Straithairn strut their stuff as more simplistic forerunners to Will Smith and Tommy Lee Jones' *Men in Black* (1997). Despite a slightly confusing dénouement, it's notable for being shot by novice cinematographer Ernest Dickerson, who'd already shot *Joe's Bed-Stuy Barbershop* (1983) and would go on to become a regular Spike Lee collaborator, and bears all the hallmarks of a cult movie. The film was nominated for the Grand Jury Prize at the Sundance Film Festival.

Further to making music videos for Bruce Springstein for 'Born in the USA', 'I'm on Fire' and 'Glory Days' (money in the bank), Sayles' next three films, *Matewan* (1987), *Eight Men Out* (1988) and *City of Hope* (1991) are played out on the more ambitious, larger canvasses that he would return to later with *Lone Star*, *Silver City* and *Sunshine State* (2002).

Shot by Haskell Wexler and edited by Sonya Polonsky, who worked on *Baby It's You*, *Matewan* is more overtly political than Sayles' previous work. Set in the past – focusing on the fight between coal miners and their bosses in 1920s West Virginia – it's as relevant to the anti-union, Reagan America of the 1980s in which it was made. Chris Cooper, excellent as Joe Kenehan, doesn't play a typical western hero, but a union leader who wants to organise the miners – white, black and Italian – by peaceful means. As with Sayles' finest work, it's utterly absorbing, full of contradictions and shades of grey; here there are no clear winners, and in business somebody somewhere always compromises or loses out.

Matewan

Next came *Eight Men Out*, an adaptation of Eliot Asinof's book, which dramatised another historical subject laden with moral conundrum: 1919's infamous Black Sox scandal, when eight players on the Chicago White Sox agreed to throw the World Series. Notable for early performances by John Cusack and Charlie Sheen, with Sayles himself particularly good as Ring Lardner, it's hard to get a handle on if you're unfamiliar with baseball. Unusually for Sayles, its moral compass is a little off, making it difficult at times to fathom the real heart of the piece.

Eight Men Out

Taking time to write a successful TV series, *Shannon's Deal*, and publish Cuban-set novel *Los Gusanos* (1991), Sayles' subsequent film, *City of Hope*, plays in many ways as a precursor to *The Wire*. It's a complex piece of screenwriting told from myriad points of view, delving into the layers of corruption and power politics in a city where an old building stands in the way of a commercial development favoured by the local mayor and his cohorts. The film ends, contrary to its title, on a decidedly discouraging note, with David Strathairn's calls for 'help' echoing those of the dying son of the property developer, and we're left with an impression of society in need of some serious reform.

Passion Fish once again proved Sayles' versatility as a writer as he shifted seamlessly from a broad, complex narrative to a compact, hothouse drama. Mary McDonnell plays a soap star wheelchair bound following a car accident, who retreats to her now-empty

Passion Fish

Louisiana family home, with Alfre Woodard as the live-in nurse who brings along plenty of her own emotional baggage. Drawing on classic melodrama tropes, the film is very funny, extremely moving and utterly absorbing. Issues of race are always present but never overplayed, and the Cajun music and mood of mystery, the latter bolstered by an ever-appealing David Strathairn as the potential love interest, adds ample atmosphere. Mary McDonnell's excellent lead performance earned her an Academy Award nomination for Best Actress, alongside Sayles' own for Best Original Screenplay.

The Secret of Roan Inish (1994), pre-dating his magical screenplay for *The Spiderwick Chronicles* by over ten years, foregrounded his ability to appeal to children as much as adults. Shot in Ireland, it's a captivating story of a young girl who moves to a small fishing village and becomes convinced of the connection of the mythical Celtic selkie, part human, part seal, to her family's past. It was nominated for Best Director and Best Screenplay at the Independent Spirit Awards.

Lone Star, his next, is probably the best known of Sayles' films, his biggest box office success and certainly one of his most accomplished and satisfying, earning him a second Academy Award nomination for Best Original Screenplay. Chris Cooper is the reluctant sheriff Sam Deeds investigating a thirty-year-old murder he suspects was committed by his 'golden boy' sheriff father. Father/son conflict resounds, echoing in the relationships between black

club owner (Ron Canada) and his aloof military son (Joe Morton), and Sam's ex, played with heartrending humour by Frances McDormand, and her overbearing father.

Interweaving the Mexican, black and white Texan experience, drawing out the truths and falsehoods of the past that stranglehold the present, he uses a simple yet effective visual device to move seamlessly from the past into the present, panning the camera away from a scene in the present so that it alights on one in the past, and vice versa. One of Sayles' very best endings, it hits a wonderfully romantic, transgressive note with Sam discovering that Pilar, the woman he's loved most of his life, is his half-sister and the pair essentially agreeing to 'forget the Alamo' and embrace their future together despite the past.

Lone Star

Set in a non-specific country with characters speaking Spanish, Nahuatl, Tzotzil, Maya and Kuna, *Men with Guns* (1997), also known as 'Hombres armadas', is one of Sayles' least-seen films. It follows the fortunes of fictional character Dr Fuentes (Federico Luppi) who unwittingly discovers the dreadful things happening in his own country.

Limbo with its 'love it or hate it' ambiguous ending, is Sayles' most enigmatic film. Strathairn is appropriately inscrutable as the former high-school basketball star and salmon fisherman burdened with secrets who falls for Mary Elizabeth Mastrantonio's worldly wise lounge singer. And Vanessa Martinez (the young Pilar in *Lone Star*) is heartbreaking as her jealous and confused daughter. Both an enjoyable portrait of small-town Alaska undergoing a tourism transformation and a nail-biting thriller, it's worth repeated viewings.

With *Sunshine State*, Sayles once again returned to a bigger ensemble, this time with the backdrop of a Florida beachside community that includes both white and black enclaves. With predatory developers wanting to turn the community into an upscale resort, locals are divided on whether to take the money or stand firm. Sly references to the harnessing of nature and the packaging of the American dream abound. Edie Falco excels as the bored daughter of local motel owner as does Angela Bassett as the woman who returns to see her mother, having left years before as a disgraced pregnant teenager. Also worthy of note is Mary Steenburgen as organiser of the annual Buccaneer Days, a local pageant, who delivers one of the funniest performances as she complains to her suicidal husband about the ungrateful townspeople: 'They don't know how difficult it is to invent a tradition.'

Casa de los Babys

With shades of *Passion Fish*, *Casa de los Babys* (2003) boasts a host of great actresses – Maggie Gyllenhaal, Daryl Hannah, Marcia Gay Harden, Lili Taylor, Mary Steenburgen and Susan Lynch – as American women in a South American hotel each desperate to adopt a baby. Pleasingly low key, Sayles avoids unnecessary sentimentality, here showing the charmless realities of their situation and the implications for mothers giving up their babies.

Silver City

In 2004's *Silver City*, the character of the Colorado Republican hopeful running for governor bears more than a passing resemblance to George W. Bush: an inarticulate, political daddy's boy with no significant experience. More satirical than Sayles' other work, it conveys some of his angry disbelief at the Bush administration, and Chris Cooper plays the part to unnerving perfection. Drawing on film noir conventions, the mystery begins with a dead body and features a shambolic, down-on-his-luck private detective (a bemused, bear-like Danny Houston), who's hired by the wrong side and soon starts to smell the whiff of corruption, and his own road to redemption. Despite some longeurs, its twisting narrative intrigues, and its theme of corporate disregard for the environment feels timely and relevant.

With *Honeydripper*, Sayles' most recent film, he places centre stage a passion for music which has been present to varying degrees in all his films. An adaptation of his own story, 'Keeping Time', which features in *Dillinger in Hollywood* (2004) (his other short-story collection *The Anarchists' Convention* was published in 1979), the movie stars Danny Glover as the proprietor of a club in 1950s Harmony, Alabama. Juggling his marriage and his livelihood, within an environment of segregation, he hires legendary musician player Guitar Sam, only to be landed with young pretender, Sammy, who fortunately knows how to play some good guitar and saves the day. Scored by regular collaborator Mason Daring, featuring a performance by blues singer Mabel John, it's one of the director's most uplifting films to date.

Honeydripper

Sayles has long professed his discomfort with the moniker of political filmmaker and some of his strongest work – *Limbo*, *Passion Fish*, *Lone Star* – is the least overtly political. Yet politics – of the personal, people kind – seems built into his DNA. 'He is the one,' film critic David Thomson has commented, singling him out amongst his contemporaries, after thirty years in the business, 'who has stood by his principles most defiantly and valiantly.' As comfortable writing for men as women, for middle class as blue collar, black as Mexican, he simply can't help but care, and that most of all is what his body of work conveys.

HANNAH PATTERSON is commissioning editor of *Kamera Books* and *Creative Essentials*, a freelance film critic and author, and documentary producer. She is also the editor of *The Cinema of Terrence Malick: Poetic Visions of America* (2007).

John Sayles filmography

[feature-film directing credits only]

1980
RETURN OF THE SECAUCUS SEVEN
Script: John Sayles. Photography: Austin De Besche. Editing: John Sayles. Players: Bruce MacDonald (Mike Donnelly), Maggie Renzi (Katie Sipriano), Adam LeFevre (J.T.), Maggie Cousineau (Frances Carlson), Gordon Clapp (Chip Hollister), Jean Passanante (Irene Rosenblue), Karen Trott (Maura Tolliver), Mark Arnott (Jeff Andrews), David Strathairn (Ron Desjardins), John Sayles (Howie), Marisa Smith (Carol), Amy Schewel, (Lacey Summers), Carolyn Brooks (Meg), Eric Forsythe (Captain), Nancy Mette (Lee). Produced by William Aydelott, Jeffrey Nelson. 110 mins

1983
LIANNA
Script: John Sayles. Photography: Austin De Besche. Production Design: Jeanne McDonnell. Editing:

John Sayles. Players: Linda Griffiths (Lianna), Jane Hallaren (Ruth), Jon DeVries (Dick), Jo Henderson (Sandy), Jessica MacDonald (Theda), Jesse Solomon (Spencer), John Sayles (Jerry), Stephen Mendillo (Bob), Betsy Julia Robinson (Cindy), Nancy Mette (Kim), Maggie Renzi (Sheila), Madelyn Coleman (Mrs. Hennessy), Robyn Reeves (Job Applicant), Chris Elliott (Lighting Assistant), Marta Renzi (Dancer). Produced by Jeffrey Nelson, Maggie Renzi. 110 mins

1983
BABY IT'S YOU
Script: John Sayles, based on a story by Amy Robinson. Photography: Michael Ballhaus. Production Design: Jeffrey Townsend. Editing: Sonya Polonsky. Players: Rosanna Arquette (Jill Rosen), Vincent Spano (Albert 'Sheik' Capadilupo), Joanna Merlin (Mrs. Rosen), Jack Davidson (Dr. Rosen), Nick Ferrari (Mr. Capadilupo), Dolores Messina (Mrs. Capadilupo), Leora Dana (Miss Vernon), Bill Raymond (Mr. Ripeppi), Sam McMurray (Mr. McManus), Liane Alexandra Curtis (Jody, High School Girl), Claudia Sherman (Beth, High School Girl), Marta Kober (Debra, High School Girl), Tracy Pollan (Leslie, College Girl), Rachel Dretzin (Shelly, College Girl), Susan Derendorf (Chris, College Girl). Produced by Robert F. Colesberry, Griffin Dunne, Amy Robinson. 105 mins

1984
THE BROTHER FROM ANOTHER PLANET
Script: John Sayles. Photography:

Ernest R. Dickerson. Production Design: Nora Chavooshian. Editing: John Sayles. Players: Joe Morton (The Brother), Rosanna Carter (West Indian Woman), Ray Ramirez (Hispanic Man), Yves Rene (Haitian Man), Peter Richardson (Islamic Man), Ginny Yang (Korean Shopkeeper), Daryl Edwards (Fly), Steve James (Odell), Leonard Jackson (Smokey), Bill Cobbs (Walter), Maggie Renzi (Noreen), Olga Merediz (Noreen's Client), Tom Wright (Sam), Minnie Gentry (Mrs. Brown), Ren Woods (Bernice). Produced by Peggy Rajski, Maggie Renzi. 108 mins

1987
MATEWAN
Script: John Sayles. Photography: Haskell Wexler. Production Design: Nora Chavooshian. Editing: Sonya Polonsky. Players: Chris Cooper (Joe Kenehan), James Earl Jones ('Few Clothes' Johnson), Mary McDonnell (Elma Radnor), Will Oldham (Danny Radnor), David Strathairn (Police Chief Sid Hatfield), Ken Jenkins (Sephus Purcell), Gordon Clapp (Griggs), Kevin Tighe (Hickey), John Sayles (Hardshell Preacher), Bob Gunton (C.E. Lively), Josh Mostel (Mayor Cabell Testerman), Nancy Mette (Bridey Mae), Jace Alexander (Hillard Elkins), Joe Grifasi (Fausto), Gary McCleery (Ludie). Produced by Mark Balsam, Ira Deutchman, James Glenn Dudelson, Ned Kendall, Amir Jacob Malin, Peggy Rajski, Maggie Renzi, Jerry Silva. 135 mins

1988
EIGHT MEN OUT
Script: John Sayles, based on the book by Eliot Asinof. Photography: Robert Richardson. Production Design: Nora Chavooshian. Editing: John Tintori. Players: John Cusack (George 'Buck' Weaver), Clifton James (Charles 'Commie' Comiskey), Michael Lerner

(Arnold Rothstein), Christopher Lloyd (Bill Burns), John Mahoney (William 'Kid' Gleason), Charlie Sheen (Oscar 'Hap' Felsch), David Strathairn (Eddie Cicotte), D.B. Sweeney (Joseph 'Shoeless Joe' Jackson), Michael Rooker (Arnold 'Chick' Gandil), Don Harvey (Charles 'Swede' Risberg), James Read (Claude 'Lefty' Williams), Perry Lang (Fred McMullin), Gordon Clapp (Ray Schalk), Jace Alexander (Dickie Kerr), Bill Irwin (Eddie Collins). Produced by Barbara Boyle, Jerry Offsay, Sarah Pillsbury, Peggy Rajski, Midge Sanford. 119 mins

1991
CITY OF HOPE
Script: John Sayles. Photography: Robert Richardson. Production Design: Dan Bishop, Dianna Freas. Editing: John Sayles. Players: Vincent Spano (Nick Rinaldi), Stephen Mendillo (Yoyo), Chris Cooper (Riggs), Tony Lo Bianco (Joe Rinaldi), Joe Morton (Wynn), Charlie Yanko (Stavros), Jace Alexander (Bobby), Todd Graff (Zip), Scott Tiler (Vinnie), John Sayles (Carl), Frankie Faison (Levonne), Gloria Foster (Jeanette), Tom Wright (Malik), Angela Bassett (Reesha), David Strathairn (Asteroid). Produced by Sarah Green, Maggie Renzi, John Sloss, Jo Throckmorton, Harold Welb. 129 mins

1992
PASSION FISH
Script: John Sayles. Photography: Roger Deakins. Production Design: Dan Bishop, Dianna Freas. Editing: John Sayles. Players: Mary McDonnell (May-Alice Culhane), Alfre Woodard (Chantelle), Lenore Banks (Nurse Quick), Vondie Curtis-Hall (Sugar LeDoux), Will Mahoney (Max), David Strathairn (Rennie), Leo Burmester (Reeves), Nelle Stokes (Therapist #1), Brett

Ardoin (Therapist #2), Nora Dunn (Ti-Marie), Michael Mantell (Dr. Kline), Mary Portser (Precious), Angela Bassett (Dawn / Rhonda), Daniel Dupont (Therapist #3), Chuck Cain (Attendant). Produced by Sarah Green, Maggie Renzi, John Sloss. 135 mins

1994
THE SECRET OF ROAN INISH
Script: John Sayles, based on a book by Rosalie K. Fry. Photography: Haskell Wexler. Production Design: Adrian Smith. Editing: John Sayles. Players: Jeni Courtney (Fiona), Pat Slowey (Priest), Dave Duffy (Jim), Declan Hannigan (Oldest brother), Mairéad Ní Ghallchóir (Barmaid), Eugene McHugh (Bar Patron 1), Tony Rubini (Bar Patron 2), Mick Lally (Hugh), Eileen Colgan (Tess), Richard Sheridan (Eamon), Micheal MacCarthaigh (Schoolmaster), Fergal McElherron (Sean Michael), Brendan Conroy (Flynn), John Lynch (Tadhg), Frankie McCafferty (Tim). Produced by Sarah Green, Glenn R. Jones, R. Paul Miller, Peter Newman, Maggie Renzi, John Sloss. 103 mins

1996
LONE STAR
Script: John Sayles. Photography: Stuart Dryburgh. Production Design: Dan Bishop. Editing: John Sayles. Players: Stephen Mendillo (Sgt. Cliff), Stephen J. Lang (Sgt. Mikey), Chris Cooper (Sheriff Sam Deeds), Elizabeth Peña (Pilar Cruz), Oni Faida Lampley (Celie), Eleese Lester (Molly), Joe Stevens (Deputy Travis), Gonzalo Castillo (Amado), Richard Coca (Enrique), Clifton James (Mayor Hollis Pogue), Tony Frank (Fenton), Miriam Colon (Mercedes Cruz), Kris Kristofferson (Sheriff Charlie Wade), Jeff Monahan (Young Hollis), Matthew McConaughey (Buddy Deeds). Produced by Jan Foster, R. Paul Miller, Maggie Renzi, John Sloss. 135 mins

1997
MEN WITH GUNS
Script: John Sayles. Photography:
Slawomir Idziak. Production Design:
Felipe Fernández del Paso. Editing:
John Sayles. Players: Federico Luppi
(Dr. Fuentes), Damián Delgado
(Domingo, the Soldier), Dan Rivera
González (Conejo, the Boy), Tania
Cruz (Graciela, the Mute Girl),
Damián Alcázar (Padre Portillo, the
Priest), Mandy Patinkin (Andrew),
Kathryn Grody (Harriet), Iguandili
López (Mother), Nandi Luna
Ramírez (Daughter), Rafael de
Quevedo (General), Carmen Madrid
(Angela, Dr. Fuentes' Daughter),
Esteban Soberanes (Raúl, Angela's
Fiancé), Alejandro Springall (Carlos,
Dr. Fuentes' Son), Maricruz Nájera
(Rich Lady), Roberto Sosa (Bravo).
Produced by Jim De Nardo, Peter
Gilbert, Lou Gonda, R. Paul Miller,
Bertha Navarro, Jody Patton, Maggie
Renzi, Eric Robison, Doug Sayles,
John Sloss. 127 mins

1999
LIMBO
Script: John Sayles. Photography:
Haskell Wexler. Production Design:
Gemma Jackson. Editing: John
Sayles. Players: Mary Elizabeth
Mastrantonio (Donna De Angelo),
David Strathairn ('Jumpin' Joe
Gastineau), Vanessa Martinez
(Noelle De Angelo), Hermínio
Ramos (Ricky), Kris Kristofferson
('Smilin' Jack Johannson), Dawn
McInturff (Audrey), Casey
Siemaszko (Bobby Gastineau),
Kathryn Grody (Frankie), Tom Biss
(Baines), Rita Taggart (Lou), Leo
Burmester (Harmon King), Michael
Laskin (Albright), Jimmy MacDonell
(Randy Mason), Mérit Carlson-van
Dort (Stacy), Monica Brandner
(Corky). Produced by Sarah
Connors, Maggie Renzi. 126 mins

2002
SUNSHINE STATE
Script: John Sayles. Photography:
Patrick Cady. Production Design:

Mark Ricker. Editing: John Sayles.
Players: Alex Lewis (Terrell),
Alan King (Murray Silver),
Cullen Douglas (Jefferson Cash),
Clifton James (Buster Bidwell),
Eliot Asinof (Silent Sam), James
McDaniel (Reggie Perry), Angela
Bassett (Desiree Perry), Edie Falco
(Marly Temple), Amanda Wing
(Krissy), Timothy Hutton (Jack
Meadows), Perry Lang (Greg),
Miguel Ferrer (Lester), Gordon
Clapp (Earl Pinkney), Kyle Meenan
(Dick Yordan), Mary Steenburgen
(Francine Pinkney). Produced by
Maggie Renzi, Nancy Schafer.
141 mins

2003
CASA DE LOS BABYS
Script: John Sayles. Photography:
Mauricio Rubinstein. Production
Design: Felipe Fernández del Paso.
Editing: John Sayles. Players: Daryl
Hannah (Skipper), Lili Taylor
(Leslie), Mary Steenburgen (Gayle),
Marcia Gay Harden (Nan), Maggie
Gyllenhaal (Jennifer), Angelina
Peláez (Doña Mercedes), Lizzie
Curry Martinez (Sor Juana),
Vanessa Martinez (Asunción),
Amanda Álvarez (Blanca), Said
Martinez (Eusebio), Abel Salas (Bus
Driver 1), Marco Mondragón (Bus
Driver 2), José Reyes (Van Driver),
Claudia Benitez (Woman on Bus),
Ignacio de Anda (Tito), José Reyes
Jr. (Grande), Emmanuel González
(Chico), Dave Baez (Rufino),
Blanca Loaria (Socorro). Produced
by Caroline Kaplan, Melissa Marr,
Jonathan Sehring, Alejandro
Springall, Lemore Syvan. 95 mins

2004
SILVER CITY
Script: John Sayles. Photography:
Haskell Wexler. Production Design:
Toby Corbett. Editing: John Sayles.
Players: Chris Cooper (Dickie
Pilager), Richard Dreyfuss (Chuck
Raven), Cajardo Lindsey (Lloyd),
John C. Ashton (Director),
Elizabeth Rainer (Leslie), Donevon

Martinez (Lazaro Huerta), James
Gammon (Sheriff Joe Skaggs),
Benjamin Kroger (Deputy Davis),
Charles Mitchell (Henry), Danny
Huston (Danny O'Brien), Alma
Delfina (Lupe Montoya), Roslyn
Washington (Hilary), David
Clennon (Mort Seymour), Mary
Kay Place (Grace Seymour), Tim
Roth (Mitch Paine). Produced by
Suzanne Ceresko, Robert Lansing
Parker, Maggie Renzi, Sam Tedesco.
128 mins

2007
HONEYDRIPPER
Script: John Sayles. Photography:
Dick Pope. Production Design:
Toby Corbett. Editing: John Sayles.
Players: Danny Glover (Tyrone
Purvis), Lisa Gay Hamilton
(Delilah), Yaya DaCosta (China
Doll), Charles S. Dutton (Maceo),
Vondie Curtis-Hall (Slick),
Gary Clark Jr. (Sonny), Mable
John (Bertha Mae), Stacy Keach
(Sheriff), Nagee Clay (Scratch),
Absalom Adams (Lonnie), Arthur
Lee Williams (Metalmouth Sims),
Ruben Santiago-Hudson (Stokely),
Davenia McFadden (Nadine), Daryl
Edwards (Shack Thomas), Sean
Patrick Thomas (Dex). Produced by
Ira Deutchman, Susan Kirr, Maggie
Renzi, Mark Wynns. 124 mins

Paolo Sorrentino by Lorenzo Codelli

Visiting the Naples set of *Il divo* on one hot summer's night, I was taken aback to meet genial actor Toni Servillo, just coming out of a lengthy make-up session, where he had been transformed into Italy's most notorious evergreen political leader, Giulio Andreotti. His menacing hump, bat ears, sceptic's eyes and rigid trunk – all exaggerated – were made even more frightening by director Paolo Sorrentino's portraying him as some kind of robotic Dracula. Using tiny paper memos, never the full script he had written, Sorrentino instructed Servillo in how to express, without words and with minimal movement, the mental maze of his unsmiling, phlegmatic character, who schemes murder while peacefully enjoying a horse race with his devoted wife. A contemporary Machiavelli, now in his late eighties, his dark legend has long fascinated Sorrentino. When the director was twenty he even attempted a short film about the politician's life. Now, at 38, he has finally achieved his ambition.

Paolo Sorrentino was born on 31 May 1970 in Naples. He studied economics at the local university but never graduated. He became involved in filmmaking at the tail-end of the so-called 'Neapolitan School', during the 1990s. An ephemeral but blazing volcano of talents, it was linked to the influential stage company, Teatri Uniti, which was founded in 1986 by Antonio Neiwiller, Toni Servillo and Mario Martone. The success of Martone's debut, *Death of a Neapolitan Mathematician* (*Morte di un matematico napoletano*, 1992), a powerful, *Citizen Kane*-style approach to the town's history and the clash between truth and myth, encouraged several other Neapolitan filmmakers to shoot there. In doing so, they avoided migration to the show business capitals, Rome and Milan, instead rooting their experiments inside their own fertile traditions. *The Vesuvians* (*I vesuviani*, 1997), a portmanteau movie co-directed by Mario Martone, Antonio Capuano, Pappi Corsicato, Antonietta De Lillo and Stefano Incerti, co-written by novelist Fabrizia Ramondino, and starring Toni Servillo, Iaia Forte, plus other homegrown 'divi', simultaneously proclaimed the movement's belated manifesto and its sad farewell.

In 1997 Sorrentino won the Franco Solinas Award, Italy's main screenwriting competition, for *Little Dragons of Fire* (*Dragoncelli di fuoco*), a gastronomic farce that was never produced. However, thanks to his win, he worked as an assistant for Antonio Capuano, with whom he co-wrote the political comedy *Neapolitan Dust* (*Polvere di Napoli*, 1998). As Sorrentino remembers: 'During that movement Naples was once again politically and economically on the rise. There was an enthusiasm, a euphoria, and a strong solidarity between filmmakers. Later on, things changed for the worse. The artistic solidarity I feel nowadays is more with Matteo Garrone and other Italian directors of my own generation.'

Sorrentino directed his first short, *Love Has No Borders* (*L'amore non ha confini*), in 1998. The story of a petty mobster and his disorganised gang, the film displayed both maturity and an enthusiasm for odd rock tunes. His second short, *The Long Night* (*La notte lunga*), made in 2001, was sponsored by the Milan municipality and written by a class of high-school pupils. It was a surprisingly ambivalent lesson in anti-drugs propaganda, again overflowing with flamboyant imagery. After *Love Has No Borders*, Sorrentino collaborated on a few scripts for *The Team* (*La squadra*), a popular Rai TV cop series, before winning the Franco Solinas Award again in 1999 for his script for *One Man Up* (*L'uomo in più*).

One Man Up

One Man Up

Neapolitan producer Nicola Giuliano and Francesca Cima of Indigo Film (the same company that financed the two shorts), in partnership with Kermit Smith, Key Films Distribution's late manager, contributed one million euros to finance Sorrentino's project. Mediatrade (Silvio Berlusconi's TV empire) also invested in the project. Sorrentino comments: 'In *One Man Up* I was dealing with two parallel worlds which fascinate me: soccer and pop music. I was inspired by the suicide of Agostino Di Bartolomei, a soccer star for Roma. And by some Italian singers who are living a very bizarre existence. The theme of the double probably came from my passion for Krzysztof Kieslowski's *The Double Life of Véronique*, without forgetting Michelangelo Antonioni's *The Passenger*.' In the 1980s, two characters bearing the same name, Antonio Pisapia – very commonplace

in Naples – a successful soccer star and a famous singer (based on Franco Califano's controversial figure), both find themselves in trouble. The former is fired, while the latter's status disappears and he descends into cocain addiction. Andrea Renzi is convincing as the sportsman too smart for his milieu, while his mirror image, played by Toni Servillo, gives a moving, bittersweet portrait of the falling minstrel. With the film, a perfect partnership was initiated: Servillo and Sorrentino. The odorous, lips-licking finale, in which Antonio the singer-gourmet smilingly cooks a fish treat in his jail cell, is one of those surprising twists of fate that have become a staple of Sorrentino's cinema. Acclaimed for its black humour and unconventional storytelling at Venice 2001 Mostra, competing in the 'Cinema of the Present' section, *One Man Up* refreshes and updates the 'Comedia alla'italiana'. 'Despite the melancholy nature of this story,' wrote David Rooney, 'the film maintains a tone that is sober and reflective without becoming maudlin, making original observations about the nature of celebrity and success, ambition and failure.' Sorrentino was voted best debutant director of the year at the Nastri d'Argento national awards.

Sorrentino spent a year travelling with the film to festivals around the globe: 'Staying in so many hotels, and spending lots of time at the bar, I was stunned to see practically the same businessmen, from Stockholm to São Paulo, hiding their unknown, mysterious backgrounds … I wanted to create a character for Servillo without limiting him, since he can

The Consequences of Love

do anything extra well. It's a kind of game – to invent things that he will be able to perform. I wrote the script in one week – I am usually a fast writer.' With *The Consequences of Love* (*Le conseguenze dell'amore*, 2004) Sorrentino peels away, layer by layer, the innermost secrets of an apparently wealthy financier staying in an anonymous Swiss hotel opposite a bank. The protagonist's philosophical voiceover further camouflages the fact that he is merely a low-level mafia accountant. As Titta Di Gerolamo (Servillo) avows, 'the bravest gesture of my life' – daring to sit at the counter, watching an enchantingly sexy hotel barmaid (Olivia Magnani) – is the beginning of his desertion of routine. Servillo's gloomy repression is an achievement equal to Alec Guinness's colonels and clerks. 'I want you to be steadfast and unbreakable,' Sorrentino instructed the actor. Several plotlines occupy the labyrinthine narration, populated by chance meetings, memories of youth and a terrifying mafia-trial climax, shot in a tour de force *plan-séquence*. Luca Bigazzi, a resourceful director of photography who had worked for Mario Martone, Gianni Amelio and Michele Placido, pushed Sorrentino to purify his baroque visual style. 'Dino Risi, Mario Monicelli and Ettore Scola are the comedy masters I am most fond of,' claimed Sorrentino. *The Consequences of Love* echoes particularly Scola's *The Most Beautiful Evening of My Life* (*La più bella serata della mia vita*, 1972), a sombre Friedrich Dürremmatt adaptation, and some of Dino Risi's merciless *I mostri* (1963). Raffaele Pisu and Angela Goodwin, playing the old couple

who finally will inherit the mafia money, are character actors from another era. Their archaic behaviour is chiselled by an admiring Sorrentino. Veteran critic Tullio Kezich wrote that 'Sorrentino's film is all murmurs and moans; even gunshots sound silenced'. Indigo Film produced the movie for €2 million, supported by Domenico Procacci's trendsetting multimedia factory, Fandango. It was critically lauded at Cannes and as a result was sold to territories around the world. 'Servillo deserved the Best Actor award,' said French reviewer Philippe Rouyer. It did receive five David di Donatello prizes, plus three Nastri d'Argento national awards. Young urban audiences found Sorrentino's style hip and hyper-real; his taste for abrasive rock soundtracks made them define him as 'our Italian Tarantino'. University film students soon began devoting their doctoral dissertations to Sorrentino's style of cinema. The literate Neapolitan writer-director's growing ambitions put him in the same class as off-beat contemporary novelists such as Sicilian Leonardo Sciascia.

The Consequences of Love

In 2004, Sorrentino directed a TV adaptation of *Saturday, Sunday and Monday* (*Sabato, domenica e lunedì*), a 1959 Eduardo De Filippo play very successfully staged for six months by Toni Servillo, who also starred in it. More than a kindly gesture by Sorrentino to his on-screen collaborator, it was a tribute to De Filippo, post-war Italian theatre's forefather and Naples' finest poet. 'I made it as a real movie, shot by shot, not simply recording the performance. It was not so easy since there were always over a dozen actors playing together,' commented Sorrentino. A witty conversation piece, it revolves around a family unsettled by the need to move on from the traditions they had adhered to during Italy's boom period. The audience, who are never seen, are important over the play's three acts, in the way the cast react to them.

The Family Friend

Sorrentino's third feature, *The Family Friend* (*L'amico di famiglia*, 2006), was budgeted at €3 million and was once again selected for competition at Cannes. However, the critical response was uneven, if not completely negative. Sorrentino stated, '*The Family Friend* was inspired by an old idea – to make a comedy about the ugliest, most socially dangerous person, a usurer. I wrote it thinking about Giacomo Rizzo.' Rizzo, a 68-year-old supporting actor, who had worked with Pier Paolo Pasolini and Bernardo Bertolucci as well as in scores of cheap quickies, projected a creepy persona ideal for the libidinous freak Sorrentino had in mind. However. his provincial Shylock, involved in cheating in order to deflower a gorgeous blonde (Laura Chiatti) before her marriage, is never truly able to convey that appealing force of evil so typical of Alberto Sordi or Ugo Tognazzi at their peak. But Sorrentino does have fun with his character, contriving a series of gags around the sexual rise and fall of his Beast. The Mussolini-built town of Sabaudia, with its fake Greek and Latin temples, provides a clean, abstract look for the dirty parable on a rotten, post-industrial society. Jonathan

Romney in his review wrote that 'for many viewers *The Family Friend* will register as one long succession of disjointed eccentricities'. Jay Weissberg said that 'unlike the fine-tuned, icy calibration of *The Consequences of Love*, here Sorrentino seems unwilling, or uncertain, how to call it a day'. Unsatisfied by the rushed 110-minute version he created for Cannes and taking on board some of his critics' advice, Sorrentino took another six months to re-edit the film. Finally released in a 99-minute cut, it presents a slightly less unhappy ending for his unrepentant brute. But some doubts still lingered: 'I think I made some mistakes with this movie. Too many visuals and not enough content, I am afraid. Today, I would not do it again!'

His manic obsession with Christian Democrat leviathan Giulio Andreotti resurfaced, not by chance, after Sorrentino played a funny cameo – alongside other top Italian film directors – in Nanni Moretti's *The Caiman* (*Il caimano*, 2006). This powerful political satire attempted to explain why, in Italy, nobody was able to get financing to make a feature film about Silvio Berlusconi. In fact, Moretti's crusade only dared to investigate a few facets of his target. 'My Andreotti project was a very old one,' says Sorrentino, 'but I had always censored myself, thinking that it would be impossible to make. I was enormously impressed by Andreotti's Curial dimension, by his Roman cynicism, and generally by the links between Vatican and politics. He was a good friend of late Roman superstar Alberto Sordi, and he even played himself in Sordi's hit comedy *The Cab Driver* (*Il tassinaro*, 1983). For decades they were rated the two most popular VIPs of our country. Andreotti is a very complex character, with a lot of faces. I tried to show all the positive and negative ones that I was aware of.' As an epigraph, Sorrentino quoted the leader's mother, Rosa Andreotti: 'If you have nothing good to say about somebody, don't talk about him.' *The Spectacular Life of Giulio Andreotti*, the subtitle of *Il divo*, whose meaning derives from ancient Rome (e.g. 'Divus Iulius [Caesar]') and which has been frequently – and without irony – accorded to Andreotti, is another bold statement from the director. He disturbs us with a bloody prologue of 'illustrious corpses'. Journalist Mino Pecorelli, bank manager Giorgio Ambrosoli, general Carlo Alberto Dalla Chiesa, bank manager Roberto Calvi, bank manager Michele Sindona and Christian Democrat prime minister Aldo Moro all died under mysterious circumstances, all linked to Andreotti. 'I was accused of everything,' the character avows in the film, 'excepting the Punic Wars.'

We witness the birth of Andreotti's seventh government in spring 1991 and his 1993–2003 Palermo trial where he was accused of supporting the Sicilian mafia and its 'boss of bosses', Totò Riina. Andreotti's entourage, Paolo Cirino Pomicino, Salvo Lima (later killed by the mafia himself), Vittorio Sbardella and Franco Evangelisti, are portrayed by a collection of comic actors cavorting like inebriated despots, accompanied on the soundtrack by a hellish electronic score. They would like to be cleverer than their 'Godfather', but Andreotti, thanks to Servillo's unflinching perfomance, always has the last word; and the last *bon mot*, because the real Andreotti is a goldmine of one-liners and aphorisms. Veteran comedian Flavio Bucci, who plays Evangelisti, was discovered in 1971 by impious political filmmaker, Elio Petri. *Il divo* steals some of Petri screenwriter Ugo Pirro's aggressive wit. Sorrentino even asked Francesco Rosi for his advice while he was editing the film. He is an admirer of Rosi's masterful *Illustrious*

Il divo

Corpses (*Cadaveri eccellenti*, 1976), part of the director's exploration into the uses and abuses of absolute power. (Interestingly, Servillo has acknowledged that Gian Maria Volontè's performance in Rosi's *Lucky Luciano* (1993) was a model for his interpretation of Andreotti.)

Compared with his predecessors, Sorrentino is less interested in redeeming the wrongdoings of his character or presenting an ideological argument to his audience. This is particularly clear in the scene where experienced leftist journalist and *Repubblica* founder, Eugenio Scalfari, played by Giulio Bosetti, interviews his 'enemy'. He launches an articulates attack on the power that Andreotti wields. A magnificent monologue, elegantly written and delivered, also reveals the journalist's old-fashioned idealism. He is easily rebuffed by the down-to-earth politician. Sorrentino leaves it to the audience to decide who is winning the sparring match.

Sorrentino does not cover the whole of Andreotti's life, nor certain well-known episodes, such as his condemnation and harsh censorship of the Neorealist movement, when he said that 'dirty laundry should be washed at home, not shown abroad'. Revisionist historians are trying to deny these words were ever spoken, whereas a few contemporary politicians have used exactly the same approach to condemn *Il divo*.

The film cost €4.3 million. One third was invested by Parco, an advertising agency that had hired Sorrentino to shoot a series of car commercials. Jay Weissberg called it 'an intensely political film so wildly inventive and witty that it will become a touchstone for years to come'. According to Mary Corliss, 'This is a film of great visual energy about an essentially static figure ... As incarnated by Toni Servillo, Andreotti has the stiff posture of Richard Nixon, but a more imperial menace.'

Months after he received the Cannes Jury Prize, Sorrentino commented, 'I was very,

Il divo

very happy about the reactions to *Il divo*. Initially I was afraid that such a story would be considered too Italian, but the Cannes jury as well as the foreign press have understood that power's strategies and weaknesses are universal. To Sean Penn, for instance, my Andreotti portrait reminded him of Henry Kissinger. Following an initial outburst of rage, Andreotti himself had to admit that my movie is "beautiful", and that I was right about his

private life – things I had mostly invented myself, lacking any concrete sources.'

The hug between Paolo Sorrentino and Matteo Garrone, minutes after they had won their awards at Cannes, was an historic event for Italian cinema. Politically engaged filmmaking of the highest quality, originality and impact, is back to stay, they exclaimed. Many issues in the film are still being debated and will probably continue to be. One can only hope that other *divi* directors will soon follow in Sorrentino's footsteps.

LORENZO CODELLI is on the board of Cineteca del Friuli, a Cannes Film Festival adviser and a regular contributor to *Positif* and other cinema-related publications.

Paolo Sorrentino filmography

[feature-film directing credits only]

2001
L'UOMO IN PIÙ (One Man Up)
Script: Paolo Sorrentino.
Photography: Pasquale Mari.
Production Design: Lino Fiorito.
Editing: Giogiò Franchini. *Players:*
Andrea Renzi (Antonio Pisapia),
Toni Servillo (Tony Pisapia), *Ninni*
Bruschetta (Genny), *Peppe Lanzetta*
(Salvatore), *Angela Goodwin* (Tony's
mother), *Nello Mascia* (Molosso),
Italo Celoro (Trainer), *Stefania*
Barca (Monica), *Clotilde Sabatino*
(Vanna). *Produced by Kermit Smith,*
Nicola Giuliano, Francesca Cima
and Angelo Curti. 97 mins

2004
LE CONSEGUENZE
DELL'AMORE
(The Consequences of Love)
Script: Paolo Sorrentino.
Photography: Luca Bigazzi.

Production Design: Lino Fiorito.
Editing: Giogiò Franchini. *Players:*
Toni Servillo (Titta Di Gerolamo),
Adriano Giannini (Valerio), *Olivia*
Magnani (Sofia), *Angela Goodwin*
(Isabella), *Raffaele Pisu* (Carlo),
Giselda Volodi (waitress), *Antonio*
Ballerio (bank manager). *Produced*
by Domenico Procacci, Nicola
Giuliano, Francesca Cima and
Angelo Curti. 99 mins

2006
L'AMICO DI FAMIGLIA
(The Family Friend)
Script: Paolo Sorrentino.
Photography: Luca Bigazzi.
Production Design: Lino Fiorito.
Editing: Giogiò Franchini. *Players:*
Giacomo Rizzo (Geremia), *Laura*
Chiatti (Rosalba), *Fabrizio*
Bentivoglio (Gino), *Luigi Angelillo*
(Saverio), *Clara Bindi* (Geremia's
mother), *Marco Giallini* (Attanasio),
Lorenzo Gioielli (Montanaro),
Giorgio Colangeli (Massa). *Produced*
by Domenico Procacci, Nicola

Giuliano, Francesca Cima and Fabio
Conversi. 99 mins

2008
IL DIVO
Script: Paolo Sorrentino.
Photography: Luca Bigazzi.
Production Design: Lino Fiorito.
Editing: Cristiano Travaglioli.
Players: Toni Servillo (Giulio
Andreotti), *Anna Bonaiuto* (Livia
Andreotti), *Piera Degli Esposti*
(Mrs. Enza), *Giulio Bosetti* (Eugenio
Scalfari), *Paolo Graziosi* (Aldo
Moro), *Flavio Bucci* (Franco
Evangelisti), *Carlo Buccirosso* (Paolo
Cirino Pomicino), *Giorgio Colangeli*
(Salvo Lima), *Lorenzo Gioielli*
(Mino Pecorelli), *Massimo Popolizio*
(Vittorio Sbardella), *Gianfelice*
Imparato (Vincenzo Scotti).
Produced by Nicola Giuliano,
Francesca Cima, Andrea Occhipinti,
Maurizio Coppolecchia, Fabio
Conversi and Stefano Bonfanti.
110 mins

Agnès Varda by Chris Darke

Never meet your heroes, they say. Not unless you're prepared to be disappointed. I beg to differ. A few years ago, I had the chance to meet someone I would happily describe as a cultural heroine and ever since she has never let me down – either in person, or in her work. In September 2000, I wandered into a Paris cinema to reacquaint myself with the films of Agnès Varda, a director whose work I had lost sight of since the late 1980s when, as a student in London, I had been beguiled by her wintry, lost-girl tale, *Vagabond* (*Sans toit ni loi*, 1985). On that September afternoon in Paris, I went to see Varda's latest film, on the strength of her name alone.

The Gleaners and I (*Les Glaneurs et la Glaneuse*, 2000) saw Varda taking to the autoroute to document the twentieth century reality of the verb 'glaner' (meaning 'to glean'). In her company, we encounter the descendants of those who, in the past, would gather leftovers after a harvest. Varda's gallery of present-day gleaners ranged from the rural and urban poor, living off what consumer society has discarded, to artists who find material for their work in scrap. *The Gleaners and I* anticipated the popular interest in big-screen documentaries that has characterised this decade's cinema. But another aspect was equally significant, best encapsulated by those moments in the film showing the diminutive septuagenarian bowling around with a mini-DV camera in hand. 'My working with digital cameras always amuses people,' she observed, 'there goes grandma with her DV!' Her embrace of new filmmaking technologies suited the film's subject matter, facilitating the access and intimacy of address that lends the film its directness and liberty of tone.

The Gleaners and I captivated me. I emerged from the cinema determined to write about it. Back in London, I was astonished to discover that there were no plans to distribute the film. So I made some calls and pitched hard to the programmers of a recently opened art cinema where I was sure it would find an audience. My proselytising paid off. Not only did I meet the filmmaker, but in January 2001 *The Gleaners and I* opened in London at the Lux Cinema, accompanied by a mini-retrospective of Varda's work, which she introduced to full houses. Dressed in chic, hippy-esque attire and fluent in English, she had the audience eating out of her hand. Nobody doubted they were in the presence of a force of nature. I learned that my experience with *The Gleaners and I* was by no means unique. So strong was the film's word-of-mouth that cinemathèques and art houses around the world requested copies. Varda was overwhelmed by the reaction. 'I've never in my entire career felt that people have loved a film of mine as much as this one,' she admitted. 'The numbers of people who've seen it and talked about it – they were our publicity because documentaries can't afford much advertising.' The success of the film's London release convinced the British Film Institute to put *The Gleaners and I* into regional circulation and it went on to harvest laurels worldwide, including the European Film Academy Award for Best Documentary in 2000, as well as several prestigious American Film Critics' awards.

Since *The Gleaners and I*, I've been a devotee; keenly awaiting Varda's new work, checking in with her when I'm in Paris and catching up with her back catalogue – something made easier since 2002, thanks to regular DVD editions released by her production company, Ciné-Tamaris. I relate these anecdotes to emphasise an aspect of her films' appeal – their emphatically first-person feel and the sense they give of Varda herself communicating with the viewer.

The Beaches of Agnès

Varda turned eighty this year and released *The Beaches of Agnès* (*Les Plages d'Agnès*, 2008), which she claims will be her last feature film. When I visited her in Paris in April 2008, she was deep in the editing stage. In a converted hardware store just across from her home on the rue Daguerre, she declared herself to be at a loss as to how to arrange her material. As well as featuring new footage, *The Beaches of Agnès* would also comprise excerpts from her previous films, unseen home-movies, paintings and photographs. With two other editors working alongside her, and another shoot for the film looming, Varda fretted about having

The Beaches of Agnès

everything pulled together in time for the premiere at the Venice Film Festival, in August. 'I invented the film day by day,' she said. 'I beat my own record in editing time.'

A fascinating and engaging self-portrait, *The Beaches of Agnès* reveals just how closely interwoven Varda's life and art have been since her cinematic debut over fifty years ago. The film covers a lot of ground – from her wartime childhood to art-student youth and her early career as a photographer working with the prestigious Théâtre National Populaire (TNP); her days as the sole woman filmmaker of the French New Wave; a sojourn in heady late-1960s Los Angeles; feminist agitation in 1970s France; marriage to fellow New Waver Jacques Demy, motherhood and loss (Demy died of AIDS in 1990); and her highly successful move into art installations, having decided to stop making fictional features in 1994. The many strands of her ciné-memoire are held together by the conceit of tying stories to particular places, namely five beaches that have been recurring touchstones throughout her life. Or, rather, four real beaches and one specially constructed for the film in the rue Daguerre, her home and workplace since the late 1950s (and a neat reversal of the old May '68 slogan 'sous les pavés, la plage!' – 'beneath the street, the beach!')

One of the beaches Varda revisits in the film was the location for her first venture in cinema, *La Pointe Courte*, made in 1954 when she was 25 years old. She shot it in the fishing neighbourhood of Sète, on the western Mediterranean coast of France, an area dear to her since childhood and where her family took refuge from her native Belgium after the outbreak of the Second World War. Despite having seen few films and knowing little about filmmaking, Varda forged ahead with her project in which the fictional story of an unhappy young couple intermingles with the real lives and locales of the fishing villages she knew intimately.

La Pointe Courte

La Pointe Courte was auspicious for a number of reasons. Not only did it mark two cinematic debuts – Varda's and that of her male lead, Philippe Noiret, then a young actor at the TNP who would become one of French cinema's best-loved screen performers – the film also pre-dated the New Wave by five years. Low-budget films made with small crews and expressing 'personal' themes were not yet a feature of French auteur cinema. With its black and white cinematography and antique aspect ratio (1.33:1), its combination of deliberate, mannered acting and stylised compositions with almost neo-realist attention to the details of everyday life, *La Pointe Courte* might today seem a cinematic curio, suspended between the Parisian bohemianism of Cocteau and the New Wave that was soon to break. Varda was ahead of her time, for which she would earn the sobriquet of 'Grandmother of the New Wave'. Or, as she tells it: 'When I was thirty, there was a magazine article with a picture of me and the caption read "The Ancestor of the New Wave". I thought "An ancestor at thirty? I won't get older than that! Great!"'

The film brought Varda into contact with New Wave figures: Alain Resnais was its editor and the critic André Bazin, co-founder of *Cahiers du cinéma*, helped to get the film shown 'off-festival' at Cannes. Despite not being publicly screened until two years later, *La Pointe Courte* established Varda and allowed her to follow up with a series of shorter films. Producers Pierre Braunberger and Anatole Dauman, key figures behind the success of New Wave films, commissioned her to make a pair of shorts for the French Tourism Office: a playful tour of chateaux in the Loire valley in *Ô saisons, ô chateaux* (1957) and a portrait of the French Riviera in *Du côté de la Côte* (1958). During the same period, she also made the more experimental personal short, *L'Opéra Mouffe* (1958), described as a 'notebook filmed by a pregnant woman' featuring documentary footage of her then-neighbourhood of rue Mouffetard. All three works were recently re-released in an indispensable DVD anthology of Varda's short films (*Varda Tous Courts*, Ciné-Tamaris, 2007).

Varda's aptitude for combining commissions with more personal projects was thus established early on and has continued ever since. She has always ranged across a variety of formats; in her fifty-year career she has made only 13 long-form fiction films and more than twice that number of documentaries, essay-films and shorts. A necessary

L'Opéra Mouffe

diversification for the jobbing filmmaker, perhaps, but in Varda's case undertaken within the context of thoroughgoing independence. Since *La Pointe Courte*, she has maintained Ciné Tamaris, which has allowed her to work from her Paris home-cum-atelier. 'I like to work in this artisan way,' she has explained. 'I'll do the editing or make up my press dossiers, go out to take some shots, come back and cook. I've always worked like that. The editing room, the production quarters and the house form the three parts of my domestic set-up. When the kids were little, Jacques also worked like that. So for me, a film is a slice of life, it's not a production.'

Cléo From 5 to 7

In summer 1961, Varda – now the mother of a three-year-old daughter – strayed no further than the *arrondissements* of the Left Bank to shoot *Cléo de 5 à 7* (*Cléo From 5 to 7*). With its luminous black and white cinematography (courtesy of Jean Rabier), romantic Michel Legrand score, bittersweet emotional tone (the story concerns the fortunes of Cléo, played by the glamorous Corinne Marchand, a singer threatened by serious illness), and its

Paris settings firmly in focus throughout, *Cléo From 5 to 7* remains one of the best-loved and most representative of New Wave films. Concentrating on an hour and a half in Cléo's life, as she awaits her medical diagnosis, the film follows her wanderings through the city in 'real time'. Varda has described the film as 'the portrait of a woman painted onto a documentary about Paris'. It is also features a short silent-film skit, starring the 'first couple' of the New Wave, Godard and Anna Karina (Varda had been the photographer at their wedding earlier that year). *Cléo From 5 to 7* was selected for Cannes in 1962 and, as Varda recalls, 'it was welcomed with great warmth. Even though we didn't win anything it was a great launching pad. The film was sold to thirty countries thanks to Cannes and it started its extraordinary life. The rights are regularly re-sold in Japan and the US for the cinema, TV or DVDs. It's incredible, after more than forty years.'

Varda made two more features in France during the 1960s before relocating *en famille* to Los Angeles for several years, where Demy had a contract to make a film with Columbia (*Model Shop*, 1969). I've only seen one of these, *Happiness* (*Le Bonheur*, 1964). Actually, that's not strictly true. I've also seen bits of *The Creatures* (*Les Créatures*, 1966), but these were the remains of the positive filmstrip that Varda had salvaged and draped over a 25-metre-square steel frame to create an installation for her first large-scale gallery show in 2006. Entitled *Ma cabane de l'échec*, the work was so named because of the commercial failure (échec) of *The Creatures*, despite the film's combined star power of Catherine Deneuve and Michel Piccoli. *Happiness* won prestigious awards, including the Golden Bear at the Berlin Film Festival in 1965, and was widely distributed. But it was received as a shocking, divisive film and was forbidden to audiences below 18 years old in France. One reviewer wrote of how 'with ravishing Impressionist imagery, Varda describes the appalling destruction of a couple'. Telling the story of a love triangle

Happiness

in which a family happily reconstitutes itself around the husband's mistress after his wife commits suicide, it remains hard to read. Is it, as some claimed, a pre-'68 plea for sexual freedom? Or a feminist assault on the institution of marriage? Watching it today, one cannot help but detect beneath its alluringly coloured surface the subversive spirit of one of Varda's favourite filmmakers; *Happiness* would have pleased Buñuel.

One of the settings that I would have liked *The Beaches of Agnès* to have lingered on for longer was that of Varda's time in Los Angeles. For while we hear about the documentaries she shot there (*Oncle Yanco*, 1967; *Black Panthers*, 1968) and the feature made independently with assorted 'superstars' on loan from Andy Warhol's Factory (*Lion's Love and Lies*, 1969), in the background is the story of her aborted project with a Hollywood major. The young Harrison Ford was cast in the lead (and turns up briefly in *The Beaches of Agnès*) but the film was nixed, it seems, by Varda's brush-off of a patronising studio executive. I think we should be told more. Perhaps we will in the five-part TV version of *The Beaches of Agnès* which is due to be aired in 2010 by ARTE and will be twice as long as the film version.

One of the most productive aspects of Varda's period in the US was her involvement with the civil rights movement, as attested by the vibrant *vérité* footage of a pro-Huey Newton rally she shot for *Black Panthers*, but also in the effect it had upon her involvement in feminist activism when she returned to France

in the early 1970s, which manifested in her quasi-musical feature *One Sings, the Other Doesn't* (*L'une chante, l'autre pas*, 1977), whose story of the intertwined lives of two women aimed to place feminist issues around reproductive rights before a mass audience.

Continuing to alternate documentaries, shorts and features throughout the 1980s, Varda delivered one of her finest films, *Vagabond*. Having won the Golden Lion at the 1985 Venice Film Festival, *Vagabond* went on to international success and established the 17-year-old Sandrine Bonnaire as one of the most charismatic French actresses of the time. Predating the focus on poverty that Varda would return to in a very different mode with *The Gleaners and I*, *Vagabond* had Bonnaire playing Mona, a young female vagrant whose death the film investigates. Like *Cléo From 5 to 7*, the film is structured around a central female character but one who remains enigmatic and defiantly unlovable. And, like many of her films, Varda imbues *Vagabond* with a tremendously evocative sense of place, in this case the rugged and inhospitable landscapes of the Languedoc region.

Vagabond

The death of Jacques Demy in 1990 resulted in Varda devoting much of the remaining decade to remembering her husband and partner-in-cinema in three films. Two of these were documentaries: *The Young Girls at 25* (*Les Demoiselles ont eu 25 ans*, 1992) revisiting Demy's 1966 film *Les Demoiselles de Rochefort* and *The World of Jacques Demy* (*L'Univers de Jacques Demy*, 1995). *Jacquot*

Jacquot de Nantes

de Nantes (1991) was perhaps the most heartfelt tribute. Combining vivid fictional reconstructions of Demy's childhood with documentary footage, it anticipates some of the qualities of *The Beaches of Agnès*: a certain nostalgic melancholy and a concern with mortality that marks Varda's work in the subsequent decade.

Since bowing out of making feature-length fictions following the commercial failure of her film celebrating the centenary of cinema, *The Hundred and One Nights of Simon Cinema* (*Les Cent et une nuits de Simon Cinéma*, 1994), Varda's long-practised talent for diversification has found new outlets. Whether in the splendid DVDs of her and Demy's films produced by Ciné Tamaris, with their lavish self-made extras (which she dubs 'boni', the plural of 'bonus'), or in her highly praised installation work, not to mention the success of *The Gleaners and I*, Varda has reinvented herself while remaining a unique and idiosyncratic filmmaker. The only comparable

models are her New Wave contemporaries, Jean-Luc Godard and Chris Marker, with whom she shares the same hunger for experimentation, dogged independence and seemingly inexhaustible creativity.

Since the beginning of her career, roughly one film per decade has had the effect of bringing – or returning – Varda to international attention. *Cléo From 5 to 7* did so in the 1960s; *One Sings, the Other Doesn't* in the 1970s; *Vagabond* in the 1980s; *Jacquot de Nantes* in the 1990s, and *The Gleaners and I* in the first decade of the twenty-first century. Not a bad tally, all things considered. But when you start to explore everything Varda has achieved in between those moments of high visibility – the shorts, documentaries, photography, installations, DVDs – only then do you realise that she's more than just a filmmaker, but a true artist with a command of various forms and media. And, what's more, with a vision. In short, what is revealed is a remarkable body of work by a truly remarkable woman.

When I last saw her, Varda was introducing *The Beaches of Agnès* to a full house at the 2008 London Film Festival. The warmth that was palpable among the audience, who were referring to her by her first name after the screening, prompted me to ask myself a question. Would British distributors make the same mistake with this film as they did with *The Gleaners and I*? Maybe it's time to make a few calls.

CHRIS DARKE is a writer and film critic based in London. His work has appeared in newspapers and magazines including *Sight and Sound*, *Film Comment*, *Cahiers du cinéma* and the *Independent*. He is the author of *Light Readings: Film Criticism and Screen Arts* (2000); a monograph on Godard's *Alphaville* (2005) and co-author of *Cannes: Inside the World's Premier Film Festival* (2007).

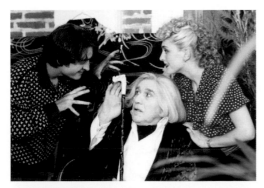

The Hundred and One Nights of Simon Cinema

Agnès Varda filmography

[documentary and feature-film directing credits only]

1954
LA POINTE COURTE
Script: *Agnès Varda. Photography: Paul Soulignac, Louis Stein. Editing: Alain Resnais. Players: Silvia Monfort* (Elle), *Philippe Noiret* (Lui). *86 mins*

1962
CLÉO DE 5 À 7 (Cleo from 5 to 7)
Script: *Agnès Varda. Photography: Paul Bonis, Alain Levent, Jean Rabier. Production Design: Jean-François Adam, Bernard Evein, Edith Tertza. Editing: Pascale Laverrière, Janine Verneau. Players: Corinne Marchand* (Florence, 'Cléo Victoire'), *Antoine Bourseiller* (Antoine), *Dominique Davray* (Angèle), *Dorothée Blank* (Dorothée), *Michel Legrand* (Bob, the pianist), *José Luis de Villalonga* (the lover), *Loye Payen* (Irma, the tarot reader), *Lucienne Marchand* (the taxi driver), *Serge Korber* (the lyricist), *Robert Postec* (Docteur Valineau). *Produced by Georges de Beauregard, Carlo Ponti. 90 mins*

1966
LES CRÉATURES (The Creatures)
Script: *Agnès Varda. Photography:*

Willy Kurant, William Lubtchansky, Jean Orjollet. Production Design: Jean Didenot. Editing: Janine Verneau. Players: Catherine Deneuve (Mylène), *Michel Piccoli* (Edgar Piccoli), *Eva Dahlbeck* (Michele Quellec), *Marie-France Mignal* (Viviane Quellec), *Britta Pettersson* (Lucie de Montyon), *Ursula Kubler* (Vamp), *Jeanne Allard* (Henriette), *Joëlle Gozzi* (Suzon), *Bernard La Jarrige* (Doctor Desteau), *Lucien Bodard* (Monsieur Ducasse), *Pierre Danny* (Max Picot), *Louis Falavigna* (Pierre Roland), *Nino Castelnuovo* (Jean Modet). *Produced by Mag Bodard. 92 mins*

1969
LIONS LOVE
Script: *Agnès Varda. Photography: Stevan Larner. Editing: Robert Dalva. Players: Peter Bogdanovich, Richard Bright, Carlos Clarens, Shirley Clarke, Eddie Constantine, Steve Kemis, Max Laemmle, Hal Landers, Jim Morrison, Peter Rafelson, Agnès Varda, Viva. Produced by Agnès Varda. 110 mins*

1976
DAGUERRÉOTYPES
Script: *Agnès Varda. Photography: Nurit Aviv, William Lubtchansky. Editing: Andrée Choty, Gordon Swire. Players: Rosalie Varda. 80 mins*

1977
L'UNE CHANTE, L'AUTRE PAS
(One Sings, the Other Doesn't)
Script: *Agnès Varda. Photography: Charles Van Damme. Production Design: Frankie D. Editing: Joële Van Effenterre. Players: Thérèse Liotard* (Suzanne Galibier), *Valérie Mairesse* (Pauline 'Pomme'), *Robert Dadiès* (Jérôme), *Mona Mairesse* (Pauline's mother), *Francis Lemaire* (Pauline's father), *Ali Raffi* (Darius), *Gisèle Halimi* (Gisèle Halimi), *Jean-Pierre Pellegri* (Doctor Pierre Aubanel), *Joëlle Papineau* (Joëlle), *Micou*

Papineau (Micou), *Doudou Greffier* (Doudou), *François Wertheimer* (François), *Mathieu Demy* (Zorro). *120 mins*

1981
MURS, MURS,
(Murals, Murals)
Script: *Agnès Varda. Photography: Nurit Aviv. Editing: Bob Gould, Sabine Mamou. Players: Juliet Berto* (the visitor). *81 mins*

1981
DOCUMENTEUR
Script: *Agnès Varda. Photography: Nurit Aviv, Affonso Beato, Bob Carr. Editing: Bob Gould, Sabine Mamou. Players: Sabine Mamou* (Emilie), *Mathieu Demy* (Martin), *Tina Odom* (Tina), *Lisa Blok-Linson* (Lisa), *Charles Southwood* (man in white room), *Chris Leplus* (the producer), *Fred Ricker* (Motel), *Delphine Seyrig* (narrator). *65 mins*

1985
SANS TOI NI LOI
(Vagabond)
Script: *Agnès Varda. Photography: Patrick Blossier. Editing: Patricia Mazuy, Agnès Varda. Players: Sandrine Bonnaire* (Mona Bergeron), *Setti Ramdane* (the Marroccan woman), *Francis Balchère* (the police officer), *Jean-Louis Perletti* (an other), *Urbain Causse* (a farmer), *Christophe Alcazar* (an other), *Dominique*

*Durand (a biker), Joël Fosse (Paulo),
Patrick Schmit (the truck driver).
Produced by Oury Milshtein.
105 mins*

**1987
KUNG-FU MASTER**
*Script: Agnès Varda, based on a
story by Jane Birkin. Photography:
Pierre-Laurent Chénieux. Editing:
Marie-Josée Audiard. Players: Jane
Birkin (Mary-Jane), Mathieu Demy
(Julien), Charlotte Gainsbourg
(Lucy), Lou Doillon (Lou), Eva
Simonet (the friend), Judy Campbell
(the mother). 80 mins*

**1988
JANE B. PAR AGNÈS V.
(Jane B. by Agnès V.)**
*Script: Agnès Varda. Photography:
Nurit Aviv, Pierre-Laurent Chénieux
Production Design: Olivier Radot.
Editing: Marie-Josée Audiard,
Agnès Varda. Players: Jane Birkin
(Calamity Jane / Claude Jade / Joan
Arc), Jean-Pierre Léaud (the lover),
Philippe Léotard (the painter), Alain
Souchon (the Verlaine reader), Serge
Gainsbourg (himself). 97 mins*

**1991
JACQUOT DE NANTES**
*Script: Agnès Varda, based on
the memoirs of Jacques Demy.
Photography: Patrick Blossier, Agnès
Godard, Georges Strouvé. Editing:
Marie-Josée Audiard. Players:*

*Philippe Maron (Jacquot 1),
Edouard Joubeaud (Jacquot 2),
Laurent Monnier (Jacquot 3),
Brigitte De Villepoix (Marilou, the
mother), Daniel Dublet (Raymond,
the father), Clément Delaroche
(Yvon 1), Rody Averty (Yvon 2).
118 mins*

**1995
LES CENT ET UNE NUITS DE
SIMON CINÉMA
(The Hundred and One Nights)**
*Script: Agnès Varda. Photography:
Eric Gautier. Editing: Hugues
Darmois. Players: Michel Piccoli
(Simon Cinéma), Marcello
Mastroianni (the Italian friend),
Henri Garcin (Firmin, the butler),
Julie Gayet (Camille Miralis),
Mathieu Demy (Camille 'Mica'),
Emmanuel Salinger (Vincent),
Anouk Aimée (Anouk). Produced by
Dominique Vignet. 101 mins*

**1995
L'UNIVERS DE JACQUES DEMY
(The Universe of Jacques Demy)**
*Script: Agnès Varda. Photography:
Stéphane Krausz, Peter Pilafian,
Georges Strouvé. Editing: Marie-
Josée Audiard. Players: Anouk
Aimée, Richard Berry, Nino
Castelnuovo, Danielle Darrieux,
Catherine Deneuve, Françoise
Fabian, Harrison Ford.
90 mins*

**2000
LES GLANEURS ET LA
GLANEUSE
(The Gleaners and I)**
*Script: Agnès Varda. Photography:
Didier Doussin, Stéphane Krausz,
Didier Rouget, Pascal Sautelet,
Agnès Varda. Editing: Laurent
Pineau, Agnès Varda. Players: Bodan
Litnanski, Agnès Varda. François
Wertheimer. Produced by Agnès
Varda. 82 mins*

**2002
LES GLANEURS ET LA
GLANEUSE...DEUX ANS APRÉS
(The Gleaners and I: Two Years
Later)**
*Script: Agnès Varda. Photography:
Stéphane Krausz, Agnès Varda.
Editing: Agnès Varda. Players:
Bodan Litnanski, Macha Makeïeff,
Agnès Varda, François Wertheimer.
Produced by Agnès Varda. 63 mins*

**2004
CINÉVARDAPHOTO**
*Script: Agnès Varda. Photography:
Per Olaf Csongova, Claire Duguet,
Jean-Yves Escoffier, John Holosk,
Rick Kearney, J. Marques, Pascal
Rabaud, Markus Seitz. Editing:
Marie-Josée Audiard, Hélène de
Luze, Jean-Baptiste Morin, Agnès
Varda, Janine Verneau. 96 mins*

**2006
QUELQUES VEUVES DE
NOIRMOUTIER**
*Script: Agnès Varda. Photography:
Eric Gautier. Editing: Jean-Baptiste
Morin, Agnès Varda. 69 mins*

**2007
LES PLAGES D'AGNÈS
(The Beaches of Agnès)**
*Script: Agnès Varda. Photography:
Hélène Louvart. Editing: Baptiste
Filloux, Jean-Baptiste Morin.
Players: Mathieu Demy, Agnès
Varda, Rosalie Varda. Produced by
Agnès Varda. 110 mins*

In Memoriam

YOUSSEF CHAHINE
1 January 1928 – 27 July 2008

Renowned as the pioneer of Egyptian Social Realism, Youssef Chahine was born in Alexandria. After attending the elite school, Victoria College, and studying acting at the Pasadena Playhouse in California, Chahine began his directorial career. His early films established his social-realist aesthetic and focused on issues of social injustice and oppression. The most famous of these works is his 1957 film, *Cairo Station* (*Bab el Hadid*), which starred Chahine as a crippled newspaper seller at Cairo's main railway station. Banned for twelve years, the feature was the first Egyptian film to create original characters rather than borrowing from Hollywood or canonical literary works.

With the arrival of Colonel Gamal Abdel Nasser's revolutionary regime, Chahine looked back to historical events to shed light on present political circumstances. However, in the 1960s, tired of the country's strict censorship, Chahine moved to Beirut, where he made films such as the musical *The Ring Seller* (*Biya el-Khwatim*, 1964). After Nasser complained about his relocation, Chahine returned to make films in Egypt. The censorship continued as filmmakers were forced to push Nasser's socialist and anti-Western views, but they also enjoyed large subsidies. Chahine continued to make films throughout his life, such as *Al-Mohager* (1994) and *Al-Massir* (1997). In 1997 he was awarded the Cannes Film Festival's 50th Anniversary Award. As his health worsened, his final film, *Chaos* (2008), was passed onto his disciple Khaled Youssef to complete.
– *Eleanor Mckeown*

MICHAEL CRICHTON
23 October 1942 – 4 November 2008

Author of *Jurassic Park* and creator of the television series *ER*, Michael Crichton had an outstanding ability to bring niche, scientific topics to the mass market. Born in Chicago, he spent his childhood in Roslyn, Long Island. It was during his time at Harvard Medical School that Crichton began to concentrate on fiction writing, producing eight novels under two pseudonyms. His 1968 sci-fi novel, *The Andromeda Strain*, and Robert Wise's hugely successful film adaptation (1971) first brought Crichton to public attention.

Indeed, Crichton's sparse prose style and linear plots led to many film adaptations, including *Terminal Man* (1974), *Rising Sun* (1992), *Sphere*

Youssef Chahine

Michael Crichton

(1998) and *Disclosure* (1994). It also sparked his own segue into screenplay writing and directing. His directorial debut, *Westworld* (1973), introduced the technology of CGI to the big screen and marked a run of directorial projects including *Coma* (1978), *The Great Train Robbery* (1975), *Looker* (1981), *Runaway* (1984) and *Physical Evidence* (1989).

The 1990s brought Crichton a new kind of stardom with Spielberg's adaptation of *Jurassic Park* (1993). The following year, *ER* debuted, which won Crichton an Emmy. Despite huge earnings, Crichton remained a driven and prolific writer throughout his life, once claiming to have as many as thirty plot ideas 'buzzing around' in his brain at any time. – *Eleanor Mckeown*

JULES DASSIN
18 December 1911 – 31 March 2008

A master of location filmmaking, Jules Dassin started out acting in theatre groups and creating radio plays. His writing skills took him to Hollywood, where he directed a few works for MGM before making his first personal feature film, *Brute Force* (1947), which starred a young Burt Lancaster. The following year, he directed *The Naked City*, an unusual experiment in American neo-realism, which followed an unknown cast on the streets of New York. Dassin made two more films, *Thieves' Highway* (1949) and the London-based *Night and the City* (1950), before being placed on Hollywood's anti-communist blacklist. He did not work again until relocating to France in 1955, when he directed the stylish heist film, *Rififi*. Having established himself in Europe, his next film, *He Who Must Die* (1957), brought him into contact with the actress and later Greek culture minister, Melina Mercouri. The couple married in 1966 and Dassin directed his wife in seven films, including the Academy Award-nominated *Never on Sunday* (1960). Dassin's later films were not able to match these early works and he stopped making films after *Circle of Two* (1980). After Mercouri's death in 1994, Dassin devoted himself to continuing her campaign for the return of the Elgin Marbles to Greece. – *Eleanor Mckeown*

ISAAC HAYES
20 August 1942 – 10 August 2008

Isaac Hayes re-entered the popular consciousness during the late 1990s as Chef, a lugubrious voice of calm amid the scatological foolery of the leads in the hit cartoon *South*

Isaac Hayes

Park and its 1999 feature-film spin-off. But it was during the 1970s that the soul icon and self-proclaimed 'saviour of Stax Records' made his most enduring contribution to the film world, writing a searing Academy Award-winning theme for the blaxploitation classic *Shaft* (1971), in which he also had a supporting role. Hayes followed it with the lead role in Jonathan Kaplan's *Truck Turner* (1974), for which he once again provided the soundtrack. As his musical output diminished during the 1980s, Hayes made further successful forays into Hollywood and off-Hollywood cinema, starring alongside Kurt Russell as the villain in John Carpenter's *Escape From New York* (1981), sending up his blaxploitation roots in Keenen Ivory Wayans' *I'm Gonna Git You, Sucka* (1988) and a charismatic turn as the narrator of *It Could Happen to You* (1994). – Benny Morgan

CHARLTON HESTON
4 October 1923 – 5 April 2008

Despite describing himself as 'shy, skinny, short and pimply' in his youth, Charlton Heston will be remembered as the quintessential Hollywood hero. Born in Michigan, Heston came from poor beginnings. After studying drama, his first big break came in the role of the ringmaster in Cecil B. DeMille's *The Greatest Show on Earth* (1952). Four years later, DeMille cast Heston as Moses in *The Ten Commandments* because of his physical likeness to Michelangelo's statue. The film defined Heston as Hollywood's primary choice for larger-than-life American heroes. In 1959, he was awarded an Academy Award for his starring role in the epic *Ben-Hur*. Looking back over these roles, Heston once said, 'I have played three presidents, three saints and two geniuses in my career. If that doesn't create an ego problem, nothing does.' Yet the performance that Heston held closest to his heart was that of the awkward, shy ranch hand in *Will Penny* (1967). Indeed, Heston liked to counter-balance heroic roles with more conflicted characters in films like *Touch of Evil* (1958) and *Soylent Green* (1973).

In later years, Heston concentrated on theatre work and his controversial position as president of the National Rifle Association. Unlike many of his peers, Heston was always vocal about his political beliefs, championing the Civil Rights Movement before switching his allegiance from the Democrats to the Republicans in the 1980s. – Eleanor Mckeown

KON ICHIKAWA
20 November 1915 – 13 February 2008

One of the key figures of post-war Japanese cinema, Kon Ichikawa was acclaimed in his home country long before an Academy Award nomination for *The Burmese Harp* (*Biruma no tategoto*, 1956) brought him to the attention of the wider world and saw him mentioned by Western critics in the same breath as the great triumvirate of Kurosawa, Ozu and Mizoguchi. Ichikawa began his career as an animator in Kyoto, before making a series of successful screwball comedies whose dark undertones anticipate the bleakness of his mature work. Japan's experiences during the Second World War, most particularly the cataclysms of Hiroshima and Nagasaki, inform the brutalised perspective of the central characters in *Conflagration* (*Enjo*, 1958), which was adapted

Charlton Heston

Kon Ichikawa

from a novel by Yukio Mishima, and *Fire on the Plain* (*Nobi*, 1959).

By the 1960s, Ichikawa's flair for allegory had secured him an international reputation as an eloquent anti-war filmmaker. It speaks volumes about his versatility as a director, then, that the films for which he is most remembered today, the ornate kabuki melodrama *An Actor's Revenge* (*Yukinojo henge*, 1963) and the documentary *Tokyo Olympiad* (*Tokyo Orinpikku*, 1965), represent distinguished anomalies in a career marked by intense engagement with the limits of human endurance and suffering. – *Benny Morgan*

ANTHONY MINGHELLA
6 January 1954 – 18 March 2008

Despite directing only six feature films, Anthony Minghella made a great impact on contemporary cinema as filmmaker, writer, producer and head of the British Film Institute. Born on the Isle of Wight in 1954, Minghella started out as a writer of radio plays and television programmes. His first feature film, *Truly Madly Deeply* (1990), a love story exploring loss and bereavement, was released to critical acclaim. After receiving a BAFTA for its screenplay, Minghella made his first foray into Hollywood with *Mr Wonderful* (1993) starring Matt Dillon. In 1996, the Second World War epic *The English Patient*, considered to be Minghella's crowning achievement, won

nine Academy Awards. Two successful and prestigious literary adaptations followed with Patricia Highsmith's *The Talented Mr Ripley* (1999) and Charles Frazier's *Cold Mountain* (2003). Whilst *The Talented Mr Ripley* was warmly received, the icy landscape featured in *Cold Mountain* was reflected in the critical response to it.

Minghella was appointed head of the BFI in 2003. He directed an English National Opera production of *Madam Butterfly* and a London-based feature film *Breaking and Entering* (2006). Before his death, he had completed work on a feature-length television pilot episode of *The No. 1 Ladies' Detective Agency*.
– *Eleanor Mckeown*

PAUL NEWMAN
26 January 1925 – 26 September 2008

More than just a handsome, blue-eyed heartthrob, Paul Leonard Newman established himself as a true Hollywood great and a humble but talented actor who, although often typecast, was an illuminating presence on

Paul Newman

screen. He worked with legendary directors, from Alfred Hitchcock and John Huston to Robert Altman and Martin Scorsese, but seemed most comfortable when playing roguish characters in crowd-pleasers such as *The Hustler* (1961), *Cool Hand Luke* (1967) and *The Sting* (1973). He was nominated for an Academy Award ten times, finally winning one for his second outing as Fast Eddie Felson in *The Color of Money* (1987), but arguably his most popular role was that of the iconic western anti-hero in *Butch Cassidy and the Sundance Kid* (1969).

Newman also worked behind the camera and earned himself acclaim (but minimal public interest) producing and directing *Rachel, Rachel* (1968), the first of six films starring his wife Joanne Woodward. Repeatedly asked how he sustained his fifty-year marriage to Woodward, he famously replied, 'Why fool around with hamburger when you have steak at home?' Not one to rest on his laurels, during his film career Newman often returned to Broadway, where he was first discovered by Warner Bros. back in 1953, and most recently earned a Tony nomination for *Our Town* in 2003. At 77 Newman was convinced by Sam Mendes to return to the screen as a mob boss in *Road to Perdition* (2002). – *Nadia Attia*

SYDNEY POLLACK
1 July 1934 - 26 May 2008

A versatile and award-winning director, Sydney Pollack originally moved to New York to look for acting jobs before turning his attention to directing. By 1971, he was directing Sidney Poitier and Anne Bancroft in *The Slender Thread* and continued to work with leading talents throughout the 1970s. He regularly collaborated with Robert Redford, whom he directed in *Jeremiah Johnson* (1972), *The Way We Were* (1973) and his biggest triumph, *Out of Africa* (1985). The film, following a love affair in colonial Kenya, was a great critical success and led to an Academy Award for best director, some sixteen years after he was first nominated for *They Shoot Horses Don't*

Sydney Pollack

They? (1969). Pollack was also shortlisted for best director for *Tootsie* (1982), starring Dustin Hoffman as a cross-dressing actor and Pollack himself as Hoffman's agent.

In the 1990s, Pollack mainly worked as an executive producer, although he did direct a couple of features including the box office hit *The Firm* (1993). More recently, he directed the crime thriller *The Interpreter* (2005) and *Sketches of Frank Gehry* (2005), a documentary about the renowned architect, as well as producing and acting in the Oscar-nominated legal thriller *Michael Clayton* (2007). – *Eleanor Mckeown*

DINO RISI
7 June 1916 – 7 June 2008

All his life, Dino Risi enjoyed poking fun at people's contradictory nature, even his own. In the late years of his prolific career he published a collection of limericks and aphorisms, plus a bestselling, award-winning autobiography, *My Monsters*. Visiting him at Aldrovandi

Residence, overlooking Rome's zoo, was like attending a session with Freud. His probing nature was well known on the sets of his films, where he would interrogate the likes of Sophia Loren, Marcello Mastroianni, or any extras or assistants for that matter, about their most intimate secrets. He directed his first feature *Vacation with a Gangster* (*Vacanze col gangster*) in 1952, followed by his first major success, the trendy comedy about Roman youths, *Poor but Beautiful* (*Poveri ma belli*), in 1956.

Risi's masterful satires of the 1960s, *A Difficult Life* (*Una vita difficile*, 1961), *The Easy Life* (*Il sorpasso*, 1962) and *15 from Rome* (*I mostri*, 1963), anatomised Italian society's ups and downs, but were scorned by critics at the time. His taste for black humour and darker tones was evident during his 'literary' period, inaugurated by the very successful *Scent of a Woman* (*Profumo di donna*, 1974). Vittorio Gassman, Ugo Tognazzi, Marcello Mastroianni, Nino Manfredi, and other popular 'monsters' of the *commedia all'italiana* genre owe him a huge debt. – *Lorenzo Codelli*

Dino Risi

ALAIN ROBBE-GRILLET
18 August 1922 – 18 February 2008

Alain Robbe-Grillet, doyen of the nouveau roman and inventor of the *ciné-roman*, once wrote of fiction that 'the true writer has nothing to say. What counts is the way he says it.' As his career at the forefront of the post-

war French avant-garde wore on, Robbe-Grillet slowly came round to an entirely new way of saying things – and renounced the novel almost completely to become a filmmaker. It all started with *Last Year at Marienbad* (*L'Année dernière à Marienbad*, 1962), his gnomic screenplay no foil for Alain Resnais' elliptical direction. Robbe-Grillet's own directorial debut, *The Immortal One* (*L'Immortelle*, 1963), borrowed heavily from Antonioni's *L'Avventura* (1960), but also set the agenda for much of the director's later work: for Robbe-Grillet, the filmmaker, like the writer, should both set ciphers and leave gaps, placing a considerable onus upon the viewer to first decode and then rewrite a large portion of the cinematic 'text' themselves. *Trans-Europ-Express* (1966) followed, starring Jean-Louis Trintignant and Robbe-Grillet himself, before the innovation began to shade into sado-erotic preoccupation (*La Belle Captive*, 1975), drawing censure from feminists, amongst others. Even if his cinematic experiments were seldom entirely successful (and often bordered on the unwatchable), Robbe-Grillet's pioneering concept of the *ciné-roman*, a form straddling film and literature and elaborated upon to great effect by Chris Marker, makes him a truly noteworthy figure in the history of film as well as literature. – *Benny Morgan*

RANDA CHAHAL SABAG
11 December 1953 – 25 August 2008

Lebanese filmmaker Randa Chahal studied filmmaking in Paris before returning to Lebanon at the start of the civil war in 1975. Her most famous documentary about the conflict there was the remarkable *Nos Guerres Imprudentes* (1995). In the 1990s, Chahal turned to feature films, making controversial works such as *Écrans de Sable* (1991), *Les Infidèles* (1997) and *Civilisées* (1999). It was with her most recent work, *The Kite* (2003), that Chahal received the attention she deserved. The film won the Silver Lion award at the Venice Film Festival and was Chahal's first general release in her native Lebanon. – *Eleanor Mckeown*

Stan Winston

STAN WINSTON
7 April 1946 – 15 June 2008

Stan Winston was the make-up and visual-effects designer behind films such as *Edward Scissorhands* (1990), *Batman Returns* (1992) and *AI: Artificial Intelligence* (2001). He attended a make-up programme at Walt Disney Studios before setting up his own studio in 1972. After his work on the 1974 tele-film, *The Autobiography of Miss Jane Pittman*, he came to the attention of Hollywood and worked with big-name directors including Steven Spielberg, Tim Burton and James Cameron. His collaboration with Cameron was particularly successful, resulting in a visual-effects Academy Award for *Aliens* (1986) and visual effects and makeup awards for *Terminator 2: Judgment Day* (1991). Despite being a master at blending physical and computer-generated effects, Winston admitted that he was more interested in 'wonderful stories and fantastic characters' than 'technology'. In 2001, he became the first special effects designer to receive a star on the sidewalk of Hollywood Boulevard. – *Eleanor Mckeown*

XIE JIN
21 November 1923 – 18 October 2008

Director Xie Jin's career spanned a turbulent period of Chinese history. He studied drama in Szechuan and was assistant director at the Datong Studio in Shanghai, and directed his first feature, *A Crisis*, in 1953. His third film, *Woman Basketball Player Number Five* (1957), marked Jin as a 'woman's director' and many of his films, such as *Red Detachment of Women* (1961) and *Two Stage Sisters* (1965), featured strong-willed heroines. During the Cultural Revolution, Jin was accused of bourgeois humanism and taken to a labour camp, but was released three times to make films.

During the 1980s, Jin answered criticisms that he had complied with the regime by making politically critical works such as *Legend of Tianyun Mountain* (1980) and *Hibiscus Town* (1986). Jin's later films were often more acceptable to the Chinese government than some of his contemporaries, but they always avoided simplistic nationalism. He was the only Chinese director to be made a member of both the Academy of Motion Picture Arts and Sciences and the Directors' Guild of America.
– *Eleanor Mckeown*

Amongst those who also passed away in 2008…

CYD CHARISSE (b. 8 March 1922)
EVA DAHLBECK (b. 8 March 1920)
GUILLAUME DEPARDIEU (b. 7 April 1971)
MEL FERRER (b. 2 August 1917)
JUN ICHIKAWA (b. 25 November 1948)
CHARLES JOFFE (b. 16 July 1929)
EDWARD KLOSINSKI (b. 2 January 1943)
HEATH LEDGER (b. 4 April 1979)
FAKIR CHAND MEHRA (b. 29 August 1923)
KEN OGATA (b. 20 July 1937)
BRAD RENFRO (b. 25 July 1982)
ROY SCHEIDER (b. 10 November 1932)
PAUL SCOFIELD (b. 21 January 1922)
NORIAKI TSUCHIMOTO (b. 11 December 1928)
RICHARD WIDMARK (b. 26 December 1914)

Country Focus: Israel

A Changing Landscape
by Dan Fainaru

Ten years ago, Israeli cinema hit rock bottom. Less than 1% of the country's audiences paid to see a domestic film, with most leaving the cinema disappointed. The same could be said for international sales or screenings at festivals.

However, in 2008, Israeli films have captured some 14% of local admissions. Ari Folman's *Waltz with Bashir* was the first film selected for Cannes and the jury's peculiar decision to ignore it was one of the most discussed issues once the festival was over. Released a month later in Paris, it attracted over half a million people.

Something radical must have happened to Israeli cinema over the course of the last decade. But then, a great deal happened to the country itself during that period. Seen as a window on the country it represents, there is a distinct connection between its political, economic and sociological state, and the cinema that it creates. Israel may not have been particularly concerned by the films being made in its own backyard – and it may not be particularly concerned now – but for the last few years, it has rightfully taken pride in their achievements.

Some reasons for this shift are obvious. Film schools were launched in the 1970s and so a new generation of filmmakers have spent time developing their skills and passing them on to the next generation. New cinematheques in Haifa, Tel Aviv and finally Jerusalem changed the perception of what cinema is for so

Ari Folman's **Waltz with Bashir**

many aspiring filmmakers. And from the first TV channel setting up operation in 1968, more channels, from commercial to satellite stations, are in existence and piped into almost every Israeli home. Though variable in terms of quality, the larger number of stations has resulted in an increased demand for material to screen.

The struggle to establish some kind of legal basis for the state support of cinema resulted in the Cinema Law, passed in 2000. After twenty years, the Fund for the Promotion of Quality Films has transformed into the more palatable Israeli Film Fund. New funds have sprung up alongside it, each supposedly specialising in just one field but more often than not stepping on each other's administrative toes, competing for the most suitable projects to invest in.

Local film festivals such as those in Jerusalem and Haifa were instrumental in encouraging the promotion of Israeli film internationally. Katriel Schori, head of the Israeli Film Fund and the person most responsible for reshaping Israeli cinema's identity, highlighted the lack of international awareness: 'When I took over the Film Fund, I realised that practically

Michael Winterbottom at the 26th Jerusalem International Film Festival

none of our films had even a flier in a foreign language, let alone well-prepared press books.' Nowadays, at least 50% of new Israeli films have some sort of international partner (often more than one) or at least a pre-sales contract. Schori's statistics indicate that in the last couple of years foreign investment in Israeli films almost double domestic contributions. The same applies to international sales. No longer is the industry happy to merely cater for Jewish communities abroad.

But as important as all these factors are, the change that took place in Israeli cinema has its roots elsewhere. It was the mood of the country that changed. In the first years after the War of Independence (1948) there were more urgent matters to attend to. Cinema was the kind of luxury not to be indulged in by a serious, determined society united together in an effort to establish the identity of a new country. The films ushered in with the change were inclined to pure entertainment, with few exceptions, for the next twenty years.

But with time, things were changing. The Six Day War in 1967 put an end to little Israel. Television, long suspected by Prime Minister Ben Gurion of poisoning the minds of his 'Golden Youth', finally came into being. It led audiences to question the need to go to the cinema when they could be entertained at home. The novelty of hearing characters on screen speaking the same language you heard on the street was also wearing off. And, on a larger scale, the country was changing.

The tightly-knit community defending its borders had become seen as colonising power, controlling alien territories which were originally supposed to be used to bargain for peace. But as the possibility of peace talks stalled, it looked like the territories would have to be kept a little longer, to scare rivals into negotiations and temporary settlements were erected between the Palestinian towns and villages, which eventually became permanent homes. The children that were born there grew up convinced this was their land and that they had a legitimate right to it. Likewise, an army created to defend its lands became a peacekeeping force within its own borders.

With the economy having improved, the self-imposed claustrophobia of the country whose regime discouraged travelling as wasteful all through the first years of its existence had eased off. A lobby of upcoming and veteran filmmakers managed to persuade several politicians that Israel should start working on having its own Bergman. The Fund for the Promotion of Quality Films was started in 1981, and the Ministry of Education and Culture was put in charge of it, with the cultural consistency not the commercial potential of the projects determining their selection.

The result was a decade of politically motivated films, attacking the official policies of the new Israeli right-wing regime with unprecedented and righteous fury. It is no wonder that towards the end of the decade, when Ariel Sharon was in charge of Industry and Trade, overseeing the Film Centre, he turned down an invitation to join the first European Media programme. Asked for the reason, he apparently said he saw no reason to help the enemies from within spread their pernicious messages abroad.

By the end of the 1990s, after the first Gulf War and the end of the first Intifada, any illusions that well-intentioned Israelis might still establish a dialogue with their neighbours were shattered. The Palestinians demands seemed to exceed anything even progressive Israelis were willing to concede. Brave liberal statements sounded lame and pointless, and since there was no discernible commercial cinema, domestic cinema looked defeated. It was in this moment that a new generation of filmmakers emerged, defining the cinematic landscape and shaping Israeli film for the future.

No one expected that on 1 January 2001, when the Cinema Law was officially implemented, events would move so fast. However, things had been moving in the period leading up to it. Arik Kaplun's *Yana's Friends* had been in the works for seven years before it won Best Film and Best Actress at Karlovy Vary in 2000. Dover Kozashvili's *Late Marriage* and Nir Bergman's *Broken Wings*, though released in late 2001 and 2002 respectively, had been in production for some time. Kozashvili and Bergman (finally Israel had its own Bergman!), and most of those who followed them, did not pretend to proffer solutions to the state of the nation. Instead they focused on small, intensely personal issues, as if inspired by the French New Wave, who had claimed forty years earlier that real cinema is not found in 'big subjects'. It was also no longer just a matter of what is said but how it is conveyed. Israeli film, to put it quite simply, had become more interesting to look at. Quite possibly because this generation had seen far more films than their elders and felt more comfortable expressing themselves in this new language.

Late Marriage confronted a young Russian emigrant with a variety of Israeli characters, all of them caught in the middle of Tel Aviv during the Gulf War. Although the sirens wail in the background, they never distracted the filmmaker or the audience from the narrative. Kozashvili's picture could almost qualify as an ethnic comedy. A Georgian family separates a favourite son from his Moroccan mistress so that he can enter into a 'decent' marriage with a nice Georgian virgin. As for Bergman's *Broken Wings*, it was a dark coming-of-age

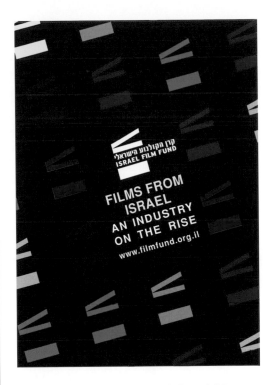

drama in which a woman, with four children, attempts to come to terms with the death of her husband. Partly autobiographical, Bergman avoided politics in favour of an emotionally engaging drama. As the film unfolds it becomes clear that the man died as the result of a bee sting, not a terrorist attack or some military operation. Far from an allegory of a state of siege, the film is a family tragedy, period.

The accent on the personal over the national, the attention paid to the individual for their own sake and not as a cipher for something else, did not deny these films their place in a larger context, but firstly made sure they existed on their own terms. Filmmakers were no longer content with issuing the 'right' statement. Their interest lay in making their point in an affecting, moving manner. So much so that, despite the growing political isolation of Israel as a state, its cinema has suddenly become more popular than ever.

Having avoided an overtly didactic approach to their work, filmmakers began to look behind the official façades characters wear. Eytan Fox's 2004 feature, *Walk on Water* (2004), upturned the cliché of the tough Mossad exterminator, with its protagonist in a state of acute crisis, questioning his identity as a secret agent and a man, even in terms of his sexuality. In the same year, Eran Riklis's *The Syrian Bride* (2004) focused on a young Druze woman who has to leave her family in the Golan Heights, as the only suitable Druze husband for her is a Syrian living in Damascus. Its deeply humanistic approach to the woman's plight, highlighting her emotional state, gave the film a universality beyond the Hollywood blueprint used three decades earlier.

Eran Riklis's **The Syrian Bride**

The new Israeli films were not turning their backs on big issues in favour of personal dramas. Rather, the big issues were reduced to human size, possessing an emotional impact that earlier Israeli films could not hope to offer. Following Amos Gitai's bitterly cynical look at religion from a purely secular point of view – a thorny subject at best – in *Kadosh* (1999), Gidi Dar's *Ushpizin* (2004) approached the same subject, but with gentle, sympathetic humour. It was followed by David Volach's painfully searing film *My Father, My Lord* (2007), and, with more than a touch of exoticism, Avi Nesher's *Secrets* (2007).

With Keren Yedaya collecting Cannes' prestigious Camera d'Or for *Or* in 2004, as well as Shira Geffen and Etgar Keret repeating the same achievement three years later with *Jellyfish*, the position of Israeli cinema as a valid new voice, both in tone

Keren Yedaya's **Or**

and content, seems to be firmly established. The tremendous success of Joseph Cedar's *Beaufort* (2007), Eran Kolirin's *The Band's Visit* (2007) and Ari Folman's *Waltz with Bashir* highlighted Israeli cinema's capacity to attract large audiences. *Beaufort*, like Clint Eastwood's *Letters from Iwo Jima*, avoided discussion of the nature of and reasons for war, but had plenty to say about the way it is waged, showing soldiers in the line of fire, victimised by generals and politicians who manipulate from a safe distance. Kolirin's film, a bittersweet, wistful comedy in which Egyptians and Israelis are divested of their national identities and allowed to act as simple human beings, was a deserved crowd-pleaser. Blessed with a touch of surrealism and a healthy dose of humour, combined with simple and yet richly imaginative visuals, it defused the eternal conflict that rears its head whenever Israelis and Arabs appear in the same frame. *Waltz with Bashir*, a resounding worldwide success, based on a premise – animated documentary – that might have

Joseph Cedar's **Beaufort**

26th JERUSALEM INTERNATIONAL FILM FESTIVAL
JULY 9-18, 2009

"Bringing a world of cinema to Israel
and Israeli Cinema to the world,
for over 25 years..."

Roberto Benigni   Robert De Niro   Lillian Gish   David Mamet
& Jean Moreau

Gila Almagor   John Malkovich   Roman Polanski   Warren Beatty

Tel: +972-2-565-4333 | Fax: +972-2-565-4335 | E-mail: beverley@jff.org.il, danielc@jff.org.il | www.jff.org.il

seemed dubious on paper, shows an Israeli soldier assuming responsibility for never lifting a finger to prevent mass murder, twenty years after the fact. Shot as a normal documentary and then transferred to animation, in its present shape it is no longer another breast-beating Israeli litany on the Middle East conflict, but one of the most potent, painful and shocking cinematic statements made this year, from any cinema.

Eran Kolirin's **The Band's Visit**

And then there is Amos Gitai, a particular case in Israeli cinema. Based in Paris for many years, where he gained an international reputation for developing a sophisticated and complex cinematic language, he is now back in Israel. Better known and respected abroad than any other filmmaker in the country, he is a prolific director whose ambitious, insistently political body of work has been acclaimed at festivals around the world, but for whom audiences at home still feel his work to be closer to lectures than drama and have yet to fully accept him.

No review of Israeli cinema would be complete without mention of the documentaries produced. Considered for many years to be just another tool to record the various achievements of a young state flexing its muscles and establishing its identity, documentaries have developed in shape, form, perspective and ambition, largely thanks to the inspiration and teachings of David Perlov. The Brazilian-born filmmaker's highly subjective six-hour long *Diary*, covering 10 years of his life (1973-83), is still considered the country's

major documentary achievement. No longer merely informative, a wave of documentaries surfaced, presenting reflections on a large variety of themes: from Orna Ben Dor's study of the second generation of Holocaust survivors, *Because of that War* (1988), and Ron Havilio's *Fragments of Jerusalem* (1997), a six-hour series that poetically ruminated on Jerusalem's past and present, to David Ben Shitrit's *Kadim Winds – A Moroccan Chronicle* (2002), dealing with the frustrations and discriminations of the Moroccan community in Israel. Interestingly, as fiction became more intensely personal and less politically militant, documentaries filled this vacuum with a series of highly relevant portraits of life in Israel.

Some documentaries were deceptively innocent of political intent, such as David Ofek's *No.17* (2003), which initially followed a police investigation searching for the last victim of a terrorist attack, but became a revealing portrait of a country under constant terrorist threat. Others were far more explicit, like Ra'anan Alexandrowicz's *Inner Tour* (2001), which looked at Israel through the eyes of Palestinians who have never seen the other side of the border before, while Yoav Shamir's *Checkpoint* showed the confrontation between young Israeli soldiers and the Palestinian population. In *Nine Star Hotel*, Ido Haar presented an uncompromising portrait of illegal Palestinian workers regularly sneaking in and out of Israel – their only way to make a living, despite the inhuman conditions they

Ido Haar's **Nine Star Hotel**

have to submit to. No filmmaker, however, is more virulently committed to his cause than Avi Mograbi, whose self-made films (from his 1997 satire *How I Learned to Overcome My Fear and Love Arik Sharon* to the recent *Z-32*) are part documentaries, part self-styled essays, all of them withering in their attack on the policies of the Israeli government.

Since Israeli cinema, both fictional and documentary, has so many references to the political situation in the region, what about the Palestinian point of view? It is doubtful whether Elia Souleiman (*Chronicle of a Disappearance*, 1996), Hany Abou Assad (*Paradise Now*, 2005) or even Tawfik Abu Wael (*Atash*, 2005) would appreciate being included in a survey of Israeli cinema. Their films deal more with internal Palestinian affairs, though they do not ignore the threatening neighbour, nor do they paint a pretty picture of it. But it is necessary to mention these films, as Israeli producers and funds were actively involved in bringing them to the screen. That all these

Tawfik Abu Wael's **Atash**

filmmakers have deservedly established a solid reputation for themselves and, in all likelihood, will not resort to the same production procedures again, does not detract from the fact that there was a collaboration of sorts, sometimes pleasant, sometimes less so, which might hint at the possibility of a dialogue between the two sides. And when or if that is ever established, perhaps a new cinema will emerge in the Middle East.

Key Players

Dan Fainru profiles some leading figures in Israeli cinema

GIORA EINI

The most unlikely key player in the Israeli film industry, Giora Eini is a lawyer with no cinematic background, who used to serve as legal adviser to the General Workers Union. Politically savvy, he became head of the Rabinowitz Foundation in the 1980s. A Tel Aviv fund, named after one of the city's ex-mayors and the main source of support for art initiatives, film was a minor focus for it until the introduction of the 2001 Cinema Law. The Cinema Project, the creation of the foundation, is now the second-largest fund in the country, disbursing an annual budget of close to US$5 million amongst six or seven productions. Titles it has funded include *Or*, *Atash*, *My Father, My Lord*, *Beaufort*, *To Take a Wife* and *Secrets*.

Giora Eini

Eini, who prides himself on having no friends in the industry, leaves artistic responsibility to cinema professionals. His area is administration, obtaining budgets from the Cinema Council, checking that none of the Fund's regulations hinders its smooth running.

Eini's organisation rarely actively seeks international partners, but is understandably happy when foreign co-producers show interest. This has made it possible for the Cinema Project to be credited on films such as the Canadian/Hungarian production of *Faceless*, Paul Schrader's *Adam Resurrected* and another Polish/Israeli co-production, *Spring of '41*, starring Joseph Fiennes.

RONIT ELKABETZ

Ronit Elkabetz is the most distinctive female movie star in Israel, with a promising directing career ahead of her. Born in Israel to a family of Moroccan emigrants, she is equally at home in Hebrew and French. Her dark, intense looks originally gained her entry into the fashion world, before her first role, in Daniel Wachsman's mystical 1990 drama, *The Appointed*. Though she never trained as an actress, she was soon entrusted with major roles, both in Israel and in France. She excels at portraying strong-willed women, struggling for their own space in a male-oriented society. She appeared as an independent divorcee engaged in a torrid affair with an unmarried man in *Late Marriage*, as an ageing prostitute who won't quit in *Or* and the improvised host of the Egyptian band in *The Band's Visit*.

In 2005, Elkabetz teamed up with her brother, Shlomi, to direct *To Take a Wife*. She plays Viviane, who attempts to escape her claustrophobic home life. Her follow-up, *Seven Days*, played in the Cannes Critics' Week in 2008.

Ronit Elkabetz in **To Take a Wife**

Ari Folman

ARI FOLMAN

Ari Folman is, without a doubt, the man of the year. Born in Haifa in 1962, Folman served with an elite unit during the Lebanon War, then went on to study filmmaking at Tel Aviv University. His graduation film, made with Ori Sivan, was the documentary *Shaanan Si*, offering an eerily surrealistic portrait of Tel Aviv during the first Gulf War. *Saint Clara*, their first feature, in which a 13-year-old girl can predict the future provided she does not fall in love, displayed the same touch of surrealism, both narratively and in terms of its strange visuals, accompanied by an aggressive soundtrack. Working again with Sivan (the psychoanalyst in *Waltz with Bashir*), Folman directed *Made in Israel*, a satirical fantasy in which the last surviving Nazi is brought before a court of justice in Israel. He has also contributed as a writer for numerous TV series.

Waltz with Bashir was not an easy film to fund. After experimenting with animation on the TV serial *The Stuff Love is Made Of*, Folman put together a short demo for HotDocs in Toronto. For a number of years, he travelled to different markets to seek funding, constantly developing his ideas along the way. Finally, he shot the entire film as a live-action

documentary, sinking his own money into
the project, even opening an animation studio
in order to painstakingly paint each frame of
the film. Vindicated by the results, he is now
looking to develop similar projects.

AMOS GITAI

Amos Gitai originally intended to follow in his
father's footsteps and studied architecture, but
then switched to film. *The House* (1980), about
a Palestinian home in Jerusalem that was
abandoned during the War of Independence
and occupied by Israelis, was commissioned
by Israeli Television. When producers disagreed
with some of the film's content, Gitai left the
country with the film. His visual style and
language, and particularly his political agenda,
which repudiated the stance of the Israeli
government, established his reputation abroad,
both as an avant-garde director and as a fierce
critic of Israel's policies. His first feature,
Esther (1986), an adaptation of the Biblical
tale with a contemporary coda, screened at
Cannes Critics' Week, and his films, alternating

between documentaries and fiction, have
played at festivals ever since. They are mostly
dedicated to the particular problems of his
homeland and the Jewish nation as a whole,
presented in a didactic style reminiscent of
Jean-Luc Godard and Jean-Marie Straub.

Gitai returned to Israel in 1993, but his films,
often featuring international stars such as
Jeanne Moreau, Juliette Binoche or Hanna
Schygulla, require budgets beyond the means
of the local industry. Therefore, although
his films are usually shot in Israel, most of
the funds come from abroad and, as such,
his works are often regarded as foreign
productions rather than domestic ones.

LIA VAN LEER

Usually referred to internationally as 'the
first lady of Israeli cinema', she was the first
person to head the Israeli Film Archive, which
became the country's first Cinematheque,
followed by a second one in Tel Aviv and a
third in Jerusalem, both of which she was
instrumental in creating. After 1967, she and
her husband Wim moved to Jerusalem and the
Film Archive moved with them.

In 1984 she set up the Jerusalem Film Festival.
Never one to delegate authority whenever she
believed she should personally take care of the
matter, Lia has proven to be an indefatigable
globetrotter, acquiring friends and acquaintances around the world and among the high and
mighty, who were always present whenever
she needed their help. She was responsible to
a great extent for establishing the Jerusalem
Cinematheque as a leading cultural centre in
the city, one of the few points of encounter between Israelis and Palestinians. She guided the
festival's rapid growth and the ever-increasing
number of competitive sections in it, insisting
on a large sidebar dedicated to Jewish-themed
films from all over the world. Having accu-
mulated prestigious awards for her activities,
both at home and abroad, she relinquished
her activities only last year, when, well into
her eighties, she stepped down as the active

Amos Gitai

Lia Van Leer

director of the Cinematheque, the Festival and the Archive, but she still retains her position as chairperson on all three boards.

AVI MOGRABI

Avi Mograbi is a one-man show, to the extent that such a thing is possible in the film industry. A filmmaker whose output is generally considered to be documentary, but is much better defined as film essay, he writes his own projects, shoots the material himself with his own digital camera, rushing out whenever the immediate events require his presence, and acts both as on- and off-camera narrator, and as himself. He is responsible for every stage of the filmmaking process and therefore needs minimum participation from funds or outside producers in order to finalise his projects.

Born in 1956, the scion of a highly respected film family (one of Tel Aviv's central squares still bears the name of the Mograbi cinema which adorned it), he studied philosophy and art. In film, he has become one of the most

irreverent spirits working in the industry. His films attack the policies of right-wing governments and their dubious achievements, not only in what he sees as the unbearable conditions meted out to Palestinians, but also in the particularities and paradoxes of life in Israel. Recognised first by international film festivals, he has already been invited to Cannes and Venice. Strangely enough, several of his films have been aided by local film funds, which might explain many of the recent successes of Israeli cinema.

EILON RATZKOVSKY

Since Eran Kolirin's *The Band's Visit* took Cannes by surprise in 2007, revealing itself as the first authentic Israeli worldwide crowd-pleaser, everyone wants to work with the film's producer, Eilon Ratzkovsky. Or, to be more precise, with July August Productions, the company he owns with TV producer Yossi Uzrad and his partner, Guy Jacoel. Ratzkovsky's golden touch was certainly a part of the film's success, but he also has a talent for creating fruitful partnerships with directors.

Eilon Ratzkovsky

After studying philosophy in Rome, Ratzkovsky returned to Israel, taking a series of jobs as an assistant director before moving gradually into production and finally setting up July August in 2003. Initially, the company filled the quota of children's features for one of the commercial channels.

With American-based Israeli producer Ehud Bleiberg they produced *Love and Dance* in 2006 and following *The Band's Visit* they worked with Bleiberg and Paul Schrader on *Adam Resurrected*. They have since produced Ronit and Shlomi Elkabetz' *Seven Days* and Eitan Green's whimsical *It all Begins at Sea*.

MAREK ROZENBAUM

Born in Poland in 1952, Marek Rozenbaum is a highly respected producer who has been closely associated with the Israeli film industry for the last 25 years. Transfax, the company he founded twenty years ago, has produced over thirty features and forty documentaries. He is currently working with Keren Yedaya on *Jaffa* and Dover Kozashvili on his third feature, *Infiltration*.

He was one of the first to realise the importance of finding audiences outside Israel, attending international festivals and markets. An active lobbyist, whose efforts brought into existence the present Cinema Law, Rozenbaum is also a realist who was quick to point out many of the shortcomings to be expected in its implementation, He is now President of the Israeli Film and TV Academy and a member of the Producers Association, which he has chaired in the past for six consecutive years. Having recently produced three films by first-time directors, he believes the only way for Israeli cinema to continue being relevant in years to come is to seek and develop new talent.

KATRIEL SCHORI

Katriel Schori's appointment as the Executive Director of the Israeli Film Fund in 1999 began the transformation of contemporary

Katriel Schori

Israeli cinema. A graduate of the NYU Film School, he returned to Israel in 1973 as head of productions for Kastel Films, the country's leading producer at the time. Involved in a large number of projects, both documentaries and fiction, he worked closely with a number of international broadcasters such as the BBC, ARD and PBS.

After three years in the US, he returned home and set up Belfilms, which, by the time he was asked to take over the Fund, had already produced over 200 documentaries and features.

Joining the Fund at its lowest ebb, he initiated a series of promotion schemes to rebuild its stature. His international links brought in potential investors, and Israel's presence at festivals and film markets increased as a result. He achieved this by creating a budget for international promotion and by assuming international responsibility not only for the films backed by the Film Fund, but also films made outside his direct remit.

DAN FAINARU is co-editor of Israel's only film magazine, *Cinematheque*, and a former director of the Israeli Film Institute. He reviews regularly for *Screen International*.

Industry Focus: Digital Platforms

The Audience Takes Control
by Liz Rosenthal

Low-cost digital tools have commoditised production and distribution. Now the most important focus should be on how to use them to build audience demand.

Out of the thousands of independent films produced around the world each year, the vast majority get little or no distribution, left to flounder in obscurity.

As several independent distribution companies shut up shop, many in the film business believe that the solution is to make fewer, but higher-quality, films. However, more films will be made, as digital tools enable filmmakers to create more easily outside the remit of the film business. An enormous wave of content is being produced around the world by an emerging generation of filmmakers who have grown up with technology and a sophisticated degree of media literacy.

The traditional theatrical-led distribution model can no longer effectively service the independent film community. With limited space in cinemas, broadcast and retail, there is no room for anything but studio films and the occasional big breakthrough independent film. And the traditional rules of holdback windows, exclusivity, territorial distribution and the 'build it and they will come' approach does little to help grow or sustain audiences. They are no longer prepared to wait for the film business to deliver content to them. Consumers want their media delivered anytime, anywhere and at an ever-lower cost, often for free.

In a congested market place where competition for audiences is fragmented over multiple new platforms, games, online activities, TV and real life, the independent film community urgently needs to find new avenues for making films easily available and engaging with their future audiences in more meaningful ways.

Thankfully, the web and Internet-based businesses have created the tools to do this. Moreover, many of these tools are free. In the last two years there has been an explosion in social media, with the rapid growth of social networking and user-generated sites, free social software and bloggers with the influence to make or break brands and political campaigns. In 2007, the audience using social networks increased by two-thirds in the Middle East and Africa, 35% in Europe and one-third in Latin America. This has resulted in the emergence of user-generated content, as well as a fan and remix culture with a whole new generation of audiences who are no longer just passive viewers of media but active creators, collaborators, distributors and even financiers.

Finding new ways of aggregating and mobilising these audiences, building communities and fanbases online, is the key to finding future ways to create, finance and distribute films. The new companies and filmmakers experimenting in this area begin with the audience and the Internet at the centre of their business model, not as the periphery to the theatrically led model.

Building and mobilising an online community around his work has been key to the success of documentary filmmaker and activist Robert

Greenwald. Over a series of four feature films, *Uncovered* (2003), *Outfoxed* (2004), *Walmart* (2005) and *Iraq For Sale* (2006), and more recently a huge number of short web films, he and his company Brave New Films have created a sustainable production and distribution model independent of traditional media. His huge online community help him to publicise his films globally and now even to finance them. After ten days of Internet fundraising, he raised US$385,000 in donations towards his last feature documentary *Iraq For Sale*. 'From the start we think from a strategic and political POV about who is our audience and how we should reach them,' he said. He even has a dedicated member of the team who builds partnerships with other groups and organisations who connect with the film's subject matter. He can subsequently tap into their communities of thousands.

Robert Greenwald

Greeenwald is not concerned about theatrical releases for his films, but about reaching the greatest number of people and getting them to act. He believes the best way to achieve this is to encourage his films to be seen in a community setting where people discuss the film. One of the key online tools on his website, Brave New Theatres, enables audiences all over the world to mobilise their own screenings in their living rooms, in community centres, in schools and even in theatres. 'House Parties', as these came to be known, are the way that his films became seeded in communities. He sends out thousands of free DVDs for those who arrange

screenings. The films are then sold on DVD from his website, other retail websites such as Amazon and partner organisation sites. Direct sales from his website often reach hundreds of thousands, with the added bonus that he gets to collect a huge email list of future audience members. His films have subsequently been sold for theatrical, broadcast and retail distribution in different territories around the world despite their free availability globally through house parties and on DVD.

Within the theatrical business model, the promise of greater variety and the long tail of unlimited digital choice seem a remote possibility, despite the promise of digital cinema.

A new Brazilian venture, Moviemobz, launched in July by the art-house digital cinema network, Rain Networks, is about to change this. Part social network, part digital content aggregator, Moviemobz allows the audience to programme screenings through their website. Co-founder Fabio Lima explains that 'audiences aren't just expecting better quality from digital cinema rollout, but better social and community aspects, flexible programming and they want to be in control like they are on the Internet'. If you join the site, you can pick your favourite cinema, choice of film and a specific screening time. You can then invite friends and family to the screenings and even form or join clubs dedicated to certain films or genres on the website. Once a certain number of people have been mobilised to a session, the cinema announces the screening and tickets are put on sale.

Today, Moviemobz/Rain Networks have a digital art-house screen network of two hundred screens in 26 cities in Brazil. By enabling extremely cost-efficient Internet delivery of digital cinema files, and grass-roots marketing of the film through audiences, Moviemobz can make a single screening of a film become profitable. To date, ninety different film titles have been programmed out of a catalogue of four hundred films. Many

Arin Crumley and Susan Buice's **Four Eyed Monsters**

titles have never been released in Brazil, such as *Sympathy for the Devil* by Jean-Luc Godard, which has been mobilised for fifteen sessions.

Arin Crumley and Susan Buice, the team behind the online cult feature film, *Four Eyed Monsters*, built awareness and a huge online fanbase by creating a podcast series around their feature film. It was posted for free on their blog and major social networks, such as MySpace. By encouraging their community to request a cinema screening of the feature by providing an email address and zip code, the filmmakers collected a vast database of fans and were able to go direct to theatres in New York, Boston, LA and San Francisco to book screenings, with proof of audience demand. They subsequently sold the DVD, digital download and merchandise directly through their website and decided to expand the audience for their film by screening the entire feature for free on YouTube, where it was viewed over a million times. The screening was monetised by a sponsorship deal of around US$60,000 by Spout.com, a new social-networking site based around film. After showing the film for free, a lucrative deal was

Wayne Wang's **The Princess of Nebraska**

then struck with the Independent Film Channel for US broadcast rights and home-video distribution.

Established filmmakers and traditional distributors are beginning to recognise that building audience demand through social media can bring new value to their features. Wayne Wang's latest feature film *The Princess of Nebraska*, a two-hour film in Mandarin, originally acquired for North America by Magnolia, was premiered in the YouTube Screening Room in October. It was viewed over 165,000 times in the first three days and was even reviewed by *New York Times* critic A.O. Scott. Roughly translated, the number of views would have placed the film around 15th on the box office charts had it premiered theatrically. Wang hopes the six-week web freebie will lead to revenue streams from DVD sales and TV companies interested in repackaging the film for ancillary markets. 'It used to be that you just had the big studios and the art houses,' he said. 'Now you have the Internet, too, which I think is going to become a third option for independent film.'

M. Dot Strange

Audience collaboration has been the cornerstone of many online success stories. M. Dot Strange, the award-winning animation director, asked his huge global YouTube fanbase to translate his film for the DVD release of his award-winning first feature *We Are the Strange*, which he self-distributed

M. Dot Strange's **We Are the Strange**

through his company, DVD Baby. Within two weeks of the request, the film had been translated (for free) into 17 languages, including the *Clockwork Orange* language Nasdat.

Finnish director Timo Vuorensola relied on volunteer fans from his 3,000-strong active online community to help create his first feature, *Star Wreck: In the Pirkinning*, a cult sci-fi comedy that has attracted a huge online following. The film had been downloaded over eight million times before it was picked up for DVD distribution by Universal. He commented, 'Without thinking about it too much, we started to ask for help from the community, which proved pretty soon to be a very good resource base, whatever was our need – when we needed people to help us out with the script, when we needed actors, when we needed 3D models and special effects, and later when we needed publicity and subtitles.' The production quality for this low-budget epic is astounding. Timo and his team have developed a special platform, Wreck a Movie, for their new film *Iron Sky*, which supports collaborative film production for themselves and other filmmakers.

Timo Vuorensola's **Star Wreck: In the Pirkinning**

As audiences begin to access stories on different media platforms and devices, we are beginning to see new possibilities for storytelling as films are no longer bound to ninety-minute formats. Film as we know it is beginning to transform. In 2003 Peter Greenaway prophesied, 'If the cinema intends to survive, I believe, it has to make a pact and a relationship with concepts of interactivity and it has to see itself as only part of a multimedia cultural adventure.'

Lance Weiler

Critically acclaimed director and digital innovator Lance Weiler has extensively experimented with creating interactive multimedia content around his films as a key part of building audiences. The release of his second feature film *Head Trauma* is a lesson in multiplatform reinterpretation and cunning marketing on a tiny budget. He created a story world that involved an interactive graphic novel, physical comics, alternate soundtracks, phone calls and text messages from characters. To create buzz for the Warners VOD release he even produced a separate web series with subliminal clues and an online game related loosely to the film that was viewed and played by over 2.5 million people.

Weiler states: 'What I've learned from the creation of these storyworlds is that they mirror the way many people are consuming their entertainment. The fragmentation of the digital space is a perfect opportunity to tell stories in new ways. And I can honestly say it has presented me with an interesting and cost-effective way to reach and engage my audience. The gaming that I've done around *Head Trauma* has been experienced by millions of people – far more than it would have reached in traditional outlets. Cross-media storytelling is exactly what traditional distribution needs. The future of media distribution resides in the ability for the audience to have total control. Not only will they help to spread the media but they will amplify and extend the story. Creating a conversation with the audience and allowing them to not only consume but to also create has the potential to develop new revenue streams for filmmakers, revenue that can be found in the cracks of what some would argue is a crumbling traditional model.'

Timo Vuorensola's **Iron Sky**

LIZ ROSENTHAL is the Founder and Director of Power to the Pixel, www.powertothepixel. com, the leading conference, think tank and cross-media project forum about digital distribution and film innovation taking place alongside The Times BFI London Film Festival. She is also the Digital Distribution Strategy Advisor for the UK Film Council.

Power to the Pixel
Hannah Patterson

Running alongside The Times BFI 52nd London Film Festival, Power to the Pixel was a two-day forum that brought together leading innovators, filmmakers and entrepreneurs to discuss new ways in which independent film and media can be financed, created and ultimately reach audiences in a multi-platform world.

A host of companies detailed their new services, such as YouTube's Screening Room, PlaceVine's branding initiatives, Tribeca's online outlet Reframe and IndieGoGo's fundraising website. Particular highlights from frontline DIY filmmakers included *The Last Broadcast* director Lance Weiler's exhaustive discussion of how to maximise awareness of your project by harnassing no-cost online tools, M. Dot Strange's account of tapping into a serious fan base to spread the word on his cult feature *We Are the Strange* and Jamie King's successful use of BitTorrrent to distribute *Steal This Film I* and *II* (over four million downloads and counting...)

The question nagging many audience members was, 'How do you produce films this way and actually make money?' Some sceptics felt that we are simply changing the distribution mechanism without really altering the industry underneath, that the Internet would inevitably go the way of TV, with corporations and big brands squeezing out the indies. But profit, it seems, wasn't the main priority for these filmmakers, who for now were proving that, with hard graft and technical savvy, they could reach audiences in the millions, bypassing distribution and exhibition gatekeepers altogether.

With such wealth of information on offer, much of it bewilderingly new, it was easy to hit overload. The key, as the experts pointed out, was to take the bits that worked best for you and your project. A must for anyone interested in new filmmaking models, the sessions can be viewed online at http://powertothepixel. com/

Special Focus: Accession to the EU

Film Industries in an 'Enlarged' Europe

by Dina Iordanova

This article was commissioned around the same time the European Union lifted restrictions on the sale of oddly-shaped fruits and vegetables in supermarkets across Europe; an action that unleashed the public's affection for gnarled carrots, bendy cucumbers and bulbous potatoes that often tasted better than the perfectly shaped but tasteless produce on offer.

Another recent development in Brussels was the admission of countries from the former Eastern Bloc to the European Union. Not without some resistance, of course. The debates over the EU's enlargement revolved around the preoccupation of how to incorporate the markets of these geographically near, yet what some saw as 'non-quite-up-to-the-mark' states, while simultaneously ensuring that the affluent and mature consumer economies of the West were not 'inconvenienced'.

The admission process took place in stages and largely reflected media concerns on the degree of the socio-cultural 'difference' that kept countries of Eastern and Southern Europe apart from what was seen as the Western norm. The first phase of the enlargement, in 2004, extended to Hungary, Poland, the Czech Republic, Slovakia, Slovenia, Cyprus, Malta, Latvia, Estonia and Lithuania. In 2007, Romania and Bulgaria were also admitted. The candidacies of countries that still remain outside the European Union, like Serbia,

Croatia, the Former Yugoslav Republic of Macedonia, Bosnia and Herzegovina, Montenegro, Albania and Turkey, are under discussion. Other countries, like Switzerland and Norway, seem to have decided that there is little benefit in joining the EU and have steered clear of any entry.

The admission to the EU put certain pressures on the new members: they now had to show that they were worthy of membership and discard any 'peculiarities' as soon as possible.

So how did the ramifications of their entry to the EU play out in the area of the film industry? What did film production and distribution gain from being part of this more affluent sphere?

The change in 2004 and thereafter was not as palpable as one would expect, mostly because the 'new' countries had embarked on the course towards 'becoming European' as early as 1989. The ascension to the EU, thus, was not the beginning of a process of strategic transformation, but its (successful) end.

Even though these national traditions could lay claim to having embraced filmmaking from the time of its very inception, they were now treated as 'emerging' cinemas. As such, it was important for them to gain visibility within the international marketplace. Having 'become European', however, the film industries and cultures of the former Eastern Bloc countries were beginning to resemble the film industries of small West European countries, even replicating their limitations and shortcomings. More and more, the previous Eastern European fare was losing its uniqueness (the equivalent of that strangely-shaped fruit), resembling instead typical European fare, which often translated as dull and lacklustre. Rather than delivering a forceful message of cultural potency and freshness, films from the 'new' Europe were marked by specific *Ostalgia* and dourness that challenged foreign mass audiences and often fell into the middle-of-the-road category. The message was that people living in the countries of the 'new' Europe were inundated with a panorama of economic disparities and social ills that were likely to persist even after Europe became 'bigger and better'.

Filmmaking in state-socialist Eastern Europe (1948–89) represented probably the best case of a vertically integrated industry. Production and distribution worked within a tightly structured framework. The capital-intensive nature of film production was underwritten by the state; film financing was centralised and generous; state-owned production facilities employed permanent teams of salaried workers. Once completed, films were first shown within the system of state-owned theatres and eventually screened on national television, as well as distributed internationally via the well-oiled channels of cultural exchange within the Eastern Bloc. Profit making was not a consideration; it was enough for the films to return the investment, which most of them did as they were made on relatively small budgets and seen by sufficiently sizable audiences. Driven by an underlying urge to rationalise and streamline the industry cycle, this model successfully maintained consistently high production outputs, comparable (and sometimes exceeding) the cinematic outputs of similarly sized countries in Western Europe.

After 1989, cinema was no longer 'the most important art' (as Lenin had reportedly termed it after the 1917 Bolshevik Revolution) and the new governments were neither willing nor able to continue bankrolling it. The state's involvement in running the cultural industries came to a halt; new legislation of a 'hands off' and 'laissez-faire' type was passed. The early

1990s saw a crisis, characterised by crumbling production routines, an abrupt fall in state funding, a sharp increase in unemployment among skilled personnel, and considerable decline in the total output. There was a concurrent crisis in distribution and exhibition. Earlier concerns over freedom of expression dissolved, taken over by worries over declining markets. Financing for film production changed profoundly, moving to producer-driven, piecemeal projects. The scarce state subsidies, competitive in some countries or automatic in others, became a hotly contested arena. The involvement of national television networks in film production and exhibition became vital, as did funding linked to international co-productions and the growing area of private finance and investment. The break-up of the Eastern Bloc also meant the collapse of the consolidated distribution operation.

In this period of hiatus, Eastern Europe's only rational economic and political choice was to turn to the West as the sole desired partner. In strictly economic terms, the capitalist economies of the West and the transitional economies of the East developed a relationship of 'haves' and 'have nots', as the funds needed to keep the film industries going could only come from the solvent West. Politically, re-orientation to the West was now at the top of the agenda for all Eastern European countries, and former partnerships within the Eastern Bloc were quickly abandoned in favour of the new alliances that prevailed in the run-up to accession.

Most of the 'new' countries joined the Council of Europe's funding body Eurimages in the early 1990s, and many took part in various editions of the EU's MEDIA programme; they also became members of exhibition (Cinema Europe) and festival networks. This access to pan-European structures, however, did not lead to a significant boost in East/West exchanges. Instead, it facilitated the revival of regional co-operations, based on geographical proximity or cultural affinity. Romance-language Romania and France, for example,

WE BRING CZECH FILMS TO THE WORLD

Laila Pakalnina's **The Hostage**

co-produce on a regular basis; many of the Eastern and Central European countries take advantage of their proximity to Germany, and the Balkan countries produce with each other. Croat-American director Rajko Grlic's *Border Post* (2006), co-produced by all the former Yugoslav republics with the participation of adjacent Hungary and Austria, is probably the best example of the prevalence of regionalism in Europe's South East. Projects that bring together partners from remote locations – like Laila Pakalnina's *The Hostage* (2006), co-produced between Latvia, Estonia and Slovenia — happen only occasionally.

One good result of the accession process was the passing of new legislation on matters related to film (a concern that otherwise would have been a low priority for governments that had more pressing economic issues to deal with). In some cases this also led to tax-incentive initiatives, often passed as a result of lobbying from film people familiar with the organisation of industries in the West who wanted to broadcast that the 'new' Europe was now open for business. In Hungary, for example, such individuals included Carolco veteran producer Andy Vajna, a returnee from the diaspora, or Andras Simonyi, a former Hungarian ambassador to the US and now CEO of the new Korda Studios.

Seen in a wider global context, the current situation in Eastern Europe is defined by the co-existence of two distinct industry strands, functioning independently of each other: the international service industry linked to Hollywood's global operations, and the domestic infrastructure linked to the national film tradition.

First, there is the well-developed and profitable operation engaged in servicing large-scale international productions, with a streamlined system of studios, service companies and below-the-line personnel, which thrives on the exploitation of skills and facilities inherited from the period of state socialism. After privatisation in the 1990s, Eastern Europe's studios entered close competition with each other for control of this lucrative business. The Czech capital, Prague, home of Barrandov studios and key service companies like Stillking Films, grew into a booming centre for production. Neighbouring countries became interested in a slice of the cinematic pie, which saw rival studios springing up across the region. The approaching European Union accession date of 2004, however, caused apprehension over the inevitable price increases and brought about fears that this business would disappear overnight. It did not play out as badly as expected, but nonetheless many productions dropped the 'new' Europe in favour of countries that were still outside the Union, like Romania (where the recently built Castel studio, near Bucharest, has hosted productions ranging from horror films to more serious shoots) and Bulgaria (where the Boyana studios near Sofia were sold to new American-Israeli owner, NuImage).

Jan Sverák

Cristi Puiu's **The Death of Mr. Lazarescu**

The other side of these 'parallel' strands comprised the remains of the national film industry, which is less present now than it was in the past. Even though it engages the cream of local talent, it employs a smaller production base that is set up ad hoc on a per-project basis. While central to the film industries of, for example, France or Denmark, in most Eastern European countries this sphere has been marginalised to open up space for the more lucrative international productions. National cinema nowadays has a lesser standing with cultural bureaucrats who need to ensure a steady flow of funds. And it is within this downsized arena that films concerned with national identity are being made.

In theory, these parallel strands could benefit from some integration, as the presence of large international productions could underwrite some of the local industry and boost its sustainability. In reality, at least for the time being, they are almost fully detached from each other.

Effectively rescued by the advent of parallel industries, which brought in a lifeline of international service demand while trimming domestic oversupply of films, by the time of the EU accession most of the film industries across the 'new' Europe had recovered from the financial crisis of the early 1990s. Output numbers had stabilised, and occasional domestic titles rose into the top ten at the box office, with commercial success stories linked to the names of directors like Jan Sverák

in the Czech Republic or Juliusz Machulski in Poland. The new generation of filmmakers can expect to enjoy reasonably productive careers at home without necessarily looking to migrate to the West.

Internationally, the most recent acclaim within the region has gone to Romania and a new generation of directors such as Cristi Puiu (*The Death of Mr. Lazarescu*), Corneliu Porumboiu (*12:08 East of Bucharest*) and Palme d'Or winner Cristian Mungiu (*4 Months, 3 weeks & 2 Days*). Awards and acclaim aside, international recognition could not remedy persisting domestic predicaments. The number of cinemas in Romania, a country of over twenty million inhabitants, had now fallen to only 38. Taking tips from self-distribution practices pioneered by Third World filmmakers, Cristian Mungiu used the proceeds of his award to rent a projection van from Germany and organised a tour of improvised screenings across the country, so that his fellow Romanians could also see his film.

Indeed, exhibition is probably the area where the new flow of funds from the EU could make the biggest difference. Most of the old

Corneliu Porumboiu's **12:08 East of Bucharest**

theatres have gradually closed their doors, often converted for usage as casinos and bingo halls, or sold off as office space. The closures came along with a move toward multiplexes, which sprung up in most capitals. Appealing to younger crowds but alienating mature audiences (who saw the hikes in admission prices as prohibitive), the new exhibition set-up works with a profoundly altered audience demographic.

What does the European future hold for people in the 'new' Europe? Two film students from Prague's FAMU, Vít Klusák and Filip Remunda, raise this question in their diploma project, the documentary *Czech Dream* (2004). A clever renunciation of the overblown media hype over Europe in the run-up to EU's accession, the film chronicles an outrageous hoax that the filmmakers pulled on their fellow citizens. As the film unravels, Klusák and Remunda put in motion a massive advertising campaign for a non-existent hyper-market which they call 'Czech Dream' and for which they erect a fake façade in the middle of an empty field outside the capital. On the appointed day, thousands of enthusiastic Prague consumers flock to the place, in anticipation of finding great promotional bargains. Their eagerness, however, soon turns into bitter consternation.

The scenes of outrage at the end of *Czech Dream* are accompanied by the filmmakers' commentary, which compares their despicable prank to the way in which Eastern Europeans sheepishly bought into unsubstantiated

'New' Europeans on the run up to accession in **Czech Dream**

Cristian Mungiu's **4 Months, 3 Weeks & 2 Days**

propaganda and flocked toward joining the European Union. Czechs and other 'new' Europeans knew well that they were not the most esteemed partners Europe wanted; they also suspected that Europe would not be as generous as it seemed. Yet they hushed whatever hesitations they had and rushed into the accession. But what if the pledge of prosperity turned out to be an empty promise? Whereas Europe felt that, by admitting these countries, it was letting in idiosyncratic oddities, the 'new' Europeans had their own concerns over its potentially deceptive façade. A few years into the joint venture, the enlarged Europe is still marked by muted mutual mistrust, either side entangled in its own subdued prejudice and caution.

DINA IORDANOVA coordinates the Leverhulme Trust-funded project *Dynamics of World Cinema*. She writes on international film at www.DinaView.com out of her home in a Scottish fishing village.

'NEW' EUROPE'S PARALLEL INDUSTRIES

International service industry

Production: Studio and other production assets are privately owned and maintained mostly for the sake of attracting international runaway business. Reliance on big-budget runaway productions. Below-the-line personnel engaged on an on-going basis; occasional opportunities for input from local creative talent.

Distribution: Mostly Hollywood subsidiaries, engaged in distributing Hollywood product, both to theatrical and ancillary markets.

Exhibition: Theatre owners mostly work in blanket-booking mode with Hollywood subsidiaries.

Audiences: Mostly engaged with Hollywood product, which is synonymous with cinema to most cinemagoers.

National cinema

Production: Handled by small companies on a per-project basis; no ownership of production assets. Small composite budgets and reliance on grants that need no repayment. Studio space and teams secured ad hoc as needed. Creative personnel closely engaged with their own projects but also contracted to work occasionally within the international service industry.

Distribution: No access to the operation of big distributors; occasional deals with small local or international distributors; reliance on guerrilla distribution.

Exhibition: Individual deals with theatres for occasional showings. Heavy reliance on TV exposure and festival screenings.

Audiences: Pleased to see the occasional domestic film but would not normally seek it out. Occasional instances of domestic blockbusters.

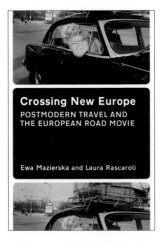

Home Entertainment by Ian Haydn Smith

A Changing World

In February 2008, Toshiba finally gave up on their bid to dominate the future, home entertainment market when they announced that they would not continue to produce their HD DVD technology. Prompted by Wal-Mart's announcement that it would only be stocking Sony's Blu-ray format, the move ended a prolonged period of speculation for both the industry and its customers, who were reticent to invest in what might become the Betamax of tomorrow.

Blu-ray players and discs have since become a ubiquitous presence in retail stores and online. Playstation 3, regarded by some as the most capable Blu-ray player on the market, best represents the demographic that studios aim their blockbuster product towards, so it was natural that big-budget mainstream releases would initially dominate availability on the new format. A riskier proposition faces smaller, niche DVD labels and their decision over whether – or when – to change. Moreover, with the dark cloud of a global recession looming, is it a greater risk for these labels to invest in this more expensive technology or in not keeping up with what is clearly the future of home entertainment?

The number of DVD labels continues to increase, as does the casualty rate. The biggest fatality in the UK in 2008 was Tartan, one of the larger labels, who had dominated Asian film releases for a number of years, as well as owning the back catalogue of many significant directors, including Ingmar Bergman.

Most mid-sized labels are experimenting with Blu-ray releases. For some, the dual-release

of new titles on DVD and Blu-ray is a short-term solution in gauging consumer interest. For many, there is no doubt about where the future lies. Having increased their output in recent months, it is likely that, within the next year and a half, all BFI releases will feature a simultaneous release.

Masters of Cinema have also entered the fray. Their Production Director, Nick Wrigley, recently offered his thoughts on why special-effects-laden blockbusters were not the only films that could profit from being released on Blu-ray: 'Regardless of the type of film, Blu-ray presents every film in higher definition and at 24fps – the same speed as projected film. There are no PAL or NTSC issues and the image resolution achievable is breathtaking. There are something like 90,000 DVD titles available in the UK, in a massively saturated market. Blu-ray has a fraction of that out there, under a thousand – so the sooner niche films are released on Blu-ray, the more likely they are to be noticed and enjoyed.'

Another avenue open to home entertainment, which Liz Rosenthal highlighted in her 'Industry Focus', is the massive potential of online screenings. Websites dedicated to showing films that might not otherwise be seen by the general public are becoming increasingly popular. So, why not embrace the opportunity to create another revenue stream for a back catalogue and also attract a new audience? That is exactly what Criterion have done.

In addition to their DVD library and initial foray into Blu-ray (an interesting selection of *Bottle Rocket*, *Chungking Express*, *The Man Who Fell to Earth*, *The Last Emperor* and *The Third*

Chungking Express

Man. And if you already own the DVD, you can upgrade for a reduced fee), Criterion have embarked on the ambitious Online Cinematheque, which offers the opportunity to download films to watch for one week, before choosing to purchase the DVD or Blu-ray (the cost of the download is deducted from the final purchase). A vast array of extras and writings on films can also be accessed. And, in conjunction with The Auteurs (www.theauteurs.com) – the 'online movie theatre and gathering place for film lovers' – there are monthly online film festivals to 'attend'.

Regional restrictions notwithstanding, Criterion's Online Cinematheque is a fantastic example of a label making the most of their library and expanding the size of their audience in an ever-diffuse environment.

DVD Round-Up

In a Silent Way

Artificial Eye follow-up last year's release of Louis Feuillade's *Fantomas* (1913) with his 1915 crime saga **Les Vampires** (Artificial Eye, R2). A criminal gang stalk the streets of Paris, led by the mysterious Irma Vep. Feuillade's ten-part serial is accompanied by a number of the director's short films. Those wanting more of the alluring femme fatale may wish to check out the re-release of Olivier Assayas' entertaining 'latex comedy' **Irma Vep** (1996; Second Sight, R2), in which Maggie Cheung plays herself in a modern remake of the crime saga, directed by Jean-Pierre Leaud's manic-depressive filmmaker.

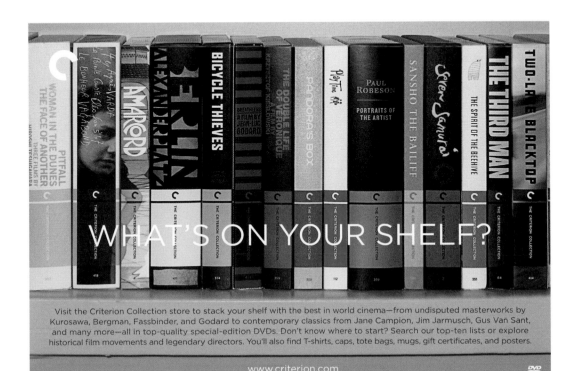

Flicker Alley surpassed themselves in 2008. Two classics by Abel Gance highlight the care and attention that has gone into the method behind the label's practice. **J'Accuse** (Flicker Alley, R1), one of Gance's most important works, is a breathtakingly ambitious film whose themes remain as pertinent now as they were when Gance directed the film 1919. A significant advance both technically and narratively, the release is accompanied by two short films and an insightful essay by Kevin Brownlow. No less remarkable is **La Roue** (1923; Flicker Alley, R1). Three years in the making and filmed almost entirely on location near Nice and on Mont Blanc, the love triangle at the heart of the narrative is explored through Gance's radical use of montage.

Saved from the Flames (Flicker Alley, R1), a collection of films shot on nitrate between 1896–1944, includes fiction shorts, animation, documentaries and musical performances. Organised across a number of themes, the pleasure of the collection lies in its ragbag quality: from the river Seine flooding in 1910 and a dirigible arriving over Los Angeles in 1924 to an early Stan Laurel comedy (*The Pest*, 1922) and the wonderful *Jazz Hot* (1939), featuring Django Reinhardt and Stéphane Grapelli.

There is little doubt, however, that the jewel of the label's collection so far is the exhaustive box set, **Georges Méliès: First Wizard of Cinema** (1896–1913) (Flicker Alley, R1). One of the best DVD releases of the year, the 13 plus hours of the director's films is a stunning achievement and, like all of Flicker Alley's output, it is immaculately presented.

Vive La France

George Franju's affectionate homage, *Le Grand Méliès* (1953) is included in the Flicker Alley box set. Not one to shy away from the fantastic, the double bill of **Judex/Nuits Rouge** (1963/1973; Masters of Cinema, R2) shows Franju at his surreal best. The former is the director's remake of Feuillade's 1916 classic (released last year by Flicker Alley) and

Les Demoiselles de Rochefort

is both beautiful and unsettling. The lesser known *Nuits Rouges* is a fine accompaniment, featuring Feuillade's grandson, Jacques Champreux, as the criminal mastermind, the Man Without a Face. Franju's horror classic, **Eyes Without a Face** (1960; Second Sight, R2), has also been made available and has lost none of its power.

The combination of Michel Legrand's score, Catherine Deneuve and Françoise Dorléac's performances, and the film's lustrous beauty, courtesy of an excellent transfer, make Jacques Demy's **Les Demoiselles de Rochefort** (1967; BFI, R2) a joy to watch. Included on the disc is Agnès Varda's 1993 film, *Les Demoiselles ont eu 25 ans*, offering an enlightening account of the film's production.

Some of Agnès Varda's best work can be found on **4 by Agnès Varda** (Criterion, R1). Featured are *La Pointe Courte* (1954), *Cléo from 5 to 7* (1961), *Le Bonheur* (1964) and *Vagabond* (1985). An excellent booklet featuring essays by Ginette Vincendeau, Adrian Martin, Amy

Taubin and Director of the Year contributor Chris Darke, makes this collection an excellent introduction to Varda's impressive body of work.

Of all the Nouvelle Vague directors, Jacques Rivette has for too long been underrepresented on DVD. Bluebell Films have gone some way to rectifying this with three films: **Love on the Ground** (1984; R2), **Wuthering Heights** (1985; R2) and **Gang of Four** (1988; R2). Although far from the director's finest period, the best of this collection is the Brontë adaptation, updated to 1930s rural France. Pared down to its essentials, the consequences of fate are accepted as inevitable, the characters playing their part with no hope of changing their destiny.

A sense of hopelessness permeates two stark accounts – both brilliant directorial debuts – of growing up. Bruno Dumont's **La vie de jésus** (1997; Masters of Cinema, R2) details the lives of a group of youths in a rural Flemish town. With its harsh view of life, frank sexual scenes and closing moments that bear the hallmark of Bresson's *Mouchette* (1967), it is a remarkable achievement. No less impressive is Maurice Pialat's **L'Enfance-nue** (1968; Masters of Cinema, R2). Michael Tarrazon plays a young boy whose violent behaviour finds him passed from one foster family to the next. This peripatetic life only serves to exacerbate his temper, until he finds himself in trouble with the law. Produced by François Truffaut, the two-disc edition includes Pialat's *L'Amour*

existe (1960), the director's fascinating short about life in the Paris Banlieues. Masters of Cinema has also released Pialat's **Police** (1985; Masters of Cinema, R2), which has many admirers, of which I am not one.

The English-subtitled release of Jean-Luc Godard's **Histoire(s) du Cinema** (1988-98; Artificial Eye, R2) finally arrived. No more does the non-French speaker have to browse the cherished ECM box set booklet that featured the film script, whilst watching a tired video recording. All eight episodes of Godard's eccentric, eclectic, frequently infuriating, but always fascinating personal history of cinema are present in this long-awaited box set. It is a reminder of just how brilliant Godard can be.

Love is the Devil

BFI at Home

With a collection of superb titles, the BFI has moved to the front rank of DVD labels. John Maybury's **Love is the Devil** (1998; BFI, R2) finally gets the release it deserves. Few films have attempted to portray the life of an artist

The Long Day Closes

as impressively as Maybury, a director with a keen visual sense. The first of two excellent trilogies, the **Bill Douglas Trilogy** (1972–78; BFI, R2) is a moving account of growing up. Also featured is the director's assured student film, *Come Dancing* (1970). One can only hope there are plans to release *Comrades* (1986) at some point.

Following last year's release of Terence Davies' *Distant Voices, Still Lives* (1988), the BFI have brought out another two DVDs of the director's work. **The Terence Davies Trilogy** (1976-83; BFI, R2) is both a brilliant and painful work of cinematic poetry. Through the life of his fictional alter ego, Davies presents an impassioned portrait of prejudice, guilt, self-doubt and sexual repression, whilst never stooping to self-indulgence or pity. **The Long Day Closes** (1992; BFI, R2) focuses on the period that Davies has often said was his happiest. Cinema is an escape to Bud (the remarkable Leigh McCormack) and Davies invests those moments with a sense of magic, a world away from the frequently brutal reality of growing up in 1950s working-class Britain. It is one of the best films ever made about childhood from one of the UK's greatest directors.

Antonioni and Pasolini

Of the Italian films released on DVD over the last year, Antonioni has fared particularly well. Mr Bongo released **L'Avventura** (1960; Mr Bongo, R2) and **Identification of a Woman** (1982; Mr Bongo, R2). However, it is **La Notte** (1961; Masters of Cinema, R2) and **Red Desert** (1964; BFI, R2) that stand out. Both have been meticulously restored to their original glory and are accompanied by informative booklets. If *La Notte* is the most immediately accessible of the two films, the spell cast by *Red Desert* lasts longer, leaving one haunted by its evocation of Italy's otherworldly industrial landscape.

Sàlo or The 120 Days of Sodom (1975; Criterion, R1 & BFI, R2) is an easier film to admire than it is to like, but both the Criterion and BFI releases offer a wealth of extras that place Pasolini's final work in the context of the director's oeuvre; outlining his reasons for making the film and documenting both the production and its reception. An unsettling, uncompromising and important film.

Red Desert

Ray and Rat-Trap

Artificial Eye have released two volumes of **The Satyajit Ray Collection** (Artificial Eye, R2). Volume one is the more accessible and arguably the most essential of the two, featuring the stunning melodrama *Mahanagar* (1963), shades of *Wild Strawberries* in *Nayak* (1966) and my favourite of the collection, *Charulata* (1964). This final film is dominated by a searing performance by Madhabi Mukherjee as a neglected wife who falls for the charms of her husband's cousin. Volume two includes one fine film, *Kaprush* (1965), which highlights Ray's skill in building tension, and two oddities, *Mahapurush* (1965) and *Joi Baba Felunath* (1978), which are lighter in tone, but lack the bite of Ray's best work.

Regarded by many as the heir to Ray, Adoor Gopalakrishnan first found international acclaim with his 1982 drama **Rat-Trap** (Second Run, R2). The story of the head of a feudal family (the excellent Karamana) unwilling to accept his place in a changing world, Gopalakrishnan presents his film as a beguilingly simple cautionary tale. The DVD includes an informative interview with the director.

Return to the German New Wave

Two directors from the German New Wave have recently had their back catalogue re-released. Axiom Films brought out the most acclaimed films of Wim Wenders, including his road trilogy, **Alice in the Cities** (1974), **Wrong Move** (1975) and **Kings of the Road** (1976), as well as **The American Friend** (1977), **Paris, Texas** (1984) and 1987's **Wings of Desire** (Axiom Films, R2). They all feature interviews with the director and limited editions include a collector's booklet with essays and articles. Most impressive of all is the **Wim Wenders Documentary Box Set** (Axiom Films, R2). It includes *Lightning Over Water* (1980), *Chambre 666* (1982), *Tokyo-Ga* (1985), *Notebook on Cities and Clothes* (1989) and *A Trick of Light* (1995), as well as an interview with the direc-

Paris, Texas

tor, articles on the films and extensive filmographies. Taken together, these films should offer ample evidence of the skills of a director who has too often been unjustly maligned.

Few directors over the course of the last year have been subject to so many re-issues as Rainer Werner Fassbinder. But very few are as deserving. For a long time it was almost impossible to find most of the director's work on DVD. Of the eight features in **Commemorative Collection 69–72** (Arrow Films, R2), *The Bitter Tears of Petra von Kant* and *The Merchant of Four Seasons* are the best known, but *Love is Colder Than Death* and *Beware of a Holy Whore* are also fine films. **Commemorative Collection 73–82** (Arrow Films, R2) includes *Effi Briest*, *Fox and His Friends*, *Chinese Roulette*, *The Marriage of Maria Braun* and the stunning *Fear Eats the Soul*. Both collections include a number of excellent documentaries, including a focus on the actresses who returned to perform for Fassbinder time and time again.

Berlin Alexanderplatz

Fassbinder Volume I (Artificial Eye, R2) features *Why Does Herr R. Run Amok?* (1970), *Martha* (1974), *Lola* (1981) and a documentary profile of the director. **Fassbinder Volume II** includes *In a Year of Thirteen Moons*, *The Third Generation* (1979), *Veronika Voss* (1981) and the portmanteau film, *Germany in Autumn*

(1978), which was made in reaction to the events surrounding the rise of the Red Army Faction. Though not as well known as the titles in the Arrow Films' collections, these volumes highlight the prodigious achievement of Fassbinder's 1970s work, not to mention his industrious work rate.

Most impressive of all is the release of Fassbinder's epic television series **Berlin Alexanderplatz** (1980; Criterion, R1 & Second Sight). No less daring in scope than Edgar Reitz's *Heimat*, it is set in Weimar Germany and encompasses the full scope of Alfred Döblin's immense novel, as it traces the attempts of Franz Biberkopf to lead an honest life following a spell in prison. Although both box sets are impressive, the ever reliable Criterion come out on top with their design (one of the year's best) and the inclusion of a 1931 adaptation of the novel, which was co-written by Döblin, as well as a booklet featuring an essay by Tom Twyker.

Other Directors

Peter Weir's **The Cars That Ate Paris** (1974, Second Sight, R2) remains one of the more eccentric debuts from a member of the Australian new wave; a cross between *Mad Max* and *Last of the Summer Wine* (a too-long-running British comedy set in the countryside). Weir's

Picnic at Hanging Rock

acclaimed sophomore feature, the dreamy, haunting **Picnic at Hanging Rock** (1975; Second Sight, R2) is treated to a three-disc edition. In addition to the Director's Cut and Original Version, there are two feature-length documentaries on the making of the film and the story that inspired it, as well as numerous interviews and *The Day of Saint Valentine* (1969), the first film version of the story, made by 13-year-old Tony Ingram.

In a short period of time, Mr Bongo, the acclaimed music label, has attracted a similar amount of praise for their DVD releases. Four films released last year justify the commendation. More discussed than seen, Glauber Rocha's **Black God White Devil** (1964; Mr Bongo, R0) is arguably the finest achievement of the Cinema Novo movement. Another classic of Latin American film, Tomas Gutierrez Alea's **Memories of Underdevelopment** (1968; Mr Bongo, R0) sidesteps a simplistic celebration of the Cuban revolution, in favour of analysing what it means to live in a post-revolutionary state.

Also available are two films by Wojciech Has. **The Saragossa Manuscript** (1965; Mr Bongo, R0) is the most famous. Acclaimed by filmmakers as diverse as Martin Scorsese and Luis Buñuel, it plays out like a cross between 'Don Quixote', 'The Adventures of Baron Munchausen' and Bergman's *The Seventh Seal*. It is an intoxicating brew that, thanks to Has's delicate balance of narrative control and wild imagination, captivates throughout. However, when compared to *The Hourglass Sanatorium* (1973; Mr Bongo, R0), *The Saragossa Manuscript* appears positively tame.

Another highlight of the last year was a sterling transfer of Miklós Jancsó's hugely influential **The Round-Up** (1965; Second Run, R0). The bridge between *My Way Home* (1964) and the more severe *The Red and the White* (1967), it is a remarkable piece of filmmaking as well as a damning indictment of the inhumanity of war. Shot on Hungary's open plains, it is rightly regarded as a classic of European cinema.

The Round-Up

Japanese Masters

Youth culture, sexuality and sexual violence permeate 1960s Japan in the early films of Nagisa Oshima. The startling **Naked Youth** (1960; Yume Pictures, R0) and its more expansive companion, **The Sun's Burial** (1960; Yume Pictures, R0), offer a bleak portrait of Japan's underbelly, whilst also revealing the director's growing dissatisfaction with his country's continued adherence to an image of itself that had long since faded. **Violence at High Noon** (1966, Yume Pictures, R0) offers an even franker view of Japanese societal norms, with an account of a real-life rapist's relationship with his wife and his only surviving victim.

Violence is not so much a fact of life as a stylistic exercise in the films of Seijun Suzuki. **Tokyo Drifter** (1966; Yume Pictures, R0) and **Branded to Kill** (1967; Yume Pictures, R0) offer a spellbinding take on the crime thriller. With their blend of cool music, 1960s kitsch, vertiginous camera angles and killers too chilled-out to care, the films remain pop-

Tokyo Drifter

culture classics. Although **Pistol Opera** (2001; Yume Pictures, R0) is something of a misfire, **Princess Raccoon** (2005; Yume Pictures, R0), starring Zhang Ziyi, is a joyful confection.

Superficially, the thematic concerns of Yasuzo Masumura might appear similar to Nagisa Oshima's. How they are presented could not be more different. **Kisses** (1957; Yume Pictures, R0) is no more sentimental than *Naked Youth*, but it avoids the nihilism of Oshima's later work. As for **Irezumi** (1966; Yume Pictures, R0), **Manji** (1964; Yume Pictures, R0) and **Red Angel** (1966; Yume Pictures, R0), their blend of eroticism and the surreal result in a heady brew that leaves the viewer wondering why Masumura has never received more attention.

Shohei Imamura's Palme d'Or winner **The Ballad of Narayama** (1983; AnimEigo, R1) is finally available, thanks to an English-language anime and samurai film specialist. Arguably one of the greatest Japanese films of the last thirty years, it features superb central performances by Sumiko Sakamoto and Ken Ogata.

Kids Return

Although Takeshi Kitano's career as a filmmaker has been somewhat erratic this decade, his output in the 1990s was something to marvel at. **Takeshi Kitano Collection** (Second Sight, R2) features most of his best work from this period. It is essential for its inclusion of the previously unavailable *A Scene at the Sea* (1993) and the semi-autobiographical *Kids Return* (1996). Their mix of tenderness and brutality prefigures Kitano's best film, *Hana-Bi* (1997), which would have been more welcome in the collection than the feeble comedy, *Getting Any* (1994).

Masters of Cinema have released a number of Kenji Mizoguchi films as double bills, the highlights of which are **Chikamatsu Monogatari/Uwasa No Onna** (1954; Masters of Cinema, R2) and **Ugetsu Monogatari/ Oyû-sama** (1953/51; Masters of Cinema, R2). The former features two accounts of a love affair, one historical and one contemporary. The better known of the two, *Chikamatsu Monogatari*, tells the tale of an affair between a merchant's wife and his employee. Through a series of misunderstandings, the pair are accused of being lovers and are forced to run away. While in hiding, their relationship develops, which Mizoguchi presents with an empathetic eye for the small moments of intimacy between the couple. One of cinema's finest ghost stories, *Ugetsu Monogatari* is based on the writings of Ueda Akinari and is rightly considered one of the best films ever

Days of Heaven

made. Employing his trademark long takes to stunning effect, Mizoguchi blends realism with the supernatural in his recreation of sixteenth-century Japan. *Oyû-sama* concerns two sisters' love for the same man and stars Mizoguchi regular, Tanaka Kinuyo (she appears in both films). The quality of the releases (as one has come to expect of all Masters of Cinema titles) – from the transfer of the film, to the wealth of extras – are exceptional.

Essential Criteria

Another label where the quality is a given is Criterion. Both **The Ice Storm** (1997; Criterion, R1) and Terence Malick's **Days of Heaven** (1978; Criterion, R1) are sterling releases. The former is arguably Ang Lee's best film to date, while Malick's film continues to bewitch. Its digitally re-mastered transfer is breathtaking, presenting Nestor Almendros's stunning images in a way that has rarely been seen since the film originally screened.

The four-disc edition of **The Last Emperor** (1987; Criterion, R1) presents fine digital transfers of the theatrical and television versions of the film, as well as a plethora of extras, including five documentaries, interviews with those involved in making the film and an illustrated booklet featuring essays, interviews and a production diary. The transfer is suitably impressive. Interestingly, it is the television version that impresses the most. Fifty minutes longer than the theatrical version, it acquires a more stately pace, allowing Bertolucci's daring character study to unfold into one of the finest films of the 1980s.

The Last Emperor

Paul Schrader's **Mishima: A Life in Four Chapters** also appears in a wonderful edition. His most visually accomplished film, Schrader was closely involved in the release and the care and attention pays off handsomely; from the eye-catching cover design to the extras, including the BBC's fascinating 'The Strange Case of Yukio Mishima'. Something of a companion piece (or vice-versa) to Schrader's film, **Patriotism**, Yukio Mishima's only film was, for me, the surprise of the year. Shot over two days in 1965 and based on the author's own short story (included in the booklet), it is a film of devastating intensity, whose blurring of the lines between death and sexual desire places this film alongside Genet's *Un chant d'amour* (1950) as one of the erotic masterpieces of world cinema.

The Ice Storm

Total Eclipse

Following last year's *Late Ozu* I wondered if Eclipse, Criterion's sister label, would bring out his early family comedy *I Was Born, But…* (1932). Lo and behold, the new year saw the release of **Silent Ozu** (Eclipse, R1), featuring that film and two others from the period, *Tokyo Chorus* (1931) and *Passing Fancy* (1933), which witness the director's vision fully formed, although their light humour might surprise anyone only used to the director's later work.

Lubitsch Musicals (Eclipse, R1) covers the same period as the Ozu and also displays a deftness of touch. The films are a pleasure to watch, particularly in the coupling of Maurice Chevalier and Jeanette MacDonald. What

Love Parade (1929), *Monte Carlo* (1930) and *One Hour With You* (1932) did was to blend a European sensibility with the best technology of the time, which created the template for the film musical. A highlight of the collection is Claudette Colbert's manic performance in *The Smiling Lieutenant* (1931), which beggars belief.

Postwar Kurosawa (Eclipse, R1) is something of a mixed bag, featuring five films in a modern-day setting. *The Idiot* (1951) is an ambitious, but only partially successful, update of the Dostoyevsky novel. *No Regrets for Our Youth* (1946), featuring the director's only female protagonist, often simmers without a sense that it is building up to anything. *One Wonderful Sunday* (1947), Kurosawa's only foray into shomin-geki, is a slice of bittersweet whimsy, as he presents a couple attempting to make ends meet, their meagre earnings allowing them a brief respite from their hardship each Sunday, which they spend in a park. But it is Toshiro Mifune's collaboration with Kurosawa on *Scandal* (1950) and *I Live in Fear* (1955) that makes the box set worthwhile. The former is an early attack on media intrusion and freedom of speech, while the last film in the collection features a searing performance from the actor as an older man living in fear of the nuclear age.

Documentary

Interest in feature documentary releases may have waned in the last few years, but, on DVD, there is a whole world to be discovered. Where better to start than with the BFI's exceptional box sets, **Land of Promise** (BFI, R2) and **Addressing the Nation** (BFI, R2). The former covers the British documentary film movement from 1930–1950, featuring over forty films from acclaimed directors such as John Grierson, Humphrey Jennings, Robert Flaherty, Basil Wright, Paul Rotha and Arthur Elton. As a document of the period the films featured are invaluable, but they also possess an impressive aesthetic quality. Likewise, the first volume of films from the GPO Film

Unit, Addressing the Nation, covering the period 1933–35, are by turns fascinating and a joy to watch. Cavalcanti's *Coal Face* (1935) perfectly blends Benjamin Britten's score and W.H. Auden's words with images from the frontline of the country's heavy industry, while Basil Wright's *Song of Ceylon* (1934) is a heady mix of the informational and exotic, filmed on location in Sri Lanka. The inclusion of the joyous A Colour Box (1934) begs just one question: will anyone ever release a collection of Len Lye's films?

Bruce Weber: The Film Collection – 1987–2008 (Metrodome, R2) offers a comprehensive retrospective of the director's career, from shorts, music videos and his feature work: *Broken Noses* (1987), *Let's Get Lost* (1988), *Chop Suey* (2000) and *A Letter to True* (2003). Accompanied by a booklet featuring a selection of Weber's photography, it is an impressive release. Amongst the highlights is one of the best jazz documentaries ever made. *Let's Get Lost's* portrait of Chet Baker is both heartbreaking and an impressive artistic achievment.

Artefact Films is a new UK documentary label. Of the impressive array of releases so far this year, two stand out. Charles Fergusson's **No End in Sight** (2007; Artefact Films, R2) is arguably the best documentary made about the Iraq conflict so far. Detailing the American occupation following the overthrow of Saddam Hussein, it presents a litany of failures and betrayals that have endangered the lives of Iraqi citizens and America's own forces.

No End in Sight

Lake of Fire (2006; Artefact Films, R2) took Tony Kaye over a decade to make and the result is a remarkable account of the abortion debate in the US. An example of the power of documentary, it presents all sides of the debate, exploring all the moral, ethical and legal arguments. It is an essential contribution to an incendiary topic.

Cult Film

Few releases can match the warts'n'all collection that is **Caligula: Imperial Edition** (1979; Arrow Films, R2). Nutty as a fruitcake and presented in three different versions, Bob Guccione's production (featuring the extensive involvement of Tinto Brass, who is credited with principle photography) is strangely hypnotic viewing. Seeing John Gielgud and Peter O'Toole one minute and hardcore pornography the next is an unsettling experience. Arrow Films have released most of Tinto Brass's distinct oeuvre.

Caligula

For those of a more sensitive disposition, **The Texas Chainsaw Massacre: Seriously Ultimate Edition** (1974; Second Sight, R2) might be to your liking. A high-definition transfer is accompanied by two discs of extras, including outtakes, interviews and deleted scenes. What surprises most when watching the film again is Hooper's adherence to the old rule of show less scare more. Compared with the recent trend for 'torture porn', the film is positively restrained, although still bloody terrifying!

The Texas Chainsaw Massacre

King of New York (1989; Arrow Films, R2), Abel Ferrara's magnificent crime drama is finally given decent treatment on DVD with a two-disc edition that features numerous documentaries and interviews. Hopefully it will be popular enough for a label to pick up many of the director's other films, which have rarely screened outside the festival circuit.

King of New York

Shorts

A focus on short films will be a regular section in the IFG from 2010. As some kind of introduction, it is worth highlighting the work of Cinema 16, which has successfully managed to bring short film collections to a larger audience. The four collections are **British Short Films**, **European Short Films**, **American Short Films** and **World Short Films** (Cinema 16, R0). Each collection features 16 shorts by world cinema's finest practitioners. In some, themes that mature in later works are already evident, whilst other films stand alone as singular pieces. The films run the gamut of style, format and genre, but all display a remarkable vision by their creators. Cinema 16 has yet to play a wrong note; let's hope it continues that way.

Finally, refusing easy categorisation is **He Who Hits First, Hits Twice: The Urgent Cinema of Santiago Alvarez** (ELF, R1), an exceptional collection of films by the Cuban agit-prop filmmaker, whose propagandist film collages bridge the gap between news reportage and art film. Of the eight films featured, *Now* (1965) and *79 Primaveras* (1969) are stunning examples of Alvarez's style.

DVD Releases of the Year
Georges Méliès: First Wizard of Cinema (1896–1913) (Flicker Alley)
L'Enfance-nue (Masters of Cinema)
Histoire(s) du Cinema (Artificial Eye)
The Long Day Closes (BFI)
Black God, White Devil (Mr Bongo)
The Ballad of Narayama (AnimEigo)
Patriotism/Mishima: A Life in Four Chapters (Criterion)
Silent Ozu (Eclipse)
Land of Promise (BFI)
Lake of Fire (Artefact Films)

Lake of Fire

Key DVD labels

Ian Haydn Smith profiles the essential distributors of world cinema in the English language

AnimEigo
The definitive Anime and Samurai film destination, which also features a number of non-animated titles.
www.animeigo.com

Arrow Films
A strong range of films across the spectrum of world cinema, some with a fine array of extras.
www.arrowfilms.co.uk

Artefact Films
A new UK documentary label, featuring an impressive roster of films.
www.artefactmedia.com

Artificial Eye
A major UK label, whose extensive catalogue reflects the best in contemporary and art-house releases.
www.artificial-eye.com

Axiom Films
High-quality presentation of new and classic releases, running the gamut of world cinema and the arts.
www.axiomfilms.co.uk

BFI
Now an essential DVD label, covering world cinema, animation, documentary and archive material, and experimental film.
http://filmstore.bfi.org.uk

Criterion
The benchmark of excellence amongst DVD labels, now spearheading the future with the impressive Online Cinematheque.
www.criterion.com

Facets
An eclectic and wide-ranging selection of films from around the world.
www.facets.org

Flicker Alley
Specialising in pre-sound and early film, this label has quickly established itself as one of the best.
www.flickeralley.com

Masters of Cinema
MoC match Criterion, both in transfer quality and the extensive extras and accompanying booklets.
www.eurekavideo.co.uk/moc

Milestone
A US label, whose recent releases are a mark of high quality.
www.milestonefilms.com

Mr Bongo
The handful of releases from this relatively new label display a refreshing daringness in choice and design.
www.buymrbongo.com

Optimum World
One of the most expansive UK labels, covering all genres and tastes.
www.optimumreleasing.com

Other Cinema
One of the best collections of underground and experimental films from North America.
www.othercinema.com

Second Run DVD
An excellent collection of must-have titles by many directors who have dropped off the cinematic radar.
www.secondrundvd.com

Second Sight
An eclectic collection of films and TV programmes, ranging from classical Hollywood to contemporary world cinema.
www.secondsightfilms.co.uk

Soda Pictures
A diverse catalogue populated with some of the best contemporary world cinema releases.
www.sodapictures.com

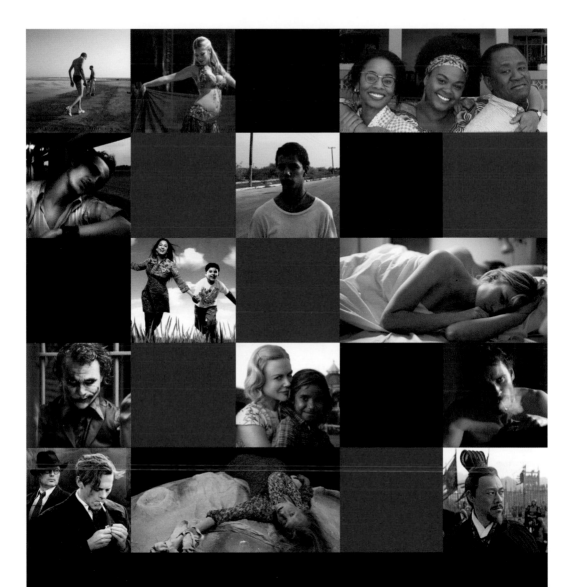

World Survey

6 continents | 123 countries | 1,000s of films......

Afghanistan Sandra Schäfer

While shooting his new film, **Opium War** (*Jang-e taryak*), the 2004 Golden Globe award winner for Best Foreign Language Film, Siddiq Barmak, found himself fighting numerous obstacles. Firstly, in 2005 poppy seeds were unable to blossom on the newly sown fields. Then, in June 2006, the government was unable to guarantee the safety of those involved in the shoot. It wasn't until 2008 that Barmak finally completed the Afghan/Japanese/South Korean co-production. He uses his own brand of humour, creating a grotesque picture of Afghan society caught between a state of survival and the West's desire to restore 'democracy'.

Diana Sageb's short documentary **25 Percent** (*25 Darsad*) contextualizes the contradictions of the current process of 'democratization' by looking at gender politics. Its title refers to the number of women now employed by the Afghan Parliament, following an article in the new constitution that permitted their entry, which was passed in 2004. Sageb, who studied film in Iran, paints an impressive portrait of six female representatives of the Parliament. She accompanies the women

Diana Saqeb's **25 Percent**

during their election campaigns in the provinces, highlighting the contradiction between the misogynistic debates taking place in parliament and the equal opportunities law being passed. The female representatives speak openly in front of the camera, not only about their political work, but also private issues and taboos such as motherhood, arranged marriage and facing societal constraints.

Alka Sadat's **Half Value Life**

Director Alka Sadat also dedicates her 20 minute documentary, **Half Value Life** (*Dar dehkadayee ke naaqesul-aqlam mikhanand*) to the situation of women. She accompanies the first female lawyer in Herat, who spends the majority of her working hours campaigning for women's rights.

Saba Sahar, who in real life works for the police, directs and acts as an undercover police-woman in the action film **Rescue** (*Nejat*). She plays Nelofer, who attepts to arrest a gang involved in the lucrative business of child abduction. Constantly placed in danger, she employs her impressive martial arts skills to protect herself. Shot in Pakistani Lollywood-style, the film was digitally produced at Homestudio and is mainly aimed at a local audience. Saba Sahar also completed the patriotic action film, **My Life, My Homeland** (*Nan-e man watan-e man*), in which she plays a military doctor and daughter of a military commander, who gains the trust of disillusioned villagers who have, for over 25 years, preferred the tyranny of a criminal gang to being ruled by government forces.

Saba Sahar, director and star of **Rescue**

Since there are little more than a dozen cinemas in Afghanistan, attended mostly by men, public exhibitions in mobile cinemas and television play a central role. Roya Sadat directs the very popular series *The House's Secret*, which has been produced by a private channel, Tolo, since 2007. It successfully captures the familiar social and political difficulties faced by Afghan society, which is mixed with a fair amount of humour. Aigela Rezaie, first known for her role in Samira Makhmalbaf's *At Five in the Afternoon*, plays the lead.

Aside of *The House's Secret*, Indian soap operas are also very popular with audiences, although five of these were banned in 2008, following pressure on the minister of culture by religious leaders, who claimed that they were immoral, un-islamic and in breach of the Media Law. Tolo and Afghan-TV are opposing the ban and an investigation into them is being conducted by authorities in Kabul. The head of Tolo has accused the government of purposefully trying to weaken politically unpopular channels and has demanded precise rules on what constitutes Islamic and un-Islamic content.

James Bond director Marc Forster shot the first Hollywood production in Afghanistan since *Rambo III*. **The Kite Runner** is based on the best selling novel by Khaled Hosseini. The film was banned in Afghanistan because of its depiction of sexual abuse and ethnic conflicts. Due to death threats, the two lead actors and their families had to be flown out of the country following the film's release.

Spring 2008 saw the first Second Take Film Festival on Gender & Society, presented in association with the artist groups Mazefilm from Berlin, CACA-Kabul and the state owned film institute, Afghan Film. 500 visitors attended daily to watch films from Afghanistan, Iran, India, Belgium, Germany and USA. Guests included the celebrated Iranian director Rakhshan Bani-Etemad. Early summer saw the third International Documentary and Shortfilm Festival take place in Kabul. It is an initiative by Afghan Film, the artist group Basa-Film, the Goethe Institute and the French Cultural Centre.

Director Roya Sadat is currently working on a sixty-minute feature about forced marriage, a Turkmenian tradition allowing the sale of girls for money. Latif Ahmadi is finalising production on the soundtrack to his feature **Roots** (*Rishe*), about an Afghan man returning from American exile.

The year's best films
Opium War (Siddiq Barmak)
25 Darsad (Diana Saqeb)

Quote of the year
'Cinema must guard against people forgetting their own tragedies. If we cannot remember the bad things, we cannot feel the renewal of life.' *Director of* Opium War, **SIDDIQ BARMAK.**

SANDRA SCHÄFER is a filmmaker and curator. With Elfe Brandenburger she made the film *Passing the Rainbow*. She co-curates the film festival SPLICE IN / SECOND TAKE.

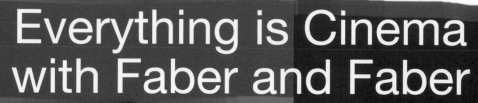
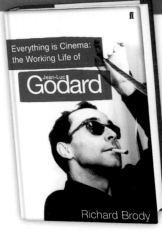

Algeria Maryam Touzani

The desire to make films is tangible in Algeria. The existing financial difficulties often mean external economic aid is necessary to help feature production. And although many of Algeria's filmmakers live abroad, their attachment to their homeland and their desire to contribute positively to the country's cinema industry is ever present. Amor Hakkar left Algeria to live in France when he was six months old. In 2002, after returning for the burial of his father, he visited the Aurès, where he was born. Inspired by his voyage, he wrote the scenario of his Berber-language feature, **The Yellow House** (*La Maison Jaune*), in which he plays the role of Mouloud who, on being informed of his son's death, sets off to collect his body. Realising upon his return that his wife will never again be the same, he does everything he can to make her happy. Through a simplistic setting and in the midst of overwhelming sadness, Hakkar creates a heartfelt drama, even managing moments of humour. It is a welcome return to the cinema for the Algerian director.

Amor Hakkar's **The Yellow House**

Lyes Salem's first feature, **Mascarades** (*Masquerades*), is Algeria's bid for Best Foreign Language Film at the Academy Awards. His

Lyes Salem's **Mascarades**

Cousines had previously won him the César for Best Short Film in 2004. In the new film, Salem plays Mounir, a proud and haughty young man who seeks recognition in his small Algerian village, but is always made fun of because of his sister Rym's narcolepsy. One night, while drunk, he announces that a wealthy foreigner has asked for her hand in marriage, failing to realise the impact his lie will have on his family's destiny. With its humour and a taste for the burlesque, *Mascarades* explores, in a surprisingly light and amusing manner, issues that are at the core of contemporary Algerian society.

Tariq Teguia's 2006 debut feature, *Rome Rather Than You*, the story of a young couple in love who desperately try to flee Algeria, attracted a great deal of attention. His second feature, **Inland** (*Gabbla*), shot in High Definition, is the story of a topographer who relocates to a remote region of western Algeria, until recently a fundamentalist stronghold. He soon meets a young black African woman who wants to return to her homeland and together they embark on a desert trip. Teguia's love of photography is clearly visible in his beautiful shots of the vast desert.

Rabah Ameur-Zaïmeche's third feature film, **Adhen** (*Le Dernier des Macquis*), completes his remarkable social trilogy. He stars as Mao, a Muslim boss in charge of a forlorn French factory, who opens a mosque and decides to designate himself as the imam. As with his other films, Ameur-Zaïmeche maintains his shrewd vision on the state of the Muslim community in France, in this symbolic analysis of the relationship between work and religion.

Rabah Ameur-Zaïmeche's **Adhen**

Through its portrayal of everyday life, French director Philippe Faucon's **In Life** (*Dans la vie*) explores the relations between Arab and Jewish communities in France. Halima nurses an elderly, ill-tempered Jewish lady, Esther. Against all odds, the two women build a strong relationship based on mutual understanding and tolerance, with Esther able to enjoy life again.

Female director Nadia Cherabi's **The Other Side of the Mirror** (*L'envers du miroir*) is the story of a taxi driver who, on finding an abandoned baby on his backseat, decides to search for its mother. A five-episode version of the film has been made for Algerian television. **Algeria, Unspoken Stories** (*Algérie, histoires à ne pas dire*) plunges the viewer deep into the country's complex past and its contemporary social realities. In Jean Pierre Ledo´s documentary, four people relate their tragic stories, drawing the audience back into the era of national liberation. Florent Emilio Siri also seeks to recreate a moment from the past with **Intimate Enemy** (*L'Ennemi Intime*), in which the moral values of a young lieutenant at the head of an outpost in Algeria, during its war for independence, are put to the test.

Algeria's past is an inveterate issue in the country's cinema, as are the complex social relations resulting from it. Having set itself apart for many years, Algeria seems to be opening to art and culture from around the world. Festivals are appearing and have attracted international recognition. The International Amazigh Film Festival and the International Film Festival of Oran are spearheading this new burst of activity. But although there is hope, the unsteady foundation of the Algerian cinema industry remains a cause for concern. Though lacking the lavish production values of some other countries, the films currently surfacing in Algeria prove that if there is passion, the rest will follow.

The year's best films
The Yellow House (Amor Hakkar)
Mascarades (Lyes Salem)
Adhen (Rabah Ameur-Zaïmeche)

Quote of the year
'I had almost forgotten I was a child of the Aurés. From all the encounters and the walks through this hostile yet beautiful region was born my very deep and intimate desire to make this film…' AMOR HAKKAR, *Director of* The Yellow House.

Directory
All Tel/Fax numbers begin (+213)
Cinémathèque Algérienne, 49 rue Larbi Ben M'Hidi, Algiers. Tel: (2) 737 548. Fax: (2) 738 246. www.cinematheque.art.dz.

MARYAM TOUZANI is a freelance journalist based in Morocco and working internationally, specialising in art and culture.

Argentina Alfredo Friedlander

I n 2008, cinema attendance remained relatively the same as the previous year, but the number of films released has gradually increased, to almost three hundred. On average, half of these releases are from the US. The rest are mainly Argentine, French, British and, to a lesser extent, Italian. A surprising presence was **Death at a Funeral**, an English production, presented in Argentina by an independent distributor, which took twelfth place, with over 550,000 spectators, even though it was a commercial failure in its own country. Annual box office returns also saw an increase due to a rise in ticket prices.

It is difficult to list the exact number of domestic theatrical releases, as some films only show once or twice a week in a single cinema for about a month. Taking this into account, the number should be around eighty, similar to 2007.

The Cannes Film Festival featured five Argentine films. This was the country's strongest participation in the festival's history and two of them, **Lion's Den** (*Leonera*) and **The Headless Woman** (*La mujer sin cabeza*), were part of the Official Selection. *Lion's Den*,

Martina Gusman in Pablo Trapero's **Lion's Den**

director Pablo Trapero's fifth film, was his third presentation at Cannes. His wife, Martina Gusmán, arguably deserving of the Best Actress award, gives a powerful interpretation of a pregnant inmate in a women's prison. Lucrecia Martel's *The Headless Woman* received mixed reviews. Like her previous films, *The Swamp* and *The Holy Girl*, the action takes place in Salta, a province in the north of Argentina, where Martel was born. The climate and atmosphere of Salta prevails over an underwhelming narrative. Martel was also appointed as a member of the jury at the recent Venice Film Festival.

The three other Argentine films shown during the festival included Lisandro Alonso's **Liverpool**, which was featured in the Director's Fortnight. This makes Alonso a record holder, as all four of his films have been screened at Cannes. It revolves around the arrival of a freighter at an Atlantic port and a seaman's return to the place of his birth, to visit his ailing mother. Pablo Fendrik's **Blood Appears** (*La sangre brota*) competed in the International Critics' Week. It tells the story of a cab driver, superbly played by Arturo Goetz, who has 24 hours to obtain US$1,000 in order to help his troubled older son, while his younger son plans to steal the money.

Argentine films were poorly represented at other international film festivals. **Café de los Maestros**, a tango documentary by Miguel Kohan, was well received by the public at Berlin. Albertina Carri's fourth movie **La Rabia** also screened there. Set in the Pampas, the film concerns two peasant families whose lives intertwine through infidelity, violence and tragedy. It was released in only two theatres in Argentina.

The San Sebastián Film Festival screened Daniel Burman's **Empty Nest** (*El nido vacío*) in its Official Competition. It depicts the life of a popular writer (Oscar Martínez) and his wife (Cecilia Roth), who decides to return to her studies at university once their adult children have left home. As with Burman's previous films, it features a strong Jewish element, particularly at the end, when the couple visit their daughter (Inés Efrón) in Israel.

Daniel Burman's **Empty Nest**

The Buenos Aires International Film Festival (BAFICI) celebrated its tenth year with over four hundred films and two competing sections, National and International. Yulene Olaizola's Mexican drama, *Shakespeare and Victor Hugo's Intimacies* won the International Competition. The National Competition prize went to Alejo Hoijman's documentary, **Unit 25**, about a penitentiary populated exclusively by people who practise evangelism.

The 23rd International Film Festival of Mar del Plata returns to its original November slot, with veteran film filmmaker José Martínez Suárez as its new director.

One of the best Argentine films of 2008 is **The Next Station** (*La próxima estación*). It is the fourth of a series of five documentaries by *The Hour of the Furnaces* director, Fernando E. Solanas. The film dramatically reflects the abandonment of the country's public transport infrastructure, focusing on the deterioration of national train services. Blame is attributed to governmental institutions, from President Menem's tenure through to the present administration under President Cristina Kirchner.

Another documentary deserving attention is **1973, a Cry of the Heart** (*1973, un grito de corazón*) by Liliana Mazure, the new president of INCAA, the National Cinema Organisation. The title refers to the dramatic moments when General Perón returned to Argentina to become President again.

Comedy has been more prevalent among recent Argentinian releases. Juan Taratuto's **A Boyfriend for My Wife** (*Un novio para mi mujer*) was seen by nearly one-and-a-half million people, enabling it to compete against Hollywood blockbusters such as *Kung-Fu Panda*, *Wall-E* and *The Dark Knight*. It ended the year as the only local (and non-American) film to appear in the box office top ten. A simple story, Adrián Suar plays a married man who decides to get rid of his wife (an excellent performance by Valeria Bertuccelli) by finding her a lover. Bertuccelli also appeared in **Rain**, a co-production with Spain, directed by Paula Hernández. It tells of a chance meeting, on a rainy day, between a woman who has left her husband and lives in her car, and an Argentinian (Ernesto Alterio) who normally lives in Spain.

Valeria Bertuccelli in Paula Hernández's **Rain**

Another comedy, Mariano Mucci's **Reasons Not to Fall in Love** (*Motivos para no enamorarse*) is the improbable love story of an elderly man and a young woman working at a call centre. It features fine performances by

Mariano Mucci's **Reasons not to Fall in Love**

Jorge Marrale and the young Celeste Cid, in her screen debut.

Leonardo Favio's **Aniceto**, a predictable love triangle, was a disappointing remake of one of his earliest films. Unlike *Nazareno Cruz y el Lobo* and *Juan Moreira*, the most successful Argentine films of the year, Favio's film only ran for two weeks.

Lamb of God (*Cordero de Dios*), partially based on real events, is an impressive debut for Lucía Cedrón. When Arthur (Jorge Marrale) is kidnapped, his granddaughter Guillermina (Leonora Balcarce) turns to her mother for the ransom. Teresa (Mercedes Morán), who lives in Paris, was also kidnapped by paramilitary forces in 1978 and immediately returns to help Guillermina. As a result, Guillermina discovers the truth about her grandfather's intervention to obtain the release of her mother.

In 2009, the number of Argentine releases should continue to be strong but their revenue share is likely to remain around, or even under, ten percent.

The year's best films
The Next Station (Fernando E. Solanas)
Lion's Den (Pablo Trapero)
Café de los Maestros (Miguel Kohan)
Empty Nest (Daniel Burman)
Lamb of God (Lucía Cedrón)

Quote of the year
'The first challenge was to shoot at more than 3,500km south from Buenos Aires, in Ushuaia, in winter and with a temperature some days of minus 12 degrees Celsius; its was something new.' *Director* **LISANDRO ALONSO**, *referring to the hardship experienced during the making of* **Liverpool.**

Directory
All Tel/Fax numbers begin (+54)
Critics Association of Argentina, Maipu 621 Planta Baja, 1006 Buenos Aires. Tel/Fax: 4322 6625. cinecronistas@yahoo.com.
Directors Association of Argentina (DAC), Lavalle 1444, 7° Y, 1048 Buenos Aires. Tel/Fax: 4372 9822. dac1@infovia.com.ar. www.dacdirectoresdecine. com.ar.
Directors of Photography Association, San Lorenzo 3845, Olivos, 1636 Buenos Aires. Tel/Fax: 4790 2633. adf@ba.net. www.adfcine.com.ar.
Exhibitors Federation of Argentina, Ayacucho 457, 1° 13, Buenos Aires. Tel/Fax: 4953 1234. empcinemato@infovia.com.ar.
Film University, Pasaje Guifra 330, 1064 Buenos Aires. Tel: 4300 1413. Fax: 4300 1581. fuc@ucine. edu.ar. www.ucine.edu.ar.
General Producers Association, Lavalle 1860, 1051 Buenos Aires. Tel/Fax: 4371 3430. argentinasonofilm@impsat1.com.ar.
National Cinema Organisation (INCAA), Lima 319, 1073 Buenos Aires. Tel: 6779 0900. Fax: 4383 0029. info@incaa.gov.ar.
Pablo Hicken Museum and Library, Defensa 1220, 1143 Buenos Aires. Tel: 4300 5967. www. museudelcinedb@yahoo.com.ar.
Producers Guild of Argentina (FAPCA), Godoy Cruz 1540, 1414 Buenos Aires. Tel: 4777 7200. Fax: 4778 0046. recepcion@patagonik.com.ar.
Sindicato de la Industria Cinematográfia de Argentina (SICA), Juncal 2029, 1116 Buenos Aires. Tel: 4806 0208. Fax: 4806 7544. sica@sicacine. com.ar. www.sicacine.com.ar.

ALFREDO FRIEDLANDER is a member of the Asociación de Cronistas Cinemato-gráficos de Argentina. He writes regularly for www.leedor.com and presents movies at the 55-year-old Cine Club Núcleo.

Armenia Susanna Harutyunyan

'The Apricot Revolution' was the title of David D'Arcy's article on Armenian cinema, published in *Screen International* on 25 July 2008. It highlights the importance of the Golden Apricot International Film Festival (GAIFF), which was founded five years ago. The festival has been seen as a revolution in overcoming the deep crisis of national film production in Armenia and in the integration of Armenian cinema within the global film community.

As D'Arcy states: 'At the Golden Apricot … international cinema is meeting the culture of this small nation whose diaspora reaches from the former Soviet Union to Paris, Santa Monica and Toronto. Armenia does not have much film production today … But it did have its own active studio under the Soviet system, and its film culture runs deep.'

In addition to a wide range of international titles, the festival played host to an ever-expanding film market, offering a gateway to an entire region's cinematic output. There was also a masterclass by acclaimed Canadian-Armenian filmmaker Atom Egoyan and a tribute to Californian-Armenian dramatist and author, William Saroyan.

Narine Mkrtchyan & Arsen Azatyan's **The Return of the Prodigal Son**

The festival also hosts a unique programme called 'Armenian Panorama', where new national film production, as well as films made globally by filmmakers of Armenian origin, are presented. The festival is growing into a major platform for Armenian directors and unlocks the doors for Armenian films to gain access to leading international festivals.

The world premiere of Narine Mkrtchyan and Arsen Azatyan's **The Return of the Prodigal Son** (*Anarak Vordu Veradardze*) took place at the 13th Pusan International Film Festival in South Korea. That festival, along with Rotterdam, are partnered with the Golden Apricot in a 'sisterhood agreement' that was signed in 2007, an arrangement that should guarantee wider coverage of Armenian films in the future.

Border (*Sahman*), the new film by GAIFF director Harutyun Khachatryan, will receive its premiere at the 38th Rotterdam Film Festival in late January 2009. This docu-drama surveys the landscape after the country's war with Azerbaijan in the late 1990s, from the perspective of a she-buffalo. The financing for the film came from various sources, including state funds, an Armenian and Netherlands co-production deal with Hubert Bals Fund participation, and other co-production deals. Such deals are typical for local Armenian features produced during the last year, but state support remains a vital source, as it sometimes covers a significant part of their budgets.

In 2009, the state subsidies for the national film industry will be about US$1.9 million. Although subsides appear to have increased over the last year, the amount allocated for film production is the same (US$825,000 for features films; US$365,000 animated films; and US$290,000 for documentaries). However, the state subsidy for the participation of Armenian films in festivals and the presentation of domestic product at leading film markets has increased. From early next year, the state will launch a new programme targeted at the development and support of alternative ways of distribution across all regions in Armenia. The programme, headed by the National Centre of Cinema and entitled 'Movie-theatre on Wheels', aims to reconnect audiences countrywide with its national cinema. This relationship had eroded over the last decade and it is hoped that this new programme will generate great interest amongst the population.

Bonded Parallels (*Khchechvatz Zugaherner*), the long-awaited feature debut by Hovhannes Galstyan, had been delayed for two years due to underfunding during post-production. The film presents two storylines, taking place during different time periods, but sharing one common theme: the fate of two heroines – mother and daughter. Shooting took place in Armenia and Norway. It was co-produced with partners from France and Norway, and features an international cast of actors from Armenia, France, Norway and Syria.

Mikayel Dovaltyan's **Landslide** (*Soghank*) is a fantasy-thriller, an unusual genre for Armenian cinema. A sudden landslide swallows up the film's protagonist and sucks him underground. What kind of life, if any, is under there? What does this underground world look like? Strangely, life appears to differ very little in this alternate world.

Suren Babayan's **A Nude** (*Bnord*) is expected to be completed by early 2009. Acclaimed Armenian actor Jean-Pier Nshanian, who has recently starred in a number of local films, plays a mentally unbalanced man whose inner turmoil results in his loss of identity, which he compensates for by an increasing obsession with spying on a stranger's family.

Director Harutyun Khachatryan speaking at the 4th Golden Apricot International Film Festival

The year's best films
Border (Harutyun Khachatryan)
The Return of the Prodigal Son (Narine Mkrtchyan and Arsen Azatyan)
Bonded Parallels (Hovhannes Galstyan)

Quotes of the year
'Donata and I had the greatest time in Yerevan and in your country. Consider us firm friends of your festival. We'll spread the word!' WIM WENDERS, *talking about the 5th Golden Apricot International Film Festival.*

'It is very powerful and full of primal emotion. In a sense, it is at the very essence of what cinema can give the viewer – a direct experience of life through a purely visual immersion into sensory worlds.' ATOM EGOYAN, *commenting on Khachatryan's* Border.

Directory
All Tel/Fax numbers begin (+374)
Armenian National Cinematheque, 25A Tbilisyan Highway, 375052 Yerevan. Tel: 285 406. filmadaran@yahoo.com.
Armenian Union of Filmmakers, 18 Vardanants, Yerevan. Tel: 540 528. Fax: 540 136.

SUSANNA HARUTYUNYAN has been a film critic for the daily *Respublika Armenia* since 1991 and is president of Armenia's Association of Film Critics and Cinema Journalists and Artistic Director of the Golden Apricot Yerevan International Film Festival.

Australia Peter Thompson

The last year has seen signs that the Australian film industry is not looking too bad. And, for a while at least, that was not the only sign of progress in the country. Before the world rejoiced at Obama, Australia had a brief moment of release late in 2007, when John Howard's bitterly divisive Liberal Party fell after eleven dismal years. Howard was replaced, however, by the no-less-conservative figure of Kevin Rudd, the leader of the Labour Party, who was quick to denounce one of Australia's leading international artists, photographer Bill Henson, when the opportunity arose. A prestigious exhibition of Henson's work, including a shadowy portrait of a nude 12-year-old girl, was raided by the police in Sydney and the pictures seized. Any illusions of genuine emancipation from a deeply entrenched Antipodean narrow-mindedness were quickly swept away.

On a more positive note, a reform of the film-financing system came into effect mid-2008. A new super-agency, Screen Australia, absorbed the long-established Australian Film Commission, Film Finance Corporation and Film Australia. In response to considerable pressure, the National Film and Sound Archive was finally given its independence.

While many see Screen Australia as yet another bloated bureaucracy and others fear its monopolistic structure, most welcomed the loosening of the purse strings signalled by various new tax incentives: the Producer Offset which guarantees a 40% rebate on qualifying expenditure; a Location Offset benefiting offshore productions shooting in Australia; and, a Post-Production, Digital and Video Offset. With its new Chief Executive Officer, Dr Ruth Harley, who has been running

the New Zealand Film Commission, Screen Australia must get to grips with investing, each year, around AUS$100 million in film, television and digital production.

Baz Luhrmann's blockbuster epic romance **Australia** was finally released, after years of heated speculation and a relentless media campaign. Promoted by 20th Century Fox as the movie that will finally knock *Titanic* off its perch as all-time box office champion (at least in Australia), it stars Nicole Kidman and Hugh Jackman. Luhrmann has an exceptional record of commercial success (*Strictly Ballroom*, *Romeo + Juliet* and *Moulin Rouge!*) and he cheerfully plundered cinema's past to create *Australia*.

Luhrmann is unique in his own country and has few peers elsewhere who can match his ability to shape audience perceptions and expectations. *Australia* is quite simply the biggest, the most ambitious and, possibly, the bravest film ever made in this country, as well as the most expensive. The production budget is rumoured to be around AUS$200 million.

Interestingly, the film's central focus is not Kidman's Lady Sarah or Jackman's Drover, but twelve-year-old Nullah, played by Brandon

Nicole Kidman and Brandon Walters in Baz Luhrmann's **Australia**

Walters. He is a so-called half-caste, son of an Aboriginal mother and a Caucasian father, the film's chief villain, Fletcher, played by David Wenham. Not only does young Brandon effortlessly steal the show, Luhrmann makes it an unambiguous tribute to the Stolen Generations: the victims of official government policy that condoned the forcible removal of Aboriginal children (especially half-castes like Nullah) from their black parents.

The film has had mixed reviews, but it is impossible to ignore its best elements: its breadth of vision; its courage; its grand theatrical gestures; and its moments of genuine emotion. *Australia* is so different from what might be described as the typical Aussie film that it will inevitably force a reconfiguring of many existing assumptions. Even if it fails to live up to the exaggerated expectations placed upon it, it has raised the bar and shone a clear light on the smallness, the self-imposed limitations, of most Australian movies.

Take *Australia* out of the equation and 2008 was a lean year. Only two films, **Unfinished Sky** and **The Black Balloon**, made much of an impression on audiences and both deserve attention. *Unfinished Sky* is an oddity, a remake of the successful Dutch film, *The Polish Bride*, which made a star of Monica Hendrickx. She also stars in *Unfinished Sky*, but this time as an Afghani woman who has come to Australia in search of her refugee husband. Adapted and directed by Peter Duncan (*Children of the Revolution*), it places Tahmeena in a contemporary country town, locked up and used as a sex slave. She escapes and is rescued by a farmer (William McInnes), a lonely man mourning the loss of his wife. There are violent elements to the drama but its great strength is the development of the relationship between the two leads, reaching out across a cultural gulf without even a shared language. Hendrickx and McInnes are impressive.

The Black Balloon signals the arrival of a strong new talent. Elissa Down draws from her own

Elissa Down's **The Black Balloon**

life, having grown up with two autistic siblings, but it is her ability to translate raw experience into engaging drama, mixed with comedy, that marks her out as a director to watch. Thomas (Rhys Wakefield) wants desperately to merge into the 'normal' adolescent world around him but it's hard when his older autistic brother, Charlie, constantly shatters the peace, rubbing faeces into the carpet, running semi-naked around the neighbourhood and even masturbating in front of guests. Thomas unexpectedly finds a sympathetic soul in fellow student Jackie (Gemma Ward) and he realizes that acceptance, rather than denial, will take him forward. Toni Collette superb as the mother and Luke Ford is totally convincing as Charlie.

Benjamin Gilmour's **Son of a Lion**

Son of a Lion, with its echoes of Siddiq Barmak's *Osama*, puts us inside the lives of a Pashtun father and son, living on the wild North West Frontier of Pakistan. Eleven-year-old Niaz (Niaz Khan Shinwari) desperately wants to go to school, but is prevented by his gunsmith father (Sher Alam Miskeen Ustad), a veteran of the Mujihadeen battle against the Soviets. Niaz finds an ally in his kindly uncle

(Baktiyar Ahmen Afridi). First-time writer, director and cameraman Benjamin Gilmour took great personal risks making the film, relying heavily on his Pashtun collaborators.

Nineteen Australian feature films were released commercially in 2008 and while most passed almost unnoticed, another, the acclaimed **Three Blind Mice**, is still awaiting distribution. Focusing on the last hours of young Navy recruits before being shipped out to Iraq, the film's lively dialogue and colourful performances give it life. Actor Matthew Newton makes his debut as director and co-writer as well as appearing alongside Ewen Leslie and Toby Schmitz. And Gracie Otto is refreshingly good.

Favourable critical response to several more films did not translate into strong box office. So is it possible to get a clear picture of current Australian cinema? There seems to be no general consensus on the status of Australian film or the challenges it faces. Each year brings a babble of voices, some bemoaning the lack of success, others blaming the usual suspects, while some look to a golden future. One thing is clear: Australians still have an appetite for cinema, if not their own product. Box-office figures for 2008 indicate a record-breaking year. More than twenty films passed the AUS$10 million mark, equivalent to Hollywood's US$100 million barrier, and at least eight will earn more than double that.

Modern technology makes it possible to produce high-quality pictures and sound very cheaply, and there has been a proliferation of no-budget or so-called credit card movies in recent years, one notable example being Shane Abbess's *Gabriel*. Couple this with the hoards of graduates from film schools and media courses, as well the growing number of alternative festivals and exhibition outlets, and it is not surprising that filmmaking activity is increasing.

Problems emerge when directors attempt to move further up the ladder. It can take years to finance a feature film through the existing agencies, which is not always a bad thing, or unique to Australia. But the AUS$5 million cap placed on budgets under the old Film Finance Corporation model probably contributed to the 'smallness' of the concepts presented. One hope for the new system is that higher budgets will become viable, especially where they involve international co-productions. Australia now has co-production treaties in place with several countries, including the UK, Canada and Germany, with more on the way.

Roger Spottiswoode's **The Children of Huang Shi**

But the common accusation that Australian filmmakers concentrate on bleak, depressing, personal stories simply doesn't stand. Of the nineteen 2008 releases, three can be described as quasi-historical epics (*Australia*, **Broken Sun** and **The Children of Huang Shi**); four as crime/thrillers (**The Square, Cactus, The Tender Hook** and **Black Water**); three as coming-of-age dramas (*The Black Balloon*, **Hey, Hey It's Esther Blueburger** and **Newcastle**, even *Son of a Lion*); and three more as romantic dramas (*Unfinished Sky*, Gillian Armstrong's **Death Defying Acts** and

Guy Pearce as Harry Houdini in **Death Defying Acts**

Monkey Puzzle). The intimate, personal or family-drama tag can be applied to **The View from Glenhaven**, **Men's Group**, **Bitter and Twisted** and **Ten Empty**, with the latter two perhaps too grim for some tastes.

I have long maintained that the perceived lack of success is directly linked to the comparatively small number of films made each year. I am also convinced that we have, for too long, pursued a mistaken 'industry' model, pretending that by fiddling with the machinery we can somehow make filmmaking financially self-sustaining.

Although the worldwide financial turmoil may take its toll, the prospects for 2009 look good. Bruce Beresford's privately financed **Mao's Last Dancer**, based on the best-selling memoir by Li Cunxin and starring Chi Cao, Principal Dancer with the Birmingham Royal Ballet, sounds very promising. Featuring Amanda Schull, Joan Chen, Kyle McLachlan, Bruce Greenwood, Jack Thompson and a huge supporting cast, it tells the improbable but true story of the poor Chinese peasant boy who negotiates the Cultural Revolution to become an international ballet star. Jane Campion is back with a period romance, **Bright Star**. Ben Whishaw plays John Keats and Abbie Cornish is Fanny Brawne, his lover and muse. High expectations also surround actress Maeve Dermody, appearing in **Beautiful Kate**, the feature debut of actress-turned-director Rachel Ward.

There's huge excitement around **Mary and Max**, the feature debut of Academy Award-winning animator Adam Elliott (*Harvie Krumpet*). With voices by Toni Collette and Philip Seymour Hoffman, it is a disarmingly simple tale of friendship between Mary, a lonely eight-year-old girl in Melbourne, and her pen pal Max, a morbidly obese Jewish New Yorker with Asperger's Syndrome. Sarah Watt (*Look Both Ways*) has completed her second feature, **My Year Without Sex**, a typically wry portrait of family life, complete with pet biographies. Closer to the political bone, **Balibo** digs into the infamous true story

of five Australian newsmen murdered during the Indonesian invasion of East Timor in 1975. It stars Anthony La Paglia and is directed by Robert Connolly, who co-wrote the script with David Williamson.

Adam Elliott's **Mary and Max**

For those still harbouring a sentimental attachment to the Australian cinema of the 1970s and 1980s, the feature documentary **Not Quite Hollywood** is a sobering, if sometimes very funny, blast from the past. Distracted by the genteel charms of *Picnic at Hanging Rock* and *My Brilliant Career* it is easy to forget that it was 'ocker' sex comedies such as *The Adventures of Barry McKenzie* and *Alvin Purple* that kickstarted filmmaking in Australia nearly forty years ago. Director Mark Hartley takes us on a chaotic, sometimes repetitive, ride through the flash trash of that era. The serious point, emphasised by Ozploitation fan Quentin Tarantino, is that *The Man from Hong Kong* and *Mad Max* as well as other films like them, had an inventive vitality that electrified audiences worldwide.

The twenty feature-length documentaries released in 2008 are marked by their diversity, ranging from Kirsty de Garis and Timothy Jolley's excellent **Celebrity: Dominick Dunne**, about the veteran American reporter now welded to *Vanity Fair* magazine, to predictable, but nevertheless powerful, environmental wake-up calls. Cathy Henkel's **The Burning Season** finds glimmers of hope in the holocaust overtaking the forests of Indonesia, while Kim Kindersley's **Whaledreamers**, produced by Julian Lennon, links the survival of the planet to the wisdom of ancient cultures. The film has won several major international awards.

As in the US, quality television production is attracting prestigious names and growing audiences. One of 2008's most significant events was the seven-part series **First Australians**, telling the story of the white invasion of the continent through the eyes of its original inhabitants, directed by Rachel Perkins who went straight into preparing the screen version of the popular stage musical, **Bran Nue Dae**. There are high hopes also for the work of another indigenous filmmaker, Warwick Thornton. His debut feature, due for release in 2009, is **Samson and Delilah**, a robust love story between Aboriginal teenagers. And Richard Frankland returns with the road movie **To Hell and Back**. It should make a nice pair with David Caesar's labour of love, **Prime Mover**, a film he has wanted to make for decades. It's the bittersweet story of a long-haul truck driver, facing up to the grim reality of the transport business.

Perhaps most exciting of all is the screen version of Nobel laureate J. M. Coetzee's scarifying South African novel, **Disgrace**. Adapted by Anna-Maria Monticelli and directed by Steve Jacobs, it has already won the FIPRESCI award at Toronto and the Best Picture Award at Abu Dhabi. The wife-and-husband team collaborated on the well-received La Spagnola in 2001, but gaining Coetzee's cooperation, in the face of stiff competition, was a significant coup. If Disgrace fulfils its promise, it may shift the debate about what constitutes an Australian film. Coetzee now lives in Australia. The screenwriter, director, cinematographer (Steve Arnold) and producer (Emile Sherman) are all Australian. But the setting is, of course, South African. John Malkovich plays the central character and South African Jessica Haines is his daughter. That's not good enough for some, who want Australian films to stay within strict, and ultimately self-defeating, guidelines. Let's hope they're wrong.

The year's best films
Australia (Baz Luhrmann)
Unfinished Sky (Peter Duncan)
Son of a Lion (Benjamin Gilmour)
The Black Balloon (Elissa Down)
Death Defying Acts (Gillian Armstrong)

Quote of the year
'The onslaught of Australian films that began in the early 1970s is still referred to as a 'renaissance' when it was in fact a naissance... I can't help seeing the glass as half full instead of half empty.' BRUCE BERESFORD, *in a recent rebuttal of the pessimism surrounding Australian film.*

Directory
All Tel/Fax numbers begin (+61)
The National Screen and Sound Archive, GPO Box 2002, Canberra ACT 2601. Tel: (2) 6248 2000. Fax: (2) 6248 2222. enquiries@screensound.gov.au. Stock: 3,800 Western Australian titles.
Australian Entertainment Industry Association (AEIA), 8th Floor, West Tower, 608 St Kilda Road, Melbourne, VIC 3004. Tel: (3) 9521 1900. Fax: (3) 9521 2285. aeia@aeia.org.au.
Australian Film Commission (AFC), 150 William St, Woolloomooloo NSW 2011. Postal address: GPO Box 3984, NSW 2001. Tel: (2) 9321 6444. Fax: (2) 9357 3737. info@afc.gov.au. www.afc.gov.au.
Australian Film Finance Corporation (AFFC), 130 Elizabeth St, Sydney NSW 2000. Postal address: GPO Box 3886, Sydney NSW 2001. Tel: (2) 9268 2555. Fax: (2) 9264 8551. www.ffc.gov.au.
Australian Screen Directors Association (ASDA), Postal address: PO Box 211, Rozelle NSW 2039. Tel: (2) 9555 7045. Fax: (2) 9555 7086. www.asdafilm.org.au.
Film Australia, 101 Eton Rd, Lindfield NSW 2070. Tel: (2) 9413 8777. Fax: (2) 9416 9401. www.filmaust.com.au.
Screen Producers Association of Australia (SPAA), Level 7, 235 Pyrmont St, Pyrmont NSW 2009. Tel: (2) 9518 6366. Fax: (2) 9518 6311. www.spaa.org.au.

PETER THOMPSON is a filmmaker and writer. He has also been reviewing and presenting movies on Australian television for 25 years.

Austria Gunnar Landsgesell

The highlight of 2008 was Stefan Ruzowitzky's success at the Academy Awards with *The Counterfeiters*, which was awarded the Best Foreign Language Film. This intriguing KZ-drama deals with 'Operation Bernhard', believed to be the biggest counterfeiting mission in history. The Oscar win increased the audience by 150,000 to 190,000 in Austrian cinemas and made the production a remarkable international success. *The Counterfeiters* also marks a shift towards genre cinema. Thus, the movement once known as the Nouvelle Vague Viennoise, featuring an introspective approach and brittle narratives, is succeeded by a collection of films that stand alongside tangible attempts at genre cinema.

Falco: Damn It, We're Still Alive (*Falco – Verdammt wir leben noch!*) exploits rather than revives the myth of Austria's late pop star in a hastily produced biopic. Thanks to the clever co-operation with newspapers and a chain of stores that sells electrical equipment (a first for Austria) granting ticket discounts, *Falco* became the most successful domestic film of the year. Less effective in terms of box office was another Austrian 'high-concept' film, Robert Dornhelm's adaptation of the Puccini opera, **La Bohème**, featuring Anna Netrebko and Rolando Villazón. The producers hoped to revive the once successful filmed opera, but with its old-fashioned look and feel, it has so far failed to attract a sizable audience.

Peter Payer's **Free to Leave** (*Freigesprochen*) played at a number of international film festivals, and was also nominated for the Golden Leopard at Locarno Film Festival. Philipp Stölzl's epic drama, **North Face** (*Nordwand*), combines spectacular images

Philipp Stölzl's **North Face**

of mountain climbers with an epic love story. It is the tragic story of two apolitical alpinists (Benno Führmann as Toni Kurz, Florian Lukas as Andreas Hinterstoisser) who follow the call of the National Socialists in 1936 to vanquish the notorious Eiger Nordwand. Following in the footsteps of Alpine filmmaker, Arnold Fanck, Stölzl moves carefully along this dangerous terrain, but knows how to entertain. Andreas Prochaska's horror sequel, **Dead in 3 Days 2** (*In 3 Tagen bist du tot 2*) is set in the snowy mountains of the Tyrol. A year after nearly all of her friends were killed by a psychopath, Nina (Sabrina Reiter) receives a terrifying call from her best friend, Mona (Julia Rosa Stöckl), whose life is in danger. Nina leaves Vienna and soon encounters a group of crazed mountaineers in Mona's hometown. Unlike the original, Agnes Pluch's screenplay and Prochaska's direction

Andreas Prochaska's **Dead in 3 Days 2**

provide deeper psychological insights and a more complex story.

Like *Dead in 3 Days 2*, the documentary **Let's Make MONEY** is being distributed by Celluloid Dreams. In a moment of financial world crisis director/writer Erwin Wagenhofer unmasks the abuses of the stock exchange and emerging markets. He has researched into how brokers and other economic players multiply money at the expense of Third World countries. Bankers are astonishingly frank in their opinions, with one expert contemplating the right moment for investment: you should invest as long as there is blood in the streets. *Let's make MONEY* is a thrilling, if didactic, documentary that remains surprisingly entertaining considering its complex subject matter.

Götz Spielmann's **Revanche**

Götz Spielmann's **Revanche** takes up two major topics in Austrian cinema: guilt and atonement. It is one of the most thrilling cinematic works of this year. Alex (Johannes Krisch) is a pimp's henchman, who is longing to start a new life with Tamara (Irina

Potapenko), a prostitute. But following a bank robbery, Tamara is killed by a policeman (Andreas Lust). When Krisch encounters the policeman and his wife, he seeks revenge. However, things turn out to be more complex than Alex thinks. Spielmann stages an understated social drama in which danger seems likely to erupt at any moment. Moreover, he elevates the narrative by linking the characters to a universal story of fate. The director of photography, Martin Gschlacht, transforms the protagonists' view of the world into a cinematic experience full of ambiguous images.

Fares Fares in Arash T. Riahi's **For a Moment, Freedom**

Arguably the most compelling film of this year is Arash T. Riahi's **For a Moment, Freedom** (*Für einen Augenblick Freiheit*). It is a story of three groups of refugees who have escaped from Iran and are stuck in a Turkish border town waiting for their visas to be authorised. It is partly autobiographical and convinces – like Arash's earlier documentaries – with its alternation between fierce humour and menacing tones. Arash had attended the Sundance script lab to help develop his screenplay, which has obviously paid dividends. *For a Moment, Freedom* was premiered at Montreal and has gone on to win numerous festival awards.

A number of interesting films are planned for release during the first half of 2009. Geyrhalter Film will release its first feature film, **The Robber** (*Der Räuber*). It tells the true story of a bank robber known as Pumpgun-Ronnie because of his Ronald Reagan mask. Young

Bavarian filmmaker Benjamin Heisenberg directs this strange story about the marathon runner who fooled a whole nation. **The Bone Man** (*Der Knochenmann*) is the third adaptation of a novel from the popular series by Austrian author, Wolf Haas. As a patron in a country inn, quirky private detective Brenner (Josef Hader) discovers human bones amongst the chicken feed. So begins another bizarre case. *The Bone Man* is once again expected to be a big success at the cinema. Austrian director Michael Haneke, after his foray into American film with the remake of his own *Funny Games*, will direct a story set in a time of conflicting ideologies. **The White Ribbon** (*Das weiße Band*) highlights a mysterious series of murders in a German village just before the First World War. Piece by piece, Haneke exposes the truth with his merciless, but precise, storytelling.

The suicide of three young men in a small village in the Tyrol is the focus of **März**, the critically-acclaimed feature début of Händl Klaus. With no explanation given for the deaths, the film details the impact on the local community. In Jessica Hausner's **Sylvie Testud** a wheelcair-bound young woman goes on a pilgrimage to Lourdes where she hopes a miracle awaits her.

The year's best films
For a Moment, Freedom (Arash T. Riahi)
Revanche (Götz Spielmann)
Free to Leave (Peter Payer)
Dead in 3 Days 2 (Andreas Prochaska)
Here to Stay! (Markus Wailand)

Quote of the year
'Sydney Pollack loved the script so much, that he wanted to realise the project himself.'
Austrian producer **VEIT HEIDUSCHKA** *on the Hollywood film director Sydney Pollack, who advised Arash T. Riahi on his screenplay* **For a Moment, Freedom** *at the Sundance script lab.*

Directory
All Tel/Fax numbers begin (+43)
Austrian Film Museum, Augustinerstr 1, A-1010

Peter Payer's **Free to Leave**

Vienna, Tel: (1) 533 7054-0. Fax: (1) 533 7054-25. office@filmmuseum.at. www.filmmuseum.at.
Filmarchiv Austria, Obere Augartenstr 1, A-1020 Vienna. Tel: (1) 216 1300. Fax: (1) 216 1300-100. augarten@filmarchiv.at. www.filmarchiv.at.
Association of Austrian Film Directors, c/o checkpointmedia Multimediaproduktionen AG, Seilerstätte 30, A-1010 Vienna. Tel/Fax: (1) 513 0000-0. Fax: (1) 513 0000-11. www.austrian-directors.com.
Association of Austrian Film Producers, Speisingerstrasse 121, A-1230 Vienna. Tel/Fax: (1) 888 9622. aafp@austrian-film.com. www.austrian-film.com.
Association of the Audiovisual & Film Industry, Wiedner Hauptstrasse 53, PO Box 327, A-1045 Vienna. Tel: (1) 5010 53010. Fax: (1) 5010 5276. film@fafo.at. www.fafo.at.
Austrian Film Commission, Stiftgasse 6, A-1070 Vienna. Tel: (1) 526 33 23-0. Fax: (1) 526 6801. office@afc.at. www.afc.at.
Austrian Film Institute (OFI), Spittelberggasse 3, A-1070 Vienna. Tel: (1) 526 9730-400. Fax: (1) 526 9730-440. office@filminstitut.at. www.filminstitut.at.
Location Austria, Opernring 3, A-1010 Vienna. Tel: (1) 588 5836. Fax: (1) 586 8659. office@location-austria.at. www.location-austria.at.
Vienna Film Fund, Stiftgasse 6, A-1070 Vienna. Tel: 526 5088. Fax: 526 5020. office@filmfonds-wien.at. www.filmfonds-wien.at.

GUNNAR LANDSGESELL is a freelance writer for *Blickpunkt: Film, FORMAT, kolik, ray film magazin* and is chief editor of the human rights magazine *MOMENT*.

Belarus Andrei Rasinski

Belarusian feature production found itself in a state of deep stagnation throughout 2008. The 'warploitation' theme once again dominated a number of films. These low-quality, poorly directed films exploit militaristic fetishism amongst certain audience members. In Dzianis' Skvartsou's state-sponsored **Shield of Fatherland** (originally titled *The Free Heaven*), characters re-enact battles through war games. Ilya Bazhko's amateurish underground short, **The Height 71** (*Vysota 71*), plays up wartime patriotism with its account of the defence of 'Stalin's Line' (the name given to the West's military border along the Soviet Union in the 1930s) during the Second World War.

Dzianis' Skvartsou's **Shield of Fatherland**

In Ivan Paulau's comedy **Riding a Black Cat** (*Na spine u chernogo kota*), two old men who live in the country win the lottery. Under the guidance of a guardian angel, the heroes make their way to the city to celebrate, along the way swearing on the name of Stalin and singing Soviet military songs. The main children's role in the film is played by Vika Lukashenko, the granddaughter of the country's leader, Alexander Lukashenko, who came to power in 1994.

Mikhail Zhdanousky's **In All Days**

In stark contrast to these celebrations of military life, director Mikhail Zhdanousky returned to the theme of Stalin's victims. The reclusive hero of his documentary **In All Days** (*Vo vse dni*) draws icons on stones at the Kurapaty memorial where, between 1937 and 1941, a vast number of people were executed by the Soviet secret police. The film was awarded the Grand Prix at the 4th Magnificat, the International Catholic Festival of Christian Films and Television.

Victor Asliuk was awarded the Best Director prize at Magnificat for his documentary **Waltz** (*Vals*). The film follows a village doctor who travels by bike to carry out his daily rounds, visiting a collection of ageing patients. By contrast, the small children in Galina Adamovich's **The Mum Will Come!** (*Mama pridet!*) appear as vulnerable as the elderly. In **Dear Dolls** (*Dorogie kukly*), Adamovich focuses on doll makers and collectors, whose objects of affection and beauty are shot in a charmingly manneristic style by Taciana Lohinava. Jury Harulou's **Edge of Blessed Dreams** (*Kraj svetlyh mrojaú*), which focuses on a gentry family, also featured exceptional camerawork.

Victor Asliuk's **Waltz**

Belarusian filmmakers are still forced to work under pseudonyms for the more Western-orientated 'Belsat' TV station, which broadcasts from Poland. **Four Symbols** (*Chatyry symbali*), whose director remains anonymous, is devoted to the architect Iosif Grigorievich Langbard's heritage and the fate of his style of design. Volha Nikalaichyk's **The Heart Behind the Bars** (*Serca za kratami*) highlighted the plight of political prisoners, while Uladzimir Kolas' **Ada's Gallery** (*Galereja Ady*) focuses on the open-air expositions organized by Ada Raichonak, a teacher based in the countryside.

Among the debutants of Belarusfilm were Alla Volskaja (**To Find Himself**), Kaciaryna Mahava (**Two Destinies**) and Volha Dashuk (**11 Coins**). The 'Belarusian Videocentre' presented 21 documentaries. Among the most interesting were **ANGELina** by Alexander Karpau, the profile of a compassionate psychologist, and Ihar Byshnou's animalistic **She-wolf Dajja** (*Volchica po imeni Dajja*).

Natalja Khatkevich, Iryna Kadziukova and Alexander Lenkin directed the animated film **The Story of Past Years – 2** (*Apoviesc' minulych hadoú – 2*), while Ihar Volchak animated more adventures of the folklore hero Nescerka, in **Nescerka-3**.

In September the first multiplex opened in Minsk. However it is practically impossible to see Belarusian documentaries or animated films there.

The Year's Best Film
Waltz (Victor Asliuk)
In All Days (Mikhail Zhdanousky)
Dear dolls (Galina Adamovich)
Edge of blessed dreams (Jury Harulou)
Four Symbols
(under the pseudonym Adam Galin)

Quote of the year
'If peasants so worked as you, all would die of famine.' ALEXANDER LUKASHENKO, *president of Belarus on meeting with filmmakers.*

Directory
All Tel/Fax numbers begin (+375)
Belarusfilm, Niezalezhnas'tsi Avenue 98, Minsk 220023. Tel/Fax: (17) 267 10 02. filmstudio@ belarusfilm.by. belarusfilm.by/eng.
Belarusian State Archives of Films, Photographs and Sound Recordings, Faminykh street 1, Dzerzhinsk, Minsk Oblast, 222720. Tel: (1716) 5 40 01, 5 47 81. Fax: (1716) 5 47 81. akffd@tut.by, akffd@bn.by.
Belarusian Video center, K.Marx street, 12a, Minsk 220030. Tel: (17) 226 09 22. Fax: (17) 227 11 81. belvc@yandex.ru. www.belvc.by.
International Catholic Festival of Christian Documentary Films and TV Programs 'Magnificat'. Tel.: (17) 216 23 65. festival@signis. by. www.magnificat.signis.by.
Ministry of Culture, Film & Video Department, Peramozhtsaú Avenue 11, Minsk 220004. Tel:(17) 203 75 74, Fax: (17) 203 90 45. ministerstvo@ kultura.by. www.kultura.by/eng.
Museum of the History the Belarusian Cinema, Svyardlova 4, Minsk 220050. Tel: (17) 227 10 75. www.sverdlova-4.joy.by.
Union of Filmmakers of Belarus, Talbukhina 18, Minsk 220050. Tel: (17) 287 31 53. roobsk@mail.ru.
Belarusian State Academy of Arts, 81 Nezavisimosti Avenue, 220012, Minsk. Tel: (1) 729 215 4. Fax: (1) 729 220 41. belam@user.unibel.by. http://www.belam.by.com.

ANDREI RASINSKI is a cinema and cultural critic and regular contributor to *Nasha Niva* newspaper, and director of two documentaries.

Belgium Erik Martens

Most Belgians will remember the past 18 months as the period in which local politicians dominated the media, proclaiming the imminent death of their country. The time when Belgium's Dutch-speaking majority (Flanders) and French-speaking minority (Wallonia and most of Brussels) were living apart together in a reasonably comfortable way would soon come to an end. From the moment the federal elections of June 2007 highlighted a separatist agenda, for most people national politics felt worse than bad cinema.

By contrast, Belgian cinema has been thriving like never before. Audience attendance for local films (especially Dutch-language releases) has grown considerably, with more films produced. Even on a film-policy level there was good news to be heard. Flemish public funding for cinema would increase and fresh money was found for combined TV/cinema projects.

Given the complex political situation of the country, an interesting project was set up by the Flemish Audiovisual Fund and the French-speaking public television station RTBF. It was labelled *TO BE OR NOT TO.be*, referring to the fact that every one of the twelve documentaries funanced by the fund would have to treat Belgium as its main theme.

There are no separatist politics in the Belgian film world. For instance, Flemish director Fien Troch's second feature **Unspoken** is in French, which is extremely unusual for a film funded by the Flemish Fund. The idea of casting French actress Emmanuelle Devos and Swiss actor Bruno Todeschini proved to be highly effective. Troch revisits a theme she already established in her first film, *Someone Else's*

Bruno Todeschini and Emmanuelle Devos in Fien Troch's **Unspoken**

Happiness: parents mourning the loss of their child. But with her new film both story and characters have gained maturity. Troch films the father and mother in extreme close-ups, thereby reducing the external world to vague backgrounds, emphasising the characters' lost contact with it. Language is sparse in this small and delicate film, which is likely to be a difficult sell for the local market. However, its artistic accomplishment is undeniably an important step in the career of this promising young director.

Unspoken wasn't the only sophomore effort to surprise its audience. Fabrice du Welz's **Vinyan** is another example of a film crossing

Fabrice du Welz's **Vinyan**

linguistic borders. Although a French speaker, du Welz had Rufus Sewell and Emmanuelle Béart speak English. They play Jeanne and Paul Bellmer, who lost their son in the 2005 tsunami. Like Devos and Todeschini in *Unspoken*, they lose sight of reality. Convinced that their child is still alive, they embark on a journey through the Thai jungle, which turns into a nightmare. Du Welz successfully shifts the film from psychological drama to straightforward genre cinema, as he did in his feature debut, *Calvaire*.

Bouli Lanners' **Eldorado**

Whereas Fabrice du Welz is a true horror-movie enthusiast, Bouli Lanners' second film **Eldorado** is clearly indebted to another genre: the road movie. Lanners' first film, *Ultranova*, made a strong impression in 2005, with its very painterly approach to widescreen landscapes and the particular kind of characters it introduced: all weird, exotic and cloaked in dark humour, yet utterly loveable. *Eldorado* pushes the envelope of the grotesque even further. Lanners himself plays Yvan, a vintage car dealer who decides to take young junkie Elie home to his parents. In doing so, the two characters and their car – a chevrolet – cross the most bewildering landscapes. It is arguably the best Belgian film of the year.

In the wonderful Jacques Tati-like pantomime **Rumba**, Bruno Romy, Fiona Gordon and Dominique Abel perfect the deadpan humour and minimalist style of their previous film,

The Iceberg. In brief, Fiona and Dominique are in love with the rumba. But one night, as the result of a car accident, Fiona loses a leg and Dominique his memory. What was once a happy life now seems to end in despair. It is difficult to prevent this kind of comedy from experiencing off moments. However, there are many scenes whose visual expression outweighs the film's weaker moments.

Both films were selected for Cannes: *Eldorado* for the Directors' Fortnight and *Rumba* the Critics' Week. Alongside *Rumba* was **Moscow, Belgium** by newcomer Christophe van Rompaey. It is a Dutch-language, or rather a Ghent-language film, because all its characters talk in local dialect, only heard in the city of Ghent. The film owes much to the simple yet effective screenplay by Jean-Claude Van Rijckeghem and Pat Van Beirs. Van Rompaey also draws out excellent performances from the ensemble cast. Once again, it is a car accident that sets the film in motion. Barbara Sarafian plays a mother deserted by her husband who literally bumps into Jürgen Delnaet's truck driver, who has also experienced unhappinesss in love. It is one of the best Flemish comedies in years.

Christophe van Rompaey's **Moscow, Belgium**

Over the last decade, television has become an important element in the production of Flemish feature films. The subject matter, actors and local celebrities who play a part in so many feature films have often been drawn from the small screen. The growing local market for Dutch-speaking film is significantly linked to this phenomenon. Even *Moscow,*

Belgium has a link with television, being part of a series of tele-fiction films, called *Faits divers*, which were co-produced by the Flemish commercial TV station, VTM.

Two other films from this series were given a theatrical release in Flanders: Geoffrey Enthoven's **Happy Together** and **Left Bank**, directed by Pieter van Hees. The former is about a seemingly happily married couple, whose relationship and family disintegrates as a result of financial misfortune. *Left Bank* is a genre piece about a young woman who falls passionately in love with the wrong man, who is clearly not who he appears to be. The film soon descends into conventional horror, along the lines of *Vinyan*.

Dimitry Kazakatsantis' **Small Gods**

Visually, Dimitry Kazakatsantis' debut feature **Small Gods** is very similar to Pieter van Hees' stylised noir universe. It is no coincidence that *Left Bank* was co-written by Kazakatsantis and filmed by his brother Nicolas. *Small Gods* is equally bizarre: a mysterious young man, played by Matthias Schoenaerts (who was also the mysterious young man in *Left Bank*), abducts a woman from a hospital and takes her with him on a trip in his van. Kazakatsantis, van Hees and directors such as Koen Mortier are part of a recent wave of filmmakers who all have a very distinct visual identity, more often than not very dark in tone. Unfortunately, they have yet to overcome the problems of narrative structure and coherence.

Jan Verheyen's **Missing** also came from a television deal. It served as pilot for a series.

A popular director with Flemish audiences, Verheyen has often based his work on television formats. *Missing* focuses on the five members of the Missing Persons Task Force as they investigate the mysterious disappearance of a young girl. Verheyen followed it with **Cut Loose**, an adaptation of the novel by popular Flemish author Tom Naegels. In it, a young newspaper journalist called Tom Naegels struggles with love amidst the joys and pains of life in modern, multi-ethnic society whilst having to deal with a grandfather who has decided to put an end to his life.

When it comes to popular appeal, there is no competition for the number one television production house, Woestijnvis, which has dominated for a decade and has established a reputation for original and rewarding small-screen entertainment. For their first feature, **Loft**, Woestijnvis teamed up with successful director Erik Van Looy, who directed the popular 2003 feature, *The Alzheimer Case*. Local television celebrity Bart De Pauw wrote the screenplay. Inevitably, the film will attract curiosity because of its central theme of adultery: five friends share a fashionable loft to accommodate their extra-marital adventures. There is lust, but also elements of the classical whodunit. After all, doesn't lust always lead to murder? The film was released at the end of 2008 and the box office results are eagerly awaited.

Returning to the language border... Once every three years the country's national pride, Jean-Pierre and Luc Dardenne, make a new

Jean-Pierre and Luc Dardenne's **The Silence of Lorna**

film. Since winning the Palme d'Or with 1999's *Rosetta*, the brothers have regularly entered the festival-circuit fray, winning at least one of the major Cannes awards for each film along the way. **The Silence of Lorna** didn't earn them a third Palme d'Or, but it did win the Best Screenplay award. Lorna is a young Albanian woman who lives in Belgium and does whatever she can to make a living, even when that means setting up sham marriages (with junkie Claudy played by Jérémie Renier) and doing business with Russian mobsters. Another tradition with the Dardennes is the revelation of a new talent. This time it undoubtedly proves to be leading actress Arta Dobroshi.

The insect cast of Ben Stassen's animation **Fly me to the Moon**

Finally, we come to Ben Stassen's animated 3D adventures in space. **Fly Me to the Moon** is nWave Pictures' first feature film and tells the story of three flies who accompany the Apollo 11 mission to the moon. The film has been sold to many territories over the world. It also contains a nice lesson that even our Belgian politicians stuck in the trenches could learn from: it may be interesting to try and see reality from a new perspective...

ERIK MARTENS is a film critic and editor-in-chief of DVD releases at the Royal Belgian Film Archive.

Bruno Romy, Fiona Gordon and Dominique Abel's **Rumba**

The year's best films
Eldorado (Bouli Lanners)
Moscow, Belgium (Christophe van Rompaey)
The Silence of Lorna
(Jean-Pierre and Luc Dardenne)
Unspoken (Fien Troch)
Rumba (Bruno Romy, Fiona Gordon and Dominique Abel)

Quote of the year
'I prefer Flemish films to have competition from other Flemish films, rather than from American films.' PIERRE DROUOT, *director of the Flemish Film Fund, about the fear that the increasing number of Flemish films might cannibalize one another.*

Directory
All Tel/Fax numbers begin (+32)
Royal Film Archive, 23 Rue Ravenstein, B-1000 Brussels. Tel: (2) 507 8370. Fax: (2) 513 1272. cinematheque@ledoux.be. www.ledoux.be.
Communauté Française de Belgique Centre du Cinéma et de l'audiovisuel, Boulevard Léopold II, 44, 1080 Brussels. Tel: (2) 413 25 19. Fax: (2) 413 24 15.
Flanders Image, Handelskaai 18/3, 1000 Brussels. Tel: (2) 226 06 30. flandersimage@vaf.be.
Flemish Audiovisual Fund (VAF), Handelskaai 18/3, B-1000 Brussels. Tel: (2) 226 0630. Fax: (2) 219 1936. info@vaf.be. www.vaf.be.
Wallonie Bruxelles Images (WBI), Place Flagey 18, 1050 Brussels. Tel: (2) 223 23 04. wbimages@skynet.be. www.cfwb.be.

Bolivia José Sánchez-H.

The grand opening of the Bolivian Film Archive (Cinemateca Boliviana) on 30 October 2007, marked a quantum leap in the preservation and exhibition of films in Bolivia. The event included a special screening of a restored print of one of the most important dramatic silent films of Bolivian cinema, **Wara-Wara** (Aymara for *Stars*), directed by José María Velasco in 1930. Based on Antonio Diaz Villamil's novel *The Flute's Voice*, it tells the story of a Spanish soldier who falls in love with a *ñusta* – a member of the Inca nobility.

Adriana Montenegro's **From the Core**

Among recently completed productions is the dramatic short, **From the Core** (*Desde el fondo*), by upcoming filmmaker, Adriana Montenegro. Lauded as Best Latino Short Film by the Directors' Guild of America, the film uses elements of magical realism to show a woman who returns to Bolivia and finds hope for life after experiencing the death of her grandfather.

Miguel Valverde Botello and Alexander Muñoz Ramirez's **Seed that Dyes** (*Airamppo*) is a comedy that moves from the comic to the absurd when the characters in the film awaken

from their drunken stupor into a cruel reality. Another comedy, **Wedding Day** (*Día de boda*), by Rodrigo Ayala Bluske tells the story of a man who kidnaps his former girlfriend with the help of his friends in order to stop her getting married.

By stark contrast, Tonchy Antezana's **Elephant Cemetery** (*El cementerio de los elefantes*), shot in the city of La Paz, deals with a dark theme of an alcoholic who, on deciding to drink himself to death, rents the presidential suite at a hotel to accomplish his goal.

Mela Márquez's **...To Know That I Have Searched for You** (*...Saber que te he buscado*), previously titled *Don't Breathe a Word... (No le digas...*), is expected to be released domestically in 2009. A visually powerful film that is presented through the character of Bolivian poet Jaime Sáenz's daughter, it tells the story of a woman returning to Bolivia in order to settle her father's estate. Sifting through the remnants of his life she gradually recovers her own sense of identity.

Gonzalo Valenzuela in Rodrigo Bellot's **Perfidy**

Rodrigo Bellot's feature **Perfidy** (*Perfidia*) is planned for a 2009 release. Bellot, who states that his film is not experimental, uses one actor and less than three minutes of dialogue. Bellot has been busy over the last year, after being appointed casting director for the Steven Soderbergh films based on the life of Ché Guevara, **The Argentine** and **Guerrilla**. He was also responsible for casting the French/German production, **The Hunt** (*La Traque*), directed by Laurent Jaoui. That film deals with the capture in Bolivia of the former SS Chief of Lyons, Klaus Barbie, known as the 'Butcher of Lyons' for his part in the murder of thousands of Jews during the Holocaust.

Benicio del Toro in Stephen Soderbergh's epic **Che: Part Two**

Film production in Bolivia continues to thrive thanks to a number of opportunities that include co-productions with other countries. Most recently, Bolivian director Paolo Agazzi has become co-producer of the German/Bolivian production **Postcards from Copacabana** (*Postales de Copacabana*), directed by Thomas Krontaler and starring Bolivian actress Carla Ortiz. It is based on a novel by German author Stefanie Kremser, who lived in Bolivia for many years. The film tells the story of three women, a mother, her daughter and her mother-in-law, who live in a town in the state of La Paz, where the lack of dynamism in their lives leaves them reminiscing about the past. *Postcards from Copacabana* is due to be released in Bolivia in 2009.

A production currently struggling to be completed is **The Forgotten Ones** (*Los Olvidados*), which looks back at repressive military

Adriana Montenegro's **From the Core**

regimes of 1970s Latin America, who were linked through a 'black ops' organisation code-named 'Operation Condor'. The story takes place in Argentina, Bolivia, and Chile and has Mauricio d'Avis L. and Carla Ortiz as producers.

The year's best films
...To Know That I Have Searched for You
(Mela Márquez)
From the Core (Adriana Montenegro)

Quote of the year
'I have tremendous debt and many problems finding financing, but I can't give up on this film, because it would be like going backwards in this dream of making films in Bolivia.'
MELA MÁRQUEZ *commenting on the difficulties of making* **...To Know That I Have Searched for You.**

Directory
All Tel/Fax numbers begin (+591)
Cinemateca Boliviana, Calle Oscar Soria, Prolongación Federico Zuazo s/n, Casilla 9933, La Paz. Tel: (2) 244 4090. info@cinematecaboliviana.org. www.cinemateca.siesis.com.
Consejo Nacional de Cine (CONACINE), Calle Montevideo, Edificio Requimia, Piso 8, La Paz. Tel: (2) 244 4759. contacto@conacine.net. www.conacine.net.

JOSÉ SÁNCHEZ-H. is a filmmaker and author of *The Art and Politics of Bolivian Cinema* (1999). He teaches in the department of Film and Electronic Art at California State University, Long Beach.

Bosnia & Herzegovina Rada Šešić

Bosnia and Herzegovina, with its average annual production of one or two features, had great cause for celebration in 2008. **Snow**, the feature debut of Aida Begic, was awarded the Grand Prix at *Semaine de la Critique* at Cannes and performed extremely well at all important festivals and with international distributors. This subtle post-war drama highlights the spirit of six women in a small remote village. The men are gone, either killed or missing. Alma, a young, modest and smart Muslim woman leads the others in their struggle to survive, selling marmalade, fruit and vegetables. A foreign investor offering to buy their land personifies a possible escape from their hardship. Alma, however, is determined to overcome the poverty and withstand the forces trying to annihilate her village, finding strength in her undying faith in God and good. The multi-layered script was written by the director and Elma Tataragic, whose Mamafilm produced the film. Zana Marjanovic excels as the withdrawn but strong Alma, playing her with tremendous credibility.

Zana Marjanovic and Jasna Ornela Beri in Aida Begic's **Snow**

Another debut was Namik Kabil's **Night Guards** (*Cuvari noci*) which was premiered

at the Venice Film Festival. The bizarre story, written by the director, takes place over one night in a furniture showroom. Young Mahir (Vahid Piralic), who is married without children and working as the night guard, is convinced he is pregnant. He seems to have the symptoms of pregnancy, including morning sickness. Into this mix enters Mahir's war-veteran neighbour. With the absurd humour of an Ionesco play, Kabil's film, taking place in post-war present-day Sarajevo, highlights his characters' inability to communicate or even lead a normal life.

Namik Kabil's **Night Guards**

Three good documentaries, all strongly connected to the war, were released in 2008. **If You Are Watching This Mum...** (*Ako ovo gledaš, Mama...*) directed by journalist Dario Novalic and respected cinematographer Mustafa Mustafic, investigates the plight of children who grew up in an orphanage in Sarajevo and who left the country during the war, finding refuge in Italy. **Srebrenica's Cenotaph** (*Srebrenički Kenotaf*) by Haris Prolic, tells the story of the discovery of a videotape, which had been buried for more than ten years. The cameraman, who was killed at Srebrenica, recorded the daily lives during the siege of the people who would later become victims of the massacre. **Diagnosis S.B.H.** (*Dijagnoza S.B.H.*) is arguably the most artistically satisfying of the three. Directed by filmmaker and musician Enes Zlatar, it questions the use of language in his homeland. Zlatar addresses his colleagues from different rock bands and investigates why they sing in Bosnian, Croatian, Serbian or English. What does language say about identity? The film impresses with its refreshing and dynamic images.

The appearance of new film festivals, from Banja Luka, Mostar and Siroki to Brijeg and Neum, has been welcome. However, they still remain in the shadow of the very well organised Sarajevo Film Festival. Joining forces with the federal government, SFF has launched an important project, *Sarajevo, City of Film*, which aims to provide production facilities for several shorts shot in Sarajevo by participants of the festival's Talent Campus. An important condition is that the film crews must represent different countries from the region. Last season, it resulted in five new, refreshing and intriguing shorts.

Sarajevo Film Festival also handed out an award to the talented young animator, Faruk Šabanović, for his almost single-handedly kick-starting a huge feature-length animation project. Although still in progress, **Birds Like Us** has been acknowledged by ANIMAFEST in Zagreb, and Sabanovic now has a small animation team of inspired youngsters working with him. This mega-project is scheduled to be completed by 2010. At the same time, another talent, Ivan Ramadan, has completed the animation short, **Tolerance** (*Tolerantia*) This award-winning film imagines the life of a Bosnian who awakens from the Ice Age.

RADA ŠEŠIĆ is a filmmaker and film critic based in the Netherlands where she helps programme of the International Documentary Filmfestival Amsterdam and International Film Festival Rotterdam. She is also head of the docu-mentary competition at the Sarajevo Film Festival as well as the main selector of the Bucharest Film Festival.

The year's best films
Snow (Aida Begic)
Night Guards (Namik Kabil)
Diagnosis S.B.H. (Enes Zlatar)
If You Are Watching This Mum....
(Dario Novalic and Mustafa Mustafic)
Srebrenica's Cenotaph (Haris Prolic)

Quote of the year
'*Night Guards* is a woman's film, without real female roles. Our men are either crazy, or they are suffering typical women problems.'
NAMIK KABIL *comenting on his feature debut,*
Night Guards.

Directory
All Tel/Fax numbers begin (+387)
Academy for Performing Arts, Obala, Sarajevo. Tel/Fax: 665 304.
Association of Filmmakers, Strosmajerova 1, Sarajevo. Tel: 667 452.
Cinematheque of Bosnia & Herzegovina, Alipasina 19, Sarajevo. Tel/Fax: 668 678. kinoteka@ bih.net.ba.

Brazil Nelson Hoineff

There was no big Brazilian film in 2008, at least not one headlining both the box office and newspapers in the way that 2007's *Elite Squad* did. However, there were some hits, most notably Mauro Lima's **My Name Ain't Johnny** (*Meu Nome Não é Johnny*). Based on the real life of João Estrela, a middle-class young man who in the 1990s became one of Brazil's most wanted drug dealers, it was a popular hit with audiences. It was adapted from Guilherme Fiúza's book and starred Selton Mello and Cléo Pires, two popular actors, who guaranteed its broad appeal. With over two million admissions, *My Name Ain't Johnny* was the only non-Hollywood movie to become one of Brazil's biggest box office attractions of the year.

Mauro Lima's **My Name Ain't Johnny**

Cult-horror director José Mojica Marins returned with **Embodiment of Evil** (*Encarnação do Demônio*), the last chapter of the trilogy that began with *At Midnight I'll Take Your Soul* (1964) and continued with *Tonight I'll Possess Your Corpse* (1967). The movie failed at the box office, despite a modest release, but pleased critics and fans of the character Coffin Joe, already a part of Brazilian pop culture.

Mark Ruffalo and Julianne Moore in Fernando Meirelles' **Blindness**

The eagerly waited adaptation of José Saramago's novel **Blindness** (*Ensaio Sobre a Cegueira*) was one of the major talking points of the year. It had a huge commercial appeal, propelled by a strong marketing campaign by distributor Fox and featuring a great ensemble cast, including Julianne Moore, Mark Ruffalo, Gael García Bernal and Alice Braga. And, of course, it was directed by Brazil's most famous filmmaker, Fernando Meirelles. Opening the Cannes Film Festival in May, it tells the story of a group of citizens who suddenly lose their sight because of a 'white blindness' outbreak. The movie failed to impress both Brazilian and international critics, but was highly debated due to its non-conventional style and controversial themes. It turned out to be a modest success, attracting almost 600,000 admissions.

The other film that attracted attention during the Cannes Film Festival was **Linha de Passe**, directed by Walter Salles and Daniela Thomas. Sandra Corveloni received the Best Actress award for her performance in a film about four brothers from São Paulo pursuing their dreams. Unfortunately, its box office performance was unimpressive, attracting little over 100,000 admissions.

Bruno Barreto's **Last Stop 174**

The official entry for the 2009 Academy Awards, **Last Stop 174** (*Última Parada 174*), is directed by Bruno Barreto, who previously directed *Four Days in September*. It is based upon the famous bus hijacking in Rio de Janeiro that shocked the nation eight years ago. The film attracted unwanted attention when it opened in the same week that another hostage situation ended in a tragic death.

A number of smaller independent films also found their way on to Brazilian cinema screens. Walter Lima Jr's much-delayed **Desafinados**, about the period of public turmoil from the 1960s to the 1970s and told through a Bossa Nova backstory, finally emerged. Jorge Fernando cast veteran actor Ary Fontoura in his comedy **A Guerra dos Rocha**. **Polaróides Urbanas** was the directorial debut of actor/writer/producer Miguel Falabella and featured an ensemble cast of TV stars, led by actress Marília Pêra. Another comedy with actors from the small screen was **A Casa da Mãe Joana**, directed by Hugo Carvana. However, like all the

aforementioned films, it did not stand a chance in such a competitive market and failed to turn a profit.

With *My Name Ain't Johnny* the only commercial success, 2008 was far from a good year for Brazil's cinema. However, the great – and varied – number of films definitely shows that the market is not slowing down.

The year's best films
My Name Ain't Johnnny (Mauro Lima)
Blindness (Fernando Meirelles)

Quote of the year
'There are different kinds of blindness. There are two billion people that are starving in the world. It doesn't need a catastrophe. It's happening, and because there isn't an event like Hurricane Katrina, we don't see.'
FERNANDO MEREILLES, *in interview at Cannes*.

Directory
All Tel/Fax numbers begin (+55)
ANCINE (National Agency for Cinema), Praça Pio X, 54, 10th Floor, 22091-040 Rio de Janeiro. Tel: (21) 3849 1339. www.ancine.gov.br.
Brazilian Cinema Congress (CBC), (Federation of Cinema Unions/Associations), Rua Cerro Cora 550, Sala 19, 05061-100 São Paulo. Tel/Fax: (11) 3021 8505. congressocinema@hotmail.com. www.congressocinema.com.br.
Cinemateca Brasileira, Largo Senador Raul Cardoso, Vila Clementino 207, 04021-070 São Paulo. Tel: (11) 5084 2318. Fax: (11) 5575 9264. info@cinemateca.com.br. www.cinemateca.com.br.
Grupo Novo de Cinema (Distributor), Rua Capitao Salomao 42, 22271-040 Rio de Janeiro. Tel: (21) 2539 1538. braziliancinema@braziliancinema.com. www.gnctv.com.br.
Ministry of Culture, Films & Festivals Dept, Esplanada dos Ministerios, Bloco B, 3rd Floor, 70068-900 Brasilia. www.cultura.gov.br.

NELSON HOINEFF is a film critic, vice president of the Association of Film Critics of Rio de Janeiro and president of the Institute of Television Studies.

Walter Lima Jr's **Desafinados**

Bulgaria Pavlina Jeleva

2008 continues Bulgaria's cinematic revival. A visible increase in local films, with strong artistic merit to match, was partly down to the help of €6 million in funding, distributed by the National Film Centre and Bulgarian National Television. Thanks to this financing, young filmmakers became more visible on the country's film scene. Bulgaria was also a minority partner on five international co-productions, most notably the Serbian **Gucha! Distant Trumpet** (*Guca!*), directed by Dusan Milic, and the Macedonian **Shadows** (*Senki*), by Milcho Manchevski.

Dusan Milic's **Gucha! Distant Trumpet**

The biggest sensation this year was theatre director Javor Gardev's provocative neo-noir debut, **Dzift**, based on Vladislav Todorov's novel and set over one wild night in Sofia, during the 1960s. The film won the Best Director prize at the Moscow Film Festival, with critics praising the radical mix of Soviet pseudo-socialist art and ironic neo-noir symbolism. Following its screening at the Toronto Film Festival, an American remake has been mooted. It also won the national Golden Rose award at the Varna National Film Festival and became the first Bulgarian film to top the local box office. *Dzift* is also Bulgaria's bid for the Best Foreign Language Film Academy Awards.

A Farewell to Hemingway (*Edinstvenata lyubovna istoriya, koyato Hemingway ne opisa*) by writer-director Svetoslav Ovcharov, best known for his beautiful *A Leaf in the Wind*, tells the fictional story of the arrival of the famous writer, by Orient Express, at a small Bulgarian railway station on 18 October 1922. Following its national premiere at Varna, the film was awarded the Best Director and Special Jury Prize. With its mood of tender melancholia, the story of a brief encounter between two solitary souls showcased the talents of American actor Chris Heuisler as young Hemingway and emerging Bulgarian star Gergana Pletnyova as a girl who works at the station.

Ernestina Chinova and Deyan Donkov perform four different roles as two couples in Andrey Slabakov's **Hindemith**. An absurdist comedy, this fresh and funny story of two similar families attempting to get along in a new neighbourhood played well with audiences.

The most ambitious co-production of the year was Stefan Komandarev's €2 million-budget **The World is Big and Salvation Lurks Around the Corner** (*Svetat e golyam i*

Stefan Komandarev's **The World is Big and Salvation Lurks Around the Corner**

spasenie debne otvsyakade). Germany-based, Bulgarian writer Ilija Troijanov's autobiographical tale narrates the journey of one family to the West during the Communist era. The Bulgarian/German/Hungarian/Slovenian co-production showed a strong ability to play to international audiences.

Forecast, by Zornitsa Sofia, was aimed at a younger audience, presenting a group of friends from different Balkan countries, who share a passion for windsurfing. Known for her earlier *Mila from Mars*, Sofia's film captures the passion of her characters' lifestyle.

Boris Despodov's **Corridor #8**

Boris Despodov's **Corridor #8** (*Korridor No. 8*) was the major Bulgarian documentary success. It focused on a decade-old EU project, which proposed a transportation link between Bulgaria, Macedonia and Albania, but as yet remains only an idea. Wittily naming his film a 'non-road movie', Despodov captures funny and revealing moments of everyday life in the Balkans.

Expectations for 2009 are high. Responding to a proposal by the National Film Council, the Ministry of Culture agreed to increase the public subsidy to more than €8 million and to help stimulate the younger generation with easier ways of financing their film projects. Four feature debuts will receive state suport of up to €300,000 and ten shorts by first-time directors will be given a total amount of €100,000. Twelve projects will receive development support of €12,500 each.

The year's best films
Dzift (Javor Gardev)
A Farewell to Hemingway (Svetoslav Ovcharov)
Hindemith (Andrei Slabakov)
The World is Big and Salvation Lurks Around the Corner (Stefan Komandarev)
Corridor #8 (Boris Despodov)

Quote of the year
'Honestly speaking, I was expecting the jury to offer me not one, but two awards, but nevertheless I forgive it.' ERNESTINA SHINOVA, *commenting on her Best Actress Award for her double role in* **Hindemith** *at the Varna Film Festival.*

Directory
All Tel/Fax numbers begin (+359)
Bulgarian National Film Library, 36 Gurko St, 1000 Sofia. Tel: (2) 987 0296. Fax: (2) 987 6004. bmateeva@bnf.bg.
Bulgarian Film Producers Association, 19 Skobelev Blvd, 1000 Sofia. Tel: (2) 860 5350. Fax: (2) 963 0661. geopoly@mail.techno-link.com.
Bulgarian National Television, 29 San Stefano St, 1000 Sofia. Tel: (2) 985 591. Fax: (2) 987 1871. www.bnt.bg/.
Ministry of Culture, 17 Stamboliiski St, 1000 Sofia. Tel: (2) 980 6191. Fax: (2) 981 8559. www.culture.government.bg/.
National Film Centre, 2A Dondukov Blvd, 1000 Sofia. Tel: (2) 987 4096. Fax: (2) 987 3626. nfc@mail.bol.bg.
Union of Bulgarian Film Makers, 67 Dondukov Blvd, 1504 Sofia. Tel: (2) 946 1068. Fax: (2) 946 1069. sbfd@bitex.com.
National Academy of Theatre & Film Arts, 108a Rakovsky Street, 1000 Sofia. Tel: (2) 9231 231/ 233. info_natfiz@yahoo.com.

PAVLINA JELEVA is a film critic and journalist, regularly contributing to many Bulgarian newspapers and magazines. Having been national representative on the boards of Eurimages and FIPRESCI, she is now artistic and foreign-relations director of her own film company.

Cambodia Anne-Laure Porée

Cambodian cinema is inextricably linked to the terrible history of the country. Under the Khmer Rouge regime, between 1975 and 1979, the majority of actors, directors, audiovisual technicians, writers and artists were executed, or died of starvation or disease. The ability to make films was almost lost. The country's cinema was eventually rebuilt, but with few means. This mainly accounts for why Cambodian filmmakers shoot their films on video and why national production is still mediocre.

The Cambodian jury of the third national film and video festival, which took place in January 2008, drew attention to the plight of its national cinema. Its members considered the quality of the films so bad they refused to hand out the first and second prize. Film production had also fallen to just ten films in 2008 (compared to 28 in 2007 and 61 in 2006). This reduction is due to both a lack of money and resources. And with piracy becoming all too common, cinemas are finding it impossible to stay open.

The greatest success of recent Cambodian cinema was back on a Phnom Penh screen. **The Crocodile's Hunter**, written and directed by Mao Ayuth, tells the story of a young man avenging villagers killed by a crocodile. The film's star, Preap Sovath, combined with a solid script containing some fine comic moments, once again attracted a young audience. The film also succeeded in conveying a rich history of culture and tradition.

The horror genre was the main staple of 2008's production slate. And of all the year's releases, only **Last or Later** (*Som bat changkraoj*) was considered acceptable. It tells the story of an orphan who discovers, ten years after the trip his father took to a distant province, that he has been killed.

There are a few signs that a better cinema is emerging. In 2007, Khmer Mekong Films (KMF) produced **Staying Single When?**, a romantic comedy about a young man looking for a wife, finally realising that the girl he loves works with him. KMF followed it with **HeartTalk** (*Vituo bes dong*), a contemporary thriller, which eschews violence in favour of a few scary moments in the unfolding narrative, which concerns a troubled radio station where two young women have disappeared. In the script, direction and performance, KMF have shown a willingness to improve the level of the production.

Tom Som and Bill Broomfield's **HeartTalk**

With **The Sea Wall** (*Barrage contre le Pacifique*), an adaptation of a Marguerite Duras novel, Rithy Panh takes an interest in the French colonial period, portraying the struggle of a mother attempting to save her land. It highlights the topical problem of land predators. Shot using a team from Cambodia and abroad, the film emphasised Panh's commitment to encouraging international co-production as a way of improving Cambodian cinema.

Rithy Panh's **The Sea Wall**

Following Rithy Panh, the Ministry of Culture recently founded the Cambodian Film Commission, whose mission is to promote the film industry in the country and to aid international film producers in shooting their films locally. Plans are also underway to build studios near Phnom Penh.

The year's best films
The Sea Wall (Rithy Panh)
HeartTalk (Tom Som/Bill Broomfield)
The Crocodile's Hunter (Mao Ayuth)
Staying Single When ?
(Tom Som/Matthew Robinson)

Quote of the year
'We have to train a generation who will be able to shoot its own images on its own country. and who will earn its living on cinema. Twenty years ago it was impossible. Now it is the right time. But it will take us 5 to 6 years.' RITHY PANH, *commenting on the challenges facing Cambodian cinema.*

Directory
All Tel/Fax numbers begin with (+855)
National Film Archive, 64 Oknha Men Street 200, Sangkat Boeung Raing, Khan Daun Penh, 12211, Phnom Penh. Tel: (0) 232 154 69. Fax: (0) 232 11004. dfladjfkjd

---

ANNE-LAURE PORÉE is a freelance journalist living in Phnom Penh, writing for national and international newspapers.

Canada Tom McSorley

The Canadian Parliament received three special guests in 2008: David Cronenberg, Sarah Polley and Paul Gross. Their reason for heading to Ottawa was to protest the Conservative government's Bill C-10, which proposed the withholding of tax credits for films deemed by government officials to be in violation of a vaguely defined set of 'community standards'. In a nation where an ever-fragile film industry relies heavily on state funding, Bill C-10 was decried as an American-style attack on artistic freedom. The trio, supported by the entire film and television industry, argued that the Bill was tantamount to censorship. The Conservatives held fast for months, but during Canada's federal election, and after much political fallout about funding cuts to other arts programmes, they backed down and promised to repeal C-10 if re-elected. They were. Stay tuned.

Julianne Moore in Fernando Meirelles' **Blindness**

Intra-Canadian politics aside, the internationalist trend continued in 2008. The highest-profile example was the Canadian co-production **Blindness**, which opened the Cannes Film Festival. Based on the dystopian novel by Portugal's José Saramago and directed by Brazil's Fernando Meirelles, the film stars Julianne Moore, Mark Ruffalo and Danny Glover.

Deepa Mehta's **Heaven on Earth**

Blindness's significant Canadian components were producer Niv Fichman, screenwriter-actor Don McKellar and actress Sandra Oh. Other examples of the border-blurring tendencies include Lea Pool's strong return to form with **Mommy is at the Hairdresser's** (*Maman est chez le coiffeur*), which features French actor Laurent Lucas in a leading role, and Atom Egoyan's **Adoration**, with American Scott Speedman. Deepa Mehta's daring drama about spousal abuse, **Heaven on Earth**, shot in India and Canada, featured Indian cinema star Preity Zinta.

On the local scene, with domestic product earning barely 4% at the box office, there has been a marked return to the modest, art-house traditions of Canadian film production, though not without a certain amount of commercial experimentation. The most prominent of these was the First World War drama, **Passchendaele**. With its massive – by Canadian standards – marketing campaign and a record-breaking production budget of CAN$20 million, the tale of a wounded soldier who falls in love with a nurse and returns to Europe to fight by her young brother's side, the film was a domestic success. Written, directed and starring Paul Gross, the film is, for all its effort and considerable craft, a disappointingly generic war melodrama.

Equally commercial in orientation, but more modest and artful, is *The Tracey Fragments* director Bruce McDonald's intriguing zombie genre film, **Pontypool**. Financed entirely without state funding and on a very short production schedule – both very rare in Canada – this is a taut, stylish tale of a jaded smalltown talk-show host confronted with hordes of zombies created by a mystery virus spread by the very words he speaks over the airwaves. Located somewhere between George Romero and David Cronenberg, *Pontypool* is an impressive achievement.

Rachel Blanchard and Noam Jenkins in Atom Egoyan's **Adoration**

Atom Egoyan's *Adoration* is the most prominent indicator of the larger trend of smaller-scale auteurist films. Egoyan's searching drama revolves around a young man named Simon (Devon Bostwick), who invents a disturbing story for his drama class about the death of his mother. The story soon

spreads virally on the Internet. An intense narrative about pretence, family history and uncertainties of identity, it recalls the best of Egoyan's 1990s work. In a similar vein and on an even lower budget is **Mothers and Daughters**, Carl Bessai's emotional, often wrenching drama about the tangled relationships between three mothers and their daughters. Veteran actress-producer Ingrid Veninger's debut feature, **Only**, a coming-of-age tale about a young man who falls in love with a guest staying at his parents' smalltown motel, cost a mere $25,000 and confirms that, as always, good Canadian films do not require big budgets.

Alison Reid's **The Baby Formula**

There were some promising first features in 2008. Alison Reid's witty comedy about a lesbian couple having a baby by very unconventional means, **The Baby Formula**, combines mockumentary and melodrama in an entertaining hybrid. Justin Simms' Newfoundland *bildungsroman*, **Down to the Dirt**, follows the turbulent life of a restless

Justin Simms' **Down to the Dirt**

Charles Officer's **Nurse. Fighter. Boy.**

twenty-something poet, Keith Kavanaugh (Joel Hynes), who leaves his small town to find himself. Charles Officer's **Nurse. Fighter. Boy.** is a moving story of a troubled boy befriended by an ex-boxer. Rounding out the impressive rookie crop is Vancouver-based Cameron Labine's **Control Alt Delete**, a wry comedy about a computer programmer whose life is complicated by his unusual love of technology.

In Quebec, too, the year was dominated by art-house fare. Veteran filmmaker Lea Pool's *Mommy is at the Hairdresser's* is a sensitive portrait of Benoit, a boy growing up in a small Quebec town and attempting to deal with his unhappy mother leaving home for a new life. The film's narrative is eerily echoed in Philippe Falardeau's **It's Not Me, I Swear!** (*C'est pas moi, je le jure!*), in which ten-year-old Leon's life is thrown out of kilter when his troubled mother suddenly decamps to Greece. New Brunswick-born director Rodrigue Jean's latest, **Lost Song**, is an art-house gem dealing with the emotional struggle of a classically trained singer spending the summer in a cottage cabin with her distant husband and newborn baby. Jean's Haneke-like precision combines tense psychological drama with a compassionate portrait of love slowly fading. Sebastien Rose's **The Banquet** (*Le Banquet*) is a ferocious assessment of a Quebec society drifting dangerously away from social cohesion. Revolving around an incident between a film professor and a troubled student, which leads to atrocity, Rose's intense, troubling film raises

unsettling questions about the corrosive, atomising influence of money on a traditionally communitarian Quebec society.

The theme of community is also explored in Benoît Pilon's **The Necessities of Life** (*Ce qu'il faut pour vivre*), the story of an Inuit man suffering with tuberculosis who is brought from his remote northern home to a Quebec City hospital in the 1950s. Culturally deracinated and unable to speak French, he is helped by an Inuit boy suffering from the same disease. While occasionally predictable and sentimental, the film's humanism is solid and engaging.

Two other notable features explore the prodigious geography of the upper reaches of North America. From Isuma Productions (*Atanarjuat: The Fast Runner*) and the Arrait Video Collective comes **Before Tomorrow**, a breathtakingly photographed tale of a powerful and resolute Inuit woman and her beloved grandson trapped on a remote island. The north also informs the return of noted Quebec auteur Robert Morin. His latest, **Papa a la chasse aux lagopedes**, involves an unnamed Montreal man driving north to escape the police, who are investigating his fraudulent business practices. It is shot mostly in the form of a video diary that the central character is creating to send to his two daughters, to explain his disappearance into the northern landscape.

Canada's strong documentary sector yielded some remarkable films: Luc Bourdon's elegiac, ghostly **The Memories of Angels** (*La Memoire des anges*) is a poetic assembly of National Film Board (NFB) footage of Montreal in 1950s, 1960s and 1970s, probing the signifance of cinema as an instrument of memory; Astra Taylor's **Examined Life** presents contemporary philosophers Cornell West, Peter Singer, Martha Nussbaum and others reflecting on twenty-first-century culture; John Walker's **Passage** explores the disastrous Franklin Expedition to find the Northwest Passage. Brett Gaylor's **RiP: A Remix Manifesto**, which captured the Audience Award at the 2008 Amsterdam documentary festival, is a formally freewheeling examination of the problematic notions of copyright in the twenty-first century through the work of remix musical artist, Girl Talk. Exploring the collision between vested commercial interests and the ideas of a cultural commons, *RiP* offers a perceptive, far-reaching challenge to the very assumptions of copyright law itself. Rounding out the documentary crop is Jean-Daniel Lafond's stunning **Folle de Dieu**, a multifaceted portrait of a woman born as Marie Guyart in France in 1599 who moved to Quebec City in 1639 to found a convent. There she became known as Marie de l'Incarnation. Lafond's film interweaves historical discussions about Marie and the process of rehearsing a play about her life. A meditation on the nature of spiritual ecstasy, identity and the documentary form itself, *Folle de Dieu* offers up yet another character disappearing into those vast, wild spaces of Canada.

The year's best films
Adoration (Atom Egoyan)
Heaven on Earth (Deepa Mehta)
It's Not Me, I Swear! (Philippe Falardeau)
The Banquet (Sebastien Rose)
Folle de Dieu (Jean-Daniel Lafond)

Atom Egoyan's **Adoration**

Quote of the year
'That's never happened to me before. From the time we think of a project to the time of shooting it, there's usually five years. It's Canada!' BRUCE MCDONALD *on the five-month production cycle of his film* **Pontypool**.

Directory
All Tel/Fax numbers begin with (+1)
Academy of Canadian Cinema & Television, 172 King St E, Toronto, Ontario, M5A 1J3. Tel: (416) 366 2227. Fax: (416) 366 8454. www.academy.ca.
Canadian Motion Picture Distributors Association (CMPDA), 22 St Clair Ave E, Suite 1603, Toronto, Ontario, M4T 2S4. Tel: (416) 961 1888. Fax: (416) 968 1016.
Canadian Film & Television Production Association, 151 Slater Street, Suite 605, Ottawa, Ontario, K1P 5H3. Tel: (613) 233 1444. Fax: (613) 233 0073. ottawa@cftpa.ca.
La Cinémathèque Québécoise, 335 Blvd de Maisonneuve E, Montreal, Quebec, H2X 1K1. Tel: (514) 842 9763. Fax: (514) 842 1816. info@cinematheque.qc.ca. www.cinematheque.qc.ca.
Directors Guild of Canada, 1 Eglinton Ave E, Suite 604, Toronto, Ontario, M4P 3A1. Tel: (416) 482 6640. Fax: (416) 486 6639. www.dgc.ca.
Motion Picture Theatre Associations of Canada, 146 Bloor Street W, 2nd Floor, Toronto, Ontario, M5S 1P3. Tel: (416) 969 7057. Fax: (416) 969 9852. www.mptac.ca.
National Archives of Canada, Visual & Sound Archives, 344 Wellington St, Ottawa, Ontario, K1A 0N3. Tel: (613) 995 5138. Fax: (613) 995 6274. www.archive.ca.
National Film Board of Canada, PO Box 6100, Station Centre-Ville, Montreal, Quebec, H3C 3H5. Tel: (514) 283 9246. Fax: (514) 283 8971. www.nfb.ca.
Telefilm Canada, 360 St Jacques Street W, Suite 700, Montreal, Quebec, H2Y 4A9. Tel: (514) 283 6363. Fax: (514) 283 8212. www.telefilm.gc.ca.

TOM McSORLEY is Executive Director of the Canadian Film Institute in Ottawa, a Sessional Lecturer in Film Studies at Carleton University, film critic for CBC Radio One, and a Contributing Editor to *POV* magazine.

Chile Hugo Diaz Gutiérrez

With fifteen released features and four waiting for a release date, 2008 has been a positive year for the Chilean film industry. However, the celebration has been marred by the possibility of an overcrowded marketplace. Distribution remains deficient, supporting a system that offers no guarantee of the commercial exhibition of any films produced.

Another issue has been a less than enthusiastic response from a more demanding audience. The domestic film industry appears to be paying a heavy price for decades of underdevelopment. Although there has been an attempt to branch out into previously unexplored genres, mediocre word-of-mouth or the lack of support from critics, who display less mercy with each season, has hindered many films' success.

Chile Can Do It, *directed by Ricardo Larrain*

A few films succeeded at the box office. Ricardo Larrain's **Chile Can Do It** (*Chile Puede*), Ernesto Díaz Espinoza's **Mirageman** and **31 Minutes, The Movie** (*31 minutos, La Película*) directed by Pedro Peirano and Álvaro Díaz all represent the search for new styles, with very different results. *Chile Can Do It* is a comedy about a businessman who is

Pedro Peirano and Álvaro Díaz's **31 Minutes, The Movie**

obsessed with sending the first Chilean into space. The candidate, chosen by a special lottery, is a simple Castilian-language teacher. The film generated significant hype before its release, which guaranteed a strong fan base, who appreciated the audacity of an FX-driven film made in Chile.

Mirageman is the story of a vigilante and his autistic younger brother, who is fascinated by a mysterious kung fu warrior who helps people fight criminals. The low-action film divided critics, but went on to win the Audience Award at the Valdivia Film Festival.

31 Minutes, The Movie is based on a popular fictional news television programme featuring puppets and a variety of second-hand toys (from ragged dolls to action figures). The comedy was released the year after the show ended and became the most successful Chilean film at the box office during 2008.

Gonzalo Justiniano's **Lokas** and Shai Agosin's **To Life** (*El Brindis*) were both co-productions with Mexico. Justiniano's film is a comedy about a homophobic man who discovers that his father is not only gay, but lives with his partner. *To Life* is a family drama about an

83-year-old Jew who is preparing a Bar Mitzvah and the daughter he has not seen for a long time. *Lokas* was the second-biggest box office hit among Chilean releases and was the first time that a gay topic had been adapted in so light a manner, particularly considering Chile is one of the most conservative countries in Latin America. *To Life* received mixed reviews, although it won an award at the San Diego Latin Film Festival. Chileans, who are mostly Catholic, were not so involved with the Jewish story, but acknowledged the solid performances by a great cast.

Undoubtedly the most important release of 2008, Pablo Larraín's **Tony Manero** was presented in the 'Directors' Fortnight' selection at the Cannes Film Festival. His second feature is an impressive thriller about a psychopath obsessed with the image of John Travolta's character in *Saturday Night Fever*. With a vicious atmosphere, strong performances and characters dancing disco music under Pinochet's dictatorship, many critics have compared Larraín with the Dardennes and lead actor Alfredo Castro with Al Pacino. It is no surprise that *Tony Manero* has been chosen as the Chilean submission for the Best Foreign Language Film category at the Academy Awards.

The Good Life (*La Buena Vida*) is also representing Chile, but at the Goya Awards. Andrés Wood's fifth feature comprises a series of interconnecting stories that have no conventional conclusion. Wood's intent is to characterise life in a grey and impersonal Santiago de Chile. It is a personal and contemplative experiment compared to his previous work. However, if compared to other films such as *Crash* or *Magnolia*, the film will suffer.

Hugo Díaz Gutiérrez is a journalist, screenwriter, film critic, and former editor of the Catalogue of the Valdivia International Film Festival.

Alfredo Castro in Pablo Larraín's **Tony Manero**

The year's best films
Tony Manero (Pablo Larraín)
Mirageman (Ernesto Díaz Espinoza)
31 Minutes, The Movie
(Álvaro Díaz and Pedro Peirano)
The Good Life (Andrés Wood)
To Life (Shai Agosin)

Quote of the year
'I am truly impressed and I don't know what to think … I hope to have just a quarter of the talent that he has, but it has been wonderful.'
ALFREDO CASTRO *talking in* Le Monde Diplomatique *about his performance in* **Tony Manero**, *when it was compared to Al Pacino's work in* Scarface *or* Serpico.

Directory
All Tel/Fax numbers begin (+56)
Consejo Nacional de la Cultura y las Artes, Fondo de Fomento Audiovisual, Plaza Sotomayor 233, Valparaíso. Tel: (32) 232 66 12. claudia. gutierrez@consejodelacultura.cl. www.consejodelacultura.cl
Corporación de Fomento de la Producción (CORFO), Moneda 921, Santiago. Tel: (2) 631 85 97. Fax: (2) 671 77 35. lordonez@corfo.cl. www.corfo.cl.
Ministerio de Relaciones Exteriores, Dirección de Asuntos Culturales, Teatinos 180, Santiago. Tel: (2) 679 44 07. Fax: (2) 699 07 83. acillero@minrel.gov.cl. www.minrel.cl.

China Luna Lin

2008 was a special year for China's film industry. Beijing was the host of the Olympic Games and became the focus of attention from all over the world. The Chinese film industry collaborated with Hollywood studios, as well as Asian countries, on numerous co-productions, many celebrating Chinese culture and history.

On the other hand, the year of the Olympics has seen art-house films or serious dramas sidelined more than previous years. In addition to struggling for a share of the box office, they also face increasing difficulty with the country's film censors. In preparing for the Olympics, authorities raised the bar in terms of security and sensitivity towards the country's national image. This posed an increasing number of problems for filmmakers seeking film permits. Filmmakers and professional film crews generally felt a cheerless atmosphere in the production sector during the first half of the year and diversity in creativity was difficult to achieve.

The year once again saw an increase in box office revenue. According to the statistics of the Chinese State Administration of Radio,

Film and Television (SARFT), the 2007 total box office revenue was US$458.6 million. In 2008, up until the end of August, the total box office revenue reached US$347.2 million, projecting an estimated total gross increase of 20% (US$586.5 million) by the end of the year. The cinema business continued to grow, with 1,502 cinemas and 3,894 screens by the end of August, an increase of 75 cinemas and 366 screens from 2007.

Peter Ho-Sun Chan's **The Warlords**

One factor that pushed the year's box office gross was the release of a series of co-produced blockbusters, or 'Da Pian'. **The Warlords** (*Tou Ming Zhuang*), directed by Peter Ho-Sun Chan and set at the time of the Qing Dynasty, is about three bandits and blood brothers who join a government army in order to suppress the Taiping rebellion. Lead actor Jet Li broke away from his usual fighter image, successfully portraying an ambitious general who sacrifices brotherhood to achieve his goal. The film successfully carried the December 2007 box office into a healthy start for 2008.

CJ7 (*Chang Jiang Qi Hao*) was co-produced by Stephen Chow's Hong Kong-based Star Overseas and China Film Group Corporation. The sci-fi comedy, about a poor labourer who

Xu Jiao in **CJ7**

finds an orb in a junkyard that later changes his life, grossed US$26.5 million in mainland China.

Maggie Q in **Three Kingdoms: Resurrection of the Dragon**

The entertaining **Three Kingdoms: Resurrection of the Dragon** (*San Guo Zhi Jian Long Xie Jia*), an historic action film about the legendary general, Zhao Zilong, in the Three Kingdom period (220–80 CE), was a co-production between China's Polybona, Korea's Taewon Entertainment and Hong Kong's Visualizer Productions. The film grossed US$9.4 million in box office. In April, Casey Silver Productions and Relativity Media collaborated with China's Huayi Brothers on the action adventure **The Forbidden Kingdom** (*Gong Fu Zhi Wang*), whose biggest draw was the on-screen face-off between Jet Li and Jackie Chan. Though less than intriguing, it has become the most successful US/Sino co-production to date, grossing US$26.64 million.

Jet Li and Jackie Chan in **The Forbidden Kingdom**

And the success of 'Da Pian' seems unlikely to end. **Red Cliff** (*Chi Bi*) is another historic film set during China's Three Kingdom period.

Dubbed the Chinese version of *Troy*, the war epic tells the story of the famous battle of Red Cliff, where two small kingdoms united to fight a powerful adversary. Directed by John Woo and billed as the most expensive production so far in Chinese film history (US$80 million), *Red Cliff* is co-produced by Japan, Korea, Taiwan and China. The film took in US$45.3 million in mainland China to become the most successful Chinese-language film ever made.

John Woo's **Red Cliff**

Smaller productions experienced unhappier times over the last year. It saw a slump for the so-called Sixth Generation directors. These filmmakers gained their fame at international film festivals, with realistic films reflecting on contemporary Chinese society. In the past three years they were the backbone of low- to mid-budget local productions. However, 2008 saw fewer films winning international recognition whilst attracting only small audiences.

In his second feature, **And the Spring Comes** (*Li Chun*), Gu Changwei focuses his beautiful but cruel lens on a music teacher in the 1980s, who is struggling to become an opera singer. Jiang Wenli was awarded the Best Actress Award at the Rome International Film Festival, but the film's box office was less than satisfying.

Wang Xiaoshuai's contemporary drama, **In Love We Trust** (*Zuo You*), won the Best Screenplay Award at the Berlin Film Festival. However, the family drama, about a divorced couple's reunion in an effort to save their leukemia-stricken daughter, earned just US$150,000, significantly less than the film's budget.

Two films witnessed the emergence of some promising new talent. Ning Jingwu's **Lala's Gun** (*Gun La La De Qiang*) is a coming-of-age story about a boy who goes in search of his father. Shot in China's Southwest Guizhou and set in the village of the Miao peoples, the unadorned performance of the actors and a detailed depiction of the affection between the boy and his grandmother make for a genuinely touching film. It has yet to be released theatrically.

Wang Jing's **End of the Year**

Wang Jing's **End of the Year** (*Yi Nian Dao Tou*) is a black comedy focusing on travel over the Chinese New Year period, the largest commuting season in the world, where more than one billion people are in transit. In order to make a trip home and enjoy a nice reunion with their families, five unrelated characters begin their New Year travel plans. Wang's humour works well with his sharp critique of a money-driven culture. However, the film made little more than US$300,000.

Behind the unfair neglect of these small dramas lies a problem for the industry. The burgeoning co-production trend may have helped local film companies build up international ties as well as boost China's box office, but it has not yet helped in developing local filmmaking talent. When established filmmakers such as Chen Kaige and Zhang Yimou are less active in 2008, new filmmaking

stars have not emerged. This presents a worry for future productions.

Leon Jay Williams and Huang Yi in Wang Yuelun's **Almost Perfect**

In terms of genre, comedy remains the most successful among local productions. More than ten comedies were released in 2008. Standouts include **Crossed Lines** (*Ming Yun Hu Jiao Zhuang Yi*), a portmanteau film, directed by Liu Yiwei, Lin Jinhe, Sun Zhou, Shen Lei and Alfred Cheung, about fate and coincidence, with events linked to mobile phones, and **Almost Perfect** (*Shi Quan Jiu Mei*), a film set in the Ming Dynasty, concerning a prince's search for a wood-carved book. Although most of these local comedies possess little potential in other territories, the high domestic returns have encouraged similar projects. The production teams of both *Crossed Lines* and *Almost Perfect* are preparing sequels for 2009.

The year also saw a significant increase in controls. In March, SARFT announced some film-censorship criteria, which listed any 'unwelcome' content. For example, films promoting pornography, gambling and violence, or any films causing harm to national security, national pride and national interests would be banned. Scenes of perverted sexual activity, rape, prostitution, homosexuality, murder, evil spirits and plots that confuse good and evil, or feature details of crime or drug abuse would be removed. Although these criteria are not part of a new policy, more a reiteration of existing regulations, there was a general concern among both local and overseas producers about project approval.

The Weinstein Company's **Shanghai**, directed by Mikael Håfström, was the most high-profile encounter between filmmakers and censors. It is reported that US$3m was spent in pre-production before authorities decided to withhold shooting permission due to problems with the script. Although approval was given three months later, producers had changed the film's location to Thailand.

Seeing fellow filmmakers' trouble in getting approval, more and more local filmmakers decided to put their pre-production work on hold until after the Olympics, when security levels would have receded and there would be less concern about China's international image.

Films and documentaries related to the theme of sports or the city of Beijing were popular. At least five sports-related films were released before the games began. **Dream Weavers – Beijing 2008** (*Zhu Meng Er Ling Ling Ba*) is a documentary about how Beijing prepared for the Olympics over the course of seven years. Filmmaker Gu Jun documented the urban renewal of the city, the demolition of traditional houses and the construction of the spectacular Bird's Nest stadium. The film also recorded the training of China's gymnasts and athletes.

Towards the end of 2008, the Chinese film industry lost the renowned filmmaker Xie Jin, who died at the age of 84. Known for his realist style and a strong sense of history, his death appears to mark an end of a filmmaking era – an era of state-owned film studios. The Chinese film industry is becoming more market oriented and privatised. Co-produced action films and comedies are the two mainstream modes of production, while investments continue to flood into the film business, despite the global recession. However, there is much room for improvement in terms of diversity. Post-Olympics, there is a general openness in Chinese society. The

country's filmmakers hope that such openness can soon feed back into the cinema.

Gu Changwei's **And the Spring Comes**

The year's best films
And the Spring Comes (Gu Changwei)
Dream Weavers – Beijing 2008 (Gu Jun)
End of the Year (Wang Jing)
Lala's Gun (Ning Jingwu)
The Warlords (Peter Ho-Sun Chan)

Quote of the year
'A film represents the passion of a filmmaker; it also crystallises a filmmaker's character and cultivation. Making a film is a burning of one's life.' XIE JIN, *commenting on filmmaking, a few months before he passed away on 18 October 2008.*

Directory
All Tel/Fax numbers begin (+86)
Beijing Film Academy, 4 Xitucheng Rd, Haidian District, Beijing 100088. Tel: (10) 8204 8899. http:www.bfa.edu.cn.
Beijing Film Studio, 77 Beisanhuan Central Rd, Haidan District, Beijing 100088. Tel: (10) 6200 3191. Fax: (10) 6201 2059.
China Film Archive, 3 Wenhuiyuan Rd, Xiao Xiao Xitian, Haidian District, Beijing 100088. Tel: (10) 6225 4422. chinafilm@cbn.com.cn.
China National Film Museum, 9 Nanying Rd, Beijing 100015. Tel: (10) 64319548. cnfm2007@yahoo.com.cn.

LUNA LIN is a Beijing-based journalist who contributes to Beijing-based *City Weekend* magazine and Shanghai-based *Modern Weekly* magazine.

Colombia Jaime E. Manrique & Pedro Adrián Zuluaga

In the five years since the groundbreaking law that benefits the Colombian film industry was approved, the nation's cinema is still trying to reconcile industry demands with riskier proposals, in order to better position the country's cinematic output globally. Film critics and specialised audiences have been critical of the quality of recent productions and are eager to see films of better artistic merit, which would better serve Colombia's film culture. However, without a solid foundation for the industry to grow from, such hopes may be premature.

John Leguizamo in Simon Brand's **Paraiso Travel**

2008 opened with an adaptation of Jorge Franco's novel, **Paraiso Travel**, directed by Simon Brand. Employing flashbacks to flesh out the central relationship of a Colombian couple who emigrate to the US, the film's incoherent narrative was littered with clichés, as well as a few too many loose ends. Ultimately, it fell short of successfully portraying the social issues surrounding immigration. Harold Trompetero's **Riverside** is also about immigrants in the US. A low-budget film shot in New York, *Riverside* is a little theatrical, but features a number of emotionally engaging scenes. **Dog Eat Dog** (*Perro come perro*) is Cali filmmaker Carlos

Carlos Moreno's **Dog Eat Dog**

Moreno's solid thriller. It displays a strong understanding of the genre's conventions, while at the same time adding local elements such as witchcraft.

For a country beset by an ongoing internal conflict, it is not surprising that so many films concern themselves with issues surrounding it. Unfortunately, many of these films have been schematic or lack drama. **Helena** by Jaime César Espinosa, **The Actors of the Conflict** (*Los actores del conflicto*) by Lisandro Duque Naranjo and Rafael Lara's **The Miracle-making Virgin** (*La milagrosa*) fail to overcome their poorly constructed presentation of events – real or fictitious – dealing with violence in Colombia.

Documentary filmmaker Óscar Campo premiered his feature debut, **I Am Other** (*Yo soy otro*). Looking at how violence affects everyone in society, the film opened to mixed reviews. **I Love You Ana Elisa** (*Te amo Ana Elisa*) by José Antonio Dorado and Robinson Díaz, creates a unique female character who struggles against a hostile environment in an intentionally kitsch film.

Diego García-Moreno's **The Heart** (*El corazón*) and Luis Ospina's **A Paper of Tiger** (*Un tigre*

Diego García-Moreno's The Heart

de papel) were two popular documentaries, although they were only released on the alternative cinema circuit (and later on DVD). A new viewpoint on the country and the formal risks that the filmmakers took to present them were appreciated. Both films have since screened at international festivals.

Colombian cinema currently runs along two courses: one plays to commercial audiences, which is necessary to support an industry financially; the other is a cinema of filmmakers who work on a smaller scale and is essential when looking for more diverse, risky and interesting representations of Colombian society.

Ciro Guerra's The Voyages of the Wind

2009 will see the opening of **The Voyages of the Wind** (*Los viajes del viento*), Ciro Guerra's follow-up to his acclaimed debut, *Shadow of the Walking Man*. It may be the independent Colombian film that can break out internationally and draw attention to a new, young breed of filmmakers.

The year's best films
Dog Eat Dog (Carlos Moreno)
Riverside (Harold Tompetero)
The Heart (Diego García-Moreno)

Quote of the year
'The greatness of a nation's cinema is to be able to show what that country has inside, its successes and errors as a society. That is a sign of maturity, intelligence and sensibility.'
DIEGO GARCÍA-MORENO, *director of the documentary* The Heart.

Directory
All Tel/Fax numbers begin (+57)
Association of Film & Video Producers & Directors, Calle 97, No 10-28, Bogotá. Tel: (1) 218 2455. Fax: (1) 610 8524. gustavo@centauro.com.
Colombian Association of Documentary Film Directors, Calle 35, No 4-89, Bogotá. Tel: (1) 245 9961. aladoscolombia@netscape.net. www.enmente.com/alados.
Colombian Association of Film Directors, Carrera 6, No 55-10, Apartado 202, Bogotá. Tel: (1) 235 9798. Fax: (1) 212 2586. lisandro@inter.net.co.
Colombian Film Archives, Carrera 13, No 13-24, Piso 9, Bogotá. Tel: (1) 281 5241. Fax: (1) 342 1485. patfilm@colnodo.apc.org. www.patrimoniofilmico.org.co.
Film Promotion Fund, Calle 35, No 4-89, Bogotá. Tel: (1) 287 0103. Fax: (1) 288 4828. claudiatriana@proimagenescolombia.com. www.proimagenescolombia.com.
Ministry of Culture, Film Division, Calle 35, No 4-89, Bogotá. Tel: (1) 288 2995. Fax: (1) 285 5690. cine@mincultura.gov.co. www.mincultura.gov.co.
National Film Council, Calle 35, No 4-89, Bogotá. Tel: (1) 288 4712. Fax: (1) 285 5690. cine@mincultura.gov.co. www.mincultura.gov.co.
Festival de Cine de Bogota, Residencias Tequendama, Centro Internacional Tequendama, Bogotá. Tel: (1) 341 7562. direccione@.bogocine.com.

JAIME E. MANRIQUE is a journalist and director of the showcases In Vitro Visual and Imaginaton. **PEDRO ADRIÁN ZULUAGA** is a journalist and the editor of *Extrabismos*, an online film magazine.

Croatia Tomislav Kurelec

The most important event in Croatia's film calendar is the National Programme at the Pula Film Festival, where films made over the last year are screened to an audience of six thousand in an old Roman arena. Six of the seven new releases received their premiere at this event.

All the films were by directors who had previously won at the festival, but there was a general agreement that those screened were below standard. Much of the criticism was levelled at the writing, which dealt inadequately with the themes being explored. Furthermore, the motivation behind certain characters' behaviour was never fully clear. However, not all the flaws were so visible.

Alen Liverić in Arsen Anton Ostojić's **No One's Son**

Within a number of films, the excellent acting, some expressionistic camerawork and original direction covered up the cracks in the script. Arsen Anton Ostojić's work on his **No One's Son** (*Ničiji sin*) displayed an articulate director at work. His film deservedly won Best Film, Best Director and the Critics' Award. Alen Liverić also walked away with the Best Actor prize for his energetic performance as Ivan, a former rock singer and soldier who, after being captured by the Serbs during the war, is now an invalid with post-traumatic stress disorder.

His wife and son leave him and he discovers that his real father is a Serb. Unable to find his place in society or the reason to carry on living, he sings Serbian songs in public, hoping he can provoke someone into killing him. Ostojić's tragic story presents a darker picture of contemporary Croatian society.

A number of other films dealt with the recent conflict in ex-Yugoslavia, which resulted, after years of fighting, in Croatian independence. In contrast to the films made during the war or immediately following it, which always portrayed Croatian soldiers as a force for good, some films show Croatian soldiers committing crimes and betraying the ideals the country was fighting for. Vinko Brešan's **Will Not End Here** (*Nije kraj*), made with Serbian co-producers, is a good example of this trend. A former Croatian sniper, years after the war, finds out that the widow of the enemy commander he shot during the war has become a porn actress. He tries to help her, but is prevented by wartime friends who have since become criminals. Unfortunately, the film is not entirely successful in its mix of action, romance and comedy. Octogenarian director Fadil Hadžić's **Remember Vukovar** (*Zapamtite Vukovar*) focuses on one of the greatest crimes committed by the Serbian

Vinko Brešan's **Will Not End Here**

Fadil Hadžić's **Remember Vukovar**

volunteers and Yugoslavian army during the conflict: the massacre of the civilians who lived in the border town of Vukovar and the soldiers who tried to defend it. Although the action scenes are well directed, the film lacks convincing characterisation. Like *Will Not End Here* and *No One's Son*, *Remember Vukovar* was more concerned with its political content than creating a well-crafted piece of cinema.

Goran Rušinović's **Buick Riviera**

Goran Rušinović's **Buick Riviera** (co-produced with Bosnia and Herzegovina) emphasised honest drama over political content. Slavko Štimac and Leon Lučev play, respectively, a Bosnian Muslim and Bosnian Serb who have relocated to the US. They meet when both are involved in a road accident. They find common ground in their desire to adapt to this strange new land, although nationalist feelings still simmer inside them. Rušinović's film adopts a bold visual style, playing up the narrative's exploration of the two complex characters at the heart of the drama. The frozen wastelands also offer strong resonance with a devastated Bosnia. It was awarded the Best Film prize in the Regional Programme of the Sarajevo

Film Festival, with Štimac and Lučev sharing the Best Actor Award. It is interesting that the most complex movie made by a Croatian director about consequences of the war in ex-Yugoslavia was made in a country not connected directly to the conflict.

Also of great importance in Croatian cinema are films that deal with contemporary issues. Tomislav Radić's ensemble drama **Three Stories About Sleeplessness** (*Tri priče o nespavanju*) presents modern life on a large canvas. Taking place over one night, the film gradually reveals the connection between its protagonists. In the first story, a young woman is distressed because of her baby's crying, a fight with her stepmother and her taxi-driver husband's failure to answer his phone. In the second story, after failing to have sex, all the problems between a married couple (he Croation, she Spanish) begin to surface. In the third story, an old woman, the mother of the Croat from the second story, is waiting for a guest from Spain (the sister of her son's wife) who arrives in a taxi cab driven by the man from the first story. Each character is defined by the stresses placed upon them, which can be seen in their body language and from the way they communicate with each other.

Tomislav Radić's **Three Stories About Sleeplessness**

In Zrinko Ogresta's **Behind the Glass** (*Iza stakla*), Nikola (Leon Lučev) is an architect whose professional and personal life is riddled by corruption and betrayal. With fine editing and regular changes in rhythm, Ogresta successfully builds a drama around his central character, whose guilt and suppressed

Zrinko Ogresta's **Behind the Glass**

emotions take a heavy toll on both him and those around him. Dalibor Matanić's **Kino Lika** combines naturalism and magical realism in an occasionally shocking critique of rural life. However, aside from a number of impressive set pieces, the film lacks coherence.

Taking into account the 'art-house' nature of the films screened, the screenings in Pula played well to large audiences. This offers hope in a country where, it seems, the majority of the population is only interested in watching comedies.

The year's best films
Three Stories About Sleeplessness
(Tomislav Radić)
Behind the Glass (Zrinko Ogresta)
Buick Riviera (Goran Rušinović)
No One's Son (Arsen Anton Ostojić)
Kino Lika (Dalibor Matanić)

Quote of the year
'The question is do we want to have an ideal picture of ourselves or not. That's exactly what I want to unmask: here, it is beautiful and ugly and great and hard ... It all exists here.'
DALIBOR MATANIĆ, *talking about* Kino Lika.

Directory
All Tel/Fax numbers begin with (+385)
Croatia Film, Katanciceva 3, 10000 Zagreb.
Tel: (1) 481 3711. Fax: (1) 492 2568.
Croatian Film Directors Guild, Britanski Trg 12, 10000 Zagreb. Tel: (1) 484 7026. www.dhfr.hr.

TOMISLAV KURELEC is a film critic, mostly for radio and television. He has directed five short films and many television items.

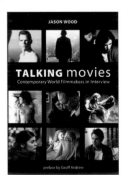

Cuba Jorge Yglesias

Once again, the films of younger talents in Cuban cinema are intent on exploring problematic areas of contemporary Cuban society, whilst also displaying a tendency towards formal experimentation, particularly in features and short-length documentaries. These works, produced independently, constitute a significant number of the Cuban films released over the last year.

Arguably the best example of this trend is Susana Barriga's **The Illusion**, in which the director's encounter with her father, for the first time in her life, takes place in a fragmented and diffused London. Successfully conveying Barriga's feeling of strangeness towards her situation, the film is reminiscent of avant-garde film and non-figurative painting. The alternation between silence and the voices of people we don't see, punctuated by the director's narration, make the film a painful testimony to an impossible reconciliation.

Laimir Fano's short film **Ode to the Pineapple** (*Oda a la Piña*), alludes to a classic piece of Cuban poetry, which narrates the anguish of a young mestizo dancer who has 'lost the rhythm' needed to impress a foreign talent scout looking for musical shows that satisfy his lust for the exotic. The film casts an ironic look at the excesses embedded in the tourist image of a Cuba that appears to want to be 'exportable' and 'exploitable'.

Laimir Fano's **Ode to the Pineapple**

Christian Torres and Hansel Leyva's animated short, **Cracks** (*Rendijas*), is an unusual departure from traditional Cuban animation. The subject of freedom is developed through a disturbing, expressionist atmosphere, with references to the work of the Quay Brothers and Phil Mulloy.

Tomás Piard's **The Immobile Traveler**

At times brilliant and occasionally bombastic, Tomás Piard's **The Immobile Traveler** (*El viajero inmóvil*) is a rare excursion for Cuban cinema. This lyrical piece is an enthusiastic narrative experiment focusing on the life and work of José Lezama Lima, one of Cuba's most acclaimed writers. Lima is represented by several actors and the spirit of his life and work is evoked by some of his intellectual friends in a beautifully assembled blend of reality and fiction. It is also the finest work of Piard's career, which began in the 1960s and has ranged from the experimental to the commercial, as well as television.

The modest independent production, **Personal Belongings**, directed by Alejandro Brugués, is ruled by the 'Strawberry and Chocolate syndrome' – a recurrent topic in Cuban cinema of the last two decades, in which a character questions whether or not to leave their family and bonds of love in order to abandon the country. Two lost souls, Ana, whose family left Cuba in a raft, and Ernesto, who lives in an automobile and has been for many years trying to leave the country, encounter each other and must decide whether they are finally going to leave Cuba.

After the success of *The Age of Peseta*, Pavel Giroud recently completed **Omertà**, a film noir homage, depicting an ageing gangster who finds himself out of touch in 1960s Cuba and discovers a way to leave the world like a real tough guy. The title refers to the sacred pact of silence within the Sicilian mafia.

Rogelio París's **Kangamba**

The long-awaited **Kangamba**, directed by Rogelio París, finally reached Cuban screens. It presents an episode in the Angola war, when FLPA forces loyal to the Angolan government and Cuban combatants resisted and finally defeated the blockade by UNITA troops, trained and armed by South Africa. Two months before the premiere, pirate copies of the film were already circulating throughout Havana, via illegal video banks.

2009 sees two significant releases: a biopic on the early years of José Martí, Cuba´s National Hero, directed by Fernando Pérez, arguably Cuba's most famous living director. And talented young filmmaker Juan Carlos Cremata will adapt the play *El premio flaco* (*The Thin*

Prize). There will also likely be innovative works by the youngest generation of film directors.

Mofo is a short film directed by Jorge Molina, arguably Cuba's most independent filmmaker. The film combines the atmosphere and film noir with scenes of explicit sex, creating a unique experience for audiences.

The year's best films
The Immobile Traveler (Tomás Piard)
The Illusion (Susana Barriga)
Personal Belongings (Alejandro Brugués)
Ode to the Pineapple (Laimir Fano)
Cracks (Christian Torres and Hansel Leyva)

Quote of the year
'I was only trying to portray the Cuba that I know in a story about the youths of my generation, it is something that I cannot help doing, because very often I have to erase of my agenda the telephone of a friend that left the country.' ALEJANDRO BRUGUÉS *on* Personal Belongings.

Directory
All Tel/Fax numbers begin (+53)
Cuban Institute of Art and Cinema Industry (ICAIC), Calle 23, No 1155, Entre 8 & 10, Vedado, Havana. Tel: (7) 552 859. Fax: (7) 833 3281. internacional@icaic.cu. www.cubacine.cu.
Escuela Internacional de Cine y TV, Finca San Tranquilino, Carretera Vereda Nueva, KM 4.5, San Antonio de Los Baños, Havana. Tel: (650) 383 152. Fax: (650) 382 366. eictv@eictv.org.cu. www.eictv.org.
Festival Internacional del Nuevo Cine Latinoamericano, Calle 2, No. 411, Entre 17 & 19, Vedado, Havana, Cuba CP 10400 festival@festival.icaic.cu, habanafest@festival. icaic.cu (World Registration). www.habanafilmfestival.com.

JORGE YGLESIAS is a poet and movie critic, and Professor of Film History and Chair of Humanities at the International School of Film and Television.

Cyprus Ninos-Feneck Mikelidis

The cinema in Cyprus is encountering a crisis. Hollywood has exiled almost all non-American films from mainstream venues and into specialised cinemas, such as the Nicosia Film Society. Although there are no official figures, the box office has continuously decreased and cinemas are closing, in both Nicosia and other towns, with only a few multiplexes remaining.

Christos Georgiou's **Small Crime**

Since 1994, the Cyprus Film Committee has co-financed approximately seventy feature films and documentaries, based on a programme approved by the European Commission: this covers 50% financing for most of these films, although it can reach 60–75% for feature debuts and low-budget films. During the past three years, the committee has approved and co-financed fifteen feature projects, as well as a number of documentaries and shorts. Of those, only three features were completed and released in 2007. Two others, **Small Crime** (*Mikro eglima*) by London-born Cypriot director Christos Georgiou, and **The Last Homecoming** (*O telefteos gyrismos*), by Corinna Avraamidou, were screened at the 2008 Thessaloniki Film Festival. Georgiou's debut, co-financed by

Corinna Avraamidou's **The Last Homecoming**

Furimages, is a comedy about a policeman transferred to an island, where he falls in love and has to investigate the appearance of a dead body. He relies heavily on visual gags to tell his story – particularly in the way he shows the various versions of how the man might have died, which recall Hitchcock's *The Trouble With Harry*. The film has strong commercial potential, something missing from many other Cypriot films.

Avraamidou's film takes place in a seaside village in Northern Cyprus during the summer of 1974, when Turkey invaded the island. It recounts the story of two brothers in love with the same woman as an amateur theatre company are preparing to stage a Greek

Corinna Avraamidou's **The Last Homecoming**

tragedy. Although the film's comic and tragic elements occasionally make for an uneasy tone, *The Last Homecoming*, notwithstanding a little naiveté, is an emotionally engaging film.

Four other films were to start shooting before the end of 2008: **Guilt** by Vassilis Mazomenos; **Nick the Knife** (*Macherovgaltis*) by Yiannis Economidis; **The Guilty Water** (*To enocho nero*) by Christos Shiopahas; and **Dinner With My Sisters** (*To deipno me tis adeldes mou*) by Michalis Hapeshi.

The recent change in government and the appointment of a new Minister of Education and Culture have brought about hopes for a new approach to the cinema and filmmaking in general. The €1 million annual budget for production is expected to rise and the Minister has promised to create the semi-independent Culture Institution, which will embrace all aspects of culture, including cinema, covering production, distribution, financing of festivals and any other related areas. Technical equipment has up until now been deficient. However, very recently some of the film and television production companies were able to equip themselves with HD cameras and other accessories. All laboratory work (film development, film transfer, optical sound processing) is still being carried out in Greece or other European countries.

The year's best film
Small Crime (Christos Georgiou)

Quote of the year
'I know that my film annoys both Greek Cypriot and Turkish Cypriot fanatics – but you cannot refer to history in black and white.' *Director* **PANIKKOS CHRYSSANTHOU** *on his 2006 film, released late 2007* **Akamas.**

NINOS-FENECK MIKELIDIS is an historian of Greek cinema and film critic for *Eleftherotypia* daily newspaper. He is also the founder and director of the Panorama of European Cinema film festival in Athens.

FILMING in CYPRUS

Locations, Incentives, Resources

There's always a new world to discover.

Cyprus lies at the crossroads of three continents, where East meets West, where deep blue seas, sandy beaches, captivating forests, breathtaking mountain, unique archeological sites, monasteries and churches and enchanting locations awaits for you discover.

Probably your next filming destination.

The "all in one" Filming Destination
One Island. One natural Studio with almost 360 days of Sunshine...

Ministry of Education and Culture of Cyprus
Cultural Department (Cinema Advisory Committee)
Kimonos and Thoukididou, 1434 Nicosia, Cyprus
Tel.: 0035722800982 Fax.: 0035722809506
Email: echristo@cytanet.com.cy / echristodoulidou@moec.culture.gov.cy
http:www.moec.gov.cy

Czech Republic Eva Zaoralovà

This isn't the first year Czech cinema has witnessed a curious paradox. While Czech films vainly try to gain entry to the most prestigious foreign festivals, back home their audiences can't get enough of them. 2007 saw audience figures increase by 11.6% over the previous year. And of the box office top ten, five were Czech. Two of them, *Empties* by Jan Svěrák and Jiří Menzel's *I Served the King of England*, even topped the list.

A major proportion of films produced during 2007 and 2008 were by new directors, most offering low-budget comedies that occasionally ingratiate themselves with audiences. Of these, the most successful were Tomáš Bařina's summer comedy **Grapes** (*Bobule*) and Jan Prušinovský's bitter-sweet comedy about an incorrigible skirt-chaser, **Womanizer** (*František je děvkař*). Household names, such as Jan Hřebejk, have stayed with the comedy genre. Over the last two years, Hřebejk has directed three films featuring his favourite actors. Last year's *Teddy Bear*, followed by **I'm All Good** (*U mě dobrý*) and, most recently, **Shameless** (*Nestyda*) all examine negative aspects of marital and extra-marital relationships within the middle-class society.

However, the reponse to his recent films was muted. Dušan Klein highlights the shortcomings of consumer society in his folk comedy, **A Wedding on a Battlefield** (*Svatba na bitevním poli*), while the equally experienced Zdeněk Troška stayed with a genre that has always found him favour with viewers: the fairy tale. His latest, **The Loveliest Riddle** (*Nejkrásnější hádanka*), is inspired by the tales of Jan Drda.

Bohdan Sláma's **A Country Teacher**

The most important films premiered during the first half of 2008 undoubtedly include the work of two directors who have just passed forty, after ten years in a business that has seen success both at home and internationally. Bohdan Sláma, whose previous film, *Something Like Happiness*, was awarded the Golden Seashell at San Sebastián in

Ivan Trojan in Petr Zelenka's **The Karamazovs**

2006, directed another study of modern society and inter-personal relationships. Living in the West Bohemian border region, the central character in **A Country Teacher** (*Venkovský učitel*) gradually comes to terms with his homosexuality. Although it was well received by Czech critics, the film was unable to establish itself in competition at major festivals, although it was invited to take part in Venice Days. While Sláma is drawn to psychological realism, Petr Zelenka has made a name for himself with his stylised combination of documentary and fiction, often employing music to great effect, such as in 2002's *Year of the Devil*. In his new film **The Karamazovs** (*Karamazovi*) we again encounter the fusion of documentary (rehearsals for a theatre production staged in a disused factory) and fiction, as actors appear on an improvised stage, playing roles in an adaptation of the Dostoevsky novel written thirty years earlier by Evald Schorm. We are also privy to the minor dramas played out by the actors between rehearsals. This complex work, requiring familiarity with the novel and considerable stamina on the part of the audience, was the only Czech film included in the first round of nominations for the 2008 European Film Academy awards.

Of the feature films that attracted positive reviews from Czech critics, animation and documentary filmmaker Michaela Pavlátová's **Night Owls** (*Děti noci*) deserves mention. The heroine of her second feature film is a girl who, after experiencing a shocking event, begins to reflect on her life and her feelings towards those around her. The two young

actors in the film, Martha Issová and Jiří Mádl, won the Best Actress and Best Actor awards at the Karlovy Vary Film Festival.

Michaela Pavlátová's **Night Owls**

Also noteworthy is the directorial debut of another female director who is already established as a screenwriter, Olga Dabrowská. **Marbles** (*Kuličky*) brings together three stories about the relationships between men and women – from childhood and early sexual encounters, to old age and death. The historical thriller **Bathory** (*Bathory*) proved to be one of the more ambitious projects seeking inspiration from the past. Featuring an international cast and costly sets, it was directed by one of the most famous members of the Czechoslovak New Wave, Slovak filmmaker Juraj Jakubisko. His film uncovers the legend of the Lady of Csejte (Čachtice) and Hungarian countess, Erzsebeth Bathory, who lived in the latter half of the sixteenth century and is said to have bathed in the blood of murdered young girls in order to preserve her youth. The director rehabilitates his heroine as a victim of political intrigue, and creates a

Anna Friel in Juraj Jakubisko's **Bathory**

fictional image of the period so suggestive that the film enjoyed uncommonly high audience figures upon its release. The critics, however, were more reticent, as they were about the new film by *Bathory*'s cinematographer, F. A. Brabec. As director, his interest lay in transferring a classic of nineteenth-century Czech culture to the screen. **May** (*Máj*) is an adaptation of the lyrical epic poem by Karel Hynek Mácha, featuring stunning images of the wonderful landscape of North Bohemia. The second film by Václav Marhoul returned to the recent past. **Tobruk** (*Tobruk*) is a psychological drama set during one of the most important battles of the Second World War.

Documentary films continue to enjoy increasing popularity. Pavel Koutecký's **Citizen Havel** (*Občan Havel*) broke all records for audience attendance. It looks behind the scenes of the political and private dramas during the period Václav Havel was president of the country. From 1992, Koutecký recorded the daily life of the president, up to the end of his tenure. After the director's tragic death in 2006, the task of editing the huge quantity of material fell to his colleague, Miroslav Janek. The resulting film is a stirring portrait of 'Havel, citizen and person', full of poignant moments and with a good degree of humour. The experienced Helena Třeštíková directed **René**, a portrait of a man who has spent two-thirds of his life behind bars as an inveterate criminal, yet is endowed with literary talent. Also remarkable is Ivan Vojnár's **Remembering the Reflection** (*Rozpomínání na Zrcadlení*),

a work linked to the films of Evald Schorm (1931–1988), who is considered a philosopher of the Czechoslovak New Wave. Here, Ivan Vojnár develops Schorm's reflections on the sense underlying our lives and his thoughts on dying. The themes of life and death, cruelty and violence, but also hope, are traced in historian Lukáš Přibyl's trilogy, **Forgotten Transports** (*Zapomenuté transporty*), which records the fate of thousands of Czech Jews interned in Nazi camps in the Baltic States.

Helena Třeštíková's **René**

Of the forthcoming releases, there is Vladimír Drha's **English Strawberries** (*Anglické jahody*), in which the director returns to the invasion of Czechoslovakia by the Warsaw Pact armies in August 1968. Representing the younger generation, David Ondříček is currently completing his crime drama **In the Shadow of the Horse** (*Ve stínu koně*), set during the period of political repression in the 1950s. His contemporary Irena Pavlásková's **An Earthly Paradise for the Eyes...** (*Zemský ráj to na pohled*) also has a political theme, focusing on the persecution of dissidents by the Communist regime after Charter 77. Ivan Vojnár traces the gradual break-up of a marriage in **Flowers of Sakura** (*Květy sakury*), and Ivan Trajkov, in **Joseph's Journey** (*Josefova cesta*), depicts an emotional crisis and the quest to make sense of life. A special attempt to break into the Western market can be seen with **The Case of Unfaithful Klara** (*Případ nevěrné Kláry*), based on the bestseller by Czech author Michal Viewegh. The film, a Czech/Italian co-production, is being shot in English by Italian director, Roberto Faenza.

Pavel Koutecký's **Citizen Havel**

WE SPEAK FILMMAKING

The year's best films
Citizen Havel (Pavel Koutecký, Miroslav Janek)
The Karamazovs (Petr Zelenka)
A Country Teacher (Bohdan Sláma)
Night Owls (Michaela Pavlátová)
Václav (Jiří Vejdělek)

Quote of the year
'Manipulation is the most dangerous antithesis of freedom. Over the course of centuries, our civilisation has developed such refined methods of manipulation that we are deprived of freedom of action without most of us realising that we´ve lost anything. Today, advertising is a huge form of manipulation, one which forces people to adopt a consumer lifestyle.' JAN ŠVANKMAJER, *surreal animation and feature director.*

Directory
All Tel/Fax numbers begin (+420)
Association of Czech Filmmakers (FITES), Pod Nuselskymi Schody 3, 120 00 Prague 2. Tel: (2) 691 0310. Fax: (2) 691 1375.
Association of Producers, Národní 28, 110 00 Prague 1. Tel: (2) 2110 5321. Fax: (2) 2110 5303. www.apa.iol.cz.
Czech Film & Television Academy, Na Îertvách 40, 180 00 Prague 8. Tel: (2) 8482 1356. Fax: (2) 8482 1341.
Czech Film Centre, Národní 28, 110 00 Prague 1. Tel: (2) 2110 5302. Fax: (2) 2110 5303. www. filmcenter.cz.
FAMU, Film & Television Faculty, Academy of Performing Arts, Smetanovo 2, 116 65 Prague 1. Tel: (2) 2422 9176. Fax: (2) 2423 0285. kamera@f. amu.cz. Dean: Karel Kochman.
Ministry of Culture, Audiovisual Dept, Milady Horákové 139, 160 00 Prague 6. Tel: (2) 5708 5310. Fax: (2) 2431 8155.
National Film Archive, Malesická 12, 130 00 Prague 3. Tel: (2) 7177 0509. Fax: (2) 7177 0501. nfa@nfa.cz. www.nfa.cz.

EVA ZAORALOVÀ is Artistic Director of the Karlovy Vary International Film Festival, editor of *Film a doba* magazine and author of books on Czech, French and Italian cinema.

pbk £18.99 / $29.50
978-1-904764-20-5

THE CINEMA OF CENTRAL EUROPE
Edited by Peter Hames
Preface by István Szabó

The cinemas of Hungary, Poland and the former Czechoslovakia can each claim their pioneers of early cinema and all attained significant levels of production between the wars. They first attracted international attention in the 1930s, confirming this with a succession of politically and aesthetically challenging films from the 1950s, through the period of Communism and into the post-1989 era. The work of directors such as Andrzej Wajda, Miklos Jancso, Jiri Menzel, István Svabó, Marta Meszaros, Krzysztof Kieslowski, Jan Svankmajer and Béla Tarr is discussed with in-depth studies of films such as *Ashes and Diamonds* (1958), *Knife in the Water* (1962), *The Round-Up* (1965), *A Shop on the High Street* (1965), *Closely Observed Trains* (1966), *Alice* (1988), *The Decalogue* (1988) and *Satantango* (1994).

'This new volume in Wallflower's superb *24 Frames* series is an authoritative text on classic and contemporary eastern European cinema ...The essays throughout are deeply felt, factually accurate, and carefully written ... ideal for both students and general readers. Essential.'
– *Choice*

'A lively, insightful and critically astute volume that offers the reader wonderfully diverse and eclectic entry-points and pathways for understanding the intellectual, cultural, political and artistic struggles, upheavals and high moments of cinematic expression in this region of Europe.'
– Daniel J. Goulding, Oberlin College

www.wallflowerpress.co.uk

Denmark Christian Monggaard

2007 was a catastrophic year for the Danish film industry. Even though the 26 Danish feature films released sold somewhere in the region of 3.2 million tickets – securing a market share of 26 percent, the second-highest share for local films in Europe after France – spiralling production costs and a greater divide between art-house and mainstream releases made it harder to profit from making films.

At the beginning of 2008, two companies closely associated with the Danish New Wave over the last 10–15 years, Zentropa and Nimbus Films, were in financial trouble. Zentropa had lost money on their last seven films and all four of Nimbus Films' releases, including former golden boy Thomas Vinterberg's return to Danish-language film-making, the comedy *A Man Comes Home*, flopped at the box office.

In May, Zentropa announced that, in order to raise money for new films, the company was selling half of its assets to Nordisk Film, making it the largest film producer, distributor and exhibitor in Denmark. In October, Nimbus Films had to scale down the company's activities, laying off a third of its staff and shutting down its commercial branch.

During the last few years, several other small production companies have closed shop and, in spite of its size, Nordisk Film has continually lost money. The situation is serious and the Danish Film Institute, which supports most films made in Denmark, as well as the organisations representing directors, producers and film workers, has been struggling to find a way out of this mess. The trend appears to be moving towards either cheaply produced

Ole Christian Madsen's **Flame & Citron**

features for the domestic market or expensive co-productions for international consumption.

Ironically, 2008 is turning out to be a very successful year for Danish films. By late October, more than 3.5 million tickets had been sold for the 22 domestic feature films released, with Ole Christian Madsen's World War Two drama **Flame & Citron** (*Flammen & Citronen*) the highest-grossing Danish film since Lone Scherfig's *Italian for Beginners*. To date, it has sold almost 700,000 tickets. But the film, which was produced by Nimbus Films on a budget of €6.4 million (more than double the average cost of a feature film in Denmark, with much of the budget coming from Germany), wasn't enough to recover the company's major losses from 2007.

Flame & Citron tells the story of two Danish freedom fighters, codenamed Flame (Thure Lindhardt) and Citron (Mads Mikkelsen), who try to navigate through the muddy waters of idealism and patriotism during the final years of Germany's occupation of Denmark. Beautifully shot and well acted, the film successfully encapsulates the heroic image

Niels Arden Oplevs' **Worlds Apart**

many people have of the Danish resistance movement. It even sparked debate prior to its release.

Niels Arden Oplevs' **Worlds Apart** (*To verdener*) opened the year. An intelligent, family-oriented drama and coming-of-age story, it was not too dissimilar in theme to the director's previous film, 2006's *We Shall Overcome*. *Worlds Apart*, which deals with a young girl's attempt to break free of her strict religious upbringing, proved to be a surprise hit, selling more than 300,000 tickets. Pernille Fischer Christensen, who debuted in 2006 with the compelling, critically acclaimed drama *A Soap*, failed with her second feature, the uneven **Dancers** (*Dansen*), which starred Trine Dyrholm and Anders W. Berthelsen as unlikely lovers. The film was only seen by 10,000 people.

Søren Kragh-Jacobsen's **What No One Knows**

After the 2003 English-language drama, *Skagerrak*, veteran director Søren Kragh-Jacobsen returned with a taut political thriller, **What No One Knows** (*Det som ingen ved*), in which the prolific Anders W. Berthelsen plays

an ordinary man who becomes embroiled in the shady world of intelligence and surveillance. Inspired by real events, as well as American conspiracy thrillers of the 1960s and 1970s – favourites of Kragh-Jacobsen's – the film asks important questions about a world in which we give up our basic rights, out of fear of terrorist attack. It sold a solid 186,000 tickets.

Kasper Barfoed's **The Candidate** (*Kandidaten*) was another thriller, in which the impressive Nikolaj Lie Kaas plays a young lawyer investigating his father's death. After two folksy family films, Barfoed aimed his sights at an older audience with a film that looked good, but was both illogical and implausible. Still, by the end of October, the film had seen over 190,000 admissions.

Henrik Ruben Genz's **Terribly Happy**

One of the year's best films, Henrik Ruben Genz's tragicomedy, **Terribly Happy** (*Frygtelig lykkelig*), was based on a book by Erling Jepsen, who also wrote the book behind one of 2007's most memorable films, Peter Schønau Fog's *The Art of Crying*. In it, the excellent Jacob Cedergren plays a cop who is transferred to a remote part of Denmark after pulling a gun on his wife when she announces she is divorcing him. In this little town, where everybody minds their own business and bitterly resents the interference of outsiders, the cop becomes romantically involved with an unstable woman whose husband is violent, and unwittingly learns the ways of the small, closed community. This witty and dramatic marshland western was awarded the top prize at the Karlovy Vary Film Festival.

New Danish Screen (NDS) is the name of the Danish Film Institute's support scheme for young talent and professional experiments. Through NDS, production companies can apply for subsidies for features and short films, documentaries and computer games. In the spring of 2008, three feature films produced with money from NDS were released to wide acclaim but attracted almost no audiences.

Christian Dyekjær's **Moving Up**

Christian Dyekjær's **Moving Up** (*Spillets regler*) is a sharp and satirical look at unbridled ambition and backstabbing at the psychology faculty of the University of Copenhagen. Niels Gråbøl's **The Gift** (*Gaven*) tells the compelling story of two sons (Jacob Cedergren and Paw Henriksen) and their estranged, mentally ill father (Hening Jensen). And Omar Shargawi's **Go With Peace Jamil** (*Gå med fred Jamil*), the most memorable and audacious of the three films, deals with bloody revenge between Shia and Sunni Muslims in a Copenhagen that more closely resembles Beirut than the capital of Denmark. Visually, Shargawi's debut was very intense, bringing us close to the characters, while asking why so many believers in the Muslim community betray their faith.

Eight films produced outside the government subsidy system were released in 2008, among them **MollyCam**, Aage Rais Nordentoft's ambitious but failed attempt to castigate society through the story of what might have been a group rape. Linda Wendel's predictable **One Shot** was filmed in one long, admittedly

impressive take, while Kaywan Mohsen's annoying **Eye for Eye** glorified gang-banger mentality over social consciousness. Christian E. Christiansen's well-acted but slight drama **Crying for Love** (*Dig og mig*), about three young women on a cancer ward, was expanded from his own short. It sold 100,000 tickets. Rasmus Heide's **Take the Trash** (*Blå mænd*) is a broad comedy with Thure Lindhardt, Sidse Babett Knudsen and stand-up comedian Mick Øgendahl, who co-wrote the script. The film has sold more than 400,000 tickets, demonstrating the possibility of producing cheap films (the budget was €1.6 million) without government support.

The rest of the year's feature films were more or less forgettable sequels in popular family franchises: Søren Frellesen's **Anja & Viktor – In Sickness and Health** (*Anja & Viktor – i medgang og modgang*), Claus Bjerre's **Father of Four – Back Home** (*Far til fire – på hjemmebane*) and Giacomo Campeotto's **The Lost Treasure of the Knights Templar III: The Mystery of the Snake Crown** (*Tempelriddernes skat III: Mysteriet om slangekronen*). There were also a couple of 3D animated features: Thomas Borch Nielsen's **Sunshine Barry & the Disco Worms** (*Disco ormene*) and Craig Frank, Thorbjørn Christoffersen and Kresten Vestbjerg Andersen's **Journey to Saturn** (*Rejsen til Saturn*).

3D adventures in **Journey to Saturn**

2008 has not been an exciting year for documentary. Carsten Søsted and Mads Kamp Thulstrup's **Danish Dynamite** (*...Og det var Danmark*), a film about the men's national soccer team and its success in the 1980s, was born out of the directors' enthusiasm for football and the period, but didn't do as well as expected at the box office, with only 36,000 admissions. However, it was the most popular Danish documentary of the year, with the others, including Ulrik Wivels' stylish **Roskilde**, about the popular music festival in Roskilde, selling less than 5,000 tickets.

Nils Malmros' **Heartaches**

The industry's economic crisis is far from over, but the impressive box office returns have made some cautiously optimistic. Looking at the list of films slated for release in 2009, it is certainly difficult to be pessimistic. Lars von Trier, who didn't exactly score a major hit with his latest, Danish-language film, *The Boss of It All*, is currently shooting another English-language feature, the horror film **Antichrist**, with Willem Dafoe and Charlotte Gainsbourg. Trier's dogme-brother, Kristian Levring, has made the psychological drama **Fear Me Not** (*Den du frygter*) with Paprika Steen and Ulrich Thomsen. Ole Bornedal is returning in 2009 with **Fri os fra det onde**, a drama about xenophobia; Nils Malmros returns to his youth with **Heartaches** (*Kærestesorger*), a sequel of sorts to his popular *Tree of Knowledge*.

CHRISTIAN MONGGAARD is the film editor at the daily Danish newspaper *Information*. He freelances for various monthly magazines, writes books on films, and in 2007 he authored a book on Nordic films for the San Sebastián Film Festival.

The year's best films
Terribly Happy (Henrik Ruben Genz)
Flame & Citron (Ole Christian Madsen)
Go With Peace Jamil (Omar Shargawi)
What No One Knows (Søren Kragh-Jacobsen)
Moving Up (Christian Dyekjær)

Quote of the year
'While other countries' national identities are closely linked to fiction, America and Great Britain for instance, we don't have the necessary national self-esteem to free ourselves of the myths and make history tangible with the help of fiction.'
OLE CHRISTIAN MADSEN, *director of the Second World War drama* Flame & Citron.

Directory
All Tel/Fax numbers begin (+45)
Danish Film Institute/Archive & Cinematheque (DFI), Gothersgade 55, DK-1123 Copenhagen K. Tel: 3374 3400. Fax: 3374 3401. dfi@dfi.dk. www.dfi.dk. Also publishes the film magazine *Film*.
Danish Actors' Association (DSF), Sankt Knuds Vej 26, DK-1903 Frederiksberg C. Tel: 3324 2200. Fax: 3324 8159. dsf@skuespillerforbundet.dk. www.skuespillerforbundet.dk.
Danish Film Directors (DF), Vermundsgade 19, 2nd Floor, DK-2100 Copenhagen Ø. Tel: 3583 8005. Fax: 3583 8006. mail@filmdir.dk. www.filmdir.dk.
Danish Film Distributors' Association (FAFID), Sundkrogsgade 9, DK-2100 Copenhagen Ø. Tel: 3363 9684. Fax: 3363 9660. www.fafid.dk.
Danish Film Studios, Blomstervaenget 52, DK-2800 Lyngby. Tel: 4587 2700. Fax: 4587 2705. ddf@filmstudie.dk. www.filmstudie.dk.
Danish Producers' Association, Bernhard Bangs Allé 25, DK-2000 Frederiksberg. Tel: 3386 2880. Fax: 3386 2888. info@pro-f.dk. www.producent-foreningen.dk.
National Film School of Denmark, Theodor Christensen's Plads 1, DK-1437 Copenhagen K. Tel: 3268 6400. Fax: 3268 6410. info@filmskolen.dk. www.filmskolen.dk.
West Danish Film Fund, Filmby Arhus, Filmbyen 23, 8000, Arhus C. Tel: 8940 4882. Fax: 8940 4852. mail@filmpuljen.dk www.filmpuljen.dk.

Ecuador Gabriela Alemán

Ecuadorian cinema shifted gear in the last year, charging full throttle into fantasy. Of the nine features that reached cinemas, five were fantasy or horror: Miguel Alvear and Patricio Andrade's **Blak Mama**; Sandino Burbano's **Black Quixotes** (*Quijotes Negros*); Wilson Burbano's **Big Bang**; Fernando Mieles' **Deported Prometheus** (*Prometeo Deportado*) and Mateo Herrera's **Impulse** (*Impulso*).

Miguel Alvear and Patricio Andrade's **Blak Mama**

Blak Mama is remarkable for the way it crosses various disciplines, from theatre and dance to film. The project was conceived as a way of reaching a wider audience than contemporary art would normally allow. Its starting point is the popular festival of the Mama Negra (Black Mama), with symbolism drawn from African, Spanish and indigenous Ecuadorian culture. *Black Quixotes* is a contemporary fable that borrows from the carnivalesque and presents us with an up-turned world where love, loyalty, friendship and honour hold a higher position than power, betrayal, avarice and corruption. Burbano's central characters are from Cervantes' *Don Quixote*, relocated to twenty-first-century Ecuador. The result is a compelling satire of political corruption and the redemptive power of love. The plot follows Sancho, who

unwittingly falls in love with the Queen and Princess of Spain. He eventually kidnaps them. An opportunistic friend realises he can profit from the venture and writes the King of Spain a letter to ask for what he considers a moderate amount: all the gold and silver that the Spaniards usurped during the conquest with an 8% interest rate back-dated to the sixteenth century. Essayistic in style, *Big Bang* runs from the oneiric and reflexive to the dark and dense. Wilson Burbano's epic film rethinks world history through the eyes of a man on death row who, by spying through the key hole of his cell door, observes some of the major events of history: the crucifixion of Christ, the Spanish Conquest, the role played by the Catholic Church in massacres, the rise of dictators and the Israel/Palestine conflict. In its powerful first scene, a hand-held camera follows the movements of an invisible condor we hear approaching the clock tower of the gothic basilica in the capital of Ecuador. The mythic bird, a symbol of power in the indigenous world, crashes into the tower and is trapped inside the mechanisms of the clock. Seconds later the hands and numbers of the clock face fall, and with them time itself disintegrates. *Big Bang* occasionally displays the influence of Jodorowsky, Terry Gilliam or even *Mad Max*. But it remains a Wilson Burbano film. *Deported Prometheus* is a forceful satire on the state of things regarding global migration. It takes place in only one location: the waiting area of a large international airport, where tourists and emigrants from Ecuador arrive, awaiting some sort of response from the authorities concerning their status. Their status never arrives, but the authorities say nothing, while more planes arrive. The passengers meanwhile begin to live their lives as though they were trapped in some strange, Kafka-esque limbo. *Impulse*, Herrera's third movie, is a horror film set in rural Ecuador. Viviana Cordero's third film, **Pieces of Life** (*Retazos de vida*), is centred around the life of fashion models in Ecuador's largest city, Guayaquil.

Alex Schlenker's **Chigualeros**, Gabriela Calvache's **The Occult Labour** (*Labranza oculta*) and Juan Martin Cueva's **This Damn Country** (*Este maldito país*) were all fine examples of Ecuador's annual documentary output. An impressive number of short fiction films were also released. Amongst them was Sebastián Arechavala's impressive **Kicked to Death** (*Un hombre muerto a punta pies*), based on Pablo Palacio's classic short story.

The year's best films
Big Bang (Wilson Burbano)
Deported Prometheus (Fernando Mieles)
Black Quixotes (Sandino Burbano)
Kicked to Death (Sebastián Arechavala)

Quote of the year
'Any attempt at constructing cinema from a place of difference, in this case from Ecuador, automatically isolates you from what is considered "normal". So why not put up a fight from the beginning and build that difference with all the cards on the table.'
MIGUEL ALVEAR, *co-director of* **Blak Mama**.

Directory
All Tel/Fax numbers begin (+593)
INCINE, Vizcaya E13-39 & Valladolid, Tel: 2904724, info@incine.edu.ec, www.incine.edu.ec
Cine Memoria Corporation, Veintimilla E8-125, Quito, Tel: 2902250, info@cinememoria.org, www.cinememoria.org
Consejo Nacional de Cine (CNC), www.cncinec-uador.blogspot.com

GABRIELA ALEMÁN is a writer and journalist with a PhD from Tulane University, where she specialised in Latin American film. She is affiliated to Andina University in Ecuador.

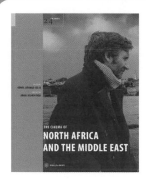

pbk £18.99 / $29.50
978-1-905674-10-7

THE CINEMA OF NORTH AFRICA AND THE MIDDLE EAST

Edited by Gönül Dönmez-Colin
Preface by Abbas Kiarostami

The appreciation of the cinema of North Africa and the Middle East has blossomed over the 1990s and 2000s with worldwide acclaim for films from such eminent directors as Abbas Kiarostami and Nuri Bilge Ceylan. *The Cinema of North Africa and the Middle East* contains twenty-four essays, each concerning an individual film, with a geographical scope that runs from Morocco all the way to Iran. The volume explores not just established film cultures such as those of Egypt, Turkey and Israel, but also nascent cinemas such as Algeria, Palestine and Syria. Some of the selected films include *Cairo Station* (Egypt, 1958), *The Runner* (Iran, 1989), *Once Upon a Time, Beriut* (Lebanon, 1994), *Ten* (Iran, 2002) and *Uzak* (Turkey, 2003). With a preface by the Cannes Palme d'Or-winning director Abbas Kiarostami, *The Cinema of North Africa and the Middle East* unveils a diverse region of filmmaking that is of interest to all consumers of global cinema.

'This excellent collection fulfils a long-standing need in scholarship on the cinema of the Middle East. By providing close readings of a number of canonical films, this work is an invaluable resource for teachers and students.' – Kamran Rastegar, University of Edinburgh

'These twenty-four films are a handful of jewels on the loosely woven and richly varied fabric of these regions. The authors, while deftly weaving their context, allow the films to shine in their own light: classic, idiosyncratic and irreducible works of cinema.'
– Laura Marks, Simon Fraser University

www.wallflowerpress.co.uk

Egypt Fawzi Soliman

In 2008, while films such as Fahhr Negeda's **Girls and Motorcycles** (*Banat We Motocyclat*) and Mo'nes Elshourbagy's **Feminine Moments** (*Lahazat Onoutha*) met the demands of the Nilesat and Arabsat satellite channels that co-produced them, there were a handful of other important mainstream Egyptian films that approached sensitive subjects: social turmoil was dealt with in Khaled El-Haggar's **Stolen Kisses** (*Kobolat Masrouka*), Youssef Chahine's last film, **Chaos** (*Heya Fawda*), Khaled Youssef's **In Time** (*Hena Maysara*) and Ahmed Atef's **Cairo Devils** (*El-Ghaba*). **The Baby Doll Night** (*Laylet El-Baby Doll*) even went so far as to deal with current political issues. Topical issues were also the subject of independent films such as Ibrahim

El-Batout's award-winning feature, **Ein Shams**, and Saad Heindawy's documentary, **Special File** (*Malaf Khas*).

Box office takings escalated due to the increase in new, state-of-the-art multiplexes and an influx of foreign as well as domestic films.

The Baby Doll Night, produced by Good News Co. with the largest ever budget for an Egyptian film (US$10 million), was the final screenplay by the late Abdel-Hay Adib, father of the head of the production company. It was directed by another of his sons, Adel Adib. The ensemble drama ties together political events across different continents, in an attempt to

describe the chaotic aftermath of the events of 11 September 2001. It also skirts comedy in one of the narrative strands, in which a man tries to deal with his over-sexed wife.

In Time, *Cairo Devils* and *Chaos* were all written by promising screenwriter Nasr Abdel-Rahman. The former featured the Gulf War as a backdrop to the lives of homeless people, one of whom is hunted by state security following his return from Iraq and accusations that he was a member of Al-Qaeda which has attempted to form a cell in Cairo. The movie also depicts the miserable and violent lives of those who exist on the city's streets. *Cairo Devils* not only portrays the lives of street children, but focuses on related problems – incest, poverty, dysfunctional families, rape and prostitution – both out on the streets and in the social centres that are supposed to help the disadvantaged. Atef, who also co-produced, found funding in Europe to make the film. *Chaos* focused on police brutality and the illegal practices of a corrupt officer in an Egyptian neighbourhood.

Youssef Chahine's **Chaos**

Hassan and Morcos, written by Youssef Maaty and directed by Ramy Imam, looks at the relationship between Muslims and Copts in contemporary Egypt. Hassan, to use the undercover name given by the police to this Coptic priest (Adel Imam), has had his life threatened by a fanatical Christian group who are in disagreement with his tolerant views. A similar fate awaits a devout Muslim, played by Omar Sharif, for his refusal to join their fundamentalist group. He now lives under

the Copt pseudonym of Morcos. A strong friendship develops between the two, until the film's climax, which suggests that unity is the only way to a peaceful solution. Although it was ultimately too superficial for the issues it dealt with, *Hassan and Morcos* may pave the way for Egyptian cinema to explore more thoroughly fundamentalist attitudes.

Amr Waked in Yousry Nasrallah's **Aquarium**

In Yousry Nasrallah's **Aquarium** (*Genenet Al-Asmak*), Laila, a radio host, and Youssef, an anaesthetist, both enjoy listening to people's confessions. It highlights a society where corruption and fanaticism battle for power.

Female filmmaker Sandra Nashaat, most famous for her action films, has returned with yet another nail-biting thriller, starring her favourite actor, the handsome Ahmed Ezz. **Transit Prisoner** (*Masgoun Transit*) is the story of a young man who wants to emigrate to Italy. To get the money he needs, he robs a safe, killing a guard. Sentenced to life imprisonment, he is approached by the secret service, who offer him the chance to work as a covert agent in a special patriotic mission.

After his acclaimed role in *That's OK!*, comic star Ahmed Helmy returned in **Sorry for the Disturbance** (*Assef Lel Eszaag*), which marks a shift to more character-driven roles. Directed by Khaled Mara'y, the story focuses on a young schizophrenic who fails to face the difficulties of reality.

Stolen Kisses was another attempt to reflect the sexual oppression of young teens who are unable to obtain immigration visas to the United States after failing to make a living in

Youssra El-Lozy and Ahmed Azmy in **Stolen Kisses**

Cairo. Among them are a girl who sells her body to feed her younger brothers and sisters, and a naïve engineer who becomes the victim of underground porn films. Surprisingly, the ensemble cast of four male and female actors was awarded Best Actor and Actress Awards at the 24th Alexandria International Film Festival.

Digital cinema has become a great outlet for new filmmakers and subjects previously never covered in Egyptian cinema. **Special File** (*Malaf Khas*) was directed by Saad Heindawy and co-produced by female journalist Amal Fawzy. The documentary discussed social issues in Arab societies, such as how the young are treated differently depending on their gender. Heindawy and Fawzy interviewed boys and girls from different groups of Egyptian society, as well as social experts who talked freely about problematic issues.

Ein Shams was the second feature by the young independent filmmaker, Ibrahim El-Batout. It was shot on digital with a very low budget with non-professional actors. In it, a young girl called Shams dreams of visiting downtown Cairo with her father, a taxi driver who can hardly make a living. She delves into a fantasy world in order to escape her miserable life. El-Batout successfully incorporates footage of a real demonstration he shot when he worked as a photojournalist for foreign news agencies. The Moroccan Film Centre helped him transfer the film to 35mm. It has since won prizes at the Taormina Film Festival and the Rotterdam Arab Film Festival.

The growth of digital filmmaking will see a new generation of Egyptian filmmakers willing to use technology to expand audiences' horizons. Likewise, mainstream producers are changing their outlook in order to appeal to ever-expanding audience tastes.

The year's best films
Hena Mayssara (Khaled Youssef)
Ein Shams (Ibrahim El-Batout)
El-Ghaba (Ahmed Atef)
Aquarium (Yousry Nasrallah)
Special File (Saad Heindawy)

Quote of the year
'I was hoping to show modern Cairo as a sort of brain-like structure, a monster that devours itself by never allowing its inhabitants to bare their souls except in moments of delirium, in anonymous nocturnal confessions, or in badly lit streets where lovers touch one another in secret.' YOUSRY NASRALLAH *discussing* **Aquarium**.

Directory
All Tel/Fax numbers begin (+20)
Central Audio-Visual Censorship Authority, Opera Ground, Gezira, Cairo. Tel: 738 1674. Fax: 736 9479.
Chamber of Film Industry, 1195 Kornish El Nil, Industries Union Bldg, Cairo. Tel: 578 5111. Fax: 575 1583.
Egyptian Radio & TV Union, Kornish El Nil, Maspero St, Cairo. Tel: 576 0014. Fax: 579 9316.
Higher Film Institute, Pyramids Rd, GamalEl-Din El-Afaghani St, Guiza. Tel: 537 7703. Fax: 561 1034. aoarts@idsc.gov.eg.
National Egyptian Film Archive, c/o Egyptian Film Centre, City of Arts, Al Ahram Rd, Guiza. Tel: 585 4801. Fax: 585 4701. President: Dr Mohamed Kamel El Kalyobi.
National Film Centre, Al-Ahram Ave, Giza. Tel: 585 4801. Fax: 585 4701.

FAWZI SOLIMAN is a journalist and critic who has contributed to magazines and newspapers in Egypt and the Arab world. He has served on the FIPRESCI jury of many film festivals.

Estonia Jaan Ruus

2007–08 was a successful period for the Estonian film industry. Ten feature films were produced, including an animated film and a theatrically released television feature.

In terms of international festivals, seventeen films were screened at 128 festivals, 26 animated films at 269 festivals, and ten documentaries at 34 festivals. The films received a total of 39 international awards and were screened in 55 countries. Far from an insignificant achievement for such a small film industry. Locally, the 22nd Pärnu Documentary and Anthropology Film Festival, 18th Pärnu Video and Film Festival, 12th Tallinn Black Nights Film Festival, 6th Matsalu International Nature Film Festival and 5th Tartu Festival of Visual Culture were all held in 2008.

Novelist Kadri Kõusaar's philosophical debut, **Magnus**, featured in 17 festival programmes and was awarded both the Grand Prix and FIPRESCI Awards at Wiesbaden. It focused on suicide and parental neglect. Based on true events, the role of the protagonist's father is played by the father of the young man who took his own life, albeit under a false name. It was denied a domestic release following a

Kadri Kõusaar's **Magnus**

court order, by the boy's mother, which stated that because it featured private details of an individual without her permission, it could not be screened publicly for seven years. By this ruling, the court subordinated the artist's freedom of expression to the constitutional right to privacy. This was the first time that the independent Estonian court ruled over an artist's freedom of expression; it was also unprecedented that a work of art should be banned by the court.

Siiri Sisask and Tõnu Oja in Ain Mäeots' **Taarka**

Taarka by Ain Mäeots, which premiered in the summer of 2008, depicts the lonely and tragic life of Estonian folk singer Darja Pisumaa (1856–1933). Confining itself within the boundaries of an ethnographic film, its static and overly moralistic view of village life is given light relief by some of the minor characters in the film. The film portrays a tiny Setu ethnic group living in southeastern Estonia, not far from the Russian border, whose lives are similar to those of the Sami of Finland, Sweden and Norway.

I Was Here (*Mina olin siin*), based on novelist Sass Henno's bestseller, was warmly received by young audiences. Director René Vilbre and screenwriter Ilmar Raag have produced a

Rasmus Kaljujärv in René Vilbre's **I Was Here**

fast-moving adventure of a student at an elite school, who comes from a troubled family and who agrees to sell drugs to make some money.

Asko Kase's **December Heat** (*Detsembrikuumus*) is a patriotic, cliché-ridden, historically based love story that depicts the failed communist coup of 1924. It is the most expensive Estonian live-action feature to date (US$2.3 million).

Asko Kase's **December Heat**

Political documentaries dominated 2008. Meelis Muhu's **Alyosha** is a detailed account of the conflict over the transfer of a bronze statue of a soldier, erected by Soviet soldiers in 1947 (popularly dubbed Alyosha), from Tallinn city centre to a military cemetery. Observational in approach, it covers three years of events, which culminated in riots and looting by Russian-speaking youths.

Estonian producers have also helped dissident filmmakers from neighbouring countries to produce films that the authorities would have suppressed domestically. **Kalinovski Square** (*Kalinovski väljak*), by Yuri Chashchavatsky, paints an ironic portrait of Belarusian president Alexander Lukashenko before and after the presidential elections of March 2006. **Revolution That Wasn't** (*Revolutsioon, mida ei tulnud*) by Aljona Polunina profiles ecstatic Russian idealists-revolutionaries during the Russian presidential campaign that culminated in Dmitry Medvedev being elected in March 2008.

Marko Raat's **Toomik's Film**

Marko Raat's convincing portrait of the artist Jaan Toomik, in **Toomik's Film** (*Toomiku film*), reveals one man's deep concern for the world, as well as showcasing his performances and video art. Mait Laas's **The Kings of Time** (*Aja meistrid*) is a clever portrait of Elbert Tuganov and Heino Pars, founders of the Estonian puppet film, reconstructing the era between the 1950s and the 1990s and blending documentary footage with animation. The grand old man of Estonian animation, Priit Pärn, this time teamed up with his wife Olga Pärn, continues to explore unexpected forms of human communication in his new film, **Life Without Gabriella Ferri** (*Elu ilma Gabriella Ferrita*).

Priit and Olga Pärn's **Life Without Gabriella Ferri**

Late 2008 saw the release of Liina Paakspuu's **Tree of Wishes** (*Soovide puu*). A pallid and faintly absurd comedy, it featured a group of young people and their struggles in life.

Altogether, Estonia produced four full-length features in 2008. With the exception of *I Was Here* all others were debuts. While the artistic levels of the films left a great deal to be desired, it does paint a hopeful future for Estonia's film industry. Of these, Jukka-Pekka Valkeapää's **The Visitor** (*Võõras/Muukalainen*) featured no dialogue in portraying a young boy's terrifying experiences trapped in a forest. It premiered in the Venice Days programme.

The Estonian film industry continues to depend on state subsidies. Despite economic recession, film subsidies increased to US$9.1 million in 2008, up 12% from 2007. Funding will be frozen at the current level for 2009. The Baltic Film and Media School will carry on its work, but with considerable financial difficulties, as the Nordic-Baltic Film Fund, which has up to now provided much of the funding for the school, will close. At present the school hosts over 300 students from thirteen countries. Thirty students graduated from the English-language Masters programme last summer.

Cinema attendance reached 1.6 million, up from 1.2 million in 2007. Despite the modest increase, the number remains significantly below that of original EU nations. On the other hand, domestic film attendance grew, reaching 14.3 percent. The first 3D cinema opened in Tallinn. Cinamon, a company building a cinema chain in all the Baltic countries, opened a 500-seat, five-screen multiplex cinema in Tartu, Estonia's second-largest city. There are now three multiplex cinemas in Estonia, with an additional one opening in Tallinn in 2009.

JAAN RUUS works as a film critic for the biggest Estonian weekly, *Eesti Ekspress*, and is the president of the Estonian FIPRESCI.

Meelis Muhu's **Aljosha**

The year's best films
Alyosha (Meelis Muhu)
Toomik's Film (Marko Raat)
The Kings of Time (Mait Laas)
Life Without Gabriella Ferri (Priit Pärn and Olga Pärn)

Quote of the year
'Some artists deal in self-admiration with much more fascinating results than others.'
Film researcher **MARI LAANISTE** *on Estonian animation.*

Directory
All Tel/Fax numbers begin (+372)
Estonian Association of Film Journalists, Narva Mnt 11E, 10151 Tallinn. Tel: (6) 533 894. Fax: (6) 698 154. jaan@ekspress.ee.
Estonian Film Foundation, Vana-Viru 3, 10111 Tallinn. Tel: (6) 276 060. Fax: (6) 276 061. film@ efsa. ee. www.efsa.ee.
Estonian Film Producers Association, Rävala pst 11-12, 10143 Tallinn. Tel: (6) 67 8 270. Fax: (6) 67 8 721. produtsendid@rudolf.ee.
Estonian Filmmakers Union, Uus 3, 10111 Tallinn. Tel/Fax: (6) 464 068. kinoliit@online.ee.
Estonian National Archive, Ristiku 84, 10318 Tallinn. Tel: (6) 938 613. Fax: (6) 938 611. filmiarhiiv@ra.ee. www.filmi.arhiiv.ee.
Union of Estonian Cameramen, Faehlmanni 12, 15029 Tallinn. Tel: (6) 662 3069. Fax: (6) 568 401. bogavideo@infonet.ee.

Finland Antti Selkokari

2008 was a year of cumulative gains for Finnish cinema. A total of 19 releases was one of the highest in decades. The main reason for this flurry of activity was the availability of production funds that had not been spent in previous years, allowing a larger number of films to be made.

Thematically, it was a good year for historical films, particularly those concerning the country's break from the Russian empire, ninety years ago. The trend began, in late 2007, with Lauri Törhönen's *The Border*, which was the personal project of veteran Finnish filmmaker, Jörn Donner. Although he had longed to make a film inspired by the journals of his father, Kai Donner, a linguist, ethnographer and activist in the early Finnish independence movement, he chose to produce the film, handing the directing reigns to Törhönen. The film was a critical and commercial success.

When puppet-animation filmmaker Katariina Lillqvist submitted her film **Far Away from Ural** (*Uralin perhonen*) to the Tampere Film Festival, the oldest short film festival in the Nordic countries, she probably had no idea how big an impact the film would have. The 26-minute love story is set in 1918 and concerns an officer's illicit affair with a beautiful young man from Kirghizia. Much of the action unfolds in the ruins of Tampere, the headquarters of the Red Brigades, who capitulated to the white troops, led by General Mannerheim. For years, there had been rumours about how the General had abandoned his male lover after conquering Tampere. Articulating this in a film released during the year that people were celebrating Finnish independence hit a nerve among those

Katariina Lillqvist's **Far Away from Ural**

conservatives who still mistook the whites and Mannerheim for saints. The film became the focus of tabloid newspaper attention. It is actually a lyrical work of art that draws heavily an the folk tales told in proletarian quarters after a brutal and bitter civil war.

A different angle on the Finnish civil war was taken by Aku Louhimies, who directed his fifth feature, **Tears of April** (*Käsky*), based on the novel by Leena Lander. It focuses on a young woman jailed for fighting in the Red Brigades and her journey to what would turn out to be an unfairly judged trial, with an idealistic white guard. Unfortunately, Louhimies loses the focus of Lander's richly detailed novel, opting instead to make a simplistic drama out of the relationship between the two soldiers and an eccentric judge intoxicated by his own power. However, the film is ravishing visually; cinematographer Rauno Ronkainen's images are the most stunning of any film released in the last year.

The intensive publicity that all these films have created only confirms how deeply the civil war scarred Finnish society.

Dome Karukoski returned with his second feature, **The Home of the Dark Butterflies** (*Tummien perhosten koti*), also based on a novel by Leena Lander. In it, two troubled youths (the impressive Niilo Syväoja and Marjut Maristo) are sent to a reformatory school located on an island, where they are expected to submit to the control of the director, played by the resident hunk of Finnish cinema, Tommi Korpela. Unfortunately, Karukoski leaves too many loose strands in the narrative and overplays the melodramatic elements of the story.

Dome Karukoski's **The Home of the Dark Butterflies**

Mika Kaurismäki also made a welcome return to Finnish cinema. The elder of the two brothers has mostly been making music-related documentaries, such as the recent **Sonic Mirror**, a documentary about Billy Cobham. His feature **Three Wise Men** (*Kolme viisasta miestä*) is an actor-driven drama about three middle-class men in their fifties, who spend Christmas Eve in a deserted karaoke bar, where they drink and discuss their lives. Inspired by John Cassavetes' work, Kaurismäki let his actors outline their own characters and then wrote a script. This allows for the

Mika Kaurismäki's **Sonic Mirror**

creation of more spontaneous situations, even achieving a gritty and affecting realism. Kaurismäki is set to return to cinemas in 2009 with **The House of Branching Love** (*Haarautuvan rakkauden talo*).

Romantic comedies proved to be the *cri du jour* at the Finnish box office. *Sex and the City* dominated the charts, but local filmmaker Lauri Nurkse, better known for his acting in film and television, made his directorial debut with **Going Solo** (*Sooloillaan*). The film attracted a respectable 187,000 admissions. Regrettably, the love story between a gossip reporter and a conductor relies too heavily on stereotypes. Nurkse's film was not the only one attempting to lure the multiplex crowd. Peter Lindholm returned to feature filmmaking after a six-year hiatus in television. In **Three in Love** (*Kolmistaan*) an urban sociologist falls for a sales clerk and finds himself in a tricky situation when his wife wants to meet the other woman. Lindholm confidently handles his material, keeping a keen eye for detail. Documentary filmmaker John Webster's amused gaze characterises his works. **Recipes**

Peter Lindholm's **Three in Love**

for Disaster (*Katastrofin aineksia*) shows how the filmmaker and his family wake up to the horrors of global warming. Reducing their oil consumption, the family abandons their car in favour of public transport. Webster goes so far as throwing away perfectly good kitchen utensils because they are made of plastic, all done to show how the modern Western lifestyle is unsustainable when its existence is based on fossil fuels. And his humour may even win over the unconverted.

Director John Webster in **Recipes for Disaster**

Two dramas about writers made their way on to the screen. **The Novelist** (*Päätalo*) tells the story of a builder who, since his childhood in the countryside, has dreamed of becoming a writer. The film chronicles the life of a burgeoning artist in painstaking detail. Hannu Kahakorpi, who is known for his works for television, must have been worried about the reaction of audiences to the film, as its protagonist is Kalle Päätalo, the most popular Finnish writer of the late twentieth century. Despite the film's calculated conservatism, Kahakorpi succeeds with a credible portrait of a writer's coming of age.

One of the quintessential post-war Finnish poets is Lauri Viita. His originality lay in his talent for puns and rhymes, producing idiosyncratic and occasionally razor-sharp observations on life. Playwright Heikki Kujanpää made a promising debut with **Falling Angels** (*Putoavia enkeleitä*), based on his stageplay. Kujanpää portrays the intensive marriage drama of two poets, one of them Viita. The relationship is intercut with the life of a fictional daughter, who blames her mother for causing her parents' divorce and the schizophrenia suffered by her father, whom she idolises. The film's visual style alternates between a 1950s Technicolour melodrama and a more sober palette. Kujanpää's control of the narrative and deft touch with his actors makes for a good, solid debut.

2009 will see Renny Harlin's long-gestating biopic, **Mannerheim**, about the military officer and statesman Carl Gustaf Emil Mannerheim. It will be Harlin's first Finnish film since 1986.

National themes look set to continue, with producer-director and all-round entertainer Timo Koivusalo's adaptation of one of Finland's best-loved novels, Väinö Linna's **Under the North Star** (*Täällä Pohjantähden alla*). It chronicles one family's life in a Finnish rural village, from the late 1800s through to the 1950s, covering the major social upheavals in the country.

The year's best films
The Border (Lauri Törhönen)
Recipes for Disaster (John Webster)
Far Away from Ural (Katariina Lillqvist)
The Home of the Dark Butterflies (Dome Karukoski)
Three in Love (Peter Lindholm)

Quote of the year
'Finnish film producers have no financial capital of their own and that makes it worse for the Finnish film business.' **Raja** *Director* **LAURI TÖRHÖNEN** *commenting on the state of things in a magazine interview.*

Directory
All Tel/Fax numbers begin (+358)
Finnish Film Foundation, Kanavakatu 12, FIN-00160. Tel: (9) 622 0300. Fax: (9) 622 0305. ses@ses.fi. www.ses.fi.

ANTTI SELKOKARI is a freelance film critic and regular contributor to the newspaper *Aamulehti* and cultural magazine *Parnasso*.

France Michel Ciment

Apparently French cinema has never had it as good as it did in 2008. For the first time in more than two decades a French film, **The Class**, by Laurent Cantet, won the Palme d'Or at Cannes and Dany Boon's **Welcome to the Sticks** (*Bienvenue chez les Ch'tis*), a comedy about the conflicts between people of the south and the north of the country, attracted more than twenty million cinemagoers, the second-biggest box office success of all time after *Titanic*.

However, there were signs of concern on the cultural front, with a sharp cut in subsidies from the ministry of culture (via the National Centre of Cinema, or CNC) towards small

Dany Boon's **Welcome to the Sticks**

Laurent Cantet's **The Class**

associations and festivals, which maintain an interest in cinema, both past and present, across all areas of France. Equally worrying was the diminishing interest in French films (177.5 million spectators – 6% less than last year). The market share was 36.6% for the national cinema (as against 44.6% in 2006), whereas American cinema attracted 49.2%. If fourteen films attracted more than two million spectators and seven more than four million, there were, respectively, only four and two French films among them. Admittedly, two French films were on top of the list (*Welcome to the Sticks* and Frédéric Forestier and Thomas Langmann's **Asterix at the Olympic Games**), but the remaining eight were Hollywood releases.

In spite of the highly vaunted diversity of distribution of foreign films in France, more than 90% of box office revenue came from domestic and Anglo-Saxon releases. Still a heaven for film buffs, art-house cinemas drew fewer patrons, as figures went down from 34.5% of total admissions in 2005 to 25.5% in 2006 and 18.8% in 2007, with only *The Lives of Others* and the animation feature *Persepolis* exceeding one million admissions. Animation is becoming an increasingly popular genre with 15.5% of the box office. If comedies fared less well than in recent years (only 16% of the total revenue), dramas enjoyed a great success with 172 releases. An increasing number of people over fifty years of age went to the cinema, with a preference for local films, while young people under 25 favoured Hollywood product. The decline in attendance was felt more in Paris (–9.6%) than in the suburbs (–5%) or in the provinces (–5.4%). Domestically, 228 films were produced (25 more than in 2006), of which 39% were feature debuts (72 as against 56 the year before). These figures are worrying, in the sense that there were only 32 sophomore features, implying that many directors were never given a second chance.

The best partners for co-productions have been (as usual) Belgium (18), Germany (10), Italy (9) and Canada (8). Film distribution was as high as ever, with 573 features released. That said, European films are in sharp decline and all the major national cinemas were represented by fewer films, while French releases were more present than ever. With twenty more screens (for a total of 5,398), exhibition is still very active, although half of the total number of tickets sold were purchased at multiplexes.

If most documentaries proved less than popular in cinemas (2% of the gross) – a genre probably linked to the small screen in the minds of most people – four of them were triumphant examples of the genre, and all with an autobiographical slant. Carmen Castillo, a Chilean exiled in France for several decades, returned in **Rue Santa Fe** (*Calle Santa Fe*)

Agnès Varda's **The Beaches of Agnès**

to the street where she lived in Santiago and where her companion, a collaborator of Salvador Allende, was killed under the order of Pinochet. Her investigation is at once an expression of her grief, a reflection on the past and a brilliant case study of Chilean politics. Sandrine Bonnaire's first feature, **Her Name is Sabine** (*Elle s'appelle Sabine*), is a heart wrenching portrait of her retarded sister. Finding the right distance – never too close or too sentimental, but never detached – she shows her compassion towards the predicament of Sabine and her rebellion against the shortcomings of medicine. Raymond Depardon's **Modern Life** (*La Vie moderne*) closes his trilogy on the peasant world (from which the great photographer and film director comes) with this beautifully shot (in Cinemascope) film, in which the director's elegiac tone expresses a vanishing world. Depardon manages to make the people interviewed – all too often silent in daily life – speak their mind with humour and feeling about the issues of work, family and the future of farmers. Agnès Varda's **The Beaches of Agnès** (*Les Plages d'Agnès*) is one of fthe inest self-portraits ever filmed. At eighty and with charm, wit and emotion, the director of *Cleo from 5 to 7* recalls her work, her friends, from Resnais to Marker, and her late husband, Jacques Demy. Constantly inventive visually, with a supreme sense of montage and commentary, it is one of her greatest achievements.

Besides this very personal trend, **Puisque nous sommes nés** by Jean-Pierre Duret

Jean-Pierre Duret and Andrea Santana's **Puisque nous sommes nés**

(one of France's best sound engineers) and Andrea Santana masterfully illustrates the Flaherty method. Following two children in the impoverished Brazilian northeast, they allow us to share their private moments and their dreams, and their obstinacy in trying to find their place in the world.

The biopic has recently become popular in France, probably due to the success of *La Vie en rose*. After the life of Édith Piaf, we had those of a painter (**Séraphine**), a criminal (**Mesrine**), a writer (**Sagan**) and a stand-up comedian (**Coluche**). *Séraphine*, by Martin Provost, about a kind of female Douanier-Rousseau who was discovered by a German art dealer living in France in the 1920s, proved the more satisfying, due particularly to the exceptional performance by Yolande Moreau, the singularity of the story and the uncanny relationship between the artist and her patron. It became the sleeper hit of the year with more than half a million visitors. The two-part *Mesrine*, by Jean-François Richet, was hailed by the national press as proof

Vincent Cassel in Jean-François Richet's **Mesrine**

that a French gangster movie could rival a Hollywood film. If it lacks focus and partly glorifies its protagonist, the film boasts a brilliant performance by Vincent Cassel and an undeniable energy in its action sequences. *Sagan*, by Diane Kurys, covers the whole life – half a century – of the famous writer who started out as a young prodigy. Its rather pedestrian direction is saved by the stunning embodiment of the novelist by Sylvie Testud, as convincing as Marion Cotillard in the role of Édith Piaf. *Coluche*, by Antoine De Caunes, is anecdotal and shallow. It failed at the box office and deservedly so, in spite of the huge popularity the comic actor once attracted, even once drawing huge scores in the polls when he was temporarily a candidate for the presidential election against Mitterrand and Giscard d'Estaing.

Abdellatif Kechiche's **Couscous**

Some of the best features of the year were made by well-known directors, while the elder statesmen of French cinema completed their films for the 2009 season. **Couscous** (*La Graine et le Mulet*), Abdellatif Kechiche's third feature, which was awarded the Silver Lion in Venice, as well as being a César winner and recipient of the Delluc Prize, was an absolute triumph. Kechiche, a middle-aged actor-turned-director of Tunisian origin, confirmed himself as one of France's top directors with this social fresco about a dockworker in the south of France who decides to open a fish restaurant with the help of his indomitable stepdaughter. Combining the humour of Pagnol and the realism of Pialat, it reveals an energy and a daring seen too rarely on the screen today.

Laurent Cantet's fourth feature, *The Class*, as its title implies, does not leave the confines of a school in a popular Parisian district. It highlights the mostly hopeless efforts of a teacher, played by François Bégaudeau (co-writer of the script and author of the original autobiographical book), to communicate with pupils of mixed origins. The film nurtured heated debate about the French educational system. The Jury in Cannes was sensitive to its vivid and sometimes hilarious description of youngsters who could not care less about their intellectual training.

Philippe Garrel's **La Frontière de l'aube** was something of a disappointment, in spite of wonderful monochrome photography by William Lubtchansky and the director's usual flair for creating a mood reminiscent of silent cinema. This story of a married man haunted by a dead woman who keeps returning to him as a hallucination fails to convince. The evocation of his relationship with his first love, who killed herself, has the usual haunting Garrel touch, in a minor key this time, but the expressionistic ghost story turns awry. Laetitia Masson's **Guilty** (*Coupable*) confirms her sophistication in combining a disquieting treatment of a couple's relationships and the use of the classical murder investigation. At once playful and passionate, stylised and emotional, the film is a strange object in the French cinematographic landscape. No less singular, **Julia** sees the return of *The Dream Life of Angels* director, Erick Zonca, after eight years of silence. It features Tilda Swinton in a vibrant performance as a distressed woman who kidnaps a young boy. Shot in English, in California and Mexico, with an energy reminiscent of John Cassavetes, the film features a strong physical quality that is rare in French cinema.

Catherine Deneuve in **A Christmas Tale**

Summer Hours (*L'Heure d'été*), perhaps Olivier Assayas's best effort so far, evokes in his usual fluid style the conflicts within a family, over the future of their recently deceased mother's country estate. A very different family drama, this time set within the black community of a Parisian suburb, is at the centre of François Dupeyron's **With a Little Help from Myself** (*Aide-toi, le ciel t'aidera*). The struggle of a dynamic mother who has lost her husband to solve the problems of her children – a pregnant teenage daughter, an eldest son's illegal activities, a younger one's depressive mood – is beautifully conveyed by Félicité Wouassi's energetic performance and the director's camera work, which recalls Spike Lee at his best. Like Mike Leigh's *Happy-Go-Lucky*, the film carries a message of hope, in spite of the predicaments of everyday life. Also family-oriented, **A Christmas Tale** (*Un conte de Noël*), one of the most satisfying films of Arnaud Desplechin and a Cannes competitor, is a complex narrative featuring a brilliant cast (Catherine Deneuve, Chiara Mastroianni, Mathieu Almaric *et al*) orchestrating the tensions inside a wealthy bourgeois family in the north of France. Desplechin's feverish direction and his love of words are displayed at their best.

Tilda Swinton in Erick Zonca's **Julia**

After an absence of several years, Jacques Doillon returned with his typically sensitive portrayal of young characters and their troubled relationships within a triangular love story. **Just Anybody** (*Le Premier Venu*), set in a bleak northern seaside landscape, has the raw edge and perverse psychology that characterise the director's view of life.

Karim Dridi's **Khamsa** is proof of the impetus within French cinema from second-generation North African immigrants. Like Kechiche's *Couscous*, it has a radiant style and a strong sense of reality as Dridi brings to life the activities of gipsy teenagers living on the outskirts of Marseille.

Two relative newcomers, Tarik Teguia and Rabah Ameur Zaïmeche, highlight the fruitful input of directors of Arab origin in French film culture. In Teguia's **Rome plutôt que vous**, we experience the feelings of two young Algerians who want to leave their homeland. A kind of road-movie, shot in an Antonioni-like style, the film portends, through micro-events, a coming disaster. More realistic, **Dernier Maquis** deals with the cultural conflict between North African and sub-Saharan African workers as their boss uses Islam to manipulate them. The building of a mosque serves as a catalyst in a film that uses music, silence and voices with a genuine aesthetic sense.

If comedy is one of the most popular genres, and is, subsequently, illustrated by a large number of films, few of them are distinguished by their style or originality. The spectacular commercial success of *Welcome to the Sticks* defies analysis. Dany Boon, the actor-director, and his fellow thespian Kad Merad, undoubtedly possess a screen presence that borrows much from the vaudeville tradition. The public loved the defence of the French way of life – at a time of national self-doubt – which reconciles a Southern man full of prejudices against his new place of work, near the Belgian border, where he has been transferred. More sophisticated was Agnès Jaoui's third feature, **Let's Talk About the Rain**

Agnès Jaoui's **Let's Talk About the Rain**

(*Parlez-moi de la pluie*), where the actress and screenwriter-turned-director proved once more that she is the true heiress to Claude Sautet. The confrontation of two incompetent TV journalists (Jean-Pierre Bacri and Jamel Debouzze – as funny as ever) with a political candidate (Jaoui), when mixed with the intricacies of their private lives, makes for a melancholy and humorous film.

Pascal Thomas's third adaptation of Agatha Christie, **Le crime est notre affaire**, does not take its whodunit structure seriously, preferring to give free rein to a group of actors (among whom André Dussollier and Catherine Frot reign supreme) in a deliberately old-fashioned, though delightful, entertainment. Emmanuel Mouret also takes pleasure in **Un baiser s'il vous plaît**, as he does his other comedies, in mixing Rohmer-like conversations and games of deception with slapstick humour.

Emmanuel Mouret's **Un baiser s'il vous plaît**

With so many first films produced, the ratio of achievements was alarmingly small. The most strident failure, however, was Michel

Houellebecq's adaptation of his bestseller **Possibility of an Island** (*La Possibilité d'une île*). The novelist-turned-director proved utterly incompetent with his new-age futurist saga full of pompous empty images and sophomoric philosophical statements.

Samuel Collardey's **L'Apprenti**

To end on a hopeful note, **L'Apprenti** (winner of the Critics' Week in Venice) by Samuel Collardey, was undoubtedly the best debut of the year. The director follows his protagonist Mathieu, a pupil in an agricultural school, as he spends part of the year working on a farm as an apprentice. The work in the fields, the lessons he is taught, his relation with the family that shelters him, are observed with a sensitive eye and a modest approach which suggest a lineage with Pialat and Raymond. A rare achievement indeed.

All in all, to continue a bucolic metaphor, the harvest this year was satisfying, and one can look with confidence to 2009 where French cinema's elder statesmen will offer their new films, from Chabrol (**Bellamy**) to Resnais (**Les Herbes folles**) and Rivette (**36 Vues du Pic Saint-Loup**). Meanwhile, their talented younger colleagues will also be heavily present: Bertrand Tavernier (**In the Electric Mist**), Cedric Kahn (**Les Regrets**), Claude and Nathan Miller (**Je suis heureux que ma mère soit vivante**), Philippe Lioret (**Welcome**), Jacques Audiard (**Un prophète**), Patrice Chéreau (**Persécution**), Robert Guédiguian (**L'Armée du crime**), Patrice Leconte (**La Guerre du Miss**) and André Téchiné (**La Fille du RER**).

The year's best films
A Christmas Tale (Arnaud Desplechin)
The Beaches of Agnès (Agnès Varda)
Modern Life (Raymond Depardon)
With a Little Help from Myself (François Dupeyron)
Summer Hours (Olivier Assayas)

Directory
All Tel/Fax numbers begin (+33)
Archives du Film, 7 bis rue Alexandre Turpault, 78395 Bois d'Arcy. Tel: (1) 3014 8000. Fax: (1) 3460 5225.
Cahiers du Cinema, 9 passage de la Boule Blanche, 75012 Paris. Tel: (1) 5344 7575. Fax: (1) 4343 9504. cducinema@lemonde.fr
Centre National de la Cinématographie, 12 rue de Lubeck, 75016 Paris. Tel: (1) 4434 3440. Fax: (1) 4755 0491. webmaster@cnc.fr. www.cnc.fr.
Cinémathèque de Toulouse, BP 824, 31080 Toulouse Cedex 6. Tel: (5) 6230 3010. Fax: (5) 6230 3012. contact@lacinematequedetoulouse.com. www.lacinematequedetoulouse.com.
Cinémathèque Française, 4 rue de Longchamp, 75116 Paris. Tel: (1) 5365 7474. Fax: (1) 5365 7465. contact@cinematequefrancaise.com. www.cinematequefrancaise.com.
Ile de France Film Commision, 11 rue du Colisée, 75008 Paris. Tel: (1) 5688 1280. Fax: (1) 5688 1219. idf-film@idf-film.com. www.iledefrance-film.com.
Images documentaires, Diffusion, 21 ter, rue Voltaire, 75011 Paris, France. Tel: (1) 4024 2131 www.difpop.com
Institut Lumière, 25 rue du Premier-Film, BP 8051, 69352 Lyon Cedex 8. Tel: (4) 7878 1895. Fax: (4) 7878 3656. contact@institut-lumiere.org. www.institut-lumiere.org.
Positif, 38, rue Milton, 75009 Paris, France Tel: (1) 4326 1780. Fax: (1) 4326 2977 posed@wanadoo.fr/www.revue-positif.net
Unifrance, 4 Villa Bosquet, 75007 Paris. Tel: (1) 4753 9580. Fax: (1) 4705 9655. info@unifrance.org. www.unifrance.org.

MICHEL CIMENT is president of FIPRESCI, a member of the editorial board of *Positif*, a radio producer and author of more than a dozen books on cinema.

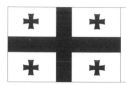

Georgia Nino Ekvtimishvili

The hundredth anniversary of Georgian cinema was met with mixed blessings. There was the first Georgian exposition at the Cannes Film Festival and the launch of the Georgian cinema online database (www. geocinema.ge). However, this was followed by the post-war financial crisis, reflected at Tbilisi International Film Festival by its reduced programme and the temporary closure of the film magazine, *Kino*. On the other hand, the number of Georgian films increased in 2008.

Three Houses, *directed by Zaza Urushadze*

Zaza Urushadze's **Three Houses** comprises three stories united by one painting. Each story, located in unnamed regions of Georgia, features different characters and presents a visual aesthetic that corresponds to the period in which they take place: the mystic nineteenth, severe twentieth and unexpectedly humane twenty-first centuries.

Unlike the present-day world of *Three Houses*, contemporary life in Dito Tsintsadze's thriller, **Mediator**, is full of brutality. In his account of a murder in Tbilisi, Tsintsadze blurs the line between cold-blooded killers and everyday people. The film is Georgia's official entry for the Academy Awards.

Dito Tsintsadze's **Mediator**

Avto Varsimashvili's **Idiocracy** is a parody of Georgian politics and democracy. While the opposition protests against a prominent minister, he indulges in a love affair with the secretary from the opposition party, in a hotel. When a body is discovered on the hotel room's balcony the minister's life is turned upside down.

Salome Jashi and Giorgi Tsikarishvili's short documentary **A Mr. Minister** focuses on the arrogant 27-year-old Georgian minister of agriculture, Bakur Kvezerely. Levan Koguashvili's documentary, **Women in Georgia**, is about Georgian women working illegally in the USA. Struggling alone, the

Levan Koguashvili's **Women in Georgia**

women work in a home caring for old people, sending what money they make to their families back in Georgia. The husbands and children receive the money, accepting the circumstances they live in, where they live without their wives and mothers.

Merab Kokochashvili's **The House of Joy**

Merab Kokochashvili's **The House of Joy** is a documentary about the creation of the film musical, *Keto and Kote*, which was called the Georgian Film of twentieth century. It reveals how the film was made, despite the strict censorship of Stalin's regime. Sasha Rekhviashvili's **The Green Lawn** was unable to escape Soviet censorship in 1972. Its aesthetics were seen to go against the grain of the Soviet project and so it was banned. An improvisation in colour, image and sound, the film will finally be released in 2009.

Two dramas, Giorgi Ovashvili's **The Other Bank** and Dato Sikharulidze's **Jako's Lodgers**, are nearing completion and will be released in 2009. Ovashvili's film is about an eleven-year-old from Abkhazia who lives in Tbilisi, who decides to return with his mother to his

home in order to find his father. *Jako's Lodgers* presents a love triangle whose narrative is used to explore the problems at the heart of contemporary Georgia.

The year's best films
Three Houses (Zaza Urushadze)
Mediator (Dito Tsintsadze)
Women in Georgia (Levan Koguashvili)
A Mr. Minister (Salome Jashi and Giorgi Tsikarishvili)
The House of Joy (Merab Kokochashvili)

Quote of the year
'The dazzling life of the centenary Georgian cinema is shining again and I'm happy that Georgian poetry will reach the spectators' eyes worldwide.' TONINO GUERRA *talking about Georgia's first exposition at the Cannes Film Festival.*

Directory
All Tel/Fax numbers begin (+995)
Ministry of Culture, Sport and Monument Protection, 4 Marjvena Sanapiro St., 0105 Tbilisi. Tel: (32) 98 74 30. info@mc.gov.ge.
Georgian National Film Center, Agmashenebeli Avenue 164, 0112 Tbilisi. Tel/Fax: (32) 342 975, Tel/Fax: (32) 342 897. office@filmcenter.ge. www.filmcenter.ge.
Film Studio – Remka, 36 Kostava st., 0179 Tbilisi. Tel: (32) 990 542. Fax: (32) 933 871. remka@remkafilm.ge. www.remkafilm.ge.
Taia Group ltd., 74, Chavchavadze Ave., 0162 Tbilisi. Tel: (32) 912 945. Fax: (32) 253 072.
Studio 99, 10 Sharashidze St., 0162 Tbilisi. Tel: (32) 220 79064. Fax: (32) 230 412. Berlin office: Greifenhagener Str. 26, D-10437 Berlin, Germany. Tel: (+49 30) 44031861. Fax: (+49 30) 44031860.
Sanguko Films, 7 Tamarashvili St., 0162 Tbilisi. Tel: (32) 22 40 61. info@sanguko.ge. www.sanguko.ge.
Sakdoc Film – 2007, 121 Zemo Vedzisi St., 0160 Tbilisi. Tel: (93) 24 32 72/(93) 32 39 29. info@sakdoc.ge. www.sakdoc.ge.

NINO EKVTIMISHVILI is a freelance journalist who specialises in cinema and art in Georgia.

Germany Andrea Dittgen

Two films – one for the heart and one for the head – dominated German cinema in 2008. **Rabbit Without Ears** (*Keinohrhasen*), a romantic comedy, attracted an audience of 6.2 million, while **The Baader Meinhof Complex** (*Der Baader Meinhof Komplex*), about Germany's brutal terrorist group, the Red Army Faction (RAF), was seen by 2.6 million people after only five weeks. The market share of 21.3% from January to September (in 2007 it was 14.4 percent) was very satisfactory. Germany's film industry is flourishing, with 99 feature films and documentaries released this year; many benefited from the new German Federal Film Fund (DFFF), whose total production fund was €60 million. Studio Babelsberg also hosted a

number of US productions, such as *Valkyrie*, *Speed Racer* and *Inglorious Bastards*. With independent production going strong and a wide range of themes and genres on view, it has been a strong and pleasantly surprising year for German cinema.

Uli Edel's The Baader Meinhof Complex

The most important film of the year was Uli Edel's *The Baader Meinhof Complex*. A unique mixture of action thriller and docu-drama, it traced the brutal rise of the iconic terrorists. Producer Bernd Eichinger (*Downfall*) wrote the screenplay in collaboration with Edel and with advice from Stefan Aust, who wrote the non-fiction bestseller on which the film is based. It is the first film to cover the entire history of the original RAF, from 1968 up to the 1977 suicide of its leaders in Stammheim prison. Edel presents one action scene after another, as if he were chronologically listing the history of the RAF with its murderous burnings, bombings, kidnappings and bank robberies, which threatened the stability of the then-fragile German democracy. Germany's most talented actors, including Moritz Bleibtreu (Andreas Baader), Martina Gedeck (Ulrike Meinhof) and Johanna Wokalek (Gudrun Ensslin) are superb, but the film falls short of explaining their motives. As a result, public reaction to the film was ambivalent; young audiences were enthusiastic, while RAF victims and those who witnessed what happened were infuriated.

Til Schweiger's **Rabbit Without Ears**

Rabbit Without Ears, the romantic comedy directed by and starring local superstar Til Schweiger was the biggest commercial success of the last year. Co-writing and producing the film, Schweiger plays a rude reporter forced to do social work in a day-care centre. It is there that he meets a cynical kindergarten teacher, eventually falling in love with her. Although superficial, Schweiger's popular film features fine comic timing and a strong performance by rising star Nora Ischirner.

Jürgen Vogel in Dennis Gansel's **The Wave**

Dennis Gansel attracted 2.7 million people to his horrifying adaptation of **The Wave** (*Die Welle*), a popular play in German schools. By reworking a high-school experiment carried out in California in 1967, transposing the action to contemporary Germany, Gansel opened up the debate on the allure of fascism (following

on from Gansel's 2004 film, *Before the Fall*, about Nazi elite schools). While working with his students on the subject of autocracy, a teacher is carried away with his own hidden fascist tendencies and creates a new group with its own shirts, salute and oppressive code of conduct. Director Max Färberböck also touched upon another sensitive spot in German history. **A Woman in Berlin** (*Anonyma – Eine Frau in Berlin*) tells the true story of women raped by Red Army soldiers in the last month of the Second World War.

Max Färberböck's **A Woman in Berlin**

Some years earlier, in 1936, two alpine climbers tried to ascend the Eiger Mountain, which is recounted in **North Face** (*Nordwand*) by Philipp Stölzl. They even joined forces with the competing climbers from the Nazi Party in order to achieve the impossible, but died from the extreme weather. Stölzl revived a unique German film genre, introduced by Arnold Fanck in the 1920s: the mountain films. With their mix of adventure and melodrama, Stölzl produced an exciting film, set against a backdrop of love and politics.

Dennis Hopper in Wim Wenders' **Palermo Shooting**

High hopes for Nicolai Müllerschön's **The Red Baron** (*Der rote Baron*), about notorious First World War pilot Manfred von Richthofen, were disappointingly dashed by a confusing script and flat direction. Another failure was Wim Wenders' **Palermo Shooting**, about a photographer faced with death who decides to find new meaning in life. Two other experienced filmmakers fared better. Doris Dörrie surprised audiences with a tense and convincing story about old people. **Cherry Blossoms** (*Kirschblüten – Hanami*) is a touching road movie about a man who travels to Japan to visit his son in Tokyo following the death of his wife. While there, he learns why his wife loved Japanese contemporary dance. Andreas Dresen (*Summer in Berlin*) presented a septuagenarian romance – with sex – in **Cloud 9** (*Wolke 9*). Hailed at Cannes and other festivals for its humorous, yet sensitively made, bedroom sequences, it was only a small domestic success (330,000 admissions).

Doris Dörrie's **Cherry Blossoms**

Seven years after winning the Academy Awards for Best Foreign Language film, Caroline Link (*Nowhere in Africa*) returned with **A Year Ago in Winter** (*Im Winter ein Jahr*). Sadly, it turned out to be no more than a well-intentioned, sophisticated art-house film about a painter helping a young dancer (rising star Karoline Herfurth) and her mother deal with a loved one's suicide.

As in 2007, Marcus H. Rosenmüller remains the only director capable of releasing two features within twelve months. And both are *Heimat*-style films in Bavarian dialect. **Beste**

Marcus H. Rosenmüller's **Beste Gegend**

Gegend, the second part of a trilogy, is a well-made road movie about two girls whose world tour ends before it begins. **Räuber Kneißl** is Rosenmüller's first period film, focusing on the dramatic life of a legendary thief of the nineteenth century. Not willing to limit himself to this feat, he has also completed another film, **Die Perlmutterfarbe**. Though working at the same speed as Rainer Werner Fassbinder once did, Rosenmüller lacks the intellectual rigour of his predecessor. Joseph Vilsmaier also put stock in a Bavarian dialect with **The Story of Brandner Kaspar** (*Die Geschichte vom Brander Kaspar*), about a farmer who cheated death. It featured German TV comedy star, Michael Herbig.

Mike Marzuk's **Summer**

Two films scored high figures with the youth market: **Summer** (*Sommer*), a teenage love-and-revenge story by newcomer Mike Marzuk, and the sequel **The Wild Soccer Bunch 5** (*DWK5 – Die wilden Kerle*), a hijack thriller directed by Joachim Masannek. Both films starred Jimi Blue Ochsenknecht. Ute Wieland's **Cheeky Girls** (*Freche Mädchen*) also performed well. However, the best children's film was **Krabat** by Marco Kreuzpaintner. An adaptation of a popular children's book set in the middle ages, it tells the story of a boy who learns the dark arts from an evil sorcerer. Rather than imitating the Harry Potter trend, the film evoked the atmosphere of the Brothers Grimm.

Ann-Kristin Reyels' **Hounds**

The long-awaited film adaptation of Thomas Mann's **Buddenbrooks**, directed by Heinrich Breloer and starring Academy Award nominee Armin Mueller Stahl, will finally come out during the Christmas period. Christian Petzold's **Jerichow**, a tense drama concerning love and money issues between two men and a woman, will be released in early 2009. Sönke Wortmann's adaptation of **Pope Joan** (*Die Päpstin*) will follow in autumn. Biopics such as **Clara** (*Geliebte Clara*), about composer Clara Schumann, by Helma Sanders-Brahms and **Hilde** by Kai Wessel (about singer Hildegard Knef) are also slated for next year. As is Tom Tykwer's thriller **The International**.

ANDREA DITTGEN is a film critic and editor of the daily newspaper *Die Rheinpfalz* and a contributor to the magazine *Filmdienst*. She is also a member of the board of the German Film Critics Association and web editor for the International Federation of Film Critics (www.fipresci.org).

The year's best films
Krabat (Marco Kreuzpaintner)
Cherry Blossoms (Doris Dörrie)
Beste Gegend (Marcus H. Rosenmüller)
North Face (Philipp Stölzl)
Two Mothers (Rosa von Praunheim)

Quote of the year
'Filming is dealing with your demons – and your angels, too.' BERND EICHINGER, *producer and co-writer of* The Baader Meinhof Complex.

Directory
All Tel/Fax numbers begin (+49)
Deutsches Filminstitut-DIF, Schaumainkai 41, 60596 Frankfurt am Main. Tel: (69) 961 2200. Fax: (69) 620 060. info@deutsches-filminstitut.de. www.deutsches-filminstitut.de.
Deutsches Filmmuseum Frankfurt am Main, Schaumainkai 41, 60596 Frankfurt am Main. Tel: (69) 2123 8830. Fax: (69) 2123 7881. info@deutsches-filmmuseum.de. www.deutsches-filmmuseum.de.
Federal Film Board (FFA), Grosse Praesidentenstr 9, 10178 Berlin. Tel: (30) 275 770. Fax: (30) 2757 7111. www.ffa.de.
Filmmuseum Berlin-Deutsche Kinemathek, Potsdamer Str 2, 10785 Berlin. Tel: (30) 300 9030. Fax: (30) 300 9313. info@filmmuseum-berlin.de. www.filmmuseum-berlin.de.
Münchner Stadtmuseum/Filmmuseum, St Jakobsplatz 1, 80331 Munich. Tel: (89) 2332 2348. Fax: (89) 2332 3931. filmmuseum@muenchen.de. www.stadtmuseum-online.de/filmmu.htm.
Umbrella Organisation of the Film Industry, Kreuzberger Ring 56, 65205 Wiesbaden. Tel: (611) 778 9114. Fax: (611) 778 9169. statistik@spio-fsk.de.

Clive Owen and Naomi Watts star in Tom Twyker's **The International**

Greece Ninos-Feneck Mikelidis

Although the number of films distributed in Greece during 2008 increased (approximately thirty films were released across the year), audience attendance decreased, both in small independent cinemas and multiplexes. Significant box office receipts were confined to large American productions, with few non-American films attracting more than 10,000 visitors. Internet downloading, the ever-increasing DVD market and rampant piracy continue to play an important part in the continuation of this downward trend.

Nicos Perakis' **Sang-froid**

This, as expected, had an impact on Greek cinema, with only seventeen films (including three documentaries) – about two thirds of the year's output – being distributed, mostly with poor box office results. Some commercial films, among them **Sang-froid** (*Psychraimia*) by Nicos Perakis and **I-4: Truancy and Acquittal** (*Ay-For, Loufa kai apallagi*) by Vassilis Katsikis, barely managed to attract ticket sales of 300,000, while a film like Thanassis Papathanasiou & Mihalis Reppas' **Strictly for All Audiences** (*Afstiros katallilo*), which was still in cinemas at the time of writing, has little hope of reaching this figure.

Nicos Panayiotopoulos's **Athens-Istanbul** was among the most interesting films of the year. A variation on the road movie, its main character

Nicos Panayiotopoulos's **Athens-Istanbul**

is depressed following a recent divorce and, in order to find a reason for living, embarks on a journey from Athens to Istanbul, accompanied by a young woman and her mysterious musician husband. An elegiac film, punctuated by moments of sadness and humour, it features lyrical scenes that capture the flavour and diversity of contemporary Greek life.

In **Female Conspiracies** (*Gynekies synomosies*), director Vassilis Vafeas presents a dying man's erotic fantasies and nightmares of encounters with women he once loved – but was unable to have – in his life. With its ironic, often surrealist imagery, the film draws on the style of *commedia all'italiana*.

Vassilis Vafeas's **Female Conspiracies**

Vassilis Douvlis' **The Return**

Vassilis Douvlis's feature debut, **The Return** (*I epistrofi*), loosely based on James M. Cain's novel *The Postman Always Rings Twice* is set in a village in northern Greece. Here we follow the love affair between a woman married to an older German ex-pat and an Albanian, which leads to tragedy when the woman's lover kills the husband. With both male characters being immigrants and the director adopting a detached, naturalistic style, not dissimilar to Theo Angelopoulos's *Reconstruction of a Crime*, the film becomes an effective commentary on immigration and the hardships of life in rural Greece.

Thanos Anastopoulos's **Correction**

Two other debuts were Thanos Anastopoulos's **Correction** (*Diorthosi*) and Konstantina Voulgaris's **Valse sentimentale**. Anastopoulos's naturalistic film is based on a real event, in which a man, following his release from prison where he served time for killing another man during a feud, goes in search of his victim's Albanian wife, in order to ask her forgiveness. Creating the

right tone for the film, Anastopoulos extracts fine performances from his actors. In *Valse sentimentale*, loneliness and the search for human contact are key to the success of this low-key, atmospheric film, directed by the daughter of veteran filmmaker Pantelis Voulgaris. The protagonists are an eccentric Athenian couple who wander aimlessly through Exarheia, an area mainly populated by anarchists. After various encounters, they decide to change their uninspired lives.

Spyros Stathopoulos's **PVC-1**

PVC-1 was shot in Colombia by Spyros Stathopoulos. It tells the story of the kidnapping of a woman turned into a human bomb by terrorists demanding a ransom from her family, in a single, suspenseful, 85-minute-long shot. In his very low-budget film **Love Lessons for Revolutionary Action** (*Erotika mathimata yia epanastatiki drasi*), Nicos Alevras analyses the driving force of 'eros' throughout mankind's history. Alevras's film is, by turns, humorous, subversive, surreal and Makavejev-like in the 'lessons' it presents. Finally, in Alexis Alexiou's claustrophobic **Story 52** (*Istoria 52*), a mentally ill character fantasises about the disappearance of his

Alexis Alexiou's **Story 52**

girlfriend, in a film that is little more than a stylistic exercise.

Notwithstanding the distribution crisis, three feature documentaries found their way into cinemas. In **Secrets and Lies** (*Mystika ke psemmata*), Stavros Stangos exposes, with harrowing images, one of the worst industrial disasters of last century when, in the early hours of 3 December 1984, the Union Carbide pesticide plant in Bhopal, India, released a toxic gas into the air, killing thousands. Athanassia Drakopoulou's **A Poet's Estate** (*Periousiaka stoicheia*) presents a loving portrait of the famous Greek poet Nikiforos Vrettakos, locating his place in the country's social and political changes over the last five decades. Annetta Papathanasiou's **Qadir – An Afghan Ulysses** traces the journey from Greece to Afghanistan of young Qadir, an Afghan immigrant who arrived illegally in Greece after the Taliban burnt down his village.

Unfortunately, the release of the second installment of Theo Angelopoulos's trilogy, **The Ashes of Time**, has been delayed because of the film's participation in the 2009 Berlin Film Festival. Paris-based Greek director Costa-Gavras shot part of his first Greek/French co-production, **East Is West**, in Crete and other parts of the mainland. The film, a commentary on immigration, narrates the long and eventful journey of an illegal immigrant (played by Italian sex idol Ricardo Scamarcio), from the moment he arrives in Greece, continuing through various countries in Europe, to his arrival in Paris, where he expects to find his Eden.

There are currently more than thirty films lined up for release during 2009, among them films by established directors (Toni Lycouresis, Thodoros Marangos, Eleni Alexandraki, Panos Karkanevatos, Petros Sevastikoglou), as well as first- and second-time directors (Philippos Tsitos, Evangelos Frantzis, Panos Koutras, Christos Georgiou, Alexandrou Avrana, Vardis Marinakis, Sofia Papachristou, Anestis Charalambidis).

The Greek Film Centre has announced its budget for 2009, which is only €5.5 million, while the Thessaloniki Film Festival's budget is €9 million, a sum strongly criticised by the Directors' Guild and the Technicians' Association, amongst others.

The most positive aspect of this year was the Culture Minister Mihalis Liapis's decision to proceed with the preparation of a new bill regarding cinema; a project that ministers have been talking about for more than a decade, but which has never materialised. At present, the ministry is preparing an updated bill, based on a report presented by Costa-Gavras, as well as an additional report prepared by representatives from various branches of the film industry (directors, technicians, actors, distributors, cinema owners and critics), which will hopefully be voted on by Parliament in March 2009. The main issues of the bill, announced during the closing ceremony of the 2008 Thessaloniki Film Festival and to be presented to Parliament shortly after, are:

a) The return, in full, of the tax applied to cinema tickets. It will be distributed among producers, exhibitors, distributors and the Greek Institute of Scriptwriting (an institute to be established by the new bill).
b) A tax shelter for anyone financing or co-financing the production of a film.
c) New measures for the development of film production (financing, subsidies, tax relief etc.)
d) A change in the way State Prizes will be distributed.

Other demands by the various sections of the industry will be dealt with individually.

NINOS-FENECK MIKELIDIS is a historian of Greek cinema and film critic for *Eleftherotypia* daily newspaper. He is also the founder and director of the Panorama of European Cinema film festival in Athens.

Nicos Panayiotopoulos's **Athens-Istanbul**

The year's best films
Athens-Istanbul (Nicos Panayiotopoulos)
Female Conspiracies (Vassilis Vafeas)
The Return (Vassilis Douvlis)
Secrets and Lies (Stavros Stangos)
Valse sentimentale (Konstantina Voulgaris)

Quote of the year
'If the Greeks go to the cinema to see stupid films it is better, I believe, that they don't go at all.' **Athens-Istanbul** *director* **NICOS PANAYIOTOPOULOS.**

Directory
All Tel/Fax numbers begin (+30)
Association of Independent Producers of Audiovisual Works (SAPOE), 30 Aegialias, 151 25 Maroussi. Tel: (210) 683 3212. Fax: (210) 683 3606. sapoe-gr@otenet.gr.
Greek Film Centre, President & Managing Director: Diagoras Chronopoulos, 10 Panepistimiou, 106 71 Athens. Tel: (210) 367 8500. Fax: (210) 364 8269. info@gfc.gr. www.gfc.gr.
Greek Film, Theatre & Television Directors Guild, 11 Tossitsa, 106 83 Athens. Tel: (210) 822 8936. Fax: (210) 821 1390. ees@ath.forthnet.gr.
Hellenic Ministry of Culture, 20 Bouboulinas, 106 82 Athens. Tel: (210) 820 1100. w3admin@culture. gr. http://culture.gr.
Union of Greek Film Directors and Producers, 33 Methonis, 106 83 Athens. Tel: (210) 825 3065. Fax: (210) 825 3065.
Union of Greek Film, TV & Audiovisual Sector Technicians (ETEKT-OT), 25 Valtetsiou, 106 80 Athens. Tel: (210) 360 2379/361 5675. Fax: (210) 361 6442. etekt-ot@ath.forthnet.gr.

Hong Kong Tim Youngs

There was some good news for the Hong Kong film industry at the beginning of 2008. Cinema attendance had risen over the previous year, thanks to the opening of a number of new cinemas and the successful run of international films. Although the local population has not given up on cinema, the outlook for domestic filmmaking is still far from rosy. By mid-2008, many in the industry were expecting the annual tally of local releases to be less than the previous year's total of fifty films. Pressure was felt on all sides: a slowdown in mainland China-backed co-productions; lukewarm enthusiasm for hometown fare; the ongoing battle against piracy; and concerns that even the distinctiveness of Hong Kong cinema was under threat.

Filmmaking partnerships with mainland China became particularly difficult after authorities there slowed prime releases to a trickle for months on end. Preceding years had seen Hong Kong's filmmakers strengthen cross-border alliances (co-productions constituted almost half the local films in 2007), eager to reach the mainland audience after hometown and regional support flagged. Yet these ventures hit trouble when Chinese approval began to stall, first after controversial mainland releases like *Lust, Caution* in early 2008, then during the lead-up to August's Beijing Olympics. To gain a cinema release or even an international premiere at a film festival, co-productions require official authorisation – a process that can delay both filming and opening dates.

Hong Kong's filmmakers, increasingly adept in sidestepping what Chinese authorities regard as unsavoury subjects, such as political and supernatural themes, found the slowdown and changes in schedule an unexpected obstacle. And all films were affected. The low-budget **A Decade of Love** (*Sup fun chung ching*), an omnibus of shorts about Hong Kong, saw its April premiere cancelled. Even mainstream titles like Alan Mak and Felix Chong's thriller **Lady Cop & Papa Crook** (*Daai sau cha ji neui*) had its release pushed back by months. The slowdown of major local releases opened up opportunities for imports, like the first part of the Chinese prestige title and Asia's most expensive film, **Red Cliff** (*Chi bi*). The historical epic, directed by Hong Kong's John Woo, set the scene for the major battle in its second part, which is set for release in early 2009. Even Hollywood blockbusters caught on to the trend of releasing films with regional ties: *Kung Fu Panda*, *Forbidden Kingdom* and *The Mummy: Tomb of the Dragon Emperor* all contained Chinese themes. The Hong Kong skyline even featured in Christopher Nolan's *The Dark Knight*.

Despite the difficulties with Hong Kong/China co-productions, filmmakers still see the business sense in aiming for the large mainland market. And when those joint ventures' increased budgets are put to good use, the results can be exceptional. Take Benny Chan's

Barbie Tsu in Benny Chan's **Connected**

Connected (*Bo chi tung wah*). A remake of the 2004 Hollywood film *Cellular*, Chan's action comedy delivered a wild ride, effectively ditching the original's plot distractions in favour of more car-chase mayhem and local humour. Earlier in 2008, Stephen Chow's kids' film **CJ7** (*Cheung Gong 7 hou*) also benefited from increased funds and went on to become the year's top-grossing local film.

Ching Siu-tung's **An Empress and the Warriors**

Expensive period epics remain one of the major trends with co-productions, such as Peter Chan's *The Warlords*, released locally in late 2007. Chan's battlefield spectacular covered darker ground than other recent epics and benefited from a top-notch cast, including Andy Lau, Jet Li, Takeshi Kaneshiro and Xu Jinglei. Daniel Lee's **Three Kingdoms: Resurrection of the Dragon** (*Saam gwok dzi gin lung se gap*) mined the same literary source as *Red Cliff* for more high-end historical action. A lighter touch was added by Ching Siu-tung to his pacifist **An Empress and the Warriors** (*Kong saan mei yan*) and Gordon Chan to **Painted Skin** (*Wa pei*), the latter a hit in China with its romance, action and supernatural elements, based on classic tales.

Censorship and creative compromise remain a major concern, as well as the dilution of Hong Kong's signature style. The anodyne *CJ7*, for instance, was set in a nondescript mainland city. Later in the year, Antony Szeto's entertaining martial arts actioner, **Wushu: A Young Generation** (*Wushu zhi shaonian xing*), possessed a distinctly mainland-Chinese feel, as too did Jacob Cheung's pleasant and scenic China-set road drama **Ticket** (*Che piao*).

Kelly Lin in Johnnie To's **Sparrow**

Mainland directors also worked on Hong Kong-backed projects, including Zhang Yibai, with the stylish Chongqing-shot art-house drama **Lost Indulgence** (*Mi guo*) and Liu Fengdou, whose crime drama **Ocean Flame** (*Yi ban hai shui, yi ban huo yan*) presented an unconvincing image of contemporary Hong Kong.

A thirst for distinctively hometown affairs was nonetheless quenched with several notable films. At the end of 2007, Johnnie To and Wai Ka-fai rekindled their fruitful co-directing partnership for the cop-psychology thriller **Mad Detective** (*Sun taam*). The dark and oppressive gumshoe drama featured the impressive Lau Ching-wan as an investigator savant. To's **Sparrow** (*Man jeuk*) was another quality diversion at home and a modest success at international film festivals. A perky, nostalgic, Euro-style pickpocket caper, *Sparrow* was a rare local box office success in the lead-up to the Olympics.

Ann Hui's social-realist **The Way We Are** (*Tin shui wai dik yat yu ye*), set in an often maligned satellite town, was produced on

Ann Hui's **The Way We Are**

Pang Ho-cheung's **Trivial Matters**

a microbudget. Hui's perceptive grass-roots drama drew rich material from everyday life, suffusing a humble story of family bonds and neighbourly spirit with wit and pathos. More local storytelling arrived in Pang Ho-cheung's nifty **Trivial Matters** (*Por see yee*), comprising seven shorts based on his own published stories, all dealing with themes pertinent to Hong Kong. Pang's mélange of comedy, nostalgia, sex and drama was positioned as the plucky Cantonese alternative to the Mandarin-language juggernaut *The Warlords* at Christmas 2007.

Maverick director Herman Yau was on fine form with the prostitute drama **True Women For Sale** (*Sing kung chok tse sup yut tam*), employing a non-exploitative and lightly comic touch to portray sex workers in a run-down district. Yau, who often uses his films to highlight social problems, included a commentary on right-of-abode seekers into the narrative. Lawrence Lau also dealt with social issues in his tough teen-delinquency drama, **Besieged City** (*Wai sing*). Towards the end of the year, he co-directed the

Herman Yau's **True Women For Sale**

urban drama **City Without Baseball** (*Mou ye chi sing*) with Scud, as well as the Taiwan-set political thriller, **Ballistic** (*Dan Dao*). Finally, actor-director Sylvia Chang presented a nostalgic overview of Hong Kong's development into her classy gangland parenting epic, **Run Papa Run** (*Yat kor ho ba ba*).

Sylvia Chang's **Run Papa Run**

In the youth market, co-directors Chan Hing-ka and Janet Chun gave their intriguing romantic comedy **La Lingerie** (*Noi yee sil nui*) a novel undergarment theme and capitalised on lead actress Stephy Tang's rising appeal. Patrick Kong continued his low-end auterist run with the 'love-hurts' melodrama **L for Love, L for Lies** (*Ngor dik dzui oi*), also starring Tang, while **See You in You Tube** (*Oi dau da*) scored decent returns with scrappy, sketch-like scenarios, made by seven unnamed directors.

Wong Kar-wai's **Ashes of Time Redux**

One of the main Hong Kong attractions at film festivals in 2008 was **Ashes of Time Redux** (*Dung che sai duk*), Wong Kar-wai's spruced-up version of his 1994 martial arts drama. For fans of the original, as well as its director, it was a welcome chance to revisit a classic. Viewers also keeping an eye on fresh directions from Hong Kong cinema had the chance to see a number of interesting films by new directors. In this regard, the springtime Hong Kong International Film Festival (HKIFF) and autumn's Hong Kong Asian Film Festival (HKAFF) remain the most important platforms for first-time directors such as Heiward Mak and Ivy Ho.

Mak made an impressive HKIFF debut, aged 23, with **High Noon**, capturing coming-of-age themes with a daring, rough-and-tumble style and a cast of newcomers. At HKAFF, acclaimed screenwriter Ho presented her directorial debut, **Claustrophobia** (*Chan mat*), which charted an awkward office romance. Carefully paced over eight scenes that play in reverse chronologically, Ho's debut offered a subtle narrative that white-collar audience members could relate to. Pierre Lam, a critic and screenwriter, also premiered his frisky youth romance, **Some Like it Hot** at HKAFF. Meanwhile, other newcomers saw their films released directly to the public. Derek Kwok's first two films, the thriller **The Pye-Dog** (*Ye. leung heun*) and the grim crime drama **The Moss** (*Ching toi*), were both ambitious features, while David Lee delivered **Yes, I Can See Dead People**, a very effective low-budget horror.

Several leading producers, like the prolific Eric Tsang, are actively supporting these rising directors, as is the government-established Film Development Fund, which backs up to a third of the production costs for low- to medium-budget commercial pictures. *Claustrophobia* was the first fund-assisted film to premiere. Privately run funds, like the pan-Asian Irresistible Films, established for mid-budget mainstream works by new directors, also launched in 2008. With the Hong Kong/China co-production route having become a mixed blessing for local filmmakers, and with economic concerns on the rise, these avenues of support offer hope to emerging talent in what remains a troubled film industry.

Johnnie To and Wai Ka-fai's **Mad Detective**

The year's best films
Mad Detective (Johnnie To & Wai Ka-fai)
The Way We Are (Ann Hui)
Trivial Matters (Pang Ho-cheung)
Connected (Benny Chan)
Claustrophobia (Ivy Ho)

Quote of the year
'Nobody knows what's happening. In that sense we don't have any idea of what's allowed and how much we can get away with.' LAWRENCE LAU, *director, on tightened mainland restrictions and stalled co-production approvals in China.*

Directory
All Tel/Fax numbers begin (+852)
Hong Kong Film Archive, 50 Lei King Rd, Sai Wan Ho. Tel: 2739 2139. Fax: 2311 5229. www.filmarchive.gov.hk.
Film Services Office, 40/F, Revenue Tower, 5 Gloucester Road, Wan Chai. Tel: 2594 5745. Fax: 2824 0595. www.fso-tela.gov.hk.
Federation of Hong Kong Filmmakers, 2/F, 35 Ho Man Tin St, Ho Man Tin, Kowloon. Tel: 2194 6955. Fax: 2194 6255. www.hkfilmmakers.com.
Hong Kong Film Directors' Guild, 2/F, 35 Ho Man Tin St, Ho Man Tin, Kowloon. Tel: 2760 0331. Fax: 2713 2373. www.hkfdg.com.
Hong Kong Film Awards Association, Room 1601–1602, Austin Tower, 22–26 Austin Ave, Tsim Sha Tsui, Kowloon. Tel: 2367 7892. Fax: 2723 9597. www.hkfaa.com.

TIM YOUNGS is a Hong Kong-based writer and a consultant on Hong Kong cinema for the Udine Far East Film Festival and the Venice Film Festival.

Hungary John Cunningham

2008 started well for the Hungarian film industry, with MAFILM announcing plans to build a US$2.5 million studio to replace the one badly damaged by fire in July 2007. However, as the year progressed and the international economic situation deteriorated, prospects have begun to look distinctly uncertain. Whether or not the cancellation of plans to build the Greenhill Studios outside the southern city of Pecs was connected to the financial downturn is, at the time of writing, speculation as hard information has been difficult to obtain. With the news in late October of an IMF-engineered deal to bail out the Hungarian economy to the tune of US$25 billion, a fuller assessment of the impact of the downturn on the Hungarian film industry may well have to wait until 2009.

In the short term, the changing economic climate may actually favour the industry at some level. The Hungarian Forint has lost around 25% of its value against the dollar and the Euro, and the favourable exchange rates for overseas customers and distributors could encourage both the export of Hungarian films and attract foreign productions to Hungary, although, in the long term, continuing devaluation of the currency can only be severely detrimental. It may be in the area of co-production that Hungarians will suffer most as companies struggle to match funding from foreign sources. The news from Brussels that the European Commission has approved €231 million for a film-support scheme (to run until 2013) was therefore very welcome. The Hungarian Film Law continues to reap benefits for foreign producers and there is evidence that, in this instance, the much-vaunted, but rarely tried and tested, 'trickle-down effect' is actually working in the interests of the domestic industry. Recent legislation to bring the Film Law into line with European law has now completed a lengthy and complex parliamentary process.

Away from the grubby world of international finance, this year's film offerings were a mixed batch. Although not as successful as the previous year, 2008 nevertheless had its moments, not least being another success for Magyar 'wunderkind' Kornél Mundruzcó with **Delta**. Set in the startling scenery of the Danube delta region, superbly captured by cinematographer Mátyás Erdély, this is a powerful but slow-moving and sparse film, showing some influence of Béla Tarr and Miklós Jancsó. Mondruczó won the Golden Reel Award in Budapest and Félix Lajkó picked up the Best Original Film Score. The film centres on the return home of Mihai (played by Félix Lajkó) and his incestuous relationship with his previously unknown half-sister (Orsolya Tóth). Ultimately, this provokes the locals (the director hired many people from the region) to kill them both in an act of primeval savagery. Much critical praise, even if it attracted few awards, was to follow at the Cannes, Toronto and London Film Festivals.

Kornél Mundruzcó's **Delta**

This film (together with his previous film-oratorio, 2005's *Johanna*) has done much to establish Mundruzcó's reputation on the international festival circuit.

Attila Gigor's The Investigator

György Szomjas's **The Sun Street Boys** (*A nap utcai fiúk*), a rather late addition to the crop of '56 'anniversary' films, was an engaging coming-of-age film about a group of football-mad kids who take up arms against the Russians and defend their local cinema. Perhaps it turned up too late to make an impact; a pity as this tale of defiant but ultimately failed heroics was everything that Krisztina Goda's *Children of Glory* – with its overladen Hollywood-infused adventure plot – was not. One can feel the hand, if not the imprint, of Dogme95 on Robert Lakatos's **Good Luck!** (*Bahrtalo! – jó szerencét!*), as the camera follows a somewhat larger-than-life Gypsy character as he wheels and deals his way around Europe (and Egypt). After a fine achievement with *Clouds Over the Ganges*, Gábor Dettre's latest offering, **Tableau** (*Tabló*), was a disappointment. This detective tale, starring popular actor Zoltán Mucsi as a Gypsy police officer, looked promising but an overloaded narrative ultimately leaves the viewer unfocused and confused. The Best Director award at the Budapest Film Week went to Elemér Ragályi with his accomplished **Without Mercy (in Memory of PD)** (*Nince kegyelem (PD emlékére)*), based on the true story of a victimised Gypsy man, badly let down by the judicial system. Attila Gigor's **The Investigator** (*A nyomozó*) was an

accomplished crime thriller by this relative newcomer. Hungarian comedy rarely travels well, but comic actor and director Róbert Koltai was on form with his **Trains Keep a Rollin'** (*Megy a gőzös*), a pleasingly silly mix of Hungarian Pythonesque and Ealing humour.

Domestically, Hungarian films still struggle with overseas (primarily US) competition and figures for the first half of 2008 show that around 16–17% of the Hungarian audiences went to see a film originating in their own country. In the world arena Hungary continues to perform well at international festivals (155 entries up to November 2008), winning numerous prizes, although this has yet to be translated into widespread distribution in the USA and the UK. Csaba Bollók's excellent *Iska's Journey*, the 2006 Golden Reel award winner, is Hungary's entry for the Academy Awards, although it faces stiff competition from a record entry of 67 films.

Away from the world of feature films, Hungary continues to turn out a remarkable number of documentaries, shorts and scientific

Péter Forgács' **Own Death**

educational films, too numerous to mention. Internationally, probably the best-known Hungarian documentary filmmaker is Péter Forgács, who did not disappoint with his experimental meditation on mortality, **Own Death** (*Saját halál*), adapted from Péter Nadás's novel of the same title, while his slightly more straightforward documentary, **I am von Höfler (Variation on Werther)** (*Von Höfler vagyok (Werther-variácio)*) was awarded the Creative Documentary Prize in Budapest. One other treasure of Hungarian film, its animation sector, was hit by the sad news of the death of Katalin Macskássy on 7 March 2008.

No doubt there are uncertain times ahead, but in 2009 the Hungarian Film Week holds its fortieth anniversary, with much to celebrate and, despite the economic gloom, much to look forward to. Watch this space!

The year's best films
Delta (Kornél Mundruzcó)
The Sun Street Boys (György Szomjas)
Without Mercy (in Memory of PD) (Elemér Ragályi)
Own Death (Péter Forgács)
The Investigator (Attila Gigor)

Quote of the year
'The trick for a national film industry like Hungary's is for its filmmakers to produce something which is culturally specific and exotic, but universal enough in its themes.'
SHANE DANIELSEN, *former director of the Edinburgh International Film Festival.*

Directory
Association of Hungarian Filmmakers, Városligeti fasor 38. Budapest, Hungary-1068, filmszov@t-online.hu
Association of Hungarian Producers, Eszter utca 7/B. Budapest, Hungary-1022, mail@mpsz.org.hu, www.mpsz.org.hu
Hungarian Directors Guild, Ráday utca 31/K., Budapest, Hungary-1092, mrc@filmjus.hu, www.mmrc.hu
Hungarian Independent Producers Associations, Róna utca 174. Budapest, Hungary-1145, eurofilm@t-online.hu
Hungarian National Film Archive, Budakeszi út 51/E. Budapest, Hungary-1021, www.filmintezet.hu
Hungarian Society of Cinematographers (H.S.C.), Róna utca 174. Budapest, Hungary-1145, hsc@hscmot.hu, www.hscmot.hu
MEDIA Desk Hungary, Városligeti fasor 38. Budapest, Hungary-1068, info@mediadesk.hu, www.mediadesk.hu
Motion Picture Public Foundation of Hungary, Városligeti fasor 38. Budapest, Hungary-1068 mmka@mmka.hu, www.mmka.hu
National Film Office, Wesselényi utca 16. Budapest, Hungary-1075, info@filmoffice.hu, www.nationalfilmoffice.hu

---

JOHN CUNNINGHAM is a Senior Lecturer in Film Studies at Sheffield Hallam University, UK. He lived in Hungary during the 1990s and is the author of *Hungarian Cinema: From Coffee House to Multiplex* (2004).

Kornél Mundruzcó's **Delta**

Iceland Eddie Cockrell

'No one's lazy in Lazy Town,' goes the Europop-y refrain of the vigorously surreal and immensely successful children's television show of that name, produced entirely in Iceland. And that's as apt a metaphor as any for 2008's production slate from Reykjavik.

Baltasar Kormákur's **White Night Wedding**

The year began with writer-director Baltasar Kormákur's much-anticipated follow-up to the global hit *Jar City*, **White Night Wedding** (*Brúðguminn*, or, literally, 'the bridegroom'). An emotionally vigorous adaptation of Chekhov's first play, *Ivanov*, it tells of a brooding professor who must overcome the suicide of his first wife to marry a headstrong student. The film showcases the breathtaking scenery of the southwestern island of Flatey, as well as

Kormákur's nimble approach to storytelling. With five features as director and many more as actor and/or producer, his strengths place him in the same league as Fatih Akin or Alexander Payne as an astute judge of narrative impact.

First-time writer-director Valdis Óskarsdóttir's mid-year release, **Country Wedding** (*Sveit-abrúðkaup*), follows the comic misadventures of a bridal party that strikes out from Reykjavik in a pair of coaches for a rustic tying of the knot. 'This is going to be a lot of fun,' says one of their number. Local audiences agreed.

Country Wedding was shot in a breakneck seven days with multiple cameras supervised by *Slumdog Millionaire* cinematographer Anthony Dod Mantle. An award-winning editor, Óskarsdóttir's resume includes the lauded Dogme production *The Celebration* (*Festen*). *Country Wedding* is cut from the same cloth, though it's funnier and far more resonant.

The third feature from lauded television director Óskar Jónasson, **Reykjavik-Rotterdam** is a sturdy, morally complex, blue-collar thriller starring Kormákur as an ex-con, average Joe who must leave his young family to run one

final smuggling scam onboard a mammoth container ship. Co-scripted by Jónasson and prominent Icelandic crime novelist Arnaldur Indridason (on whose immensely popular novel *Jar City* was based), the film opened strongly on seven screens in early October and is primed for high-profile festival exposure.

Alongside *White Night Wedding*'s seven end-of-year Edda awards, including Best Film and Best Cinematography, *Reykjavik-Rotterdam* won in five categories, including Best Director and Best Screenplay. Tellingly, both films were produced by Kormákur's Blueeyes Productions.

Hulda Rós Guðnadóttir and Helga Rakel Rafnsdóttir's end-of-an-era retail meditation **Corner-shop** (*Kjötborg*) won the feature documentary award, with Rúnar Rúnarsson's emotionally brave coming-of-age drama **2 Birds** (*Smáfuglar*) taking shorts honours. Beyond those, Ari Alexander Ergis Magnusson and Bergsteinn Björgúlfsson's **At the Edge of the World** (*Syndir feðranna*) is an unflinching look at the brutal practices at a mid-twentieth-century boys' reformatory, while Grímur Hákonarson's short film **Wrestling** (*Bræðrabylta*), about middle-aged athletes grappling with their mutual affection, could well have been called 'Brokeback Floorboards' – and has travelled to 19 international festivals, after winning the best-short Edda in 2007.

Olaf de Fleur Johannesson's **The Amazing Truth About Queen Raquela**

Combining documentary elements and sexual identity, **The Amazing Truth About Queen Raquela** was the year's most unclassifiable

Sólveig Anspach's **Back Soon**

film. Executive produced by Kormákur and described as a 'visiomentarie' by director Olaf de Fleur Johannesson, this improvised, scripted documentary profiles a Filipino transsexual 'ladyboy' who realises her dream of visiting Paris via a working stint at an Icelandic fish factory ('it's freezing and Björk is from there' represents the sum of her geographic knowledge). Dazzlingly assured, the film won the best-feature Teddy at the Berlin Film Festival.

Rounding out the year's feature roster: Sólveig Anspach's whimsical, critically praised stoner comedy **Back Soon** (*Skrapp út*), winner of a *Variety* award in Locarno and the Sevilla Film Festival's main prize; the rural community comedy-drama **Small Mountain** (*Heidin*), which plays like Kevin Smith's *Clerks* without... well, without New Jersey; and Johannesson's *Queen Raquela* follow-up, the more dramatically straightforward criminal-underworld comedy, **The Higher Force** (with former *Sopranos* cast member Michael Imperioli imported for a small role).

Though the global economic crisis has hit Iceland particularly hard, the local film business immediately found the cloud's silver lining. 'Shooting in Iceland today is an outstanding option,' film commissioner Einar Tomasson told trade paper *Variety*, 'since our currency is so weak that producers are getting much more value for their money.'

And it's true. Recent visitors from Hollywood included Brendan Fraser with *Journey to the Center of the Earth* (aka *Journey 3-D*), Clint Eastwood for *Flags of Our Fathers* and the big-budget fantasy *Stardust*.

The future looks equally bright. Kormákur is finishing **Inhale**, which was shot in New Mexico and features playwright-iconoclast Sam Shepard (now there's a meeting of the minds). Also in English is **The Good Heart**, from *Noi Albino* director Dagur Kári, co-starring Brian Cox and Paul Dano. And on the genre front, Júlíus Kemp's **Reykjavik Whale Watching Massacre** leaves little doubt as to its intentions.

With a nod to Iceland's recent film history, the traditional honorary Edda Award went to Fridrik Thór Fridriksson, whose 1991 drama *Children of Nature* put Iceland on the movie world's map. That Fridriksson is the executive producer of *Reykjavik-Rotterdam* and is finishing a documentary, **The Sunshine Boy**, on the global reactions to autism, suggests that, less than twenty years later, in Reykjavik, laziness is the last thing that can be said about the Icelandic cinema.

The year's best films
Reykjavik-Rotterdam (Óskar Jónasson)
Country Wedding (Valdis Óskarsdóttir)
White Night Wedding (Baltasar Kormákur)

Quote of the year
'Even Iceland is out of money.' *Variety Editor-in-Chief* PETER BART, *24 October 2008*.

Directory
All Tel/Fax numbers begin (+354)
Association of Icelandic Film Directors, Leifsgata 25, 101 Reykjavík. Tel: 588 6003/898 0209. ho@ismennt.is.

Association of Icelandic Film Distributors, SAM-Bíóin, Álfabakka 8, 109 Reykjavík. Tel: 575 8900. Fax: 587 8910. thorvaldur@sambio.is.
Association of Icelandic Film Producers, Túngötu 14, PO Box 5367, 125 Reykjavík. Tel: 863 3057. Fax: 555 3065. sik@producers.is. www.producers.is.
Icelandic Film Centre, Túngata 14, 101 Reykjavík. Tel: 562 3580. Fax: 562 7171. info@icelandicfilm-centre.is. www.icelandicfilmcentre.is.
Icelandic Film Makers Association, PO Box 5162, 128 Reykjavík. Tel: 562 6660. Fax: 562 6665. bjorn@spark.is.
Icelandic Film & Television Academy/EDDA Awards, Túngötu 14, 101 Reykjavík. Tel: 562 3580. Fax: 562 7171. bjorn@ spark.is.
National Film Archive, Hvaleyrarbraut 13, 220 Hafnarfjordur. Tel: 565 5993. Fax: 565 5994. kvikmyndasafn@kvikmyndasafn.is. www.kvikmyndasafn.is.

EDDIE COCKRELL is an American film critic living in Sydney, Australia.

Valdis Óskarsdóttir's **Country Wedding**

India Uma Da Cunha

While India held on to its title as the top film-producing country (1,146 titles in 2007, with more forecast for 2008), its successes were vastly outnumbered by its failures. Not even Diwali, the national Festival of Lights, marking the new business year, could dispel the gloom. Big-budget releases failed to muster support, continuing a worrying trend since 2005, the last good year in terms of box office.

After the glory of his 2007 hit, *Go for it, India*, top producer Aditya Chopra endured a drubbing early in 2008 for his much-heralded **Style** (*Tashan*), about a call-centre romance, which performed poorly despite its star cast (Akshay Kumar, Saif Ali Khan and Anil Kapoor). It followed the fate of his *Dance with Me* (*Aaja Nachle*), which was planned as the comeback film for Madhuri Dixit, and his heavily publicised **A Little Love, A Little Magic** (*Thoda Pyar, Thoda Magic*), about a rich, reclusive bachelor left to care for four orphans and a heaven-sent nanny who comes to his aid.

Akshay Kumar, Saif Ali Khan and Anil Kumar in Style

Other big names also suffered. Three releases featuring brooding star Ajay Devgan collapsed in quick succession, including his directorial

Ravi Chopra's Lord of Ghosts

debut, **You, Me and Us** (*U, Me aur Hum*), about the effect of Alzheimer's on a young married couple. Charismatic director Ram Gopal Verma also bombed with **Rule of the Overlord** (*Sarkar Raj*), a remake of the popular 2005 film *Overlord*, linking crime, politics and industry. Ravi Chopra's star vehicle **Lord of Ghosts** (*Bhoothnath*), on a child's relationship with his dead grandfather and a benevolent ghost, also failed to spark at the box office.

Other big-budget failures included Goldie Behl's **The Warrior** (*Drona*), a film that fused Indian mythology with contemporary fantasy; Satish Kaushik's **Debt** (*Karzzz*), about a man reincarnated to seek vengeance on the wife who killed him for his money; Sanjay Gadhvi's **Kidnap**, about the confrontation between a young lad and the father of the girl he kidnaps; and Harry Baweja's **Love Story 2050**, a love story that fast-forwards to Mumbai in 2050.

Content, style and innovation appear to be of little concern at the moment and box office statistics are all that concern the industry. Of the 66 Hindi films released in the first half of

Mukesh Bhatt's **Heaven**

2008, only two were successful. They were Abbas Mastan's **Race**, a fast-paced account of two very different brothers who must jointly manage the South African stud farm they inherited, and producer Mukesh Bhatt's **Heaven** (*Jannat*), about a cricket bookmaker lured into crime. Significantly, both were made on reasonable budgets with lesser-known stars and unusual themes.

Reassuringly, originality in smaller films was rewarded. Notable examples were Abbas Tyrewala's **Whether You Know... or Not** (*Jaane Tu... Ya Jaane Na*), tracing the burgeoning love between teenaged friends; Ram Gopal Varma's **A Black Magic Story** (*Phoonk!*), about a confirmed atheist whose beliefs are shaken when his loved ones face terrifying ordeals; and Abhishekh Kapoor's look at today's alternative music culture, **Rock On!**.

Abbas Tyrewala's **Whether You Know... or Not**

As belated balm came Anees Bazmee's **Singh is King**. It rode high on the huge appeal of a new muscled hero figure, Akshay Kumar. Aamir Khan's directorial debut, **Stars on Earth** (*Taare Zameen Par*), about a troubled eight-year-old who is discovered to be dyslexic, also performed well. As did Ashutosh Gowarikar's period saga, **Jodhaa Akbar**, earning US$10 million. It recalled the great Emperor Akbar's fabled love for his Hindu queen, extolling his secular values and starred the alluring leads, Aishwaria Rai Bachchan and Hrithik Roshan. This visual feast earned a ban in the state of Rajasthan and parts of Madhya Pradesh, both with princely antecedents, where its historical veracity was questioned. By the time the courts lifted the ban, audiences had seen the film on DVD.

The unfortunate circumstances of Gowarikar's film did highlight the ongoing problem of piracy, which eats into the profits of the film industry.

Even with a 4% drop over recent years, the domestic box office revenue in 2007 was estimated at US$145 million, a growth of 12% over the previous year. The overseas collections are even more promising, at US$17 million in 2007, a growth of 21% over 2006.

The paradox is that, despite an unpredictable box office, India's film and entertainment sector is experiencing an astonishing boom, thanks to the adoption of effective management techniques and profits linked to spin-offs and lucrative tie-ins. By mid-2008, corporate branding was *de rigueur* for the industry. The names of these production companies and studios are as well known as the talent they sponsor: Reliance Entertainment, Eros Entertainment, Studio 18, UTV Motion Pictures, the Percept Group, PVR, Fame Cinemas and Pyramid Saimara Group, among many others. They join the ranks of long-standing, family-owned studio houses led by names such as Yashraj Films, Rajshri Productions, Dharma Productions, Tips Group, Mukta Arts and more recent entrants into film production: Pritish Nandy Communications, Padmalaya Telefilms and Zee Telefilms Limited.

Ashutosh Gowarikar's **Jodhaa Akbar**

Representatives of the American studios, Warner Bros., Fox, Universal and Columbia Tristar also maintain a steady presence in India.

Filmdom approves of corporate involvement. It brought sound funding, which helped widen the global market for Indian film. However, there have been downsides. Corporations bank on stars, who raised their already astronomical fees several times over, sending budgets soaring into often loss-making space. High operational costs menace the small, independent filmmaker, and those making films rooted in India's different regions and languages – that is, those making the most promising product. They barely surface now. Except, surprisingly, for films in Marathi, the language of Mumbai, capital of Bollywood. They are original, lively and have not deserted their grassroots. Another language with an increasing number of films each year is Bhojpuri, from eastern India. The home of art-house cinema, Bengal, now has little to show.

It is often puzzling why corporations bankroll stars and big-budget films when both, more often than not, are loss makers. One view is that the money paid for publicity and marketing papers over the cracks in content. Another is satellite rights, which bring in further revenue. The proliferation of movie-driven TV channels help recover initial costs regardless of box office performance. 2008 saw a significant amount of available funds in the Indian money market.

The increasing number of multiplexes (PVR, Adlabs, Inox and Fame Cinemas lead) has changed cinema-going habits and the amount spent on seeing a film. Cinema owners look beyond box office as the sole revenue stream, focusing on the impressive profit margins of food and beverage sales, computer games and children's zones. Cinemax, which already has 95 screens in 23 properties and plans to open 400 screens over the next three years, has installed in their cinemas twenty bowling alleys, purchased from Thailand's Blue Bowling.

This surging business has prompted some sensational predictions. The business, it is said, will double its profits, rising to around US$10 billion over the next three years and will likely create six million jobs by 2010. Some 1,200 films will be produced annually, in different languages and dialects.

What is unfolding in India pales compared with the global view of the larger businesses. In Cannes, movie moguls from India made it abundantly clear that their eye was now on the world market. Amit Khanna, Chairman of Reliance Big Entertainment (RBE), told a press conference that '4.2 billion people watched Indian films in 2007. But our share of world revenue was only 5%. We plan to change that.' He announced that, by the end of 2009, his company will have invested US$1 billion in production, distribution and exhibition. The very next day, RBE announced that it will provide development finance to Hollywood by striking separate development deals with companies owned by Tom Hanks, Brad Pitt, Nicolas Cage and George Clooney.

Adlabs Films, the Indian film and exhibition division of the Reliance ADA Group has struck a deal with DreamWorks worth US$1.5 billion, tying in with around thirty movies. Yash Raj Films has teamed up with Walt Disney Studios to exclusively create a series of computer-animated feature films.

UTV Motion Pictures featured among the top twenty film distributors in North America during the period January–June 2008, becoming the first Indian film studio to cross the US$5 million revenue mark over this period. The feat was achieved with only three releases: *Jodhaa Akbar* (US$3.44 million), *Race* (US$1.37 million) and *Whether You Know… or Not* (US$ 539,857 and counting). These totals were supported by Aamir Khan's *Taare Zameen Par* performing strongly well into the new year.

India as a location for overseas producers hit new heights, triggered in 2007 by two films: Michael Winterbottom's *A Mighty Heart* and Wes Anderson's *Darjeeling Limited*. In 2008, international accolades were awarded to Danny Boyle's extraordinary **Slumdog Millionaire**, set in the grubby dog-eats-dog backstreets of Mumbai. Planned for next year is **Racing the Monsoon**, a period-set Catherine Zeta Jones and Michael Douglas vehicle, co-produced by Douglas and Shailendra Singh of Percept Pictures.

Post-Diwali, the cinema landscape offered more hope than at the start of the year. Two films on which expectations rode high, UTV-produced **Fashion**, directed by Madhur Bhandarkar, and Studio 18's **Golmaal Returns**, a sequel to the hit *Golmaal* (literally, 'mayhem'), performed well at the box office.

Shyam Benegal's **Welcome to Sajjanpur**

Smaller films continued to perform well, particularly those funded by UTV. 'We have had six back-to-back successes,' commented UTV's CEO, Siddharth Roy Kapur. Three of these were refreshingly different in content. Shyam Benegal's **Welcome to Sajjanpur** focused

on off-beat characters in smalltown India and was received enthusiastically, raising a warm 'huzzah' to this gifted director's return to popular fiction. Neeraj Pandey's **A Wednesday**, in which a man doles out justice when all other means fail, was popular amongst urban audiences. Nishikant Kamath's perceptive study of the destructive pressures of a metropolitan city on its people, **Mumbai, My Love** (*Mumbai Meri Jaan*), was also a hit.

Nandita Das' **Firaaq**

Percept Picture Company showed its mettle when two recent films were accepted at the Toronto International Film Festival: actor Nandita Das's commendable directorial debut, **Firaaq**, on the impact of genocide on individuals' lives; and **Kanchivaram**, an art-house film from the king of commercial cinema, Priyadarshan. The title comes from the city known for its superb hand-woven silk. In the film, local craftsmen are bought out by rich industrialists, leading to revolt.

Priyadarshan's **Kanchivaram**

The world recession may be a warning against India's immediate plans for global expansion. One film, Vipul Shah's **London Dreams**, has already suffered, when Studio 18's India Film Company retracted their offer to pay US$200,000 for the world rights. Reliance's Big Pictures has reportedly delayed two projects and Eros Entertainment has stopped all new projects until March 2009.

The huge budgets invested in flashy Indian blockbusters will almost certainly shrink. It could presage a time to think small and be sensible, perhaps to even look back to the great and creative cinema of India's past.

The year's best films
Kanchivaram (Priyadarshan)
Welcome to Sajjanpur (Shyam Benegal)
Firaaq (Nandita Das)
Valu – The Bull (Umesh Kulkarni)
The Prisoner (Pryas Gupta)

Pryas Gupta's The Prisoner

Quotes of the year
'2008 has finally confirmed what production houses like ours have been saying for years. That Bollywood desperately needs a facelift. You cannot be the world's largest film-producing country and proudly produce so much trash.' PRITISH NANDY, *Chairman, Pritish Nandy Communications.*

'The idea that Bollywood is doing anything radically different is a notion spread by people who have no idea of the history of Indian cinema.' *Film director* SUDHIR MISHRA.

'It is not entirely correct to say that films have not worked this year. The more

Umesh Kulkarni's Valu – The Bull

serious problem is of sustaining a film with sometimes five to seven films releasing in one week.' *Film director* SUDHIR MISHRA.

Directory
All Tel/Fax numbers begin (+91)
Film & Television Institute of India, Law College Rd, Pune 411 004. Tel: (20) 543 1817/3016/0017. www.ftiindia.com.
Film India Worldwide, Confederation of Indian Industry, 105 Kakad Chambers, 132 Dr Annie Besant Rd, Worli, Mumbai 400 018. Tel: (22) 2493 1790. Fax: (22) 2493 9463. www.ciionline.org. www.ciiwest.org.
Film Federation of India, B/3 Everest Bldg, Tardeo, Bombay 400 034. Tel/Fax: (22) 2351 5531. Fax: (22) 2352 2062. supransen22@hotmail.com.
Film Producers Guild of India, G-1, Morya House, Veera Industrial Estate, OShiwara Link Road, Andheri (W), Mumbai 400 053. Tel: (22) 5691 0662/2673 3065. Fax: (22) 5691 0661. tfpgoli1@vsnl.net. www.filmguildindia.com.
National Film Archive of India, Law College Rd, Pune 411 004. Tel: (20) 565 8049. Fax: (20) 567 0027. nfai@vsnl.net.
National Film Development Corporation Ltd, Discovery of India Bldg, Nehru Centre, Dr Annie Besant Rd, Worli, Bombay 400 018. Tel: (22) 2492 6410. www.nfdcindia.com.

UMA DA CUNHA is based in Mumbai, where she works as a casting director, researcher and freelance journalist and edits the quarterly, *India Film Worldwide*. She is also a programmer for international film festivals, specialising in new Indian cinema, and organises film industry PR events.

Indonesia Lisabona Rahman

Indonesian cinemagoers are able to enjoy a wide variety of films these days, with over a hundred local productions released since early 2008. Film producers literally have to fight over screening slots at local cinemas to get their films shown. In terms of the successes of the last year, two local films dominated the box office. However, upcoming filmmakers are entering the industry with more original story ideas, as well as their own distribution strategies.

February's release of Hanung Bramantyo's **Verses of Love** (*Ayat-Ayat Cinta*) created an unusual sight at Indonesia's cinemas. Instead of the usual teenager groups hanging around at theatre lobbies, long lines of veiled women were queuing up for tickets. Based on a popular novel of the same title, the tearjerker is about a young man involved in a love triangle. Muslim leaders and politicians obliged their followers to see the film, resulting in audience figures that topped four million.

Hanung Bramantyo's **Verses of Love**

In September, a new box office record was set by director Riri Riza's **The Rainbow Warrior** (*Laskar Pelangi*). It is likely to continue to play into the new year, exceeding *Verses of Love*'s

total viewership. The film is a didactic piece about a poor Muslim school on the mining island of Belitong in early 1980s. Once again, it is based on a bestselling novel.

Riri Riza's **The Rainbow Warrior**

Like Bramantyo's film, *The Rainbow Warrior* was marketed to highlight its representation of Muslim identity, which appeals to a broad cross-section of Indonesian society. At the other end of the scale, younger, less established filmmakers are addressing another side of identity issues in Indonesia. Films like **May**, **Karma** and **Our Flag** (*Kita Punya Bendera*) focus on the repressed identity of Chinese Indonesians. These films were critically acclaimed, but not as successful at the box office.

A group of young filmmakers and artists, called Proyek Payung, who focus on equally critical issues, created a different distribution concept to reach more viewers with their work. They released **9808**, an omnibus of short documentaries and fiction films, which are all about the filmmakers' personal experiences of the political upheaval in Indonesia, in 1998. The omnibus delivers a mix of comedy, visual poetry and very strong political commentary on corruption, state violence and discrimination towards Indonesian Chinese. Instead of a conventional cinema release, it is currently touring different communities and film festivals in Asia and in Europe.

Indonesian films have also enjoyed great acclaim at international festivals. Director Nan T. Achnas's **The Photograph** won the Special Jury Prize at the Karlovy Vary Film Festival in July. Director Aryo Danusiri's documentary **Playing Between Elephants** (*Bermain di antara gajah-gajah*) and Riri Riza's **Three Days to Forever** (*3 hari untuk selamanya*) were awarded Best Documentary and Best Film at Brussels' Independent International Film Festival in November. Director Ravi Bharwani's second feature film, **Jermal** and Edwin's **Blind Pig Who Wants to Fly** (*Babi buta yang ingin terbang*) have also been selected for competition at international festivals. An atypical Indonesian entry at an international festival was Mouly Surya's suspenseful feature debut, **Fiction** (*Fiksi*), which was screened at the Pusan Film Festival. The film not only represents a new generation of Indonesian filmmakers, it offers a new view of the country.

Mouly Surya's **Fiction**

The documentary film scene became more lively this year. MetroTV, a news TV station set up in 2005, continues to fund productions by young filmmakers through a competition called the Eagle Award. Several workshops have also offered new possibilities to documentary filmmakers. The Kalyana Shira Foundation created a workshop for short documentaries on women's reproductive issues, while the Goethe-Institut Indonesien initiated a production workshop for feature-length documentaries. The omnibus of short cinema documentaries from Kalyana Shira Foundation, titled **At Stake**, will be released in early 2009.

With its unprecedented success over the last year, the Indonesian government has begun to pay more attention to the film industry. Indonesian Minister of Trade and Industry Mari Pangestu encouraged investors to start making films. One sign of movement from investors was the initiation of Movieland, a new film/TV studio complex in West Java, which was opened in August 2008. It was a joint investment project between the film company PT Tripar Multivision and industrial estate company PT Jababeka Tbk. Movieland is said to have US$320 million of investment and is planned to begin its operation in 2011.

The year's best films
Sugiharti Halim (Ariani Darmawan)
Trip To The Wound (Edwin)
They Say I'm A Monkey (Djenar Maesa Ayu)
Love (Khabir Bhatia)

Directory
All Tel/Fax numbers begin (+62)
Ministry of Information for Film & Video, Departement Penerangan RI, Jalan Merdeka Barat 9, Gedung Belakang, Jakarta Pusat. Tel: 384 1260. Fax: 386 0830.
Ministry of Tourism, Art and Culture, Jalan Medan Merdeka Barat 17, Jakarta 10110. Tel: 383 8000/381 0123. Fax: 386 0210. http://gateway. deparsenibud.go.id.

LISABONA RAHMAN is a Jakarta-based freelance writer on film. She is Programming Manager of community cinema *kineforum The Jakarta Arts Council*.

Iran Kamyar Mohsenin

Iran's cinematic year begins in early February with the Fajr International Film Festival, focusing on new productions in the national competition section, which presents a perfect showcase for contemporary Iranian cinema.

A total of 105 feature submissions set a new record in 2008, showing how important the festival is to filmmakers. However, due to a fundamental change in the mood and language of the films, many national and international participants were not satisfied with the festival. It was a deviation from what had previously been presented, which had been acclaimed internationally for two decades.

The Song of Sparrows, *directed by Majid Majidi*

Without the familiar themes, with their social-realist undertones and naturalistic, almost documentary style, this new trend is characterised by its accessibility. Although aiming for a wider audience, a necessity for an industry that thrives on success, some films have still won critical favour at prestigious festivals. For example, after winning four prizes in Fajr, Majid Majidi's **The Song of Sparrows** (*Avaz-E Gonjeshk-Ha*) picked up the Best Actor award for Reza Naji at the Berlin Film Festival, (*There Will Be Blood* Oscar-winner Daniel Day-Lewis was also a contender). Iran's

submission to the Academy this year, Majidi's film attempts to recapture the emotional elements of his earlier *Children of Heaven*, the only Iranian film to be nominated for an Academy Award. Dealing with a decent poor man's decline in a material world, it highlights Majidi's classic approach to a morality tale and his personal vision in telling it.

The Iranian entry in the Berlinale's Forum section, Manhjeh Hekmat's **Three Women** (*Seh Zan*), also displays a critical attitude towards the material world. A keenly observed film, it features three generations of female carpet weavers who are lost in a world of forgotten values. A double winner at the Moscow Film Festival, Reza Mir-Karimi's **As Simple As That** (*Beh Hamin Sadegi*) was also a favourite at Fajr, winning two awards in the Asian Competition and three in the National Section. Delving into the life of a housewife who longs for change, Mir-Karimi's film is a turning point in his career, adopting a new style in order to reflect the frustration of his central character, combining elements of Iranian 'cinema d'art' with more post-modern concepts. Saman Salour's **Lonely Tune of Tehran** (*Taraneh-ye Tanhaiy-e Tehran*), which premiered in the 'Directors' Fortnight' section at the Cannes Film Festival, deals with two marginal characters searching desperately for love and wealth.

Venice welcomed Abbas Kiarostami, the internationally acclaimed director who is recognised as one of the leading forces in New Iranian Cinema. Also present was Amir Naderi, creator of *The Runner* and *Water, Wind, Dust*. While Naderi presented an American independent film, *Vegas: Based on a True Story*, in the official competition, Kiarostami premiered his new experimental venture, **Shirin**, out of competition. Beginning with an extratct used in the '*Where is my Romeo?*' segment of the portmanteau project *Chacun son cinema* for the 60th anniversary of Cannes, Kiarostami expanded his video-art piece into a full-length gallery of portraits, who are witnessed watching something on an unseen screen. However presence of the most famous Iranian actresses as the audience initially does not impress the real audience, including Juliette Binoche as a face in the crowd provides an unknown code for the eccentric experience. Debates surrounding Kiarostami's latest work continue, both inside and outside Iran. However, there is no doubt that the filmmaker is playing a key role in the promotion of digital cinema as means for more personal, experimental and abstract expression, and as a way to escape the trappings of the film industry.

Best known for his *The Girl in the Sneakers* and *I'm Taraneh, 15*, Rasoul Sadr-Ameli presented **Night** (*Shab*) at the Montreal World Film Festival and **Every Night, Loneliness** (*Har Shab Tanhaie*) at a number of European film events, focusing on the salvation of its characters during the pilgrimage.

Mohammad Ali Talebi's **The Wall** (*Divar*), an outdated redoing of a Iranian social drama, spiced with some feminist pretense, screened at the Taormina Film Festival. Meanwhile, Mehrshad Karkhani's **The Loose Rope** (*Risman-e Baz*) was shown in London. An inspirational little film, focusing on two men taking a cow to an unknown destination, it is a modern parable of how men's lives reflect the absurd condition Camus relates in 'The Myth of Sisyphus'.

Two extraordinary discoveries of Fajr 2008 did not enter the festival circuit. The Best Film in the international competition, **Wind Blows on the Meadow** (*Bad Dar Alafzar Mi-Pichad*) by Khosrow Masoumi, completes his snowy forest trilogy of love and violence. The Best National Film, **The Earth's Child** (*Farzand-e Khak*) by Mohammad Ali Ahangar, depicts

a moving tale of post-war body searchers, recalling haunting visions of great westerns. Right now, Iranian cinema faces a decisive challenge in controlling its business more efficiently. To this end, a national movement for the construction of new cinemas is seen as essential – symbolised by the opening of Tehran's Azadi Cineplex, which burned down due to a technical problem twelve years ago.

The year's best films
The Song of Sparrows (Majid Majidi)
The Earth's Child (Mohammad Ali Ahangar)
Wind Blows on the Meadow
(Khosrow Masoumi)
Night (Rasoul Sadr-Ameli)
As Simple As That (Reza Mir-Karimi)

Quote of the year
'A film is global, only when preserving its own localness and nationality. Thus it is a strategic debate that a global film is rooted in its national identity. Everywhere, it is independent identities that mark great filmmakers and great film movements.'
Filmmaker **MAJID MAJIDI.**

Directory
All Tel/Fax numbers begin (+98)
Institute for Intellectual Development of Children & Young Adults. Tel: 871 0661. Fax: 872 9290. info@kanoonparvaresh.com.
National Film Archive of Iran, Baharestan Sq, Tehran 11365. Tel: 3851 2583. Fax: 3851 2710. crb@kanoon.net.
Sahra Film Cultural Institute, 39 Corner of 6th Alley, Eshqyar St, Khorramshahr Ave, Tehran. Tel: 876 5392/6110. Fax: 876 0488. modarresi@dpir.com.
Tamasha Cultural Institute, 124 Khorramshahr Ave, Tehran 15537. Tel: 873 3844/876 9146. Fax: 873 3844/9146. info@tamasha.net.

KAMYAR MOHSENIN has worked as a film critic (now in *Cinema Weekly*) and TV host in film programmes for the last fifteen years. He is also in charge of Research in International Affairs at the Farabi Cinema Foundation.

PROMOTING
IRANIAN CINEMA

FARABI
CINEMA FOUNDATION

PRODUCTION, CO-PRODUCTION, ACQUISITION, SALES, DISTRIBUTION

HEADQUARTER
75, Sie Tir Ave., Tehran 11358, Iran.
Tel: +98 (21) 66708545, 66705454
Fax: +98 (21) 66720750
E-mail: info@fcf.ir

INTERNATIONAL AFFAIRS
19, Delbar Alley, Toos St., Valiye Asr Ave., Tehran 19617, Iran.
Tel: +98 (21) 22741252-4, 22734939
Fax: +98 (21) 22734953
E-mail: fcf1@dpi.net.in

Ireland Michael Dwyer

The mood was celebratory in January 2008, when Irish talent received five nominations for the eightieth Academy Awards. The Irish Film Board organised a trade delegation visit to Los Angeles in the week leading up to the Oscars. Meetings with studio executives, producers, financiers and agents were arranged for the 25 Irish producers in the delegation led by IFB chairman James Morris, chief executive Simon Perry, and the board's Los Angeles-based film commissioner, Jonathan Loughran.

On the eve of the Oscars, John Carney's micro-budget Dublin musical, *Once*, saw off formidable competition when it was voted Best Foreign Film at the US Independent Spirit Awards. *Once* won again on Oscar night, with leading actors Glen Hansard and Markéta Irglova winning Best Original Song for their composition 'Falling Slowly'. More good news came when Irish citizen and resident Daniel Day-Lewis collected his second Best Actor Oscar for *There Will Be Blood*.

In Dublin, the Irish Film Censor's Office became the Irish Film Classification Office, ending an era during which Ireland operated one of the most draconian film censorship systems in the world. There was more good news for distributors and exhibitors when the dismal Irish summer weather boosted attendances significantly. The principal beneficiaries were *Mamma Mia!* (which now ranks second to Ireland's all-time box office champion, *Titanic*) and *The Dark Knight*.

The biggest Irish cinema hit over the first four months of 2008 was **In Bruges**, a UK/Irish co-production featuring Brendan Gleeson and Colin Farrell as a couple of Irish professional

Brendan Gleeson and Colin Farrell in Martin McDonagh's **In Bruges**

assassins hiding out in the eponymous Belgian medieval city. Both actors are on top form in this exuberant comedy-thriller, whose distinctive visual style and jet-black humour marked an assured feature debut for writer-director Martin McDonagh, who won an Oscar for his taut 2004 short, *Six Shooter*, which was shot in Ireland and also featured Gleeson.

Taking on a highly emotive and politically charged subject, Turner prize-winning British artist Steve McQueen has produced a thoughtfully considered and unflinching Northern Ireland drama with his first feature, **Hunger**. It deals with the ten IRA hunger strikers who died protesting against British rule in 1981. The dramatic focus is the group's

Michael Fassbender and Liam Cunningham in Steve McQueen's **Hunger**

leader, Bobby Sands, played by rising Irish actor, Michael Fassbender, in a powerfully expressive performance. McQueen and Enda Walsh, the Irish playwright who collaborated with him on the screenplay, approach the issues with clear concern for the human cost on both sides of the political divide. In its fascination with the human body as the final weapon of protest, *Hunger* takes on an inevitable contemporary relevance in the age of the suicide bomber. It earned McQueen the Camera d'Or award at Cannes.

Eileen Walsh in Declan Recks' **Eden**

Unusually, **Eden** went on Irish cinema release after its television debut. Opening out his stage play for the screen, writer Eugene O'Brien reveals the disintegrating marriage of an Irish couple (emotionally raw performances from Eileen Walsh and Aidan Kelly) over the week before their tenth wedding anniversary. Director Declan Recks dissects this relationship with subtlety and frankness in a film rooted in honesty and realism. Walsh received the Best Actress award when *Eden* received its US premiere at the Tribeca Film Festival in May 2008.

The annual Galway Film Fleadh, one of Ireland's three leading film festivals, was awash with new Irish features, shorts and documentaries. To nobody's surprise, its award for best new Irish feature went to writer-director Lance Daly for his endearing **Kisses**, which artfully blends tension and humour. Impressive newcomers Kelly O'Neill and Shane Curry play pre-teen neighbours impulsively escaping their drab Dublin housing estate and their dysfunctional families for an eventful long night's journey into day.

Ian FitzGibbon's **A Film with Me in It**

Replete with movie references and streaked with humour that turns pitch black, Ian FitzGibbon's **A Film with Me in It** was another Galway favourite. Mark Doherty, who scripted it, plays Mark, a luckless actor auditioning for a minor role in a Neil Jordan film. In a perfectly deadpan cameo, Jordan brusquely turns him down. Dylan Moran plays Pierce, Mark's best friend, a dissolute aspirant screenwriter and film director addicted to alcohol and gambling. Through an entertainingly outlandish series of coincidences, the odd couple find themselves caught up in a real-life drama more extreme than any of Pierce's pretentious screenplays.

Gerard Stembridge's **Alarm**

The protagonist of writer-director Gerard Stembridge's **Alarm** is a young woman, played with conviction by Ruth Bradley, who becomes unhinged by a series of creepy incidents after she buys a house on the outskirts of Dublin. Adrian Turner is engaging as the amorous young man she regards as her protector until her trust in him is also shaken. The consequences are not as compelling as the premise and are curiously lacking in tension.

Martin Duffy's **Summer of the Flying Saucer**

On a lighter note, Martin Duffy's **Summer of the Flying Saucer** takes place in rural Ireland in 1967, when teen student Danny (Robert Sheehan) shocks the conservative villagers with his new hippie appearance. They get much more to bother them when Danny befriends two aliens and introduces them to the locals as Janis Joplin and Jimi Hendrix. The scene is set for conflict between the prejudice and fear of difference in the village and the values of peace, love and understanding represented by Danny and the aliens in this amiable coming-of-age fantasy.

In a year that started so promisingly, the mood was distinctly less upbeat as 2008 drew to a close. Ireland's so-called Celtic Tiger economy, which had boomed for years, shuddered to a halt and the country headed towards recession. Although the Irish government introduced a harsh end-of-year financial budget, the Irish Film Board fared better than many state-supported bodies.

Chairman James Morris welcomed 'the retention of funding to the level of 2007' and said the board 'expects to maintain the current levels of production' in 2009. He estimated that IFB-funded film and TV projects contributed over €70 million to the Irish economy during 2008. These included the third series of Showtime's TV drama, *The Tudors*, with Irish actor Jonathan Rhys Meyers as the young King Henry VIII, and two new feature films starring Colin Farrell: as a war photo-journalist in Danis Tanovic's **Triage** and in Neil

Jordan's sixteenth feature, **Ondine**, in which Farrell plays a fisherman who finds a young woman (Alicja Bachleda) in his net.

The year's best films
Hunger (Steve McQueen)
In Bruges (Martin McDonagh)
Eden (Declan Recks)
Kisses (Lance Daly)
A Film with Me In It (Ian FitzGibbon)

Quote of the year
'I lost about 14 kilos and weighed 59 kilos by the end. It was the only way we could possibly do it and make it convincing. I felt as if I was anorexic. I became obsessed with food and counting calories.' *Irish actor* MICHAEL FASSBENDER *on playing IRA hunger striker Bobby Sands in* **Hunger**.

Directory
All Tel/Fax numbers begin (+353)
Film Institute of Ireland, 6 Eustace St, Dublin 2. Tel: (1) 679 5744. Fax: (1) 679 9657. www.fii.ie.
Irish Film Board, Rockfort House, St Augustine St, Galway, Co Galway. Tel: (91) 561 398. Fax: (91) 561 405. www.filmboard.ie.
Screen Directors Guild of Ireland, 18 Eustace St, Temple Bar, Dublin 2. Tel: (1) 633 7433. Fax: (1) 478 4807. info@sdgi.ie.

Lance Daly's **Kisses**

MICHAEL DWYER has been Film Correspondent of the *Irish Times* since 1988. He is chairman and co-founder of Dublin International Film Festival. In 2006 the French government appointed him as a Chevalier des Arts et des Lettres.

Israel Dan Fainaru

I f 2007 was the year of *The Band's Visit*, 2008 will most certainly go down as the year of **Waltz with Bashir**. Four years in the making, this unusual project was first shot as a documentary and then painstakingly transformed, frame by frame, into animation. On paper it looked suspicious. However, it turned out to be one of the most emotionally charged and powerful films released anywhere this year. Everything in it, from its look – more in the tradition of graphic books than film animation – its soundtrack, and of course the ever-increasing anguish generated by its narrative, makes the film quite unique.

Ari Folman's **Waltz with Bashir**

On the surface, it is the personal story of producer-director Ari Folman coming to terms with his own horrific memories of the Lebanon War in the 1980s; memories he has supressed for over twenty years and is now trying to recall through a series of interviews with friends and acquaintances who served with him at the time. But beyond that, it is an uncompromising indictment by an Israeli against himself, as he faces the fact that neither he nor any of his colleagues and friends did anything to stop the massacre of Palestinian refugees at the hand of the Christian Lebanese forces. No scoop, to be sure, but a public confession of well-known

facts, which was troubling enough to cause several Israeli exhibitors to refrain from showing it, at least for the first few months of the film's domestic distribution. Of course, no such reticence was noticed abroad, where Folman has been the toast of every festival at which the film has screened. Its commercial release in France was a triumph and, judging by the interest displayed around the world, it is likely to become one of the most successful Israeli films ever.

As eloquent, though less immediately effective, Avi Mograbi's documentary **Z-32** takes the premise of Folman's film one step further. It is no longer about Israeli soldiers watching others commit genocide; it is about confessing the crimes they have committed themselves. Mograbi interviews a member of an elite unit who gives a detailed account of how he executed a number of unsuspecting Palestinian policemen, in order to avenge the shooting of several Israeli soldiers. Interspersed with the interview are sequences of the soldier discussing with his girlfriend whether he deserves to be called a murderer, as well as Mograbi's own signature addresses to camera. Throughout the film, the faces of both the interviewee and his girlfriend are hidden by digital masks to prevent their being

The masked subjects of Avi Mograbi's documentary **Z-32**

identified. Interestingly, this effect places the film within a much larger context, where such tragedies are not exclusive to the conflict in the Middle East.

Lemon Tree, *directed by Eran Riklis*

Still on political issues, Eran Riklis's **Lemon Tree** (*Etz Limon*), acclaimed at the Berlin Film Festival but less appreciated at home, is an eminently worthy film. However, the story of a poor Palestinian widow deprived of her lemon grove by absurd Israeli security measures, following the Israeli Minister of Defence's relocation to land across the border from her, never extends beyond its manipulative plot, in which supreme Israeli arrogance is no match for a traditional Palestinian. However, a powerful performance by Hiam Abbass as the widow lends some scenes an emotional depth beyond the original reach of the script.

On a much more personal level, Eitan Green's whimsical three-part family portrait, **It All Begins at Sea**, displays the skill of a filmmaker who believes that the best direction is the direction you never notice.

Eitan Green's **It All Begins at Sea**

Green skilfully takes the viewer on a journey through three stories, several years apart, each featuring the same characters. It could be defined as a coming-of-age picture, a family drama or even a reflection on life and death. Avoiding pretention or unnecessary complexity, the film presents a series of subtly drawn relationships. However, this approach has previously limited the appeal of Green's films to audiences seeking more in character development than the banality of a conventional soap opera, instead revealing the intricate layers of emotion that both define and connect his characters.

Ronit and Shlomi Elkabetz's **Seven Days**

Ronit and Shlomi Elkabetz returned to the same formula and background, the Moroccan community in Israel, that worked so well for them in their 2004 hit, *To Take a Wife*. **Seven Days** (*Shiva*) even uses many of the same characters. The result is an ensemble piece that plays like a stage adaptation. It follows on three years after *To Take a Wife*, when one of the heroine's brothers has died and the family gather together for the traditional seven-day wake. Tradition does not permit anyone to leave the house, creating a claustrophobic environment. When politics is introduced into the mix, passions overflow and the characters' frustrations and jealousies are aired with a bitterness and anger. Expanding the canvass of their previous film, with each character given their own set-piece, it looks and sounds terribly authentic. Although they cover the territory with confidence, there are ultimately too many characters in the drama to satisfy as a whole.

The stellar cast, including Ronit, Moshe Ivgi, Alon Aboutboul, Keren Mor, Yael Abecassis and Hana Azoulay, show that star power is still a major factor with Israeli audiences. The film notched up 100,000 admissions in its first fortnight. Initial screenings in France indicate that the picture may also prove solid outside its own territory.

However, if this report sounds unusually upbeat, a final, darker note needs to be added. The Film Law, introduced in 2001 and seen as responsible for the tremendous upsurge of Israeli cinema, is under threat. Until recently, it was regulated by agreement between the Treasury and the Film Council. That expired in December and the Treasury has intimated that they intend to cut up to 60% of the budget. With the impending Israeli election and the state of the global economy, a solution to this potential crisis is no longer clear.

The year's best films
Waltz with Bashir (Ari Folman)
Z-32 (Avi Mograbi)
It All Begins at Sea (Eitan Green)
Seven Days (Ronit and Shlomi Elkabetz)
Lemon Tree (Eran Riklis)

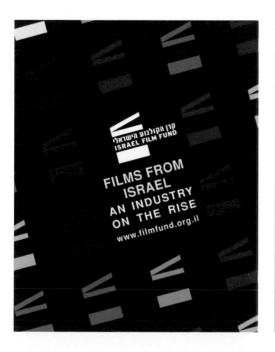

Ari Folman's **Waltz with Bashir**

Quote of the year
'If we wish to go on being relevant on the international scene, our only hope is to uncover new talent. There is plenty of it around, all it needs is to be given the chance to express itself.' *Producer* MAREK ROZENBAUM.

Directory
All Tel/Fax numbers begin (+972)
Israel Film Archive, Jerusalem Film Centre, Derech Hebron, PO Box 8561, Jerusalem 91083. Tel: (2) 565 4333. Fax: (2) 565 4335. jer-cin@jer-cin. org.il. www.jer-cin.org.il.
Israel Film Fund, 12 Yehudith Blvd, Tel Aviv 67016. Tel: (2) 562 8180. Fax: (2) 562 5992. info@filmfund. org.il. www.filmfund.org.il.
Israeli Film Council, 14 Hamasger St, PO Box 57577, Tel Aviv 61575. Tel: (3) 636 7288. Fax: (3) 639 0098. etic@most.gov.il.
Tel Aviv Cinema Project, 29 Idelson St, Tel Aviv 65241. Tel. (2) 525 5020. info@cinemaproject.co.il. www.cinemaproject.org.il.
The New Fund for Cinema and Television, 112 Hayarkon St, Tel Aviv. Tel. (3) 522 0909. info@nfct. org.il. www.nfct.org.ilx

DAN FAINARU is co-editor of Israel's only film magazine, *Cinematheque*, and a former director of the Israeli Film Institute. He reviews regularly for *Screen International*.

Italy Lorenzo Codelli

Attracting international accolades and two major awards at the Cannes Film Festival, Matteo Garrone's **Gomorrah** and Paolo Sorrentino's **Il divo** spearheaded an uplifting year for Italian cinema, one very much at odds with the country's social and political turmoil.

The market share for local films rose from 23% in 2007 to almost 33% in 2008. The commercial successes notwithstanding, unflinching films like *Gomorrah* and *Il divo* had a huge impact, attracting audiences of two million and 800,000 respectively. However, this success failed to prevent Silvio Berlusconi's government from cutting funds for the film industry, as well as many other cultural sectors; nor did it accelerate a film law that has been in discussion for some time.

The Rome International Film Festival – whose management, like Rome's municipality, suddenly shifted from centre-left to far-right – organised a series of panels called 'General States of Italian Cinema' as a way to postpone any real decisions and to paper over more cuts carried out by ministries and public institutions. Paradoxically, both the Rome and Venice festivals, spendthrift rivals separated by only a few weeks, were ordered 'to support and herald Italian cinema' by the same politicians who are trying to bury it. These same politicians protect, with the utmost diligence, their omnipotent boss's TV empire. Which is not to say that our beloved plutocrat doesn't enjoy films. Berlusconi himself declared that he was very fond of Giuseppe Tornatore's €25 million-plus Sicilian extravaganza **Baaria**, which will be released in spring 2009. Interestingly, the company that made the film, Medusa, belongs to him.

Matteo Garrone's **Gomorrah**

The mighty Medusa has updated its strategy, choosing to release in mid-summer and November – two of the quieter periods in the Italian film calendar – the same kind of cheap farces that made tycoon Aurelio de Laurentiis the 'King of Christmas' ('Cinepanettoni'). Aimed squarely at low-brow audiences, **A Summer at Sea** (*Un'estate al mare*), directed by Carlo Vanzina and starring a group of comedians, and Enrico Oldoini's **Daddy's Fiancée** (*La fidanzata di papà*) were heavily advertised and released simultaneously in multiplexes across the country. De Laurentiis's veteran yes-man Neri Parenti directed frantic jester Christian De Sica in **Christmas in Rio de Janeiro** (*Natale a Rio de Janeiro*), a film more predictable and tiresome than any yuletide customs.

The teen weepie, another mini-trend popular at the box office, scored another success with debutant director Silvio Muccino's **Let's Talk About Love** (*Parlami d'amore*), adapted from his autobiographical novel. Ex-pat filmmaker Gabriele Muccino's younger brother Silvio also stars, as a poor youngster tormented by his mature lover. Despite the lousy performance and direction, the blond Casanova was enthusiastically endorsed by his mostly female

fan base. The relationship between an older man and younger woman drove Federico Moccia's **Sorry But I Call You Love** (*Scusa ma ti chiamo amore*). At least Moccia, Italy's bestselling novelist and son of late comedy director Pipolo, employs an unpretentious approach to pulp that his many imitators fail to grasp. He has little to say about generational differences but knows how to coat his stories. Carlo Verdone, the official inheritor of Alberto Sordi's Roman humour, returns to his comic roots with the satirical **Big, Bad and... Verdone** (*Grande, grosso e... Verdone*). The chameleon-like writer-actor-director once again plays three of his favourite characters, although the film shows how the previously biting comedian has mellowed, in a film whose success owes much to Aurelio De Laurentiis's marketing campaign.

With its Academy Award hopes high, *Gomorrah* may not be the 'Neorealism Redux' as Martin Scorsese has claimed. However, Matteo Garrone's film expertly translates to cinema Roberto Saviano's daring pamphlet against the Camorra, the criminal organisation that is devastating Naples and much of the country. It was shot in the "hoods' where boy killers and drug lords dominate, at times making them play themselves, and is narrated through five parallel stories, similar to Roberto Rossellini's classic *Paisà* (a sixth story was written, but Garrone did not shoot it). With its violent prologue, a massacre shot in garish white, blue and yellow, and non-stop action, a sense of doom prevails over all the film's

characters, who are struggling to survive the daily inferno. Toni Servillo's episode in particular underlines the connections between industry, corruption and the insidious cancer of the Camorra's influence.

By complete contrast, Paolo Sorrentino instead chooses a Honoré Daumier pencil to shape the narrative of *Il divo*, his vengeful, larger-than-life caricature of diabolical politician Giulio Andreotti and his cohorts (for more on this, read the profile of Sorrentino in the 'Directors of the Year' section earlier in this volume).

Gianni Di Gregorio's **Mid-August Lunch**

Garrone also produced *Gomorrah* co-screenwriter Gianni Di Gregorio's **Mid-August Lunch** (*Pranzo di ferragosto*). Premiered at Venice Critics' Week, it received the De Laurentiis Award for the best first work from any section. Costing less than €500,000, it stars Di Gregorio himself as an ageing alcoholic taking care of his elderly mother in a decaying Rome apartment. To pay off some debts he agrees to nurse three more old women, whose relatives are leaving town to enjoy August bank holiday. Following a series of amusing misunderstandings, the female community becomes protective of their guardian. It is a charming portrait of senility, masterfully played by non-professional actors and directed with aplomb by Di Gregorio. The sleeper of the year, earning €2 million in its first two months of release, Di Gregorio was also awarded the Satyajit Ray Award at the London Film Festival.

Toni Servillo as Giulio Andreotti in Paolo Sorrentino's **Il divo**

Marco Pontecorvo's **PA-RA-DA**

Marco Pontecorvo, son of late filmmaker Gillo Pontecorvo, debuted with **PA-RA-DA**, a moving drama about a brave French circus clown (Jalil Lespert) trying to save homeless children in post-Ceausescu Bucarest. Tiro Stefano Tummolini produced and directed the zero-budget **One Day in a Life** (*Un altro pianeta*), an unconventional dramedy about a group of homosexuals and heterosexuals stranded on a Roman beach. Renowned Turinese novelist Alessandro Baricco's **Lesson 21** (*Lezione 21*), shot with a large English-speaking cast, voices the author's deep admiration for Beethoven's music and fame, as well as for Peter Greenaway's kind of art cinema. *Full Monty* producer Uberto Pasolini's directorial debut, **Machan**, is set in Sri Lanka and follows a group of poor people desperate to emigrate, who pretend to be a professional handball team in order to be invited to play in Germany. It is based on a true story. Chile-born Marco Bechis' visually striking **Birdwatchers** (*La terra degli uomini rossi*), obviously influenced by Werner Herzog's Latin American expeditions, deals with conflicts between Mato Grosso natives and land exploiters. Sadly, Bechis simplifies both sides, losing both narrative and pathos deep in the Brazilian jungle.

Nanni Moretti received a tribute and comprehensive retrospective at the Locarno Film Festival, where he premiered his new short, **Filmquiz**. It is an impressive account of a life spent inside cinemas. Moretti's performance in Antonello Grimaldi's **Quiet Chaos** (*Caos calmo*) was something of a novelty, considering he wasn't directing or playing himself. He is understated as a widower unable to cope with his wife's sudden death. Inspired by Sandro Veronesi's psycho-erotic bestseller, the movie would have been served better by Moretti the director than Grimaldi's flat style. Booed at the Berlin Film Festival, *Quiet Chaos* sold more than one million tickets domestically.

Antonello Grimaldi's **Quiet Chaos**

Ferzan Özpetek's **A Perfect Day** (*Un giorno perfetto*), and Pupi Avati's **Giovanna's Dad** (*Il papà di Giovanna*) both played out like the kind of bland melodrama normally associated with TV. Whereas Özpetek falls into clichés and bathos describing a husband's (Valerio Mastandrea) revenge against his ex-wife, Avati piously chronicles the tragedy of a father (Silvio Orlando) helping his murderous daughter (Alba Rohrwacher) to endure life in 1930s Italy. Orlando's candid performance earned him the Best Actor award at the Venice Film Festival.

Giulio Manfredonia's exuberant and heartwarming **You Can Make It** (*Si può fare*) sees the inmates of Italian asylums released into society and forming a tile-making co-operative. In **All of the Life Ahead** (*Tutta la vita davanti*) Paolo Virzì peppers his account of short-term workers at a pitiless call-centre with unnervingly kitsch musical numbers, his broad asides attacking employers but sparing those working for them. As well as playing a repressed manager in Virzì's film, 28-year-old Elio Germano was busy this year, appearing as a droll radio DJ in Francesco Patierno's **The

Early Bird Catches the Worm (*Il mattino ha l'oro in bocca*), a greedy poker player in Daniele Vicari's **The Past is a Foreign Land** (*Il passato è una terra straniera*) and a half-wit misfit in Gabriele Salvatores' **As God Orders** (*Come Dio comanda*). This fractious, fragile icon appears ideal for uncertain times like ours.

Vulnerable immigrants' topics are superficially grazed by Cristina Comencini's **Black and White** (*Bianco e nero*) and by Francesco Munzi's **The Rest of the Night** (*Il resto della notte*). However, *Gomorrah* remains the film that digs deeper into the barriers that exist between foreigners and Italians.

93-year-old *maestro della commedia* Mario Monicelli received an extensive retrospective at the San Sebastián Film Festival. His first documentary, **Near the Coliseum There is Monti** (*Vicino al Colosseo c'è Monti*), devoted to the ancient Roman neighbourhood named Monti (where the director lives in a Spartan flat), is a wonderful, all-too-short hymn to life and its many pleasures. Marco Tullio Giordana presented an ambitious fresco on the Fascist era, its catastrophes and its 'divi' with **Wild Blood** (*Sanguepazzo*). Luca Zingaretti and Monica Bellucci are convincing as Osvaldo Valenti and Luisa Ferida, movie stars who were executed by partisans in the final hours of the Second World War. A clever allegory, questioning contemporary mass-media myths and their forgotten roots, Giordana's political analysis is as elaborate as it was in *The Best of Youth*. *Wild Blood* performed poorly, but is

likely to attract a larger audience as a TV mini-series, longer in length and widening its scope even more.

Among 2009's most awaited titles are Pupi Avati's **Margherita Bar's Friends** (*Gli amici del bar Margherita*), Giorgio Diritti's **The Man Who Will Come** (*L'uomo che verrà*) and Marco Bellocchio's **To Win** (*Vincere*).

The year's best films
Gomorrah (Matteo Garrone)
Il divo (Paolo Sorrentino)
Wild Blood (Marco Tullio Giordana)
Mid-August Lunch (Gianni Di Gregorio)

Quote of the year
'It's aesthetics which produces ethics.'
Gomorrah director MATTEO GARRONE.

Directory
All Tel/Fax numbers begin (+39)
Audiovisual Industry Promotion-Filmitalia, Via Aureliana 63, 00187 Rome. Tel: (06) 4201 2539. Fax: (06) 4200 3530. www.aip-filmitalia.com.
Cineteca del Comune, Via Riva di Reno, 40122 Bologna. Tel: (051) 204 820. www.cinetecadibologna.it.
Cineteca del Friuli, Via Bini 50, Palazzo Gurisatti, 33013 Gemona del Friuli, Udine. Tel: (04) 3298 0458. Fax: (04) 3297 0542. cdf@cinetecadelfriuli. org. http://cinetecadelfriuli.org.
Cineteca Nazionale, Via Tuscolana 1524, 00173 Rome. Tel: (06) 722 941. www.snc.it.
Fondazione Cineteca Italiana, Villa Reale, Via Palestro 16, 20121 Milan. Tel: (02) 799 224. Fax: (02) 798 289. info@cinetecamilano.it. www.cinetecamilano.it.
Fondazione Federico Fellini, Via Oberdan 1, 47900 Rimini. Tel (0541) 50085. Fax: (0541) 57378. fondazione@federicofellini.it. www.federicofellini.it/.
Museo Nazionale del Cinema, Via Montebello 15, 10124 Turin. Tel: (011) 812 2814. www.museonazionaledelcinema.org.

Monica Bellucci in Marco Tullio Giordana's **Wild Blood**

LORENZO CODELLI is on the board of Cineteca del Friuli, a Cannes Film Festival adviser and a regular contributor to *Positif* and other cinema-related publications.

Japan Katsuta Tomomi

Over four hundred local films were released across three thousand screens in 2008, a similar number to 2007. Last year's box office share of 47.7% for domestic releases has also remained more or less the same. After a decade in which studios frequently joined forces with TV networks on large-scale mainstream films, the audience's desire to see more adventurous fare has influenced cautious producers to approach less conventional material.

Sakamoto Junji's **The Children of Dark**

Sakamoto Junji's **The Children of Dark** (*Yami no Kodomotachi*) tackles paedophilia and illegal organ transplants in Thailand. Based on the novel by Yan Sogil, a journalist's investigation into a liver transplant donation to a seriously ill Japanese child uncovers the merciless reality of impoverished young children in Thailand, who are forced into prostitution and even giving up their organs. Filmed in documentary style and based on detailed research, the film shocked Japanese audiences. Opening modestly at five cinemas, strong reviews and word-of-mouth led to screenings at over a hundred venues. Thai censors banned the film from the Bangkok International Film Festival just prior to its screening.

Kadoi Hajime's **Vacation**

72-year-old Wakamatsu Koji sheds light on the history of the leftist students' movement in **United Red Army – The Path to Asama Mountain Lodge** (*Jitsuroku rengô sekigun: Asama sansô e no*). It is an account of the notorious shootout between several members of theUnited Red Army, who were besieged at a mountain lodge in 1972 by police. Wakamatsu's three-hour film, based on an account by a participant in the siege, offers audiences the chance to hear the revolutionaries' side of the story for the first time. The death penalty was the subject of Kadoi Hajime's **Vacation** (*Kyuuka*). Although obfuscating the debate over capital punishment, Kadoi was effective in capturing daily life in the prison and presenting details

Hyugaji Taro's **Grave of the Fireflies**

of how executions are carried out, which had previously not been known outside the system. Hyugaji Taro directed **Grave of the Fireflies** (*Hotaru no Haka*), about young siblings' struggle for survival during the Second World War. Based on a novel by Nosaka Akiyuki, the story is famous because of the animated adaptation directed by Takahata Isao. Hyugaji's version remains faithful to the original story while skilfully avoiding sentimentality.

Departure, *directed by Takita Yojiro*

Departure (*Okuribito*) is a story of a man employed to clean dead bodies and place them in their coffins. Motoki Masahiro plays the *nokanshi*, whose daily routines are examined in their every detail by prolific director Takita Yojiro. Exploring Japanese attitudes to life and death, the film surprised its distributor, Shochiku, when it earned US$19 million at the box office. It went on to win the Grand Prix at the Montreal World Film Festival.

The controversy over the modest documentary **Yasukuni** revealed that there were still areas some considered too sensitive to be covered by a film. Yasukuni is Japan's war shrine, dedicated to the soldiers killed during the Second World War, including war criminals executed by the Allies after the conflict had ended. For right-wing elements it is a sacred place for war heroes, but for victims of the Japanese army it is a symbol of their humiliation. Chinese director Li Ying, who has worked in Japan for more than a decade, filmed people visiting the shrine, from fanatical worshippers to rabid protestors. Just before its opening in April, a conservative politician

commented that 'it could be anti-Japanese'. One cinema was picketed by a member of a rightist group, harassing anyone who entered it. Soon after, all five of the cinemas that planned to show the film cancelled it, fearing a backlash by protestors. The media and organisations, such as the Directors' Guild of Japan, spoke out against such intimidation and the film was eventually screened at twenty other cinemas. Athough state- or industry-sponsored censorship does not exist in Japan, the controversy highlighted the precarious situation filmmakers can find themseles in.

Younger filmmakers seem less interested in carving their own signature style in film than appealing to the broadest of audience tastes. Tanada Yuki's **One Million Yen Girl** (*Hyakuman yen to Nigamushi Onna*) is an endearing and light-hearted comedy about a young woman's (Aoi Yu) refusal to lead a life of apathy and indifference. **After School** (*Afutâ sukûru*) is Uchida Kenji's follow-up to the successful *A Stranger of Mine*. A fast-paced crime comedy, the 36-year-old director keeps the audience's attention with a series of clever twists. Born in 1980, Ikeda Chihiro studied under Kitano Takeshi and Kurosawa Kiyoshi. His remarkable debut, **The Woman in the Room at the South-east Corner Upstairs** (*Tonan Kadobeya Nikai no Onna*), features outstanding performances from a cast of newcomers and veterans (including Nishijima Hidetoshi, Kase Ryo, Kagawa Kyoko and Takahashi Masaya) as occupants of an old apartment building who are trying to make their way in the world.

Aoi Yu in Tanada Yuki's **One Million Yen Girl**

At the 65th Venice Film Festival, three internationally acclaimed Japanese masters, Miyazaki Hayao, Oshii Mamoru and Kitano Takeshi, presented their new films. Miyazaki's **Ponyo on the Cliff by the Sea** (*Gake no ue no Ponyo*) is about a five-year-old boy's friendship with a fish princess who longs to become human. Lacking the multi-layered ethical complexity of *Princess Mononoke* or the ambivalent attitude towards civilisation in *Spirited Away*, the film tells a more conventional story. Nevertheless, its stunning imagery and strong emotional content make for irresistible entertainment. With ten million admissions and topping the domestic box office for seven weeks, the film's US$144 million revenue made it the most successful film of the year.

Mamoru Oshii's **The Sky Crawlers**

Oshii's animated **The Sky Crawlers** (*Sukai kurora*) is a sci-fi drama about a young pilot, fighting in a corporate-sponsored reality wargame, who never grows up. Contrary to *Ponyo on the Cliff by the Sea*, whose hand-drawn imagery is full of optimism, Oshii's colour-drained, computer-generated visuals are bleakly pessimistic. As creatively brilliant as Miyazaki's film, *The Sky Crawlers* failed to ignite the Japanese box office.

Kitano's **Achilles and the Tortoise** (*Akiresu to Kame*) is the final part of his self-reflective trilogy. With a more linear narrative than *Takenshis'* or *Glory to the Filmmaker!*, telling the tragicomic story of a talentless painter, the film was welcomed more by critics than audiences.

Kabei – Our Mother, directed by Yamada Yoji

Other internationally renowned directors released new films that grapple with family virtue in a harsh and gloomy reality. One of the most popular and celebrated directors in Japan, Yamada Yoji's eightieth film, **Kabei – Our Mother** (*Kabei*), is a portrait of a woman who lived alone with her little daughters during the Second World War. Starring box office attraction Yoshinaga Sayuri, Yamada presented audiences with an emotionally involving film whose anti-war sentiment was unmistakeable. Kurosawa Kiyoshi's **Tokyo Sonata** moved away from the director's conventional horror fare, instead exploring the unsettling world of a family on the brink of collapse and how even the closest relationship can draw out feelings of alienation.

Kurosawa Kiyoshi's **Tokyo Sonata**

Kore-eda Hirokazu's **Still Walking** (*Aruitemo, Aruitemo*) is another accurate portrait of an average Japanese family. A middle-aged brother and sister accompany their family on a visit to their ageing parents, on the fifteenth anniversary of their brother's death. Kore-eda expertly depicts the love, resentment and

Kore-eda Hirokazu's **Still Walking**

secrets that bind a family together. And in Hashiguchi Ryosuke's **All Around Us** (*Gururi no Koto*), a courtroom artist and his wife, suffering from depression following a miscarriage, struggle to keep their relationship alive.

Toho continue to dominate the Japanese market. Their total box office revenue for 2008 is estimated at a record US$576.9 million, nearly a third of the Japanese total. Franchised animation such as *Doraemon* and *Pokemon* remained strong, each with more than US$28.8 million in revenue. As for the adaptations of popular mangas, Ishii Yasuharu's **Boys Over Flowers** (*Hana yori Danshi F*), based on Kamio Yoko's long-selling manga, earned US$72 million, while Tsutsumi Yukihiko and Urasawa Naoki's **20th Century Boys** (*20 Seiki Shonen*) earned more than US$38 million. Besides these pre-formatted projects, Mitani Kouki's hilarious screwball comedy, **The Magic Hour** (*Za majikku awâ*) drew US$38 million in ticket sales. Toei, the smallest of the three major corporations, scored with Izumi Seiji's **The Partners: The Movie** (*Aibo; Gekijouban*), a TV spin-off that grossed US$42 million.

2009 will likely continue the current trend, in terms of both mainstream and independent film. Popular screenwriter Kimizuka Ryoichi will release his second feature **Nobody to Watch Over Me** (*Daremo Mamotte Kurenai*), which was awarded the Best Screenplay Award at the Montreal World Film Festival. Acclaimed cinematographer Kimura Daisaku has directed

his first feature, **Tsurugidaki; Recording the Controlling point** (*Tsurugidake; Ten no Ki*), and internationally renowned actor Yakusho Koji recently completed his directorial debut, **Frog's Oil** (*Gama no Abura*).

The year's best films
Still Walking (Kore-eda Hirokazu)
Tokyo Sonata (Kurosawa Kiyoshi)
The Magic Hour (Mitani Kouki)
The Children of Dark (Sakamoto Junji)
One Million Yen Girl (Tanada Yuki)

Quote of the year
'I shot this film from the point of view of the suppressed people, not the authorities. When the incident happened, the police controlled all the information and manipulated the mass who watched it live into detesting the activists. However, I wrote the script based on what I heard from the person at the actual scene and I tried to tell the true story of what happened inside the lodge.' WAKAMATSU KOJI, *explaining the intention of making United* **Red Army – The Path to Asama Mountain Lodge**

Directory
All Tel/Fax numbers begin (+81)
Kawakita Memorial Film Institute, Kawakita Memorial Bldg, 18 Ichiban-cho, Chiyoda-ku, Tokyo 102-0082. Tel: 3265 3281. Fax: 3265 3276. info@ kawakita-film.or.jp. www.kawakita-film.or.jp.

Kanako Higuchi, star of Takeshi Kitano's **Achilles and the Tortoise**

KATSUTA TOMOMI is a reporter for *The Mainichi Shimbun*, one of the largest-circulation newspapers in Japan.

Kazakhstan Gulnara Abikeyeva

Following the Kazakh film industry's 7% share of the domestic market in 2007, two recent releases were seen as symbolic of how local revenue is growing. Akhan Sataev's crime drama **The Racketeer** doubled in box office revenue what was spent on its budget. Secondly, Rustem Abdrashev's **A Gift to Stalin** was pre-sold to eleven countries at Berlin's Film Market before it had even been completed. Both are unprecedented, with investors looking favourably on the profit that can be generated from the film industry. However, films made for international audiences differ significantly from those aimed at a domestic release.

Ashat Kuchinchirekov in Sergey Dvortsevoi's **Tulpan**

Independent Kazakh film producers have understood the lessons of entering international markets. Whether for festival entry or distribution, co-productions are a preferable form of film financing. Though no less a 'Kazakh' film than any other release, Sergey Dvortsevoi's **Tulpan** benefited greatly from the support of Karl Baumgartner (Germany) and Sergey Selyanov (Russia), as well as Kazakh producer Gulnara Sarsenova. An account of the harsh life experienced by a group of villagers who live in the deserts of Betpak-Dala, it won the 'Un Certain Regard' award at the Cannes Film Festival. It is also Kazakhstan's Oscar entry for Best Foreign

Language Film. Gulnara Sarsenova, who produced *Mongol*, was awarded the 'Female of the Year in Asian Cinema' at the Pusan Film Festival in South Korea.

A Gift to Stalin opened the Pusan festival. Abdrashev's Kazakhstan/Russia/Israel co-production tells the story of a young Jewish boy surviving on the Kazakh Steppes at the end of the 1940s. Other films aimed at the international market are Ardak Amirkulov's adaptation of Chingiz Aitmatov's novel, **Farewell, Gulsary** and Marat Sarulu's psychological drama about the relationship between two families, **Songs from the Southern Seas**.

Films for the domestic market are either commercially oriented, such as Sataev's *The Racketeer* and Sabit Kurmanbekov's comedy, **Auerelen**, or draw on national themes and receive significant support from the state.

Satybaldy Narymbetov's two-part **Mustafa Shokai** was made over five years. Financed entirely by the Kazakh government, the film was shot in France, Turkey, the Czech Republic, Azerbaijan and Kazakhstan. The film tells the story of Mustafa Shokai, a major political figure in Turkestan during the first

Satybaldy Narymbetov's **Mustafa Shokai**

half of the twentieth century and is seen as crucial to understanding Kazakh identity. He opposed Soviet intervention in Kazakhstan and later refused to join Hitler. Danyar Salamat's **Together with the Father** is a touching psychological drama about a boy whose relationship with his father develops following his mother's departure with a wealthier man.

Films for 2009 include Ermek Tursynov's mountain-set drama **Kelin**, Gaziz Nasyrov's **FEF**, Aktan Arym Kubat's Mohsen Makhmalbaf-scripted **Winter, Fall** and Doskhan Zholzhaksynov's nineteenth-century historical drama, **Birzhan-sal**.

Ermek Tursynov's **Kelin**

The year's best films
A Gift to Stalin (Rustem Abdrashev)
Tulpan (Sergey Dvortsevoi)
Together with the Father (Danyar Salamat)
Mustafa Shokai (Satybaldy Narymbetov)

Quote of the year
'The basket can never be empty. It is filled with emptiness. Enough of reading Harry Potter and watching American films. Our young generation, finally, has to start reading our Kazakh books and watching our Kazakh films.' *Screenwriter* ERMEK TURSYNOV.

GULNARA ABIKEYEVA is a Kazakh film researcher and film critic, and an author of five books about the cinema of Central Asia. She is Art Director of the 'Eurasia' film festival in Almaty, Kazakhstan.

pbk £18.99 / $29.50
978-1-903364-83-3

THE CINEMA OF RUSSIA AND THE FORMER SOVIET UNION

Edited by Birgit Beumers
Preface by Sergei Bodrov

This volume explores the cinema of the former Soviet Union and contemporary Russia, ranging from the pre-Revolutionary period to the present day. It offers an insight into the development of Soviet film, from 'the most important of all arts' as a propaganda tool to a means of entertainment in the Stalin era, from the rise of its 'dissident' art-house cinema in the 1960s through the glasnost era with its broken taboos to recent Russian blockbusters. Films have been chosen to represent both the classics of Russian and Soviet cinema as well as those films that had a more localised success and remain part of Russia's cultural reference system. The volume also covers a range of national film industries of the former Soviet Union in chapters on the greatest films and directors of Ukrainian, Kazakh, Georgian and Armenian cinematography. Films discussed include *Strike* (1925), *Earth* (1930), *Ivan's Childhood* (1962), *Mother and Son* (1997) and *Brother* (1997).

'Typically, the Russian volume ... avoids, where possible, the too obvious, or too voluminously written-about ... Typically, too, the thematic content is rich, if – in the context of ten-page articles – succinct and introductory.' – Wally Hammond, *Time Out*

'The analysis of the twenty-four listed films gives the reader a look into the progress of the Soviet film industry. It is lucidly written and imaginative [making] a great addition to other volumes on the subject.' – David A. Ellis, *Cinema Technology*

www.wallflowerpress.co.uk

Latvia Andris Rozenbergs

The past remains a rich area for Latvian cinema. **Defenders of Riga**, by Aigars Grauba and Andrejs Ēķis, is the first Latvian feature to be shot in High Definition. It takes place during a crucial moment in Latvian history when, in 1918, a small army liberated Riga from German and Russian forces. A success at home, it is only the second Latvian film in sixteen years to be submitted for consideration in the Best Foreign Language Film category at the Academy Awards.

Aigars Grauba and Andrejs Ēķis's **Defenders of Riga**

Together with the aid of editor Maija Selecka, Romualds Pipars' **Other Side of the Coin** recreates Latvian life prior to independence. Using 8mm amateur film – the only footage free from censorship at the time – the documentary recalls long-forgotten details of how things used to be.

In a number of documentaries, Dzintra Geka has recorded the testimonies of people who were deported to Siberia as children. **Igarka and Taurenis** is perhaps the best of these, due in no small part to Nadježda Ariņa, a woman of overwhelming sincerity and kindness. She embarks on a trip to Igarka, a Siberian town in the very north of the Arctic Circle – where temperatures can reach minus seventy

Dzintra Geka's documentary **Igarka and Taurenis**

degrees – where she was born and her mother is buried. There, she meets her childhood friend, Anatoly Taurenis, who is unemployed and an alcoholic. 'Taurenis' means 'butterfly' in Latvian, and the character looks equally as fragile. During Nadježda's stay, he pulls himself together and, on their parting, dedicates a poem to her, intimating that he was once in love with her.

In **The Soviet Story**, supported by the European Nation Group of the EP, Edvīns Šņore uses previously unseen footage to examine the philosophical and political relationship between the Soviet Union and Nazi Germany. It received the Mass Impact Award at the Boston Film Festival, while in

Edvīns Šņore's **The Soviet Story**

Russia demonstrators burned an effigy of the director outside the Latvian Embassy.

Peteris Krilovs' **Deconstruction of an Artist** is dedicated to the Latvia-born constructivist artist Gustav Klucis, who contributed much to the style of Soviet propaganda art, but due to his national origin was executed in 1938. The director's father – a member of independent Latvia's clandestine provisional government – was also executed by the Soviets, and Peteris, like Klucis's son, had to change his family name in order to escape persecution. The resulting film is a painfully personal reflection on both the role of artists and national identity.

Peteris Krilovs' **Deconstruction of an Artist**

Even animators engaged with history. Jānis Cimmermanis's bitterly ironic **Latvian** presents a potted history of Latvia from the thirteenth century to the present. In it, the Latvian is a naïve lad, sitting on his doorstep and playing a zither, while battling invaders from East and West force him to side with them, always to his misfortune. Weary of conflict, he builds a fence around his hut, hanging a sign on the door: 'Don't disturb!'

Signe Baumane's **The Vet**

One other animated film is worth mentioning: Signe Baumane's **The Vet**. With simple drawings she presents a parable about a veterinary surgeon whose heart is broken by the violence and hatred in the world. What is most important is treating your fellow creatures well. Perhaps she's right.

The year's best films
Deconstruction of an Artist (Peteris Krilovs)
Other Side of the Coin (Romualds Pipars)
Igarka and Taurenis (Dzintra Geka)
John Dored's Island (Dzintra Geka)
Stuck in Stikine (Ugis Olte)

Quote of the year
'I cannot be in a state of permanent erection for five and more years uninterruptedly.' *Film director* **PETERIS KRILOVS** *on the long periods one has to wait to get a project financed.*

ANDRIS ROZENBERGS is Head of the Film Registry at Latvia's National Film Centre, and has directed seven fiction films and a dozen documentaries.

Luxembourg Boyd van Hoeij

Luxembourg is one of the few countries where international co-productions are the lifeblood of the film industry and local films are very rare. The subsidised film sector attracts international talent to its sound stages and magnificent outdoor locations. Most of the films in which Luxembourg is the primary producing nation are documentaries or shorts, with fiction features amounting to no more than one or two a year.

But things are slowly changing. Films produced in Luxembourg are now more often European co-productions rather than US/Luxembourg productions. The revamped financing law of 2007 should keep Luxembourg competitive, as it has abolished the rule that part of the film has to be shot on Luxembourg soil in order to qualify for rebates (it now only needs to have Luxembourg residents on the payroll). This helps keep talent closer to home, as countries such as Belgium, France, the Netherlands and Switzerland are now the main co-production partners on foreign films. International titles such as *Bride Flight*, *JCVD*, *Diamant 13*, *Ne te retourne pas*, *Humains*, *Vampire Party*, *Robber Girls*, *Dragon Hunters* and *The Children of Timpelbach* were recently co-produced by Luxembourg.

It is telling of the size of Luxembourg that even local features often have a foreign component. The most successful Luxembourg film of the year was **Charlotte: A Royal at War** (*Léif Lëtzebuerger*), a documentary about the period the Luxembourg Grand-Duchess Charlotte spent in exile during the Second World War. It follows in the tradition of another box office success from 2004, *Heim ins reich – L'échec d'une annexion*, which looked at Nazi Germany's annexation of the country.

Roy Tostevin's **Charlotte: A Royal at War**

Co-produced with the UK and directed by Roy Tostevin, *Charlotte: A Royal at War* alternates between talking heads and polished re-enactments of historical events, presenting a good introduction to the subject, albeit superficial.

More challenging dramatically is the fiction feature **Arabian Nights** (*Nuits d'Arabie*) from director Paul Kieffer. As it follows a train conductor from his staid life at home to a voyage into the North African desert in search of a girl, the narrative swerves from realism to the fantastic. The film's second half, shot on location in Algeria, is more successful than its first, which lacks credibility. The film is noteworthy because it is one of the very few

Jules Werner in Paul Kieffer's **Arabian Nights**

Geneviève Mersch's **Plein d'essence**

features to feature Luxembourgish, one of the official languages of the country, besides German and French.

On the documentary front, Geneviève Mersch's **Plein d'essence** looked at one of the biggest petrol stations in the country, while Christophe Wagner's **Luxemburg, USA** looks up descendants of Luxembourg immigrants in the US. Both were produced with aid from the 2007 European Capital of Culture initiative, but are strictly local fare. Shot on video, these films have little cinematic value, despite being shown in cinemas. Both directors have new fiction projects in development.

Christophe Wagner's **Luxemburg, USA**

The pool of local talent has been steadily growing in the last couple of years. Beryl Koltz, who made the 2005 short *Starfly*, is in pre-production on her feature debut **Hot Hot Hot**, and Max Jacoby, who directed the 2005 short *Butterflies*, has started shooting his first feature **Dust**. Several other talented youngsters are waiting in the wings, including Jeff Desom, Fred Neuen and Adolf El-Assal.

Also noteworthy are two shorts with a gay theme: Laura Schroeder's **Senteurs** and Jacques Molitor's **En Compagnie de la poussière**. Schroeder's film focuses on a housewife who embarks on a passionate affair with a woman (which echoes some of the same escapist themes – and problems – as *Arabian Nights*), while Molitor's explores the feelings of two male friends. It was selected for the Locarno Film Festival and shows a fine grasp of visual language and non-conformist narration that makes him a name to watch.

The year's best films
Arabian Nights (Paul Kieffer)
Charlotte: A Royal at War (Ray Tostevin)
En Compagnie de la poussière
(Jacques Molitor)

Paul Kieffer's **Arabian Nights**

Quote of the year
'*Arabian Nights* proposes a compromise in which the locals speak to each other in Luxembourgish and speak French when they are with French speakers, much like in real life. This helps the Luxembourg audiences to identify with the hero while the film should also be accessible for those who do not speak the language.' **Arabian Nights** *director*, **PAUL KIEFFER.**

BOYD VAN HOEIJ is a freelance film writer specialising in contemporary European cinema. He runs the website www.european-films.net, is a contributing critic for *Variety* and a correspondent for www.cineuropa.org.

Malaysia Hassan Abd Muthalib

The average domestic output in Malaysia has hovered around 25 films per year. In 2008, a record 31 films were produced or are in the final stages of production. The year is also remarkable for the arrival of 13 first-time directors, many with stories and styles that break away from the usual fare. That said, Malaysian mainstream cinema is still dominated by films littered with clichés and stereotypes and many are typical genre fare: comedy, romance, horror and action.

More reason then to celebrate Yasmin Ahmad's **The Convert** (*Muallaf*), and Mamat Khalid's **When the Moon Waxes Full** (*Bila Kala Malam Mengambang*), which adopt an

Mamat Khalid's **When the Moon Waxes Full**

art-house sensibility. Both these directors are part of a movement that, since 2003, has caught the attention of international festivals for its articulate and socially conscious cinema. The last few years have also seen the rise of a group of young, brash digital filmmakers, whose features and shorts have been critically acclaimed, winning awards at prestigious festivals.

Malaysian mainstream cinema is profit-driven. With formulaic films scoring at the box office, producers continue to invest in the tried and tested, which often feature popular comedians from television. Ahmad Idham's **Senario the Movie: Episode 1** made almost US$1 million in its first two weeks. A sequel is already in the offing. **Cicakman 2: The Dark Planet** (*Cicakman 2: Planet Hitam*) premiered at the Pusan International Film Festival, under the 'Superheroes in Asia' section, and looks set to repeat Yusry Kru's first *Cicakman* success, which earned US$2 million in 2006.

The high quality of the CGI and visual effects in these films attracted international attention, resulting in production company KRU Films' collaboration on a Hollywood feature. Another CGI-laden film, Azizi Chunk's **Ghost Fighter** (*Antoo Fighter*), a local version of *Ghostbusters*, is also likely to be a hit. Ahmad Idham's **Kid's Game** (*Congkak*), a horror movie, crossed the US$1 million mark despite its emphasis on sound effects and jarring editing rather than narrative.

Other films continued to cash in on the demand for light entertainment. Hans Isaac's debut, **Cleaning** (*Cuci*), is about a group of friends who vie with rivals to acquire the rights to clean the windows of the Petronas

Hans Isaac's **Cleaning**

Twin Towers. A modest effort, it won the Best Screenplay Award at the Malaysian Film Festival. The prolific Razak Mohaideen continued to produce his audience-oriented entertainment with **Mermaid** (*Duyung*), **Otai** and **U-Turn Love** (*Cinta U-Turn*). Though panned by critics, his films have continuously made money.

Razak Mohaideen's **Mermaid**

It is the new wave of Malaysian filmmakers that are employing subtext to articulate their feelings about identity, belonging and responsibility in a multi-racial country. Quirky director Mamat Khalid shot his best film to date, *When the Moon Waxes Full*, in black and white. In style, it is reminiscent of film noir and the gothic genre, while paying tribute to the Malay films of the 1950s. In it, a detective is investigating the disappearance of villagers, who become absent whenever the moon is full. It was screened at the Udine Film Festival and won the Best Picture and Best Director Awards at this year's Malaysian Film Festival, giving Khalid the recognition that he deserved.

Other new talents include Amir Muhammad, who made Malaysia's first digital feature, *Lips to Lips*, in 2000. His **Susuk** was co-directed with Naeim Ghalili, an Iranian-American who runs a post-production house in Malaysia. Touted as a horror-thriller, the film was in reality a satire about the current political landscape. It tells the story of singers who are past their prime and resort to black magic to maintain their youthfulness. Yasmin Ahmad, the only Malay filmmaker to articulate issues of a multi-racial society, continued in the same vein with *The Convert*, ostensibly a romance between a Muslim girl and a Catholic teacher, but is actually about how children should be brought up – a constant theme in all her films. Anuar Nor Arai's 1995 feature, **Johnny Makes a Film** (*Johnny Bikin Filem*), was finally released. A movie about gangsters in 1950s Singapore, with mise-en-scene and cinematography as good as any Hollywood production, plans are underway to enter it in a major film festival in its original five-and-a-half-hour version. Hatta Azad Khan's **Shadows** (*Wayang*) is a melodrama whose strong subtext is concerned with the future of the Malay shadow play.

James Lee's **Before We Fall in Love Again** (*Nian ni ru xi*) is about a man's search for his missing wife. It is an oblique critique of the alliance between Malaysia's Chinese community and the country's dominant political party, and how they have gained little out of the relationship. In **This Longing** (*Punggok Rindukan Bulan*), Azharr Rudin uses the demolition of some dilapidated flats to focus on working-class Malays for whom the country's economic development has made no difference to their lives. Yasmin Ahmad is more optimistic, signalling hope for family, race and nation with her film, **Talentime**. The country's three dominant races, represented by Malay, Chinese and Indian youths, are seen interacting and discovering a common ground. The film ends the way it began, with images of empty spaces in the school, leaving the audience to ponder: is school the right place to learn about the world and how to live life?

Long before the 'tsunami' at the 2008 elections, which heralded the emergence of a new generation of Malaysians seeking to transform the social and political landscape, the new wave of Malay filmmakers were already active in calling for change. Digital cinema and satellite television have made their films more accessible to a wider audience. But to have a greater impact on the local audience, there is a need for the films to be less personal, less ambiguous and more engaging. Only then can they hope to truly make it into the mainstream.

Wan Azli Wan Jusoh's feature debut, **Kelantan Boys** (*Budak Kelantan*), tells the story of two childhood friends, Jaha (Asrulfaizal) and Buchek (Danny X. Factor). When they meet some years later in the city, Buchek kas maintained his religious beliefs and practices while Jaha lives a wild lifestyle. Shot verité-style, it focuses on unemployment amongst graduates, race relations and questions the role of religion in society's development.

Mamat Khalid's **When the Moon Waxes Full**

The year's best films
Susuk (Amir Muhammad/Naeim Ghalili)
When the Moon Waxes Full (Mamat Khalid)
The Convert (Yasmin Ahmad)
Johnny Makes a Film (Anuar Nor Arai)
Before We Fall in Love Again (James Lee)

Quotes of the year
'Making films in Malaysia is like building arks for carpenters. They will only look at the wood.' MAMAT KHALID, *director of* **When the Moon Waxes Full**, *lamenting the criticism of his style of filmmaking.*

'I search and search for clues from God in the things I see, the people I love, the feelings I have, and the films I make.' YASMIN AHMAD, *director of* **The Convert**, *reacting to a question from a film student about her approach to films.*

Directory
All Tel/Fax numbers begin (+603)
National Film Development Corporation (FINAS), Studio Merdeka Complex, Hulu Kelang, 68000 Ampang, Selangor. Tel: 41041300. Fax: 41068509. finas@po.jaring.my. www.finas.gov.my.
Malaysia Institute Of Integrative Media, Centre for Film and Broadcasting, No. 1, Jalan 9/27 A, Section 5 Wangsa Maju, Kuala Lumpur 53300. Tel: 41422422 Fax: 4142 8422

HASSAN ABD MUTHALIB is an animator and scriptwriter who now researches, lectures and writes about Malaysian cinema. His writings appear in international film and academic journals, and also on the Internet.

Azharr Rudin's **This Longing**

Mexico Carlos Bonfil

Against all odds, Mexican cinema managed to produce seventy films in 2008, 41 of which were state supported, while the remaining 29 were funded by private investors. Of these, only 43 films were released. Foreign features, most of which were American productions (143), brought the total to 262 films.

While the above figures should indicate the steady recovery of the Mexican film industry, particularly when one considers that in 2002 only 14 films were actually produced, an endemic problem still hampers the healthy development of its national cinema; namely, the poor distribution and exhibition of most of these films. Hollywood productions occupy nearly 90% of the screening space available, precisely during the months when public attendance is at its peak. The absence of any film legislation to secure the fair distribution of Mexican films and apply fixed quotas to the number of foreign films in the national market has had direct consequences for new productions. It particularly affects newcomers, who face unfair competition and whose films disappear after one or two weeks in cinemas. Domestic films that manage to survive in this environment and which eventually constitute box office hits are generally formulaic comedies or thrillers; as innocuous as the commercial films from Hollywood.

It has been argued that one important obstacle to any development of a Mexican film industry stems from the fact that, contrary to Canada, during the ratification of NAFTA (the North American Free Trade Agreement), Mexico did not exclude culture from its negotiations. As a result, cinema is just another merchandise in a competing, unrestrained market. The possibility of renegotiating NAFTA, as proposed by President-Elect Barack Obama during his campaign, may open the way to providing Mexican cinema with more effective tools to defend its own productions and to propose legislation that guarantees better distribution and exhibition of local films.

Rigoberto Castañeda's **KM 31: Kilometre 31**

The best films Mexico has produced in the last couple of years – those that have attracted the most international acclaim – are precisely the artistic achievements that Mexican audiences have not had the chance to appreciate at home. When one of these films is released, few exhibitors take the risk of a widespread marketing campaign and release, giving the film very little opportunity to succeed. The common argument for not encouraging the distribution of these films is that there is not a significant audience for them, either because of the film's subject matter or because of its innovative style. These films do not entertain large audiences the way Hollywood films do and therefore would have little impact at the box office. The films that do correspond to the accepted commercial criteria are precisely those that are rarely seen or appreciated abroad, which are aimed at domestic

Robert Sneider's **Arráncame la vida**

consumption. These are the commercial hits that erroneously offer the impression of a resurgence of the Mexican film industry: Rigoberto Castañeda's **KM 31: Kilometre 31** (*Kilómetro 31*), Gabriel and Rodolfo Riva Palacio Alatriste's **Una película de huevos** and Roberto Sneider's **Arráncame la vida**. There is bitter irony in the idea that the more films a country produces, the healthier its film industry appears. This consideration naturally overshadows the quality of those films and ignores the fact that good, low-budget films are currently screened at international film festivals but are ignored at home.

Amat Escalante's **The Bastards** (*Los bastardos*) was recently awarded the Best Fiction Film award at Mexico's Morelia International Film Festival. It is a disturbing story set in Los Angeles and features two illegal immigrants who are trapped in a spiral of violence after breaking into a suburban home and taking a middle-aged American housewife as a hostage. On understanding the inoffensive intentions of her young captors, she begins to befriend them, until things turn sour and lead to an unexpected tragedy. Minimalist in style and beautifully shot, featuring non-professional actors, there is a sense of immediacy and truth to the film's compelling narrative. It does not have a commercial distributor in Mexico.

Lake Tahoe is the second feature by successful young director, Fernando Eimbcke (*Duck Season*). Both the narrative and style of the film are simple, with long takes employed to tell of the coming-of-age of teenager, Juan. After a car accident, he meets various larger-than-life characters, who help him to overcome a feeling of aimlessness and distress following the death of his father. An impressive exploration of a young man's thoughts and feelings, it unfolds with discreet humour and an air of melancholy.

Diego Cataño in Fernando Eimbcke's **Lake Tahoe**

Laura Amelia Guzmán and Israel Cárdenas, adopted a less-is-more approach to **Cochochi**, which is set in rural Mexico. It recounts the experience of two children in a small village, commissioned to deliver medicine to an ill relative in another town, who lose their horse and experience countless hardships before they can return home. Similar in tone to Abbas Kiarostami's *Where is the Friend's House*, it plays out using an indigenous dialect and with disarming simplicity. **Cumbia callera**

Amat Escalante's **The Bastards**

Laura Amelia Guzmán's **Cochochi**

is the directorial debut of fifty-year-old René Villarreal, for a long time the first assistant to some of the finest filmmakers in Mexico. An original social drama set amongst the neighbourhoods of Monterrey in northern Mexico, it features two youngsters in pursuit of the same woman. It has practically no dialogue, but is suffused with Caribbean music, allowing the romance between the small-time thieves and the object of their desire a carefree sensuality.

Staying in rural Mexico, two documentaries deal directly with the issue of immigration into the United States: Juan Carlos Rulfo's **Those Who Remain** (*Los que se quedan*) and Eugenio Polgovsky's **The Inheritors** (*Los herederos*). Both describe the daily routine of people who have witnessed their relatives' forced migration in order to alleviate their extreme poverty. Children express their desire to follow their father, while absorbed in the task of earning money. It is fascinating in its lyrical depiction of these tough lives, which are only occasionally alleviated by civil and

Eugenio Polgovsky's **The Inheritors**

religious festivities. Other documentaries include Alejandra Sánchez's **Under Juarez** (*Bajo Juárez*), a harsh chronicle of the mysterious execution of hundreds of working women in the bordertown Ciudad Juarez, which remains largely unresolved due to official corruption; Juan Sepúlveda's **Endless Frontier** (*La frontera infinita*) highlights the problems faced by Central American immigrants attempting to enter Mexico from the south and whose mistreatment differs little from that experienced by Mexicans at the American border; and Christiane Burkhard's **Sketching Aleida** (*Trazando Aleida*), the portrait of a woman who, after losing her parents in the so-called dirty war in the 1970s, eventually found her long-lost brother decades later in New York.

Juan Sepúlveda's **Endless Frontier**

With an increase in short film and documentary production over the past two years, it is gratifying to see that better fiction films are being made. There is novelty and diversity in the choice of subject matter, accompanied by a relentless quest for aesthetic freedom, even with a tendency to favour simpler, even minimal, narratives over conventional storytelling techniques. Filmmakers are exploring alternative ways of financing and distributing their own low-budget productions and, as they gain international recognition, their efforts may be partially rewarded in the mainstream market. This happened with *The Bastards*, which profited from private investment that was able to claw back money through tax-deductible incentives. The global financial crisis may well discourage these investments in the near future and the question still remains of whether the state will do its best to honour the long-standing promise to defend Mexican cinema.

The year's best films
The Bastards (Amat Escalante)
Lake Tahoe (Fernando Eimbcke)
The Inheritors (Eugenio Polgovsky)
Cochochi (Laura Amelia Guzmán and Israel Cárdenas)
Cumbia callera (René Villarreal)

Quote of the year
'When it comes to cinema, there is in Mexico a changing reality that has turned video, DVD and TV series into a key reference in daily conversations, more so than the old habit of reading.' *Writer* CARLOS MONSIVÁIS.

Directory
All Tel/Fax numbers begin (+52)
Cineteca Nacional, Avenida México-Coyoacán 389, Col Xoco, México DF. Tel: 1253 9314. www.cinetecanacional.net.
Association of Mexican Film Producers & Distributors, Avenida División del Norte 2462, Piso 8, Colonia Portales, México DF. Tel: 5688 0705. Fax: 5688 7251.
Cinema Production Workers Syndicate (STPC), Plateros 109 Col San José Insurgentes, México DF. Tel: 5680 6292. cctpc@terra.com.mx.
Dirección General de Radio, Televisión y Cine-matografía (RTC), Roma 41, Col Juárez, México DF. Tel: 5140 8010. ecardenas@segob.gob.mx.
Instituto Mexicano de Cinematografía (IMCINE), Insurgentes Sur 674 Col del Valle, CP 03100, México DF. Tel: 5448 5300. mercaint@institutomexicanodecinematografía.gob.mx.

CARLOS BONFIL is a film critic, contributing a weekly article on cinema to *La Journada*, a leading Mexican newspaper. He is the author of *Through the Mirror: Mexican Cinema and its Audience* (1994).

Morocco Maryam Touzani

Moroccan cinema aspires to becoming a leader in the Arab and African world. The last decade has seen it overcome many obstacles and it is at last making headway.

Although a new generation of filmmakers are making their presence felt, the old guard are still producing films. More than two decades after her first and only feature *Embers*, Farida Bourquia made a welcome return with **Women's Road** (*Deux Femmes sur la Route*). The film focuses on the female condition in Morocco and the Arab world through an unexpected encounter between two women. Pioneer Latif Lahlou also reappeared after more than twenty years with his third feature, **Samira's Gardens** (*Samira Fi Adayaa*). It is the story of a woman who, on accomplishing her goal of getting married, discovers her husband's impotence. In a desperate quest for affection she embarks on an affair with her husband's young nephew. The film offers a glimpse into feminine sexuality in a society ruled by taboos. In the same vein, Abdelkader Lagtaâ's **Yasmine and the Men** (*Yasmine et les Hommes*) relates the story of a young woman who, after a serious accident, decides to change her life.

Mohamed Ismail, another characteristic figure of Moroccan cinema, returned with **Goodbye Mothers** (*Adieu Mères*), which represented Morocco at the Academy Award. The story relates the unyielding bonds between a Jewish and a Muslim family in 1960s Casablanca. Hassan Benjelloun has long attempted to reconcile the Moroccan population with its history. His eighth feature, **Where Are You Going Moshé?** (*Où vas-tu Moshé?*), takes place in the little town of Bejjad. As Jews secretly plan their departure, a Muslim bar owner tries desperately to find a way to keep the law from closing him down. With this humane depiction of an often neglected episode in the country's history, Benjelloun illustrates how loss of diversity is a disadvantage for any society.

Contemporary issues are also a concern for filmmakers. Ahmed Boulane's **Satan's Angels** (*Les Anges de Satan*) is based on the shocking story of fourteen young 'hard-rockers' imprisoned for Satanism in 2003. In Daoud Aoulad-Syad's **Waiting for Pasolini** (*En Attendant Pasolini*), Thami, a satellite-dish salesman and former film extra waits for forty years for the return of his 'friend', the director Pier Paolo Pasolini. Souad El-Bouhati's

French Girl (*Française*) analyses the problem of immigration through the experiences of a young girl born in France to Arab parents and obliged to return to Morocco. Aziz Salmy's **Veiled Love Stories** (*Amours Voilées*) is a tale of love in which the issue of the Muslim veil becomes an issue in the relationship. In Zinoun Lahcen's **The Lost Beauty** (*Oud L'Ward*), a young girl sold into slavery is liberated by her musical talent, only to be defeated by the hand of destiny. Saâd Chraïbi's **Islamour** (*Islam ya Salam*) features a Moroccan-American family who return to Morocco because of the hostilities they face after 9/11. Nourredine Lakhamri's **Casa-negra** depicts a chaotic yet enthralling Casablanca in which two childhood friends who live by their wits take different paths in their search for fulfilment. In Mohamed Zineddaine's **Do You Remember Adil?** (*Tu te Souviens d'Adil?*), a young man leaves the country for Bologna, where he leads a double life. Izza Genini traces the history of the nûba – fourteenth-century Arab and Andalusian music – in her documentary, **Nûba of Gold and Light** (*Nouba d'or et de Lumière*). French director Jérôme Cohen Olivar explores Moroccan myths for his feature, **Kandisha**, in which a legendary spirit inhabiting the body of certain women is at the heart of an unsolved murder case. Yassine Fennane made his debut with **Skeleton** (*Squelette*), in which a young man returns to his village and announces that he wants to sell his body to science. Nabil Ayouch has created an innovative and ambitious project, which aims to produce thirty films a year in order to stimulate local cinema. *Skeleton* is part of this enterprise and reflects the vital importance of such initiatives to the country's cinematic landscape .

Although it is an undeniable fact that Moroccan cinemas are closing at an alarming rate, some films offer hope for the commercial future of film in the country. Ayouch's **Whatever Lola Wants** was an impressive box office hit. The young filmmaker came to symbolise the new generation with his first feature *Mektoub*, returning a few years later with the inspirational cult film, *Ali Zaoua, Prince of*

Nabil Ayouch's **Whatever Lola Wants**

Casablanca. Both were chosen to represent Morocco at the Academy Awards. His latest is the unusual story of a New York postal worker obsessed with dancing, who moves to Egypt to follow the man she loves. Once there, she relentlessly pursues the legendary dancer Ismahan. An uplifting and original approach to cultural exchange, the story is a lyrical bridge between different worlds.

Morocco attracted a record amount of investment in 2008. Although video piracy and the closure of cinemas are a problem, the country's film industry has finally taken flight, with the aspiration of becoming a major point of reference on the map of world cinema.

The year's best films
Where Are You Going Moshé?
(Hassan Benjelloun)
Goodbye Mothers (Mohamed Ismail)
Satan's Angels (Ahmed Boulane)
Whatever Lola Wants (Nabil Ayouch)

Quote of the year
'I wanted to make a film where the humane finds its true place at the heart of the identity problems that preoccupy East and West; where communication is at the base of any form of exchange, where what unites us and separates us is no longer terrorism or bombs, but what we are with all our differences, and beyond, our capacity to transcend them.'
Whatever Lola Wants *director* **NABIL AYOUCH.**

MARYAM TOUZANI is a freelance journalist based in Morocco and working internationally, specialising in art and culture.

Netherlands Leo Bankersen

Do Dutch filmmakers look beyond their borders? The jury of the Netherlands Film Festival in Utrecht in September had its doubts, causing a bit of a stir by rhetorically asking themselves, 'Do some filmmakers from the Netherlands ever take a look at foreign films.' They expressed their dissatisfaction with the variable quality of content and production of the films they had to judge, suggesting that more should be done to keep Dutch cinema in step with international developments.

Pieter Verhoeff's **The Letter for the King**

On the other hand, quite a few of the thirty or so feature films produced in 2008 found their inspiration or location in other countries. Five of them are (partly) set in Africa, while Pieter Verhoeff's handsomely produced adventure of a young knight-to-be, **The Letter for the King** (*De*

Ben Sombogaart's **Bride Flight**

brief voor de koning), made good use of Scottish scenery. Ben Sombogaart, director of the Academy Award-nominated *Twin Sisters*, filmed his ambitious new drama, **Bride Flight**, about the emotional secrets of three young Dutch immigrant brides in New Zealand. Featuring fine performances from two generations of Dutch actresses, it attracted a large audience.

Perhaps the most striking example of a Dutch filmmaker in search of adventure is David Verbeek, a young director fascinated by Asian cinema. Fresh from the Amsterdam Film Academy, he lived in Shanghai for two years. There, he captured the anxieties of present-day adolescents in **Shanghai Trance**, in which three love stories criss-cross in a style that, even for a local audience, proved hard to distinguish from the works of his Chinese contemporaries. After limited release in the Netherlands, a Chinese distributor bought the rights to the film (in a censored version).

Another daring enterprise, albeit in a very different direction, is the children's adventure story, **The Seven of Daran – The Battle of Pareo Rock** (*De Zeven van Daran, de strijd om Pareo Rots*). First-time director Lourens Blok attracted little praise for his old-fashioned villains and a young hero attempting to prevent a tribal war in Africa, but the film at least displays a degree of daring and features its fair share of breathtaking African scenery. Made without the support of the usual funding bodies and with English dialogue, it is aimed firmly at the international market.

The Netherlands was modestly represented at major international festivals. Berlin's youth competition selected Dana Nechushtan's lively road movie, **Dunya & Desie**, the Dutch entry

Dana Nechushtan's **Dunya & Desie**

for this year's Academy Awards. It is about two teenage girls who face a turning point in their lives when their friendship is put to the test on a trip to Morocco, where Dunya's parents live.

In Cannes, Margien Rogaar's short film **Breath** (*Zucht*) was screened in a side section and Jos van Ginkel's short, **Sand** (*Zand*), was selected for the Venice Film Festival.

Theo Maassen in Pieter Kuiper's **Nothing to Lose**

The Dutch auteurs' films are not completely absent from the international scene either. **Left** (*Links*), a quirky low-budget love story by Froukje Tan, was selected for Pusan and a number of other festivals. Arno Dierickx's **Blood Brothers** (*Bloedbroeders*), based on a notorious murder case in the 1960s, was invited to the New Directors Competition in San Sebastián, while Pieter Kuijpers' gripping thriller **Nothing to Lose** (*TBS*), with Theo Maassen scary in the lead as a mentally disturbed kidnapper, received a Best Film award in Philadelphia.

Mijke de Jong went to Locarno and Toronto with **Katia's Sister** (*Het zusje van Katia*), a sensitive drama about a 13-year-old girl,

neglected by her stripper sister and prostitute mother, who struggles for affection. Not as sharp as his previous film, *Stages*, but still one of the highlights of the year.

Mijke de Jong's **Katia's Sister**

The critics' prize at the Netherlands Film Festival went to another small film, the highly original **Calimucho** by Eugenie Jansen. She used real circus people to improvise a drama, resulting in a fascinating blend of fiction and reality.

Two outstanding documentaries came from filmmakers with a foreign background. For **Recycle**, director Mahmoud al Massad went back to his former hometown, Zarqa in Jordan, the same place where notorious Al Qaida leader Al Zarqawi came from. There he found the material for this beautifully shot, unpredictable and humane film about a former mujahedeen, who is now trying to earn a living for his family by collecting cardboard.

Mahmoud Al Massad's documentary **Recycle**

Renowned documentarist Heddy Honigmann went back to her roots in Lima, Peru for **El olvido**. In a deceptively relaxed way she integrates intimate portraits into a telling picture about the hardship of life under a succession of corrupt governments.

Another fine example of non-fiction is **Carmen Meets Borat**, the Dutch Academy Award entry for feature documentaries. Mercedes Stalenhoef went to the poor Romanian village which was used by Sacha Baron Cohen as stand-in for Kazakhstan in his comedy *Borat*. There she filmed a sensitive portrait of teenager Carmen dreaming of a better life, in the meantime registering the troublesome aftermath of Cohen's intrusion.

2008 has been a year of optimism and concern. Dutch film seems to hold its ground at the box office. The market share is expected to reach 14–15%, a figure we haven't seen in many years.

Martin Koolhoven's **Winter in Wartime**

Monique van de Ven's **Summer Heat**

Although we did not see a smash hit like last year's *Love is All*, the number of films that performed well appears to be on the rise. Most of these releases were lightweight fare, like springtime favourite **Summer Heat** (*Zomerhitte*), the directorial debut of actress Monique van de Ven. Based on a story by famous Dutch writer Jan Wolkers, it featured lots of sun, sex and crime.

One November release that will continue to perform well into the New Year is Martin Koolhoven's **Winter in Wartime** (*Oorlogswinter*), which transforms a famous book for children into an adult story about a 14-year-old boy's loss of innocence in the final days of the Second World War. Hopes are also high for the African-set thriller **White Light**, by Jean van de Velde. It stars Marco Borsato, arguably the Netherlands' most popular singer.

Youth and family films still constitute the solid base of Dutch popular film. Among the best in this genre are *Dunya & Desie* and *The Letter for the King*, as well as Nicole van Kilsdonk's moving and funny **How Do I Survive Myself?** (*Hoe overleef ik mezelf?*) about the growing pains of a 13-year-old girl, and Barbara Bredero's **Morrison Gets a Baby Sister** (*Morrison krijgt een zusje*) in which a five-year-old fears a tragedy with the arrival of his baby sister.

Nicole van Kilsdonk's **How Do I Survive Myself?**

Although the audience share for Dutch film is growing, the number of people who go to see the more artistic or specialist films is not. A small gem like **Winter Silence** (*Winterstilte*) by visual artist and first-time filmmaker Sonja Wyss, in which secrets of life unfold amidst Swiss mountains, even had a hard time finding a distributor.

Sarah Bühlmann in Sonja Wyss' **Winter Silence**

Meanwhile, the Netherlands Film Fund, which funds the majority of domestic releases, published a new policy plan called *Room for Talent*, as well as a reorganisation plan that has to counteract past criticism of the Fund's sometimes inefficient and not particularly transparent operations. However, as the budget of the Fund is unlikely to increase very much, significant changes are not expected. Will focus on the development of talent really be the key to seeing a Dutch film in competition in Cannes or another major festival, as Fund director Toine Berbers is hoping for? We'll wait and see.

The year's best films
Recycle (Mahmoud al Massad)
Shanghai Trance (David Verbeek)
Winter in Wartime (Martin Koolhoven)
Katia's Sister (Mijke de Jong)
Bride Flight (Ben Sombogaart)

Quotes of the year
'Go make yourself useful and write a novel, that will be better for literature and better for the art of cinema.' PETER GREENAWAY *on the overestimated value of the screenplay, after being invited by the Dutch scriptwriters' guild to their annual meeting.*

'The Netherlands is a country in confusion, but I see very little of it in the films we make.' Producer FRANS VAN GESTEL, *after receiving the Golden Calf for best feature film* **Love is All.**

Directory
All Tel/Fax numbers begin (+31)
Circle of Dutch Film Critics (KNF), PO Box 10650, 1011 ER Amsterdam. Tel: (6) 2550 0668. Fax: (6) 627 5923. knfilm@xs4all.nl.
Cobo Fund, PO Box 26444, Postvak M54, 1202 JJ Hilversum. Tel: (35) 677 5348. Fax: (35) 677 1995. cobo@nos.nl. Contact: Jeanine Hage.
Dutch Film Fund, Jan Luykenstraat 2, 1071 CM Amsterdam. Tel: (20) 570 7676. Fax: (31) 570 7689. info@filmfund.nl. Contact: Toine Berbers.
Filmmuseum, Rien Hagen, Vondelpark 3, PO Box 74782, 1070 BT Amsterdam. Tel: (20) 589 1400. (20) Fax: 683 3401. info@filmmuseum.nl. www.filmmuseum.nl.
Netherlands Institut voor Beeld en Geluid, PO Box 1060, 1200 BB Hilversum. Tel: (35) 677 2672/7. Fax: (35) 677 2835. klantenservice@naa.nl. www.naa.nl.
Netherlands Film & Television Academy (NFTA), Markenplein 1, 1011 MV Amsterdam. Tel: (20) 527 7333. Fax: (20) 527 7344. info@nfta.ahk.nl. www.nfta.ahk.nl. Contact: Marieke Schoenmakers.
Ministry of Education, Culture & Science, Arts Dept, Sector Film, Europaweg 4, PO Box 25000, 2700 LZ Zoetermeer. Tel: (79) 323 4321. Fax: (79) 323 4959. j.j.cassidy@minocw.nl.
Netherlands Cinematographic Federation (NFC), Jan Luykenstraat 2, PO Box 75048, 1070 AA Amsterdam. Tel: (20) 679 9261. Fax: (20) 675 0398. info@nfc.org. Contact: Wilco Wolfers.
Netherlands Institute For Animation Film, PO Box 9358, 5000 HJ Tilburg. Tel: (13) 535 4555. Fax: (13) 580 0057. niaf@niaf.nl. Contact: Ton Crone.
Rotterdam Film Fund, Rochussenstraat 3C, 3015 EA Rotterdam. Tel: (10) 436 0747. Fax: (10) 436 0553. info@rff.rotterdam.nl. Contact: Jacques van Heijnigen.

LEO BANKERSEN is a freelance film critic who writes regularly for the Netherlands Press Association. He also contributes to the monthly film magazine *de Filmkrant*.

New Zealand Peter Calder

It is universally accepted that director Roger Donaldson was responsible for kick-starting the modern New Zealand film industry with his 1977 political thriller *Sleeping Dogs*.

So it is fitting that Donaldson's most recent New Zealand-based film, *The World's Fastest Indian*, should have been responsible for sparking renewed audience interest in the local business. The story of a backyard mechanic who set land-speed records on a homebuilt motorcycle perfectly captured this country's uniquely can-do spirit, and Kiwis responded, making it the most successful domestic release ever.

Paul Murphy's **Second-Hand Wedding**

That success seemed to spawn a renewed interest among domestic audiences, who have long avoided local films. Seven films consecutively attracted over 50,000 admissions, an impressive number for a small market. And 2008's biggest hit, Paul Murphy's **Second-Hand Wedding**, passed the 200,000 mark.

The popularity of such an anodyne family comedy was arguably attributable to the public's appetite for feel-good films (this year's winter was one of the wettest on record)

and the fact that the plot played up to a local custom – rummaging around Saturday-morning garage sales.

Melody Wihapi in Vincent Ward's **Rain of the Children**

Second-Hand Wedding led the charge in a relatively good year for local films. Even tormented New Zealand auteur Vincent Ward returned to the screen. The director's keenly awaited follow-up to the fraught *River Queen* revisited the subject of *In Spring One Plants Alone*, a fly-on-the-wall documentary he made when he was at arts school thirty years ago. **Rain of the Children** interweaves the troubled history of a Maori tribe and the story of the earlier film's major figure, Puhi, a woman regarded by some of her people as cursed. Although it was praised by some critics, the film is clumsy and a little patronising. That said, it is technically accomplished and highlights a shameful episode in New Zealand's history.

More culturally assured is **Apron Strings**, the debut feature by the talented Samoan-born, theatre-trained director Vaele Sima Urale, who has long been one of the Pacific community's more vibrant talents. It focuses on the clash between European and Indian cultures, reflected in co-writer Shuchi Kothari's background. Urale provided sensitive direction for a film whose feminine sensibility was, if anything, a little too low key.

Gareth Reeves in Gregory King's **A Song of Good**

A clutch of other, more modest, productions came and went during the year. Athina Tsoulis's **Jinx Sister**, a micro-budget drama about a woman returning from Los Angeles and discovering the meaning of family, seemed overstretched at feature length, but Gregory King's **A Song of Good** was an accomplished little melodrama. King, whose debut, *Christmas*, was a clammy family-gathering meltdown, focused on a young man's struggle for redemption after committing a horrific crime. **Rubbings from a Live Man** was a very creditable documentary by Florian Habicht (*Kaikohe Demolition*), about Warwick Broadhead, one of the local arts scene's more flamboyant and outré figures. And writer-director Anthony McCarten adapted his own novel for the end-of-year release, **Show of Hands**. Based on a world-record contest in which participants held onto a car for more than 109 hours in a bid to win it, it featured Melanie Lynskey (who co-starred with Kate Winslet in Peter Jackson's *Heavenly Creatures*), but its characters lacked conviction and the romantic ending was implausible.

Anthony McCarten's **Show of Hands**

Soon to be released is the new film by *Whale Rider* director, Niki Caro. **The Vintner's Luck**, based on a New Zealand magical realist novel and shot both here and in France, stars Keisha Castle-Hughes and Vera Farmiga. **Dean Spanley**, the second feature by Toa Fraser (*No. 2*), which screened at Toronto, is an Edwardian-set yarn about an old man healing his stilted relationship with his son. The story's English focus and star line-up (Peter O'Toole and Jeremy Northam are joined by antipodeans Sam Neill and Bryan Brown) suggests the co-production might favour its British backers, although New Zealanders occupied all the key creative posts.

Peter O'Toole in Toa Fraser's **Dean Spanley**

Whether 2009 will deliver on the expectations encouraged by 2008 is unclear. The company behind Justin Chadwick's **Mark of the Lion**, a drama based on the biography of Second World War hero Charles Upham, the only soldier to have twice won the Victoria Cross, went into liquidation in October and the production now seems doomed. Meanwhile, Jonathan King's **Under the Mountain**, a big-screen adaptation of the famous New Zealand novel (and iconic 1970s TV show) about two boys battling dark forces beneath Auckland's volcanoes, wrapped in October, but only after being thrown a budget lifeline by a new Government initiative called the Screen Production Incentive Fund.

The fund, which refunds 40% of local spend, is intended to complement a five-year-old scheme for larger-budget (read foreign) productions, which gave a 15% rebate on money spent in New Zealand. The larger fund has assisted the country in attracting international productions for shooting or post-production and was particularly important in the first half of 2008, when the New Zealand dollar was at US$0.80. But the national location office, Film New Zealand, reports that overseas producers also praise the splendid locations, the high standard of technical talent and the confidence in the post-production environment, exemplified by the Peter Jackson empire in Wellington. James Cameron's **Avatar** and Roland Emmerich's **10,000BC** were noted titles that employed local skills. Meanwhile, there has been a promising spike in Asian interest. The Korean comedy **Laundry Warrior**, written and directed by Sngmoo Lee, was shot in the Henderson Valley studios, a new production facility with a soundstage, just west of Auckland. And post-production work on John Woo's two-part, third-century Chinese epic, *Red Cliff*, was also carried out there.

New Zealand still remains a small player. The centre-left, Labour-led government, which was voted out during an end-of-year election, was arts- and film-friendly. The new administration, less sentimental and more pragmatic, is unlikely to increase funding for the Film Commission, the state-funded film bank, which celebrated its thirtieth anniversary in 2008.

Increasingly, the commission, which operates on a modest annual budget, has turned away from production funding and focused on assisting writers at an early stage and then picking winners to assist through development. With the departure of vociferous chief executive Ruth Harley, who has taken the top position at Screen Australia, the industry has lost a powerful advocate. That, combined with the fact that the economy is officially in recession, might give even the most sanguine observer a moment's reflection.

Vaele Sima Urale's **Apron Strings**

The year's best films
Apron Strings (Vaele Sima Urale)
Rubbings from a Live Man (Florian Habicht)
Second-Hand Wedding (Paul Murphy)

Quote of the year
'What we want in New Zealand cinema are more voices – different voices.' *Departing Chief Executive of the New Zealand Film Commission,* **RUTH HARLEY**, *on the need for more diversity.*

Directory
All Tel/Fax numbers begin (+64)
Film New Zealand, PO Box 24142, Wellington. Tel: (4) 385 0766. Fax: (4) 384 5840. info@filmnz.org.nz. www.filmnz.com.
New Zealand Film Archive, PO Box 11449, Wellington. Tel: (4) 384 7647. Fax: (4) 382 9595. nzfa@actrix.gen.nz. www.filmarchive.org.nz.
New Zealand Film Commission, PO Box 11546, Wellington. Tel: (4) 382 7680. Fax: (4) 384 9719. marketing@nzfilm.co.nz.
Ministry of Economic Development, 33 Bowen St, PO Box 1473, Wellington. Tel: (4) 472 0030. Fax: (4) 473 4638. www.med.govt.nz.
Office of Film & Literature Classification, PO Box 1999, Wellington. Tel: (64) 471 6770. Fax: (4) 471 6781. information@censorship.govt.nz.
Screen Production & Development Association (SPADA), PO Box 9567, Wellington. Tel: (4) 939 6934. Fax: (4) 939 6935. info@spada.co.nz.

PETER CALDER has been a film critic for the *New Zealand Herald*, the country's largest circulation newspaper, since 1984.

Nigeria Steve Ayorinde

The Nigerian motion-picture industry, otherwise called Nollywood, spent the best part of 2008 recovering from the '2007 debacle' – a glut in production that was attributed to the new distribution framework from the National Film and Video Censors Board. There was also the sex scandal that rocked the Hausa film sector, in the northern part of the country, which further alienated it from the mainstream.

Convinced that the industry could not sustain the profusion of movies being released annually (literally in their thousands), the head of the Censors Board, Emeka Mba, championed a revolutionary reform process that sought to streamline the distribution network by increasing the capital base of distribution companies and separating national players from the opportunistic – and ever-expanding – market distributors. While it offered a lasting cure for a regulated production and distribution regime, it was initially resisted.

The resulting lull in the industry was similar to the 'meltdown' of 2005, when market distributors unilaterally banned the ten highest-paid actors in the industry and reduced production activities.

The face-off between the Censors Board and the independents coincided with the sex scandal that almost halted filmmaking activity in the northern part of the country (known as Kannywood). The bubble burst when an eight-minute sex video appeared of popular actress Maryam Kiyana with her boyfriend, apparently filmed using a cell phone. The Kano State Government responded with a sweeping crackdown on all feature productions in the area. The actress went into hiding and eventually left the industry. Many professionals moved to more liberal states to escape sanctions.

Aside of the flamboyant fourth edition of the African Movie Academy Awards (AMAA), where the industry's finest were celebrated, the year progressed at a measured pace. Kannywood, having caved in under heavy government sanctions and threats of *sharia* law, produced Mohammed Auwal's documentary, **Bakan Dabo**, about the life of the Emir of Kano, Ado Bayero, and the vaunted Kano Emirate. In the southern part of the country, where Nollywood has taken root, notable productions came mainly from producers funded by the market distributors, with a few 'independent' directors continually exploring other avenues of distribution.

One of the most remarkable films of 2008 is Izu Ojukwu's **White Waters**, a romantic thriller set in northern Nigeria. It dominated both the home-video markets and the AMAA awards. Justifying his position as Nigeria's most respected director, Tunde Kelani scored again with his latest feature, **Arugba**, a broadly

Tunde Kelani's **Arugba**

traditional drama that explores the relevance of myths and old beliefs within modern life. His exploratory short film about child survival, **Life in Slow Motion**, which was shot in Ghana, is also a trailblazer in a year that did not record many great successes. As usual, Kelani's films were released in cinemas first, with a general video release not likely until some time in 2009.

One thousand completed films in 2008 may look like a huge number, but the figure is relatively quiet for Nollywood, which has recorded an annual average of almost two thousand titles for the last couple of years. Fearing audience apathy towards a cinema that is often predictable, a few directors tried some new ideas in order to spark their viewers' interest. Daniel Ademinokan's outstanding romantic drama, **Modupe Temi**, featured just two actors. In a market saturated with 'exploitation' films, this template provides a fascinating insight into how Nollywood has reached out to live theatre for inspiration.

Nollywood still continues to attract interest from abroad, albeit primarily with its documentaries. One such film is Dorothee Wenner's **Peace Mission**, which presents the evolution of the new Nigerian cinema through the perspective of one of the industry's most passionate and eloquent voices, Peace Anyiam-Fiberesima, a producer and the Chief Executive Officer of AMAA. The film, co-produced with Germany, was the only Nigerian entry at the Toronto International Film Festival and has already been invited to other festivals in 2009.

But the industry seems to be acutely aware that interest from abroad may be short-lived if the quality of films fails to improve. This is why many prominent figures appear eager to channel a new course for the industry. The collaboration between writer-producer Emem Isong and directors Lancelot Imasuen and Onyeka Okeychukwu has already shown fine results with films like Imasuen's **When the**

Heart Lies, a romantic adventure, and the action thriller **Reloaded**. Veteran filmmaker Zen Ejiro also returned with **Sakobi Returns**, a horror adventure set in eastern Nigeria and the sequel to his 1994 hit, *Sakobi the Snake Girl*.

However, if there is any consensus in the industry at all, from many of the small film festivals and conferences that were held in 2008, it is the resolution to collectively lobby for the passing into law of the bill that will set up the Movie Practitioners Council (MOPICON).

The year's best films
White Waters (Izu Ojukwu)
Arugba (Tunde Kelani)
Modupe Temi (Daniel Ademinokan)
State of the Heart (Kingsley Omoife)
When the Heart Lies (Lancelot Imasuen)

Quotes of the year
'What we are doing is African magic because we have been able to do so much with so little. Critics should know that a movie takes three or four million Naira to make, which is what a Minister gives his girlfriend for a car. That is what I make a whole film with.' T-CHIDI CHIKERE, *writer-director criticising critics of Nollywood for comparing its low-budget movies with Hollywood films.*

'A good film starts from thinking it has to be good. When you think well, you get good scripts. We all know that without good scripts, there are no good movies.' GABS OKOYE (Gabosky), *film producer, stressing the importance of good scripts and planning in filmmaking.*

STEVE AYORINDE is a film critic and Editor of *The PUNCH*, Nigeria's largest circulation daily newspaper. He is a member of FIPRESCI. He is also a Jury member of the African Movie Academy Awards (AMAA).

North Korea James Bell

Choe Ik-kyu's **The Flower Girl**

N orth Korea's isolation from the international community means that reliable and accurate details on recent film production are difficult to obtain. However, it is clear that the years since 2000 have been lean ones for film production: at this year's Pyongyang International Film Festival, a biannual event held in the country's showcase capital in September, there was only one new locally made feature film screened.

The current situation is a stark contrast to that of the period between the late 1950s and the early 1990s, when, buoyed by financial and technical investment from friendly Communist regimes in China and the USSR, film production was high. As ever, precise figures for annual output during these years differs, but the best estimates agree that on average twenty feature films were made each year during the period. Some sources claim that as many as a hundred films were made in given years, but it is likely that these figures include shorts, documentaries, cartoons and educational films.

Virtually all of the country's studios and film archives were destroyed by the aerial bombing of the three-year-long Korean War, and following the war's end in 1953 the studios had to be rebuilt from scratch. North Korea's president Kim Il-sung was astute in recognising the propaganda potential of cinema, ordering that it 'should play a mobilising role in the revolutionary struggle', and all films produced in the country in some way must serve to support the regime or reinforce resistance to perceived external aggressors such as Japan and the United States. Several films made during this period enjoyed considerable success across the Communist territories:

Choe Ik-kyu's anti-Japanese melodrama *The Flower Girl* (1970) was a hit in China, and took the Special Prize at the 1972 Karlovy Vary Film Festival, and the martial arts movie *Hong Kil Dong* (1986) was a box office hit in Bulgaria.

This close interest in cinema has continued under the rule of Kim Jong-il, Kim Il-sung's son and successor following his death in 1992. Well known as a film fan, Kim Jong-il reportedly has a personal collection of over 20,000 films, and has written extensively on cinema, such as in his 1973 book, *On the Art of Cinema*. It is said he harboured ambitions to be a director himself, and North Korean filmmakers and actors interviewed by this writer at the Pyongyang International Film Festival proudly shared anecdotes about his frequent visits to film sets where he offered crucial advice on troublesome scenes.

The economic realities of the post-Soviet world have not favoured film production in North Korea. The 1990s saw a sharp decline in annual output, as Soviet investment dried up overnight and the country faced hardships such as the devastating famine of the mid-

1990s. The belt-tightening has been reflected in films produced since the early 1990s, which have moved away from large-scale, overtly didactic productions towards a more realist aesthetic, with family dramas especially popular.

Production has declined still further since 2000. One official figure states that an average of five features has been made annually, but the number of local features screened at the past two Pyongyang Film Festivals suggests that the numbers are lower still. The only local feature screened at this year's festival was Phyo Kwang and Kim Hyon-chol's **The Kites Flying in the Sky**, based on the true story of a woman who abandons her promising marathon running career to care for orphaned children. The film was popular locally, where it previewed in February on Mansudae, the country's only television channel, before opening in cinemas in June. In 2007 the Korean Civil War drama *Kang Ho Yong* was the only feature released, while in 2006 two features were released: the anti-Japanese period drama *Pyongyang Nalpharam*, by Phyo Kwang, and Jang In-hok's *A Schoolgirl's Diary*, about a teenage student unsure whether to follow her father into a life devoted to scientific research in the interests of the country. The film became the first North Korean feature to be bought by a Western distributor when the Paris-based Pretty Pictures secured international rights. Pretty Pictures are planning a DVD set featuring the North Korean films

Jang In-hok's **A Schoolgirl's Diary**

A Schoolgirl's Diary, *The Flower Girl*, *Bell-flower* and the two-part *The Tale of Chun Hyang*.

Interviewed at this year's Pyongyang Film Festival, a spokesman from Korfilm, the state film distribution organisation, stated that one reason for the low output of the past two years was that Kom Jong-il, dissatisfied with the quality of recent films, in 2005 personally shut down all film production and ordered every North Korean director to undergo an eight-month training programme, part of which involved watching a selection of 250 foreign titles hand-picked by Kim Jong-il himself, and including films by the likes of Steven Spielberg and Zhang Yimou. According to Korfilm, the fruits of this intervention will be seen in 2009, with six or seven productions completed and awaiting approval from the State, and several more in production. Two confirmed titles are a historical drama from Phyo Kwang, and Jang In-hok's **The Village Beyond the Mountain**, an autobiographical story written by Bae Byeong-jun, a wealthy Korean resident in California, about a Korean soldier in the Civil War who ends up in the Netherlands, where he lives for forty years before returning to Pyongyang. According to the director Jang In-hok, shooting has been completed in North Korea, the Netherlands and Austria.

Feature-film production in North Korea is almost exclusively handled by the State-run Korean Film Studio, whose premises are on the outskirts of Pyongyang. There is also the Korean documentary studio, the April 25 Film Studio of the Korean People's Army, the Korean Science and Educational Film Studio, and an anime production house called the April 26th Children Film Studio, also known as SEK. Interest in anime is strong in the country, and it has also been an area where rare co-productions have been allowed with foreign production companies: 2005's *Empress Chung*, by director Nelson Shin, was a co-production between North and South Korea, and the first film to get a simultaneous release in both countries.

This year's Pyongyang Film Festival screened 108 films from 46 foreign countries. The final selection was whittled down from an initial number of five hundred chosen by Korfilm representatives who had attended the Shanghai and Berlin festivals. The final selection was made by a panel that included North Korean directors, academics and government officials. Founded in 1987, the festival was initially known as the Pyongyang Film Festival of Non-Aligned and Other Developing Countries, and its selection limited to films from nations with friendly diplomatic relations. Since the fall of the Soviet Union the festival has gradually become more open; the 2008 edition included titles from France, Britain, Iceland, Germany, Italy, Singapore and more. Chinese director Feng Xiaogang's *Assembly* took the Best Film prize. For the vast majority of North Korean people, the festival offers their only opportunity to see films from the West, their access to foreign films at other times restricted to mainly Russian, Chinese or Cuban titles that occasionally screen on the Masudae channel, or can be bought on the Mokran DVD label. The festival took place in six of Pyongyang's 14 cinemas, and attracted roughly seventy foreign guests.

Quotes of the year

'Actors should pursue their political study and skills training intensively, in order to raise their ideological level and steadily improve their artistic ability, so that they will not be tempted to envy or imitate others when acting.'
KIM JONG-IL, *leader of North Korea and published film theorist.*

Directory

Korfilm (Korea Film Export & Import Corporation), Central District, Pyongyang, Democratic People's Republic of Korea. Tel: 850 2 18000 (381 8034). Fax: 850 2 3814503. korfilm@co.chesin.com

---

JAMES BELL James Bell is Assistant Editor at *Sight & Sound* magazine

pbk £18.99 / $29.50
978-1-904764-11-3

THE CINEMA OF JAPAN & KOREA

Edited by Justin Bowyer
Preface by Jinhee Choi

The Cinema of Japan and Korea focuses on the continuing vibrancy of Japanese and Korean film. The 24 concise and informative essays each approach an individual film or documentary, together offering a unique introduction to the cinematic output of the two countries. With a range that spans from silent cinema to the present day, from films that have achieved classic status to underground masterpieces, the book provides an insight into the breadth of the Japanese and Korean cinematic landscapes. Among the directors covered are Akira Kurosawa, Takeshi Kitano, Kim Ki-duk, Kenji Mizoguchi, Kinji Fukusaku, Kim Ki-young, Nagisa Oshima and Takashi Miike. Included are in-depth studies of films such as *Battle Royale, Killer Butterfly, Audition, Violent Cop, In the Realm of the Senses, Tetsuo 2: Body Hammer, Teenage Hooker Becomes a Killing Machine, Stray Dog, A Page of Madness* and *Godzilla*.

'An introduction to two national cinemas that covers an impressive range of films, from international successes to lesser-known works. Both the academic and journalistic approaches are sure to widen the spectrum of potential readers for this fine volume.'
– Mitsuyo Wada-Marciano, Carleton University

'The essays themselves are all of excellent quality and take a varied approach to their subjects ... If you are new to Japanese and Korean cinema or want to look at your favourite films in more depth then this is, without doubt, the place to go.'
– *www.kamera.co.uk*

www.wallflowerpress.co.uk

Norway Trond Olav Svendsen

The winter season of 2007/08 saw both Bent Hamer and Nils Gaup release new films. Hamer's **O'Horten** was very well received. The eponymous hero is a railway engineer on the verge of retirement, whose adjustment to the life of a pensioner is the film's main focus. Horten is initially seen as an ordinary man with a somewhat unimaginative personality. He lives alone and spends his last working days at the helm of the passenger train that crosses the mountains, from Oslo to Bergen. Scenes in a public bath further suggest his loneliness. But Horten is liked by his colleagues and people trust him. We gradually discover that this ordinary fellow also has dreams and ambitions. Hamer's stories work both on the surface level, as 'slice of life' storytelling, and on a more ambiguous metaphorical level. His sensibilities when shooting in Norway (he has also made films abroad) is linked to the landscape, history and mentality of the nation in ways recognised by his audience. At the same time, the characters in his films have a deeper significance. The supporting characters are often a reflection of certain aspects of Horten's personality: a small boy lonely in his bed at night; an elderly

Bent Hamer's **O'Horten**

tobacco-shop customer with dementia; a dying eccentric posing as his own, more successful brother. All these characters are somehow tied to Horten's own regrets, anxieties and desires. There is a profound longing, mixed with a sense of danger, underneath the daily routines and behind the good-natured facades people project. Baard Owe is excellent as Horten, suggesting the dreamer beneath the ordinary man.

Nils Gaup's The Kautokeino Rebellion

Gaup's **The Kautokeino Rebellion** (*Kautokeino-opprøret*) was a disappointment. Gaup has a Sami background and his account of the famous events that took place in the Sami village of Kautokeino in 1852 was looked forward to with high expectations. A group of Sami men and women killed a sheriff and local trader who was selling liquor to the Sami men and enslaving them in debt. The two leaders of the gang were later executed. The way the film deals with the colonial attitudes of civil servants and traders was too obvious and lacked insight. The rebellion was fuelled by the revivalist teachings of Lars Levi Læstadius, whose followers, even today, are a puritanical group fighting not only the abuse of alcohol, but denying its members the pleasures of radio, TV and cinema. The film does perhaps betray Gaup's intolerance towards this form of religious doctrine and there can be

no denying the director's talent for storytelling. And Anni-Kristiina Juuso was impressive in her screen debut.

Stian Kristiansen's **The Man Who Loved Yngve**

With an increase in the number of films produced, some new directors have won the praise of critics. Thanks to the film school at Lillehammer and the lively Norwegian short-subject scene – the Grimstad short film festival certainly deserves kudos for its part in this development – many of the directorial debuts are remarkably assured. Stian Kristiansen's **The Man Who Loved Yngve** (*Mannen som elsket Yngve*) is a coming-of-age story set in the director's home town of Stavanger, on the west coast, commonly referred to as Norway's North Sea oil capital. Based on a popular novel by Tore Renberg, who also adapted it for the screen, the simple tale of how main protagonist Jarle discovers his possible homosexuality, focusing on the interplay between a group of friends and the choices they face, is impressive. The performances of the young actors, Rolf Kristian Larsen, Ole Christoffer Ertvaas, Arthur Berning and Ida Elise Broch, who are all relatively new to the screen, offer a fresh take on growing up.

In his film **Troubled Water** (*DeUsynlige*), Erik Poppe tells the story of a young man who has killed a small boy by throwing him into a river after he had stumbled and knocked himself unconscious. Poppe tells the story twice, from the viewpoint of the perpetrator and the boy's mother, impressively played, respectively, by Pål Sverre Valheim Hagen and Trine Dyrholm.

Ultimately, the film is rather better in its separate parts than its whole. Poppe's mise-en-scene is often vague and the story would have profited from a less improbable finale. But Poppe's handling of such a difficult subject is admirable. His sincerity is visible throughout and the film attracted a significant audience.

Poppe is not the only Norwegian director who attracts an audience these days. Norwegian cinema is, on the whole, progressing with energy and optimism. The current government, a Labour/Socialist/Centre coalition, has received praise from most quarters for its film initiatives. The number of feature releases has increased to around 25 per year (including documentaries). Norwegian films have doubled their local audience share, reaching up to 25%. Some complain that the growing number of features has turned the filmmaking scene into something of a young man's business. Only two films were directed by women in 2008, a surprisingly low number in equality-minded Norway. Although the number of young directors is significant, directors who have been around for some time (Bent Hamer, Hans Petter Moland, Petter Næss, Eva Isaksen, Knut Erik Jensen and Pål Sletaune) do seem to be able to make the films they want. If these trends are maintained, it looks like there will be exciting times ahead.

In Eva Sørhaug's impressive **Cold Lunch** (*Lønsj*) a hairdresser's selfish behaviour causes an accidental death and sets in motion a tragic series of consequences. Per Schreiner's script brings out the frustrations with refreshing clarity, while Sørhaug, previously a director of short films, transforms here into a fine director of actors who can deftly balance drama and humour.

TROND OLAV SVENDSEN is a historian from the University of Oslo. He has worked as a newspaper film critic and an editor in the Oslo publishing house of Kunnskapsforlaget. Among his publications is a Theatre and Film encyclopedia.

The year's best films
O'Horten (Bent Hamer)
The Man Who Loved Yngve
(Stian Kristiansen)
Troubled Water (Erik Poppe)
The Kautokeino Rebellion (Nils Gaup)
Cold Lunch (Eva Sørhaug)

Quote of the year
'We are so trendy in Norway. When you finally acquire some film experience, your career is suddenly over.' *Actor* HELGE JORDAL.

Directory
All Tel/Fax numbers begin (+47)
Henie-Onstad Art Centre, Sonja Henie vei 31, 1311 Høvikodden, Tel: 6780 4880, post@hok.no
Norwegian Film Fund, PO Box 752 Sentrum, 0106 Oslo, Tel: 2247 8040, Fax: 2247 8041, www.filmfondet.no, Contact: Stein Slyngstad
Norwegian Film Institute, PO Box 482 Sentrum, 0105 Oslo, Tel: 2247 4500, Fax: 2247 4599, post@ nfi.no, www.nfi.no, Contact: Lise Gustavson
Norwegian Film Development, PO Box 904 Sentrum, 0104 Oslo, Tel: 2282 2400, Fax: 2282 2422, mail@nfu.no, Contact: Kirsten Bryhni
Norwegian Film and TV Producers Association, Dronningens gt. 16, 0152 Oslo, Tel: 2311 9311, Fax: 2311 9316, pf@produsentforeningen.no, Contact: Leif Holst Jensen
Norwegian Film Workers Association, Dronningens gt. 16, 0152 Oslo, Tel: 2247 4640 , Fax: 2247 4689, post@filmforbundet.no, Contact: Sverre Pedersen
Norwegian Media Authority, Nygata 4, 1607 Fredrikstad, Tel: 6930 1200, Fax: 6930 1201, post@medietilsynet.no, Contact: Tom Thoresen

Eva Sørhaug's **Cold Lunch**

pbk £18.99 / $29.50
978-1-904764-22-9

THE CINEMA OF SCANDINAVIA

Edited by Tytti Soila
Preface by Jacob Neiiendam

This volume in the 24 Frames series focuses on 24 key films from Scandinavia – Denmark, Sweden, Norway and Finland. Each national cinema is able to boast directors of worldwide renown, such as Ingmar Bergman, Carl Theodor Dreyer, Victor Sjöström and more contemporary filmmakers such as Lukas Moodysson, Aki Kaurismäki and the co-founders of the Dogme 95 movement, Lars von Trier, Thomas Vinterberg and Soren Kragh-Jacobsen. This book deals with the impact that these and other filmmakers have had on both their national cinema as well as the world of film and looks in detail at the styles, movements and influences from this region. Includes detailed coverage of a wide range of films including *Operation Swallow* (1948), *The Unknown Soldier* (1955), *Ebba the Movie* (1982), *The Idiots* (1998) and *Ballroom Blitz* (2001).

'*The Cinema of Scandinavia* offers insights with both scholarly acumen, and a respectful approach to Scandinavian cinema … It is an important book that clarifies and illuminates the state of Scandinavian cinema, and makes a genuine contribution to the field of cinema studies.' – **Jarmo Valkola, University of Jyväskylä**

'Gives a more broad and varied account of Swedish, Norwegian, Danish, and Finnish films than any other internationally published volume before it.'
– **Erik Hedling, Lund University**

'The book is accessible yet expert, broad yet detailed, useful yet delightful … A necessary, useful, and excellent book.' – **Andrew Nestingen, University of Washington**

www.wallflowerpress.co.uk

Pakistan Aijaz Gul

The picture emerging from the Pakistani film industry may have its share of gloom, but it's far from doom. There may have been few films in 2008, but there were some impressive releases amongst them. With the official import of Indian films (they have actually been available in Pakistan for decades, on illegal video, DVD and VCD, as well as cable TV), new cinemas are being built.

Director Shoaib Mansoor's *In the Name of God*, the biggest success of 2007, continued to play successfully throughout 2008. Received well by critics, its appearance at many film festivals brought a degree of prestige to Pakistani cinema.

Mehreen Jabbar's **Ramchand Pakistani**

Mehreen Jabbar's feature debut, **Ramchand Pakistani**, opened to great success in July. Filmed in the desert of Thar, which adjoins Rajasthan in India, the Pakistan/US co-production's tag line was 'He crossed one line and three lives changed forever'. When the seven-year-old Pakistani Hindu, Ramchand, crosses the unmarked border into India, his father goes in search of him. Both are caught and imprisoned in a film that deals with their struggle, as well as the helplessness of the mother who awaits their return. The film

profits from two exceptional performances by Fazal Hussain as Ramchand and Indian actress Nandita Das as his mother. Jabbar's direction is sparse, but engages the audience with its emotional impact. Certain scenes of incarceration were actually filmed in an Indian prison, with the help of local authorities. Their permission was secured by producer-writer Javed Jabbar and took just six hours to complete. *Ramchand Pakistani* has so far screened at Tribeca, Seattle, Osian's Cinefan and Rhode Island film festivals.

Four young independent filmmakers presented their work at the Osian's Cinefan Festival, which takes place every July in Dehli. It was significant that so many Pakistani films were featured at an Indian festival. Director Ehteshamuddin's **This is India That is Pakistan** (*Yeh Hindustan Woh Pakistan*), set during the 1947 Partition, stresses the importance of friendship and human relations over politics and religious bias. Sharjil Baluch's **The Will of Gurmukh Sing** (*Gurmukh Singh Ki Virasat*) is about closely-knit Sikh and Hindu families in a predominantly Sikh village in 1947.

Producer-director Omar Khan's digitally-shot teen slasher, **Hell's Ground** (*Zibahkhana*), was screened theatrically with a special projection system set up at selected cinemas. It also appeared at a number of film festivals. Made on a shoestring budget, the UK co-production is about a teen gang who take a short-cut through some woods on their way to a rock concert. The gang encounters the living dead and other nasty creatures in a film that even the director refers to as a 'midnight cheesy movie'.

Producer-director-actor Javed Sheikh's much awaited **Sky** (*Khuley Aasman Key Neechey*) was mostly filmed in India and featured Humayun Saeed, Nadeem, Sana and Meera. A weak plot and weaker songs could not save it, even with widespread media publicity and promotion.

Government control of piracy remains inadequate, with both Pakistani and Indian films widely available on all formats. However, the appearance of Bollywood films in cinemas is a new move. The flow of films has increased, from six features last year to twelve by August this year. *Goal*, *Race* and *Singh Is King* all performed well, supporting the revenues of the multiplexes in Karachi, Lahore, Rawalpindi and Islamabad. But significant business for both Pakistani and Indian films will only increase when the government takes a strong stand against piracy.

The year ended on a sad note with the passing of two major figures in Pakistan's film industry: Badar Munir and Pervaiz Malik. Munir began his career as a rickshaw driver and then a lighting operator in Karachi's film studios. He made his debut as the leading man in the first Pakistani Pushto film, *Eternal Love*, but was best known for his action roles. Director-screenwriter-producer Malik earned his MA in Cinema from the University of Southern California. He made 26 films in a career that spanned 28 years from 1964 to 1992. In recent years he worked on TV serials. The winner of numerous awards, he was the recipient

of the President's Pride of Performance. His films looked at social issues such as poverty, planned parenthood and the remarriage of young widows. He will be rmostly emembered for the films *Wish*, *Favour* and *Anonymous*.

Muhammed Saife Hassan's adaptation of a Rohinton Mistry short story, **The Victoria's Stamp** (*Victoria Ka Ticket*), reflects both the fears and fantasies of a child. 'It is difficult to adapt short stories,' he said. 'The plot made me cry. The film is true to the spirit but after that it takes its own twists and turns.'

Fazal Hussain in Mehreen Jabbar's **Ramchand Pakistani**

The year's best films
Ramchand Pakistani (Mehreen Jabbar)
This is India That is Pakistan
(Ehteshamuddin)
Hell's Ground (Omar Khan)
The Victoria's Stamp (Saife Hasan)

Quote of the year
'That's the revolution that I want – a revolution of ideas. It feels great that a Filipino film is being noticed abroad because of its story and how well made it is.' *Director* MEHREEN JABBAR *on the realism of her first feature,* **Ramchand Pakistani**.

AIJAZ GUL is a film critic who went to USC, Los Angeles from where he earned his BA and MA in Film. He has published four books, the latest on singer-actress Noorjehan which has been published in Delhi. He is a member of FIPRESCI and NETPAC (Network for the Promotion of Asian Cinema).

Omar Khan's **Hell's Ground**

Peru Isaac Léon Frías

Compared to previous years, film activity increased in Peru during 2008. Between September and December, five domestic films were released – an unusually high number over such a short period of time.

However, the year did not start off well. Eduardo Mendoza's **I'll Tell You Tomorrow 2** (*Mañana te cuento 2*) and David Bisbano's **Valentino and the Klan of the Dogs** (*Valentino y el clan del can*) did not perform as well as the directors' previous films. Inca Cine, the most active production company in Peru, produced Mendoza's film. His original, released three years ago, followed the adventures of three young friends who encounter high-class prostitutes. The sequel adds some police intrigue, which fails to work. Even its target audience, the youth market, saw through the weak plotting. *Valentino* was the third digital animated feature released by Alpamayo Entertainment, but lacked the attraction of *Pirates in Callao* and *Dragoons: Destiny of Fire*.

The skilful management of the National Cinematography Council (CONACINE), presided over by Rosa María Oliart, saw greater support from the government, which should see its involvement in feature projects increase in 2009. This atmosphere of progress can be seen in five productions released this year, although not all of them were recipients of awards issued by CONACINE juries.

Rocío Lladó's debut, **Parallel Lives** (*Vidas paralelas*), looks at the terse relationship between the military and the violent terrorist organisation, Sendero Luminoso (Shining Path). Sadly, the weak narrative and a strange point of view undermine the film.

Jorge Cesti and Mónica Sánchez in Andrés Cotler's **Passengers**

Another new director, Andrés Cotler, looked at migration amongst the young in **Passengers** (*Pasajeros*). Unlike *Parallel Lives*, the film benefited from fine plotting and strong direction from Cotler. **Gods** (*Dioses*), the second film by Josué Méndez, did not repeat the success of his debut, *Santiago's Days*. The film focuses on the lives of a powerful and influential Peruvian family.

A Naked Body (*Un cuerpo desnudo*) is the latest film from Francisco Lombardi, the most prolific Peruvian director. Its point of reference is *Friends*, which Lombardi directed thirty years ago and which the filmmaker also used in *Immoral Tales*. In the original, the main characters were four friends gathered together

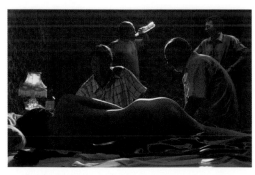

Francisco Lombardi's **A Naked Body**

Miguel Iza in Daniel Ró's **El Acuarelista**

in a bar. Now they are four veterans who meet in one of the characters' houses. Tightly directed and well acted, the film increases the tension of the situation as the drama unfolds.

Finally, **El acuarelista** is Daniel Ró's (Rodríguez is his last name) account of a painter who rents an apartment in an old building in Lima and whose imagination gets the better of him. Having cut his teeth on short films after his studies, Ró's feature debut is something of a disappointment, lacking the energy and warmth of his previous work.

With so much activity over the last year, 2009 looks set to be a productive time for filmmaking.

Rocío Lladó's **Parallel Lives**

ISAAC LÉON FRÍAS is a film critic and Professor of Language and Film History at the University of Lima. From 1965 to 1985 he was director of *Hablemos de Cine* magazine and from 1986 to 2001 ran Filmoteca de Lima.

pbk £18.99 / $29.50
978-1-903364-83-3

THE CINEMA OF LATIN AMERICA

Edited by Alberto Elena and Marina Díaz López
Preface by Walter Salles

The Cinema of Latin America focuses on the vibrant practices that make up the traditions of filmmaking in this complex and diverse region. A historically significant regional cinema, Latin American film is increasingly returning to popular and academic appreciation. Through 24 concise and insightful essays that each consider one significant film or documentary, the editors of this volume have compiled a unique introduction to the cinematic output of countries as diverse as Brazil, Argentina, Cuba, Mexico, Bolivia and Chile. The work of directors such as Luis Buñuel, Tomás Guitérrez Alea, Glauber Rocha and Walter Salles is discussed and the collection includes in-depth studies of seminal works such as *Los Olvidados*, *The Hour of the Furnaces*, *Memories of Underdevelopment*, *The Battle of Chile*, *Foreign Land* and *Amores Perros*.

'A must-have for anyone who professes admiration and enthusiasm for Latin American cinema. Seldom has a selection of films done such a competent job of synthesising the nature and virtues of a body of cinema; this anthology manages to grasp the genuine character of Latin American film.' – **Héctor D. Fernández l'Hoeste, Georgia State University**

'A very useful book. Not only are the contributions of a high standard, but by providing close readings of films in historical sequence – and it's a very well made selection – it amounts to an extremely useful survey for anyone teaching, learning of just interested in the cinema of Latin America.' – **Michael Chanan, Roehampton University**

www.wallflowerpress.co.uk

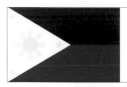

Philippines Tessa Jazmines

On the surface, there has been little action in Filipino cinema. Look again, however, and you will find a great deal of underground activity. Although mainstream films were once again kept to a minimum, independent productions made 2008 a breakthrough year. More than ever, Filipino filmmakers circumnavigated the globe, exhibiting their product at international film festivals including Rotterdam, Berlin, Cannes, Paris, Bangkok and Montreal. (For the first time in the 49-year existence of the Thessaloniki International Film Festival, a Filipino film, Ellen Ramos and Paolo Villaluna's **The Inmate** (*Selda*), was featured in competition.)

For the most part, the burgeoning digital technology has made it difficult to keep up with all aspects of film production in the country. What is clear is that established directors and budding filmmakers are all producing films outside the major studios. Big-name actors have also launched their own film projects, making bold moves with left-field scripts and taking risks with their own money – all in search of independence within the market.

For the first time, **Urduja**, a full-length Tagalog animated movie made by Reggie Entienza, was a success at the local box office. Not bad for an industry described as 'dead' or 'dying'.

Independently-produced films are now responsible for reviving the Philippine film industry. 'Budding directors are turning to [independent films] because they need less money to produce,' says Brillante 'Dante' Mendoza, the director of **Service** (*Serbis*), the first full-length Filipino film to compete in Cannes since 1984. 'You don't need a production team. You don't even need actors. All you need to have is your camera,' Mendoza

added. *Service* is the story of a family who run a dilapidated porn theatre. It was awarded two prizes at the 6th International Pacific Meridian Film Festival in Russia, as well as the Golden Kinnaree Award in the Southeast Asian competition at the Bangkok Film Festival. Mendoza's other films, *Slingshot*, *Summer Heat*, *Foster Child* and *The Masseur* have all won critical acclaim both locally and abroad.

Brillante 'Dante' Mendoza's **Service**

The 31-year-old Manunuri ng Pelikulang Pilipino (The Filipino Film Critics Circle) did not nominate any studio films for the 2008 Gawad Urian award. The popularity of independent films amongst the Manunuri jury suggests 'Pinoy indie' films are enjoying wider acceptance than ever before. Could it also be a hint that the movie industry is finally moving in the right direction?

Even the mainstream studio, Star Cinema, produced Chito S. Roño's **Caregiver**, an 'alternative' film starring Sharon 'the Mega Star' Cuneta, one of the Philippines' top actresses. This story of an overseas worker taking care of sick patients in Britain, who is torn between work and her family back home, delivered a meaningful message and played well to local audiences.

Judy Ann Santos in Dante Nico Garcia's **Ploning**

Dante Nico Garcia's **Ploning** was produced by and starred another bankable leading actress Judie Ann Santos (described in entertainment pages as 'the most influential actress of [her] generation'). A haunting story of a provincial woman who waits patiently for the return of her one true love on the idyllic island of Cuyo, it is the Philippines' foreign-language entry for the 2009 Academy Awards. It received an 'A' Rating from the Cinema Evaluation Board, which automatically gave it a tax reprieve and a cash incentive, a reward from the government to local filmmakers who make world-class films. It was also a success at the local box office.

Twenty new digital films competed in the 2008 Cinemalaya Independent Film Festival and Competition. **100**, Chris Martinez's winning film, is about a cancer victim with a hundred things to do. Francis Xavier Pasion's **Jay** is about a TV producer who creates a documentary about a homosexual teacher. John Torres' **Years When I Was a Child Outside** (*Taon Noong Ako'y Anak Sa Labas*)

John Torres' **Years When I Was a Child Outside**

weaves autobiography and fictional vignettes with a documentary approach to make and impressive and engrossing feature.

Despite their limited output, mainstream studios fared well throughout the year. The big winners were romantic dramas and stories targeted at younger audiences: Mark A. Reyes' **My Best Friend's Girlfriend** (GMA Films), Cathy Garcia-Molina's **A Very Special Love** (Star Cinema) and Joyce E. Bernal's **For the First Time** (Star Cinema).

Another Metro Manila Film Festival opened in the capital on Christmas Day. The two-week festival features only Filipino films. This year's batch was dominated by comedy, followed by drama and horror. It was also the first time that a feature-length animated film (Robert Quilao's **Dayo**) participated. The Christmas Day parade is a sight to see, with movie fans lining the parade path six-deep just to see their favourite stars up close.

Overall, piracy, poverty and taxes continued to be the major challenges facing the film industry. But the constant creative flow from older and younger artists offers hope that the complex and challenged Filipino cinema will one day strengthen its position in the region. The question is not if, but when.

The year's best films
Ploning (Dante Nico Garcia)
Service (Brillante 'Dante' Mendoza)
100 (Chris Martinez)
Jay (Francis Xavier Pasion)
Caregiver (Chito Rono)

Quote of the year
'You just go out, write your script and shoot the film.' BRILLANTE MENDOZA, *on making digital films.*

TESSA JAZMINES teaches advertising, public relations, thesis writing and sports writing at the University of the Philippines College of Mass Communication.

Poland Barbara Hollender

After tough times at the beginning of this decade, Polish cinema has left the doldrums and is currently looking healthier. Thanks to the new system of financing, the Polish Film Institute (PISF), which was set up in 2005, has shown its effectiveness in supporting domestic production. By the end of August 2008, the annual operational programme budget for the production of feature films had reached €22 million, almost double the amount set aside in 2006. In 2004, thirteen films were shot in Poland. In 2007, sixty had been produced and all showed a marked increase in quality. The participants of the 2008 Polish Feature Films Festival were unanimous that the programme was the best overview of Polish films for some time.

Michał Rosa's **The Scratch**

Diversity remains key to success for Polish cinema. One of the most interesting titles of the season is **The Scratch** (*Rysa*) by Michał Rosa. The Polish equivalent of *The Lives of Others*, the film looks at the period of Polish 'decommunisation', when people were accused, not always correctly, of being informers for the secret police. A professor of biology is informed that her husband of forty years had informed on her dissident father.

Małgorzata Szumowska's **33 Scenes from Life**

Although there is no evidence available, she cannot cope with the information and suffers a breakdown. Rosa shows the loneliness experienced by those accused of collaboration. The film was invited to screen at Venice Days.

Małgorzata Szumowska's **33 Scenes from Life** (*33 sceny z życia*) is a study of suffering. An exhibitionist, aggressive work, transcending safety limits and unwilling to make the viewer feel comfortable, Szumowska focuses on those moments in life when everything falls apart, with a sharp and unsentimental eye. A young woman loses both her parents over a short period. Shortly after, her marriage fails and she descends into alcohol abuse and parties with abandon, all in an effort to escape her life. Whether audiences like the film or not, whether they accept its philosophy, it is impossible to stay indifferent to it.

Jerzy Skolimowski returned after seventeen years with **Four Nights with Anna** (*Cztery noce z Anną*). A delicate and surprising story of an obsessive, but pure, love, it is a characteristically difficult film, close in style to Skolimowski's work from the 1980s. It was presented in the 'Directors' Fortnight' section

DMITRIJ
ULIANOV

SVETLANA
KHODCHENKOVA

GRAND PRIX - GOLDEN LIONS
at the PFF GDYNIA 2008
Svetlana Khodchenkova
- BEST ACTRESS

LESŁAW
ŻUREK

A FILM BY WALDEMAR KRZYSTEK

LITTLE MOSCOW

MAŁA MOSKWA

114', colour, 35 mm, Dolby Digital, 1:2.35, Poland 2008

Producer:

SKORPION
ART

skorpion@softmark.com.pl
www.skorpionart.republika.pl

TELEWIZJA POLSKA

World sales & co-producer:

sales@tvp.pl
www.international.tvp.pl
tel. +48 22 547 38 07

Jerzy Skolimowski's **Four Nights with Anna**

of the Cannes Film Festival and later – in the autumn of 2008 – at a dozen important festivals, including Toronto, New York, London and Tokyo.

Waldemar Krzystek's **Little Moscow** (*Mała Moskwa*) presented an interesting romance set around a Soviet base in Legnica, a town in southwestern Poland, in 1968. An illicit love affair between the wife of a Soviet officer and a Polish soldier allows Krzystek the opportunity to explore life on a Soviet base. Ultimately, the film is about the corrupting power of a totalitarian system.

Documentary filmmaker Jacek Bławut's noble film **Before Twilight** (*Jeszcze nie wieczór*), looks at life inside an old actors' home in Skolimow. The actors stage *Faust* for the last time in their lives for the inmates of a nearby prison.

Offsiders (*Boisko bezdomnych*) is Kasia Adamik's second film. It is about a group of homeless people from the Warsaw Central railroad station, who decide to field a football

Kasia Adamik's **Offsiders**

team in an attempt to enter the World Cup. Interestingly, it displayed an atypically optimistic tone for Polish cinema.

Polish immigrants are the subject of Dariusz Gajewski's **Mr Kuka's Advice** (*Lekcje pana Kuki*), while Magdalena Piekorz presented a series of character studies in **Drowsiness** (*Senność*). Both are the fruits of cooperation between the new generation of directors and writers. Gajewski adapted Radek Knapp, while Piekorz teamed up once again with Wojciech Kuczok, the winner of one of Poland's most prestigious literary awards, the Nike.

Magdalena Pierkorz's **Drowsiness**

The lives of young people and the future they can look forward to was seen in **O_1_0**, by the recently deceased Piotr Łazarkiewicz. A similar mood is found in **Splinters** (*Drzazgi*) by Maciej Pieprzyca. The central characters of both films are lost and unfulfilled in life.

Polish cinema also succeeded at the box office. The biggest draw in 2008 was **Lejdis**, directed by Tomasz Konecki, with a script by Andrzej Saramonowicz. It is the story of four female friends in their thirties. A Polish version of *Sex and the City*, it was disliked by critics but attracted more than 2.5 million people. Piotr Weresniak's romantic comedy **Don't Lie, Dear** (*Nie klam, kochanie*) also performed well. It was written by Ilona Łepkowska, who also writes for some of Polish television's most popular soaps. **Testimony** (*Swiadectwo*), Pawel Pitera's documentary about Pope John Paul II, also looks set to attract a huge audience.

Polish cinema still shows a strong affinity for history. After Andrzej Wajda's *Katyn*, the Polish press discussed the issue of other uncovered events in Polish history. The 1944 Warsaw Uprising is often mentioned. The PISF set up a contest to find the perfect script to cover this event. Two were finally chosen. One attracted the attention of Juliusz Machulski, and the other Dariusz Gajewski.

Other directors are also interested in this period of history. Anna Jadowska and Lidia Kazen are preparing a film about the death of General Sikorski during the Second World War. Waldemar Krzystek wants to make a film about Lower Silesian Solidarity activists. There are also projects about Polish soldiers fighting in Afghanistan and the invasion of Czechoslovakia by Warsaw Pact forces in 1968. However, the budget for such movies is likely to be too large.

International co-productions are becoming more popular. *33 Scenes from Life* was made in cooperation with Germany, Gajewski's *Mr Kuka's Advice* included Austrian funding and Skolimowski's *Four Nights with Anna* had support from France. Poland is also the destination of many foreign filmmakers. Christopher Doyle directed the thriller *Warsaw Dark* and Petr Zelenka's *The Karamazovs* was partly shot in Kraków. Autumn saw the first Polish/Israeli production, **Spring 1941** (*Wiosna 1941*), by Uri Barbash. And in September *Waltz with Bashir* director Ari Folman was negotiating the terms of yet another Polish/Israeli co-production – an adaptation of one of Stanisław Lem's novels.

The co-production hit of 2008 was **The True Story of Janosik**, directed by Agnieszka Holland and Kasia Adamik. A Slovak/Czech production, it was suspended three years ago due to a lack of funds, but was re-launched last year with PISF subsidies. Next year will see a joint venture by Krzysztof and Joanna Krauze. **Birds Singing at Kigali** (*Ptaki spiewaja w*

Malgorzata Szumowska's **33 Scenes from Life**

Kigali) is based on a story by Wojciech Albiński and produced in co-operation with Canada. Dariusz Jabłoński also wishes to work in Canada, where he wants to make a film about the tragedy at Vancouver Airport, when police killed a Polish immigrant with a tazer gun.

One of the most awaited films over the next year will be Andrzej's Wajda's **Sweet Flag** (*Tatarak*), based-Polish writer Jaroslaw Iwaszkiewicz's novel.

The Polish market shows an ever-growing division between viewing figures for commercial and artistic films. Local comedies, backed with heavy advertising and released on 150–180 prints, can count on an average audience of 700–900,000, even reaching into the millions. More ambitious films are an unprecedented success if they attract 60–80,000 viewers, but most of them face attendance figures of 15–20,000. The fundamental question is, how can these films reach a wider audience? Agnieszka Odorowicz, the director of the Polish Film Institute hopes that digital exhibition will resolve the problem. This technological change will be carried out on a mass scale in the near future, with funding from the Ministry of Culture and National Heritage.

BARBARA HOLLENDER is a Warsaw-based journalist and film critic for the daily *Rzeczpospolita*. She covers the Berlin, Cannes, Venice and Karlovy Vary film festivals, and has written, amongst other works, a study of *Studio Tor* (2000).

The year's best films
33 Scenes from Life (Malgorzata Szumowska)
The Scratch (Michal Rosa)
Four Nights with Anna (Jerzy Skolimowski)
The Karamazovs (Petr Zelenka)
Before Twilight (Jacek Bławut)

Quote of the year
'Nearly every day I find in a newspaper an article about problems and events that would attract the world. Nobody has made a serious film about Polish Catholicism, about anti-semitism, about the attitude of our society towards minorities - for example, towards homosexuals. And there is no true art without dealing with difficult issues.' MALGORZATA SZUMOWSKA, *talking about Polish cinema.*

Directory
All Tel/Fax numbers begin (+48)
Muzeum Kinematografi, Pl Zwyciestwa 1, 90 312 Lódz. Tel: (42) 674 0957. Fax: (42) 674 90006.
National Film Library, Ul Pulawska 61, 00 975 Warsaw. Tel: (22) 845 5074. filmoteka@filmoteka.pl. www.fn.org.pl.
Association of Polish Filmmakers, Ul Pulawska 61, 02 595 Warsaw. Tel: (22) 845 5132. Fax: (22) 845 3908. biuro@sfp.org.pl. www.sfp.org.pl.
Film Polski, Ul Mazowiecki 6/8, 00 048 Warsaw. Tel: (22) 826 0849. Fax: (22) 826 8455. info@filmpolski.com.pl. www.filmpolski.com.pl.
Film Production Agency, Ul Pulawska 61, 02 595 Warsaw. Tel: (22) 845 5324. info@pakietyfilmowe.waw.pl. www.pakietyfilmowe.waw.pl.
National Board of Radio and Television (KRRIT), Skwerks Wyszynskiego 9, 01 015 Warsaw. Tel: (22) 635 9925. Fax: (22) 838 3501. krrit@krrit.gov.pl. www.krrit.gov.pl.
National Chamber of Audiovisual Producers, Ul Pulawska 61, 02 595 Warsaw. Tel: (22) 845 6570. Fax: (22) 845 5001. kipa@org.pl.
Polish TV Film Agency (TVP), Ul JP Woronicza 17, 00 999 Warsaw. Tel: (22) 547 9167. Fax: (22) 547 4225. www.tvp.pl.
WFDIF Film Studio, Ul Chelmska 21, 00 724 Warsaw. Tel: (22) 841 1210-19. Fax: (22) 841 5891. wfdif@wfdif.com.pl. www.wfdif.com.pl.

Portugal Martin Dale

A land of sunshine, warm friendly people, charming natural and cultural heritage, imbued with a spirit of discovery and standing at the cutting edge of new technology. This is the image Portugal projects via lavish international marketing campaigns, funded by the Portuguese Tourism Board, under the brand image 'Europe's West Coast'.

Portuguese cinema, by contrast, which is heavily dependent on state funding, projects a very different image of the country. Corruption, prostitution, bribery, blackmail, murder, adultery, meddling politicians, incompetent policemen, jealousy, bickering, drug addiction, domestic violence, shadowy interiors and despair are the main themes emanating from recent Portuguese films, whether 'auteur' or 'commercial' fare.

Portuguese cinema's 'downbeat' outlook on life is undoubtedly rooted in the country's genuine problems and also linked to the nation's strong Catholic tradition, which views sex as sinful, power as corrupting and life as a vale of tears. Portugal's two biggest hits in 2008 – João Botelho's **Corruption** (*Corrupção*) with over 230,000 admissions and António-Pedro Vasconcelos's **Call Girl** with 232,000 – both revolve around the worlds of politics, prostitution and corruption.

António Pedro Vasconcelos' **Call Girl**

Corruption was produced by Portugal's new kid on the block, Alexandre Valente, who cut his teeth in advertising and TV movies. In 2004, he launched Utopia Filmes. The following year, it opened with Portugal's biggest domestic hit, *The Crime of Father Amaro* (380,000 admissions), starring veteran actor Nicolau Breyner and hot starlet, Soraia Chaves.

Valente's production approach differs from the majority of his colleagues. Whereas most Portuguese film producers wait for a non-reimbursable grant from the national film institute, ICA, Valente has made most of his films without subsidies. This market-orientated approach garnered him €5 million in seed funding from the recently launched public/private venture-capital fund, FICA.
Key ingredients of Valente's productions are slick photography, hip soundtracks and a strong dose of eroticism. He also insists on final cut. In the case of *Corruption*, the original director - renowned auteur João Botelho – was dismissed during postproduction and Valente re-edited the film with a new soundtrack. Once again starring Nicolau Breyner, it performed well at the box office but is confused and lacks soul. Valente is now preparing an erotic thriller, **Second Life**, to be co-directed by Breyner and Miguel Gaudêncio.

João Botelho's latest feature is the sprawling family drama, **The Northern Land** (*A Corte do Norte*), produced by veteran producer António da Cunha Telles. Based on the novel by Agustina Bessa-Luís and starring Ana Moreira, the film premiered at the New York Film Festival. **Call Girl**, directed by António Pedro Vasconcelos and produced by Tino Navarro, shares certain surface similarities with Alexandre Valente's productions –

including stars Nicolau Breyner and Soraia Chaves. But there the similarities end. *Call Girl* is an accomplished film noir, featuring a mesmerising central performance by Chaves.

At the other end of the spectrum, Europe's oldest working director, Manoel de Oliveira, celebrated his hundredth birthday with a series of exhibitions and retrospectives. In early 2009, Oliveira will begin shooting his next feature **The Peculiarities of a Young Blonde Girl** (*Singularidades de uma Rapariga Loira*), about a young man who falls in love with a mysterious blonde, based on a short story by Eça de Queiroz and produced by Filmes do Tejo.

Filmes do Tejo also released Paulo Marinou Blanco's love triangle film, *Goodnight Irene*, in 2007 and is currently working with Ivo Ferreira on his second feature, **Downpour** (*Águas Mil*), about a young boy on the trail of his lost father, a former revolutionary agitator.

Portugal's most prolific producer, Paulo Branco, has revamped his approach over the last two to three years. In the wake of the death of auteur João Cesar Monteiro and following a parting of ways with Oliveira, he now focuses on new filmmaking talent. Business difficulties have also obliged Branco to cut back drastically on his exhibition activities. He now operates through two new production companies: Clap Filmes in Portugal and Alfama Filmes in France.

Luís Filipe Rocha's **The Other Side** (*A Outra Margem*) recounts the emotional rebirth of a transvestite who rediscovers the joy of

Luis Filipe Rocha's **The Other Side**

life by spending time in the company of an adolescent with Down's Syndrome. Lead actors Filipe Duarte and Tomás Almeida won Best Actor *ex aequo* at the Montreal World Film Festival. José Nascimento's **Wolves** (*Lobos*) portrays the flight from justice of Joaquim (Nuno Melo) through the remote mountains of northern Portugal, accompanied by his niece (Catarina Wallenstein), with whom he develops a moving relationship.

João Canijo's **Misbegotten**

Talented young directing duo Tiago Guedes and Frederico Serra followed their previous horror film, *Wicked Thing*, with the black-and-white **Noise** (*Entre os dedos*), a bleak portrayal of a man trying to make sense of his life after losing his job. The pair are now working on the biopic **D. João II – The Perfect Prince**. Paulo Branco's long-time collaborator, João Canijo, produced an equally glum view of Portugal in **Misbegotten** (*Mal Nascida*), about a widow who attempts to avenge her husband's murder. It was inspired by the Greek myth of Electra.

Miguel Gomes' **Our Beloved Month of August**

Upcoming production outfit, O Som e a Furia, released the second feature by Miguel Gomes, **Our Beloved Month of August** (*Aquele querido mês de Agosto*), which screened as part of the 'Directors' Fortnight' at Cannes. It has since clocked up over 17,000 admissions in Portugal and has been chosen as the country's candidate for the Best Foreign Language Film Academy Award. The film follows a musical band during popular summertime festivities. O Som e a Furia also produced Sandro Aguilar's powerful debut feature, **Uprise** (*A Zona*), which premiered at the London Film Festival. An atmospheric search for identity, set in a hospital, it features masterful visual and sound design.

At an institutional level, the main change this year was the launch of the long-awaited film fund, FICA, which has secured €83 million in financing for the next five years.

FICA's board members include the State and main national broadcasters. The fund is shared equally between film and audiovisual productions, investing in individual projects and in companies. The fund's principal initial investments include €2.5 million in a 26-part TV series, **Ecuador**, €5 million in Utopia Filmes and €4 million in Valentim de Carvalho Filmes. The latter is a vertically integrated operation, topped by former SIC programming director, Manuel Fonseca. Its first two feature productions are biopics of seminal figures from recent Portuguese history: Jorge Queiroga's **Private Life of Salazar** and Carlos Coelho da Silva's **Amália**. The latter premiered in December and will be an interesting test to see if Portugal's new institutional focus on 'commercial films' will be successful.

The year's best films
Call Girl (António Pedro Vasconcelos)
Our Beloved Month of August (Miguel Gomes)
Uprise (Sandro Aguilar)
The Other Side (Luís Filipe Rocha)
Misbegotten (João Canijo)

Quote of the year
'I don't have a pessimistic outlook on life, but I have a completely pessimistic vision of Portugal.' JOÃO CANIJO, *director of* **Misbegotten**.

Directory
All Tel/Fax numbers begin (+351)
Cinemateca Portuguesa, Rua Barata Salgueiro 63, 1269-059 Lisbon. Tel: (21) 359 6200. Fax: (21) 352 3180. www.cinemateca.pt.
Institute of Cinema, Audiovisual & Multimedia (ICAM), Rua de S Pedro de Alcântara 45, 1°, 1250 Lisbon. Tel: (21) 323 0800. Fax: (21) 343 1952. mail@icam.pt. www.icam.pt.

MARTIN DALE has lived in Lisbon and the north of Portugal since 1994 and works as an independent media consultant and a contributor to *Variety*. He has written several books on the film industry, including *The Movie Game* (1997).

Coelho da Silva's **Amália**

Puerto Rico Raúl Ríos-Díaz

In 2008, Puerto Rican film production rose for the third year in a row. With few exceptions, though, these films experienced a few weeks of limited release and attracted little money at the box office. Some local producers believe that the sudden spurt in production may have had a negative effect on the public, which had previously viewed any new domestic release as a 'must-see event'. On the positive side, two 2008 releases began reversing that trend, with one becoming Puerto Rico's top-grossing film.

Carlos Ruiz-Ruiz and Marie Pérez-Rivera's **Lovesickness**

Following a brief 2007 Academy Award-qualifying run, Carlos Ruíz Ruíz and Mariem Pérez Riera's **Lovesickness** (*Maldeamores*) debuted in February to favourable reviews and solid box office. Executive produced by Puerto Rican Oscar winner Benicio del Toro, the film's three storylines present an ironic take on love.

Local reggaetón figure, Raymond Ayala, known internationally as 'Daddy Yankee', produced and starred in **Talent from the Barrio** (*Talento de Barrio*), directed by José Iván Santiago. The film follows the efforts of a young man who gives up his thuggish life in order to become the 'Big Boss' of reggaetón. The film scored

an opening-day record audience of 12,000 when it premiered on fourteen screens in August (versus the reported opening day ticket sales of 6,000 for *Lovesickness*). It also took in an impressive US$515,575 in its opening weekend and topped US$1 million before the end of its first month in cinemas (a box office accomplishment previously achieved by only two other local productions). Still screening, the film is well on its way to becoming the highest-grossing locally produced film in Puerto Rican history. It is scheduled to be released theatrically in the US by Maya Entertaiment.

Another reggaetón-themed film, the low-budget thriller **Death in Paradise** (*Muerte en el Paraíso*), opened a few weeks after *Talent from the Barrio* and featured the local reggaetón star Arcángel. The film was directed by Abimael Acosta and deals with two brothers struggling to succeed along different paths.

Three comedies premiered in 2008, although none found a significant audience. **Manuela and Manuel** (*Manuela y Manuel*) was directed by Raúl Marchand Sánchez and scripted by Chilean-born screenwriter José Ignacio Valenzuela. This gender-reversal farce focuses on the misadventures of Manuela, a transvestite who reinvents himself as Manuel when his best friend suddenly needs a fake fiancé. **My Summer with Amanda** (*Mi verano con Amanda*) follows the summertime misadventures of an insecure teen who falls head-over-heels for a beautiful model. It was directed by Benjamin López. Actor Bruno Irizarry's first feature, **Shut Up and Do It!**, is a charming comedy about the hellish experience of an out-of-work actor when he becomes fed up with the stereotypical portrayal of Latinos

Raúl Marchand's **Manuela and Manuel**

by Hollywood and decides to make his own independent film.

Films scheduled for release at the end of 2008 include three new music-themed projects. **Kabo & Platón** (*Kabo y Platón*), a coming-of-age urban drama, is directed by Edmundo H. Rodríquez, from a screenplay by award-winning Puerto Rican novelist Mayra Santos-Febres. It focuses on two teenagers struggling to become Puerto Rico's next rap superstars. **Party Time** is a teen musical comedy written and directed by local film critic Juan Fernández-Paris, which centres on the 1980s Puerto Rican high school rivalry between 'Cocolos' (fans of Puerto Rican urban music) and 'Rockeros' (fans of US rock music). Pedro Perez Rosado and Lilian Rosado Gonzalez's **The Bad One** (*La Mala*) is Spanish husband-and-wife directing team Pedro Pérez-Rosado and Lillian Rosado-González's story of a woman obsessed with turning her daughter into a musical icon, modelling her on the notorious Cuban singer, La Lupe. The film is co-produced by Puerto Rico's Viguié Films.

Out of Darkness (*Fuera de Tinieblas*) is inspired by the growing Christian independent film movement. This ultra micro-budget film, directed by Julio Román, deals with a father's efforts to bond with his son while fending off a mysterious stalker.

In October, a new film festival, the San Juan International Film Festival, sponsored various industry events to continue inspiring local producers as well as to showcase the best films from around the world.

Three new films were released at the end of the year. Francisco Serrano's **Seva Vive** is promoted as the first local documentary be given a theatrical run. **Chiquito pero Juquetón**, a comedy based on the stand-up routine of local comedian Luis Raúl, was directed by Raúl Marchand Sánchez and produced by Rafo Muñiz. Finally, **Contraseña**, written and directed by Luis Freddie Vazquez, is a thriller that tackles the problem of film piracy.

With increased film production and the commercial success of *Lovesickness* and *Talent from the Barrio*, 2008 should prove to be a banner year in the development of the Puerto Rican film industry.

Quote of the year

'The economic rule of thumb in Hollywood holds that only one out of every ten movies makes money, so it's important to the survival and continued growth of the local film industry that Puerto Rico's explosion of film production over the past few years has finally come up with a couple of moneymakers in *Maldeamores* and *Talento de Barrio*.' JAMES STEVENS-ARCE, *Puerto Rican writer-producer-director.*

RAÚL RÍOS-DÍAZ is a Puerto Rican filmmaker and writer. He heads the production company ALT165 and is the author of the book *Dominio de la Imagen: Hacia una Industria de Cine en Puerto Rico* ('Mastering the Image: Towards a Puerto Rican Film Industry', 2000)

Romania Cristina Corciovescu

For Romanian cinema, 2008 was not a year of the big surprises it has grown accustomed to. Let's consider it simply as a brief hiatus from the highs of Cristian Mungiu's Palme d'Or win for *4 Months, 3 Weeks & 2 Days*. On the other hand, we should bear in mind what the Romanian Culture Minister said in a press conference: that the Romanian film industry is significantly healthier, with 13–15 new features produced every year. The biannual contest the Cinematography National Centre organises each spring and autumn is the main source of financing for this industry and the loans it offers make it possible for all types of films (long and short feature films, long and short documentaries, animated features) to reach the production stage. Consequently, at the 2008 spring session there were 72 winning projects, which were awarded a total of €7,895,000.

The best feature of 2008 was an independent production. **Elevator**, directed by George Dorobantu, an ex-Navy officer, is the tragic story of two teenagers – a girl who wishes to lose her virginity and a boy who is no expert on sex – caught in the elevator of an old, deserted factory and whose desperate cries for help remain unheard. The drama of their situation, the tenderness of their feelings and Dorobantu's confident handling of the narrative all make for an outstanding debut film.

*Iulia Veres and Cristi Petrescu in George Dorobantu's **Elevator***

The other two debuts build on long-established careers. Horatiu Malaele is a well-known theatre and film actor who ventured into directing with **Silent Wedding** (*Nunta muta*). In March 1953, the death of Stalin forced Romania to go into mourning. In a village where a wedding is about to take place, the guests decide that everything must go ahead as planned, but without the utterance of a single word or vow. Even though Malaele has some interesting solutions for the enactment of the ceremony, the film is too theatrical and suffers from the appearance of too many stars from Romanian theatre (many of them used merely as extras). Anca Damian, a director of photography and, more recently, a documentary filmmaker, directed **Crossing Dates** (*Intalniri incrucisate*), featuring three separate narratives told in succession. It is a solidly directed but little more than average film.

*Ioana Bulca in Nae Caranfil's **The Rest Is Silence***

The return of Nae Caranfil was highly anticipated. However, **The Rest is Silence** (*Restul e tacere*) was not a success. In his familiar, highly ironic style, the writer/director turns the making of the first Romanian feature film, *Romania's Independence* (1912), into some kind of Grand Guignol event, rather than present an account of a long-gone era. The outcome was a tedious epic.

The busiest member of the new wave, Radu Muntean, directed his third film, **Boogie**, which plays out like *I Vitelloni*, Romania style. Three former high school friends meet by chance and wish, if only for one night, they could re-live their youth. Drinking, womanising, and bad jokes – nothing is as good as it used to be.

Radu Muntean's **Boogie**

Among the films made by the veteran directors, Radu Gabrea's **Gruber's Journey** (*Calatoria lui Gruber*), a drama based on a real event, with a script by Alexandru Baciu and Razvan Radulescu, was particularly impressive. Curzio Malaparte visits Moldavia as a war correspondent, but arrives during the anti-Jewish pogrom of June 1941. Suffering from a severe case of allergy, he is placed under the supervision of a Jewish doctor, whom he eventually searches for on the death trains. The merits of this fine film should be shared

Radu Gabrea's **Gruber's Journey**

equally between the young writers and the veteran director. **Exchange** (*Schimb valutar*) was directed by Nicolae Margineanu. Sadly, Margineanu's directional skills were unequal to Tudor Voican's promising script, in which a gullible man, tricked by a swindler, has no choice but to become a criminal himself in order to survive.

Thomas Ciulei's **The Flower Bridge**

The most important award won by a Romanian film this year was the Palme d'Or won by Marian Crisan at Cannes for her short film, **Megatron**. The award for best Romanian film at the Transylvania International Film Festival was given to Thomas Ciulei for **The Flower Bridge** (*Podul de flori*). A beautiful feature documentary, it focuses on a father who cares for his children in a small village in the Republic of Moldova.

The year's best films
Elevator (George Dorobantu)
The Flower Bridge (Thomas Ciulei)
Boogie (Radu Muntean)
Gruber's Journey (Radu Gabrea)
Megatron (Marian Crisan)

Directory
Romania Film, Str Henri Coanda 27, Bucharest. Tel: (40 1) 310 4499. coresfilm@hotmail.com.
Centrul National al Cinematografiei, Str. Dem. I. Dobrescu nr. 4-6, Sector 1, 010026, Bucuresti. Tel: 310 430 1. Fax: 310 430 0. cnc@cncinema.ro. www.cncinema.abt.ro.

CRISTINA CORCIOVESCU is a film critic and historian, and the author of several specialised dictionaries.

Russia Kirill Razlogov

The film industry in Russia is growing steadily. In 2008, there were more than a hundred domestic releases. The number of modernised cinemas has reached 700, with almost 1,900 screens. The 2007 box office reached US$565 million, 37% more than in 2006, and the first time in post-Soviet history that more than 100 million tickets were sold. Experts foresee a stabilisation of the number of films produced, with a strong but dangerous tendency towards fewer films with larger budgets. The slogan 'less but better' was used in the USSR in the late 1940s, with obvious negative results. Nevertheless, producers hope to secure higher budgets if fewer films are made.

The average budget for a feature film is estimated to be US$2–3 million, with another US$1 million spent on prints and advertising. Only four out of 85 Russian films released in 2007 recovered their initial investment. This means that state support remains essential. Private investment in the industry sky-rocketed when a couple of highly successful Russian films became box office champions, surpassing Hollywood blockbusters. Timur Bekmambetov's **Irony of Fate: The Sequel** (*Ironiya sud'by: Prodolzhenie*) attracted almost US$50 million in box office receipts, playing well to the youth market and mature audiences who remembered the original *Irony of Fate* (1975), a New Year's Eve tale made by the charismatic El'dar Ryazanov and played on several channels around the end of the year. The sequel destroyed the romanticism of the original, presenting younger characters – the progeny of the stars of the earlier film – in a similar story.

Kirill Kuzin's **The Best Movie** (*Samyy luchshiy fil'm*), featuring a popular group of entertainers,

Comedy Club, was initially a success, but soon word spread about how awful a film it actually was. Nevertheless, it still grossed US$27.5 million and a sequel – another parody of popular movies – will be released in 2009.

Officials were happy with the results for 2008 (the domestic market share has increased from 2% in 2004 to almost 30% last year), but the investors were disappointed by the takings – the average revenue for each release was still under US$1 million. The only exceptions were: Vladimir Toropchin's animated feature **Ilya Muromets and the Robber** (*Il'ya Muromets i Solovey Razboynik* (US$9.7 million)); Marius Balchunas' tasteless parody, **Hitler Kaput!** (US$9.5 million); **We Are From the Future** (US$8.2 million); Aleksandr Chernyaev's **Kings Can Do Anything** (US$7.5 million); Oleg Fesenko's **Streetracers** (*Stritreisery*, US$6 million); Dimitriy D'yachenko's **Day of the Radio** (*Den' Radio*, US$5.7 million); Roman Prygunov's **Indigo** (US$4.7 million) and **Alexander: The Neva Battle** (*Aleksandr. Nevskaya Bitva*, US$2.9 million).

Of these only *We Are From the Future*, by Andrei Malyukov deserves a separate mention. A group of modern teenagers find themselves in the middle of the Second World War and discover what patriotism really means. *Alexander* is another version of Eisenstein's classic, but director-producer Igor Kalyonov failed dismally in its realisation. It is important to mention that these films are part of an official quest for a 'National Idea' and national identity, to unite the new Russian state. Its historical and mythological background is supported by military victories from the Neva battle in the thirteenth century to the Great Patriotic War in the twentieth.

Lisa Boyarskaya and Konstantin Khabensky in **Admiral**

The future is anticipated in **Terra Nova** (*Novaya Zemlya*), a political blockbuster by Alexander Mel'nik, owner of the company Andreyevskiy Flag (the ensign of St. Andrei Pervozvannyi, which was adopted by the Russian imperial fleet in the seventeenth century). Combining excessive violence, cannibalism, religious symbols and anti-Western sentiments, the film opens with the Council of Europe recommending the abolition of the death penalty and that all criminals from around the world be banished to the far north, presumably Russia. On a more academic note, a similar National idea appears in **Admiral**. Andrei Kravchuk (*The Italian*) tells the story of one of the leaders of anti-Bolshevik civil war, Admiral Alexandre Kolchak, with an emphasis on personal tragedy and impossible love. The shorter theatrical version will be followed by a TV mini-series.

Nikita Mikhalkov is still working on **Burned by the Sun 2** (*Utomlyonnye Solntsem 2*), which is shaping up to be even more ambitious than the original. It is set during the Great Patriotic War and will comprise two features, each about three hours long, which will eventually be integrated into a longer TV version.

The result of this support for propagandist blockbusters will be direct commissioning by the State of several super-productions. They will cost approximately US$40 million, and begin production in 2009/10. Another innovation, announced in September by Aleksandr Golutva, President of the Producers' Guild and Vice-Minister of Culture, and more or less confirmed by Vladimir Putin at the opening of a private studio complex in St Petersburg in October 2008, was the official consecration of Russian majors – film-producing companies that have proven their commercial (and sometimes artistic) potential. Among them will be Nikita Mikhalkov's Tri Te, Sergei Selyanov's STV, Central Partnership, Mosfilm and Lenfilm, as well as companies created by two or three of the main TV channels. About US$40 million will be divided among them for new productions, to be decided by the companies themselves.

Another US$40 million will be given, project by project, to all the other production companies with the same amount reserved for children's films, documentaries, animation and 'auteurs'. This last group is responsible for more than 50% of international festival entries.

After the stunning festival and award success of 2007, the results for 2008 look less spectacular. The leader appears to be **The Mermaid** (*Rusalka*) by Anna Melikyan, which won the World Cinema Direction Award at Sundance and is the official Russian entry for the 2009 Academy Awards. This tragic transposition of a fairy tale to contemporary society fascinated critics but failed to attract large audiences. Alexei German Jr's **Paper Soldier** (*Bumazhnyi Soldat*) was awarded the Best Director and Best Cinematography prizes at Venice, adopting his signature

Anna Melikyan's **The Mermaid**

poetic naturalist style for a story linked to Yuri Gagarin's first space journey. Alexei Uchitel's **The Captive** (*Plennyi*), an adaptation of Vladimir Makanin's brilliant story about friendship during wartime, received the Best Direction Award at Karlovy Vary.

Sergei Dvortsevoy's **Tulpan**

Co-productions with former Soviet republics (especially Kazakhstan) gave life to a number of dramas, including the tale of a simple traditional magician in Gulshat Omarova's **Baksy**. The first feature by documentary filmmaker Sergei Dvortsevoy, **Tulpan**, made with Russian, German and Swiss involvement, went on to win the 'Un Certain Regard' award at Cannes.

The young Valeriya Gai Germanika continued her shocking career with the teenage drama, **Everybody Dies But Me** (*Vse umrut, a ya ostanus*), which premiered in Cannes' Critics' Week. The eccentric director announced to the press that next year she will come back to collect the Palme d'Or. Her film curiously resonates with a feature-length documentary

Valeria Gui-Germanica's **Everybody Dies But Me**

by producer-director Vitaliy Manskiy, the controversial **Virginity** (*Devstvennost*), about very young girls trying to sell their virginity to the highest bidder.

The Moscow International Film Festival presented two stylistically opposed films: the horribly pessimistic **Once in the Province** (*Odnazhdy v provintsii*) by Ekaterina Shagalova, and a comical version of Chekhov's **The Orchard** (*Sad*), by Sergei Ovcharov. Georgian Bakur Bakuradze, after his underestimated chronicle of *gastarbeiter* (guest workers) in *Moskva*, made **Shul'tes**, presented in the 'Directors' Forthnight' at Cannes and winner of the main prize at the Kinotavr National Film Festival. This Bressonian film told the story of a pickpocket suffering a partial loss of memory. The second-best film at Kinotavr was **Wild Field** (*Dikoye pole*) by Mikhail Kalatozishvili, who dared to adapt a famous script by the late geniuses, Alexei Samoryadov and Pyotr Lutsik. Written more than ten years ago, this 'eastern', relocated to the Kazakh steppes, details life in the barren region.

In documentary, Renata Litvinova mixed concert footage and interviews with popular singer Zemfira (Ramazanova) in **The Green Theatre Inside Zemfira** (*Zelenyi Teatr v Zemfire*).

While everybody is waiting for Fyodor Bondarchuk's Hollywood-like adaptation of the brothers Strugatsky's anti-utopian **The Inhabited Island** (*Obitayemyy Ostrov*), the same writers' **It is Difficult to be God** (*Trudno byt' Bogom*) has still not been finished by Alexei German Sr. Valery Todorovsky reconstructs the 1950s in **Stylish Guys** (*Stilyagi*), an early response to Karen Shakhnazarov's 1970s-set **The Vanished Empire** (*Ischeznuvshaya imperiya*). Vladimir Naumov, working from a screenplay by Tonino Guerra, has the elderly and middle-aged play aesthetic games in **Gioconda on the Asphalt** (*Dzhokonda na asfal'te*). **Live and Remember** (*Zhivi i pomni*) is an adaptation of a once-

Darya Moroz in Alexander Proshkin's **Live and Remember**

controversial novel by Valentin Rasputin, about a deserter during the Second World War, by Aleksandr Proshkin. Meanwhile, in **Yuri's Day** (*Yuriev den*), Kirill Serebrennikov conjures up a religious parable.

Oksana Bychkova's comedy **Plus One** (*Plyus odin*) had little success in matching the popularity of her debut, *Piter FM*. Andrei Libenson's **Sovereign** (*Tot, kto gasit svet*) Russifies a conventional thriller, while Yuliya Kolesnik explores the geographical mysticism of the Volga river in **Lower Caledonia** (*Nizhnyaya Kaledoniya*). Igor Voloshin succumbs to psychedelic charms in **Nirvana**, while, in **Mukha**, Vladimir Kott continues the tradition of social realism. Meanwhile, Natalia Uglitskikh's winning short, the eccentric comedy **Tag** (*Pyatnashki*), was screened at Telluride.

Maria Shalaeva in Igor Voloshin's **Nirvana**

The future looks bleak if it is dominated by patriotic themes. But with US$18 million promised to the Russian film industry in 2010 to do exactly this, it seems that this is the course Russian cinema is likely to take for the time being.

The year's best films
The Mermaid (Anna Melikyan)
Tag (Natalia Uglitskikh)
Wild Field (Mikhail Kalatozishvili)
Lower Caledonia (Yulia Kolesnik)
Nirvana (Igor Voloshin)

Quote of the year
'The decision was taken to allocate important amounts of money to support our national cinema, whose aim is to promote values corresponding to social needs and strategic goals of the country's development.'
Prime Minister VLADIMIR PUTIN, *talking to filmmakers in St Petersburg.*

Directory
All Tel/Fax numbers begin (+7)
Alliance of Independent Distribution Companies, Tel: 243 4741. Fax: 243 5582. felix_rosental@yahoo.com.
Federal Agency of Culture & Cinema of the Russian Federation, Film Service, 7 Maly Gnezdnikovsky Lane, Moscow 103877. Tel: 923 2420/229 7055. Fax: 299 9666.
Ministry of Culture & Mass Communication of the Russian Federation, 7 Kitaisky Proezd, Moscow. Tel: 975 2420. Fax: 975 2420/928 1791.
National Academy of Cinema Arts & Sciences, 13 Vassilyevskaya St, Moscow 123825. Tel: 200 4284. fax: 251 5370. unikino@aha.ru
Russian Guild of Film Directors, 13 Vassilyevskaya St, Moscow 123825. Tel: 251 5889. fax: 254 2100. stalkerfest@mtu-net.ru.
Russian Guild of Producers, 1 Mosfilmovskaya St, Moscow 119858. Tel: 745 5635/143 9028. plechev@mtu-net.ru.
Union of Filmmakers of Russia, 13 Vassilyevskaya St, Moscow 123825. Tel: 250 4114. fax: 250 5370. unikino@aha.ru.

KIRILL RAZLOGOV is Director of the Russian Institute for Cultural Research and Programme Director of the Moscow International Film Festival. He has written fourteen books on cinema and culture and hosts Kultura's weekly TV show, *Movie Cult*.

Serbia & Montenegro Goran Gocić

The most anticipated release of 2008 was **Tears for Sale** (*Carlston za Ognjenku*), the debut of director Uros Stojanovic and writer Aleksandar Radivojevic. With its lavish budget, the film features two enterprising young women who accidentally kill the only man in their village. Agreeing to find a replacement, they embark on a journey across a Serbia whose male population has been decimated by the First World War. Stojanovic is allegedly in discussions with a Hollywood studio for his next film.

Srdja Penezic's **Film Noir**

Uros Stojanovic's **Tears for Sale**

Writer-director Milorad Milinkovic opted for a dark comedy set amongst contemporary Belgrade's criminal underworld in the ridiculous **An Obituary for Escobar** (*Citulja za Eskobara*). In it, a pretty boy undergoes a sex change and seduces a mafia capo who used to abuse him in his school days.

Tears for Sale and *An Obituary for Escobar* were the two most popular domestic releases of the last year. Two other projects aimed as high, but with less success. The first was a American/Serbian joint venture, **Film Noir**, a feature-length black-and-white animated thriller, written and directed by Srdja Penezic and animated by Risto Topaloski. The second

film was a Serbian/Croatian co-production, **Will Not End Here** (*Nije kraj*), written and directed by Vinko Bresan. Employing a mixed cast and featuring various locations, it told an odd love story about a Serbian prostitute and Croat war veteran.

Other films also relied heavily on sexual provocation. **Change Me** (*Promeni me*), by theatre director Milan Karadzic and written by Stevan Koprivica, was a toned-down sex romp in which an ageing dentist falls for a young girl. More explicit and highlighting Belgrade's transitional mess was Darko Bajic's **On the Beautiful Blue Danube** (*Na lepom plavom Dunavu*), based on the stage play by Nebojsa Romcevic. It is about a floating brothel, upon which good-looking eastern Europeans pamper

Darko Bajic's **On the Beautiful Blue Danube**

Nebojsa Radosavljevic's **Who the Fuck is Milos Brankovic**

and serve their rich Western compatriots. **Who the Fuck is Milos Brankovic** (*Milos Brankovic*), written and directed by Nebojsa Radosavljevic, is about an idealistic architect who is abused by most of the people in his life.

Stefan Arsenijevic's **Love and Other Crimes**

Stefan Arsenijevic, considered a major talent thanks to his excellent short, *Atorsia*, wrote and directed **Love and Other Crimes** (*Ljubav i drugi zlocini*), about an ageing petty criminal and set in the depressing New Belgrade projects. It was premiered at Berlin and has been popular at festivals. **Lost & Found** (*Biro za nadjene stvari*), in which a young writer is trying to find his soul, was written and directed by veteran Svetislav Prelic, returning after a nineteen-year absence. Strangely, *Lost & Found* felt as though it had been directed by a youngster and *Love and Other Crimes* by someone middle-aged.

Ljubisa Samardzic's **Pale Moon** (*Bledi mesec*), like 2007's *Black Horses*, failed to capture the power of the original film in her series, 2006's *Goose Feather*. The unlucky but resilient hero,

Sava Ladjarski, survives a loveless marriage, alcoholism, poverty, the First World War and several attempts on his life. The whole series is planned to screen as a TV series, which will no doubt win admirers. Similarly, **Masa**, about a poor girl whose life spirals out of control due to drug use, which was written and directed by Sinisa Kovacevic, is a feature culled from an epic thirty-episode television series directed in the style of soap opera. Both *Pale Moon* and *Masa* starred Kalina Kovacevic. **Black Gruja** (*Crni Gruja i kamen mudrosti*), directed by Marko Marinkovic, also grew out of a TV series, set during the Ottoman Empire. Its crude, ridiculous humour, recalling *Black Adder*, helped at the box office. On the other hand, comedy veteran Slobodan Sijan still struggles to find his way back into the industry, as his comedy **SOS – Save Our Souls** (*Spasite nase duse*) was not even released.

The season's sweetest comedy was **The Paper Prince** (*Princ od papira*), which premiered at the Sarajevo Film Festival in 2007 and was invited to over a dozen other festivals. Previously a short feature and then a novel, it is a simple family drama in which an eight-year-old outwits a burglar and her parents. The film stands as a stark contrast to other, more apocalyptic narratives that were popular with audiences and marks a promising debut for director Marko Kostic.

Marko Kostic's **The Paper Prince**

Tears for Sale, backed by Luc Besson's EuropeCorps, and *Film Noir*, supported by Wild Bunch, might have a chance of reaching international audiences. The season's inclination towards sex and violence is perhaps seen as a way to reverse low cinema attendance, but they remain a relative novelty in conservative Serbia.

The trend of audiences abandoning cinemas continues: in 2007, the admissions per capita figure of 0.18% hit the lowest mark since 2002, despite the fact that Star Cinema Multiplex recently opened in Belgrade, featuring six screens and 1,100 seats.

People in the film business remember better times; between 1955 and 1985 Serbian films performed comparatively well at home and abroad (the USSR was a profitable market), returning an average 65% on an investment. This decade, cinemas and studios have seen revenues plummet.

Kennedy Gets Married is the final segment of Zelimir Zilnik's documentary-feature trilogy, which began with *Kennedy is Going Back Home* in 2003 and the short *Where Was Kennedy for Two Years?* from 2005. Zilnik deals with problems faced by the Roma community, returning home to Serbia from other EU countries. In the film, young gypsy Kennedy Hassani has taken out a number of loans to built a house. To repay the debt, he provides sexual services to male and female clients. Because of liberal laws in the EU, he is interested in finding a potential groom, who would enable him to gain legal status in the West.

Mention should be made of Dejan Zečević's *The Fourth Man*, which premiered at the 2007 Sarajevo Film Festival. With shades of Robert Ludlum's Bourne series, it is a slick, convoluted thriller that draws on this region's recent past whilst delivering enough twists to keep any viewer engaged.

The year's best films
Kennedy Gets Married (Zelimir Zilnik)
The Paper Prince (Marko Kostic)
The Fourth Man (Dejan Zecevic)
On the Beautiful Blue Danube (Darko Bajic)

Darko Bajic's **On the Beautiful Blue Danube**

Quote of the year
'As long as I remember, those who don't shoot movies claim that Serbian cinema is in crisis. But that a film festival days before opening gives a statement that this year's production is below average, is something new.' *Director* DARKO BAJIĆ, *commenting on the statement made by the festival selector at the Nis Film Festival.*

Directory
All Tel/Fax numbers begin (+381)
Association of Film Producers, Kneza Viseslava 88, 11000 Belgrade. Tel: 323 1943. Fax: 324 6413. info@afp.yu. www.afp.co.yu.
Faculty of Dramatic Arts, Bulevar Umetnosti 20, 11070 Belgrade. Tel: 214 04 19. Fax: 213 08 62. fduinfo@eunet.yu.
The Film Center of Serbia, Zagrebacka 9/III, 11000 Belgrade. Tel: 262 51 31/262 87 47. Fax: 263 42 53. fcs.office@fcs.co.yu. www.fcs.co.yu.
Yugoslav Film Archive, Knez Mihailova 19, 11000 Belgrade. Tel/Fax: 622 555. kinoteka@eunet.yu. www.kinoteka.org.yu.
Yugoslav Film Institute, Cika Ljubina 15/II, 11000 Belgrade. Tel: 625 131. Fax: 634 253. ifulm@eunet.yu.

GORAN GOCIĆ is a broadcast and print journalist whose works have been published by over thirty media outlets in eight languages. He has contributed to many on the mass media, edited several magazines, authored studies on Warhol, Kusturica and pornography and directed two feature-length documentaries.

Singapore Yvonne Ng

Singapore's feature production appears to be growing steadily. Most of the mainstream output has come from the de facto state studio, MediaCorp Raintree Pictures.

The studio's Chinese New Year release, **Ah Long Pte Ltd** (*Lao shi jia lao da*), was directed by Jack Neo. A Singapore/Malaysia co-production, it is a forgettable comedy about the loan-shark business, starring the popular Fann Wong as a new triad boss who tries to reform the family business and Mark Lee as her effeminate, dance-teacher husband.

Dance of the Dragon (*Long zhi wu*), by Australians John Radel and Max Mannix, was produced by Silk Road Pictures and Easternlight Films. Set in Singapore, this sumptuously photographed, sentimental love triangle sees Fann Wong transformed into a ballroom dance teacher caught between her jealous martial arts champion boyfriend (Jason Scott Lee) and her new student (Korean heartthrob Jang I Iyuk).

Raintree's romantic drama **The Leap Years**, directed by Jean Yeo, is an uninspired adaptation of Catherine Lim's novella *Leap of Love* about a young teacher Li-ann (Wong Li-Lin) falls in love with Jeremy (Thailand's Ananda Everingham), who is already engaged. They promise to meet once every four years on 29 February.

Singapore's first English-language animated feature, **Sing to the Dawn**, is about a young village girl's dream to study in the city. Made by Raintree with Infinite Frameworks and the Media Development Authority for US$5 million it is directed by Canadian filmmaker Philip Mitchell, who has tried to endow the animation with a Southeast Asian flavour.

Raintree also co-produced Kelvin Tong's **Rule #1**, a supernatural crime thriller shot in Hong Kong for US$2 million. Starring Hong Kong's Shawn Yue and Ekin Cheng, its story about two cops in charge of investigating supernatural incidents is probably Tong's best horror film to date.

Jack Neo's **Money Not Enough 2** (*Qian bu gou yong 2*), co-produced by Neo Studios and Raintree Pictures, is the sequel to Tay Teck Lock's top-grossing 1998 satirical comedy *Money Not Enough. Money 2* focuses on the financial woes of three brothers (played by the original trio of Jack Neo, Mark Lee and Henry Thia) and, more poignantly, the treatment of their elderly mother who is shunted from one family to another. It grossed US$3 million, becoming the most successful domestic production of 2008.

Another Raintree sequel, Royston Tan's **12 Lotus** (*Shi Er Lian Hua*), is the follow-up to his 2007 musical hit *881*. The film relates, through a Hokkien-dialect stage song, the tragic life of Lian Hua (Lotus), a young female singer ill-used by the men around her. As with *881*, the best moments are the musical numbers.

Eric Khoo's **My Magic**

Singapore's independent cinema is also progressing. Eric Khoo's **My Magic** became the first Singapore film to compete for the Palme d'Or at Cannes. The mostly Tamil-language production tells of an alcoholic who returns to his former profession as a magician to regain the respect of his son. Bosco Francis and Jathishweran Naidu give commendable performances in their first acting roles as father and son respectively. The 75-minute film was shot over nine days for US$135,000.

The experimental **Lucky 7** is a surreal game of 'exquisite corpse' by a group of seven directors (Sun Koh, K. Rajagopal, Boo Junfeng, Brian Gothong Tan, Chew Tze Chuan, Ho Tzu Nyen and Tania Sng). Lim Mayling's feature-length documentary boldly explored lesbian lives in **Women Who Love Women: Conversations in Singapore**.

A dominant subject of home-grown documentaries in the last two years has been football. Cheng Ding An wrote and directed **Kallang Roar**, expanded from his eponymous short, a nostalgic tribute to Singapore's legendary coach, 'Uncle' Choo Seng Quee. It was shot at the Singapore National Stadium in Kallang, earmarked for demolition in order to make way for the new Sports Hub.

Increasingly, Singapore's independents are venturing beyond their shores. In **Homeless FC** James Leong and Lynn Lee followed the Dawn Team in Hong Kong, a group of homeless men who aspire to compete in the Homeless World Cup in South Africa. **Veil of Dreams**, the directorial debut of Zaihirat Banu Codelli, records the struggles of the Iranian national women's football team to exist and to compete internationally amidst deep-seated social disapproval.

Ng Khee Jin's **Feet Unbound** tells the remarkable and virtually unknown story of the teenage female soldiers in the Chinese Red Army's Long March. **Mad About English** is a well-made and entertaining production directed by broadcast journalist, Pek Siok Lian. It provides a humourous and insightful account of the

English-language fever in China, particularly in the lead-up to the Beijing Olympics.

The Singapore Film Commission, under its new director, Kenneth Tan, celebrated its tenth anniversary by launching the New Feature Film Fund to encourage the efforts of aspiring film-makers. Nine directors working across a range of genres were awarded up to US$170,000 to make their first or second feature. The grant, which includes guidance by experienced production companies and a commitment by Golden Village to distribute their films, is expected to give a boost to the country's independent filmmakers.

The year's best films
Mad About English (Pek Siok Lian)
Feet Unbound (Ng Khee Jin)
Homeless FC (James Leong, Lynn Lee)
Veil of Dreams (Zaihirat Banu Codelli)
My Magic (Eric Khoo)

Quote of the year
'It was a proud moment for Singapore film. We were overwhelmed by the encouraging response because *My Magic* was an underdog competing in the World Cup of films.' ERIC KHOO, *on the screening of his film for the Palme d'Or competition in Cannes.*

Directory
All Tel/Fax numbers begin (+65)
Cinematograph Film Exhibitors Association, 13th & 14th Storey, Shaw Centre, 1 Scotts Rd, Singapore 228208. Tel: 6235 2077. Fax: 6235 2860.
Singapore Film Commission, 140 Hill St, Mita Bldg #04-01, Singapore 179369. Tel: 6837 9943. Fax: 6336 1170. www.sfc.org.sg.
Singapore Film Society, 5A Raffles Ave, #03-01 Marina Leisureplex, Singapore 039801. Fax: 6250 6167. ktan@sfs.org.sg. www.sfs.org.sg.

YVONNE NG is on the editorial board of *KINEMA*. She is co-author of *Latent Images: Film in Singapore* (2000) and *Latent Images: Film in Singapore CD-ROM* (2003).

Slovakia Miro Ulman

The Slovak film industry can rightfully regard 2008 as one of the most successful years in the era of an independent Slovak Republic (the last 15 years). And that can be said despite the fact that nearly a half of the 21 projects planned for release in 2008 have been postponed, mostly for financial reasons. In the first and second rounds of the state Audiovisual Grant Programme, AudioVision 2008, chosen projects received only €3,888,236 – almost one-third less than the amount allocated in 2006.

On 1 January 2008, the Audiovisual Law came into force. A more vital provision will be the Audiovisual Fund law, the goal of which is to ensure the continuing support and development of Slovak film production, culture, and industry. The Slovak Parliament passed the law on 5 November 2008.

Juraj Nvota's **Music**

In spring, Juraj Nvota's **Music** (*Muzika*), a tragicomic story of three musicians in Czechoslovakia during the late 1970s and early 1980s, won nine National Film Awards. **Blind Loves** (*Slepé lásky*), the directorial debut of Juraj Lehotský, was selected for Cannes. A documentary about relationships amongst

Juraj Lehotský's documentary **Blind Loves**

blind people, it is a touching, humorous film that avoids cheap sentimentality. It received the Art Cinema Award 2008.

Juraj Jakubisko, the recipient – along with another Slovak director, Dušan Hanák – of a Crystal Globe Award for Lifetime Contribution at Karlovy Vary, presented his latest film **Bathory** (*Bathory*), starring Anna Friel as Countess Erzebet Bathory. The director's aim was to cast doubt on supposedly horrible acts of the 'bloody countess'. The film was premiered on 10 July and within twelve weeks had grossed €1.32 million. It has become the most popular film in Slovak box office history (*Titanic* only grossed €960,000.

Juraj Jakubisko's **Bathory**

Anna Gurji in **Gypsy Virgin**

In the eighteenth century, some hundred years after Countess Bathory, lived another famous figure of Slovak history. Dušan Rapoš's **Gypsy Virgin** (*Cinka Panna*) is a story of the legendary violin player, who became the first Roma band leader. Zdeněk Tyc's **Small Festivities** (*Malé oslavy*) is a contemporary story of a mother and her 14-year-old daughter. Peter Beňovský's documentary, **Last Caravan** (*Posledná maringotka*), tells the story of the last traditional comedians in Central Europe.

Peter Beňovský's **Last Caravan**

Two documentaries are scheduled for release at the end of 2008. Ján Oparty's **The Rock of Shelter** (*Skala útočišťa*) is a story of a group of people who decided to reconstruct a medieval monastery in the region of Slovenský Raj. Slovak-based Afghan director Sahraa Karimi's **Afghan Women Behind the Wheel** (*Afganské ženy za volantom*) shows the gradual break-down of taboos in Afghanistan.

Minor co-productions constitute an important part of the Slovak film industry. Czech director

Václav Marhoul's **Tobruk** is a drama about soldiers from the Czechoslovak Infantry Battalion fighting in the Libyan desert in 1941, while Polish director Dariusz Jablonski made the documentary **War Games** (*Vojnové hry*), about a Polish colonel who rescued Europe from atomic disaster.

Robert Nebřenský in Václav Marhoul's **Tobruk**

For the moment, the future of the Slovak film industry looks bright. A number of forthcoming releases look set to continue the trend. Peter Kerekes's **Cooking History** (*Ako sa varia dejiny*), Miloslav Luther's **Mosquitos' Tango** (*Tango s komármi*), Jiří Chlumský's **Broken Promise** (*Nedodržaný sľub*) and Vladimír Balko's **Soul at Peace** (*Pokoj v duši*) are all slated for release in spring 2009.

The year's best films
Blind Loves (Juraj Lehotský)
Music (Juraj Nvota)
Bathory (Juraj Jakubisko)

Quote of the year
'It will be me who brings Slovak viewers back to movie theatres, because the attendance at screenings, of Slovak films mainly, has been a real disaster.' JURAJ JAKUBISKO, *director of* **Bathory**, *when his film became a blockbuster.*

MIRO ULMAN is a freelance journalist. He works for the Slovak Film Institute and is a programmer for the Bratislava International Film Festival.

Slovenia Ziva Emersic

The second half of 2007 was not a happy period for the fragile Slovenian film industry. The system of public subsidies, controlled by the National Film Fund, began to strain under heavy criticism from almost all professional associations, including directors and producers. The film industry is also ridiculously underestimated as a promotional tool for the young state. In the last decade, Slovenian film managed to score significant international recognition. Thankfully, by the end of the year, things began to look better.

Marjuta Slamic in Damjan Kozole's **Forever**

The year started successfully, with the world premiere at the Rotterdam Film Festival of **Forever** (*Za vedno*), the eighth feature by Damjan Kozole. Shot in the director's own apartment, it is an intense study of marital relations. Tina returns home late one night to face her husband's accusations that she is having an affair. Kozole accurately portrayed the problems facing modern relationships in his small drama. Almost immediately after promoting *Forever*, Kozole began shooting **Slovenian Girl** (*Slovenka*), a drama that takes place in Ljubljana during the Slovenian presidency of the European Union. A young student tries to improve her material situation by offering sexual services to elderly wealthy men. When a European diplomat dies in her bed, the police begin looking for her.

Marko Mandic in Vinko Moederndorfer's **Landscape No.2**

Another Slovenian director with an appetite for harsh social issues is Vinko Moderndorfer, who made a memorable debut in 2005 with *Suburbia*. His second film, **Landscape No.2** (*Pokrajina st. 2*), screened at the Venice Film Festival. It looks at the crimes committed in the civil conflict that immediately followed the Second World War. Moderndorfer, who is also a theatre director and writer, approached his politically incendiary subject matter as a thriller, evoking elements of film noir.

Blaz Kutin, who received the Best Young Scriptwriter award at Cannes in 2006, debuted with **We've Never Been to Venice** (*Nikoli nisva sla v Benetke*), which was shot on digital. Under pressure from the Sarajevo Film Festival, who picked the film for competition, the Slovenian Film Fund covered the costs of the film's transfer to 35mm. Bleak and admittedly quite weak, the story of a young couple on a road trip that becomes therapy following the loss of their child is unlikely to please many audience members.

Blaz Kutin's **We've Never Been to Venice**

Martin Turk's short **Every Day Is Not the Same** (*Vsak dan ni vsakdan*) was chosen for the 'Directors' Fortnight' section at Cannes, while Jan Cvitkovic's short **I Know** (*Vem*) appeared at Locarno. Dull and gloomy, it is unlikely to repeat the success of his previous short, *Heart is But a Piece of Meat*. Igor Sterk took his short **Every Breath You Take** (*Vdih*) to Venice. The film underlined the thematic tendency for the year: death, loss and grief.

Martin Turk's **Each Day is Not Every Day**

Slovenian producers were involved in a number of co-productions, thanks to a modest sum from the Film Fund. Of these, the film with the highest profile was Serbian director Srdjan Karanovic's **A Given Word** (*Besa*), an intriguing love story between an Albanian man and a Slovenian woman, staring Serbian legend Miki Manojlovic and young Slovenian actress Iva Krajnc.

Domestic films are poorly represented in local distribution, which is still flooded by American product. Branko Djuric's **Tractor, Love and Rock'n'Roll** (*Traktor, ljubezen in Rock'n'Roll*)

was successful, but couldn't match the record set in 2007 by *Rooster's Breakfast*.

Documentary production saw a serious attempt to influence a change in the political situation in Sudan, with Maja Weiss and Tomo Kriznar's **War for Water**.

The positive shift in the Slovenian film landscape can be seen in the rise in the number of independent productions, mostly by young filmmakers. This niche cannot establish complete independency from the Film Fund, considering the size of the market, but it can help develop independent artistic spirit and ambition, even beyond national borders.

The year's best films
Forever (Damjan Kozole)
Landscape No.2 (Vinko Moderndorfer)
War for Water (Maja Weiss and Tomo Kriznar)

Quote of the year
'I couldn't say what is in the heads of the decision-makers in the Slovenian Film Fund. Maybe they stick to harsher criteria than the selectors at Cannes.' BLAZ KUTIN, *the 'new EU talent' screenwriter on being turned down three times, when he applied for production support for his projects.*

Directory
All Tel/Fax numbers begin (+386)
Association of Slovenian Film Makers, Miklošičeva 26, Ljubljana. e-mail. dsfu@guest. arnes.si.
Association of Slovenian Film Producers, Brodišče 23, Trzin, 1234 Mengeš. dunja.klemenc@ guest.arnes.si
Slovenian Cinematheque, Miklošičeva 38, Ljubljana. Tel: 434 2520. silvan.furlan@kinoteka.si.
Slovenian Film Fund, Miklošičeva 38, 1000 Ljubljana. Tel: 431 3175. info@film-sklad.si.

ZIVA EMERSIC is a journalist and film critic, former director of the Slovenian National Film Festival in Portoroz, currently head of documentary programming at TV Slovenija.

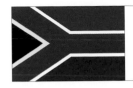

South Africa Martin P. Botha

The South African film industry is in a slump. Compared to three years ago, the number of features has decreased significantly. As an important national institution for the development and promotion of the South African film and video industry, the South African National Film and Video Foundation (NFVF) works with a tiny budget of US$3.6 million, with which it has to cover its administrative expenditure, as well as funding obligations.

As a result, some of the most significant features of the last year received no funding from the NFVF. A good example is Darrell Roodt's neorealist jewel, **Girl** (*Meisie*), about a girl in a rural community who is prevented from attending school by her father, believing that she should spend her days tending goats, which won several awards at local film festivals. Ralph Ziman's **Jerusalema**, a realistic and unwavering look into the gritty underbelly of crime, corruption and transgression in the new South Africa, was also made without backing from the Fund. It chronicles the rise and fall of Lucky Kunene (Rapulana Seiphemo) who rises out of poverty to become a crime boss. By September 2008, the film had made US$120,000 at the local box office. It is one of the few South African films, aside of Leon Schuster's comedies, to earn over US$100,000.

Acclaimed Zimbabwean director Michael Raeburn also couldn't rely on the NFVF to finance **Triomf**. Taking place just prior to South Africa's first democratic elections in 1994, the film tells the story of a dysfunctional family living in Triomf, a poor white suburb built on the ruins of Sophiatown, a black community. The film was praised at Cannes, as well as the Durban International Film Festival, where it received the Best South African Feature award. Rejected by Ster-Kinekor, one of South Africa's film distributors, *Triomf* finally secured domestic distribution for February 2009.

Over the past few years, Ster-Kinekor has rejected most local films dealing with apartheid and has focued instead on contemporary comedies. Some performed very poorly at the box office. **Running Riot** (*Koos Roets*), a comedy about the antics of two men during the Comrades marathon, opened on 83 prints and sold a meagre 91,974 tickets. John Barker's **Bunny Chow Know Thyself**, about a trio of stand-up comics spending a weekend at a rock festival, fared worse with just 20,197 tickets sold against its 16-print run.

Rapulana Seiphemo in Ralph Ziman's **Jerusalema**

By contrast, some Afrikaans-language films performed very well. Willie Esterhuizen's **Poena is Koning**, a very crude farce about secondary school pupils and their obsession with sex, grossed US$250,000 by the end of August. Henk Pretorius's **Bakgat!**, an Afrikaans equivalent of an American school comedy, grossed US$290,000. Apart from *Jerusalema* and these two Afrikaans-language comedies, only *Faith Like Potatoes* (reviewed in IFG 2008) grossed more than US$100,000 at the local box office. Regardt van den Bergh's film earned US$360,000.

Shamim Sharif's **The World Unseen**

Despite Ster-Kinekor's reluctance to distribute historical dramas, filmmakers continued to explore South Africa's painful past in a number of impressive productions. Shamim Sarif's **The World Unseen** is a sensitive story of two Indian-South African women who fall in love in the racist, sexist society of 1950s South Africa. Junaid Ahmed's **More Than Just a Game** is a touching drama that tells the story of how political activists who were unjustly imprisoned on Robben Island in the 1960s rose above the problems of their incarceration through the creation of a football league. For years, political prisoners had to fight for the right to play football on the island, with men secretly playing the game in their cells with balls made of paper, cardboard and rags, held together with string. The island's authorities finally gave in, granting inmates the right to play football in 1965. The prisoners then built their own goals and every Saturday would swap their drab prison outfits for their team colours. Anthony Fabian's **Skin** is based on the true story of Sandra Laing, a black girl born of two white Afrikaner parents, Abraham and Sannie (Sam Neill and Alice Krige). As a child, her parents try to integrate Sandra into a South African educational system that doesn't allow the inclusion of black children. Given that her birth certificate indicated a 'white' status, she was able to attend school initially but was later classified as 'coloured' and rejected.

Fortunately, Nu Metro, another important film distributor, seems less reluctant to screen South African films. Amanda Lane's award-winning **Confessions of a Gambler**, a fascinating portrait of a Muslim woman who struggles with her gambling addiction, enjoyed a successful theatrical release thanks to them. They are now the venue of choice for the organisers of the annual Encounters International Documentary Film Festival, as well as the Out in Africa Gay and Lesbian Film Festival, events that were hosted on the Ster-Kinekor theatrical circuit.

Amanda Lane and Rayda Jacobs' **Confessions of a Gambler**

During the past year, Ster-Kinekor received harsh criticism for a lack of films from a diversity of film cultures on the so-called Cinema Nouveau circuit. As a result, specialised DVD rental venues and film festivals have become important platforms for world cinema. In this regard, the first edition of the Cape Winelands Film Festival in Cape Town was an important development in ensuring that South Africans are exposed to quality films from around the globe. The festival included successful retrospectives of the work of Ingmar Bergman, Ousmane Sembene, François Ozon and Youssef Chahine, and was the first film festival in South Africa to award an M-Net Lifetime Achievement Award to the late master, Ousmane Sembene.

The year's best films
Girl (Darrell Roodt)
The World Unseen (Shamim Sharif)
Jerusalema (Ralph Ziman)
Triomf (Michael Raeburn)
Confessions of a Gambler
(Amanda Lane and Rayda Jacobs)

Quote of the year
'By immersing itself into the often sordid world where poverty, and the educational gaps that attend it, meet an arrogant sense of entitlement, Triomf exposes a series of universal truths. The dirty secrets of capitalism, of racism, of manipulative politics, of the human heart are mirrored in the secrets of one family, whose disintegration reminds us that a nation's history is written by individuals.' *A comment by the jury of the Durban International Film festival who awarded Triomf the Best South African Feature Award*

Directory
All Tel/Fax numbers begin (+27)
Cape Film Commission, 6th Floor, NBS Waldorf Bldg, 80 St George's Mall, Cape Town 8001. Tel: (21) 483 9070. Fax: (21) 483 9071. www.capefilmcommission.co.za.

Michael Raeburn's **Triomf**

Independent Producers Organisation, PO Box 2631, Saxonwold 2132. Tel: (11) 726 1189. Fax: (11) 482 4621. info@ipo.org.za. www.ipo.org.za
National Film & Video Foundation, 87 Central St, Houghton, Private Bag x04, Northlands 2116. Tel: (11) 483 0880. Fax: (11) 483 0881. info@nfvf.co.za.. www.nvfv.co.za.
South African Broadcasting Co (SABC), Private Bag 1, Auckland Park, Johannesburg 2006. Tel: (11) 714 9797. Fax: (11) 714 3106. www.sabc.co.za.

MARTIN P. BOTHA has published five books on South African cinema, including an anthology on post-apartheid cinema entitled *Marginal Lives and Painful Pasts: South African Cinema After Apartheid* (2007). He is a professor of film studies in the Centre for Film and Media Studies at the University of Cape Town.

South Korea Nikki J. Y. Lee

The recent staggering growth of the South Korean film industry appears to have suffered a setback over the last two years. The market share for domestic releases fell from 50.8% in 2007 to 41.5% by October 2008. A total of 124 Korean films were released in 2007. Only 11% of domestic titles turned a profit. By October 2008, 89 domestic films had been released, while the market share for American films surpassed 50% for the first time since 2003. In such circumstances, the industry eventually decided to take active measures in preventing illegal downloading from the Internet. Downloading is believed to ruin the ancillary market for Korean films at whose cost the high-speed Internet industry has developed. Ironically, the new financial resources for the Korean film industry are large Korean IT and telecommunication conglomerates such as KT, KTF and SKT, who want to secure a stable supply of content for such new and increasingly popular media as IPTV and DMB.

The top box office hit of the year was Kim Ji-woon's **The Good, the Bad and the Weird** (*Joeun Nom, Napeun Nom, Isanghan Nom*), whose mysterious marketing campaign held back any coverage of the film until its release

Kim Ji-woon's **The Good, the Bad and the Weird**

in mid-July, even though it had received its world premiere at Cannes in May. The film is set in 1930s Manchuria and most of its action scenes were shot in China. Often dubbed a 'Kimchi-western', it is in fact an homage to 1970s' Korean 'Manchu-western' films as well as to Sergio Leone's 'spaghetti westerns', which its title makes clear. The film is about three tough guys, played by top Korean stars Lee Byung-heon, Jung Woo-sung and Song Kang-ho, who chase after one another in an attempt to gain possession of a map.

Ha Jung-woo in Na Hong-jin's **The Chaser**

The second-biggest hit was Na Hong-jin's **The Chaser** (*Chugyeokja*). An unexpected success, it concerns an ex-cop who runs a 'massage service' (in reality a sex service), who pursues a brutal serial killer over one night in an attempt to stop him murdering one of his vulnerable female employees. In the context of a national cinema that generally prefers melodrama over hard-boiled logic, the thriller has historically been one of the weakest genres at the Korean box office. Yet *The Chaser* demonstrates the Korean film industry's ability to churn out riveting thrillers for an ever-expanding legion of fans, whose ranks are swelling thanks to the popularity of

US TV dramas such as *24*, as well as Japanese mystery and thriller novels. The intense performances by Ha Jung-woo and Kim Yun-suk – arguably Korean cinema's leading talents over the last year – helped sustain adrenaline levels to the very end.

Won Shin-yeon's *Seven Days*, which stars Kim Yun-jin (who plays Sun in the US TV drama *Lost*) as a lawyer forced to defend a rapist and murderer after her young daughter is kidnapped, initiated the thriller boom when it was released towards the end of 2007. The trend continued with Yun In-ho's **The Devil's Game** (*Deo ge-im*), an adaptation of a Japanese *manga*, about a dangerous relationship between a rich old man and a poor young man.

Kwon Chil-in's **Hellcats, I Like it Hot**

Another unexpected hit was Yim Soon-rye's **Forever the Moment** (*Uri saengae choego-ui sungan*), inspired by the true story of the Korean women's handball team who won the silver medal at the 2004 Athens Olympic Games. The film chronicles how the main characters joined the national team in their thirties, overcoming obstacles and prejudice. The success of this women-themed drama was followed by a crop of impressive romantic dramas and female coming-of-age sagas, which moved beyond the confines of conventional romantic comedies and melodramas. With a realistic but light touch, Kwon Chil-in's **Hellcats, I Like it Hot** (*Ddeugeoun-geosi joh-a*) focuses on the dilemmas of romance and sexuality faced by three women of different generations.

Ha Jung-woo and Jeon Do-yeon in Lee Yoon-ki's **My Dear Enemy**

Adapted from a Japanese novel, Lee Yoon-ki's **My Dear Enemy** (*Meotjin haru*) presents one day in the life of an odd couple. A woman calls upon her ex-boyfriend, who owes her a small sum of money, who then takes her to many of his ex-girlfriends to pay back his debt. Min Gyu-dong's **Antique** (*Antikkeu: Seoyanggol Dongyang Gwajajeom*), released in October, was eagerly awaited by female fans of the Japanese manga of the same name, whose story revolves around four 'flower beauty' men working in a cake shop. Young female director Kim Tae-hee's debut feature, **Share Living and Joy** (*Donggeo, Dongnak*), employs a taboo as its main motif – a mother sleeps with her daughter's boyfriend. Another female director, Lee Kyoung, debuted with **Crush and Blush** (*Misseu Hongdangmu*), the comic story of a young female school teacher who is unable to hide her true emotions because of her blushing face.

Kim Tae-hee's **Share Living and Joy**

A key recurring trend is Korean films' desire to travel back to points in the past that have hitherto been unexplored in Korean popular culture. Kyung-seong, the old name of the country's capital city during the Japanese occupation period, is a favoured historical and geographical location in which the modern and the pre-modern co-existed, and Western and Japanese cultures intersected, amid the nationalist struggle for independence. Ha Gi-ho's **Radio Dayz** (*Ra-deui-o De-i-jeu*) is a comedy about the production of the first radio drama on a station in Kyung-seong in the 1930s, while Jung Ji-woo's **Modern Boy** (*Modeon Boi*) – also set in Kyung-seong in the same period – is a melodrama about how one carefree, fun-loving modern boy turns into a nationalist fighter after he falls for a mysterious woman. Jeong Yong-ki's **Once Upon a Time** (*Wonseu-eopon-eo-taim*), also set in Kyung-seong but this time just before National Liberation in the 1940s, is a comic action film about a hustler and a thief in pursuit of a jewel that is about to be shipped to Japan.

Jung Ji-woo's **Modern Boy**

The 1970s, often labelled a dark period of repressive military rule, is also being explored in recent Korean films. Lee Jun-ik's **Sunny** (*Nim-eun-meon-go-sae*) brings back memories of the Vietnam War and the popular music of the 1970s. Choi Ho's **Go Go 70s** (*Go Go Chilgong*) celebrates the burning energy of the first generation of Korean rock bands and youth culture under brutal rule. The band presented in the film is modelled after a real-life band, The Devils, with the musical numbers performed by the actors.

Shin Min-a in Choi Ho's **Go Go 70s**

Gangster-themed melodramas and comedies used to dominate the box office, but are now showing signs of fatigue. The only current survivor from this genre is Kang Woo-suk's **Public Enemy Returns** (*Kang Chul-jung: Gonggongui jeog 1-1*), the third sequel in the *Public Enemy* series, which features fearless wild cop Kang Chul-jung. By contrast, cool and intelligent gangster films are being widely hailed. Kwak Kyung-taek and Ahn Kwon-tae's **Eye for an Eye** (*Noon-e-neun noon I-e-neun i*) entertainingly plays on the clichés of the heist film, while Jang Hun's account of the making of an action film, **Rough Cut** (*Yeonghwaneun Yeonghwada*), blurs the line between fictional filmmaking and fighting for real.

Kwak Kyung-taek and Ahn Gwon-tae's **Eye for an Eye**

Jeong Byeong-gil's **Action Boys** (*Urin Aeksyeon Baeuda*) is an interesting documentary that looks at the hardship experienced by young men who shed tears, sweat and blood to become stuntmen. The sole example of the horror genre is Chang's **Death Bell** (*Gosa: Piui Junggangosa*), in which high school students must solve some math or literature questions within a given time in order to stop their friends being killed.

Kim Ki-duk's **Dream**

Kim Ki-duk wrote the script for *Rough Cut* and his production company produced **Beautiful** (*Arumdabda*), directed by Juhn Jaihong, from an original idea by Kim himself. Kim also directed **Dream** (*Bi-mong*) featuring Japanese actor Odagiri Jô. Hong Sang-soo's **Night and Day** (*Bam gua nat*) features a womaniser wandering through Paris.

A small group of period dramas set in the Chosun period (AD 1392–1910) were released in autumn and winter 2008. Kim Yu-jin's **The Divine Weapon** (*Shin ge jeon*), about the development of a powerful new weapon, was a box office success. It was followed by Jeon Yun-su's **Portrait of a Beauty** (*Mi-in-do*), which was adapted from a novel that has already been made into a popular TV

Jeon Yun-soo's **Portrait of a Beauty**

drama. It fictionalises the true stories of two renowned painters of the period by imagining one of them as a woman disguised as a man. Yeo Kyun-dong's **1724 Hero** (*Ilchilisa Gibang Nandong Sageon*) is a comic action film set in 1724 and concerns gangsters fighting over a beautiful courtesan.

Park Chan-wook's vampire film, **Bat** (*Bagjeui*), co-produced with Universal Pictures International, and Bong Joon-ho's **Mother** (*Madeo*), about a mother trying to clear her son of a murder charge, are two much-anticipated titles scheduled for release in 2009.

The year's best films
Action Boys (Jeong Byeong-gil)
Forever the Moment (Yim Soonrye)
Go Go 70s (Choi Ho)
Light My Fire (Lee Jong-pil)
My Dear Enemy (Lee Yoon-ki)

Quote of the year
'The first time I met him, I told him he looked better without the cap. As he always appears in photos wearing a military cap, he looks like a criminal. Then later he wore a wool cap. Then he just looked like a monk.' *Lee Na-young, an actress appearing in Kim Ki-duk's* **Dream**, *commenting upon her impression of director Kim.*

Directory
All Tel/Fax numbers begin (+82)
Korean Film Archive, 700 Seocho-dong, Seocho-gu, Seoul 137-718. Tel: (2) 521 3147. Fax: (2) 582 6213. www.koreafilm.or.kr.
Korean Film Council (KOFIC), 206-46, Cheongnyangni-dong, Tongdaemun-gu, Seoul 130-010. Tel/Fax: (2) 958 7582. www.kofic.or.kr.

NIKKI J.Y. LEE is a film researcher based in Seoul and London. She contributed to *Cine21*, a weekly Korean film magazine, from 2001 to 2005 and has written articles on Korean directors Park Chan-wook and Im Kwon-taek. She currently teaches at Yonsei University in Seoul.

Spain Jonathan Holland

Spain is famously a nation of extremes and nowhere is this more apparent than in the current state of its film industry. Seen from abroad, Spanish cinema has a higher profile than ever before, with actors such as Javier Bardem, Penélope Cruz and Eduardo Noriega, alongside directors like Pedro Almodóvar and Alejandro Amenábar, making regular appearances on the world's cinema screens and in the international media. Woody Allen's next three films will be part-financed with Spanish money. But such success abroad may be symptomatic of the serious problems the industry is facing at home, with talented directors such as Juan Carlos Fresnadillo (*28 Weeks Later*), Gonzalo López Gallego (*King of the Hill*) and Àlex Pastor (the forthcoming apocalypse thriller *Carriers*) having left Spain to seek their fortunes in the US.

At home, all is not well. Cinema attendance is down 20% since the beginning of the decade, with only 116.9 million tickets sold in 2007. Of Europe's big five, only Germany had worse figures. Ticket sales mid-way through 2008 were down six million on 2006. The reasons are threefold: changes in consumer habits, especially among the young, mean that potential audiences are watching their films at

Miguel Bardem's **Mortadelo and Filemón: Mission Save the Planet**

home; city-centre cinemas are closing down; and piracy is rife, with an estimated 53% of Internet users in Spain involved in illegal downloading.

There is also the fact that Spanish audiences are famously sceptical about the quality of their own films; Spain lacks a middle-class that is prepared to encourage its own culture. Despite investment by the state TV channel and its campaigns to generate interest, including an increase in primetime screenings of Spanish films, cinemagoers emerge too often from a screening feeling that the trip simply wasn't worth it. Local market share in 2008 opened strongly, but, as ever, it was a small number of box office hits – namely

Miguel Bardem's knockabout **Mortadelo and Filemón: Mission Save the Planet** (*Mortadelo and Filemón: Mision: salvar la tierra*) and Álex de la Iglesia's English-language philosophical thriller, **The Oxford Murders** – making the numbers look better than they really were. However, by the end of August 2008, attendance was up by two million compared with 2007.

Nacho Vigalondo's **Timecrimes**

Artistically, the last twelve months have brought little of distinction. There were few films from major figures, with younger talents falling into one of three camps. The first of these is the clutch of genre directors reworking Hollywood genres and motifs into a Spanish style (i.e. lower budget). Dany Saadia's Spanish/Mexican co-production **3:19** mixed romantic comedy, melodrama and maths into a visually stunning film that festival audiences and juries rightly warmed to, whilst highlighting the talents of Miguel Angel Silvestre, an upcoming actor who supplies a combination of brain and looks that could generate international appeal. Nacho Vigalondo's **Timecrimes** (*Cronocrímenes*),

Manuela Velasco in Paco Plaza's **[Rec]**

a witty time-travel piece about a man who travels back in time an hour, offered a carefully worked-out script and was snapped up by United Artists for a US remake, while Luis Piedrahita and Rodrigo Sopeña's **Fermat's Room** (*La habitación de Fermat*) had four mathematicians struggling to solve math problems as the room around them shrank in size. Again, the word 'remake' was being bandied about. Indeed, Spain is currently a hub for such edgy genre fare. One of the box office smashes of the year, Jaume Balagueró and Paco Plaza's horror item **[REC]**, also generated a US remake.

Nacho García Velilla's **Chef's Special**

In a bid for bigger audiences, comedy producers have been importing proven TV talent into film, creating films that are basically showcases for small-screen talent. Surprisingly, two such films were more than watchable. Peris Romano and Rodrigo Sorogoyen's **8 Dates** (*8 citas*) looked at the struggles faced by people across generations, dealing elegantly with their problems, smoothly changing its emotional register as it did. The enjoyably vulgar **Chef's Special** (*Fuera de Carta*) is Nacho García Velilla's tale about a gay chef which, despite being a throwback to less sophisticated times, entertained Spanish audiences and sold well abroad. It featured the considerable talents of perhaps Spain's finest working actor, Javier Cámara.

Other younger actors are busy mining the gritty social-criticism seam, often with a dramatic success that is almost invariably unmatched at the box office; these are

Irene Cardona's **A Boyfriend for Yasmina**

projects that screen for a few days in art-house cinemas and are then gone. The year's standout debut in this category was Xavi Puebla's **Welcome to Farewell-Gutmann** (*Bienvenido a Farewell-Gutmann*), a savage satire about life in the corporate jungle, featuring a ruthless trio, practised in the art of humiliation, who then find themselves sacrificed on the altar of their own ambition. The lively, perceptive **Under the Snow** (*Nevando voy*), a micro-budget piece about four people discovering true happiness in the unlikely surroundings of a factory that makes snow chains, marked out its directors, Candela Figueira and Maitena Muruzabal, as two to watch for the future. Irene Cardona's **A Boyfriend for Yasmina** (*Un novio para Yasmina*) dealt with immigration problems faced by a Moroccan woman in southern Spain. It is peopled with warm, memorable characters, displaying Cardona's talent for blending social critique with comedy.

It was heartening that some of the year's best debuts came from women. The claustrophobic but compelling **Pretexts** (*Pretextos*), by actress Silvia Munt, unflinchingly examined

Juan Sanz and Marian Álvarez in Roser Aguilar's **The Best of Me**

the dynamics of family relationships as seen through the eyes of a theatre director. In **The Best of Me** (*Lo mejor de mí*), Roser Aguilar deftly and charmingly unpicked the emotions of a couple whose lives are torn apart by a medical problem.

Although women still account for too small a percentage of Spain's film output, many of the films they make are of a higher quality than those of their male counterparts. Ángeles González Sinde's **One Word from You** (*Una palabra tuya*) sympathetically examines the conflicted relationship between two emotionally dissatisfied street cleaners and features one of the year's great traumatic scenes, following the women's appalling roadside discovery. Gracia Querejeta's **Seven Billiards Tables** (*Siete mesas de billar francés*) had Maribel Verdú (*Pan's Labyrinth*) reuniting a team of oldies for one final game, whilst dealing with the unwanted attentions of her ex-husband. Though not particularly innovative, the film revealed Querejeta's increasingly sure directorial touch.

Angeles González-Sinde's **One Word from You**

Veteran directors turned out work which, in many cases, appeared weary – a fact implicitly recognised by Manuel Gutiérrez Aragón when he announced his retirement from filmmaking in August. His swansong was the worthy, if a liitle dull, **Who's Next** (*Todos estamos invitados*). It deals with the way that Basque politics affects the emotional life of the inhabitants of that troubled region. Antonio del Real, best known for poor comedies, made **The El Escorial Conspiracy**

Manuel Gutierrez Aragón's **Who's Next**

(*La conjura de El Escorial*), a sixteenth-century gowns'n'skullduggery drama, which flopped at the box office, despite the presence of Jason Isaacs and Julia Ormond. Octogenarian Vicente Aranda, with **Songs of Love in Lolita's Club** (*Canciones de amor en Lolita's Club*), showed that his ideas have evolved little since his best work in the 1970s, not unlike the maverick Gonzalo Suárez, with his **Oviedo Express**. Few audience members under the age of fifty any longer are taking an interest in the work of these ageing auteurs, and, indeed, the most interesting new film by a mature director, Jaime de Armiñán's **14, Fabian Road**, remains unreleased in Spain. It deals with the kidnapping of a writer by an obsessive fan and their ensuing, troubled relationship. It showed that the 81-year-old Armiñan, has not lost his touch.

The last twelve months have seen a renewed interest in issues of Spanish history, in part motivated by the current public debate about whether to bring the horrors of the country's recent past to light or to let sleeping dogs lie. José Luis Cuerda's **The Blind Sunflowers** (*Los girasoles ciegos*), Spain's Oscar nomination, was a clumsy, disappointing adaptation of Alberto Méndez's masterly novel about a priest torn between his religious beliefs and his physical urges. José Luis Garcí, a former Oscar winner, provided the year's most visually spectacular historical piece with **Blood in May** (*Sangre de Mayo*), set in Madrid during the Napoleonic invasion of Spain. It must be said that the film works better as a cinematic love letter to the Spanish capital than as a drama. More recent Spanish history was also examined in Dunia Ayaso and Félix Sabroso's lively **The Naked Years: Classified S** (*Los años desnudos: clasificada S*), an entertaining feminist fable dealing with the film industry in post-Francoist 1970s Spain, when the democratic freedoms led to everyone shedding their clothes.

Dunia Ayaso and Félix Sabroso's **The Naked Years: Classified S**

Recent conversation about film has been dominated by two controversial entries at the San Sebastián Film Festival. Jaime Rosales followed up his well-received *Solitary Fragments* with **Bullet in the Head** (*Tiro en la cabeza*), a challengingly experimental film about a day in the life of a Basque terrorist. The dialogue consisted of one word and the lengthy shots in which little happens provoked admiration in some and tedium in others. Livelier by far was Javier Fesser's genre-defying **Camino**, the troubling tale, based on real life, of a dying young girl whose parents are members of Opus Dei. Powerful, memorable and thoroughly distinctive, it marks

José Luis Cuerda's **The Blind Sunflowers**

Jaime Rosales' **Bullet in the Head**

Fesser out as one of depressingly few Spanish directors who are committed to developing their own unique style.

As ever, the year has provided a clutch of fine documentaries, among them **Flores de luna** (*Night Flowers*), Juan Vicente Córdoba's politically charged study of the growth of a working-class Madrid suburb; Carla Subirana's **Nedar**, which welds one man's fight with Parkinsons Disease onto a wider story about Spanish history; and **El Somni**, in which Christophe Farnarier – the cameraman on Albert Serra's internationally lauded *Honor de cavalleria* – tells his life story, with compelling results. These worthy items occasionally make it into the country's art-house cinemas, before disappearing.

2009 will reveal whether Alejandro Amenábar, who has yet to make a false step, can follow up on the Academy Award-winning success of **The Sea Inside**. He is directing **Agora**, an English-language film, with Rachel Weisz playing a fourth-century philosopher. Meanwhile, the other member of Spain's two-man A-team, Pedro Almódovar, waits in the wings with the four-way love story, **Broken Embraces** (*Los abrazos rotos*), starring Penélope Cruz. Is the moment for the Almodóvar backlash finally upon us? Don't hold your breath.

JONATHAN HOLLAND has lived in Spain for nearly twenty years. He is a university lecturer and *Variety*'s critic in Spain.

The year's best films
Welcome to Farewell-Gutmann (Xavi Puebla)
Camino (Javier Fesser)
One Word from You (Angeles González-Sinde)
A Boyfriend for Yasmina (Irene Cardona)
Timecrimes (Nacho Vigalondo)

Quote of the year
'In American films, having a Spanish accent no longer means you have to be the person who runs in screaming or who does the cleaning.'
PENÉLOPE CRUZ

Directory
All Tel/Fax numbers begin (+34)
Escuela de Cinematografia y de la Audiovisual de la Comunidad de Madrdid (ECAM), Centra de Madrid a Boadilla, Km 2200, 28223 Madrid. Tel: (91) 411 0497. www.ecam.es.
Federation of Associations of Spanish Audiovisual Producers (FAPAE), Calle Luis Bunuel 2-2º Izquierda, Ciudad de la Imagen, Pozuelo de Alarcón, 28223 Madrid. Tel: (91) 512 1660. Fax: (91) 512 0148. web@fapae.es. www.fapae.es.
Federation of Cinema Distributors (FEDICINE), Orense 33, 3ºB, 28020 Madrid. Tel: (91) 556 9755. Fax: (91) 555 6697. www.fedicine.com.
Filmoteca de la Generalitat de Catalunya, Carrer del Portal de Santa Madrona 6-8, Barcelona 08001. Tel: (93) 316 2780. Fax: (93) 316 2783. filmoteca. cultura@gencat.net.
Filmoteca Espanola, Calle Magdalena 10, 28012 Madrid. Tel: (91) 467 2600. Fax: (91) 467 2611. www.cultura.mecd.es/cine/film/filmoteca.isp.
Filmoteca Vasca, Avenida Sancho el Sabio, 17 Trasera, Donostia, 20010 San Sebastián. Tel: (943) 468 484. Fax: (943) 469 998. www.filmotecavasca. com. andaluciafilmcom@fundacionava.org.

Nerea Camacho in Javier Fesser's **Camino**

Sweden Gunnar Rehlin

I n 2008, vampires conquered Sweden. The best domestic film of the year was **Let the Right One In** (*Låt den rätte komma in*), directed by Tomas Alfredson, which was awarded Gothenburg Film Festival's Nordic film prize. It is based on is based on John Ajvide Lindqvist's bestselling novel about the friendship between a bullied young boy and a girl who turns out to be a vampire. Combining impressive technical skill with sensitive characterisation and a mastery of the genre, Alfredson has come up with the perfect combination of art and horror. The film also picked up awards at Tribeca, Puchon, Copenhagen, Edinburgh and Fant-Asia film festivals. It attracted widespread acclaim and Hollywood is already looking to remake it.

Tomas Alfredson's **Let the Right One In**

Sadly, the editing on Lukas Moodysson's highly anticipated English-language debut, **Mammoth** (*Mammut*), has taken longer than planned, pushing the release date back to January 2009. As always with Moodysson, the project is shrouded in secrecy, but the advance word on a rough cut is very positive.

The year opened with its biggest box office hit, Peter Flinth's **Arn: The Knight Templar** (*Arn: Tempelriddaren*). It received tepid reviews, but

Peter Flinth's **Arn: At the End of the Road**

that did not stop this epic about a Swedish knight in the crusades from attracting an audience in excess of one million. Part two of the tale, **Arn: At the End of the Road** (*Arn: Riket vid vägens slut*), opened to slightly better reviews and strong box office once again at the end of August. Internationally, the two films will be edited into one two-hour feature, to be presented at the film markets in 2009. The films' total budget was US$30 million, so it could do with selling well.

Josef Fares experienced his first commercial failure with **Leo**, a well-made and thought-provoking anti-violence film. It received good reviews, but its bleak tone, with its downbeat ending, could not attract an audience.

Josef Fares' **Leo**

Simon Staho's **Heaven's Heart**

Jens Jonsson's offbeat coming-of-age comedy, **The King of Ping Pong** (*Pingpong-kingen*), is about the relationship between two brothers who live in northern Sweden. Jonsson's shorts have been highly praised and his feature debut went on to win the Grand Jury prize at the Sundance Film Festival before travelling to Rotterdam and Brisbane.

Danish director Simon Staho presented his ascetic Swedish chamber drama, **Heaven's Heart** (*Himlens hjärta*). It was proof that the spirit of Ingmar Bergman lives on. Daniel Alfredson, the brother of *Let the Right One In*

Peter Stormare in Daniel Alfredson's **Wolf**

director Tomas Alfredson, had a well-deserved hit with **Wolf** (*Varg*). Hollywood Swede Peter Stormare played the lead in this exotic drama about a reindeer handler who refuses to give up his profession, even though modern times suggest he should.

Another previously successful director, Colin Nutley, experienced his first real failure with the drama **Angel**. The film, about a singer who tries to stage a comeback by deceiving the audience, was poorly reviewed by critics and shunned by the public. Nutley has taken a break from filmmaking, instead staging a version of *Cabaret* at a Stockholm theatre.

Ruben Östlund's **Involuntary**

Ruben Östlund's episodic comedy drama, **Involuntary** (*De ofrivilliga*) made a successful debut in the 'Un Certain Regard' section in Cannes. The film went on to win the main award at the Brussels Film Festival.

Even though they had their first screenings at festivals in the spring, both *Let the Right One In* and *Involuntary* did not have their Swedish premieres until late in the year. They joined a strong line-up, which included Maria Blom's charming comedy **Fishy**, Ella Lemhagen's poignant adoption comedy **Patrik Aged 1.5** (*Patrik 1.5*) and master director Jan Troell's **Everlasting Moments** (*Maria Larssons eviga ögonblick*). The latter was screened at the Toronto Film Festival, where it was bought for US distribution. It is also Sweden's entry for the Academy Awards. Troell has been nominated three times before. A fourth nomination would beat Ingmar Bergman (although he did go on to win each time).

Jan Troell's **Everlasting Moments**

The Bergman legacy has been prominent throughout the year. Several exhibitions opened, depicting him at work and at play. A representative from the Academy of Motion Picture Arts and Sciences was in Sweden to start preparing an extensive Bergman exhibition in Los Angeles, in 2010. The debate still rages about what to do with the late filmmaker's estate on the island of Fårö. Will it be sold privately or will it become a museum and a place for young filmmakers to develop their craft? A decision will be taken in 2009.

The year ahead looks very interesting. Aside from Moodysson's *Mammoth*, there is also Tarik Saleh's animated **Metropia**, Måns Herngren's synchronised-swimming comedy, **Allt flyter**, Carl Åstrand and Mats Lindberg's sci-fi comedy **Kenny Begins**. Ulf Malmros deals with life in the upper classes in **The Wedding Photographer** (*Bröllopsfotografen*), while Niels Arden Oplev's **The Girl with the Dragon Tattoo** (*Män som hatar kvinnor*) is the first film based on late author Stieg Larsson's best-selling 'Millennium' trilogy.

Tarik Saleh's **Metropia**

The year's best films
Let the Right One In (Tomas Alfredson)
Involuntary (Ruben Östlund)
Everlasting Moments (Jan Troell)
Fishy (Maria Blom)
Patrik Aged 1.5 (Ella Lemhagen)

Quote of the year
'Once in a lifetime...' PETER STORMARE's *reaction to* Wolf *receiving good reviews.*

Directory
All Tel/Fax numbers begin (+46)
Cinemateket, Swedish Film Institute, Box 27126, SE-102 52 Stockholm. Tel: (8) 665 1100. Fax: (8) 666 3698. info@sfi.se. www.sfi.se.
Swedish Film Distributors Association, Box 23021, SE-10435 Stockholm. Tel: (8) 441 5570. Fax: (8) 343 810.
Swedish Film Institute, Box 27126, SE-10252 Stockholm. Tel: (8) 665 1100. Fax: (8) 666 3698. info@sfi.se.
Swedish Film Producers Association, Box 27298, SE-102 53 Stockholm. Tel: (8) 665 1255. Fax: (8) 666 3748. info@frf.net.
Swedish National Archive for Recorded Sound & Moving Images, Box 24124, SE-10451 Stockholm. Tel: (8) 783 3700. Fax: (8) 663 1811. info@ljudochbildarkivet.se.

Lukas Moodysson's **Mammoth**

GUNNAR REHLIN is a Swedish film journalist, working for several Scandinavian media. He is also the Nordic correspondent for *Variety*. He once had his face melted by acid in a Swedish horror film.

Switzerland Marcy Goldberg

2008 turned out to be a lacklustre year for Swiss cinema, with the industry failing to match the exceptional box office and critical successes of 2006/07. Chronic under-funding and mediocre scriptwriting are two factors that continue to handicap Swiss film. But most of the blame for the current situation has been directed at the country's film funding policies. For the past three years, the federal film fund in Berne has pumped the largest share of its modest budget into a handful of genre productions aimed at mass audiences, all of which have flopped. The biggest disappointment of 2008 was Frédéric and Samuel Guillaume's animated children's film **Max & Co** which received the highest subsidy ever paid out by Berne but attracted little at the box office and lukewarm reviews. At the Locarno Film Festival in August, Nicolas Bideau, Head of the Cinema section of Office Federal de la Culture and architect of the current funding policies, expressed a new interest in supporting more author-driven projects in the future.

Silvio Soldini's **Days and Clouds**

ole), about a bourgeois family's economic and emotional free fall after the husband loses his job, and Denis Rabaglia's **Marcello, Marcello**, an amusingly retro coming-of-age romance set in a picture-book Italian fishing village. The year's highest hopes have been pinned on Ursula Meier's **Home**, a Swiss/French/Belgian co-venture starring Isabelle Huppert. This tense drama, about the disintegration of a lower-middle-class family after a superhighway is

Frédéric and Samuel Guillaume's **Max & Co**

Switzerland still managed to be present on the international scene this year, thanks mainly to a number of feature-film co-productions with neighbouring countries. Two noteworthy films of the year were Swiss/Italian co-productions: Silvio Soldini's **Days and Clouds** (*Giorni e nuv-*

Denis Rabaglia's **Marcello, Marcello**

Isabelle Huppert leads the cast of Ursula Meier's **Home**

built next to their home, premiered as a special screening at the Cannes Critics' Week and has already done well in cinemas in French-speaking Switzerland.

It will come as a surprise to many that the Kazakh drama **Tulpan** – veteran documentary director Sergei Dvortsevoy's first feature, which won the 'Un Certain Regard' award in Cannes and picked up a half-dozen prizes at other festivals including Karlovy Vary, Montreal, São Paulo and Tokyo – is also a Swiss film, co-

Sergei Dvortsevoy's **Tulpan**

produced by Zurich's Cobra Film with support from the Swiss public broadcaster SF TV.

Cobra's penchant for unlikely cross-cultural connections has also resulted in the much-anticipated **Tandoori Love**: a romance between an Indian chef and a rustic Swiss beauty, filmed as a tongue-in-cheek mix of Alpine drama and Bollywood musical. Since many Bollywood films are indeed shot in the Swiss Alps, the combination is not as far-fetched as it might at first seem. But it remains to be seen whether director Oliver Paulus's handling of genre and parody can satisfy the tastes of audiences at home and abroad.

Oliver Paulus's **Tandoori Love**

Meanwhile, the unexpected success of smaller Swiss films continues to demonstrate how unpredictable success in the cinema can be. One of the surprise winners of the year was Micha Lewinsky's unassuming debut feature **Der Freund** (the title can be translated as either 'the friend' or 'the boyfriend'), which picked up the Swiss Film Prize for Best Film and Best Actor, in addition to several other

awards. The melancholy story of a young misfit's unrequited love for a suicidal singer also helped launch the career of the talented singer-songwriter Sophie Hunger.

Micha Lewinsky's **Der Freund**

Even more unpredictable has been the box office success of Hans Haldimann's documentary **Bergauf, Bergab**. This sympathetic portrait of a family of mountain farmers, shot single-handedly over an entire year by former schoolteacher Haldimann without any support from the film funds, seems set to become one of the most popular Swiss films of 2008/09.

Hans Haldimann's **Bergauf, Bergab**

Indeed, documentary continues to be a mainstay of the Swiss film industry, although it has been somewhat neglected by funding policy of late. Perhaps the strongest non-fiction contender of the year is Fernand Melgar's **The Fortress** (*La Forteresse*), which takes a hard look at Swiss refugee policy by examining, in direct-cinema style, the workings of one asylum centre. Melgar's film premiered in Locarno, where it won the Golden Leopard in the Cinéastes du présent section, and is

Fernand Melgar's **The Fortress**

currently racking up festival awards abroad and good box office figures at home.

A much-anticipated documentary that did not live up to expectations was Eric Bergkraut's homage to the Russian journalist Anna Politkovskaya, who was murdered in 2006. **Letter to Anna** (*Ein Artikel zu viel*) premiered at a privately organised screening during the 2008 Berlinale and has had some success in human rights circles. Somewhat choppy and repetitive, *Letter to Anna* is nevertheless worth watching for its rare interview footage of Politkovskaya and her colleagues, and for its examination of the Chechen war and the dire state of journalism and civil rights in Russia.

Another festival success worth mentioning is Reto Caffi's short film **On the Line** (*Auf der Strecke*), at last count winner of 33 awards including a Student Academy Award for Best Foreign Film. A recent graduate of the Academy of Media Arts in Cologne, Caffi is clearly a name to watch for in future.

Reto Caffi's **On the Line**

Generally, the mood in Switzerland at the end of 2008 seems to be one of anticipation. As the film funds on federal and cantonal levels pledge to fine-tune their funding policies, and a new generation of producers and directors continues to pursue alternative or additional methods for funding and distribution, a number of promising filmmakers are currently at work on new projects. Anna Luif (*Little Girl Blue*), Andrea Štaka (*Das Fräulein*), Thomas Imbach (*Lenz*), Bettina Oberli (*Late Bloomers*) and Michael Steiner (*Grounding; My Name is Eugen*) are all planning releases for 2009/10. Veteran documentary filmmaker Richard Dindo is currently in post-production with two non-fiction projects, and art-world superstar Pipilotti Rist is preparing to launch her first feature film **Peppperminta**. Peter Liechti (*Signer's Suitcase; Lucky Jack*) has announced a release in early 2009 for his feature **The Sound of Insects: Record of a Mummy**, an innovative adaptation of a short story by Shimada Masahiko, which is itself based on a true story.

The year's best films
On the Line (Reto Caffi)
Bergauf, Bergab (Hans Haldimann)
The Fortress (Fernand Melgar)
Marcello, Marcello (Denis Rabaglia)

Quote of the year
'Swiss film funding is very weak in comparison with similar small countries like Denmark or Norway. Those countries invest about three times as much money in national film production as Switzerland does.' *Filmmaker* EDGAR HAGEN, *quoted in 'Cash Daily', August 2008.*

Silvio Soldini's **Days and Clouds**

Directory
All Tel/Fax numbers begin (+41)
Swiss Films, Neugasse 6, P.O. Box, CH-8031 Zurich. Tel: (43) 211 40 50. Fax: (43) 211 40 60. info@swissfilms.ch.
Swiss Films, Maison des Arts du Grütli, 16, rue Général Dufour, CH-1204 Genève. Phone Tel: (22) 308 12 40. Fax: (22) 308 12 41. geneva@swissfilms.ch.

MARCY GOLDBERG is a film historian and independent media consultant based in Zurich.

Taiwan David Frazier

As Taiwan's famed auteurs have increasingly found their niches internationally, local critics have continued to applaud politely while domestic audiences have focused their cinemagoing – more than 90% of it – on Hollywood fare. The situation in recent years has left Taiwan's film industry in search of new homegrown heroes – 'heroism' implying commercial success. In 2008, Taiwan's film industry found its best candidate in Wei Te-sheng, whose surprise hit **Cape No. 7** (*Hai Jiao Qi Hao*) achieved the second highest grossing figure in Taiwanese box office history. The comedy attracted sales of US$6.8 million in the first twelve weeks following its early August debut. The last film to gross more in Taipei theatres was *Titanic* back in 1997. (Taiwan only keeps statistics for theatres in Taipei, whose metro region includes about a quarter of Taiwan's 23 million people and a disproportionate number of the nation's cinemas.) Comparing *Cape No. 7*'s success to other Taiwanese produced films, not one since at least 1996 (when statistics began) has topped annual sales in Taipei cinemas, including last year's universally feted *Lust, Caution* from Ang Lee, which managed formidable local sales of US$4.1 million.

On *Cape No. 7*'s strength, Taiwanese film secured 8.4% of the island's total box office through to the end of September, compared to 8.1% for films from China and Hong Kong and 83.5% for other, mainly Hollywood, imports. Wei Te-sheng's success marked the second year of local resurgence (last year was driven by *Lust, Caution*). Between 2001 and 2006, the Taiwanese segment of the local market had never accounted for more than 2.2% of box office receipts. By the end of October 2008,

26 local films had been released, compared to 25 for the whole of 2007.

Wei shot *Cape No. 7* on a budget of about US$1.6 million, without stars, but featuring several indie rockers, a first-time octogenarian actor, and some locally-known talent. The film used a multi-cultural, multi-lingual cast that included major Taiwanese ethnic groups, in a story about a beach concert in southern Taiwan. Pop star Atari Kousuke (who plays himself), wants a local band to open his concert and some locals decide to form a band and write the three songs required to appear at the concert.

Wei first came to attention three years ago for a five-minute, US$60,000 trailer he produced for a war epic, *Seediq Bale*, about the battle between Japanese colonials and Taiwan's aborigines. With a budget in the range of US$10 million, he was never able to complete the film. However, following *Cape No. 7*'s success, funding is reportedly now in place.

In the political sphere, local identity has been increasingly emphasised by the island's first pro-independence government, which has encouraged this trend through cultural policies and increased subsidies for the arts and film. Virtually every film mentioned in this report has received government funds, from established directors such as Hou Hsiao-hsien to the younger generation of filmmakers. In 2007, US$1.8 million in subsidies were awarded to eleven productions, while the government also helped with publicity. Private sector investment remains very limited and directors borrowing money from friends and family to finish their films remains common.

Jack Kao in Singing Chen's **God Man Dog**

Taiwanese identity dominated a number of films, including Singing Chen's **God Man Dog** (*Liu lang shen gou ren*), which received an Audience Choice award at the Berlin Film Festival. Like *Cape No. 7*, it uses a light touch to present a cross-section of Taiwanese society, but it differs in its more serious engagement with social issues and themes of error and redemption. Jack Kao received a nomination for Best Actor in the Asian Film Awards for his excellent performance as the crippled caretaker of a portable Buddhist shrine. He will soon appear in his first non-Asian project, directed by Monica Truet. Singing Chen has since moved on to making a documentary about a dance troupe, while scriptwriter Lou Yi-an is working on **Yi Xi Zhi Di**, the feature follow-up to his comically apocalyptic short, *Waterfront Villa Bonita*.

Billed as Taiwan's first historical epic in two decades, **1895** (*Yi Ba Jiu Wu*) might have been hoping to draw comparisons with Hou Hsiao-hsien's landmark of Taiwanese cinema,

Hong Zhiyu's **1895**

City of Sadness. The claim was as misleading as the film was disappointing. **The Wall** (*Qiang Zhi Yan*) is about a Japanese Communist agitator hunted by China's Nationalist military government after it took control of Taiwan in 1949. It won Best Film at the International Film Festival of India.

Taiwanese history was addressed a little more obliquely in **Soul of a Demon** (*Hu Die*), by veteran director Chang Tso-chi. A gritty and superbly acted tale of gangster life in a small and starkly beautiful Taiwanese harbour town, its excessively convoluted plot stood in the way of critical or popular success.

Yang Ya-che's **Orz Boys**

Two school dramas, Ya-che Yang's **Orz Boys** (*Jung Nan Hai*) and Tom Lin's **Winds of September** (*Jiu Jiang Feng*), also hit nostalgic notes. The better of the two, *Orz Boys* was a quirky, endearing tale of the elementary school friendship between boys dubbed Liar No. 1 and Liar No. 2. It came in second in Taiwan's annual box office, with US$500,000 but was still playing at the end of the year.

With nativism thick in the air, Hou Hsiao-hsien's **The Flight of the Red Balloon** (*Hong Qi Chiu*) was barely an event in Taiwan, even though the homage to the 1953 Albert Lamorisse

Hou Hsiao-hsien's **Flight of the Red Balloon**

classic precipitated the requisite hagiographies from international critics. Perhaps infected by the desire for commercial relevance, Hou has unexpectedly announced that with his next film, he will follow his fellow dons of Greater Chinese cinema – Ang Lee, Chen Kaige and Zhang Yimou – in producing his own martial arts epic, **Assassin** (*Nie yin niang*). The budget now stands around US$9 million, with production set to begin in early 2009.

Lee Kang-sheng – the lead in every Tsai Ming-liang film to date – failed to provoke any scandal with **Help Me, Eros** (*Bang Bang Wo Ai Shen*), despite a scene with three B-list pop stars writhing naked on a rooftop while designer fashion logos were projected on their nude bodies. Tsai, who runs his production company like a theatre troupe, chipped in as executive producer and production designer on the film, and the surreal kitsch symbolism screams of his style, even if it lacks his subtlety. In November, Tsai began shooting **Visages** on a commission from the Louvre, which is sponsoring a film series and allowing Tsai to shoot inside its august galleries. The US$4.7 million project will be based on the Biblical story of Salome and star Lee alongside French model-actress Laetitia Casta.

Taiwan's oddball critical success came in **What on Earth Have I Done Wrong?** (*Qing Fei De Yi Zhi Shengcun Zhi Dao*), an autobiographical mockumentary by actor-director Doze Niu, which won Best Asian Film in Rotterdam. It's about everything that's wrong with Taiwan cinema.

The year's best films
God Man Dog (Singing Chen)
Flight of the Red Baloon (Hou Hsiao-hsien)
What on Earth Have I Done Wrong?
(Doze Niu)
Cape No. 7 (Wei Te-sheng)
Soul of a Demon (Chang Tso-chi)

Quote of the year
'A lot of people have gone to work in China because there's more attention there, but I still think there are a lot of stories to tell here in Taiwan.' *writer/director* **LOU YI-AN**.

Directory
All Tel/Fax numbers begin (+886)
Chinese Taipei Film Archive, 4F, 7 Chingtao East Rd, Taipei. Tel: 2392 4243. Fax: 2392 6359. www. ctfa.org.tw.
Government Information Office, Department of Motion Picture Affairs, 2 Tientsin St, Taipei 100. Tel: 3356 7870. Fax: 2341 0360. www.gio.gov.tw.
Motion Picture Association of Taipei, 5F, 196 Chunghwa Rd, Sec 1, Taipei. Tel: 2331 4672. Fax: 2381 4341.

DAVID FRAZIER has written on Taiwanese art, film and music for the *International Herald Tribune*, *Art in America*, *Art AsiaPacific*, the *South China Morning Post* and other publications. He is director of Taiwan's Urban Nomad Film Fest, a roving event for underground and indie film.

Tseng Yi-che in Chang Tso-chi's **Soul of a Demon**

Thailand Anchalee Chaiworaporn

In 2008, Thai cinema moved in two contradictory directions. While local insiders complained about the decline in production budgets, films continued to garner acclaim at international markets and on the festival circuit.

The number of domestic releases rose to approximately 54 titles, compared to 47 in 2007. Despite the domination of comedy, horror and action, a variety of other themes emerged; from romance and animation to children's films. Sadly, the thematic diversity was merely the release of older productions that had been shelved in recent years.

In the first ten months, only six films earned more than US$1.5 million. They included the sequel to 2004's box office hit, **The Holy Man 2** (*Luang Phee Theng 2*), about a monk who tries to develop a rural community; Banjong Pisanthanakun, Paween Purikitpanya, Youngyooth Thongkonthun and Parkpoom Wongpoom's portmanteau horror film, **4Bia**; Songyos Sugmakanan's **Hormones** (*Pidtermyai huajai wawoon*), which presents four stories about teen love; Prachya Pinkaew's **Chocolate**, about an autistic Japanese-Thai girl with martial arts skills; Tony Jaa's troubled **Ong Bak 2**, and festival favourite Nonzee Nimibutr's **Queens of Lungkasuka** (*Puen yai jom salad*).

Two main factors caused this dip in cinema attendance: the global rise in petrol prices and the political tension over ex-premiere-in-exile, Thaksin Shinawatr, who still exerts some political influence in the country. The cost of living increased, affecting many companies, who were forced to downsize or even close down operations. Some films looked promising revenue-wise, but any box office success was stymied by growing violence on the streets.

People preferred to follow political news than be entertained. And if they wanted to watch a film, it was cheaper to wait for a few months and watch it on DVD.

Most studios chose to reduce their operating budgets, offering few opportunities for new directors. Thus, the emphasis on films that had previously been completed, but not released: *Chocolate*, *The Holy Man 2*, *Queens of Lungkasuka* and *Ong Bak 2*.

Nonzee Nimibutr's **Queens of Lungkasuka**

Queens of Lungkasuka, made by the vanguard of the Thai new wave, was finally unveiled at the Venice Film Festival. The film blended fantasy, history and action in an epic that tells the story of three queens attempting to protect their kingdom from various enemies in the late sixteenth century.

Martial arts star Tony Jaa's directorial debut, *Ong Bak 2*, was finally released, despite the long months of disputes with the studio producing it, Sahamongkol Film International. News of the dispute caused American and Japanese buyers to cancel their purchase of territorial rights to the film.

Other films, even by well-known directors or featuring big stars, experienced budget cuts.

Ekachai Eukrongtham's **The Coffin**

It even affected Songyos Sukmaganan, who cast all of the country's teen heartthrobs in *Hormones* and commerical darling Yuthlert Sippapak who directed the love triangle **The Last Moment** (*Rak Sam Sao*) and **E-Tim Tay Nae**, a romantic comedy featuring Thai comedian Udom Taepanich.

In addition to *The Holy Man 2*, there were two other high-profile sequels. Bhandit Rittakol's **Boonchoo 9** takes place twenty years after the original comedy, about a country boy who struggles to live in the city. This time the story shifted to the relationship between the main character and his son. Tanit Jitnuku's **Art of Devil 3** is a prequel, showing how the main protagonist, Pa-nor, was abused by people around her and forced to use black magic. The film made little off the back of its previous instalments.

Staying with horror, Ekachai Uekrongtham's **The Coffin**, a Hong Kong/Japan/Singapore/Thailand co-production, plays on the Thai ritual of cheating death by sleeping a night in a

coffin. Sopon Sukdapisit, the co-writer of the most successful Thai supernatural film, *Shutter*, returned with the inventive **Coming Soon**, in which a ghost exists in a cinema screen.

Several independent production companies in competition with each other were established by producers or directors. A fair proportion of them have merely emulated the studios, with a slate of action and horror releases. Companies such as Nangnuk, Frame Production, Alangkarn Studio, Pacific Island Film and 54321 Action Film appear motivated solely by profit, seeking a short theatrical release before reaping rich dividends from the home entertainment market.

Aditya Assarat's **Wonderful Town**

The other production companies appear to want to make a difference with their films and it is generally their films that are acclaimed, both at home and internationally. Aditya Assarat and his Pop Pictures was the most successful, with his directorial debut **Wonderful Town**, which focuses on life in a village following the 2004 Tsunami. The film

Hiro Sano and Sinitta Boonyasak in O Nathapon's **A Moment in June**

has been sold to over twenty-five countries and invited to more than forty festivals, winning ten awards. O. Nathapon's directorial debut, **A Moment In June** is the melancholy tale of three couples in 1972 and 1999, who are linked together through the use of a song, 'Tha Charom', sung by Charoen Nathanakorn.

Uruphong Raksasad's **Agarian Utopia**

Extra Virgin is responsible for producing films by the likes of Pimpaka Tohveera, Jakrawal Nilthamrong and Uruphong Raksasad. They also provided local distribution for *Wonderful Town*. In 2009, they will see the completion of Raksasad's second film, **Agarian Utopia**, an experimental documentary about the future of agriculture.

Panu Aree, Kong Rithdee and Kaweenipon Ketprasit's **The Convert**

Chookiat Sakweerakul's **The Love of Siam** (*Rak Hang Siam*) is both a family drama and a teen romance between two boys. A departure for the director from his previous film, the thriller *13 Beloved*, Sakweerakul presents the story of two school friends who reunite when they are at college. Set over the Christmas period, the lengthy film traces the growing affection between the two leads as they set

about soothing the pain caused by an earlier family tragedy.

Two of the major documentaries of the year focused on elements of Islamic culture. Panu Aree, Kong Rithdee, and Kaweenipon Ketprasit's **The Convert** explores the life of a woman who converted from Buddhism to Islam. Pioneering filmmaker Ing K. returned, after ten years, with a four-hour-documentary, **Citizen Juling** (*Polamuang Juling*), on the death of a Buddhist art teacher, who lived in an Islamic area in the South of Thailand.

The year's best films
Wonderful Town (Aditya Assarat)
Love of Siam (Chookiat Sakweerakul)
The Last Moment (Yuthlert Sippapak)
A Moment in June (O Nathapon)

Directory
All Tel/Fax numbers begin (+66)
Film Board Secretariat, 7th Floor, Public Relations Dept, Soi Aree Samphan, Rama VI Rd, Bangkok 10400. Fax: 618 2364/72. thaifilmboard@hotmail.com.
National Film Archive, 93 Moo 3, Phutthamonton 5 Rd, Salaya, Nakorn Prathom 73170. Tel: 441 0263/4 ext 116.

ANCHALEE CHAIWORAPORN contributes to both local and international journals, and won 2000's Thai Best Film Critic award. She is now running a bilingual website on Thai cinema www.thaicinema.org.

Chookiat Sakweerakul's **Love of Siam**

Tunisia Maryam Touzani

It is debatable whether or not one can truly make reference to a Tunisian cinema industry. Although the majority of films produced in the country are indisputably co-productions, Tunisia is striving to create a cinema of its own. However, due to the scarcity of funding from state institutions, the evolution is slow and uncertain. Moreover, Tunisian cinema seems to be a stranger in its own country. The unpopularity of local productions means the already sparse cinemas prefer to screen more lucrative international features. Festivals, which are currently flourishing at a steady rate, offer the only chance for films to break through.

Successful co-productions are beneficial for aspirational Tunisian cinema, but may be polemical when determining the film's 'identity'. **Khamsa**, entirely produced by France and directed by French-Tunisian Karim Dridi, revolves around Marco, an eleven-year-old boy who flees the foster family he was placed in, returning to the gypsy camp where he was born. There, he forms a friendship with two other boys, increasingly finding themselves in trouble. From cockfighting and petty theft to

Marco Cortes in Karim Dridi's **Khamsa**

burglary, fortune is not on Marco's side. Using real gypsy children as actors, Dridi presents a realistic, albeit occasionally crude, vision of marginalised lives.

Enriched by the cross-cultural perspective of filmmakers, Tunisian cinema is a vehicle for social commentary, often analysing issues such as the quest for a cultural identity and reconciliation between colonial histories.

Hafsia Herzi in Abdellatif Kechiche's **Couscous**

Diasporic filmmaker Abdellatif Kechiche marked a powerful return to the cinema with **Couscous** (*La Graine et le Mulet*), which was awarded four Césars, including Best Film and Director. It relates the story of Mr Slimani, a divorced man in his sixties who, after having dragged himself to his shipyard job for years, decides to fight an overwhelming feeling of uselessness by opening a couscous and fish restaurant on an old boat. His family gradually reunites around him and invest themselves in realising a dream that has come to symbolise the quest for a better life. Kechiche succeeds in making his story touching and humane.

Co-produced by Morocco and Tunisia, Rachid Ferchioui's **The Accident** (*L'Accident*) is the tale

Sana Kassous in Rachid Ferchioui's **The Accident**

of Fares, a university graduate and occasional taxi driver whose wife has just given birth. However, he has no idea the turn his life will take the moment he admits a beautiful and mysterious woman into his cab.

Nadia el Fani's documentary, **The Story of a Militant** (*Ouled Lenin*), depicts the story of her own father, a chief of the Tunisian Communist Party. She attempts to shed light on a story that is both personal and far-reaching. Working in a similar vein, Lassaad Oueslati's **Memories of a Woman** (*Mémoires d'une femme*) focuses on a woman of Italian Jewish descent who converted to Islam in the 1950s and married a militant. Searching for her Jewish origins, the woman enthusiastically relates her enthralling story.

Férid Boughédir's **Villa Jasmine** is the gripping story of a French-Tunisian Jewish family whose son returns with his wife to his birthplace, in search of his roots. Based in 1942, Karin Albou's second feature, **The Wedding Song** (*Le Chant des Mariées*), is the story of two childhood friends, one Jewish and the other Muslim, as they experience their first contact with love, remaining united regardless of the way society perceives and underlines their differences. Khaled Ghorbal's second film, **Such a Beautiful Voyage** (*Un Si Beau Voyage*), recounts the tale of Mohamed, a retired builder living alone in the suburbs of Paris who, due to illness, returns to a changed Tunisia, where he feels thoroughly estranged.

Although the Tunisian public is indifferent to domestic releases, two films were eagerly awaited. Brahim Letaïef's **Cinecittà**, made under precarious conditions and without the support of the Ministry of Culture, is a witty portrayal of the financial difficulties filmmakers encounter. Disappointed by the refusal of funds for his police comedy, director Chahin decides to rob a bank to make his dream come true. Opening with experiences from Letaïef's own professional life, then pushed to the extreme, the story manages to provoke while remaining light-hearted. Fadhel Jazirin's **Thirty** (*Thalathoun*) closed the Journées Cinématographiques de Carthage. Looking back at Tunisia's shift into the modern world in the 1930s, it relates the story of three young men who became mythic figures in their country's history. With its huge budget and technical virtuosity, *Thirty* has set the benchmark for what Tunisian cinema can achieve.

More challenges lie ahead, such as finding new economic opportunities to support cinema production and ways in which Tunisian film can better reach its local audience. The Tunisian public is at heart avid and cinema-hungry. With the appropriate backing, Tunisian cinema can conquer its people and flourish within its own borders and beyond.

The year's best films
Couscous (Abdellatif Kechiche)
Khamsa (Karim Dridi)
Thirty (Fadhel Jazirin)

Quote of the year
'Making an energetic and liberated pledge for the right to difference, without falling into the reducing stigma of exotic representation, constitutes an essential double stake to which my emotionally implicated vision predisposes me.' **Couscous** *director* ABDELLATIF KECHICHE.

MARYAM TOUZANI is a freelance journalist based in Morocco and working internationally, specialising in art and culture.

Turkey Atilla Dorsay

The years 2007–08 will be remembered as a rebirth of Turkish cinema. The share of the local market has been remarkable, with more than 50% of the box office generated by Turkish films, which occupied the first five places in the top-ten-grossing films of the year. And Turkish cinema has been a presence at every major international film festival.

The successes were hardly impressive on a creative level, but some managed to score outside the domestic market, amongst Turkish communities internationally. Togan Gökbakar's **Recep İvedik** is a vulgar tale about an impoverished man who, upon finding a wallet, books into a luxury hotel. A blend of *Borat*, *Mr Bean* and some local humour made the film indigestible to some, but due to the presence of popular local comedian, Sahan Gökbakar, it scored at the box office. Other financial successes included Murat Aslan's **The Masked Five: The Cyprus Adventure** (*Maskeli Besler: Kibris*), Faruk Aksoy's **The Crazy Class Goes to the Camp** (*Çilgin dersane kampta*) and Murat Saraçoglu's **Sons of the Bitch** (*O... Çocuklari*). The latter was written by Sirri Süreyya Önder, who might have brought to the film the intelligence that he invested in his earlier – and more successful – *International*, had he made it himself. Murat Saraçoglu, working with Özhan Eren, also directed **120**, which attempts to depict some events of the First World War from a nationalistic viewpoint. Although an attempt was made to be intelligent and objective, the film fails on both counts.

Of the popular cinema of a higher quality, Ömer Vargi's **For Love and Honour** (*Kabadayi*) attempts to repeat the success of Yavuz

Ömer Vargi's **For Love and Honor**

Turgul's *The Bandit*, which Vargi produced. Both films feature Sener Sen in similar stories of people defending the ancestral and feudal values of eastern Turkey within the heart of modern Istanbul. Çagan Irmak also failed to achieve the success of his earlier film, *My Father, My Son*, with **The Messenger** (*Ulak*). Taking place in an unspecified period, the film is overburdened with symbolic meaning.

Nuri Bilge Ceylan dominated the artistic scene with **Three Monkeys** (*Üç maymun*), for which he won the Best Director award at Cannes. It is darker and more melodramatic than his previous work, seeing him forge new ground. Semih Kaplanoglu, a successful follower of Ceylan, completed the first part of a planned trilogy with **Egg** (*Yumurta*). It is about a

Nuri Bilge Ceylan's **Three Monkeys**

Semih Kaplanoglu's **Milk**

bookseller and poet who, after his mother's death, returns to his native village to look for meaning in his life. Stylish and lyrical, it was a treat for festival audiences. Kaplanoglu followed it immediately with **Milk** (*Süt*), which focuses on the younger years of *Egg*'s main character. It premiered at Venice and possesses the same qualities as the first film, albeit with fewer surprises.

Dervis Zaim's **Dot** (*Nokta*) took as its inspiration the art of calligraphy, in its story of revenge, lust and guilt. Shot against the blinding white of the famous Salt Lake in the east, the film, not for everyone, but is will charm passionate lovers of experimental cinema.

So-called political directors also had a good year. Reis Celik directed **Refugee** (*Mülteci*), a lucid account of political refugees in Germany. Handan İpekçi's **Hidden Faces** (*Sakli Yüzler*) focused on honour crimes and tackled the exploitation of women in general in present-day Turkey and Germany. The eternal warrior of the Kurdish cause, Kazim Öz, presented a long film, **Storm** (*Firtina*), about young Kurdish students in Istanbul, stuck between 'the cause' and their personal lives. Tayfun Pirselimoglu followed the excellent *In Nowhereland* with **Riza**, an interesting but ultimately unconvincing portrait of life in a poorer area of Istanbul. Yesim Ustaoglu's **Pandora's Box** (*Pandoranin kutusu*), which was awarded the Grand Prix at San Sebastián, tells the story of two sisters visiting their

mother, who suffers from Alzheimers. It is the director's best film since *Journey to the Sun*.

Ümit Ünal's third film, **Ara**, appeared in search of something new, but left audiences unconvinced. Aydın Sayman's **Janjan** was a unusual love story set in a remote town. Though nicely played, it left too much untold. Cemal San filmed his trilogy, **Zeynep's Eight Days** (*Zeynep'in 8 Günü*), **Ali's Eight Days** (*Ali'nin 8 Günü*) and **Dilber's Eight Days** (*Dilber'in 8 Günü*) back-to-back. With them he succeeded in presenting something unique in a surprisingly short time: three approaches to three portraits of modern Turkish life, featuring three excellent actors.

Hüseyin Karabey's **My Marlon and Brando**

The last year also witnessed a number of fine debuts. Well-known documentary filmmaker Hüseyin Karabey made **My Marlon and Brando** (*Gitmek*). The love story between a Turkish actress and a Kurdish fighter in Iraq, the film's charms attracted festival audiences. Dersu Yavuz Altun's **Murky Waters** (*Münferit*) tries to combine a political story with a thriller. Theatre director Berkun Oya's **Happy New Year London** (*Iyi Seneler Londra*) has a group of Turks and British people meet in a sordid hotel, where they experience a grotesque and sad adventure. Both Mehmet Eryilmaz's **A Fairground Attraction** (*Hazan Mevsimi*) and Mehmet Güleryüz's **Havar** lacked some much-needed maturity.

Mehmet Güreli's first feature, **Shadow** (*Gölge*), is an adaptation of Peyami Safa's novel and displays a keen period sense and a literary taste. Seyfi Teoman's **Summer Book** (*Tatil Kitabi*) and Özcan Alper's **Autumn** (*Sonbahar*) are two wonderful films. The first is an account of family life in the Mediterranean, while *Autumn* follows a young man, just released from prison, who pays a visit to his home town on the Black Sea coast. *Summer Book* is a contender for this year's FIPRESCI European Discovery prize.

Semih Kaplanoglu's **Egg**

The year's best films
Three Monkeys (Nuri Bilge Ceylan)
Autumn (Özcan Alper)
Egg (Semih Kaplanoglu)
Pandora's Box (Yesim Ustaoglu)
Summer Book (Seyfi Teoman)

Directory
All Tel/Fax numbers begin (+90)
Association of Actors (CASOD), Istiklal Caddesi, Atlas Sinemasi, Pasaj- C Blok 53/3, Beyoglu, Istanbul. Tel: 251 9775. Fax: 251 9779. casod@ casod.org.
Association of Directors (FILM-YON), Ayhan Isik Sokak 28/1, Beyoglu, Istanbul. Tel: 293 9001.
Association of Film Critics (SIYAD), Hakki Sehithan Sokak-Barlas Apt 33/13, Ulus, Istanbul. Tel: 279 5998. Fax: 269 8284. al.dorsay@ superonline.com. Contact: Atilla Dorsay.
Istanbul Culture & Arts Foundation (IKSV), Istiklal Caddesi, Louvre Apt 146, 800070 Beyoglu, Istanbul. Tel: 334 0700. Fax: 334 0702. film.fest@ istfest-tr.org.
Turkish Cinema & Audiovisual Culture Foundation (TÜRSAK), Gazeteci Erol Dernek Sokak, 11/ 2 Hanif Han, Beyoglu, Istanbul. Tel: 244 5251. Fax: 251 6770. tursak@superonline.com.
Turkish Film & Television Institute, 80700 Kislaönü-Besiktas, Istanbul. Tel: 266 1096. Fax: 211 6599. sinematv@msu.edu.tr.

Seyfi Teoman's **Summer Book**

Documentaries and shorts also had a good year, with a large documentary section at the Istanbul Film Festival and both documentary and short awards at the Ankara, Bursa, Antalya and Adana festivals.

Erden Kiral, director of *A Season in Hakkari*, made his comeback with **Conscience** (*Vicdan*). Unlike his previous films, with their influences of Angelopoulos and Tarkovsky, his new film, a fiery melodrama set amongst the working class, was a welcome surprise from this prestigious filmmaker.

ATILLA DORSAY has been a film critic since 1966 and has published over thirty books, including biographies of Yilmaz Güney and Türkan Soray. Founder and honorary president of SIYAD-Association of the Turkish critics, he is also one of the founders and consultants of the Istanbul Film Festival.

Özcan Alper's **Autumn**

Ukraine Volodymyr Voytenko

The last year saw some interesting movement in the Ukrainian film industry. Ten feature films were released theatrically, twice as many as last year. And for the first time since the country gained its independence a Ukrainian film, Robert Crombie's **Sappho**, earned over US$1 million at the local box office. Another significant moment was the government's decision regarding compulsory dubbing (or subtitling) of foreign films into the country's official language. This has led to a relative decrease in cinema attendance, but further contributed to the Ukraine market's independence from Russia. The Multiplex-Holding Company, who dominate the exhibition market in the Ukraine, opened its largest cinema to date, the twelve-screen megaplex in Kiev.

As for the most prolific Ukrainian director, Oleksandr Shapiro managed to complete three features within the last year. **Bes Porno** is about a group of school children who enter the shady world of pornographic filmmaking, while **Casting** and **Pick Up** are two low-budget art-house films. Of these two, *Casting* was one of a number of films featured at the Cannes Film Market. The premise involves thirty-six actors who appear at a casting session, unaware that material shot in each session will become part of a single, thirty-six scene feature. The aim of the film is to present a mosaic of Kyiv life.

Ukrainian art-house cinema boasted a number of films from different generations. Kira Muratova, who films under her self-described style known as 'critical surrealism', completed the Christmas social tragic-comedy **Melody for a Barrel Organ** (*Melodiya dlya sharmanki*), about two orphans wandering through an immense city. Ihor Podolchak, the popular

Kira Muratova's **Melody for a Barrel Organ**

Ukrainian graphic artist, made his feature debut with **Las Meninas**, a postmodern take on the famous canvas by Velásquez. It received its world premiere at the Rotterdam Film Festival. Presently, the director is editing his next film, **Space** (*Kosmos*), inspired by Witold Gombrowicz's work.

In terms of production, *Melody for a Barrel Organ* and *Las Meninas* are related to Oleh Kokhan, the chief of Sota Cinema Group. Together with Polish co-producers, Kokhan also produced the existential drama **With a Warm Heart** (*Serce na dloni*) by Krzysztof Zanussi. It starred one of Ukraine's top actors, Bohdan Stupka, whose performance was awarded a prize at the Rome Film Festival. Sota also produced Roman Balayan's **Birds of**

Serhiy Bukovskiy's **The Living**

Paradise (*Rayski ptakhy*), a tragic reflection on the period of totalitarian rule when Ukrainian writers in their search for freedom desired to fly, like birds, to escape the Soviet Union.

The history of the Holodomor genocide of 1932–33 is piercingly told by Serhiy Bukovskiy in his documentary **The Living** (*Zhyvi*). During this period, the communist regime exterminated approximately seven million peasants, the largest class of the Ukrainian nation.

Oles Yanchuk's **Metropolitan Andrey**

Oles Yanchuk, who on the dawn of Ukrainian independency filmed *Holod 33*, completed a bio-pic on the life of Andrey Sheptycky, the Metropolitan of the Ukrainian Byzantine denomination of the Catholic Church, forbidden at the times of the USSR. Unfortunately, the sketchiness of **Metropolitan Andrey** (*Vladyka Andrey*) reduced the impact of the film on this extraordinary character.

The world economic crisis will certainly influence film production. Already the proposed increase by 100% of the budget for film production has been shelved, leaving the 2009 budget the same as 2008. However, independent producers are showing no signs of slowing down.

Early 2009 will see the completion of a number of films by new directors. In particular, Valentyn Vasyanovych, the prize-winner of Clermont-Ferrand Film Festival, with his social tragicomedy **Matter of Course** (*Zvychayna sprava*), about an intellectual coping with the realities of Ukraine's consumer society, a

Ihor Podol'chak's **Las Meninas**

society that appears to be edging towards an acute ecomnomic and ideological crisis.

The year's best films
The Living (Serhiy Bukovskiy)
Melody for a Barrel Organ (Kira Muratova)
Las Meninas (Ihor Podol'chak)
Pick Up (Oleksandr Shapiro)
Birds of Paradise (Roman Balayan)

Quote of the year
'The crisis can hardly influence the Ukrainian film industry, which is in its embryonic state. One fact is obvious: the one who would find now resources and ideas for creation of high-quality film product and would overcome crisis difficulties, in two years will lay a claim to leadership in the whole domestic film industry and will be able to easily enter the international market.' *Producer* OLEH KOKHAN *discussing the world economic crisis.*

Directory
All Tel/Fax numbers begin (+380+
Central State Archives of Film, Photo & Sound Documents, 24 Solomyanska St, Kiev 252601. Tel: 277 3777. Fax: 277 3655.
Ministry of Culture & Art, 19 Franka St, Kiev 252030. Tel: 226 2645. Fax: 225 3257.

VOLODOMYR VOYTENKO is a film critic, editor-in-chief of the analytical quarterly *KINO-KOLO* and presenter of the weekly programme about art cinema on national TV.

United Kingdom Philip Kemp

To British filmmakers, feeling insecure is nothing new. Indeed, some would say that the UK industry has existed in a precarious state almost from its inception. Which may explain why – at least so far – the global financial crisis seems to have alarmed British filmmakers less than might be expected; to them, the sense of gazing into the abyss has become almost a matter of routine. Though such calmness might also be ascribed to the industry's habitual blissful indifference to anything outside its immediate vicinity. According to *Screen International* it was at the Edinburgh International Film Festival in late June, with financial institutions around the globe tottering and crashing on an almost daily basis, that a seasoned producer was heard to advise an eager young hopeful, 'If you want stability, go and run a bank.'

But in any case, there was plenty more to worry about than a few crumbling banks. When Hollywood sneezes, the rest of the movie world catches cold, and 2008 started with the Hollywood writers' strike still holding. Potentially lucrative US overseas productions planned for the UK – Ron Howard's *Angels and Demons*, Ridley Scott's *Nottingham*, Jerry Bruckheimer's *Prince of Persia* – were withdrawn or postponed, and the then strong

sterling/dollar exchange rate wasn't helping any. By the end of the year the writers were back at work, but there came ominous rumblings that the Screen Actors Guild was now contemplating industrial action. And then, of course, there was that perennial bugbear of the industry, the UK Treasury.

It is, within the UK film world, a truth universally acknowledged that any fiscal intervention by the British Government into the affairs of the industry – however well meant – will result in disaster. This year, filmmakers have been living in the aftermath of the decision to clamp down on the tax loophole known as Section 42, which had allowed investment partnerships to offset expected losses on film investments against their other tax liabilities. At the same time, the Government (nudged by the EU's diktat on 'cultural specificity') drastically tightened up the rules previously laid down in Section 48, under which films could be classified as 'British' to qualify for tax incentives.

The general opinion in the industry is that the demise of Section 42 was, on balance, perhaps no bad thing. The previous dispensation encouraged the involvement in production of a horde of dubious middlemen

with absolutely no interest in film but a deep devotion to tax avoidance, and led (so it's generally believed) to a lot of films being made that never achieved a release even on video – and were probably never intended to. But at the same time the change has meant that funding for British films, elusive at the best of times, has become yet harder to secure. According to Alex Brown, a partner at the UK production company Studio 8, 'Before, we could look at up to 45% relief on a film. Now, you would be lucky to receive 18% on a British film. It's been a big blow.'

The new ruling on 'Britishness' has been widely deplored. In an editorial Michael Gubbins, the editor of *Screen International*, observed that, 'In the UK, the restrictions on the kind of film that unlocks [tax] incentives are ridiculous. British culture is nothing if not international. This is a country whose history, for better or worse, is inextricably tied to the rest of the world. Yet a film struggles once it crosses the English Channel, meaning that anyone who wants soft money needs to be insular.' As a result, it seems that productions that might have brought work and income to the British industry are going elsewhere. Michael Hoffman's *The Last Station*, about the final days of Leo Tolstoy, is an English-language film; most of the cast and crew are Brits. Yet it was shot and post-produced in Germany. As producer Chris Curling explained, 'In the days of Section 48, we might have shot it in Russia, Germany or Prague… We would have done all the post-production in the UK and maybe the studio work too; we'd have qualified as British in that way… But with the new tax credit it doesn't work for us at all, because the film is not set in the UK.'

With co-productions dwindling, inward investment faltering and costs spiralling, discontent was widespread in the industry. ('When isn't it?' a cynic might add.) A new lobby group, Directors UK, was formed to agitate for the status of the director, alleged to have been seriously eroded. 'Over the past few years,' announced the group's chairman,

Charles Sturridge, 'we have seen a decline in both the creative and economic rights of the director… We need to argue and fight when the creative process is inhibited by mismanagement and wrong judgement.'

Independent distributors, as always in the UK, found themselves engaged in an uphill battle against the power of the Hollywood majors, an unequal match underlined by the collapse in June of Tartan Films, one of the country's best-established and best-regarded independents. According to Mark Batey, MD of the Film Distributors' Association, in 2007 73 companies released films in the UK; of these, 63 accounted for at most 5% of the market. Independent exhibitors, too, feared being squeezed out, this time by new technology. The imminent changeover to digital distribution should bring evident benefits to many in the industry, not least to production companies who will no longer bear the expense of striking multiple prints, and the cost of the digital changeover can easily be absorbed by the multiplex chains. But for small independent screens, already struggling to compete, the necessary expenditure may be the last straw unless Euro-funding can be secured.

Given such widespread gloom, it might be expected that 2008 would be a poor year for British films. Certainly the UK made a sparse showing at Cannes, although the acclaim for Terence Davies' **Of Time and the City** (shown as a special screening), and the award of the *Caméra d'Or* to Steve McQueen's **Hunger** (in

Terence Davies' **Of Time and the City**

the 'Un Certain Regard' section) partially made up for it. But the Cannes spotlight famously doesn't pick up everything, and elsewhere signs of vitality and originality were to be found, from the black comedy of **In Bruges** to the clear-eyed anger of Nick Broomfield's *Battle for Haditha*.

Martin McDonagh's **In Bruges**

It's a standing reproach to the British film industry – and to those, including the UK Film Council, who pulled the plug on his projected adaptation of *Sunset Song* – that it's been nearly a decade since Terence Davies, our finest living cinematic poet, has found funding to complete a film. With any luck, the enthusiastic reception accorded to *Of Time and the City* may signal an end to the long drought. Even so, it feels like something of a stopgap since so little of it was shot by Davies himself. A wry ode to his native Liverpool, the film assembles mostly found footage to present a highly idiosyncratic post-war history of the city, linked together by an eclectic range of music – everything from Liszt to Peggy Lee – and Davies' own nostalgic, disillusioned voice-over commentary. Comparisons with Humphrey Jennings are wholly justified.

Davies' film is perhaps too personal and *sui generis* to be classified as a documentary. Nick Broomfield, whose documentaries have often been criticised for being too personalised, with the director intruding into frame in the guise of a naïve bumbler, stays discreetly behind the camera for *Battle for Haditha* – and the result is his finest and most hard-hitting film to date. As with his previous film, *Ghosts*, Broomfield

semi-fictionalises recent events, in this case the planning and aftermath of a bomb attack on American troops in the Iraqi city of Haditha in 2005. By casting non-professionals whose backgrounds, Iraqi no less than American, are similar to those of the people they're portraying, he achieves a level of authenticity and conviction that recent Hollywood films on the Iraq conflict have rarely approached. The film conveys a vivid sense of the fear, incomprehension and intolerance that fuels both sides of the conflict – and its lethal effect on those caught in the middle – and creates a microcosm of the whole disastrous campaign.

In a very different register, though creating a comparable mood of tension, James Marsh's **Man on Wire** recounts how a Frenchman, Philippe Petit, crossed between the twin towers of the World Trade Center on a high wire in August 1974. Combining interviews and dramatised sequences with footage of the actual crossing, Marsh reconstructs the way Petit set up his 'illegal, but not wicked or mean' stunt with all the care and rehearsal of a well-organised heist. Nor did he simply wire-walk from A to B, but stayed on the wire for a barely credible 45 minutes, strutting and dancing, before delivering himself into the hands of the irate authorities. Marsh never conceals Petit's rampaging ego, nor the callous way he used people, but the beauty and exhilaration of his feat are irresistible.

All three of these films were made by experienced directors. In British feature films, though, some of the year's best work came

Steve McQueen's **Hunger**

from first-time directors. Most striking in its originality and uncompromising regard was *Hunger*, the feature debut of video artist Steve McQueen. With a cool, relentless gaze he leads us through the final weeks in the life of Bobby Sands, first of the IRA prisoners to die on hunger strike in the Maze prison in 1981. McQueen is not concerned with whatever acts of terrorism Sands may have committed outside. He takes that as read. Instead he gives us some idea what it was like being an inmate (prisoner or guard) of the Maze at the height of the Troubles. Drawing parallels with Abu Ghraib and Guantánamo, he noted that 'people have short memories, and we need to remember that things like this happened in Britain'. Scenes where naked prisoners are mercilessly beaten by riot guards spare us no details – their brutality is painful to watch. But the reprisal wreaked on a warder is no less horrifying – and totally unexpected.

McQueen shoots much of his film almost without dialogue, heightening its bleak intensity. However, the key central scene, where dialogue dominates – an encounter between Sands and a Catholic priest as the prisoner embarks on his hunger strike – is shot in one extraordinary, twenty-minute-long, fixed-camera take of the two men sitting opposite one another at a table. This takes us to the heart of McQueen's attempt to understand why an intelligent, articulate man should condemn himself to a lingering, agonising death. No sides are taken: each man's arguments are given due weight and it's clear why, despite mutual respect and even liking, there's an unbridgeable gulf between them. As Sands, the German-born, Irish-raised actor Michael Fassbender gives a performance of total dedication and conviction.

As original, in its very different way, was **Unrelated**, Joanna Hogg's first feature. Anna (Kathryn Worth), a fortyish, childless woman whose marriage is foundering, comes to stay at a villa in Tuscany where her old schoolfriend's family, plus another family, are spending the summer. All too conscious of

the ticking of her biological clock, Anna finds herself increasingly drawn not to her fellow-adults but to the youngsters in the party, a boozy, bantering crowd in their late teens, and especially to the rangy, good-looking Oakley (Tom Hiddleston). They tolerate her presence until, as the outsider, she falls foul of unspoken assumptions within the group and things turn sour. Hogg takes a naturalistic, intriguingly oblique approach – remarks are half-heard, things happen just offscreen – so that we, like Anna, are often left wondering quite where we stand. It feels like the kind of film that Eric Rohmer might make if he were British.

Outsiders in continental Europe also populate *In Bruges*, the feature debut from playwright Martin McDonagh. Two Irish hitmen – the brash, sulky Ray (Colin Farrell) and the older and more reflective Ken (Brendan Gleeson) – who botched an assignment in London have been sent by their Essex-Cockney boss (Ralph Fiennes) to lie low in Belgium until the heat dies down. Much of the comedy derives from the tension between the two – Ray moaning about Bruges as 'a fockin' shithole' while Ken

Joanna Hogg's **Unrelated**

finds himself unexpectedly delighted by the art and culture on display. Factor in a pretty Belgian drug dealer, a racist dwarf, grossly overweight American tourists and accidental child-killing, and it seems McDonagh (who also wrote the script) is out to offend as many people as possible. But the film is shamelessly funny, with – especially as regards Gleeson's character – an unexpected undertow of quiet melancholy. It's also the best thing Farrell has done for years.

Garth Jennings' **Son of Rambow**

After his underwhelming film version of the cult fantasy *The Hitchhiker's Guide to the Galaxy*, Garth Jennings' **Son of Rambow** came as a welcome surprise. Fortuitously released in the UK the same month as the latest and weariest entry in the clapped-out *Rambo* franchise, the film is set in a precisely recalled 1982 England where two boys – one the movie-forbidden son of Plymouth Brethren parents, the other the school tearaway – bond over a project to make their own action movie. The view of childhood is warm, clear-eyed but never sentimental, and the mix of humour and poignancy led several reviewers to invoke Shane Meadows.

Meadows himself, meanwhile, caused some astonishment by accepting a commission from Eurostar to make a sponsored feature. But **Somers Town**, the director's first venture outside his Midlands stamping-ground, rarely feels like a commercial. Like *Son of Rambow* it centres round an odd-couple pair of boys: a young runaway from Nottingham (Thomas Turgoose, from *This Is England*) arriving in

Thomas Turgoose in Shane Meadows' **Somers Town**

London, and the son of a Polish builder who is working on the huge St Pancras refurbishment. Performances are semi-improvised and there's a gentle, unforced humour about the dialogue and characters. A minor Meadows work, but an appealing one. Mike Leigh also astonished his fans – by making a cheerful film. The protagonist of **Happy-Go-Lucky**, Poppy (Sally Hawkins), is an inveterate optimist, determined to see the best in everyone and everything – and this despite teaching in a London state school. Even her embittered driving instructor (Eddie Marsan) can't get her down. Reviewers divided on the film; some found Poppy's sunny outlook uplifting, others were exasperated by her relentless cheeriness.

Sally Hawkins in Mike Leigh's **Happy-Go-Lucky**

No surprises, alas, from Woody Allen, whose dispiriting run of British movies concluded with **Cassandra's Dream**, the weakest and least convincing yet. And **Puffball**, a piece of mystical Irish whimsy adapted from a novel by Fay Weldon, continued the long, slow, sad decline of Nicolas Roeg. Paul Andrew

Williams, whose debut feature *London to Brighton* impressed with its edgy, downbeat realism, disappointed with his sophomore effort, **The Cottage**; the mix of gangland slapstick and Chainsaw Massacre-style rural horror failed to gel. The master of Cockney knockabout violence, Guy Ritchie, made a slight return to form with **RocknRolla** – but London teen-gang thriller **Adulthood**, sequel to 2006's *Kidulthood*, with screenwriter and lead actor Noel Clarke taking over direction, felt even more tritely sensationalist than its predecessor.

Saul Dibb's The Duchess

Gerard Butler in Guy Ritchie's **RocknRolla**

That reliable old standby of British genres, the costume drama, continues to thrive. Sumptuously – if a little too cleanly – staged and costumed, Saul Dibb's **The Duchess** starred Keira Knightley as Georgiana, Duchess of Devonshire, a leading society beauty of eighteenth-century London. Knightley showed more acting skill and range than she's generally credited with, but the picture was stolen by Ralph Fiennes as her emotionally frozen consort. Knightley also showed up, to less effect, as Dylan Thomas's mistress in

Jessica Biel in Stephan Elliott's **Easy Virtue**

John Maybury's *ménage à trois* biopic, **The Edge of Love**. But Jessica Biel, against all expectations, proved well up to the polished witticisms of Noël Coward adaptation **Easy Virtue**, holding her own against such distinguished thesps as Colin Firth and Kristin Scott Thomas.

Easy Virtue emanated from the revamped Ealing Studios, whose relatively modest size (four acres, with its biggest stage 10,000 sq. ft) ensures that even in hard times it can count on staying almost fully booked. But even the larger studios – Pinewood, Shepperton, Leavesden – have stayed busy despite the financial downturn, partly thanks to the no-ill-wind effect of the pound having weakened against the dollar, making the UK once again attractive for co-productions. (As ever, the unsinkable James Bond and Harry Potter franchises contributed substantially to the kitty.) Box office admissions, having fallen off slightly in 2005 and 2006, started to rise again in 2007, reaching GB£163 million, up 4% on the previous year; and at the time of writing, they look likely to increase again in 2008. British-made films (if you include co-productions) increased their market share by 10%, up to 29% of the market by value. Encouragingly, foreign-language films – and especially French-language releases – are also increasing their market share, though admittedly from a fairly modest base.

Uncoupling itself from the main festival, the Edinburgh International Film Festival shifted its slot from August to June, a move generally agreed to have been a complete success. The London International Film Festival stayed where it was in calendar terms, but a lively debate was started – and still continues – over whether it should become more glamorous. Stewart Till, chairman of the UK Film Council (the overall governing body which also controls the British Film Institute (BFI)) has expressed a desire for a 'bigger, louder festival' with 'more impact on the worldwide film stage'. Not everyone agrees, not by a long way. Producer Jeremy Thomas, a former BFI chairman, is typical of those deploring the idea of added glitz and red carpets. 'The festival does a very good job on its limited resources,' he says. 'All it needs is a little more money.'

In a year less doom-laden than might have been anticipated, one event cast a deep shadow: the sudden, totally unforeseen death in March of writer-director Anthony Minghella at age 54, just after completing his first film for television, **The No. 1 Ladies Detective Agency**. Fellow-director Alan Parker, Minghella's predecessor as chairman of the BFI, wrote a heartfelt tribute: 'This was a man whose abilities as a consummate filmmaker – as writer, director, and producer – were always intermingled with his qualities as a man... He was also kind, gentle, thoughtful, generous and humble. Now, trite as these words might appear, I have to remind myself that I'm talking about someone in the film industry – a world where such attributes are far from plentiful.'

PHILIP KEMP is a freelance writer and film historian, and a regular contributor to *Sight & Sound*, *Total Film* and *DVD Review*.

The year's best films
Hunger (Steve McQueen)
Of Time and the City (Terence Davies)
In Bruges (Martin McDonagh)
Battle for Haditha (Nick Broomfield)
Unrelated (Joanna Hogg)

Quotes of the year
'This isn't a dignified business. It's an absurd business. There is no dignity in this business, you just have to go with that and accept it.' *Director* **ALEX COX** *on working as second unit director on a Mexican TV soap*.

'If we are going to have a national cinema, we have got to make stories which arise from our islands. The American template is very often lousy. Why do we want to imitate it?' *Director* TERENCE DAVIES.

Directory
All Tel/Fax numbers begin (+44)
British Academy of Film & Television Arts (BAFTA), 195 Piccadilly, London, W1J 9LN. Tel: (20) 7734 0022. Fax: (20) 7734 1792. www.bafta.org.
British Actors Equity Association, Guild House, Upper St Martins Lane, London, WC2H 9EG. Tel: (20) 7379 6000. Fax: (20) 7379 7001. info@equity. org.uk. www.equity.org.uk.
British Board of Film Classification (BBFC), 3 Soho Square, London, W1D 3HD. Tel: (20) 7440 1570. Fax: (20) 7287 0141. webmaster@bbfc.co.uk. www.bbfc.co.uk.
British Film Institute, 21 Stephen St, London, W1T 1LN. Tel: (20) 7255 1444. Fax: (20) 7436 7950.

sales.films@bfi.org.uk. www.bfi.org.uk.
Directors Guild of Great Britain (DGGB), Acorn House, 314-320 Grays Inn Rd, London, WC1X 8DP. Tel: (20) 7278 4343. Fax: (20) 7278 4742. guild@ dggb.org. www.dggb.org.
National Film & Television Archive, British Film Institute, 21 Stephen St, London, W1P 1LN. Tel: (20) 7255 1444. Fax: (20) 7436 0439.
Scottish Screen Archive, 1 Bowmont Gardens, Glasgow, G12 9LR. Tel: (141) 337 7400. Fax: (20) 337 7413. archive@scottishscreen.com. www. scottishscreen.com.
Scottish Screen, 249 West George St, 2nd Floor, Glasgow, G2 4QE. Tel: (141) 302 1700. Fax: (20) 302 1711. info@scottishscreen.com. www. scottishscreen.com.
UK Film Council, 10 Little Portland St, London, W1W 7JG. Tel: (20) 7861 7861. Fax: (20) 7861 7862. info@ukfilmcouncil.org.uk. www. ukfilmcouncil.org.uk.
UK Film Council International, 10 Little Portland St, London, W1W 7JG. Tel: (20) 7861 7860. Fax: (20) 7861 7864. internationalinfo@ukfilmcouncil. org.uk. www.ukfilmcouncil.org.uk.

United States Shane Danielsen

If 2007 was all champagne and back-slapping, then 2008 was the bleary morning after: such, at least, ran the conventional wisdom. In their end-of-year summations, many critics had taken pains to hail the preceding year's post-summer releases as a vindication of faith: the long-awaited triumph of smart, ambitious filmmaking. A new day was dawning, it was implied – whether as a reaction to the manifest iniquities of the Bush administration, or a natural corrective to the pervasive idiocy of mainstream culture. Either way, a perceptible shift had occurred. And there was no going back.

Twelve months later, however, the story was very different. The year rallied in its final stages, thanks to the usual glut of A-list, pre-Christmas releases. But for the most part, it was a period characterised by discontent (why weren't this year's films as good as last year's?), unease (where were the audiences?), and a deepening, all-pervasive sense of dread. Which only grew as first the US and then the world economies slid – abruptly, alarmingly – into recession.

In fact, the terms of this argument were skewed from the outset. If 2007 had been the year of *There Will Be Blood* and *No Country For Old Men*, it was also the year of *License To Wed* and *The Number 23* and *Good Luck Chuck*. Hollywood had not changed; the lotus-eaters had not taken over. Its supposed

renaissance was actually just propitious timing, a rare confluence of good projects made well: brainy, haunting conundrums like *Zodiac*; old-fashioned corporate conspiracy thrillers like *Michael Clayton*; elegiac westerns like *The Assassination of Jesse James by the Coward Robert Ford* and *3:10 to Yuma*. Scattered like jewels amid the usual dross.

Nor, for that matter, were this year's statistics quite as frightening as they appeared. By Labor Day – the US industry's film traditional yardstick – the summer box office had reached US$4.2 billion, a decline of 1% from the previous year. Overall admissions were down by almost 7%. Yet what seemed at first glance to offer further proof of a shrinking market, turned out, upon closer examination of the figures, to be a solid, if not quite buoyant, year for the majors.

Part of this, admittedly, was simple bookkeeping: the end of New Line as an independent distributor, and its annexation by Warner Bros., meant that some of the former's biggest titles (notably, Michael Patrick King's **Sex in the City: The Movie**) were folded into the latter's accounts, boosting its numbers considerably. Yet total box office figures for the majors saw an increase of approximately 14% from 2007, despite a slump after the first few weeks of summer – precisely the opposite of the previous year, which had recovered in August after a sluggish start. The real casualties were smaller studio films and the independent sector, each of which failed to match their 2007 incomes.

Various hypotheses were advanced to explain this shortfall. The most commonly invoked was the Writers' Strike, the 100-day stoppage by the Writers Guild of America which ended in February 2008, and whose onset was heralded by Eddie Cockrell in his article for last year's edition of this publication. (That capitalisation is intentional: the Strike was rendered thus in most press reports, conferring upon a simple industrial dispute an historical significance akin to the Gunpowder Plot or the Six Day War.)

Michael Patrick King's **Sex and the City: The Movie**

Thereafter it filtered, with slippery expedience, down to the trenches. Cannes disappointing? Blame the Writers' Strike. Venice a damp squib? Ah, those damned writers… By the time Toronto's line-up was drawing weary sighs, you could almost imagine Piers Handling, that festival's long-serving director, shaking a fist at the idle dreamers of the Golden West.

But in fact the industry's woes were not so easily explained. Certainly, the Writers' Strike presented a hurdle to production – but far more so in television, where a number of series were postponed and a few actually cancelled. In terms of actual production quotas, much of the film industry was barely affected.

Still, there were casualties – and, ironically, it was the very heart of 'quality filmmaking', the specialty arms of major studios, which accounted for most of the corpses. Given their recent high-profile successes with *No Country For Old Men* and *There Will Be Blood* – which they co-produced with Miramax – one would not have thought Paramount Vantage would be folded, just four months after the Academy Awards, into Paramount's main operation. Yet so it transpired. Nor would we have expected Warner Independent to be shut down, along with fellow Time Warner affiliate Picturehouse. Yet that, too, occurred.

Not everyone was saddened by this development, however: 'There were too many players,' said Miramax CEO Daniel Battsek, of the specialty sector. 'There are probably still too many players. Even with the slight reduction of companies operating in this space, there are still too many movies being released.' The problem, it turned out, was not shortage at all, but abundance.

If 2008 was notable for anything, it was the unlikely convergence of art and commerce. In terms both of box office returns and critical opprobrium, the year belonged to **The Dark Knight**, Christopher Nolan's latest addition to Warners' Batman franchise. Scripting with his brother Jonathan, Nolan crafted a dense, complex, frequently harrowing treatise on the blurred lines between good and evil, and the limits of personal and social responsibility. In doing so, he displayed a keen reading of recent history: its second act, in particular, conveyed a sense of the reeling chaos of urban terrorism, analogous to and reminiscent of 9/11.

Heath Ledger in Christopher Nolan's **The Dark Knight**

It also featured a performance by the late Heath Ledger that actually surpassed the considerable hype which followed his death. Licking his lips, twitching convulsively, his Joker seemed to be corrupt in the literal sense, rotting from the inside out. It was a big performance, determinedly iconic, and would have utterly capsized a less confident film. In Nolan's hands, however, it was merely the crowning glory.

By contrast, the year's other big superhero flick, **Iron Man**, attested to a more old-fashioned Hollywood virtue: the power of a charismatic leading man to elevate, more or

Robert Downey Jr in Jon Favreau's **Iron Man**

less single-handedly, an otherwise routine production. As millionaire playboy-turned-superhero Tony Stark, Robert Downey Jr held the film in the palm of his (newly steady) hand – his performance so apparently effortless, so amused and amusing, that one barely noticed the strictly workmanlike nature of Jon Favreau's direction, or the efficient but unremarkable script.

You could see the appeal, at least on paper, of **Hancock**: an attempt to apply director Peter Berg's rough-hewn, handheld style – developed in films like *Friday Night Lights* and *The Kingdom* – to the more balanced equations of the superhero movie. And it was a bold choice for actor Will Smith: a chance to play against type, as a character of monumental selfishness and minimal self-awareness. And if the film never quite gelled, undone not only by uncertainties of tone, but by some of the most pronounced script issues of the year, it performed well at the box office nevertheless, attesting to the dependable appeal of its star. In early December came reports that a sequel had been green-lit. Another franchise might yet result.

Less a narrative than a post-production show-reel, **Speed Racer** – the Wachowski Brothers' first directorial credit since 2003's *The Matrix Revolutions* – updated Tatsuo Yoshida's 1967 cartoon classic, buffing it to a dazzling hi-definition sheen. So much so, that one friend, a British critic, compared the experience of watching it to being pummeled with a thousand brightly coloured hammers… for 135 minutes.

Which begs the question: why exactly was *Speed Racer*, a film ostensibly made for pre-teens, two-and-a-quarter hours long? One might as well ask, why did **Synecdoche, New York**, the directorial debut of acclaimed screenwriter Charlie Kaufman, cost US$25 million – in the process, all but guaranteeing that it would never recoup its investment? The film looked, and played, like an indie, albeit one of unusual ambition. And while its cast was excellent (Phillip Seymour Hoffmann, Samantha Morton, Emily Watson, Hope Davis, Catherine Keener), it could hardly be called a costly ensemble.

Charlie Kaufman's **Synecdoche, New York**

Cerebrally, if not aesthetically, Kaufman's film was every bit as flashy as the Wachowskis': a series of infinitely receding perspectives that recalled the Borges of 'Tlön, Uqbar, Orbis Tertius'. Less predictable (though not wholly unexpected, at least for those who recalled *Eternal Sunshine of the Spotless Mind*) was its anguish. What appeared, at first glance, to be boilerplate Kaufman surrealism, swiftly deepened into a meditation on the writer's perennial themes: the swift implacability of time, the toll extracted by artistic temperaments on the lives of those around them. The result was at once dizzying, profound and heartbreaking.

Standing onstage at the Kodak Theatre last February, Hollywood's other reigning intellectuals, Joel and Ethan Coen, had looked characteristically unimpressed by their Oscar win for *No Country for Old Men*, perhaps believing that to display any actual pleasure,

much less gratitude, would reduce them to the level of an industry they patently despise. So it should not have come as a surprise that they chose to follow that film – one of their very best – with something markedly different, in terms of both tone and content.

Set in and around the world of espionage, and allegedly a comedy, **Burn After Reading** managed – against fairly stiff competition – to be their most purely contemptuous film to date. Barely a single character in it was less than venal – and the few that were (Brad Pitt's gym instructor; Richard Jenkins' besotted boss) were defined instead by a cluelessness verging upon the moronic. Apart from feeling it marked a backwards step for these talented if perennially contrary filmmakers, there was something deeply depressing about watching an ensemble of talented actors (George Clooney, Tilda Swinton, John Malkovich) so cynically ill used.

Meanwhile, Clooney's own feature, **Leatherheads** – a romantic comedy, set in the hectic world of 1920s American football – failed to equal the artistic or critical heights of his previous directorial efforts: even its maker's vast reserves of charm (on display, since he also starred) were not enough to compensate for its creakily old-fashioned feel.

His friend and occasional co-star Brad Pitt fared much better, with David Fincher's **The Curious Case of Benjamin Button**, loosely adapted from an F. Scott Fitzgerald story by Eric Roth. The tale of a man who ages in reverse (played by Pitt, with the assistance

Ethan and Joel Coen's **Burn After Reading**

Brad Pitt in David Fincher's **The Curious Case of Benjamin Button**

of some incredible CGI effects), this was an unabashedly prestige production: meticulously crafted, packed with memorable set-pieces and arresting imagery, and breathtakingly shot – on HD digital – by cinematographer Harris Savides. But it also had a swooning sense of melancholy, which lifted it from seeming merely virtuosic. Beneath its surface glitter lurked a rumination on death and loss, whose ironies, though playful, never quite eclipsed its not-inconsiderable sadness.

Coming as it did after the grungy hyper-realism of *Requiem for a Dream*, and the utopian sci-fi of *The Fountain*, **The Wrestler** seemed a strange choice of project for Darren Aronofsky. Yet working for the first time from another's script (Robert D. Siegel, better known as a writer for satirical website The Onion), he crafted something special: an unexpectedly tender ode to a C-list celebrity, and the difficulty of making a life in the shadows, once the bright lights have faded.

Mickey Rourke in Darren Aronofsky's **The Wrestler**

Ultimately, though, the film belonged to Mickey Rourke. Playing a pro wrestler – Randy 'The Ram' Robinson – some twenty years past his prime, it was hard to not hear the actor speaking through his character. 'I'm slower now,' he says. 'I don't hear so good. An' I ain't as pretty as I used to be.' This was undeniable: disfigured by years of booze, beatings and steroid abuse, he seemed unrecognisable as the handsome, mysterious Motorcycle Boy from *Rumble Fish*. But here his off-screen tribulations were finally, triumphantly vindicated. He owned the movie from its very first frame, and, come February, should rightfully claim a Best Actor Academy Award.

M. Night Shyamalan's **The Happening**

Muddled and hokey – despite a suitably unnerving opening sequence – **The Happening** did not arrest M. Night Shyamalan's critical and commercial decline, much less reverse it. And **10,000 BC** failed to provide Roland Emmerich with a tentpole hit to equal *Independence Day* or *The Day After Tomorrow*; however dire our present-day situation might become, it appears audiences do not yearn for the simpler pleasures of the Epipalaeolithic.

Steven Spielberg's **Indiana Jones and the Kingdom of the Crystal Skull**, meanwhile, seemed as laboured as its title, with a visibly irritable Harrison Ford communicating little of the hero's former rakish charm. Essentially a string of set-pieces, of varying ingenuity and success, it also provided conclusive evidence that Shia LaBeouf is no more a leading man –

which is to say, capable of holding the screen, of urgently compelling the viewer's attention – than was Orlando Bloom.

But *Crystal Skull* was also indicative of a puzzling new phenomenon: a film that everyone anticipated, but no one actually desired. Did even the most diehard Indie fan seriously crave a further instalment of this franchise, more than eighteen years after the last? What point did it serve, except to devalue our memories of the originals? Audiences came, certainly – the film wound up grossing some US$785 million worldwide, the second-highest of the year – but more out of a sense of duty, one suspects, than pleasure. Most reviews were favourable, but hardly enthusiastic; likewise, viewers' reactions.

The Women offered another example of this trend. A remake of the Claire Booth Luce play, first brought to the screen in George Cukor's 1939 classic, it had languished in development for almost two decades; at one time or another, virtually every major Hollywood actress had been attached to star. In the end, it fell to Diane English, better known as a writer for TV sitcom *Murphy Brown*, to serve up this turkey. Meg Ryan, unsurprisingly, proved to be no Norma Shearer – and Eva Mendes was most definitely no Joan Crawford.

Shrill, crass and almost defiantly unfunny, the result made a convincing case for cultural decline, with Anita Loos' sparkling witticisms replaced by crude profanity ('What do you think she sells, Chanel Number Shit?' inquired one character, charmingly), and its distaff cast in thrall to the same reflexive brand-envy as the fem-bots of *Sex in the City*. What possible conclusion could one draw, except that neither the movies nor the times were quite what they used to be?

Yet it was a dire time for 'women's movies' in general. Anne Fletcher's **27 Dresses** was agreeable fluff, but *Sex and the City* played precisely like what it was – four or five episodes of the TV series stitched together,

with no visible concessions to cinema beyond an extended budget. Worse, it continued to patronise its audience with the same equation of consumerism with empowerment. In the absence of dissenting voices, one feels obliged to point out that the ladies of the Seraglio were beautifully outfitted, too – *and* had a lot of sex. But that didn't make them free.

James McAvoy in Timur Bekmambetov's **Wanted**

On the other side of the aisle were the guys' films – of which, typically, there were no shortage. Notwithstanding games-inspired shoot-em-ups like John Moore's **Max Payne**, the biggest, loudest bang of the year belonged to Universal's **Wanted**, which set the inexplicably popular James McEvoy opposite Angelina Jolie – perhaps the most uneven screen pairing since Danny Kaye romanced Gene Tierney in *On the Riviera*.

Michael Brandt and Derek Haas's adaptation considerably diluted the cold-blooded nihilism of Mark Miller's original graphic novel – so much so, in fact, that its source was practically unrecognisable – yet, if nothing else, this tedious, cacophonous revenge-fantasy provided a 110-minute showcase for the visual invention of Russian-Kazakh émigré Timur (*Night Watch*) Bekmambetov, a director so enamoured of all things kinetic, he made Michael Bay look like Eric Rohmer.

Jolie's other starring role could hardly have been more different. Written by *Babylon 5* creator J. Michael Straczynski, and directed by Clint Eastwood, **Changeling** premiered

Angelina Jolie in Clint Eastwood's **Changeling**

in competition at Cannes, and drew reviews ranging from the respectful to the reverent.

One would be hard pressed, perhaps even hard hearted, to call *Changeling* a bad movie. It was made with rigour and care; its intentions were noble. Yet it lacked something indefinable, some crucial spark of life. Everyone in it, from the evil police captains to John Malkovich's crusading churchman to, in particular, Ms Jolie's suffering mother – a veritable paragon of martyrdom, so ravishing in her anguish she might have been carved by Canova – seemed to be merely fulfilling their assigned function, subordinated to the schematics of its plot, and its trapped-in-varnish look. The result was the finest example of immaculate production design stifling a drama since Sam Mendes' *Road to Perdition*.

That same overweening good taste threatened to unbalance Mendes' latest film, an adaptation of novelist Richard Yates' 1962 masterpiece **Revolutionary Road**, which reunited Leonardo DiCaprio and Kate Winslet for the first time since the big ship went down, back in 1997. Its timing was both fortuitous and regrettable: the Emmy Award-winning *Mad Men*, on the AMC network, had recently provided a window into much the same world and many of the same themes. (In fact, there's a strong case to be made that the best American movie of 2008 was the second season of that series – it just happened to be delivered in weekly instalments, and ran to somewhere in excess of twelve hours.

Nevertheless, it displayed an acuity of vision, an overall excellence of performance, and a level of screenwriting that put most of its big-screen counterparts to shame.)

Actually it was very fine indeed, communicating its concerns – a study, not merely on the woe that is in marriage, but of that uniquely American preoccupation: the sense of personal failure that can dwell, like a cancer, at the heart of success – via oblique dialogue, careful compositions, and some beautifully nuanced acting. Faithful to its source text, handsomely mounted, it managed to achieve something of the humanity, if not the emotional intensity, of Yates' novel. In his *Variety* review, Todd McCarthy speculated that, in its well-crafted way, the film represented the limits of cinema's ability to capture essentially literary qualities. What it truly lacked, perhaps, was the transcendent quality of a Naruse or a Bergman, the intimation of something – be it spiritual or temporal – trembling just outside the frame.

Opening in the first weeks of 2008, **Cloverfield** presented something unique: a first-person vision of apocalypse, as New York (and possibly the rest of the world; one of the film's virtues is that we never know for sure) succumbed to what appeared to be some kind of alien invasion. In rejecting the omniscient perspective of conventional filmic storytelling, and proposing instead a series of partial and subjective 'nodes', the film not only conformed to our own fragmentary experiences of catastrophe, but also offered

Matt Reeves' **Cloverfield**

a thoroughly immersive experience, whose occasional contrivances (Manhattan proved surprisingly easy to traverse!) did not detract in the least from the panicky terror of unfolding events. Its lurching visuals inspired genuine nausea in filmgoers: its producer, J. J. Abrams, suggested its true milieu was not the cinema, but DVD, where it would fulfill its supposed role as a 'found text', watched after the events it describes by survivors.

For those seeking lighter fare, however, 2008 was a lousy year. Despite apparently note-perfect casting (Ann Hathaway and Steve Carell), Peter Segal's **Get Smart** demonstrated the perils of the Robert McKee school of scriptwriting: in giving Maxwell Smart a credible set of human concerns (and, worse still, an actual *backstory*), it radically diminished his effectiveness as a comic avatar; you want to laugh at Agent 86, not empathise with him. And **Pineapple Express**, despite the pictorial elegance of David Gordon Green's direction – far removed from the TV-derived, utilitarian blankness of most post-Apatow comedy movies – perhaps best conveyed its stoner ethos by conjuring a state of foggy forgetfulness: an hour after it was done, you struggled in vain to recall the first thing about it.

Kevin Smith's **Zack and Miri Make a Porno**

Indie kingpin Kevin Smith returned with **Zack and Miri Make a Porno**. It showed how decisively the baton had been passed, and how comprehensively the pupil had outstripped the teacher, in terms of raunch as well as profile, that Kevin Smith was effectively reduced to making a Judd Apatow movie. Its two leads (Seth Rogan and Elizabeth Banks) were members of Apatow's rep company, as were a number of the supporting players; its mixture of sweetness and profanity occupied precisely the same territory Apatow has mined since *The 40 Year Old Virgin*. Unsurprising, then, that the film marked Smith's biggest commercial success to date.

Sean Penn in Gus Van Sant's **Milk**

Milk, directed by Gus Van Sant from a script by Dustin Lance Black, charted the life and times of the onetime San Francisco city supervisor, America's first openly gay politician, who was assassinated in 1978. A timely biopic, released in the US just days after the passage of Proposition 8 banned gay marriage in California, it made its political points adroitly and well, and its fairly conventional structure saw Van Sant return to the mainstream, after more experimental works like *Elephant* and *Paranoid Park*. Perhaps most remarkably of all, it featured a beguiling, even joyous, lead performance from Sean Penn, typically one of the most visibly humourless and self-important of American actors.

To my mind, though, the finest American film of the year was an animation: Andrew Stanton's **WALL-E**. Ferociously modern in execution, indisputably state-of-the-art – has CGI ever looked more dazzling? – its early scenes nonetheless harkened back to cinema's early days, the silent classics of Chaplin and Keaton. This push-and-pull – between slick surface and bumpy, beating heart, comedy and

Andrew Stanton's **WALL-E**

sentiment – characterised and distinguished the entire movie. Unreal, in the strict sense, its protagonist might have been – no more than a collection of zeroes and ones, when all is said and done. Yet he made a far more convincing romantic hero than the legions of skin-puppets who crowd the pages of *InStyle* or *People*; his longing for Eve was as moving as Léon's courtship of Ninotchka – even as the film's vision of a depopulated earth, of vast empty canyons strewn with trash, offered an unusually strident environmental polemic. Little wonder that a number of conservative critics condemned the film as 'Malthusian fear-mongering'.

WALL-E was hailed as a groundbreaking work: digital wizardry imbued with the weight and texture of human drama. This is true, but it was also something more – a reminder that movies can move us, provided the viewer is willing to surrender to them.

As Philip Larkin once observed, in his poem 'An Arundel Tomb', we are predominantly visual creatures, easily seduced by the surface of things, and conspicuously blind to the deeper meanings beneath. Yet sometimes that illusion suffices – achieving, almost by accident, a deeper truth. Forget its dire prophecies, however appropriate they may seem to this desperate time: if *WALL-E* proved anything, it was a simple thing. What will remain of us is love.

The year's best films
WALL-E (Andrew Stanton)
The Dark Knight (Christopher Nolan)
Synecdoche, New York (Charlie Kaufman)
The Wrestler (Darren Aronofsky)
The Curious Case of Benjamin Button (David Fincher)

Quotes of the year
'Taken together, *Sex and the City*, *Mamma Mia!*, and *The Women* add up to a spectacular trilogy of the inane, and to point that out is not the prerogative of the misogynist or the killjoy. It's the view of someone who thinks that women deserve better from the movies, and who sees no joys to kill.' ANTHONY LANE, *The New Yorker*

Directory
All Tel/Fax numbers begin (+1)
Academy of Motion Picture Arts & Sciences, Pickford Center, 1313 North Vine St, Los Angeles, CA 90028. Tel: (310) 247 3000. Fax: 657 5431. mpogo@oscars.org. www.oscars.org.
American Film Institute/National Center for Film & Video Preservation, 2021 North Western Ave, Los Angeles, CA 90027. Tel: (323) 856 7600. Fax: 467 4578. info@afi.com. www.afi.com.
Directors Guild of America, 7920 Sunset Blvd, Los Angeles, CA 90046. Tel: (310) 289 2000. Fax: 289 2029. www.dga.org.
Independent Feature Project, 104 W 29th St, 12th Floor, New York, NY 10001. Tel: (212) 465 8200. Fax: 465 8525. ifpny@ifp.org. www.ifp.org.
International Documentary Association, 1201 W 5th St, Suite M320, Los Angeles, CA 90017-1461. Tel: (213) 534 3600. Fax: 534 3610. info@documentary.org. www.documentary.org.
Motion Picture Association of America, 15503 Ventura Blvd, Encino, CA 91436. Tel: (818) 995 6600. Fax: 382 1784. www.mpaa.org.

SHANE DANIELSEN was Artistic Director of the Edinburgh International Film Festival from 2002 to 2006; he now lives in Berlin..

Uruguay Jorge Jellinek

I f the number of films released in one year can be taken as a reflection of the strength of a national cinema, then 2008 has been a good year for Uruguay. Twelve new features and documentaries were shown at multiplexes and independent cinemas, and although none of them achieved the unqualified success of Enrique Fernández and César Charlone's endearing *El baño del Papa*, the total box office was nonetheless one of the best in recent years.

This year was also a turning point in the government's policies regarding the audiovisual industry. Last May, a new law was finally approved unanimously by the Parliament and its impact will be registered in the months to come. It creates the Institute for Cinema and the Audiovisual (ICAU), with an annual budget of more than US$1 million, most of it dedicated to promoting film production and distribution. Also, with the help of a special government initiative for small industries, the production companies formed the Audiovisual Chamber, to develop and consolidate a sector that has created hundreds of new jobs.

The new harvest of Uruguayan films was varied and, in general, of good quality, with a few garnering prizes at international festivals. Some of these works explored the country under the rule of the military dictatorship in the 1970s and early 1980s. In the case of **Masangeles** (*Polvo nuestro que estás en los cielos*), the new feature by Beatriz Flores Silva (*In This Tricky Life*), it is the first Uruguayan film to tackle the political turmoil at the end of the 1960s, when the confrontation between a conservative government and the left-wing militants of the Tupamaros urban guerrillas eroded a fragile democracy and cleared the path for the military coup. With its strange mix of grotesque comedy and political testimony, the film attempts to reflect the chaos that enveloped the country during those years. It follows the misadventures of a young girl, Masangeles, who goes to live with her political-leader father following her mother's suicide. Employing an all too obvious metaphor, the large, crumbling house the girl goes to live in reflects the decay at the heart of the country. Although it misfires at certain moments, this Belgian co-production impresses with its audacity, honesty and for its production values (it is one of the largest Uruguayan productions in recent years).

More temperate and precise is **Kill Them All** (*Matar a todos*), a political thriller directed by Esteban Schroeder (*The Vineyard*). It is an account of Eugenio Berrios, the Chilean chemist who devised the lethal and traceless Sarin gas for Pinochet, who used it to eliminate enemies. When he became a potentially dangerous witness, he was sent to Uruguay, where he was killed in an undercover operation. The assassination involved the Condor Plan, part of a dark chapter in South American history. They coordinated the collaboration of military dictatorships in

Esteban Schroeder's **Kill Them All**

the region and were still active in certain democratic regimes as late as the early 1990s. This sober and well-made film, in the tradition of Costa-Gavras, introduces the fictional lawyer Julia Gudari, who discovers the kidnapping and uncovers the conspiracy behind it. As a result, she is alienated from her military family. The excellent Roxana Blanco received the Best Actress prize at the Havana Film Festival for her intense performance.

Federico Veiroj's **Acne**

Also set in the early 1990s, but with a totally different tone, is newcomer Federico Veiroj's subtle comedy about the growing pains of a Jewish adolescent, **Acne**. Produced by Control Z, the same young team that marked a fresh style in local production and who gained international recognition with *25 Watts* and *Whisky*, *Acne* is a light-hearted portrait of the adolescent universe, in an age before the mobile phone and Internet.

Gabriel Bossio's **Jewel** (*Joya*) is a bittersweet comedy featuring an almost improvised style and quick pace in its account of the misadventures of a young and errant couple in the process of separation.

Documentaries were one of the highlights of the year and proved to be a surprise success at the box office. One of the best, Aldo Garay and José Pedro Charlo's **The Circle** (*El círculo*), is an austere but emotionally charged portrait of Henry Engler, the hard-line leader of the Tupamaros movement, who remained in jail, in harsh conditions, during the thirteen years of the military regime. He was one of the nine

'hostages' that the military held in order to prevent further activity by left-wing guerrillas. After his release, he continued his medical studies in Sweden and is now a respected human rights investigator, even mentioned as a possible candidate for the Nobel Prize. The film traces his many lives, focusing on the process that allowed him to recover from his mental breakdown. Intense and absorbing, it won the first prize at film festivals in Bahia and Trieste.

Covering the same issues, but with a more general perspective, **Tell Mario Not to Come Back** (*Decile Mario que no vuelva*) is a personal film by veteran filmmaker Mario Handler, famous for his political films in the 1960s. His return to the country and to his past is a voyage through memory, in an attempt to heal and reconcile. Occasionally lacking focus, the most interesting section features the testimony of a member of the military, now in jail for human rights violations. Another personal account of the period was presented in **Final Destiny** (*DF: Destino Final*), directed by Marcos Gutierrez, the youngest son of the political leader Héctor Gutierrez Ruiz, who was assassinated in 1976 whilst in exile in Buenos Aires. The clandestine operation, still being investigated, also killed left-wing leader Zelmar Michellini and two other leftists. With detailed testimonies, including Gutierrez's mother and brothers, as well as archive material, the director constructs an intimate and reflexive homage to his father, whom he was too young to remember.

Visiting the past in a different way, the captivating documentary **Hit**, directed by two young film students, Claudia Abend and Adriana Loeff, digs into the memories of the past fifty years, through the story of five songs that became popular hits. Following a long trail, from the phenomenon of the 1960s local rock 'n' roll group The Shackers, created in the image of The Beatles, to the more recent success of Jaime Roos, with his recycling of the carnival tradition, the film investigates the mystery of what makes a song so popular that

Claudia Abend and Adriana Loeff's **Hit**

it transcends time. It attracted an audience of over twenty-five thousand. Sebastián Bednarik's **Cachila** (*La Matinée*) continued his attempt to rescue the carnival cultural tradition. Meanwhile, **Stranded: I Have Come from a Plane That Crashed in the Mountains** (*Vengo de un avión que cayó en las montañas*), directed by Gonzalo Arijón, brought back the intense memories of the sixteen survivors of the famous plane crash in the Andes, in 1972. This well-constructed testimony won the first prize at the Amsterdam International Documentary Festival.

Gonzalo Arijón's **Stranded: I Have Come from a Plane That Crashed in the Mountains**

Of the new directors' films, **Giant** (*Gigante*), a comedy by Adrián Biniez, **Leo's Room** (*El cuarto de Leo*), the out-of-closet drama by Enrique Buchichio, and **Bad Day to Go Fishing** (*Mal dia para pescar*) by Álvaro Brechner, based on the short story by Juan Carlos Onetti, are

all expected to be released early in 2009. And with the help of the new funds created by the government, the outlook for Uruguayan cinema looks brighter than ever.

The year's best films
The Circle (Aldo Garay & José Pedro Charlo)
Acne (Federico Veiroj)
Hit (Adriana Loeff & Claudia Abend)
Kill Them All (Esteban Schroeder)
Masangeles (Beatriz Flores Silva)

Quote of the year
'The film is essentially about truth, a truth that hurts but also heals.' ESTEBAN SCHROEDER, *director of* **Kill Them All.**

Directory
All Tel/Fax numbers begin (+598)
Asociación de Productores y Realizadores de Cine y Video del Uruguay (ASOPROD),
Maldonado 1792, Montevideo. Tel: 418 7998. e-mail: info@asoprod.org.uy. www.asoprod.org.uy.
Cinemateca Uruguaya, Lorenzo Carnelli 1311, 11200 Montevideo. Tel: 418 2460. Fax: 419 4572. cinemuy@chasque.net. www.cinemateca.org.uy.
Fondo Para el Fomento y Desarrollo de la Producción Audiovisual Nacional (FONA),
Palacio Municipal, Piso 1°, Montevideo. Tel: 902 3775. fona@prensa.imm.gub.uy. www.montevideo.gub.uy/cultura/c_fona.htm.
Instituto Nacional del Audiovisual (INA),
Reconquista 535, 8° Piso, 11100 Montevideo. Tel/Fax: 915 7489/916 2632. ina@mec.gub.uy. www.mec.gub.uy/ina.
Asociación de Críticos de Cine del Uruguay (ACCU), Canelones 1280, Montevideo.
Tel: 622 0085. Fax: 908 3904. criticosuruguay@yahoo.com.

JORGE JELLINEK has been a film critic and journalist for over twenty years, contributing to newspapers, magazines and radio. He is vice-president of the Uruguayan Critics' Association and in the last two years the Artistic Director of the Punta del Este Film Festival.

Venezuela Martha Escalona Zerpa

There is no doubt that, over the last three years, film production in Venezuela has taken a significant leap. Not only due to increased financial and promotional support for new documentary and feature films from the Centre for National Cinematography (CNAC), Villa del Cine and Amazonia Films, but through the appearance of a new generation of Venezuelan film directors.

For decades, Venezuelan cinema was represented by a handful of filmmakers: Román Chalbaud, Carlos Azpúrua, Alfredo Lugo, Fina Torres and Solveig Hoogesteijn. Today, there are a growing number of new directors. In addition to this development, there is an increase in co-productions with other Latin American countries, including Argentina, Bolivia, Chile and Cuba. Another aspect is the continuous participation of Venezuelan productions in regional and international film festivals. This cross-border presence enhances the image of Venezuelan cinema around the world.

Recent Venezuelan films focused on issues relating to delinquency and violence. However, looking at the films produced by Villa del Cine, the state-of-the-art production house that is changing the face of Venezuelan cinema, patriotic and nationalist themes have also made an appearance. The films released display a diverse range of topics, but all are specific to the Venezuelan people, dealing with life, religious beliefs, the conflicts between women and men, as well as the role of women both in the countryside and urban areas. And not forgetting that these issues are approached with typical Venezuelan humour.

However, only in the future will it be possible to see where these films fit into the complex and controversial political reality that is Venezuela under the government of Hugo Chávez.

If anything, 2008 was a better year than 2007. By the end of September, 38 films had been released, 16 of which were features and 22 documentaries. They were financed by the CNAC, with an annual budget that was extended to US$28 million. The selected projects can receive support at any stage of their development, production and distribution, including marketing and publicity. The most expensive production to date was *Miranda Regresa*, in 2006, costing US$2 million.

The following films are some of the outstanding releases of the year: **Postales de Leningrado** by Mariana Rondón; **La virgen negra** by Ignacio Castillo Cottin; **Despedida de Soltera** by Antonio Llerandi; the comedy **Comando X** by José Antonio Varela; **Cyrano Fernández** by Alberto Arvelo; **El infierno perfecto** by Leonardo Henríquez; **Libertador Morales, el justiciero** by Efterpi Charalambidis; and **1, 2 y 3 Mujeres** by Andrea Herrera, Andrea Rios and Anabel Rodriguez. An exceptional short film was **Cunaro** by Alexandra Henao. Of the documentaries, the most noteworthy were Ana Cristina Henríquez's docuentary **A los pies de Canaima**, **María Lionza, aliento de Orquídeas** by John Petrizzelli and the co-production with Observatorio de Cine de Buenos Aires, **Colores del Alma**, by Elena Pastor and Xaviert Sureda.

María Lionza, aliento de Orquídeas and *La virgen negra* recreate Venezuelan magic-religious beliefs. In *Maria Lionza*, the main character is a bucolic goddess in the cosmogonía story (a mythical story regarding the origins of the world) of the Creole Venezuelans, who is an icon of faith and devotion, not dissimilar to the Virgin Mary. *Commando X*, *Cyrano Fernández* and *Libertador Morales, el justiciero* feature heroes who promote nationalistic values. For some critics and audience members, these films were merely government propaganda. *Despedida de Soltera* and *1, 2 y 3 Mujeres* view the world through the history of different women and their destinies. *Cunaro* focuses on the patriarchal and misogynistic mentality of a fishmongers' town on Venezuela's central coast. *Postales de Leningrado* is a critical reflection on the Venezuelan guerrilla movement of the 1960s, narrated from a girl's point of view. Finally, *A los pies de Canaima* is about bio-tropical diversity from one of the most beautiful regions of Venezuela.

Alberto Arvelo's **Cyrano Fernández**

With the approval of the Law of National Cinematography in 2005 and with the budget increase for the CNAC, the Venezuelan government has tried to expand Venezuelan cinema at a national level. The number of cinema screens has been increased and the national film library now has offices around the country. At the moment, the distributor National Amazonia Films can achieve its goal of positioning Venezuelan films in many cinemas, in order to compete with Hollywood films, which continue to be the major preference of

the Venezuelan public. Having the stamina to continue competing will be important for the future of Venezuelan cinema.

The year's best films
Postales de Leningrado (Mariana Rondón)
A los pies de Canaima
(Ana Cristina Henríquez)
Maria Lionza, aliento de orquídeas
(John Petrizzelli)
Cyrano Fernández (Alberto Arvelo)
1, 2 y 3 Mujeres (Andrea Herrera, Andrea Rios and Anabel Rodriguez)

Quote of the year
'I am here for a few days to see a project [the Bolivarian Revolution in Venezuela] with which I agree. I believe in the human inclination towards social justice. This country [Venezuela] is the opposite to the fatalistic vision of the world, where everything is oriented towards materialism and objects. I wanted to spend some days immersed in a social process that reflects my ideals.'
EMIR KUSTURICA, *well-known director and Bosnian musician, during his visit to Caracas in March 2008.*

Directory
All Tel/Fax numbers begin (+58)
Centro Nacional Autónomo de Cine-matografia (CNAC), Avenida Diego Cisneros, Piso 2, 1071 Caracas. communicación@cnac. org.ve. www.cnac.org.ve.
Consejo Nacional de la Cultura (CONAC), Centro Simón Bolivar, Piso 15, Caracas. www.conac.org.ve.
Cinemateca Nacional, Centro Simón Bolívar, Torre Norte. Tel: 212 481 3247. www.cinemateca.gob.ve.

MARTHA ESCALONA ZERPA is a Berlin-based freelance journalist, a researcher and a psychologist . She writes regularly for www.analitica.com.

Vietnam Sylvie Blum-Reid

With more relaxed regulations, private film studios are able to compete against State-owned studios and have contributed to the revival of Vietnamese cinema. Directors are increasingly producing films with an eye on the international market. Among some of the criteria designed to please film critics abroad, one may find more 'artsy' films. However, few of the films produced are commercially successful outside the international film festival circuit.

Co-productions are on the rise, with America dominating the scene. Foreign capital is also flowing into the country, contributing to a better infrastructure and an increase in the number of cinemas. Vietnamese film-production houses have also been working on bettering their sound system, and on implementing English subtitles. The Korean exhibition complex, Lotte Cinema, has expanded its facilities into Vietnam, where it has acquired multiple screens in Ho Chi Minh City and Danang.

Several ex-pat Vietnamese directors and actors are returning to the country to make films, contributing to the revitalisation of Vietnamese cinema in a year rich with box office successes. The topics of these films has varied, ranging from action-packed war epics, to horror and psychological drama. More realist films also tackle social issues related to drugs, prostitution and other health-related concerns that are common to contemporary Vietnam.

Truc Charlie Nguyen's **The Rebel** (*Dòng Máu Anh Hùng*) stars Johnny Tri Nguyen, Ngo Thanh Van and Dustin Nguyen and unfolds in 1920s colonial Vietnam, where rebel forces unite to combat the French colonial rulers. Apparently the most expensive Vietnamese film ever made, it won the Grand Jury award for best feature at the Los Angeles Asian Pacific Film Festival. A major box office success at home, it received mixed reviews from party officials.

Vinh Son Nguyen's directorial debut, **Moon in the Bottom of the Well** (*Trang noi day gieng*), was co-produced by Giai Phong Film Studio and Alliance Studio, and received French backing from Fonds Sud cinema. A happily married high school professor, unable to bear children, allows her husband to have a child with another woman in order to continue the family lineage. This is kept secret until she discovers that her love and trust were abused. Nguyen was assistant director on Jean-Jacques Annaud's 1992 film, *The Lover*.

The Vietnamese-Korean horror film, **Muoi, the Legend of a Portrait**, was written and directed by Kim Tae-Kyeong. It is the first horror film produced in Vietnam and had its release delayed by the Vietnamese Bureau of Cinema, who took umbrage at its 'unsuitable content'. It opened at the end of 2007 and has since been screened in the US.

Othello Khanh's **Saigon Eclipse** (*Sài Gòn nhat thuc*), starring Dustin Nguyen, Truong Ngoc Anh, Nhu Quyen and Marjolaine Bui, is a contemporary drama based on a nineteenth-century epic poem, *The Story of Kieu*, about a young woman who sacrifices her life for her family and country. Nguyen Thanh Van's **The Little Heart** (*Trái Tim Bé Bong*) tells the story of 17-year-old girl Mai, who leaves her Central Vietnam village in order to find employment in Saigon, but finds herself trapped in a prostitution ring.

Following on from his earlier *Wood Cutters*, veteran director Vuong Duc returned with **Black Forest** (*Rung Den/Forêt Noire*), which depicts the disintegration of a family of wood cutters who, by cutting down sacred trees, have violated the spirit of the forest.

Huynh Luu's **The White Silk Dress** (*Áo lua Hà Đông*) is set in colonial Vietnam prior to the French collapse in 1954 and follows the plight of two lovers, servants of two different households, in the town of Ha Dong. This epic war drama pays tribute to Vietnamese women and stars Truong Ngoc Anh and Nguyen Quoc Khanh. Another period drama, **The Life** (*Sinh Menh*), is directed by Dao Duy Phuc and set in 1970s Vietnam.

Huynh Luu's **The White Silk Dress**

In Bui Trung Hai's directorial debut, **When Autumn Sunlight Comes** (*Khi Nang Thu Ve*), a young Vietnamese college graduate, Trung, who can only find work as a taxi driver, hopes to find true love. The film was screened at the Houston WorldFest Independent Film Festival and was awarded the Golden Remi award for best first film.

Of the documentaries released, Nguyen Trinh Thi's **Love Man, Love Woman** looks at gay men in Vietnam or 'dong co', a term used to describe effeminate gay men. The film focuses on Master Luu Ngoc Duc, a male medium at the Dao Mau temple in Hanoi. The medium channels a female deity during trance ceremonies. It is a rare insight into homosexuality in contemporary urban Vietnam.

Doan Hoang's **Oh Saigon**

Doan Hoang's **Oh Saigon** premiered at the 24th Los Angeles Asian Pacific Film Festival and was co-awarded the Grand Jury prize for Best Documentary Feature. It traces Hoang's story; of her family being airlifted from Saigon in 1975 to arrive in the USA, and her return to Vietnam 25 years later. The film also aired on PBS television.

Tran Anh Hung returns in 2009, after an eight-year absence, with **I Come with the Rain**, an English-language film starring Josh Hartnett. The film was shot in Hong Kong, the Philippines and Los Angeles. His next project is an adaptation of Haruki Murakami's 1987 novel, *Norwegian Woods*. Pham Linh Dan, the Franco-Vietnamese actress who starred in *Indochine* and *The Beat That My Heart Skipped*, returns to Vietnam to star in **Without an Anchor** (*Choi Voi*), directed by Bui Thac Chuyen.

Quote of the year
'People are used to seeing Vietnam as rice fields and misery…We want to create a new Vietnam realism. We want to show this county in the midst of renewal, how it is now, how people live.' **Saigon Eclipse** *director* OTHELLO KHAN.

SYLVIE BLUM-REID is Assistant Professor of French and Film at the University of Florida, and has published widely on French cinema and post-colonial studies.

Additional Countries

ANGOLA

Following the end of the civil war in 2002 and after a significant period of inactivity, there has been a revival in Angolan cinema. During 2004, three films, including Zeze Gambao's *The Hero*, were released. That film sensitively explored the country's painful past. The main character, Vitório, returns from the front lines, where he lost his leg because of a land mine. He stumbles, both literally and figuratively, in his attempt to build a new life for himself in the capital, Luanda.

Vitório's recovery is symbolic of the film industry in Angola, which lacks any film studio and where any suitable auditorium screens videos. Angolan cinema originated during the 1970s with the 'guerrilla-films' of Sarah Maldoror, about the battle for independence. They were mainly documentaries produced on cheap video format.

Although in ruins for many decades, the Angolan film institute IACAM was recently given a new lease of life. The first task in hand for the institute is to build more cinemas and to assist in developing Angolan film productions.

As part of national efforts to revive its film industry, Angola is to build a 'cinematographic campus' in Luanda. The campus will comprehensively cover all aspects of production and exhibition. The space to build this complex has already been secured and a project plan has been submitted.

The campus is one of a number of projects planned by the ministry, aimed at the rehabilitation of the country's cultural infrastructure. These projects are outcomes of the Third Symposium on National Culture, held in September 2006 in Luanda, which were endorsed by the Head of State, Jose Eduardo dos Santos. The Minister of Culture, Boaventura Cardoso, called for the intervention of the private sector in the development of the country's cinema, as this was a feat that could not be achieved by government alone. He stressed that the country had 'great human potential' in the film industry, but needed to boost its production and distribution circuit. – *Martin P. Botha*

BANGLADESH

Mainstream cinema in Bangladesh is passing through a critical period. Although it is the main source of entertainment for the majority of Bangladesh's working classes, with many mainstream films produced every year, cinemas are closing with alarming regularity. Approximately 400 of the 1,200 cinemas in the country have been torn down. In their place are multiplexes whose prohibitive pricing is beyond the reach of the traditional cinemagoer.

Last year the Bangladeshi government handed out awards for the best films of the last four years. The government has also ensured that there are funds to make films, with funding given to three films, which are currently in production.

Television networks have also crossed over into film production, broadcasting features on TV channels, alongside their regular programming. The Bangladesh Film Development Corporation recently announced its intention to find new screen stars and Channel 1 produced a number of award-winning films.

Abu Syeed, director of critically acclaimed *Nirontor*, recently completed **The Flute** (*Ban-*

shi), which is set in the village of Sonamukhi and features a dispute between two powerful families. At the centre of it is Arif, a young filmmaker in search of the right location. On his way to the traditional fair at Sonamukhi, he meets Shaila, who is visiting her relatives. The story unfolds from this point. Syeed's film suggests that enmity cannot be resolved with violence but with peace and love.

AHA! was written, directed and scored by Enamul Karim Nirjhar. It focuses on people living in a congested area of Dhaka. The protagonist gives shelter to a stranger in his palatial house only to have that good gesture lead to the discovery of a murder.

The Cycle (Ghani), by screenwriter-director Kazi Morshed, is about the struggles of a Bangladeshi mill family whose sole source of revenue is the oil products yielded from a mill. After their ox is stolen, the family resorts to pulling the yoke of the hand-mill themselves.

Forthcoming films include Morshedul Islam's **Beloved One** (Priyotomeshu), based on a story by Humuyun Ahmed; the government funded **Rabeya**, directed by Tanvir Mokammel;

Shamim Akhter's **Twilight Sonata**

Golam Rabbany Biplob, **Another World** (Onno Bhubon), based on a story by Anisul Haque; Shamim Akhter's **Twilight Sonata** (Kaal Purobi), which draws parallels between the independent war in 1971 and the post-9/11 world; Humayun Ahmed's **Amar Achhe Jol**; Mostafa Sorwar Forooki's **Third Person Singular Number** and Khalid Hassan Mithu's **Gohin Shobdo**.

AHMED MUZTABA ZAMAL is Secretary General of Rainbow Film Society and Director of the Dhaka International Film Festival.

BENIN

The Republic of Benin finally followed neighbouring Nigeria, Ghana and Cameroon in embracing the home-video concept as a cheaper alternative to 35mm feature films, which the country's economy obviously cannot sustain. It has experienced a dry spell since the phenomenal success of Paris-based Sylvestre Amoussou's African Paradise, a comical fantasy tale about the future of Africa.

Local heroes like Hakeem Amzat are championing the video revolution in a country where many cinemas have now been converted into churches. His Laha Productions bankrolled the year's big-budget production, **Why Me?** (Pourquoi Moi?). Directed by Nigeria's Tunde Kelani, the broad drama featured actors from Benin, Nigeria, and Cote d'Ivoire.

The biggest hit of the year was the fascinating thriller **The Dupes** (Djibiti), Prince Ogujobi's two-part film exploring the theme of corruption, set against the background of growing foreign influence in major cities like Cotonou and Porto Novo. Its style of filming and distribution is undeniably modelled on Nollywood.

More than ten home-video productions were completed in the first half of 2008, not bad for a country that made a mere dozen 35mm feature films in 25 years. The government is already warming up to the new video format as a thriving alternative, according to Akambi Akala, Benin's Director of Cinematographic Censorship, who is himself an actor. But while actors like Noelle Agbondegba and Oncle Bazar have accepted the new industry, funding and distribution outlets for the DVDs are still proving to be a major challenge.

On 1 August, Hollywood star Djimon Hounsou returned to Benin for the country's 48th anniversary of independence. Celebrating his career, the Benin film industry was also able to celebrate a new lease of life, knowing it is now a choice location for Nollywood. – *Steve Ayorinde*

BHUTAN

The Kingdom of Bhutan, located in the eastern Himalayas, bordered to the south, east and west by India and to the north by China, is one of the most mysterious and poor countries in the world. The Bhutanese call their home Druk Yul (Land of the Thunder Dragon).

The most famous Bhutanese filmmaker is Khyentse Norbu, one of the most important incarnate lamas in the Tibetan Buddhist tradition and a member of one of Bhutan's noblest families. His films, *The Cup* and *Travellers and Magicians*, screened at the recent Cinemaya Cinefan Film Festival, in New Delhi.

His first feature, *The Cup*, was shot in a Tibetan refugee colony in the Himalayan foothills of northern India. It is the semi-autobiographical tale of a group of young monks obsessed with the World Cup soccer final. Made by a cast and crew of monks and novices, it received international recognition at festivals and helped humanise the image of Tibetan monks. The average scene required only three takes, which Khyentse Norbu attributed to the power of meditation.

In *Travellers and Magicians*, a young government official, Dondup, dreams of escaping to America while stuck in a beautiful but isolated village. Matters go awry when he heads to town to await his visa. Missing the bus, he hitchhikes with an elderly apple seller, a sage young monk, and an old man travelling with his beautiful daughter, Sonam. The film is a beautiful portrait of the country.
– *Ahmed Muztaba Zamal*

BOTSWANA

Botswana has a long history of filmmaking, but it is comprised largely of wildlife documentaries. It is best known internationally as the subject of Jamie Uys's South African feature film, *The Gods Must Be Crazy*, which was not actually made in Botswana.

During 2007, the government invested approximately US$5 million in the production of the late Anthony Minghella's BBC drama feature, **The No. 1 Ladies' Detective Agency** and the ensuing television series. The film is based on Alexander McCall Smith's internationally best-selling series of novels. Minister of Environment, Wildlife and Tourism, Mr Kitso Mokaila argued the production would not only help to promote the tourism sector, but should create employment opportunities for the country.

Anthony Minghella's **The No. 1 Ladies' Detective Agency**

The No.1 Ladies' Detective Agency is a passionate story chronicling the adventures of Precious Ramotswe, the sensible and wise proprietor of the only female-owned detective agency in Botswana. She investigates cases, helps people solve problems in their lives, and falls in love with the highly respectable owner of a local garage.

When Precious Ramotswe was young, she spent her days with Obed, her father, in the wilds of Botswana, learning the secrets of nature. With that upbringing came her natural inquisitiveness and intuition. When Obed dies, Precious is left with 180 cows. With her bad marriage to jazz musician Note Makoti behind her, she decides to become her country's first female detective. – *Martin P. Botha*

BURKINA FASO

Although there are many films in production, art-house films, which have made Burkina Faso's reputation, are becoming increasingly rare.

Sam, the Boss (*Sam le caïd*), Boubacar Diallo's eighth film, premiered in July. This comedy-drama immerses audiences in the African underworld, a place not often shown on the big screen. A fine cast, including such great names from the Burkinabé cinema as Joseph Tapsoba, Eugène Bayala and Ildevert Méda, made the most of the script's humour.

Boubakar Zida Sidnaba's **A Ghost in the City** (*Un Fantôme Dans La Ville*) plays with mysticism when, following a forced marriage, a deceased woman mysteriously returns to life. Certain people who encounter her become insane.

The second edition of the *Semaine du Cinéma Contre l'Oubli* (Cinema Week against the Forgotten) took place from 10–13 July in the capital, Ouagadougou. The *Ciné Droit Libre* (Free Rights Cinema Film Festival) on human

rights and freedom of expression is now in its fourth year and has extended to the Ivory Coast where screenings took place between 2–6 July.

FESPACO (The Pan-African Film and Television Festival of Ouagadougou), the most important cinema event on the continent, has a new Managing Director in Michel Ouédraogo. Baba Hama, who headed up the festival for twelve years, passed the reins on to the former journalist and 'figure of the establishment', ready for the next festival, which is planned for 28 February through 7 March 2009.

HONORÉ ESSOH is a journalist who works for media outlets from West Africa. He has started a filmmaker career a year ago and has directed his first short film about clandestine immigration in Senegal in 2008.

BURUNDI

Cinematically, little has happened in Burundi since Leonce Ngabo made the country's first and only feature film, *The Ungrateful Gito*, in 1991 and then relocated to Canada. Gito is an idealistic young African who returns home from France with the political ambition to make his country better but whose ideals are crushed by the contradictions of his country.

When fate brought together Canadian filmmaker Christopher Redmond and Raymond Kalisa, a Rwandan CNN freelancer who had been working on a proposal to train aspiring filmmakers in Burundi, Redmond knew he was in Africa to stay. He returned to Bujumbura with two other Canadian filmmakers, Bridget Farr and Sabrina Guerrieri, to set up the Burundi Film Centre (BFC) in 2007. They began by training 36 students aged 18–25 years in the basics of film production, which has resulted in a number of short dramatic films.

Burundi is a politically unstable nation that is entering a new era of cultural understanding, tolerance and education. However, the absence of developed media has crippled the nation's ability to operate as a proper democracy and exposed the need for professional journalism and artistic expression through audio-visual storytelling. According to Redmond, the BFC's vision is to develop Burundi into a film- and video-producing nation as well as a location for foreign films.

OGOVA ONDEGO is a Nairobi-based writer and cultural practitioner who specialises in socio-cultural and audiovisual media issues. He publishes ArtMatters.Info and runs Lola Kenya Screen film festival for children and youth in eastern Africa.

CAMEROON

In 2008, Daniel Kamwa successfully returned to the cinema after a ten-year hiatus with **Don't talk about it** (*Mâh Saah-Sah*). This charming and sentimental comedy reveals, through the circumcision ritual and the dance of seduction between characters, specific traits and traditions of the Bamoun people of West Cameroon. It presents a love story between two young people compromised by the financial difficulties of the girl's family. The father is forced to promise her to their benefactor, an old man who wants her as his fourth wife.

Serge Alain Noa's **Involuntary Gift** (*Don Involontaire*) opened at the beginning of the year in Yaoundé, the political capital. Also writing the screenplay, Noa tackles corruption, a topical subject in Cameroon. An agent of the state feigns his death following a hijack, an act that eventually causes him to lose his mind.

In **On the Border of Life** (*Aux frontiers de la vie*), Narcisse Mbarga deals with the thorny question of heritage. Based on a true story, Cathy, played by the promising Appolonie Vega, battles against her in-laws who want to allow her chronically ill husband to die.

Central Africa's biggest film event, the *Ecrans Noirs* (Black Screens) festival, took place from May 31 to June 7 and featured a competition for the first time. Despite the gathering of acclaimed Congolese filmmakers, young Cameroonians Hélène Patricia Ebah and Ghislain Amougou emerged successful. Of more than fifty films shown, around thirty were from Cameroon.

Despite the initial uncertainty, the new festival *La Nuit du Court Métrage* (Short Films Night) launched on March 15 and proved to be a success.

The veteran director Jean-Pierre Bekolo has begun preparations for a documentary on the life of the musician Manu Dibango and plans to make another on the footballer Samuel Eto'o Fils. – *Honoré Essoh*

CHAD

The film industry in Chad is still dominated by internationally renowned directors such as Mahamat Saleh Haroun, Issa Serge Coelo and Zara Yacoub.

With his films *BYE BYE Africa*, *Abouna* and *Daratt*, Mahamat Saleh Haroun has been referred to as 'one of the leading lights in African cinema' by the Harvard Film Archive. His new film, **Sex, Okra and Salted Butter** (*Sex Gombo et Beurre Salé*), presents a comical take on the lives of Africans living in Europe, yet who are insistent on maintaining their traditions rather than embracing European culture. At the heart of the film is Hortense, a 40-year-old nurse from the Ivory Coast, who leaves her husband and children for her lover, Jean-Paul a French oyster farmer.

France-based filmmaker Issa Serge Coelo will follow up his history of Chad in the 1980s and 1990s, *Tartina City*, with a film about one of the great flutists from the Fula ethnic group. The film is scheduled to be released in 2009.

Zara Yacoub produced her last film in 2007 on refugees in Sudan. She has yet to announce her latest project.

AGNES THOMASI has over 15 years of experience as a media practitioner. She trained at Radio Deutsche Welle Training Centre in Koln, Germany, the International Institute of Journalism in Berlin, AACC Communication Training Centre in Nairobi and the Leeds Metropolitan University in the United Kingdom.

COSTA RICA

The past two years have been the most productive in Costa Rican film history. For the first time, the government, private industry and a group of audiovisual producers have come together to create a development strategy that promotes foreign investment through the creation of a film commission. The promotion of local production has also been aided by the setting up of a fund, Proartes, and by the joining of Ibermedia, the main fund for film co-production in Latin America. The support of Doctv-Iberoamerica, which Costa Rica joined two years ago, has also been of benefit, as has Cinergia, the fund for audiovisual development in Central America and the Caribbean.

2008 saw two feature premieres. Ishtar Yasin's **The Way** (*El camino*) blends documentary and fiction as it tells the story of two children who run away from Nicaragua to Costa Rica, via the path that many immigrants walk daily, in order to find their mother. The film premiered

Ishtar Yasin's **The Way**

at the Berlin Film Festival and went on to win two awards at Fribourg and two at Guadalajara International Film Festival. In addition to being the most awarded Costa Rican film, it also screened – out of competition – at the Cannes Film Festival. It premiered in Costa Rica in August.

Isabel Martínez and Vicente Ferraz's **The King of Cha-cha-cha**

The second film to premiere locally in August was Miguel Gómez's **Red Sky** (*El Cielo Rojo*). A stark contrast to *The Way*, it was filmed in digital with a budget of US$4,000. It is a youth-oriented film that genuinely attempts to talk to the younger generation about problems that concern them: relationships, drugs, education and the future. A box office success, the film was also popular with critics.

There are currently six more films in post-production. **The King of Cha-cha-cha** (*El rey de cha-cha-cha*) by Isabel Martínez and Vicente Ferraz, which follows the path of Paco Jarquin, a former Sandinista major who left his revolutionary principles to begin a solitary life. Francisco Gonzáles's **Three Mary** (*Tres Marías*) is an urban drama set in contemporary San Jose, focusing on three women and their problems with drugs, violence and prostitution. César Caro's **Third World** (*Tercer mundo*) looks at identity across three countries: Chile, Bolivia and Costa Rica. Hernán Jiménez's **Closing Eyes** (*A ojos cerrados*) looks at loneliness experienced in old age, while Esteban Ramírez's **Pregnancy** (*Gestación*) presents the story of a teenage couple faced with a an undesired pregnancy.

Hilda Hidalgo's **About Love and Other Demons** (*Del amor y otros demonios*) recently completed shooting. An adaptation of Gabriel García Márquez's novel, the co-production with Colombia and Spain is the most ambitious project yet undertaken in Costa Rica. The Sundance/NHK award finalist, Paz Fábrega, began shooting his new project, *Agua fria de mar*, in December.

MARIA LOURDES CORTÉS teaches film at the Universidad de Costa Rica and directs the Film and Television School of the Veritas University and the Cinergia audiovisual foundation. The most recent of her numerous books on Costa Rican and Central American cinema is *La pantalla rota: Cien años de cine en Centroamérica* (2005).

DEMOCRATIC REPUBLIC OF CONGO

Eastern Congo's best-known filmmaker and festival organiser, Petna Ndaliko Katondolo, operates between his base, Kampala, and Goma. He has made numerous experimental films, mainly for younger audiences. His latest fiction film is the short **True Story**, which was made on High Definition Video. Shot in Goma, North Kivu, it starrs Sperantia Sikuli, Christine York, Prince Agakhan and Jean-Pierre King Kembwa. Katondolo also wrote, shot, edited and produced it.

True Story is about the real experience of a woman and the man who values her but cannot protect her, his career in the army notwithstanding. Katondolo says one cannot be neutral on the sexual violence women face in the war-torn Congo. 'We have to react to the atrocity of sexual violence against women. But how do I convey what I see, hear, and witness around me without falling into voyeurism? This is not the first time I have tried to make a film on the subject, but I have abandoned it each time for fear of telling it wrongly and trivialising such a terrible crime,' Katondolo says. 'Must a horrific story be told in a horrific way? Must a bloody story be written with blood for people to understand it? How do you make a film about rape without raping the victim once again?'

True Story also tells of soldiers who join the army in the hope of protecting their loved ones but only discover that the army is 'an arbitrary and unjust world in which the leaders use their power with complete impunity to serve their own personal interests and commit atrocities against society'.

Katondolo, a multi-talented artist and activist, works as a correspondent for the Metropolitan programme of the Dutch TV station, VPRO. Katondolo previously made the documentary *Raise the Flag* and the feature *Agreement of Treaty* in 2007. In 2008, Katondolo was Second Director on Franck Piasecki Poulsen's *Blood in the Mobile*, about the Congolese minerals used in making mobile phones, while the ordinary Congolese die, starve and are tortured. The mineral is the Democratic Republic of Congo's equivalent of Sierra Leone's Blood Diamonds. – *Ogova Ondego*

EL SALVADOR

The major success of this or any year, which also highlighted the problem of piracy, was Roberto Dávila's **Surviving Guazapa** (*Sobreviviendo Guazapa*). It was seen by 11,718 people in its first weekend, across eleven of the country's major cinemas, amassing a box office total of US$37,785. The figure might have been higher had the film not been available on the streets for the price of US$1. However, the film still outsold the Hollywood films on release at the same time.

Filmed in high definition, *Surviving Guazapa* tells the story of two men, a soldier and a guerrilla, trapped in the Guazapa volcano. They decide to work together when they encounter a girl who has escaped the conflict. Although the context of the film is the civil war that raged from 1980 to 1992, the theme is

Roberto Dávila's **Surviving Guazapa**

brotherhood, the little girl's role a metaphorical one, a bridge at the centre of a war between countrymen.

Many critics, as well as former guerrilla members, commented that the film's context was wrong, it was overly idealistic and completely distorted history.

However, it is the first domestic feature film seen in cinemas since José David Calderón's 1969 film, *Fish Out of the Water*. With the creation of a filmmakers' association, offering courses and workshops, it is hoped that audiences will not have to wait so long again.
– *Maria Lourdes Cortés*

ERITREA

Like Ethiopia, Eritrea's cinema appears to be based in 'Diaspora America'. But unlike Ethiopia, there is very little documentation of the country's filmmaking sector. This has led critics to conclude that Eritrean cinema does not exist. Which may account for why **Teza**, a film by US-based Eritrean academic and filmmaker Haile Gerima, which won both the Special Jury Prize and the Best Screenplay Award at the 65th Venice Film Festival, was such a surprise. The film is an Ethiopian, German and French production that revisits Ethiopia under Marxist dictator Mengistu Haile Mariam.

It is admittedly rare to come across Eritrean productions, save for Bereket Yowhannes' *Gun Smoke 77* (1996) and Efrem Kahsay and Tesfarehan Mehari's *Can I Divorce Her and*

Marry You? (2000), which has only been seen at festivals. *Gun Smoke 77* is a tragedy about love and politics, which takes place during Ethiopia's struggle for political independence. *Can I Divorce Her and Marry You?* deals with the difficulties of two couples in Asmara, whose inability to resolve their problems, as well as a passionate affair between two of the people, is a portent of disaster in their relationship.

One of Eritrea's better known and professionally trained US-based filmmakers, Ambessa jir Berhe, is critical of the predictability of the small output of Eritrean film. Berhe contends that Eritrean cinema will never grow out of infancy unless filmmakers steer clear of such formulaic narratives. He argues that films made in the 1990s were all about the Ethiopian occupation and the effect on Eritrea's people. After the 1998 war with Ethiopia, Berhe says, many films switched to stories about Ethiopians and their evil deeds, after which the focus moved to 'clichéd love stories', which always tend to parody Hollywood romances. He claims that he hasn't seen any Eritrean filmmakers 'doing something interesting and revolutionary'.

For his part, Berhe wrote, directed, and edited several short films between 1998 and 2008. His latest thirty-minute film, **Fragmented Lives**, is about an Eritrean family living in the United States. Berhe's other films include *Africa* (1998), *Wondering* (1999), *My Fate* (2000), *Spice my What?* (2001), *Last Night* (2003), *Shigara* (2005), *Shikorina's Date* (2006), and *A-Weight-With-Words* (2007). The many screenings of his films at festivals in the US have given his works a great deal of exposure, something that the older generation of Eritrean filmmakers seem not to understand.
– *Ogova Ondego*

FIJI

Top local filmmaker Vilsoni Hereniko has recently been appointed director of the Center for Pacific Island Studies at the University of Hawaii, in Manoa. Consequently, the enchanting Fiji archipelago has lost one of its strongest creative figures.

Recent activity includes projects such as a Fiji-shot episode of CBS' *Survivor* and the annual competition among schoolchildren for the Kula Film Awards. **An Island Calling**, a New Zealand feature documentary, premiered at the 2008 Sydney Film Festival. Directed by Annie Goldson and inspired by Owen Scott's book *Deep Beyond the Reef*, it deals with the brutal murder in Suva of a gay couple by a fundamentalist Christian. Goldson explores the complex religious and political background of Fiji following a series of coups.

The likelihood of an international film festival in Fiji seems to have been cancelled, at least temporarily. The Fiji Audio Visual Commission (www.fijiaudiovisual.com) has proudly supported a TV series for children, *Pirates Island: Lost Treasures of Fiji*, 13 half-hour episodes starring Sera Tikotikuivatu and Wame Valentine, together with a group of Australian actors. Its US$16m budget was financed under the tax incentives administered by the Commission. According to Australian co-producer Jonathan M. Shiff, this lavish computer-game fairy-tale swashbuckler should boost Fiji filmmaking as well as its tourist trade. – *Lorenzo Codelli*

GABON

The film and television industry in Gabon has been consistently active since Philippe Mory directed *The Tam Tams Are Silent* in 1972. 'Documentaries in Transit' (Les Escale Documentaire), established three years ago, will return again in November, according to the director of the Libreville French Cultural Centre. The festival screens African documentaries and also invites special guests to attend. Last year, Cameroonian documentary filmmaker Jean Marie Teno visited. It is hoped that Moussa Touré from Senegal will attend this year. There will also be a conference and

training workshop for young filmmakers, who will produce three documentaries by the end of the festival.

There was no feature production in 2008. The last film from Gabon was 2007's *The Shadow of Liberty*, directed by Imunga Ivanga. However, the Gabonese Centre of National Cinema, in collaboration with the French production company Play Film, has implemented a project for the production of six short documentaries. The project, started in 2007, has so far screened three films by young Gabonese filmmakers, dealing with the life of artists in Gabon: Joel Moundounga's portrait of painter **Georges Mbourou**, Fernand Lepoko on musician **Vyckos Ekondo** and Pol Minko's account of designer **Chouchou Lazare**. The final three films will be screened at the festival in November. They will focus on the cartoonist Lybek, actor Michel Ndaot and singer Naneth. – *Agnes Thomasi*

GHANA

Although it has trailed its Anglophone Western African neighbour in video-film production for almost a decade, 2008 was the year that Ghana finally proved its mettle against the dominant Nigerian presence in the region. And it was at the African OSCARS, Nigeria's African Movie Academy Awards (AMAA), that Ghollywood, as Ghana's video-film industry is now known, showed that it could beat the Nigerians at their own game. For the first time since the awards ceremony was instituted five years ago, Ghana won the AMAA's top three awards – Best Picture, Best Director and Best Screenplay of the year, for Emmanuel Apea's **Run Baby Run**, a cross-continental drama set against the background of drug trafficking between England and Ghana.

Run Baby Run's success achieved two things for Ghollywood: it endorsed Ghana's modest attempt to emulate the Nigerian template, promoting low-budget melodramatic movies as a cheap but acceptable alternative to big-budget celluloid films; and it set in motion a new wave of digital filmmaking. Added to this is the increased presence over the last year of both Ghanaian and Nigerian producers in Accra, the Ghanaian capital, which is fast becoming a choice destination for location hunters.

One of the most popular films of the year was Agya Koo's **Fire For Fire**, a comedy drama that shows how the contentious subject of witchcraft can be treated with a degree of taste. Equally popular were Rajah's **Princess Tyra**, a fairytale romantic adventure, which won the Best Make-Up and Best Costume awards at AMAA, and his **Darkness of Sorrow**, an allegorical drama exploring the age-old conflict between morality and wealth. Both were produced by Rajah's Zenith Productions.

Short films such as the documentary **Not My Daughter**, which documents the growing concern about health challenges facing young girls, has shown that trained professionals can enjoy some degree of attention in the increasingly competitive industry. It was produced by Akofa Edjeani-Asiedu and directed by one of Ghana's most talented young filmmakers, Bikpe Cosby.

The most popular films remain the more flamboyant 'exploitation' video-films, often serialised, which have firmly established a strong following. They have helped create a new generation of celebrities and have also increased cross-production and distribution between Ghana and Nigeria.

Veteran filmmaker Kwah Ansah, who redefined the art of cinema in Ghana in the 1980s with *Heritage Africa* and *Love Brew in an African Pot*, which were both produced on 35mm and presented as pan-African commentaries on the post-colonial region, has returned to filmmaking. His project, slated for release in 2009, is the romantic drama **The Good Old Days**. It will likely be given a theatrical release before it hits the video market.

Laila Daisy's **Tulips**, a dramatic account of the harmful effects of female circumcision, as well as Salam Abdulahi's **Agony of the Christ**, a pseudo-religious action drama, will also be released in 2009. – *Steve Ayorinde*

GUATEMALA

Since 2003, after almost a decade without a national cinema, the Guatemalan film industry has gradually been growing. Nowadays, there is at least one production per year – a record for the region.

In 2007, Casa Comal, the producer of Elías Jiménez's *The Opposite House* and Rafael Rosal's *Las Cruces, Next Town*, returned with *Vip, The Other House*, once again directed by Jiménez, dealing with political corruption. The film was premiered on 1 November attracting 125,000 spectators.

In 2008, Julio Hernández Cordón's **Petrol** (*Gasolina*) was screened at the Locarno and San Sebastian Film Festivals, after successfully participating in last year at San Sebastian's

Julio Hernández Cordón's **Petrol**

Cinema Under Construction section. It has yet to open domestically.

A road movie, *Petrol* features three teenagers who spend their time stealing gasoline in order to go out at night in their car. A series of conflicts puts their friendship to the test, forcing them to face up to the reality of their situation. Typical of a 'road movie', the characters' journey is more important than their destination.

Alejo Crisóstomo's **Faith** (*Fe*) participated in the Open Doors programme at the Locarno Film Festival, where it received one of three awards. Both *Petrol* and *Faith* have been supported by Cinergia, the only fund for audiovisual development in Central America and the Caribbean. Although the Guatemalan film industry does not receive state subsidies or support, the Guatemalan Audiovisual and Film Association (AGAcine) was recently created – a first step towards the creation of a real film industry for the country.
– *Maria Lourdes Cortés*

GUINEA

Although the film industry in Guinea has produced more than one hundred films, the majority of them were made between the 1960s and 1980s. Since then, Guinea's film industry, once the pride of Africa, has dried up. Between 1989 and 2008, less than ten feature films were made. Among them, two were international successes: Cheick Doukouré's *Paris According to Moussa* (*Paris selon Moussa*), released in 2000, and Cheikh Fantamady Camara's **Clouds over Conakry** (*Il va pleuvoir sur Conakry*). It was only last October, two years after it was made, that Camara's film was screened domestically.

Clouds over Conakry tells the story of a conflict between a father who is both an Imam and a traditional leader – the caretaker of the ancestral tradition of his village – and

his young son, a journalist whose roots are firmly entrenched in modern life. With his first feature, Camara successfully placed Guinea back on the map of world cinema, winning the Grand Prix at the 2008 Festival of African Cinema, at Khouribga, in Morocco; the Special Jury Prize at the 2008 Film Festival Quintessence in Benin; the Audience Award at the 2007 African Film Festival of Verona; and the Audience Award at the FESPACO 2007, in Burkina Faso.

The country's new film institute saw its first students graduate in 2008. With these new filmmakers, as well as the burgeoning career of Cheikh Fantamady Camara, lies hope for the future of film in Guinea. – *Agnes Thomasi*

IRAQ

For reasons all too obvious, filmmaking in Iraq has suffered for much of the last three decades. Moving from pro-Saddam Hussein propaganda throughout the 1980s to near-total collapse during the United Nations sanctions of the 1990s, which banned the importation of celluloid, and most recently virtual standstill in the wake of the 2003 invasion of the country by coalition forces, Iraq's film industry is – like the country itself – re-building from scratch.

Oday Rasheed, who made Iraq's first post-Saddam film with *Underexposure* in 2004, and Mohammad al-Daradji, whose debut feature **Ahlaam** won the top prize at the Gulf Film Festival in 2008, are both working on their follow-up projects. Rasheed is working on **Heaven's Road**, a psychological thriller looking at non-Iraqi Arab fighters who decide to join the insurgency against coalition troops. Al-Daradji is preparing **Um Hussein**, about a mother in modern-day Iraq searching for her son, an Iraqi soldier imprisoned by Saddam after the 1991 Gulf War, which he intends to shoot on location in Iraq in 2009.

With a number of powerful shorts also being produced by other young, aspiring Iraqi filmmakers, the future holds great promise that a talented group of Iraqi filmmakers are simply awaiting the opportunity to blossom.

ALI JAAFAR is *Variety*'s Europe and Middle East correspondent. He is also a regular contributor to *Sight & Sound*, *Time Out* and is a programme advisor to The Times BFI's London Film Festival.

IVORY COAST

The advent of digital technology has revived Ivorian cinema. Films have increased due to the efforts of local producers. Even if the quality of films had previously been acceptable, this stimulation proved to be very welcome.

In recent years, a wave of actresses have become directors. Marie-Louise Asseu and Léa Dubois presented their sophomore features, while Bleu Brigitte and Clémentine Papouet began their careers with solid debuts. Papouet's film, **Amah Sahoua**, is a melodrama about a couple caught up in the AIDS crisis. The wife is abandoned by her husband and his family when they discover she has been diagnosed as HIV positive.

Bernard Massili's **Lost Illusion** (*Illusion Perdue*), an attack on spurious religious leaders, features one of the finest performances of the year by a male actor. Guy Kalou is excellent as Kobi, an ex-con who sets up a church where black magic, swindling and money laundering reins.

Idrissa Diabaté, with around twenty documentaries to his credit, is one of Ivory Coast's veteran directors. In **The Woman Carries Africa** (*La Femme Porte l'Afrique*), he describes his admiration for five women who cope with having to work and take care of their families.

The two festivals for short films, the Clap Ivoire and the International Festival for Short Films of Abidjan, benefited this year from the support

of the Government. Moreover, it has promised to create a support fund for cinema, which will generate €1.5 million for the industry.

Sadly, Yéo Kozoloa, the director of *Petanqui*, passed away on 14 September.
– Honoré Essoh

JORDAN

2008 was a landmark year for Jordanian cinema. Amin Matalqa's debut feature **Captain Abu Raed**, a heart-warming tale about an airport janitor who pretends to be an airline pilot so he can regale the poor neighbourhood kids with imagined tales of his worldly travels, won the World Cinema Audience award at the Sundance Film Festival and has since secured distribution in all English-speaking territories via a deal with Neoclassics. The film was Jordan's first feature film to gain international recognition in decades. Also generating a lot of praise was Mahmoud Al-Massad's beautifully shot documentary **Recycle**, a powerful portrayal of a former Mujahideen attempting to rebuild his life in the Jordanian town of Zarqa (also the birthplace of notorious insurgent Abu Musab Al-Zarqawi). That film won Sundance's World Cinema cinematography prize.

Amin Matalqa's **Captain Abu Raed**

With both Matalqa and Al-Massad working on follow-up projects, as well as the opening of the Middle East's first proper film school in the Aqaba-based Red Sea Institute for Cinematic Arts in partnership with the University of Southern California, Jordanian cinema looks like it can only grow in the years to come. Throw in a number of high-profile Hollywood films to have been filmed in Jordan recently, including Michael Bay's mega-budget *Transformers 2* and Kathryn Bigelow's Iraq drama *The Hurt Locker*, and you now have a skilled indigenous pool of film technicians to draw on to help make the country's film industry expand. – *Ali Jaafar*

KENYA

The Kenya Film Commission has established an online film directory on local industry members as well as an email list for networking and regular meetings for stakeholders in the audio-visual media sector. The Commission is also planning to host the annual red-carpet Kalasha Television and Film Awards to recognise local talent from March 2009.

Kenya has witnessed a proliferation of low-budget, fast-made, stand-up-comedy-style productions, both for television and home-video consumption.

Samora Michelle creates **Little Knowledge is Dangerous**

Lola Kenya Screen, the annual audio-visual media platform for children and youth in East Africa, went truly regional in 2008, by attracting participants from Zimbabwe, Zanzibar, Uganda, Rwanda and Tanzania to its screenings and skill-development programmes. For the second year, a Lola Kenya Screen production, **Little Knowledge is Dangerous**, beat films from Zimbabwe, South Africa, and the Democratic Republic of Congo to the 2nd Kids for Kids Africa Grand Prize in Nairobi. In 2007, Films by Children for Children won the inaugural prize at the 5th World Summit on Media for Children/Kids for Kids Africa in Johannesburg, South Africa. Additionally, Lola Kenya Screen produced **Africa-i-Motion** (a compilation of five animated shorts by children) and **Children and Doc**, six-short documentaries for children and youths, by practising filmmakers from the two annual production workshops.

Due to the fast pace of producing films with digital technology, it is almost impossible to keep track of the films made in Kenya over the last year. However, one can confidently single out a few that were screened at festivals and at Nu-Metro West Gate's Cinema. (Kenya now has 28 screens, courtesy of Nu-Metro Cinemas.)

Steve Ominde's **Formula X** tells the story of a Kenyan scientist who discovers the antidote for HIV/AIDS but is robbed of the formula by a huge pharmaceutical firm. Cajetan Boy's **All Girls Together** is about a woman who is hell-bent on seducing married men and her friend who changes her personality in order to get the man she desires. Boy also directed **Obohoz**, which revolves around the struggles of a young unemployed graduate and how she resists the temptations that come her way. Simiyu Barasa's **Toto Millionaire** is about a boy who becomes a millionaire after winning the lottery. Rob Bresson and Mburu Kimani's **Pieces for Peace** deals with the suspicion and mistrust that preceded and followed the violence that rocked Kenya following the disputed presidential poll on 27 December 2007. Wanuri Kahiu directed **From a Whisper**, which tells the story of an artist and a security intelligence officer who are direct victims of the 1998 terrorist bombing of the US embassy in Nairobi and how they survive the tragedy. Finally, there was Billy Mbilkimo's **R2 Security**, about two Mafia boys from Greece who are forced by circumstances to take a holiday in Kenya, where they set up a security firm.

South Africa's satellite television DSTV and pay-channel M-Net became more involved in the Kenyan film industry by having local representation to scout for talent, in order to feature Kenya's films 'on the continental map' by 2010, when South Africa hosts the FIFA World Cup.

Nectel, a new Kenya-based pay channel, is dedicating a channel to East African productions. It goes on air in 2009. A24 Media, Africa's first online delivery site 'designed to bring the African voice to a global audience hungry for an authentic perspective on African issues', was launched in September 2008 as an 'online delivery site for material from journalists, African broadcasters and NGOs from around the Continent'.
– *Ogova Ondego*

KYRGYZSTAN

Every new feature film made in Kyrgyzstan is not only a cultural event, it is one of the country's major political events, be it a film's content or its success on the local market.

Temir Birnazarov's **The Unknown Route** places different generations and social classes together on one bus trip. Lost in a thick fog, the bus becomes a microcosm of Kyrgyz society, with the lost driver representative of President Askar Akaev.

Another film with strong political connotations is Marat Alykulov's **Adep Akhlak**. It is a youth drama about three young men, friends since childhood, who share an apartment. Every detail of their lives is known by each of

Marat Alykulov's **Adep Akhlak**

them, from their personal interests to their love affairs. Against this backdrop unfolds the Presidential election campaign. The title of the film, literally translated, means 'the moral canons of human behaviour', a subject that one of the friends uses to question their existence.

Of the few studio films, one of the most successful was Erkin Ryspbaev and Aktan Arym Kubat's **Love Has Its Own Sky**. A tragic love story, it was shot on digital and transferred to 35mm.

Films currently in production include Aktan Arym Kubat's drama **The Light** and Ernest Abdyzhaparov's **A Thief in Love**.
– *Gulnara Abikeyeva*

LEBANON

As the most liberal of all Arab countries, Lebanon has long had a vibrant cultural scene. That has translated into the film world with Lebanese filmmakers such as Ziad Doueiri with his civil war coming-of-age drama *West Beirut* and, most recently, Nadine Labaki with **Caramel** (*Sikar Banet*) delivering cross-over hits with commercial appeal and cultural integrity. The international success of *Caramel*, a warm-hearted tale about a group of women working in a Beirut fashion salon, which grossed over US$10 million worldwide against a budget of only US$1.5 million, has helped open the door for other Lebanese directors.

Philippe Aractingi's powerful drama **Under the Bombs**, which follows a young Lebanese mother's desperate search for her missing son during the 2006 war between Israel and Lebanon, performed strongly in the country, where it amassed some 40,000 admissions and also sold well internationally, with distributors in the UK and US both acquiring it. The film is Lebanon's official entry for the 2009 Foreign Language Academy Award and marks a dramatic change of direction for Aractingi, whose previous feature *Bosta*, a musical comedy about a Lebanese dance group coming up against disapproving traditionalists, out-grossed the likes of *Harry Potter* and *King Kong* when it was released in 2006.

Elsewhere, Lebanese director Chadi Zeneddine, who made his feature debut with *Falling From Earth* in 2007, has now been enlisted by Walt Disney Studios to make their first-ever Arab-language feature **The Last Storyteller**, a family drama inspired by Arabian folklore.

A slew of Lebanese directors have also recently completed new projects. Samir Habchi's **Beirut Open City**, a dark, twisting thriller set in the mid-1990s, at the height of the Syrian occupation of Lebanon, was selected in 2008 for international festivals in both London and Abu Dhabi. The film, which stars Egyptian actor Khaled Al-Nabawy as a photojournalist attempting to expose torture cells used against political detainees by the feared intelligence forces, has much to commend it, particularly its recreation of Beirut's smoky, twilight clubs and air of unpredictability.

Hany Tamba's melodrama **Habibi**, a comedy about a Lebanese one-hit wonder from the 1970s who now works as a receptionist in a Paris hotel, will have its world premiere at the Dubai International Film Festival before its eagerly anticipated opening in Lebanon in 2009.

For all the undoubted glamour of Lebanese high society, the country has remained bedev-illed by the effects of the Lebanese civil war between 1975–1990 and the ongoing Arab-Israeli conflict, as seen in 2006 with the 33-day-long war with Israel, the aftermath of which was captured hauntingly by both Aractingi in *Under the Bombs* and husband-and-wife film-making team Joana Hadjithomas and Khalil Joreige with *I Want To See*. That film, which stars French icon Catherine Deneuve playing herself as she is taken on a tour of war-affected areas in the country, is a dreamy cinematic hybrid of documentary, road movie and art installation.

2009 also seems to hold plenty of potential for Lebanese cinema, with new films expected from Ghassan Salhab, Dima Al-Horr, Simon El-Habre, the long-awaited comeback of Ziad Doueiri and Nadine Labaki's second feature. Labaki has resisted all the offers from abroad and plans to make her next film in Lebanon and in Arabic. 'I had a good experience with *Caramel*. It went all over the world and it was a good example of something Lebanese that would work worldwide,' says Labaki. 'I can repeat that. Why not do the same adventure again on a bigger scale?' – *Ali Jaafar*

MALI

Mali, formerly a dominant country in French-speaking cinema, is now in woeful decline, despite several government and private initiatives.

Kadiatou Konaté, a great campaigner for women's causes, is responsible for one of the year's best films. Her documentary **The Yellow Mirage** (*Mirage Daman Da*/*Le mirage jaune*) shows life in the country's small-scale gold-washing sites. She succeeds in presenting the human face of the men and women who live in a difficult environment, detailing their everyday lives of prostitution, violence and human sacrifice.

The country's major cinematic event was the announcement of a project about Da Monzon Diarra, the legendary ruler of the Kingdom of

Segou. Directed by Sidi Diabaté and set to begin shooting at the end of 2008, it will be produced on a scale previously unheard of in the country: 500,000 extras, of which 500 soldiers will come from the army. Completely financed by the Malian state, the film's budget is €450,000.

Veteran filmmaker Adama Drabo's **Power of the Poor** (*Faatan Fagan*) focuses on the human sacrifice made as the country's elections approach. Fatoumata Sidibé, part of a new generation of filmmakers, won the Grand Prize for **Travelling Pharmacies** (*Les Pharmacies ambulantes*) at the West-African Clap Ivoire Festival, held in the Ivory Coast.

Bamako's 5th African National Film Week (SENAFAB) was held in the Malian capital from 28–30 March. During this annual event, around fifty participants visited from different West African countries, discussing the theme 'the African problem with audiovisual production: a sub-regional issue' as a way of finding means to revive the sector. – *Honoré Essoh*

MALTA

The Maltese film industry in 2007–08 was dominated by the visit of Alejandro Amenábar's ancient-Egyptian epic, **Agora**, an English-language, Spanish production billed as the largest independent European feature ever. The story of Greek philosopher, astrologer and mathematician, Hypatia (Rachel Weisz), who must battle to save the library of Alexandria

*Alejandro Amenábar & Rachel Weisz during the filming of **Agora** in Malta*

from religious riots, it was completely filmed on Malta, with huge sets built on the island's coast at Fort Ricasoli (previously home to *Gladiator* and *Troy*), ahead of a twelve-week shoot from March to June 2008. An average of more than 200 extras were used daily and local actors filled three principal roles.

Malta Film Commissioner Luisa Bonello said: '*Agora* should have a major local impact, because, more than on other productions of this scale, many Maltese were employed in crew positions usually taken by non-Maltese, giving them unprecedented experience on a top-quality production.' The Maltese government's cash rebate of up to 22% on EU-eligible expenditure in Malta was a significant factor in securing *Agora*, against competition from Turkey, Tunisia, Morocco and Spain.

Though there were no significant indigenous fiction productions in 2008, a Maltese documentary, *The Darkness We Know*, with a €118,000 budget (high by local standards) filmed in October 2008. It follows a Maltese

family whose son suffers from Photosensitive Epilepsy, obliging them to live in perpetual darkness.

Other visiting projects included two Russian features. **Terra Nova** (*New Land*), directed by Alexander Melnik, follows four prisoners battling the elements in the Arctic; critical scenes were filmed at Mediterranean Film Studios' (MFS) water tanks. Eugeny Solokov's fact-based **Anakop** (*Ascent of Aphon*) dramatises the quest for a golden statue of Simon the Apostle (six days underwater and location shooting in Malta). Based on a celebrated 1970s animated series about Viking boy Vicky, **Vicky and the Mighty Men** (*Wickie und die Starken Männer*), from hugely popular German director Michael 'Bully' Herbig, filmed on Malta for 25 days, mostly at MFS, where two Viking ships and other sets were built.

DANIEL ROSENTHAL was Editor of *International Film Guide* from 2002 to 2006. He is the author of *100 Shakespeare Films* (2007) and is currently writing *The NT Story*, a history of the National Theatre of Great Britain.

MAURITANIA

Mohamed Ould Idoumou's documentary **Sagné… The Little World** (*Sagné… Le petit monde*) is about a Mauritanian village close to the Senegalese border and a Senegalese town that both have the same name. The film highlights how much they have in common, from their culture and language, to their dreams and even a mobile-phone network.

Acclaimed filmmaker Abderrahmane Sissako directed the segment **Tiya's Dream** (*Le Rêve de Tiya*) as part of the film **8**. Looking at the problems facing our planet, Sissako's film is about a young Ethiopian girl who, before going to school, has to work to help her parents and finance her studies. The film was part of a promotion of the United Nations' Millennium Development Goals.

In 2006, the Film Centre, known locally as the 'Filmmakers' House', organised another film week to promote local filmmakers. This year's third edition took place from 23–29 June. In January, the House also organised the Dromedary Screen (Ecran Dromadaire) – a caravan screening films in regions of the country where the people do not have access to a cinema. This year, films were screened in 18 locations and reached more than 5,000 people.

The House of Films (La Maison de cineaste) selected young filmmakers in Mauritania to produce twelve short films, each lasting six minutes. The project is called 'Do you speak the picture's language?'

Although there have been few locally produced films, two Western filmmakers shot their films in the country: Bettina Hassen from Germany and Pierre-Yves Vandeweerd from Belgium.
– *Agnes Thomasi*

MOZAMBIQUE

During May 2008, South Africa experienced horrific xenophobic attacks that ignited in informal settlements in Gauteng and other provinces. By 21 May, the death toll stood at 42, with 16,000 people displaced. Images of foreigners being burnt alive, dead bodies in the streets and homes ablaze made their way around the world.

Mozambican film producer Pedro Pimenta sent an email out to the South African film industry, denouncing the killing of fellow Africans, including people from Mozambique, by South Africans. He announced that he was breaking off all communication with South Africans and would not welcome them to Mozambique.

Filmmakers Against Racism (FAR) was formed on 23 May, in response to these attacks. The collective, involving prominent South African directors such as Rehad Desai, Richard Green and Xoliswa Sithole, made six 24-minute

Adze Ugah's **The Burning Man**

documentaries. One of the films focuses on Ernesto Alfabeto Nhamavue, a Mozambican national who was attacked and set alight on 18 May. A picture of his gruesome death was to become a reference point for the violence. The media dubbed him the Burning Man. Adze Ugah's film **The Burning Man** explores who Ernesto really was and tracks his last minutes, from where he lived in Johannesburg, to his family compound in Mozambique, where his remains were finally laid to rest.

The films were screened at the Tri Continental Film Festival and the Durban International Film Festival. At the Durban event, Rogerio Manjate's Mozambican production, **I Love You**, won the Best Short Film Award. It focuses on a young boy naively in love with his neighbour, who is a prostitute. It received praise for telling a relevant story – the danger of HIV infection – in a direct way, as well as showing how effective the short film form can be.
– Martin P. Botha

NAMIBIA

Namibia continues to be an attractive location for international film productions. During the past year, the Namibian Film Commission (NFC) launched Film Location Namibia, a public-private sector partnership programme formed out of an alliance between the German Development Service, DED, and four private-sector business entities (Pilots Paradise Video Productions, Namib Films, LemonReel.com and SMES Compete).

'Namibia has huge potential for filmmaking with its cosmopolitan cities, colonial buildings and ghost towns, desert landscapes, river canyons and the Atlantic Ocean as well as a uniquely diverse population and bountiful wildlife' stated Edwin Kanguatjivi of NFC. He added, 'Namibia can still be described as the world's undiscovered film location.'

Kanguatjivi announced that the NFC will also participate at various international film location fairs. Film production in Namibia has become popular over the past decade and in turn has made a significant contribution to the country's economy. It is projected that through this initiative even more international film production houses will consider Namibia as a filmmaking destination. Kanguatjivi pointed out that this in turn holds numerous benefits, such as the promotion of the tourist sector by showcasing the country's beauty and diversity.

Some of the recent international films shot in Namibia include a controversial feature film about Sam Nujoma, **Namibia: Struggle for Liberation**, Sanjay Gadhvi's action thriller **Dhoom:2** and Roland Emmerich's prehistoric epic, **10,000 BC**. *– Martin P. Botha*

NEPAL

The Nepalese film industry has been surprisingly more experimental this year. However, from a business perspective, traditional, formula-based, commercial films continue to be more successful.

Kaagbeni, based on a story about unemployed youths, was released early in 2008 and failed to attract audiences in significant numbers. Bhusan Dahal was not able to replicate his success as a music-video director with the film. Another music-video director, Alok Nembang, also found it hard to attract an audience with **Tiny World** (*Sano Sansar*).

The love story **Keep Waiting** (*Parkhee Base*) proved popular with audiences, whereas the

Biraj Bhatta and Rekha Thapa in Ujwaal Ghimire's **Exertion**

Deepak Raj Giri comedy **My Name is Sunder** (*Sundar Mero Naam*) failed to light up the box office.

Actress Rekha Thapa also took on the role of producer for the successful romantic drama **Exertion** (*Kismat*), while Gyanendra Deuja directed **Dewarbabu**. Veteran actor Bhuwan K.C. saw **I Can't Be Alive Without You** (*Ma Timibina Marihalchhu Ni*) play well with audiences and attract critical acclaim for its portrayal of Nepali armed forces working in areas of conflict with the UN.

Das Dhunga, based on the accidental death of the leftist leader Madan Bhandari, popularly known as the Karl Marx of Nepal, was much talked about even before its release. Likewise, **Maina**, based on the sad story of the death of a female insurgent, attracted a fair amount of controversy prior to its opening.

In recent years, films about indigenous nationalities have found strong support amongst audiences. Last year alone, there were more than half a dozen films made on such subjects. In response to this, an international festival of these films was held in Kathmandu. It was a new and exciting experience for Nepal, drawing international attention to its growing film industry.

Pokhara, a hive of tourist activity, played host to the Film Journalists' Association (FIJA), who organised the National Film Festival and also FIJA's first short film festival. Of the thirty competitors, **Petrol**, a film based on the oil crisis, was voted the winner.

PRABESH SUBEDI is a reporter with *Kantipur Daily*, Nepal's largest circulation newspaper. He is an editor of e-magazine: Filmnepal.com.

NICARAGUA

Although Nicaraguan film was most prolific during the Sandinista period (1979–89), the last full-length drama made in the country was Ramiro Lacayo's *The Spectre of War*, in 1988. During subsequent years, numerous high-quality documentaries and short films have been produced, many of which received recognition at an international level, but the cinema appeared to have died.

Which is why Florence Jaugey's **La Yuma** is cause for celebration. It is the story of Yuma, a young girl who finds an outlet in boxing. In her poor neighbourhood, gangs fight for control of

Florence Jaugey's **La Yuma**

the street. At home, her family is indifferent to her. The boxing ring is her dream and her only hope.

La Yuma highlights the sense of abandonment and marginalisation, as well as violence, felt by Nicaragua's young population. It is supported by Mexico and Spain and received two awards from the Cinergia Fund for audiovisual development in Central America and the Caribbean. The film participated in the *Cinema under Construction* section at San Sebastian Film Festival and will be released in 2009.

Rossana Lacayo is also preparing to film **Transitory Madness** (*Locura transitoria*), which might also be co-produced with Mexico.
– *Maria Lourdes Cortés*

NIGER

Cinematic activity remains sparse in the country, with the education of young people clearly lacking.

The country's most experimental director, Djingarey Abdoulaye Maiga, completed his sixth feature, **Fourth Black Night** (*Quatrième Nuit Noire*). In production since 2003, it deals with conflict within a military regime that takes power following a coup d'état.

One of the most promising filmmakers of the new generation, Abdou Malah, directed the documentary **The New Directors** (*Les Nouveaux Maîtres de Scènes*). It depicts the difficult conditions of the lives of young talented dancers from Niger, who take pleasure in practising this art despite their low income and opposition from family members.

Malam Sanguirou's 52-minute **The Dress of Time** (*La Robe du temps*) is set in the village of Zinder, in the north of the country. A man is confronted by numerous difficulties when he is placed in charge of a conservative corporation of butchers and attempts to improve its productivity.

Malam Sanguirou's **The Dress of Time**

The third edition of the *Festival International du Film d'Environnement de Niamey* (FIFEN) was held 3–8 June. This year's theme was 'Africa and its technical, scientific and cultural knowledge of the service of water management for man and his environment'. The award winners of the FIFEN will represent Africa at the next international 'Water and Film Meetings' in Turkey, in March 2009.
– *Honoré Essoh*

PALESTINE

While the Palestinians continue to struggle in their attempts to achieve statehood and reach a lasting peace with Israel, Palestinian filmmakers have enjoyed remarkable success internationally for much of the last decade. Ever since the first Palestinian feature film was made – generally recognised to be Michel Khleifi's 1987 *Wedding in Galilee* – the likes of Elia Suleiman (*Divine Intervention*) and Hany Abu-Assad (*Paradise Now*) have eloquently and artfully captured the elusive existence of a people rendered homeless on their own land.

A young generation of directors such as Tawfiq Abu-Wael, Annemarie Jacir, Sameh Zoabi and Najwa Najjar are now ensuring that Palestinian cinema remains at the forefront of Arab filmmaking. 2008 and 2009 are already shaping up to be banner years for Palestinian cinema.

Palestinian filmmakers completed an unprecedented number of features in 2008. Annemarie Jacir premiered her debut feature

Annemarie Jacir's **Salt of This Sea**

Salt of This Sea, about Soraya, an American-Palestinian woman returning to the Palestinian territories to reclaim her past, at Cannes. Jacir's debut burns with righteous indignation as Soraya, played by Palestinian-American poet Suheir Hammad, decides to rob a bank, together with local waiter Emad (Saleh Bakri), embittered at discovering his visa application to study in Canada – where a full scholarship awaits him – has been rejected. More importantly, the film succeeds in capturing the beauty of a troubled land, as these two young lovers fight to create a home for themselves amongst a people denied a state.

Rachid Masharawi's **Leila's Birthday**, about a Palestinian judge-turned-taxi driver played by Mohammed Bakri, struggling to stay sane in the West Bank, received its world premiere at Abu Dhabi's Middle East International Film Fest in October. Bakri's performance as an honourable man slowly driven crazy by his surroundings is at once affecting, powerful and utterly unforgettable. Eschewing didactic sermonising, Masharawi instead creates an indelible portrait of ordinary people living in impossible circumstances.

Najwa Najjar's debut **Pomegranates and Myrrh**, about a Palestinian dancer who has to cope with her husband being sent to an Israeli prison, received its premiere at the Dubai International Film Festival.

There are also a slew of projects set for completion in 2009 that is likely to keep Palestinian cinema very much on the agenda for international film festivals and cineastes. Elia Suleiman, whose *Divine Intervention* won the 2002 Jury Prize at Cannes, is busy filming **The Time That Remains**, an epic account of a Palestinian family's journey from 1947 through to the present day. Tawfiq Abu Wael, whose *Thirst* won the Cannes Fipresci prize in 2004, is currently filming his sophomore feature, loosely based on Palestinian writer Ghassan Kanafani's 1968 novel **Return to Haifa**. Hany Abu Assad, who won the Golden Globe for foreign film and received an Oscar nomination for *Paradise Now*, is also prepping his English-language debut, an adaptation of Paolo Coelho's erotic thriller **Eleven Minutes**.

And while the dire political and economic situation in the Palestinian Territories means that theatrical box office there remains negligible, these filmmakers' efforts are ensuring that Palestinian culture continues to have a voice around the world. Film 'allows us to tell our stories in our voices to the Arab world, and to international and professional audiences attending, to present another story not often seen or heard in the barrage of nightly, usually violent, news from our part of the world,' says Najwa Najjar. – *Ali Jaafar*

PANAMA

Though hard to believe, Panamanian cinema has not seen a full-length domestic film since the middle of the last century: Carlos and Rosendo Ochoa's *When Hope Dies* from 1949. Even that film has not even survived. Nevertheless, the country has been the location for numerous North American super-productions, the most recent being the continuation of the James Bond franchise, *A Quantum of Solace*.

Fed up with this situation, local filmmakers grouped together to form Asocine, the Panamanian Association of Cinematography, which has had a positive impact. They were instrumental in the introduction of a law which finances the development of the industry and also encouraged the country's membership of Ibermedia, the most important co-production fund in Latin America, as well as its documentary development programme, DocTV-Iberoamerica.

Abner Benaim's *Chance* is a co-production between Panama and Colombia. A 'macabre tropical comedy' about two maids who take over their employer's house, it is based on a real incident that took place in Brazil, although Benaim milked the drama more for its comedy potential. In addition to *Chance*, there are seven projects in the pipeline, thanks to the support of Ibermedia.

Abner Benaim's **Chance**

Luis Franco's **The Sigh of the Ugly One** (*El suspiro de la fea*) stars the current Minister of Tourism, Ruben Blades. Producer José Macías will soon begin shooting **The Plasma State** (*El estado plasma*), while Eduardo Verdum's **Rex Angelorum** and Luis Palomo's **The Time that Goes By** (*El tiempo que se va*) are in development.

In a country more used to being treated as a stopover for big Hollywood productions, these projects already anticipate the growth of a domestic market, with hopes for international distribution in the future.
– *Maria Lourdes Cortés*

RWANDA

Though lacking an infrastructure, the audiovisual media sector in Rwanda has enormous support from President Paul Kagame, who even attends international film festivals. Present at the Tribeca Film Festival in 2007, he equated the 'story of the Rwandan film' with that of 'the story of Rwanda itself', in solidarity with his country's emerging filmmakers.

The President has encouraged governmental, inter-governmental, non-governmental organisations and even the corporate sector to help support film initiatives, even if the involvement is merely to curry favour with the country's leader.

The most prominent film organisation is the non-governmental Rwanda Cinema Centre, which conducts workshops, facilitates the work of foreign crews and hosts the annual Rwanda Film Festival. Also known as Hillywood or Inflatable Cinema, this festival has operated both a mobile cinema in the country and a sedentary one in Kigali for two weeks every March since 2005.

The genocide that rocked Rwanda in 1994 has been the subject of many films, most recently Lee Isaac Chung's *Munyuragambo* and *Shake Hands with the Devil* by Roger Spottiswoode, both of which were made in 2007. Even as it services big-budget international films, it should be noted that Rwanda has yet to make a full feature film.

Belgian Guido Convents has written a book that traces the history of cinema in Rwanda and Burundi called *Les Rwandais et les Burundais face au cinema et a l'audiovisuel. Une histoire politico-culturelle de la Deutsch OstAsrik jusqu'aux republiques du Rwanda et du Burundi: 1896–2007.*

Another interesting initiative is that of the Cameroonian, Francois Wouokoache, who has been running Kemit, a film training programme for young people, for more than ten years. Kemit's aim, Wouokoache says, is to 'ensure the emergence of a new generation of filmmakers aware of the need to become involved in thinking about the big issues in their country, with the technical and artistic means at their disposal to show these realities through the medium of cinema.'

Some of the recent films made in Rwanda include Joseph Muganga's **The Kadogo Brothers**, Richmond Ruhanira's short **Better in than Out**, Nicole Kalisa's **The Consequence** and Daddy Yousouf Ruhorahoza's **Confession**. – *Ogova Ondego*

SENEGAL

Even though the Senegalese film industry has been in the doldrums for the last decade, hope has arrived with a talented new generation. However, they are currently unable to produce feature-length films due to a lack of means. As a result, they are limited to documentaries, television series and shorts.

Angèle Diabang Brener's documentary **Yandé Codou, the Singer of Senghor** (*Yandé Codou, la Griotte de Senghor*) profiles the octogenarian Senegalese performer. A living legend, she was an inspiration to Léopold Sédar Senghor, the country's first president.

Fatou Kandé Senghor sensitively documents 'bukut', an initiation ceremony that celebrates the passage from adolescence to adulthood in the Diola population of southern Senegal. **Diola Tigui** shows what has become of this practice.

Angèle Diabang Brener's **Yandé Codou, the Singer of Senghor**

Aïssatou Bah's **Mambéty for Ever** commemorates the tenth anniversary of the death of one of the fathers of the Senegalese cinema, Djibril Diop Mambéty. However, the film lacks substance, despite those involved, such as the journalist Catherine Ruelle and film directors Mahamat-Saleh Haroun, Abderrahmane Sissako and Mahama Johnson Traoré.

Although more than half of Senegal's cinemas have closed in recent years, there is now a travelling cinema that will hopefully allow many more people to watch films. – *Honoré Essoh*

SWAZILAND

During recent years, Swaziland was the subject and location for Richard E. Grant's autobiographical drama *Wah-Wah*, a co-production between the UK, South Africa and France. The film sensitively chronicled Grant's childhood experiences at the end of the 1960s, as Swaziland was about to become independent from Great Britain.

Aside of *Wah-Wah*, Swaziland has also been the subject of a documentary, **Dear Francis** by Jason Djang and Brent Gudgel. The United Nations has declared Swaziland to be the world's most HIV-infected nation with nearly 40% of its adult population carrying the virus. Experts say that within fifty years the Swazi people may become extinct unless profound change is realised. Shortly after the official declaration, Lance and Kelly, two Texas college students with high ideals, great hopes, and a degree of naiveté, join on an AIDS-prevention programme to Swaziland.

Dear Francis puts a face to the AIDS pandemic as it chronicles the personal stories of two strangers and the Swazis they befriend. Through these relationships, they discover that the causes of this epidemic are much more complex than they could have ever imagined. Included are interviews with local and international officials working on the front lines of the battle. *Dear Francis* confronts audiences with the stark reality of the AIDS pandemic.

Swaziland also hosts the Gold Lion Film Festival, which focuses on short films and videos from around the world.
– *Martin P. Botha*

TAJIKISTAN

The Tajikistan film industry is in a paradoxical situation. On one hand, there are almost no cinemas and people are watching films on DVD. On the other hand, there is a significant number of low-budget films that could be shown in cinemas. These films are eventually screened on local TV channels. Ten full-length films were made in the last year.

Ethno mythological elements have a significant presence in a number of films, including **Life**, directed by Radzhabali Pirov. Playing on the story of Sleeping Beauty, a girl in a coma is brought back to life after twenty years by the devotion of her lover.

Radzhabali Pirov's **Life**

Yunus Yusupov's **Love to Live** features a legend about a lonely hunter in the mountains who gives shelter to a young man who has escaped from prison. The young man claims that he is innocent, but when the hunter gives a gun to him, the young man kills the hunter. Later, the convict discovers that the hunter was his father.

In Orzumurod Sharipov's psychological drama, **A Source of Hope**, events take place in the most beautiful area of Tajikistan – the Obi-Garm canyon – where people of different nationalities and ages gather together in winter. According to the legend, there is a water well that can make wishes come true, if one drinks from it. In reality, the beauty, calmness and closeness to God make people think of what they would really like to do and realise what they really want from life.

With **The Mask** director Ozod Malikov faces the problem of migration, as well as slavery and violence, in today's world.

Although the last year saw a significant increase in the number of films made, many were extremely poor. However, the quantitative growth of the market offers hope for the development of Tajikistan's cinema.
– *Gulnara Abikeyeva*

TANZANIA

Tanzania, like the rest of East Africa, does not have a film industry. The country lacks the basic audio-visual media infrastructure from production to distribution facilities and has almost no understanding of the global film market.

According to Daniel Nyalusi of the Zanzibar International Film Festival, Tanzania lacks the coordination mechanisms between government policy-makers, the private sector and civil society. Lack of capital is perhaps the biggest obstacle to filmmaking. Piracy further suffocates any emerging film production, while the Copyright Society of Tanzania, COSOTA, sits by impotently.

The closest Tanzania comes to having a production and distribution channel is GMC, a private monopoly that pays producers to make films which GMC then distribute. Such producers receive a one-off fee and no royalties.

Tanzania is deluged with Nigerian home videos, making consumers dependent on them for entertainment and shunning any local film that they take to be inferior to the West African productions. This, in turn, tempts locals to copy the Nollywood template for making films. All too often they fall short of the standards of their Nigerian counterparts.

Faced with no local films to show, television is dominated by foreign series, soaps, films, and documentaries. And no new cinemas have been built in the last two years.

Dr Martin Mhando, the director of Zanzibar International Film Festival, has conducted some research within the film sector and published a series of critical papers on it: 'Film Value Chain Study – ZIFF' (2007), and 'The Development of Indigenous East African Video Industry' (2008). – *Ogova Ondego*

THE GAMBIA

The film industry in the Gambia could be described as youthful. There are a number of production companies, such as Vinasha Productions, the first production house, which was set up in the 1990s. Headed by Nana Ofori–Atta, Vinasha's first production was *Banjul Cops*, written and directed by Segun Oguntola, which focused on police practices.

2008 saw the emergence of 31-year-old producer/director Mariama Khan, who has so far produced two films and recently completed a third. The first film, **The Journey Up the Hill**, is based on the experiences of international students in the US. It looks specifically at students attending the Heller School for Social Policy and Management, at Brandeis University. **The Professor** continues on the same theme, presenting a profile of Henry Felt, Mariama's film professor at Brandeis University.

Khan's forthcoming film is **Secret** (*Sutura*), which looks at rape in Senegal. Featuring testimonies from victims, it analyses how the

law deals with rape, highlighting the distance between theory and practice. The film has already premiered in Dakar, the Senegalese capital. It was also screened at a conference of judges in Accra, Ghana. The film should provide the opportunity for further discussion on the need for victims to speak up. – *Agnes Thomasi*

TURKMENISTAN

Since the Turkmenfilm studio in Ashgabad was closed in 1998, there has been no film activity in Turkmenistan. However, in 2007, President Gurbanguly Berdymuhammedov agreed to revive Turkmenfilm. The studio was given the name of the legendary father of all Turkmen – Khan Oguz. Eurasia Trans Limited brought in new equipment to the studio, including High Definition cameras and sound and lighting equipment.

In 2007, three features were completed on video format. **Melody of the Soul** was directed by Oraz Orazov and based on four legends from the book, *Rukhnama: Reflections on the Spiritual Values of the Turkmen*. It was made in a very basic, televisual style. Basim Agaev's **This is called life** is another melodrama, which opens in a maternity hospital. One woman loses her child, while another woman gives birth to twins and generously gives one of her babies to her neighbour. The secret is hidden for a long time and the women remain friends, until their children grow up and fall in love with each other. **Penance** (*Pokayanie*) is directed by

Oraz Orazov's **Melody of the Soul**

Durdy Niazova. A grittier film, it is about an ex-drug addict who, upon his release from prison, seeks his mother's forgiveness.
– *Gulnara Abikeyeva*

UGANDA

Kampala has only one cinema and more than 600 make-shift video halls, mainly in the densely populated informal settlements. Rather than adopt the Western model of film distribution, pundits argue that a new model based on the video halls be expanded in Uganda.

With less than 300,000 DVD/VCD/VHS players, selling videos may not make good economic sense – the producer would not make enough money to break even. It is therefore recommended that producers adopt the mobile cinema model by taking locally produced films directly to audiences at play grounds, community centres and town halls.

Uganda's best-known film in 2007/2008 is **DivizionZ**, co-directed and produced by Donald Mugisha and James Tyler. Musicians Bobi Wine and Eunice Baguma also helped in the writing. Besides being screened widely in the numerous video halls in Kampala, *DivizionZ* was also shown abroad at festivals in Germany, Holland, and South Africa. The film portrays the class separation in Kampala and Mugisha, whose short experimental film, *610*, won the Golden Impala Award at the 3rd Amakula Kampala International Film Festival in 2006, claims the lack of interest and funding from the government makes life difficult for filmmakers.

DivizionZ was popular because it featured popular local musicians such as Bobi Wine, Mark 'Buchaman' Bugembe, Peter Miles, Menshan, Bonny 'Lot' Olem and Catherine 'Scarlet' Nakyanzi. It is about life in central Kampala and how the people living in this area survive the lack of amenities and frequent muggings, stabbings and a high usage of illegal drugs. The film follows the stories of four

Shooting **DivizionZ**

youths who come from the four administrative regions of Uganda to seek a better life in the capital. Stereotypes associated with various regions in terms of speech and temperament are also highlighted.

The film is set in a time when graduated tax was still part of the Ugandan culture. Back then, it was not uncommon to see well-dressed people dragged out of their cars and forced to sit on the ground for not having paid their tax. The biggest victims were the jobless youths who live in the poorer sections of the city. They never paid their taxes and thus were always on the lookout for the officers.
– *Ogova Ondego*

UZBEKISTAN

There is a pattern of the most popular films in Russia having Uzbek directors. *Turkish Gambit* was directed by Djagankhir Faiziev, while *Nightwatch* and *Daywatch* were presided over by Timur Bekmambetov, who later made his English-language debut with the action spectacular, *Wanted*. This trend is unique and does not exist in any other country of Central Asia.

Up to 90% of the films shown in local cinemas are Uzbek. The mechanism for producing cheap films is successful and the return on investment is, on average, quite quick. Most films are made by private studios. Only a small fraction (no more than one fifth) are produced by the official film body, Uzbekkino. As a result,

Aub Shakhobiddinov's **Idiot**

there is a dynamic commercial cinema built on the interests of the Uzbek population who go to see its product.

Melodrama is the most popular genre in Uzbekistan. In **Zumrad and Kimmat**, Bahrom Yakubov refashioned the 'Cinderella' story. **Zabordzhat** is the story of a woman who falls in love with a married man, while Bahrom Yakubov's **Podkidish** is a sad family story presented in the style of an Indian musical.

The most popular melodrama of 2008 in was **Idiot** (*Telba*), directed by Aub Shakhobiddinov. Producer Avaz Tadjikhanov said at a press conference that the film had a budget of US$35,000 and his company earned US$350,000. It is a story of a girl from a rich family who falls in love with a boy hired by her parents to take care of the dogs.

Three independent production companies – Shark Cinema, Daur S and Zamin Film – supply the Uzbek market with commercial films. This year the most popular comedy was Zhagongir Pazildzhonov's **Boivacha**. Pazildzhonov, a popular singing star himself, humorously presents the problems facing his character, who is in search of a soul-mate. Another successful comedy was Khotam Faiziev's **Small People**, which is set in a small Uzbek village.

Abduvokhida Ganieva's science fiction feature, **Sevginator**, concerns a young scientist who creates a female robot that is able to cook

Uzbek food and address him with due respect. But the robot wants to have more – love. Timur Musakov's **The Sky Is Near** features a ghost, whose mission is to save those near to him before his time is up. – *Gulnara Abikeyeva*

ZAMBIA

On 8 September 2008, filming of the first Zambian feature by a Zambian director and crew ended. Jabbes Mvula's **Bad T!ming** is the story of Chiku, a respected Zambian social activist, who is invited to head the United Nations' Task Force looking into the future of African children. Chiku is a respected member of his community, but after being accused of rape, he struggles to avoid prison and desperately tries to clear his name. A tale of failure, corruption, forgiveness and redemption, *Bad T!ming* is based on renowned Zambian playwright Samuel Kasankha's stage play.

Bad T!ming is a watershed in the country, which has virtually no film industry. The country has two television channels and 15 cinemas that predominantly screen films from the West. Several attempts by independent filmmakers to produce Zambian features were unsuccessful due to equipment and technology limitations. Mvula has also helped to launch the National Association of Media Arts to support the growth of a Zambian film industry.

Cynthia Greening, the executive producer of *Bad T!iming*, completed a documentary about the making of the feature. **Voice of an African Nation** is more than a behind-the-scenes documentary; it explores the educational and creative journey of Mvula, as well as the cultural exchange between Zambians and Americans, who collaborated on these projects. (Mvula studied filmmaking in Arizona, before returning to Zambia.)

Another notable documentary of the past year is **Tikambe**, which means 'Let's talk about it'. Made with USAID (United States Agency for International Development) funding, the focus is on people with HIV/AIDS and the stigma attached to their condition. The film, developed for the Zambia Integrated Health Programme, a project run by Johns Hopkins University's School of Public Health for USAID, will be shown throughout Zambia, including local television. – *Martin P. Botha*

ZIMBABWE

Zimbabwe's protracted political crisis and economic meltdown have stifled the local film industry. In a climate of the world's highest inflation rate, chronic shortages of foreign currency and food, skyrocketing unemployment and widespread hunger, cinema is something of a luxury.

The most significant film of the past year to emerge out of these dire circumstances is South African Darrell Roodt's **Zimbabwe**. Armed with only a Sony PD150 camera and no budget whatsoever, Roodt successfully made a film about an 18-year-old AIDS orphan who travels to South Africa in an effort to support herself and her two siblings. Roodt's

recent films (*Yesterday*, *Faith's Corner*, *Meisie*, *Lullaby*) have all explored marginalised female characters. *Zimbabwe* continues the director's studies about vulnerable women challenged by social and political circumstances.

The film was made with no script or professional actors. The crew consisted of Roodt and his camera, making up the film along the way. He shot chronologically over 14 days and the story evolves in real time. Aside from the main character's traumatic story, the film vividly reflects the bleakness of a Zimbabwe in ruins. It also highlights a very serious phenomenon: every day, 1,000 people illegally cross the border between Zimbabwe and South Africa, falling victim to exploitation and abuse. The film screened at the Rotterdam and Durban film festivals.

Hopefully a unity government and very fragile power-sharing agreement between the main political parties will end the political and economic crisis in Zimbabwe, and also contribute to the revival of a once vibrant film culture. – *Martin P. Botha*

World Box Office 2007

ALBANIA

		$
1.	Pirates of the Caribbean: At World's End	40,633
2.	Spider-Man 3	34,609
3.	300	24,184
4.	Harry Potter and the Order of the Phoenix	17,387
5.	Mr. Bean's Holiday	16,924
6.	Night at the Museum	14,334
7.	Norbit	13,752
8.	Rush Hour 3	13,395
9.	No Reservations	13,000
10.	Knocked Up	11,614

Population	2.5 million
Total box office	$340,000
Local films' market share	2 films per year
Admissions	95,000
Sites	4
Average Ticket Price	$2.50

Source: Kinema Millenium

ARGENTINA

		Admissions
1.	The Simpsons Movie	2,493,000
2.	Shrek the Third	1,936,000
3.	Pirates of the Caribbean: At World's End	1,559,000
4.	Harry Potter and the Order of the Phoenix	1,480,000
5.	Spider-Man 3	1,400,000
6.	Ratatouille	1,338,000
7.	Night at the Museum	1,115,000
8.	300	874,000
9.	Transformers	835,000
10.	Incorregibles	735,000

Population	39.5 million
Total box office	$110 million
Local films' market share	9.5%
Admissions	34 million
Screens	850
Average Ticket Price	$3.20

Source: Instituto Nacional de Cine y Artes Audiovisuales (INCAA), Sindicato de la Industria Cinematográfica Argentina (SICA)

AUSTRALIA

		AUS$
1.	Harry Potter and the Order of the Phoenix	35.5m
2.	Shrek the Third	33.7m
3.	Pirates of the Caribbean: At World's End	33.1m
4.	The Simpsons Movie	31.4m
5.	Transformers	27.9m
6.	Spider-Man 3	24m
7.	The Bourne Ultimatum	22m
8.	Happy Feet	20.7m
9.	Night at the Museum	17.6m
10.	Wild Hogs	17.2m

Population	21.2 million
Total box office	$895.4 million
Local films' market share	4%
Admissions	84,708 million
Sites/screens	485/1,941
Average cinema ticket price	$10.57

Source: Australian Bureau of Statistics, MPDAA, Screen Australia

AUSTRIA

		Admissions
1.	Pirates of the Caribbean: At World's End	715,922
2.	Ratatouille	701,290
3.	The Simpsons Movie	676,432
4.	Harry Potter and the Order of the Phoenix	632,925
5.	Casino Royale	586,395
6.	Shrek the Third	494,530
7.	Lissi und der Wilde Kaiser	477,880
8.	7 Zwerge – Der Wald ist nicht genug	468,655
9.	Mr. Bean's Holiday	436,194
10.	The Devil Wears Prada	408,804

Population	8.3 million
Total box office	€95.9 million
Local films' market share	12.31%
Admissions	15.7 million
Sites/screens	163/570
Average cinema ticket price	€6.29

Source: Fachverband der Audiovisions- und Filmindustrie (FAFO), Austrian Film Commission, WKO

BELGIUM

		Admissions
1.	Pirates of the Caribbean: At World's End	987,664
2.	Harry Potter and the Order of the Phoenix	979,889
3.	Ratatouille	957,251
4.	Shrek the Third	844,374
5.	The Simpsons Movie	580,331
6.	Spider-Man 3	577,007
7.	Night at the Museum	419,007
8.	Mr. Bean's Holiday	359,614
9.	Live Free or Die Hard	339,077
10.	The Departed	315,220

Population	10.7 million
Total box office	€134.4 million
Local films' market share	7%
Admissions	22,326,000 million
Sites/Screens	123/520
Average cinema ticket price	€5.87

Source: European Cinema Yearbook, Federation of Belgian Cinema Owners

BOLIVIA

		Admissions
1.	Spider-Man 3	151,300
2.	Harry Potter and the Order of the Phoenix	121,800
3.	The Simpsons Movie	121,000
4.	Pirates of the Caribbean: At World's End	95,000
5.	Transformers	66,200
6.	Night at the Museum	70,000
7.	300	59,900
8.	Ratatouille	54,100
9.	Enchanted	51,100
10.	Fantastic Four: Rise of the Silver Surfer	51,100

Population	10 million
Total box office	$5.3 million
Local films' market share	3%
Admissions	1.9 million
Sites/Screens	7/47
Average cinema ticket price	$2.60

Source: Manfer Films

BRAZIL

		$m
1.	Spider-Man 3	20.5
2.	Shrek the Third	15.1
3.	Harry Potter and the Order of the Phoenix	13.3
4.	Pirates of the Caribbean: At World's End	12.9
5.	Night at the Museum	9.6
6.	300	9.5
7.	Elite Squad	8.5
8.	The Simpsons Movie	7.2
9.	Ratatouille	7.1
10.	Fantastic Four: Rise of the Silver Surfer	6.9

Population	183.9 million
Total box office	$295.1 million
Local films' market share	11.3%
Admissions	87.9 million
Sites/Screens	2,159/20,321
Average cinema ticket price	$3.30

Source: Agência Nacional do Cinema (ANCINE), Filme B, IBGE

BULGARIA

		$m
1.	Pirates of the Caribbean: At World's End	8.7
2.	300	8.4
3.	Live Free or Die Hard	6.4
4.	Ocean's Thirteen	5.9
5.	Harry Potter and the Order of the Phoenix	4.4
6.	Rush Hour 3	4.2
7.	Shrek the Third	4.1
8.	Ratatouille	3.6
9.	Ghost Rider	3.5
10.	Blood Diamond	3.4

Population	7.7 million
Total box office	$92.9 million
Local films' market share	1.17%
Admissions	2.6 million
Sites/Screens	62/107
Average cinema ticket price	$3.80

Source: National Film Centre, National Statistic Institute, Union of Bulgarian Filmmakers

CANADA

		CAN$m
1.	Harry Potter and the Order of the Phoenix	32.7
2.	Spider-Man 3	31.6
3.	Transformers	29.8
4.	Shrek the Third	28.4
5.	Pirates of the Caribbean: At World's End	27.6
6.	The Bourne Ultimatum	23.1
7.	300	22.5
8.	The Simpsons Movie	20.9
9.	Ratatouille	14.9
10.	Superbad	14.4

Population	32 million
Total box office	$857.6 million
Local films' market share	3.5%
Admissions	104.4 million
Screens	3,200
Average cinema ticket price	$7.35

Source: Motion Picture Theatre Associations of Canada

CHILE

		$m
1.	The Simpsons Movie	3.1
2.	Harry Potter and the Order of the Phoenix	2.6
3.	Spider-Man 3	2.4
4.	Pirates of the Caribbean: At World's End	2.3
5.	Shrek the Third	2.3
6.	Transformers	1.8
7.	Ratatouille	1.7
8.	Night at the Museum	1.6
9.	Radio Corazón	1.4
10.	300	1.2

Population	16.8 million
Total box office	$42.9 million
Local films' market share	7.8%
Admissions	11.5 million
Sites	298
Average cinema ticket price	$3.74

Source: Camara de Comercio Cinematográfico, Instituto Nacional de Estadísticas

CHINA

		$m
1.	Transformers	37.6
2.	Warlords	26.5
3.	Assembly	24.8
4.	Spider-Man 3	19.8
5.	Harry Potter and the Order of the Phoenix	19.4
6.	Lust, Caution	18.9
7.	Pirates of the Caribbean: At World's End	17
8.	Casino Royale	12.6
9.	Night at the Museum	8.8
10.	Curse of the Golden Flower	8.3

Population	1.32 billion
Total box office	$475 million
Local films' market share	54.13%
Admissions	114 million
Sites/Screens	1,427/3,527
Average cinema ticket price	$3.49

Source: State Administration of Radio, Film and Television (SARFT)

COLOMBIA

	Admissions
1. Shrek the Third	1,087,490
2. Spider-Man 3	1,012,683
3. The Game Plan	971,061
4. The Simpsons Movie	967,445
5. The Golden Compass	912,126
6. Night at the Museum	874,843
7. Pirates of the Caribbean: At World's End	815,047
8. Harry Potter and the Order of the Phoenix	684,363
9. Ratatouille	681,198
10. Transformers	622,466

Population	42 million
Total box office	$73 million
Local films' market share	10.4%
Admissions	22.7 million
Sites/Screens	157/487
Average cinema ticket price	$3.37

Source: Proimágenes en Movimiento.

CROATIA

	$m
1. Harry Potter and the Order of the Phoenix	5.7
2. Shrek the Third	5.4
3. Mr. Bean's Holiday	5.1
4. Pirates of the Caribbean: At World's End	4.5
5. Ocean's Thirteen	3.1
6. Arthur and the Minimoys	2.9
7. Spider-Man 3	2.7
8. Night at the Museum	2.5
9. Transformers	2.3
10. The Simpsons	2.2

Population	4.4 million
Total box office	$108.1
Local films' market share	2.08%
Admissions	2.3 million
Sites/Screens	86/123
Average cinema ticket price	$4.40

Source: Croatian Audiovisual Centre

CZECH REPUBLIC

	$m
1. Vratné lahve	6.5
2. Obsluhoval jsem anglického krále	4.3
3. Harry Potter and the Order of the Phoenix	3.6
4. Shrek the Third	3.2
5. Medvídek	2.5
6. Gympl	2.4
7. Pirates of the Caribbean: At World's End	2.3
8. The Simpsons Movie	2.2
9. Ratatouille	1.7
10. Bestiář	1.4

Population	10.4 million
Total box office	$63.1 million
Local films' market share	32.4%
Admissions	12.8 million
Sites/Screens	668/821
Average cinema ticket price	$4.90

Source: Union of Film Distributors (UFD)

DENMARK

	Admissions
1. Harry Potter and the Order of the Phoenix	645,000
2. Pirates of the Caribbean: At World's End	586,000
3. Shrek the Third	543,000
4. Ratatouille	427,000
5. Anja and Viktor - Flaming Love	339,000
6. Live Free or Die Hard	326,000
7. The Simpsons Movie	316,000
8. Temporary Release	309,000
9. Spider-Man 3	288,000
10. The Gold of Valhalla	251,000

Population	5.5 million
Total box office	€110.5 million
Local films' market share	26%
Admissions	12.1 million
Sites/Screens	167/394
Average cinema ticket price	€9.12

Source: Danish Film Institute

EGYPT

	$m
1. Morgan Ahmed Morgan	4.7
2. That Is Enough	4.6
3. Artificial Bump	4.1
4. Taymour and Shafika	3.3
5. Justified Betrayal	2.9
6. The Chaos	2.1
7. The Ghost	1.9
8. The Island	1.8
9. The Hostage	1.7
10. Nightingale of Dokki	1.5

Population	76 million
Total box office	$53.1 million
Local films' market share	80%
Admissions	22.3 million
Sites/Screens	175/281
Average cinema ticket price	$0.18

Source: United Motion Pictures - Cairo

ESTONIA

	Admissions
1. Pirates of the Caribbean: At World's End	83,664
2. Shrek the Third	75,618
3. 186 Kilometres	73,336
4. The Simpsons Movie	64,488
5. Ratatouille	57,714
6. Mr. Bean's Holiday	50,520
7. Harry Potter and the Order of the Phoenix	49,670
8. Georg	49,423
9. Autumn Ball	37,859
10. Surf's Up	37,204

Population	1,34 million
Total box office	$9.6 million
Local films' market share	14.3%
Admissions	1,63 million
Sites/Screens	12/67
Average cinema ticket price	$5.90

Source: Estonian Bank, Estonian Film Foundation

FINLAND

		€m
1.	The Simpsons Movie	3.3
2.	Pirates of the Caribbean: At World's End	3.1
3.	Harry Potter and the Order of the Phoenix	2.9
4.	Mr. Bean's Holiday	2.4
5.	Ratatouille	1.9
6.	Shrek the Third	1.8
7.	Christmas Story	1.7
8.	V2 Dead Angel	1.5
9.	Ganes	1.4
10.	Casino Royale	1.1

Population	5.3 million
Total box office	€50.8 million
Local films' market share	20%
Admissions	6.5 million
Screens	316
Average cinema ticket price	€7.8

Source: Finnish Film Foundation, Statistics Finland

FRANCE

		Admissions
1.	Ratatouille	7,640,000
2.	Spider-Man 3	6,320,000
3.	Harry Potter and the Order of the Phoenix	6,090,000
4.	Pirates of the Caribbean: At World's End	5,620,000
5.	Shrek the Third	5,510,000
6.	La Môme	5,210,000
7.	Taxi 4	4,550,000
8.	The Simpsons Movie	3,510,000
9.	Ensemble, c'est tout	2,310,000
10.	Night at the Museum	2,260,000

Population	58.5 million
Total box office	€1 billion
Local films' market share	36.6%
Admissions	177.5 million
Sites/Screens	2,122/5,398
Average cinema ticket price	€5.95

Source: Centre National de la Cinématographie

GERMANY

		Admissions
1.	Harry Potter and the Order of the Phoenix	7,076,615
2.	Pirates of the Caribbean: At World's End	6,048,259
3.	Ratatouille	5,911,416
4.	The Simpsons Movie	4,592,790
5.	Shrek the Third	3,923,908
6.	Mr. Bean's Holiday	3,412,945
7.	Spider-Man 3	3,170,560
8.	Live Free or Die Hard	2,628,206
9.	Die wilden Kerle 4	2,454,325
10.	Night at the Museum	2,330,862

Population	82.3 million
Total box office	€768 million
Local films' market share	18.9%
Admissions	125.4 million
Sites/Screens	1,812/4,832
Average cinema ticket price	€6.12

Source: Filmförderungsanstalt FFA (German Federal Board)

HONG KONG

		$m
1.	Spider-Man 3	7.1
2.	Harry Potter and the Order of the Phoenix	6.76
3.	Lust, Caution	6.28
4.	Pirates of the Caribbean: At World's End	5.39
5.	Transformers	5.12
6.	Night at the Museum	4.84
7.	Protégé	3.42
8.	Ratatouille	3.26
9.	The Warlords	2.99
10.	Shrek the Third	2.72

Population	6.95 million
Total box office	$132.8 million
Local films' market share	22.4%
Admissions	19.4 million
Sites/Screens	49/192
Average cinema ticket price	$6.83

Source: Hong Kong Theatres Association, Motion Picture Industry Association (MPIA)

HUNGARY

		Admissions
1.	Shrek the Third	736,550
2.	Harry Potter and the Order of the Phoenix	609,802
3.	Ratatouille	543,659
4.	Pirates of the Caribbean: At World's End	437,754
5.	Live Free or Die Hard	257,404
6.	SOS Szerelem	238,849
7.	Taxi 4	221,854
8.	Train Keeps A Rollin'	209,359
9.	Transformers	192,317
10.	300	190,122

Population	10 million
Total box office	$53.7 million
Local films' market share	9.6%
Admissions	10.9 million
Sites/Screens	184/400
Average cinema ticket price	$4.1

Source: Hungarian Central Statistical Office, National Film Office

INDIA

		$m
1.	Om Shanti Om	28.2
2.	Welcome	25.2
3.	Chak de India	21.3
4.	Partner	20.4
5.	Taare Zameen Par	18.1
6.	Bhool Bhulaiyaa	17.7
7.	Heyy Babyy	16.8
8.	Guru	13.5
9.	Ta Ra Rum Pum	12.4
10.	Namastey London	12.1

Population	1.13 billion
Total box office	$1.5 billion
Local films' market share	95%
Admissions	3 billion
Screens	14,250
Average cinema ticket price	$0.02

Source: www.boxofficeindia.com

JAPAN

		$m
1.	Pirates of the Caribbean: At World's End	104
2.	Harry Potter and the Order of the Phoenix	90.3
3.	Hero	78.4
4.	Spider-Man 3	68.5
5.	Letters from Iwo Jima	49
6.	Pokemon: The Rise of Darkai	48.3
7.	Always Sunset on Third Street 2	43.8
8.	Monkey Magic	42
9.	Love and Honor	39.5
10.	Transformers	38.6

Population	127.7 million
Total box office	$1.91 billion
Local films' market share	47.7%
Admissions	163.1 million
Screens	3221
Average cinema ticket price	$11.7

Source: Motion Picture Producers Association of Japan

KOREA

		Admissions
1.	The Host	13,019,740
2.	Tazza: The High Rollers	6,847,777
3.	My Boss, My Teacher	6,105,431
4.	Mission: Impossible III	5,740,789
5.	Pirates of the Caribbean: Dead Man's Chest	4,628,903
6.	Hanbando	3,880,308
7.	200 Pounds Beauty	3,561,866
8.	Marrying the Mafia 3	3,464,516
9.	The Da Vinci Code	3,339,082
10.	Maundy Thursday	3,132,320

Population	48.5 million
Total box office	$63.5 million
Local films' market share	50.8%
Admissions	158.9 million
Sites/Screens	348/2,085
Average cinema ticket price	$4.80

Source: Korean Film Council (KOFIC)

MEXICO

		$m
1.	Spider-Man 3	34.4
2.	Harry Potter and the Order of the Phoenix	24.7
3.	Shrek the Third	23.6
4.	Pirates of the Caribbean: At World's End	23.5
5.	Tranformers	17.7
6.	Fantastic Four: Rise of the Silver Surfer	16.2
7.	Ratatouille	15.8
8.	The Simpsons Movie	15.2
9.	Kilómetro 31	10.7
10.	300	9.8

Population	103 million
Total box office	$618 million
Local films' market share	$46 million
Admissions	175 million
Screens	3,907
Average cinema ticket price	$3.60

Source: Imcine, Nielsen Edi Mexico

NEW ZEALAND

		NZ$
1.	Shrek the Third	7,025,286
2.	Transformers	6,955,274
3.	Casino Royale	6,000,790
4.	Pirates of the Caribbean: At World's End	5,930,719
5.	Harry Potter and the Order of the Phoenix	5,742,138
6.	The Simpsons Movie	4,381,014
7.	Happy Feet	4,314,548
8.	Spider-Man 3	3,726,276
9.	The Bourne Ultimatum	3,553,223
10.	Mr. Bean's Holiday	3,229,828

Population	4.2 million
Total box office	$151.7 million
Admissions	15.4 million
Screens	403
Average cinema ticket price	$ 9.88

Source: Motion Picture Distributors' Association of New Zealand (MPDA)

NORWAY

		$m
1.	Pirates of the Caribbean: At World's End	6.7
2.	Harry Potter and the Order of the Phoenix	6.5
3.	Shrek the Third	4.7
4.	The Simpsons Movie	4.3
5.	Ratatouille	3.6
6.	Live Free or Die Hard	3.4
7.	Spider-Man 3	3.1
8.	Olsenbanden jr Sølvgruvens hemmelighet	2.6
9.	Mr. Bean's Holiday	2.4
10.	The Bourne Ultimatum	2.3

Population	4.7 million
Total box office	$112 million
Local films' market share	16.4%
Admissions	10.8 million
Sites/Screens	229/426
Average cinema ticket price	$10.40

Source: FILM&KINO

POLAND

		Admissions
1.	Shrek the Third	3,352,469
2.	Katyn	2,735,777
3.	Testosterone	1,356,163
4.	Harry Potter and the Order of the Phoenix	1,129,621
5.	Dlaczego nie!	1,151,998
6.	Ratatouille	1,074,697
7.	Pirates of the Caribbean: At World's End	1,070,462
8.	Swiadek koronny	959,569
9.	Rys	808,873
10.	Bee Movie	767,710

Population	38.5 million
Total box office	€134.4 million
Local films' market share	24.7%
Admissions	32.6 million
Sites/Screens	65/985
Average cinema ticket price	€4.12

Source: www.boxoffice.pl

PORTUGAL

		€m
1.	Shrek the Third	3.5
2.	Ratatouille	2,792,881
3.	Pirates of the Caribbean: At World's End	2,188,053
4.	Mr. Bean's Holiday	2,058,382
5.	Harry Potter and the Order of the Phoenix	2,033,461
6.	Spider-Man 3	1,713,277
7.	Bee Movie	1,680,324
8.	The Simpsons Movie	1,457,301
9.	Blood Diamond	1,403,596
10.	Ocean's Thirteen	1,282,444

Population	10.6 million
Total box office	€69.1 million
Local films' market share	2.8%
Admissions	16.3 million
Sites/Screens	176/546
Average cinema ticket price	€4.24

Source: Instituto do Cinema e Audiovisual (ICA)

ROMANIA

		Admissions
1.	Pirates of the Caribbean: At World's End	98,961
2.	4 luni, 3 saptamani si 2 zile	88,684
3.	Shrek the Third	85,258
4.	300	80,098
5.	Harry Potter and the Order of the Phoenix	78,757
6.	The Heartbreak	74,851
7.	Apocalypto	68,412
8.	Ocean's Thirteen	54.379
9.	Mr. Bean's Holiday	50,882
10.	Spider-Man 3	48,790

Population	21.5 million
Total box office	$14.1 million
Local films' market share	3.38%
Admissions	2.9 million
Sites	72
Average cinema ticket price	$4.94

Source: Statistic Report of Romanian Cinematography

RUSSIA

		$m
1.	Pirates of the Caribbean: At World's End	31.8
2.	Shrek the Third	24.1
3.	Wolfhound	22.7
4.	Harry Potter and the Order of the Phoenix	16.7
5.	The Heat	16.5
6.	Transformers	15.7
7.	Spider-Man 3	14.3
8.	Night at the Museum	13.6
9.	Taxi 4	12.6
10.	Love-Shmove	12.2

Population	142.8 million
Total box office	$560.4 million
Local films' market share	28%
Admissions	124.5 million
Sites/Screens	649/1510
Average cinema ticket price	$4.50

Source: www.film.ru

SERBIA

		Admissions
1.	Black Gruja	131,699
2.	The Simpsons Movie	81,258
3.	The Fourth Man	73,259
4.	Harry Potter and the Order of the Phoenix	71,226
5.	Seven and a Half	59,029
6.	Change Me	57,990
7.	The Trap	50,128
8.	300	47,599
9.	Casino Royale	43,406
10.	Mr. Bean's Holiday	42,249

Population	7.6 million
Total box office	$4.6 million
Local films' market share	26.53%
Admissions	1.4 million
Sites/Screens	129/149
Average cinema ticket price	$3.34

Source: Film Distributors Association of Serbia

SINGAPORE

		$m
1.	Spider-Man 3	5.27
2.	Transformers	4.76
3.	Harry Potter and the Order of the Phoenix	3.78
4.	Pirates of the Caribbean: At World's End	3.51
5.	Ratatouille	2.87
6.	Mr. Bean's Holiday	2.64
7.	Fantastic Four: Rise of the Silver Surfer	2.56
8.	Rush Hour 3	2.43
9.	Shrek the Third	2.39
10.	881	2.36

Population	4.6 million
Total box office	$103 million
Admissions	18 million
Screens	117
Average cinema ticket price	$5.73

Source: Screen International, Singapore Film Society, The Straits Times

SLOVAKIA

		€
1.	Harry Potter and the Order of the Phoenix	612,895
2.	Shrek the Third	577,878
3.	The Simpsons Movie	481,892
4.	Pirates of the Caribbean: At World's End	404,574
5.	Empties	320,627
6.	Ratatouille	282,644
7.	I Served the King of England	209,022
8.	Perfume: The Story of a Murderer	163,136
9.	Spider-Man 3	155,062
10.	Bridge to Terabithia	122,037

Population	5.5 million
Total box office	€8.2 million
Local films' market share	1.06%
Admissions	2.8 million
Sites/Screens	207/251
Average cinema ticket price	€3.36

Source: Media Desk Slovakia, Slovak Film Institute

SLOVENIA

		€
1.	Petelinji Zajtrk	478,509
2.	Mr. Bean's Holiday	477,555
3.	Pirates of the Caribbean: At World's End	472,250
4.	Shrek the Third	356,535
5.	Ratatouille	324,002
6.	Harry Potter and the Order of the Phoenix	304,542
7.	Night at the Museum	226,015
8.	The Heartbreak	217,627
9.	Ocean's Thirteen	195,911
10.	Apocalypto	185,740

Population	2 million
Total box office	€9.7 million
Local films' market share	5.65%
Admissions	2.4 million
Sites/Screens	55/108
Average cinema ticket price	€5.00

Source: Slovenian Film Fund

SOUTH AFRICA

		$
1.	I Am Legend	1,300,000
2.	Enchanted	1,100,000
3.	Bee Movie	960,000
4.	Surf's Up	810,000
5.	Alvin & The Chipmunks	780,000
6.	The Golden Compass	710,000
7.	Stardust	650,000
8.	Heartbreak Kid	620,000
9.	American Gangster	580,000
10.	Knocked Up	570,000

Population	47 million
Total box office	$58.1 million
Local films' market share	0.7%
Admissions	27.1 million
Sites/Screens	130/743
Average cinema ticket price	$2.10

Source: Ster-Kinekor Distribution

SPAIN

		€m
1.	The Orphanage	24.3
2.	Pirates of the Caribbean: At World's End	22.8
3.	Shrek the Third	22.1
4.	The Simpsons Movie	18.4
5.	Spider-Man 3	18.3
6.	Harry Potter and the Order of the Phoenix	17.2
7.	300	15
8.	Ratatouille	14.3
9.	Night at the Museum	12.7
10.	The Golden Compass	10.7

Population	45.2 million
Total box office	€643.7 million
Local films' market share	13.4%
Admissions	116.9 million
Sites/Screens	907/4,296
Average cinema ticket price	€5.50

Source: Spanish Ministry of Culture

SWEDEN

		Admissions
1.	Pirates of the Caribbean: At World's End	845,208
2.	Harry Potter and the Order of the Phoenix	731,714
3.	Ratatouille	676,891
4.	Gothia Canal 2	606,423
5.	Shrek the Third	542,314
6.	The Simpsons Movie	473,379
7.	Arn: The Knight Templar	469,913
8.	Spider-Man 3	429,202
9.	Night at the Museum	322,662
10.	Live Free or Die Hard	288,784

Population	9.1 million
Total box office	$151.6 million
Local films' market share	21.6%
Admissions	14.9 million
Sites/Screens	710/1,049
Average cinema ticket price	$10.17

Source: The Swedish Film Institute

SWITZERLAND

		Admissions
1.	Ratatouille	736,282
2.	Pirates of the Caribbean: At World's End	609,794
3.	The Simpsons Movie	441,583
4.	Shrek the Third	417,644
5.	Spider-Man 3	330,318
6.	Ocean's Thirteen	260,863
7.	Live Free or Die Hard	254,806
8.	The Bourne Ultimatum	239,080
9.	The Golden Compass	227,663
10.	Night at the Museum	217,223

Population	7.6 million
Total box office	$181.8 million
Local films' market share	5.06%
Admissions	13.8 million
Sites/Screens	307/550
Average cinema ticket price	$13.10

Source: Office Fédéral de la Statistique (OFS)

TURKEY

		Admissions
1.	Beyaz Melek	1,702,144
2.	Kabadayi	1,485,735
3.	Maskeli Besler I.R.A.K	1,238,023
4.	Son Osmanli – Yandim Ali	1,084,448
5.	Pirates of the Caribbean: At World's End	970,414
6.	300	807,443
7.	Spider-Man 3	737,889
8.	Ciglin Dersane	783,199
9.	Harry Potter and the Order of the Phoenix	687,184
10.	Shrek the Third	662,034

Population	71.2 million
Total box office	$200.2 million
Local films' market share	35.29%
Admissions	31.1 million
Sites/Screens	434/1,454
Average cinema ticket price	$3.40

Source: ANTRAKT- Sinema Dergisi (Entre'acte- Cinema Magazine)

UNITED KINGDOM

	£m
1. Harry Potter and the Order of the Phoenix	49.43
2. Pirates of the Caribbean: At World's End	40.65
3. Shrek the Third	38.74
4. The Simpsons Movie	38.66
5. Spider-Man 3	33.55
6. The Golden Compass	26
7. I Am Legend	25.52
8. Ratatouille	24.8
9. The Bourne Ultimatum	23.72
10. Transformers	23.5

Population	60.8 million
Total box office	£821 million
Local films' market share	29%
Admissions	162.4 million
Sites/Screens	727/3,514
Average cinema ticket price	£5.05

Source: UK Film Council

UNITED STATES OF AMERICA

	$m
1. Spider-Man 3	336.5
2. Shrek the Third	322.7
3. Transformers	319.2
4. Pirates of the Caribbean: At World's End	309.4
5. Harry Potter and the Order of the Phoenix	292
6. I Am Legend	251.7
7. The Bourne Ultimatum	227.5
8. 300	210.6
9. Ratatouille	206.4
10. National Treasure: Book of Secrets	205.7

Population	301 million
Total box office	$9.63 billion
Admissions	1.47 billion
Sites/Screens	6,356/40,077
Average cinema ticket price	$6.88

Source: Motion Picture Association of America (MPAA)

WORLDWIDE TOP 25

	$m
1. Pirates of the Caribbean: At World's End	958.4
2. Harry Potter and the Order of the Phoenix	937
3. Spider-Man 3	885.4
4. Shrek the Third	791.4
5. Transformers	701.1
6. Ratatouille	615.9
7. I Am Legend	584
8. The Simpsons Movie	525.5
9. 300	456.6
10. National Treasure: Book of Secrets	454
11. The Bourne Ultimatum	440.9
12. Live Free or Die Hard	377.5
13. The Golden Compass	364.1
14. Alvin and the Chipmunks	357.5
15. Enchanted	339.9
16. Ocean's Thirteen	311.1
17. Bee Movie	283.2
18. American Gangster	264.7
19. Ghost Rider	223.8
20. Wild Hogs	223.2
21. Mr. Bean's Holiday	222
22. Beowulf	190.8
23. Juno	185.5
24. Knocked Up	148.7
25. Meet the Robinsons	146.1

Source: www.worldwideboxoffice.com

Festival Focus: Sundance

Sundance Goes International
by Sandy Mandelberger

As the Sundance Film Festival celebrates a milestone 25th anniversary this year, the prestigious event continues to move beyond its status as a mecca for American independent filmmaking, embracing the entire world of art cinema. Along with Toronto, Sundance has made North America an important and vital showcase for international producers and distributors to premiere their titles and generate international press and industry attention.

Founded by Robert Redford in 1982, Sundance has done something that no other festival has been able to do – create a brand name that almost defines a genre of film. Through the festival, the accompanying Sundance Film Institute, the Sundance Cinemas theatrical chain and the cable/satellite network The Sundance Channel, Sundance has become synonymous with films that have a stylistic edge, a social conscience or that push the envelope in storytelling technique. The best of them have an instant 'cool' status that gives audiences a self-satisfied feeling that they too are on the cutting edge. No other festival has quite been able to pull off this hattrick of branding and image association.

While the world premieres of the latest crop of American indies remains the main draw, the festival, under the helm of Geoffrey Gilmore and John Cooper, has consciously expanded its remit to include international cinema. 'While Sundance is not a formal market like Cannes or Berlin, the energy and excitement generated here and the access to North American industry and press is highly productive for international films and filmmakers,' offered Caroline Libresco, Senior Programmer. 'During the festival, we host the Sundance International Meetings, where international filmmakers meet with movers and shakers in the American industry,' Libresco added. 'We believe Sundance can and should play a vital role in awakening the appetite for foreign cinema in the US and actively encourage the American indie movement to be in a vigorous dialogue with international cinema.'

While non-American cinema has always been part of the mix, it clearly had sidebar status until 2005. However, that year the festival increased its focus on the 'World Cinema' section, moving it out of its non-competitive slot and creating two parallel competition sections for 'Dramatic Features' and 'Documentaries'. 'Sundance has become extremely important to us for international film promotion,' said Hengameh Panahi, head of French international distributor Celluloid Dreams. 'Given its position in the calendar and important buyer attendance, it has become the first major market of the year.'

Anna Melikyan's **The Mermaid**

Jens Jonsson's **King of Ping Pong***, photo by Askild Wik Edvardsen*

Not everyone is so big a fan. 'Sundance is very expensive and very difficult for us to get to,' a well-known sales agent commented. 'There is no formal market where you can meet people, and you are stuck in this tiny ski town without public transportation, good restaurants or ways that you can properly promote your film. The attending press is almost strictly American, so they like to write about the movie stars that are in town, and smaller films are literally left out in the cold.'

With American independent films of recent years not quite creating the spark of their forebears, the festival realised it was limiting its future clout by being pegged as a largely American-only event. As a result, it began to place more stock in world cinema. With the launch of the competition strands in 2005, films arrived from 25 countries, from Angola to Zimbabwe. Important winners that year included *The Hero*, an Angolan/Portugese/French co-production directed by Zézé Gamboa; Dane Susanne Bier's *Brothers*; Dutch documentary *Shape of the Moon* by Leonard Retel Helmrich; and *Wall*, an Israeli/French co-production directed by Simone Bitton.

The following year international representation expanded to 32 countries, hailing from as far afield as Belgium, Hungary, Iceland, Kenya, Lebanon, Morocco, Palestine, The Philippines, Georgia, Switzerland and Thailand. Films that made their mark include Géla Babluani's *13 Tzameti*, Juan Carlos Rulfo's humanistic documentary *In the Pit*, and Toa Fraser's *No. 2*.

By 2007, nearly one-third of the films shown at the festival arrived from outside the United States. Major prize winners included Eva Mulvad and Anja Al Erhayem's Jury Prize-winner *Enemies of Happiness*, Dror Shaul's Drama Grand Jury Prize-winner *Sweet Mud*, David Sington's *In the Shadow of the Moon* and John Carney's sleeper hit *Once*. New to the festival were entries from Azerbaijan, Colombia, Haiti, Iran, Jordan, Pakistan and Panama. While Jens Jonsson's *King of Ping Pong* won the Feature Documentary Prize, the real 'find' of the Festival was James Marsh's *Man on Wire* (which won both the Documentary Prize and the Audience Award), which has gone on to score at box offices around the world.

Yung Chang's **Up the Yangtze***, photo by Jonathan Chang*

Other stand-outs from last year's international crop include Amin Matalqa's Dramatic Audience Award winner *Captain Abu Raed*, Tanaz Eshaghian's *Be Like Others*, Ernesto Contreras' *Blue Eyelids*, Ole Bornedal's *Just Another Love Story*, Anna Melikyan's *The Mermaid*, Carlos Moreno's *Perro Come Perro*, Gonzalo Arijon's *Stranded*, Erez Tadmor and Guy Nattiv's *Strangers*, Phillipe Aractingi's *Under the Bombs*, Yung Chang's *Up the Yangtze* and Dennis Gansel's *The Wave*.

Finding acclaim at the festival is one thing… finding distribution yet another. 'There is never enough time to see all the films we want to, and the world premieres of American independent films definitely take precedence over the international titles,' Jon Gerrans, Co-President of specialty art-house distributor Strand Releasing stated. 'That said, the festival

James Marsh's **Man on Wire**

has made great strides to give international films equal footing to the American films, but now it is up to the industry to pay attention.'

Emily Russo, whose New York-based art-house distribution company Zeitgeist Films picked up the documentaries *Up the Yangtze* and *Stranded* at last year's festival commented that 'we generally track what is there and catch up with it in Berlin or elsewhere'. Lacking a formal market has its advantages. 'Sundance is a place where I can informally meet with key theatre exhibitors and press so I can get invaluable intelligence on how best to position a prospective acquisition before finalising a commitment to buy a film,' said Richard Lorber, President of the art-house theatrical and DVD company, Koch Lorber Films.

Carlos Moreno's **Perro Come Perro**

While all acknowledge its continued importance, the festival is not without controversy. The positioning of a major film festival in what is essentially a one-street ski

resort has been a source of contention for years. While the festival is building several new state-of-the-art screens with advanced digital projection systems, the current infrastructure is rather rickety and somewhat improvised. Press and industry screenings, which are often the first place where films are unveiled for visiting critics and professionals, are mostly held in converted hotel ballrooms with inadequate seating. And mobile communications are frequently hampered by the rugged, mountainous terrain. Add to that the rigors of sub-freezing temperatures and the current controversy about the Mormon funding of a California state election proposition that bans gay marriage (Park City is largely Mormon-owned and managed) and the festival faces its silver anniversary with calls for a move to more embracing and temperate climes.

Amin Matalqa's **Captain Abu Raed**

But in the end, it's the films that matter and there is no doubt that Sundance has launched many a career: the Coen Brothers (*Blood Simple*, 1985), Jim Jarmusch (*Stranger Than Paradise*, 1985), Steven Soderbergh (*sex, lies and videotape*, 1989), Todd Haynes (*Poison*, 1991), Bryan Singer (*Public Access*, 1993), Kevin Smith (*Clerks*, 1994), Edward Burns (*The Brothers McMullen*, 1995), Todd Solondz (*Welcome to the Dollhouse*, 1996), Neil LaBute (*In the Company of Men*, 1997), Kenneth Lonergan (*You Can Count On Me*, 2000), John Cameron Mitchell (*Hedwig and the Angry Inch*, 2001), Christopher Nolan (*Memento*, 2001), Tom McCarthy (*The Station Agent*, 2003), Noah Baumbach (*The Squid and the Whale*,

2005) and Jonathan Dayton and Valerie Faris (*Little Miss Sunshine*, 2007).

The festival relishes its 'kingmaker' status, even in the face of harsher industry realities that have seen recent Sundance winners (*Girlfight, The Believer, Personal Velocity, American Splendor, Primer, Forty Shades of Blue, Quincanera, Padre Nuestro* and *Frozen River*) meet with anaemic box office returns upon theatrical release. By casting its net wider to find hidden gems from the four corners of the globe, Sundance not only provides a cushion for its continued

relevance but also makes it clear that independent cinema is not solely an American phenomenon. It remains the mountain peak for the kind of cinema that needs all the buzz and cachet it can generate. It's cold out there for artistically inventive films of any stripe... and we don't just mean in Park City.

SANDY MANDELBERGER is Web Editor of www.internationalfilmguide.com. He is also the Founder and President of International Media Resources, a marketing, promotion and editorial services company based in New York.

SUNDANCE 2009 COMPETITION ENTRIES

World Cinema Dramatic Competition

Before Tomorrow (*Le Jour Avant Lendemain*, Canada, Madeline Piujug and Marie-Helene Cousineau)
Bronson (UK, Nicolas Winding Refn)
Carmo, Hit the Road
(Spain, Murilo Pasta)
The Clone Returns (Japan, Kanji Nakajima)
Dada's Dance (China, Zhang Yuan)
An Education
(UK, Lone Scherfig)
Five Minutes of Heaven
(UK, Oliver Hirschbiegel)
A French Gigolo
(*Cliente*, France, Josiane Balasko)
Heart of Time (*Corazon Del Tiempo*, Mexico, Alberto Cortes)
Louise-Michel (France, Benoit Delepine and Gustave Kervern)
Lulu and Jim (*Lulu und Jimi*, Germany, Oskar Roehler)
Maid (*La Nana*, Chile, Sebastian Silva)
One Day in a Life
(*Un Altro Pianeta*, Italy, Stefano Tummolini)
Unmade Beds (UK, Alexis Dos Santos)
Victoria Da (Canada, David Bezmozgis)
Zion and His Brother
(Israel/France/Israel, Eran Merav)

World Cinema Documentary Competition

211:Anna (Italy, Paolo Serbandini and Giovanna Massimetti)
Afghan Star
(Afghanistan/UK, Havana Marking)
Big River Man
(Slovenia/USA, John Maringouin)
Burma VJ (Denmark, Anders Ostergaard)
The End of the Line (UK, Rupert Murray)
The Glass House
(Iran/USA, Hamid Rahmanian)
Kimjongilia (France/USA, N.C. Heikin)
Let's Make Money
(Austria/China/South Africa/Spain/Switzerland, Erwin Wagenhofer)
Nollywood Babylon (Canada, Ben Addelman and Samir Mallal)
Old Partner (South Korea, Chung-ryoul Lee)
Prom Night in Mississippi
(Canada, Paul Saltzman)
The Queen and I
(Sweden, Nahid Persson Sarvestani)
Quest for Honor
(Kurdistan/USA, Mary Ann Bruni)
Rough Aunties (UK, Kim Longinotto)
Thriller in Manila (UK, John Dower)
Tibet in Song
(China/USA, Ngawang Choepel)

Festival News

BIFF Celebrates its 10th Anniversary in October 2009

Bergen, Norway's beautiful capital of the Fjords, celebrates **Bergen International Film Festival**'s 10th anniversary in October 2009. BIFF has become one of the largest and most important film festivals in the Nordic region. 44.000 admissions were registered at the 2008 edition of the festival, which screened 140 titles.

The festival is screening a great mix of new international fiction and documentary films. The competition section Cinema Extraordinaire is dedicated to discoveries and innovative fiction films. The festival also has a competition section for documentaries. In addition BIFF also screens upcoming theatrical releases and several domestic productions.

The strong 2008 documentary section consisted of about 70 productions – half of the programme, and many of these were linked to educational purposes in schools, as well as panel discussions and seminars. To curate the programme content in different sections has become BIFF's hallmark. For instance, BIFF 2008 presented a special sidebar devoted

Anna Melikyan's **Mermaid**

to the U.S. presidential election with eight films about former presidential candidates and presidents. Also, a seminar about the Americanization of Norwegian politics was arranged.

The sidebar Checkpoints is a collaboration with The Rafto Foundation – which annually grants the prestigious Rafto Prize to individuals or organizations working for human rights. At BIFF 2009 the Rafto jury, consisting of former Rafto Prize winners, will grant an award to the best film in competition.

The festival also has a strong focus on music, and invites bands to play live as well as screening music films. BIFF 2008 hosted gigs and films with Canadian heavy metal band Anvil and Chinese punk rockers Subs, and ten other music docs were presented.

News from Copenhagen

Two prominent Danish festivals will emerge as one in 2009, offering local audiences a dynamic and vibrant overview of world cinema, and international directors, producers and studios an exciting platform to exhibit their films. CPH:PIX will take place between 16–26 April 2009, in the place of the NatFilm Festival and Copenhagen International Film Festival.

The artistic profile of CPH:PIX is drawn up by Festival Director Jacob Neiiendam and Head of Programming Niels Lind Larsen, who used to be the programme heads of Copenhagen IFF and Natfilm respectively. 'This has given us a unique opportunity to start from scratch and ask ourselves what a new festival anno 2009 should strive for,' says Neiiendam. 'It was obvious to us that we should look to the future, which is also why we chose the name we did - celluloid is a thing of the past, but visual storytelling and the filmmaking craft is used across a constantly expanding range of new media platforms. The role of the film festival is changing along with the technology, and we aim to be on the forefront of this development.' However, computer games, 3-D and collaborations across artistic genres and cultural institutions will not overshadow the backbone of the festival, which continues to be a strong and varied film programme. It is highlighted by a Competition Programme dedicated to feature directing debuts. The 10-12 films will compete for a cash prize of 50.000 Euros, which goes to the director. 'A substantial cash prize can make all the difference to a first time filmmaker, and it is our hope that the money is used to kick start their next project,' Jacob Neiiendam adds. The festival's other main award is a distribution prize of 15.000 Euros sponsored by the national newspaper, Politiken. This audience award goes to a film that hasn't already secured distribution in Denmark.

A fascinating strand of the new structure, CPH:PIX are proud to premiere the exciting FILM-ART-FILM project during its first edition in April 2009. Five Danish acclaimed filmmakers will create five different films in collaboration with five equally renowned visual artists. The pairings will include: Pernille Fischer Christensen (*A Soap*) and Cathrine Raben Davidsen; Christoffer Boe (*Reconstruction*) and Kristian von Hornsleth; Dagur Kari (*Dark Horse*) and Christina Hamre; Lone Scherfig (*Italian For Beginners*) and Ulrik Møller; and Martin de Thura (*Young Man Falling*) and Peter Callesen.

GL Strand, the modern exhibition hall in the heart of Copenhagen, will for two weeks be transformed into an installation that will be part cinema and part exhibit. The FILM-ART-FILM project will reflect the challenging process the filmmakers and artists have gone through and how it has worked as a creative dynamo. The result will be exciting unpredictable fusions between the two artists, who each have a strong artistic expression themselves, but together they also become a manifest for the Danish creativity, innovation and high quality.'We are thrilled to be able to present this unique project at CPH:PIX,'says Neiiendam. 'GL STRAND is famous for presenting audiences with new art and for putting art into new contexts and different framesets, not unlike what we will strive to do

CPH:DOX 2008 (photo: Kristoffer Horn)

Buster 2008 (photo: Hasse Ferrold)

with films at our new festival. Danish art is on the brink of a major international breakthrough and we hope we can help raise awareness around these extraordinary artists.'

When the Danish capital's two feature film festivals merged into CPH:PIX, two already established and popular film festivals also became part of the same family: BUSTER – Copenhagen International Film Festival for Children and Youth and CPH:DOX – Copenhagen International Documentary Film Festival. These strong brands continue unchanged but strengthened under the new umbrella organisation: Copenhagen Film Festivals. Thus this new festival power station today house Denmark's three major international film festivals: CPH:PIX (late April); BUSTER (late September) and CPH:DOX (early November). The organisation also hosts two film markets. September's COPENHAGEN FILM MARKET, exclusively for invited film professionals, has a section for new Danish feature films and one for Nordic films for Children and Youth. DOX MARKET for international documentaries is held during the festival in November.

European Film Awards

In his welcome speech to the audiences gathered for the European Film Awards, European Film Academy President Wim Wenders admitted to a secret agenda behind the location for the event. After years of trying to persuade Lars von Trier to travel to previous awards at other European locations, it was conceded that they

would come to him instead. And von Trier did indeed attend, where he and his other Dogme cohorts, Thomas Vinterberg, Kristian Levring and Søren Kragh-Jacobsen accepted an award for European Achievement in World Cinema.

In the presence of Their Royal Highnesses The Crown Prince Frederik and Crown Princess Mary of Denmark, Danish Prime Minister Anders Fogh Rasmussen and EU Commissioner Viviane Reding, Danish news anchorman Mikael Bertelsen played host to the 1,400 guests gathered for the 21st awards at the prestigious Copenhagen Forum. Guests presenting the awards included Marianne Faithfull (UK), Julia Jentsch (Germany) and Paprika Steen (Denmark), as well as Andrzej Chyra (Poland), Mads Mikkelsen (Denmark) and Santiago Segura (Spain).

Matteo Garrone, European Director 2008 for **Gomorra** *(photo: Rune Evensen/ScanPix)*

The evening was dominated by the stark, brutal and disturbing Italian crime drama, *Gommorah*. It picked up five awards, included European Film 2008, Best Director for Matteo Garrone, Best Screenplay (Maurizio Bracci, Ugo Chiti, Gianni di Gregorio, Matteo Garrone, Massimo Gaudioso and Roberto Saviano) and Best Cinematography (Marco Onorato). Tony Servillo's European Actor Award was given both for his performance in *Gommorah* and for his startling transformation into Giulio Andreotti in Paolo Sorrentino's *Il divo*.

The European Actress Award went to Kristen Scott Thomas for her searing performance in *I've Loved You So Long*, although theatre

Steve McQueen European Discovery 2008 for **Hunger** *(photo: Jens Dige/ Polfoto)*

commitments prevented her from attending. Another English actress who was present, Dame Judi Dench, received one of the evening's largest ovations when she accepted the European Achievement in World Cinema.

Certainly one of the most striking debuts of the year, Turner Prize-winning artist Steve McQueen's *Hunger* earned its director the European Discovery Award, while this year's Prix FIPRESCI went to Abdellatif Kechiche for *Couscous.*

Magdalena Biedrzycka deservedly received the European Film Academy Prix D'Excellence with her costume designs for *Katyn*, Andrzej Wajda's powerful examination of the Soviet slaughter of thousands of Polish officers and citizens in the Katyn forest in 1940. Helena Trestikova's *René*, an account of the life of

habitual offender René Plášil, was awarded the European Film Academy Documentary Award, while the Prix UIP for the best short film went to *Frankie* by Darren Thornton.

Arguably the most moving moment of the evening was the announcement of the Award for European Composer. Instead of the usual announcement, the envelope was rushed over to the orchestra who then began playing the haunting music to *Waltz with Bashir*, which filled the auditorium as composer Max Richter walked up to the podium to accept his award.

The 2009 awards ceremony will take place in Essen, in Germany's Ruhr region in North Rhine-Westphalia. The unique move is a change from the regular system that brings the European Film Awards to Berlin, home of the European Film Academy, every two years. In the years in-between the awards ceremony is held in different European film capitals such as London, Paris, Rome, Barcelona, Warsaw and now Copenhagen. Berlin's contribution of the European Film Awards 2009 to Essen are a first highlight of the European Capital of Culture year 'RUHR 2010'.

Abdellatif Kechiche, European Film Academy Critics' Award 2008- Prix FIPRESCI for **Couscous** *(photo: Rune Evensen/ScanPix)*

5 DECEMBER 2009

THE 22ND EUROPEAN FILM AWARDS

ESSEN / GERMANY

The IFG Inspiration Award

A special award was launched in 2008 to honour independent filmmakers at the start of their careers. **The International Film Guide Inspiration Award** is presented by Wallflower Press, leading independent specialist publishers of books and magazines devoted to cinema and the moving image, and the Criterion Collection, the leading distributor of classic world cinema on DVD. The recipient, a native of the festival's country hosts, is chosen by that festival's jury. The Award was given out in 2008 at four leading North American film festivals.

A profile of the winning filmmaker and their film is included below and on the IFG website (www.internationalfilmguide.com). The four festivals featuring the prize were: Vancouver International Film Festival (www.viff.org), Montreal's Festival du Nouveau Cinema (www.nouveaucinema.ca), Fort Lauderdale International Film Festival (www.fliff.com) and Santa Fe Film Festival (www.santafefilmfestival.com).

The winner at Vancouver International Film Festival, in late September, was Canadian filmmaker **Cameron Labine** for his debut,

Cameron Labine's **Control Alt Delete**

the comedy **Control Alt Delete** (www.controlaltdeletemovie.com), which screened in the 'Canadian Images' section of the Festival. The film was chosen from among nearly a hundred Canadian films for its 'unique visual style, daring content and expansive execution'. It tells the amusing tale of a loveable computer geek who is dumped by his longtime girlfriend and becomes obsessed with internet porn. In time, the young man discovers that the website images no longer turn him on ... and thus begins his strangely satisfying sexual relationship with the machine itself. His desire for newer, sexier models grows until he finds himself copulating with co-workers' CPUs, while his boss vows to identify the 'computer rapist'.

Guy Édoin's **The Beat**

Quebec-based short filmmaker **Guy Édoin** won the award at the Festival du Nouveau Cinema for his 19-minute drama **The Beat** (*La Battue*). It screened in the 'Fictions Quebec' section of the Short Film Focus programme.

The beautifully shot film takes place on a few acres of snowy woods in northern Quebec, where a group of women are out hunting. Lost in the forest, a teenage girl tells her mother she is leaving the family farm. *The Beat* is the final film in Guy's rural trilogy, which also includes *The Bridge* (2004) and *The Dead Water* (2006). All of the films were shot on the director's farm and dedicated to the region and its people.

The prize then moved to the Fort Lauderdale International Film Festival, where American director **Brian Hecker** was awarded for his feature debut, **Bart Got a Room**, which had premiered at the Tribeca Film Festival. A winning family comedy shot in south Florida, it has been picked up for distribution by Plum Pictures (http://www.plumpic.com).

Brian Hecker's **Bart Got a Room**

Danny Stein, played by newcomer Steven J. Kaplan, is a somewhat geeky high school senior whose biggest challenge is finding the right date for his senior prom. Danny wants what any young man wants on his prom night … a little lovin' from a cute girl. The film also stars William H. Macy and Cheryl Hines. Hecker based the story on his own adolescence, with his hometown of Hollywood, Florida serving as the setting for the film. Currently, Hecker and his business partner Craig Sherman are writing a biopic for Leonardo di Caprio and Paramount Pictures about the rebel-genius Nolan Bushnell who started the video game revolution in the early 1970s.

The fourth and final North American film festival where the Award was given out was at the Santa Fe Film Festival, which celebrated its ninth edition in the first week of December. It honored director **Tony Barbieri** for **EM**, which had its world premiere at the Seattle International Film Festival, where it won the Grand Prize.

In this twenty-first-century variation on Hitchcock's *Vertigo*, up-and-coming actor Nathan Wetherington gives a riveting performance as a dazed everyman who falls for a woman who becomes a ghostly presence in his life. Barbieri's earlier film *The Magic of Marciano*, starring Robert Forster and Nastassja Kinski, was a festival hit eight years ago. The director is known for his Bergman-like directorial style, particularly his use of close-ups to suggest shifting emotions.

'What initially inspired me to write *EM* was my experience watching someone I loved grappling with mental illness', Barbieri explained. 'The fine line between the illness and normal behaviour compelled me to tell this story, where the audience can see the full effect of it.'

Tony Barbieri's **EM**

For the directors who have been honoured, **The International Film Guide Inspiration Award** will hopefully serve as a guidepost to measure the development and enrichment of their careers. With the publicity surrounding the award and the support from their peers and the industry they work within, the hope is that these young directors will find the courage, the perseverance and indeed the inspiration to expand their careers and adhere to their artistic inspirations. Such is the hope of this award, which will increase its profile at major international festivals around the world in the months to come.

Film Festivals Calendar

Leading Festivals

American Film Market
November 4–11, 2009

The business of independent motion picture production and distribution – a truly collaborative process – reaches its peak every year at the American Film Market. Over 8,000 leaders in motion picture production and distribution – acquisition and development executives, agents, attorneys, directors, financiers, film commissioners, producers and writers – converge on Santa Monica for eight days of screenings, deal making and hospitality. The AFM plays a vital role in global production and finance. Each year, hundreds of films are financed, packaged, licensed, and green lit, sealing over $800 million in business for both completed films and those in pre-production. With the AFM – AFI FEST alliance, attendees capitalise on the only festival-market combination in North America. *Inquiries to*: 10850 Wilshire Blvd, 9th Floor, Los Angeles, CA 90024-4311, USA. Tel: (1 310) 446 1000. Fax: 446 1600. e: afm@ifta-online.org. Web: www.americanfilmmarket.com.

Amiens International Film Festival
November 13–22, 2009

Discovery of new talent, new cinematography and the reassessment of film masters. A competitive festival in northern France for shorts, features, animation and documentaries. Also, retrospectives, tributes and the 'Le monde comme il va' series, which includes works from Africa, Latin America and Asia. 'Europe, Europes', an expanding section for more than ten years, presents new works from Young European Talents (shorts, documentaries and animation). *Inquiries to*: Amiens International Film Festival, MCA, Place Léon Gontier, 80000 Amiens, France. Tel: (33 3) 2271 3570. Fax: 2292 5304. e: contact@filmfestamiens.org. Web: www.filmfestamiens.org.

Amsterdam-International Documentary Film Festival (IDFA)
November 19–29, 2009

The world's largest documentary festival, built up over two decades, IDFA 2008 opened with Renzo Martens' *Episode 3 – Enjoy Poverty*. Over the following ten days, IDFA screened 309 documentaries and sold over 150,000 tickets. Apart from regular sections, IDFA has several competition programmes. The big winner of the 2008 festival was *Burma VJ - Reporting from a Closed Country* by Anders Østergaard, winning both the VPRO Joris Ivens competition for feature-length docs and the Movies that Matter Human Rights Award. A new section was the DocLab programme, in which the relationship between new media and documentary is examined. In addition to the screenings there were daily talk shows, a special performance by Youssou Ndour, debates and three masterclasses by, amongst others, Steve James, Nikolaus Geyrhalter

IDFA is located in the heart of historical Amsterdam (photo: Ramon Mangold, © Bram Belloni)

and Avi Mograbi. IDFA has two markets: the FORUM, a market for international co-financing, and Docs for Sale, which stimulates the sales and distribution of creative documentaries. From December 2008, Docs for Sale also boasts an online marketplace where new as well as older documentaries can be viewed all year long. Docs for Sale Online is a place where sales agents and producers can show their documentaries to potential buyers and exhibitors online, even after IDFA is over. *Inquiries to*: International Documentary Film Festival-Amsterdam, Kleine-Gartmanplantsoen 10, 1017 RR Amsterdam, Netherlands. Tel: (31 20) 627 3329. Fax: 638 5388. e: info@idfa.nl. Web: www.idfa.nl.

AWARDS 2008
VPRO Joris Ivens Award for the best documentary film longer than 60 minutes: **Burma VJ-Reporting From a Closed Country** (Denmark/Sweden/Norway/UK), Anders Østergaard.
Joris Ivens Special Jury Award: **Forgetting Dad** (Germany), Rick Minnich and Matthew Sweetwood.
Silver Wolf Award for the best documentary film shorter than 60 minutes: **Boris Ryzhy** (The Netherlands), Aliona van der I Iorst.
First Appearance Award for the best documentary debut: **Constantin and Elena** (Romania/Spain), Andrei Dascalescu.
IDFA Student Award: **Shakespeare and Victor Hugo´s Intimacies** (Mexico), Yulene Olaizola.
Dioraphte Audience Award: **RiP - A Remix Manifesto** (Canada), Brett Gaylor.
Movies that Matter Human Rights Award: **Burma VJ-Reporting From a Closed Country** (Denmark/Sweden/Norway/UK), Anders Østergaard.
DOC U! Award: **Kassim the Dream** (USA), Kief Davidson.
The Dutch Cultural Broadcasting Fund Award for Documentary: **Monsters Under the Bed** (Netherlands), Sarah Mathilde Domogala.

Report 2008
The 21st IDFA showed an increase in visitor numbers compared to 2007 (145,000 tickets

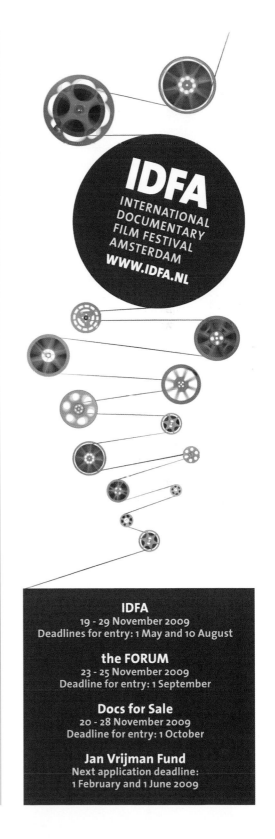

IDFA
19 - 29 November 2009
Deadlines for entry: 1 May and 10 August

the FORUM
23 - 25 November 2009
Deadline for entry: 1 September

Docs for Sale
20 - 28 November 2009
Deadline for entry: 1 October

Jan Vrijman Fund
Next application deadline:
1 February and 1 June 2009

sold), with at least 157,500 tickets sold. Net receipts rose from €623,000 in 2007 to at least €700,000 this year. The number of international guests was less than last year: 2,469, as opposed to 2,700 last year. The new website was visited almost 20% more frequently than in 2007. A striking note was the success of IDFA TV; the hundreds of video reports, recordings, trailers and short films were viewed some 4,000 times a day during the festival. Another factor in the increased online interest in the festival was the presence of IDFA on platforms such as YouTube, Facebook and Brightcove.
– **Laura van Halsema**, Press Officer.

Austin Film Festival
October 22–29, 2009

Celebrating its sixteenth year, an internationally recognised Film Festival and Screenwriters' Conference – one of the select few in the US accredited by the Academy of Motion Picture Arts and Sciences. It brings together a broad range of established and up-and-coming writers, directors and industry professionals for screenings, panels and high-profile networking. *Inquiries to*: Austin Film Festival, 1145 W 5th St, Ste 210, Austin, TX 78703, USA. Tel: (1 512) 478 4795. Fax: 478 6205. e: info@austinfilm.com. Web: www. austinfilmfestival.com.

Bergen International Film Festival
October 21–28, 2009

Norway's beautiful capital of the fjords launches the tenth BIFF in 2009. The festival, which is largest of the Norwegian film festivals in content, has a main International Competition of about 15 films, as well as an International Documentary Competition. The documentary section makes BIFF one of the Nordic countries' largest annual documentary events. The festival has sidebars with international art-house films, Norwegian Shorts Competition as well as premieres of the upcoming Christmas theatrical releases, through extensive collaboration with Norway's distributors. Also hosts seminars and other

events. *Inquiries to:* Bergen International Film Festival, Georgernes verft 12, NO-5011 Bergen, Norway. Tel: (47) 5530 0840. Fax: 5530 0841. e: biff@biff.no. Web: www.biff.no.

AWARDS 2008
Jury Award-Cinema Extraordinaire
Competition: **The World Is Big and Salvation Lurks Around the Corner** (Bulgaria/Hungary/Germany/Slovenia), Stefan Komandarev.
Documentary Award: **War Child** (USA), Christian Karim Chrobog.
Audience Award: **Young@Heart** (UK), Stephen Walker.
Visjon Vest Award for Young Talent: Olav Øyehaug, Norway.
Youth Documentary Award: **Yodok Stories** (Norway), Andrzej Fidyk.
Norwegian Short Film Award: **The Squirrel** (Norway), Stian Einar Forgaard.

Berlin –
Internationale Filmfestspiele Berlin
February 5–15, 2009

Interest in the Berlinale 2008 among visitors from both the film industry and the general public has been greater than ever: More than 20,000 accredited visitors from 125 countries, including more than 4,100 journalists, attended the 58th Berlin International Film Festival. Approximately 450,000 cinemagoers have attended the festival, including roughly 240,000 audience tickets. Altogether, 384 films were shown in 929 screenings. Besides the 'regular sections' – Competition, Panorama, Forum, Generation, Perspektive Deutsches

Berlin-Internationale Filmfestspiele (photo: Jan Windzus)

Kino and Berlinale Shorts – there were special events including the comprehensive Luis Buñuel Retrospective and the Homage to Francesco Rosi, as well as the Berlinale Special and the Culinary Cinema events, which were almost completely booked out. Under Jury President Costa-Gavras, Uli Hanisch, Diane Kruger, Walter Murch, Shu Qi and Alexander Rodnyansky brought glamour, passion and expertise to the Berlinale 2008. *Inquiries to:* Internationale Filmfestspiele Berlin, Potsdamer Str 5, D-10785 Berlin, Germany. Tel: (49 30) 259 200. Fax: 2592 0299. e: info@berlinale.de. Web: www.berlinale.de.

AWARDS 2008
Golden Bear: **The Elite Squad** (Brazil/Argentina), José Padilha
Jury Grand Prix: **Standard Operating Procedure** (USA), Errol Morris.
Best Director: **There Will Be Blood** (USA), Paul Thomas Anderson.
Best Actor: Reza Najie for **The Song Of Sparrows** (Iran), Majid Majidi.
Best Actress: Sally Hawkins for **Happy-Go-Lucky** (UK), Mike Leigh.
Best Short: **A Good Day For A Swim** (Romania), Bogdan Mustata,

Bermuda International Film Festival
March 20–28, 2009

The festival features the best of independent film from around the world in three competition categories: features, documentaries and shorts. Q&A sessions with directors, and the festival's popular lunchtime 'Chats with…' sessions give filmgoers and filmmakers a chance to mix. A competition victory earns each film's director an invitation to sit on the festival jury the following year. Submission deadline: October 1. *Inquiries to:* Bermuda International Film Festival, Broadway House, PO Box HM 2963, Hamilton HM MX, Bermuda. Tel: (441) 293 3456. Fax: 293 7769. e: info@biff.bm. Web: www.biff.bm.

AWARDS 2008
Best Narrative Feature: **Caramel** (France/Lebanon), Nadine Labaki.
Best Documentary Feature: **Saving Luna** (Canada), Michael Parfit and Suzanne Chisholm and **Souvenirs** (Israel), Shahar Cohen and Halil Efrat.
Bermuda Shorts Award: **Toyland** (Germany), Jochen Alexander Freydank.
Audience Choice: **Red Dust** (South Africa), Tom Hooper.

Bilbao International Documentary and Short Film Festival
November 23–28, 2009

This festival for shorts and documentaries, heading for its 51st edition in 2009, has established itself for its speciality on the international film festival circuit. A brief look at the names in international cinema who have received awards in Bilbao reveals a list featuring outstanding figures such as Jacques Demy, Pierre Perrault, Michel Brault, Claude Lelouch, Gian Vittorio Baldi, Fernando Birri, James Blue, Santiago Álvarez, Robert L. Drew, Felipe Cazals, Peter Watkins and Peter Mullan. In this sense, it can be stated that the festival has fulfilled

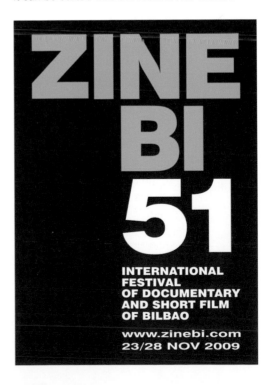

beyond all expectations the main function that can be attributed to a cultural event of its characteristics: to act as a testing ground for new trends and ways of understanding cinema, offering shelter to its most intrepid exponents and offering them the opportunity of having their work seen in a specialised context. At least three generations have emerged from this festival, for example: Carlos Saura, Ramón Masats, Basilio M. Patino, Pío Caro Baroja, José Val del Omar, Javier Aguirre, Gabriel Blanco, Jaime Chávarri, Francisco Betriu, Imanol Uribe, Montxo Armendáriz, Julio Medem, Juanma Bajo Ulloa, Javier Rebollo and Santiago Segura. Featuring over 2,600 films from over eighty countries in 2008, with nearly a hundred films selected for the International competition which encompasses three categories for fiction, documentary and animation. The number of countries, geographical areas and cultures participating once again underlined the truly universal character of the competition. *Inquiries to:* Bilbao International Documentary and Short Film Festival, Colón de Larreátegui, 37-4° Derecha, 48009 Bilbao, Spain. Tel: (34 94) 424 8698. Fax: 424 5624. e: info@zinebi.com. Web: www.zinebi.com.

AWARDS 2008

Grand Prize: **Le Feu, Le Sang, Les Etoiles** (France), Caroline Deruas.
Best Spanish Film: **One Goal**, Sergi Agusti.
Best Basque Film: **FGM** (Euskadi), Jon Garaño.
Gold Mikeldi for Animation: **DIX** (France), Fabrice Le Nezet, François Roisin and Jules Janaud.
Silver Mikeldi for Animation: **Sagan Om Den Lille Dockpojken** (Sweden), Johannes Nyholm.
Gold Mikeldi for Documentary: **Clean-Up** (Germany), Sebastian Mez.
Silver Mikeldi for Documentary: **Ghosts and Gravel Roads** (Canada), Mike Rollo.
Gold Mikeldi for Fiction: **The Door** (Ireland), Juanita Wilson.
Silver Mikeldi for Fiction: **Hemel Boven Holland** (The Netherlands), Rolf van Eijk.
Silver Caravel: **Tierra Roja** (Cuba/Switzerland), Heidi Hassan.

St George Bank Brisbane International Film Festival
July/August, 2009

Since its inception in 1992, this annual celebration of film has evolved to become one of Australia's most highly respected and celebrated festivals, delighting the Brisbane community with quality programming and cutting-edge events. BIFF showcases a range of entertaining and thought-provoking films from Australia and around the world. The critically acclaimed programme offers a feast of over 200 films that includes features, documentaries, shorts, experimental and retrospectives. It showcases a number of awards and competitions, including the Chauvel and Kinetone Awards, as well as the Queensland Short Film Competition and Queensland New Filmmakers Awards. In addition, BIFF hosts three major film Juries including FIPRESCI, NETPAC and Interfaith. Cine Sparks – the Australian Film Festival for Young People – provides quality world cinema and Master Classes to school-groups and young people. *Inquiries to:* St George Bank BIFF, GPO Box 15094, Brisbane City East, Queensland 4002 Australia. Tel: (61 7) 3007 3003. Fax: 3007 3030. e: biff@biff.com.au. Web: www.stgeorgebiff.com.au.

Report 2008
This year the Festival presented more than 110 feature-length films from across the world. While much is made of where the films come from – this year 56 countries were represented – just as important is the mix of genre, the

Film-maker Morgan Spurlock was a very special guest at the 2008 St.George Bank Brisbane International Film Festival opening night (photo: Jimmy Malecki).

variety of themes, and the depth of challenge. With the Festival's focus on terrorism – understanding became an important theme of this year's Festival. Certainly, the Opening Night film – *Where in the World is Osama Bin Laden?* (Morgan Spurlock, 2008) – was made with the intention of breaking down cultural and religious misconceptions. Spurlock was in attendance and entertained and engaged with patrons into the early hours of the morning. **– Catherine Miller**, Publicist.

Buenos Aires International Independent Film Festival
March 25–April 5, 2009

The Buenos Aires International Independent Film Festival was created in 1999. Sections include the two Official Competitions, for features and shorts. 'Argentina – Brand-New Novelties' has, since 2001, highlighted the increasing production of independent films in Argentina, complemented by the 'Work in Progress' section. BAFICI also programmes sections dedicated to outstanding directors. *Inquiries to:* Buenos Aires Festival Internacional de Cine Independiente, Saenz Peña 832, 6 Piso, 1035 Capital Federal, Buenos Aires, Argentina. Tel: (54 11) 4328 3454. e: produccion@bafilmfest.com. www.bafici.gov.ar.

BUFF
March 10–14, 2009

In 2009, BUFF will celebrate its 26th annual Film Festival. BUFF shows about 100 films and the screening sections are: Competition, Short Film Competition, Panorama, New

Grethe Bøe with her award for The Ten Lives of Titanic the Cat

Nordic, Documentary, School Cinema Project, and Short Films. BUFF 2009 also sets focus on a SCREEN and we will focus on young people by screening their own films and create meeting points. BUFF:FF Financing Forum was organised for the first time 2007 and this event was a success. For BUFF 2009 we will organise the third edition of BUFF:FF, a new niche of importance to the festival, making the arena for professionals much larger. *Inquiries to:* BUFF - Filmfestival, PO Box 4277, SE 203 14 Malmö, Sweden. Tel: (46 40) 239211. e: info@buff.se. Web: www.buff.se or www. financingforum.eu.

AWARDS 2008
City of Malmö Film Award: **The Ten Lives of Titanic the Cat** (Norway), Grethe Bøe.
Swedish Church Award: **Fighter** (Denmark), Natasha Arthy.
Youth Jury Award: **Keith** (USA), Todd Kessler.

County Council of Skåne Shortfilm Award:
Doggie (The Netherlands), Simone van
Dusseldorp.
Sydsvenskan and BUFF Achievement Award:
Lennart and Ylva Li Gustafsson, Sweden.

Report 2008
Danish film *Fighter* by Natasha Arty opened
the 25th BUFF Film Festival. Malmö City
hosted the anniversary party at City Hall.
Director Ella Lemhagen and producer Tomas
Michaelsson took part in the seminar 'Work
in Progress' talking about their new film *Patrik
1,5.* Young filmmakers experienced special
effects and other activities through workshops
at SCREEN. The Swedish Film Institute
introduced the director Jan Troell as the guest
of honour at School Cinema Day. – **Cecilia
Grubb**, Festival Producer.

Cairo International Film Festival
November 2009

The festival is organised by the General Union
of Arab Artists and is the oldest film festival in
the Middle East with competitions for feature
films, feature digital films and Arab films.
Inquiries to: Cairo International Film Festival,
17 Kasr el Nile St, Cairo, Egypt. Tel: (20 2) 2392
3562. e: info@cairofilmfest.com. Web: www.
cairofilmfest.com.

Cannes International Film Festival
May 13–24, 2009

Cannes remains the world's top festival,
attracting key films, personalities and industry
professionals. The official selection includes
the Competition, films out of competition,
special screenings, 'Un Certain Regard',
short films in competition, Cinéfondation and
Cannes Classics (created 2004). The Marché
du Film, with facilities improved and extended
since 2000 (Producers network, Short Film
Corner) is part of the official organisation.
Inquiries to: Festival de Cannes, 3, rue Amélie,
75007 Paris, France. Tel: (33 1) 5359 6100. Fax:
5359 6110. e: festival@festival-cannes.fr. Web:
www.festival-cannes.com.

Cannes International Film Festival – International Village

AWARDS 2008
Palme d'Or: **The Class** (France), Laurent Cantet.
Grand Prix: **Gommorah** (Italy), Matteo Garrone.
Best Director: **Three Monkeys** (Turkey), Nuri
Bilge Ceylan.
Best Screenplay: **The Silence of Lorna**
(Belgium), Jean-Pierre & Luc Dardenne.
Best Actress: Sandra Corveloni, Argentina.
Best Actor: Benicio Del Toro, Puerto Rico
Jury Prize: **Il divo** (Italy), Paolo Sorrentino
Vulcain Prize: **Il divo** (Italy), Paolo Sorrentino
Special Prize: Catherine Deneuve, Clint
Eastwood

Cartagena International Film Festival
February 27–March 8, 2009

Since 1960, the festival has become the
focus for Latin American films that compete
for the India Catalina Award. The festival
comprises features, shorts, documentaries,
tributes to Latin American directors and a
film and TV market. *Inquiries to:* Cartagena
International Film Festival, Centro, Calle San
Juan de Dios, Baluarte San Francisco Javier,
Cartagena, Colombia. Tel: (57 5) 664 2345. e:
prensa@festicinecartagena.org. Web: www.
festicinecartagena.org.

Chicago International Film Festival
October 8—21, 2009

The Chicago International Film Festival is
among the oldest competitive events in North
America. It spotlights the latest work by established international directors and newcomers
showcasing over a hundred features and more

than forty short films during the festival. It bestows its highest honour, the Gold Hugo, on the best feature in the International Competition, with separate prizes for documentaries, student films and shorts. Chicago is one of two US sites to award the FIPRESCI prize for first- and second-time directors, judged by top international critics. *Inquiries to:* Chicago International Film Festival, 30 E Adams St, Suite 800, Chicago, IL 60603, USA. Tel: (1 312) 683 0121. Fax: 683 0122. e: info@chicagofilmfestival.com. Web: www.chicagofilmfestival.com.

Cinekid Festival
October 18–25, 2009

Cinekid Festival is an annual film, television and new media festival for children that is held in Amsterdam. Every year, during the autumn break, more than 40,000 children are given an opportunity to attend one or more of the two hundred media productions that Cinekid presents: feature films, children's documentaries, short films, animation, TV series and single plays, cross-media productions, interactive installations and workshops. The main festival is held in Amsterdam, but approximately thirty satellite festivals are held in cities all over the Netherlands. Cinekid for Professionals is the place to be for anybody involved with children and media. Readings, seminars, a chance to meet fellow professionals and viewings of the best and latest international productions – plus all the information about them. *Inquiries to:* Cinekid Festival, Korte Leidsedwarsstraat 12,

Excited children enjoying a really successful Cinekid Festival

1017 RC Amsterdam, Netherlands. Tel: (31 20) 531 7890. Fax: 531 7899. e: info@cinekid.nl. Web: www.cinekid.nl

AWARDS 2008
Film
Cinekid Lion Jury Award: **Niko** (Finland), Michael Hegner and Kari Juusonen.
Cinekid Lion Audience Award: **Niko** (Finland), Michael Hegner and Kari Juusonen.
Television
Cinekid Kinderkast Jury Award Fiction: **De Daltons, de jongensjaren** (The Netherlands), Rita Horst.
Cinekid Kinderkast Jury Award Non-Fiction: **Overleven in Nederland: RAUW** (The Netherlands), Anneloek Sollart.
Cinekid Kinderkast Audience Award Fiction: **Het Huis Anubis** (The Netherlands), Dennis Bots.
Cinekid Kinderkast Audience Award Non-Fiction: **Taarten van Abel, Zomerspecial** (The Netherlands), Onno Krijnen.
De Golden Cinekid Kinderkast: **De Daltons, de jongensjaren** (The Netherlands), Rita Horst.
New Media
Cinekid New Media Jury Award: **Klokhuis Game Studio** (The Netherlands), IJsfontein Interactive Media, NPS.
Cinekid New Media Audience award: **Mario Kart Wii**, Wii, Nintendo.

Report 2008
Cinekid 2008 opened with the latest Miyazaki Hayao film, *Ponyo on the Cliff by the Sea.* The film competition programme consisted of fifteen films from thirteen different countries. Within the television programme, Dutch chil-

dren's television series like *Sterke verhalen uit Zoutvloed*, *De avonturen van Pim en Pom* and *Kikker & Vriendjes* premiered. The Cinekid New Media Lab was bigger than ever (1,200 square metres), housing around thirty interactive installations, games and workshops for children. The festival welcomed important guests from all over the world, including Mark Walsh, Supervising Animator at Disney and Pixar, and Michael DiMartino and Bryan Konietzko, the creators of the successful series *Avatar – The Last Airbender*. Walsh, DiMartino and Konietzko spoke at seminars for professionals, but also attended the Cinekid Media Lab for children. The members of the Cinekid 2008 juries were: Film Jury: Kasper Barfoot (Denmark), Rock Demers (Canada), Firoze Bulbulia (South Africa), Maria Bollini Lucisano (Italy) and Sabine Veenendaal (The Netherlands). Television Jury: Dany Deprez (Belgium), Mieke de Jong (The Netherlands), Walter van der Kooi (The Netherlands), Chris Silos (The Netherlands) and Signe Zeilich-Jensen (The Netherlands). New Media Jury: Corné van Delft (The Netherlands), Marinka Copier (The Netherlands), Michael van Eeden (The Netherlands), Carla Hoekendijk (The Netherlands) and Ilone Bloemen (The Netherlands). – **Elvira Pouw**, Assistent Marketing & Communicatie.

Cinéma Tous Ecrans
November 2–8, 2009

Cinéma Tous Ecrans featured amongst the world's fifty best film festivals, labelled 'indispensable and unmissable' by Variety. Cinéma Tous Ecrans will be celebrating its 15th edition in Geneva from November 2 to November 8, 2009. In 2008, Cinéma Tout Ecran became Cinéma TouS EcranS, a festival for all screens. Renowned for their groundbreaking aspirations from day one, the festival's organisers remain convinced that visual supports are beyond artistic hierarchy. Because of this, the festival continues to open itself up to all existing types of screens, those of today and tomorrow - television screens, cinema screens, computer screens and even mobile phones. *Inquiries to:* Leo Kaneman,

Director, Cinéma Tous Ecrans, Maison des Arts du Grütli, 16 rue Général Dufour, CP 5730, CH – 1211 Geneva 11, Switzerland. Tel: (41 22) 800 1554. Fax: 329 3747. e: info@cinema-tous-ecrans.ch. Web: www.cinema-tous-ecrans.ch.

AWARDS 2008
International Competition
Reflet d'Or for Best Film: **Chega de Saudade** (Brazil), Laís Bodanzky.
Reflet d'Or for Best Direction: Ruben Östlund for **Involuntary** (Sweden).
Prix Tudor Best Female Performance: Ursula Werner for **Wolke 9** (Germany).
Prix Tudor Best Male Performance: Yiorgos Symeonidis for **Correction** (Greece)
Prix Titra Film SA for the Encouragement of Theatrical Distribution: **Correction** (Greece), Thanos Anastopoulos.
FIPRESCI Award: **Frozen River** (USA), Courtney Hunt.
Youth Jury Award: **Hunger** (UK), Steve McQueen.
Youth Jury Special Mention: **Yo Soy Otro** (Colombia), Oscar Campo.
Audience Award: **Brothers** (Switzerland), Igaal Niddam.
Regards d'Aujourd'hui Competition
Reflet d'Or for Best Film: **Skin** (The Netherlands), Hanro Smitsman.
Actua Films Award: **Girls** (Hungary), Anna Faur.
International Series, Collections & Long Dramas Competition
Reflet d'Or for Best Series: **Capadocia** (Mexico), Javier Patrón.
Reflet d'Or for Best Collection & Long Drama: **Album** (Denmark), Hella Joof.
Audience Award for Best Series: **Ashes to Ashes** (UK), Matthew Graham and Ashley Pharoah.
New Screens for Drama Competition
Reflet d'Or for Best Online Series: **Quarterlife** (USA), Marshall Herskovitz.

Reflet d'Or for Best Self-Produced Film for the Internet: **4960** (USA), Wing-Yee Wu.
Reflet d'Or for Best Interactive Multimedia Fiction: **Meanwhile** (Canada), David Clark.
Exceptional Award for New Screens-TSR: **La Planque** (France), Akim Isker.
Grand Prix Cinéma Tout Mobile: **Phone or Fun** (Switzerland), Loïc Oswald.
Jury Award Cinéma Tout Mobile: **Mobile Game** (Switzerland), Alexandre Caniglia.
TV5 Monde Award for Best French-Speaking Film Cinéma Tout Mobile: **Mobile Game** (Switzerland), Alexandre Caniglia.
Audience Award Cinéma Tout Mobile: **L'Amour C'est...** (Switzerland), Didier de Iaco.
Swiss Short Films Competition
Reflet d'Or for Best Swiss Short Film: **Heaven**, Mohcine Besri.
Swisscom Audience Award for Best Swiss Short Film: **Big Sur**, Pierre-Adrian Irlé and Valentin Rotelli.
Other Awards
Reflet d'Or for Lifetime Achievement: Charles Burnett.

Reflet d'Or for best film: Laís Bodansky's **Chega de saudade**

Prix TV5 Monde for Best French-Speaking Fiction: **Fortunes** (France), Stéphane Meunier.
Swissperform Award for Best TV Film: **Jimmie** (Switzerland), Tobias Ineichen.
Swissperform Award for Best Female Performance: Stephanie Japp for **Jimmie** (Switzerland).
Swissperform Award for Best Male Performance: Joel Basman for **Jimmie** (Switzerland).

Report 2008

An ideal international meeting place between television, cinema and multimedia, Cinema Tous Ecrans this year again captivated its public thanks to the quality and diversity of its programme. No less than 14 feature films within the International Competition and ten feature films within the Regards d'Aujourd'hui section took us on an exhilarating world tour of cinemas. The International Series, Collections & Long Dramas section displayed a diverse and original selection of television premieres. Not forgetting nearly twenty Swiss short films, a day of promising Nouveaux Ecrans, together with special events and the presence of many international actors and directors all contributed to the success of this 14th edition. After being considered last year by *Variety* magazine as one of fifty film festivals not to be missed, Cinema Tous Ecrans once again proves how appealing it is and that it knows how to generate keen interest (with 29,000 visitors), thanks to its specificity: the multiplicity of screens. **– Jeffrey Hodgson**.

Clermont-Ferrand Short Film Festival
Late January–early February 2010

International, National and 'Lab' competitions for 35mm films and digital works on DigiBeta and Beta SP, all completed after January 1, 2009, of forty minutes or less. All the entries will be listed in the Market catalogue. Many other side programmes (retrospectives and panoramas). *Inquiries to:* Clermont-Ferrand Short Film Festival, La Jetée, 6 Place Michel-de L'Hospital, 63058 Clermont-Ferrand Cedex 1, France. Tel: (33 473) 916 573. Fax: 921 193.

e: info@clermont-filmfest.com. Web: www.
clermont-filmfest.com.

AWARDS 2008
Grand Prix
International: **Auf der Stecke** (Germany/
Switzerland), Reto Caffi.
National: **Como Todo el Mundo** (France),
Franco Lolli.
Lab: **Pikapika, Lightning Doodle Project**
(Japan), Takeshi Nagata and Kazue Monno.
Audience Prize
International: **The Wednesdays** (Ireland),
Conor Ferguson.
National: **C'est Dimanche!** (France), Samir
Guesmi.
Lab: **45cm** (Denmark), Charlotte Sieling and
Annette Kristina Olesen.

Copenhagen Film Festivals
BUSTER September 18–27, 2009
CPH:DOX November 6–15, 2009
CPH:PIX April 16–26, 2009

Copenhagen Film Festivals is the result of the
merger between the Danish capital's major film
festival organisations: Copenhagen International
Film Festival and the NatFilm Festival. The new
festival power station today houses Denmark's
three major international film festivals: CPH:PIX
– the highly anticipated new feature-film
festival focusing on new filmmaking talents
and new technology; BUSTER – Copenhagen
International Film Festival for Children and
Youth; CPH:DOX – Copenhagen International
Documentary Film Festival. The organisation
also hosts two film markets: September's
Copenhagen Film Market, exclusively for
invited film professionals, has a section for
new Danish feature films and one for Nordic
films for Children and Youth; DOX Market for
international documentaries is held during
the festival in November. *Inquiries to:* Øster
Farimagsgade 16B, DK-2100 Copenhagen Ø,
Denmark. Tel: Buster (45) 3312 0005, CPH:DOX
(45) 3393 0734, CPH:PIX (45) 3312 0005. e:
buster@buster.dk, info@cphdox.dk, info@
cphpix.dk. Web: www.cphfilmfestivals.dk.

AWARDS 2008
CPH:DOX
DOX:AWARD: **Burma VJ** (Denmark), Anders
Østergaard.
BUSTER
Best Children's Film: **Dragon Hunters** (France/
Germany), Guillaume Ivernel and Arthur Qwak.
Best Youth Film: **The Tracey Fragments**
(Canada), Bruce MacDonald.

Cork Film Festival
Early November 2009

Cork Film Festival is Ireland's largest and oldest film festival. Founded in 1956, the eclectic
programme includes a World Cinema strand,
a Documentary Panorama, an Irish showcase,
live cinema, and experimental work. Latterly
the festival has platformed New Arab Cinema.
In particular the festival celebrates the art of
the short film. In 1970 Cork was the founding
city of the International Short Film Conference
and in 2005 the festival organised an International Short Film Symposium, a major gathering of short filmmakers, programmers, academics and industry professionals. *Inquiries
to:* Corona Cork Film Festival, Emmet House,
Emmet Place, Cork, Ireland. Tel: (353 21) 427
1711. Fax: 427 5945. e: info@corkfilmfest.org.
Web: www.corkfilmfest.org.

AWARDS 2008
Best Irish Short: **Driving Lesson**, Cecilia
McAllister.
*Claire Lynch Award for Best First-Time Irish
Director:* **The Door**, Juanita Wilson
Best International Short: **2 Birds** (Iceland),
Rúnar Rúnarsson.
Prix UIP Cork for Best European Short: **14**
(UK), Asitha Amaresekere.
Audience Award for Best International Short:
On The Line (Switzerland), Reto Caffi.
Audience Award for Best Irish Short: **Out Of
The Blue**, Michael Lavelle.
Award of the Festival for Best Short: **Journey
To The Forest** (Germany), Jorn Staeger.
Youth Jury Award for Best International Short:
Giants (Italy), Fabio Mollo.
Outlook Award for Best Lesbian LGBT Short:

Terence Davies with Festival director, Mick Hannigan, at Cork Opera House during the Corona Cork Film Festival in 2008 (photo: Rose Gowan)

James (Ireland), Connor Clements.
Gradam Gael Linn for Best Short in the Irish Language: **Foireann Codladh**, Danann Breathnach.
'Made In Cork' Award for Best Short: **Matty Kiely's Last Day**, Ed Godsell.

Report 2008

The 53rd edition of Cork Film Festival attracted some 30,000 admissions to a wide-ranging programme of screenings, talks and events. The festival welcomed 250 guests, among whom was Terence Davies who participated in a retrospective of his work. Other guests included Rahmin Bahrani (*Goodbye Solo*), Enda Walsh (*Hunger*), Peter Greenaway (*Nightwatching*), Paul Merton and Neil Brand (*Silent Clowns*), John 'super8' Porter, cinematographer Robbie Ryan and a host of documentary and short filmmakers. New Arab Cinema was highlighted in a special strand and four programmes of Mexican shorts were screened. Some 46 programmes of shorts were screened over the eight days of the festival. The latest Irish productions of shorts, documentaries and features were premiered. 'Meet the Filmmaker' sessions, talks and masterclasses were opportunities for discussion between audiences and filmmakers. The festival was the occasion of the world premiere *BC/AD*, the final work by the late artist and filmmaker Ian Breakwell.
– Mick Hannigan, Festival Director.

Crossroads Film Festival
April 2–5, 2009

The Crossroads Film Festival is the largest film festival in Mississippi and commemorates its tenth anniversary in 2009. Founded in 1999 in the Capital city of Jackson – known as 'The Crossroads of the South' – the four-day festival was designed as a meeting place where the strands and influences of art, themes and culture come together. Every event celebrates film, music, and food, along with the great culture and heritage of Mississippi. Each year the festival provides a cross-cultural backdrop of screenings, concerts and receptions. Over the years, the festival has celebrated filmmakers with ties to Mississippi, beginning with Robert Altman in its premiere year and continuing to native Morgan Freeman, new resident Joey Lauren Adams, and Vicksburg native Charles Burnett. Crossroads has been the first Mississippi stop for most films made in Mississippi: *Ballad*, *Big Bad Love*, *The Rising Place*, *I'll Fly Away*, *Cries of Silence*, *Red Dirt* and *Blossom Time*. In addition to young filmmakers' workshops and filmmaker forums, the Mississippi Film Office Summit of independent filmmakers from across the state is also presented. *Inquiries to:* Crossroads Film Festival, PO Box 22604, Jackson, MS 39225, USA. Tel/fax: (1 601) 510 9148. e: crossroadsfilmfest@yahoo.com. Web: www.crossroadsfilmfest.com.

AWARDS 2008

Feature: **Disappearances** (USA), Jay Craven.
Documentary: **Beyond the Call** (USA), Adrian Belic.
Short Documentary: **Hero, Wings Are Not Necessary to Fly** (Spain), Angel Loza.
Short: **Spider** (Australia), Nash Edgerton.
Student: **Last Day of December** (Romania), Bogdan George Apetri.
Animation: **The Hunger Artist** (USA), Tom Gibbons.
Experimental: **Doxology** (USA), Michael Langan.
Music Video: **Fashionable** (USA), Cameron McCasland.
Youth: **What's Up?** (USA), Curtis Everitt.
The Ruma: April Grayson for **Another Word For Family** (USA).
Director's Choice Award: **Of All the Things** (USA), Jody Lambert.
Audience Choice Award: **Pretty Ugly People** (USA), Tate Taylor and **Control** (USA), Anton Corbijn.

Starz Denver Film Festival
November 12–22, 2009

The Starz Denver Film Festival presents over 200 films from around the world and plays host to more than 150 filmmakers. Including new international features, cutting-edge independent fiction and non-fiction works, shorts and a variety of special programmes, the Starz Denver Film Festival also features the best in student work with the inclusion of the First Look Student Film section. SDFF pays tribute to established film artists with retrospective screenings of their works. Entry fee: $40 ($20 for students). The Denver Film Society also programmes the Starz FilmCenter, Colorado's only cinematheque, daily throughout the year. *Inquiries to:* Denver Film Society at the Starz FilmCenter, 900

Auraria Parkway, Denver, Colorado 80204, USA. Tel: (1 303) 595 3456. Fax: 595 0956. e: dfs@denverfilm.org. Web: www.denverfilm.org.

AWARDS 2008

John Cassavetes Award: Bill Pullman.
Stan Brakhage Vision Award: Carolee Schneemann.
Emerging Filmmaker Award: **Sita Sings the Blues** (USA), Nina Paley.
The Maysles Brothers Documentary Award: **Another Planet** (Hungary), Ferenc Moldoványi.
Krzysztof Kieslowski Award for Best Feature Film: **Moscow, Belgium** (Belgium), Christophe van Rompaey.
Starz People's Choice Award (Feature): **Katyn** (Poland), Andrzej Wajda.
Starz People's Choice Award (Documentary): **They Killed Sister Dorothy** (USA), Daniel Junge.
Starz People's Choice Award (Short): **Grandma O'Grimm's Sleeping Beauty** (Ireland), Nicky Phelan.

Report 2008
The 31st Starz Denver Film Festival kicked off

with a Red Carpet premiere of Rian Johnson's newest caper, *The Brother's Bloom*, and played host to over 150 filmmaker guests for the following eleven days. With notable directors such as James Gray and Don Hertzfeldt and tribute guests Majid Majidi, Thomas Imbach, Carolee Schneemann and Wally Pfister, the 2008 Festival set new records for screening attendance. The festival concluded with the presentation of the 2008 John Cassavetes Award to actor Bill Pullman. **– Neil Truglio**, Director of Marketing.

Dubai International Film Festival
Mid December 2009

Reflecting Dubai's cosmopolitan and multi-cultural character, the festival showcases a wide selection of features, shorts and docu-mentaries from around the world. The festival aims to establish itself as a major international festival, while continuing to act as a platform for showcasing excellence in Arab Cinema and simultaneously contributing to the develop-ment and growth of the regional industry and talent. As one of the world's fastest-growing business and tourist destinations, Dubai provides an ideal meeting point for industry friends and colleagues from around the globe. The festival creates an exciting atmosphere for exchanging ideas among a group of progres-sive film industry professionals. In addition, the networking initiatives hosted by DIFF provide participants and guests with a favourable set-ting for conducting business. The festival con-sists of twelve distinct programming sections, featuring a total of approximately a hundred films. *Inquiries to:* Dubai Media City, PO Box 53777, Dubai, United Arab Emirates. Tel: (971 4) 391 3378. e: diffinfo @dubaimediacity.ae. Web: www.dubaifilmfest.com.

Edinburgh International Film Festival
June 17–28, 2009

The festival devotes itself to discovering and promoting the very best in international cinema - and to embracing, celebrating and de-bating changes and developments in the global film industry. Key to the EIFF mission is the identification, exposure and development of the filmmaking legends of the future. *Inquiries to:* Edinburgh International Film Festival, 88 Lothian Rd, Edinburgh EH3 9BZ, Scotland. Tel: (44 131) 228 4051. Fax: 229 5501. e: info@ed-filmfest.org.uk. Web: www.edfilmfest.org.uk.

AWARDS 2008
Standard Life Audience Award: **Man On Wire** (UK), James Marsh.
Michael Powell Award for Best New British Feature: **Somers Town**, Shane Meadows.
Skillset New Director's Award: **Marianna Palka** (UK), Dick Good.
UK Film Council Award for Best British Short Film: **Son**, Daniel Mulloy.
McLaren Award for Best New British Animation in Partnership with BBC Film Network: **Space Travel According to John**, Jamie Stone and Ander Jedenfors.
European Film Academy Short Film - Prix UIP: **2 Birds** (Iceland), Rúnar Rúnarsson.
Short Scottish Documentary Award Supported by Baillie Gifford: **Christmas With Dad** (UK),Conor McCormack.
PPG Award for Best Performance in a British Feature Film: Robert Carlyle for **Summer**.
Best Documentary Award: **Encounters at the End of the World** (USA), Werner Herzog.

Espoo Ciné International Film Festival
August 21–30, 2009

Espoo Ciné has established itself as the annual showcase of contemporary European, primarily long feature, cinema in Finland. This year Espoo Ciné is celebrating its 20th

celebrates the 20th anniversary edition
21.–30. August 2008
www.espoocine.fi

Executive director Jenni Ukkonen with actor Greg Timmermans representing **Ben X** *at the opening reception of the 19th Espoo Ciné IFF on 19th August 2008 (photo: Pauli Vanhala)*

anniversary with a ten-day festival. The traditional section should appeal to every movie buff in Finland, and the growing fantasy selection should attract those hungry for stimulation of the imagination. Annual special programmes present, for example, Spanish and Italian gems, films from Eastern Europe, documentaries, gay films and US indies, not to forget the best of contemporary Finnish cinema, outdoor screenings, retrospectives, sneak previews, seminars and distinguished guests. *Inquiries to:* Espoo Ciné, PO Box 95, FI-02101 Espoo, Finland. Tel: (358 9) 466 599. Fax: 466 458. e: office@espoocine.fi. Web: www.espoocine.fi.

Report 2008
The six-day festival gathered 23,000 film enthusiasts and professionals together. The festival hosted the annual Méliès d'Argent Competition for the best European fantasy films. The jury, chaired by the Finnish director Hanna Maylett (*Sisters Apart*, 2008), chose the winners: the feature films competition was won by *The Substitute* by Danish Ole Bornedal and the short films competition by *Curse of the Remote Island* by the Finnish animator Chrzu. **– Jenni Ukkonen**, Executive Director.

Fajr International Film Festival
January 31–February 10, 2009
Iranian International Market for Films and TV Programmes
January 30–February 3, 2009
Apart from the International Competition, the programmes include 'Festival of Festivals' (a selection of outstanding films presented at other international festivals),

'Special Screenings' (films of documentary or narrative content which introduce cinema or cultural developments in certain geographical regions) and retrospectives. The newly created Competition of Spiritual Cinema emphasises cinema's role as a rich medium for the expression of the essence of religious faith. Another new addition is the Competition of Asian Cinema, organised with the aim of promoting film art and industry in Asian countries. Festival Director: Majid Shah-Hosseini. During the festival, the Farabi Cinema Foundation also organises the Iranian International Market for Films and TV Programmes. *Inquiries to:* Fajr International Film Festival, 2nd Floor, 19 Delbar Alley, Toos St, Valiye Asr Ave, Tehran 19617-44973, Iran. Tel: (98 21) 2273 5090/4801. Fax: 2273 4801. e: office@fajrfestival.ir. Web: www.fajrfestival.ir.

AWARDS 2008

Best Film: **Wind Blows in the Meadow** (Iran), Khosro Masoumi.
Special Jury Prize: **Very Well Thank You** (France), Emmanuelle Cuau.

Rohollah Hejazi receives the Crystal Simorgh Award for Best Debut Film

Best Director: Semih Kaplanoglu for **Egg** (Turkey).
Best Script: Francisco Vargas for **The Violin** (Mexico).
Best Performance: Galina Vishnevskaya for **Alexandra** (Russia).
Best Technical or Artistic Achievement: Ozgur Eken for **Egg** (Turkey).
Best Short Film: **LHO** (Germany), Jan Zabiel and Kristof Kannegeisser.

Report 2008

Events included a tribute to the Swedish

Hengameh Qaziani, winner of the Best Actress Award

master of cinema, Ingmar Bergman, with the screening of nine of his films plus a retrospective of the Russian director Nikita Mikhalkov, including the films *At Home Among Strangers*, *The Barber of Siberia*, *Burnt by the Sun*, *Five Evenings*, *Unfinished Pieces for the Piano Player*, *Without Witness* and *Several Days from the Life of Oblomov*, and finally a Panorama of Georgian Cinema with films by Sergei Parajanov, Eldar Senglaya, Nikoloz Sanishvili, Rezo Chkheidze and Tengiz Abuladze. – **Masoud Ahmadian**, Festival Manager.

Fantasporto
February 20–28, 2009

The 29th edition of the Oporto International Film Festival takes place in theatres of Oporto and the North of Portugal, mostly at the Rivoli – Teatro Municipal, Teatro Sá da Bandeira and Warner Lusomundo Theatres (a total of about 5,000 seats). Apart from the Competitive Sections (Fantasy, Directors Week, Orient Express) the Festival will also includes the Sections 'Panorama of the Portuguese Cinema', 'Anima-te' for younger audiences, 'Première' for previews and vintage features and 'Love Connection' section. The Retrospectives will include the Portuguese director José Fonseca e Costa, among others. Director: Mário Dorminsky. *Inquiries to:* Fantasporto, Rua Anibal Cunha 84, Sala 1.6, 4050-048 Porto, Portugal. Tel: (35 1) 222 058 819 Fax: 222 058 823. e: info@fantasporto. online.pt. Web: www.fantasporto.com.

AWARDS 2008

Fantasy Section
Film: **REC** (Spain), Jaume Balagueró and Paco Plaza.
Special Jury Award: **How to Get Rid of Others** (Denmark), Anders Ronnow Klarlund.
Director: Juan Antonio Bayona, **El Orfanato** (Spain).
Actor: Marc Borkowski, **The Ungodly** (USA).
Actress: Belen Rueda, **El Orfanato** (Spain).
Screenplay: Luis Piedrahita and Rodrigo Sopeña, **La Habitacion de Fermat** (Spain).
Best Cinematography: Gabor Medvigy, **Dolina** (Hungary).
Best Short: Rojo Red (Colombia), Juan Manuel Betancourt.
18th Director's Week
Film: **Opium, Diary of a Madwoman** (Hungary), Janos Szasz.
Director: Roy Andersson, **You, The Living** (Sweden).
Special Jury Award: **The Lovebirds** (Portugal), Bruno de Almeida.
Actor: Sassom Gabai, **The Band's Visit** (France/Israel).
Actress: Kirsti Studo, **Opium, Diary of a Madwoman** (Hungary).
Screenplay: Steve Buscemi and David Schechter, **Interview** (USA).
Orient Express Competitive Section
Film: **Triangle** (Hong Kong), Ringo Lam, Johnnie To and Tsui Hark.
Special Jury Award: **Breath** (South Korea), Kim Ki Duk.
Méliès D'Argent: **Habitacion de Fermat** (Spain), Luis Piedrahita and Rodrigo Sopeña.
Méliès D'Argent Short Film: **Ark** (Poland), Grzegorz Jonkajtys.
Critics Jury Award: **The Band's Visit** (France/Israel), Eran Kolirin.
Audience Award: **REC** (Spain), Jaume Balagueró and Paco Plaza.

Report 2008

With general praise for the quality of the selection, the latest edition of Fantasporto, Portugal's leading film festival has just ended. So much said the members of the jury of the three competitive sections (Fantasy,

Directors Week and Orient Express). Director Bruno de Almeida, whose career started in Fantasporto with the award-winning short *The Debt* followed by *On the Run*, came back with his latest, *The Lovebirds*, with Michael Imperioli, Ana Padrão and John Ventimiglia, to win the Special Award of the Directors Week. But it was in the Fantasy competition that the recent production of Spanish cinema came to full glory. *REC*, by Jaume Balagueró and Paco Plaza, received a six-minute ovation at the end of the screening, and became soon afterwards the winner of the Fantasporto 2008 Grand Prix-Best Film Award. Confirming the present vitality of the Spanish, *El Orfanato* by Juan António Bayona and produced by Guillermo del Toro and *La Habitacion de Fermat* by Rodrigo Sopeña and Luis Piedrahita will both be theatrically released very soon in Portugal. A frequent winner in Fantasporto, Danish cinema did not disappoint with *How to Get Rid of Others* by Anders Klarlund, receiving the important Fantasy Special Award. Visitors to Fantasporto included real icons of the film world, namely an actor who has played in his long career both God and the Devil, Max von Sydow, the celebrated Kelly LeBrock who came to Oporto for the opening of *The Mirror* in which she plays the leading role, and a Portuguese director, Fernando Lopes, whose body of work includes, among others, a film about boxing, a few good scoundrels and some women on the verge of many breakdowns. Fernando Lopes was, like Max von Sydow, the recipient of a Fantasporto Career Award. A second-time visitor to Oporto, a city she loved the first time, was Academy Award-nominated actress Karen Black.

Portuguese directors Manoel de Oliveira and Fernando Lopes, with the cinema critic João Lopes.

Fernando Lopes, one of the directors of the Cinema Novo, received a Career Award. His films *Crónica dos Bons Malandros*, *Belarmino*, *O Delfim* and *98 Octanas* were shown in a retrospective. The director also became an accidental actor in *The Lovebirds* by Bruno de Almeida, screened in the Directors Week Competition, rightfully playing the role of a film director. The list of guests included most of the directors of the films in the competitions, with 99-year-old and Oporto-born director Manoel de Oliveira leading the way. Also a noted presence was Jack Sholder, a former winner of the Best Film Award in Fantasporto 1988 with *The Hidden* and, this year, doing jury duty. Around 115,000 visitors and spectators animated the streets of downtown Oporto, walking to the Rivoli Theatre or to the nearby Sá da Bandeira Theatre and filling the city with great enthusiasm. The festival closing party, the Vampires Ball, brought, once again, many impersonators who danced to the sound of live music and DJs. The 2009 Fantasporto will be held, as usual, from the last week of February until the beginning of March in the

World Heritage City of Portwine. Welcome to Fantasporto 2009! – **Mário Dorminsky**, Festival Director.

Far East Film Festival
April 24–May 2, 2009

Annual themed event which, since 1998, has focused on Eastern Asian cinema. *Inquiries to:* Centro Espressioni Cinematografiche, Via Villalta 24, 33100 Udine, Italy. Tel: (39 04) 3229 9545. Fax: 3222 9815. e: fareastfilm@cecudine.org, Web: www.fareastfilm.com.

AWARDS 2008
Audience Award First Prize: **Gachi Boy, Wrestling With a Memory** (Japan), Koizumi Norihiro.
Audience Award Second Prize: **Adrift in Tokyo** (Japan), Miki Satoshi.
Audience Award Third Prize: **Fine, Totally Fine** (Japan), Fujita Yousuke.
Black Dragon Award First Prize: **Mad Detective** (Hong Kong), Johnnie To and Wai Ka Fai.
Black Dragon Award Second Prize: **Fine, Totally Fine** (Japan), Fujita Yousuke.
Black Dragon Award Third Prize: **Crows-Episode 0** (Japan), Miike Takashi.

Report 2008
The 10th Anniversary of Far East Film confirmed the great success of this Festival. The audience this year exceeded 50,000 spectators, including a large number of additional visitors, more than the event has ever hosted: 1,100 present from a dozen countries ranging from the United States to the Czech Republic plus almost 200 journalists

From left: Johnnie To, Wai Ka Fai, Kelly Lin, Lam Suet e Lau Ching Wan awarded for the film **Mad Detective** *(photo: Ricky Modena)*

and 42 representatives from international festivals. – **Sabrina Baracetti**, President.

Festival Des 3 Continents
November 24–December 1, 2009

The only annual competitive (with fiction and documentary) festival in the world for films that originate solely from Africa, Asia and Latin and Black America. It's one of the few festivals where genuine discoveries may still be made. From Hou Hsiao-hsien or Abbas Kiarostami in the 1980s, to Darejan Omirbaev or Jia Zangke, great filmmakers have been screened and acknowledged in Nantes. For 28 years, F3C has also charted the film history of the southern countries through retrospectives (genres, countries, actors and actresses), showing more than 1,200 films and bringing to light an unrecognised part of the world's cinematographic heritage. Festival Director: Philippe Reilhac. *Inquiries to:* Guillaume Marion, General Delegate, Festival des 3 Continents, BP 43302, 44033 Nantes Cedex 1, France. Tel: (33 2) 4069 7414. Fax:

4073 5522. e: festival@3continents.com. Web: www.3continents.com.

Filmfest Hamburg
September 24–October 1, 2009

Under the direction of Albert Wiederspiel, the renowned film festival takes place every year in the fall. Around 130 international films are screened as German or world premieres in the following sections: Agenda, KinderFilmfest Hamburg (Children's Filmfest Hamburg), TV Movies in cinema, Eurovisuell, Voila!, Vitrina, Nordlichter and Deluxe. The many facets of the programme range from art-house films to innovative mainstream cinema. The Douglas Sirk Award honours outstanding contributions to film culture and business. There are 40,000 admissions and about 1,000 industry professionals attend. Filmfest Hamburg also sees itself as a platform for cultural exchange and dialogue: in the past years, the festival has, among others, shed light on productions from Asia (from Iran to Japan and Korea) and Europe (from the UK and Scandinavia to France, Spain and Eastern Europe). *Inquiries to:* Filmfest Hamburg, Steintorweg 4, 20099 Hamburg, Germany. Tel: (49 40) 3991 9000. Fax: 3991 90010. e: info@filmfesthamburg.de. Web: www.filmfesthamburg.de.

Fort Lauderdale International Film Festival
Mid October–early November 2009

The festival features more than 200 films from 40 countries during the world's longest film event, with screenings in Miami, Palm Beach and Fort Lauderdale. Awards include Best Film, Best Foreign-Language Film, Best American Indie, Best Director, Actor, Screenplay, Best Florida Film and Kodak Student prizes for Narrative (over 20 minutes), Short Narrative (20 minutes or under), Documentary and Experimental. *Inquiries to:* The Fort Lauderdale International Film Festival, 1314 East Las Olas Blvd, Suite 007, Fort Lauderdale, FL 33301, USA. Tel: (1 954) 760 9898. Fax: 760 9099. e: info@fliff.com. Web: www.fliff.com.

Fribourg Film Festival
March 14–21, 2009

Features, shorts and documentaries from Asia, Africa and Latin America unspool at this Swiss event, with a competitive section. *Inquiries to:* Fribourg International Film Festival, Ancienne Gare, Case Postale 550, CH-1701 Fribourg, Switzerland. Tel: (41 26) 347 4200. Fax: 347 4201. e: info@fiff.ch. Web: www.fiff.ch.

AWARDS 2008
Grand Prix Le Regard d'Or: **Flower in the Pocket** (Malaysia), Liew Seng Tat.
Special Jury Award: **El Camino** (Costa Rica), Ishtar Yasin.
Swiss Oikocredit Award: **He Fengming** (China), Wang Bing.
General Public Award: **La Zona** (Mexico), Rodrigo Plà.
Ecumenical Jury Award: **El Camino** (Costa Rica), Ishtar Yasin.
FIPRESCI Jury Award: **With a Girl of Black Soil** (South Korea), Jeon Soo-il.
IFFS Jury 'Don Quijote Award': **With a Girl of Black Soil** (South Korea), Jeon Soo-il.
Ex-Change Award: **God Man Dog** (Taiwan), Singing Chen.

Ghent International Film Festival
October 6–17, 2009

Belgium's most prominent annual film event which attracts an attendance of 110,000 plus and is selected by *Variety* as one of the fifty 'must attend' festivals due to its unique focus on film music. This competitive festival awards grants worth up to $120,000 and screens around 130 features and 50 shorts, most without a Benelux distributor. Besides the official competition focusing on the impact of music on film, the festival includes the following sections: Festival Previews (World, European, Benelux or Belgian premieres), World Cinema (films from all over the world, mainly without a distributor), retrospectives, a programme of media art, film music concerts, seminars and a tribute to an important international film maker.

The festival's Joseph Plateau Awards are the highest honours in Benelux. Presented for the first time in 2001, the festival also hands out the World Soundtrack Awards, judged by some 270 international composers. Every year in October, the Ghent Film Festival is the meeting point for film music composers and fans worldwide. *Inquiries to:* Ghent International Film Festival, 40B Leeuwstraat, B-9000 Ghent, Belgium. Tel: (32 9) 242 8060. Fax: 221 9074. e: info@filmfestival.be. Web: www.filmfestival.be. and www.worldsoundtrackawards.com.

AWARDS 2008

Impact of Music on Film Competition
Grand Prix for Best Film: **The Market** (Germany/Turkey), Ben Hopkins.
Georges Delerue Prize for Best Music: Tolibhon Shahidi, **Two-Legged Horse** (Iran).
SABAM Award for Best Screenplay: Sylvie Verheyde, **Stella** (France).
Robert Wise Award for Best Director: Bent Hamer, **O'Horten** (Norway).
Special Jury Mention for Acting: Yolande Moreau for her role in **Seraphine**, Hadji Gul for his role in **Kabuli Kid**, Genco Erkal for his role in **The Market** and Karole Rocher for her role in **Stella**.
Prix UIP/Ghent for Best European Short: **Zwemles** (Belgium), Danny De Vent.
Xplore! Award: **Hunger** (UK), Steve McQueen.
National Lottery Award for the Best Belgian Short: **Songes d'Une Femme de Menage**, Banu Akseki.
Special Mention: **Jazzed** (Belgium), Anton Setola.
Ace Award for Flemish Student Shorts:

35th Ghent International Film Festival (photo: Luk Monsaert)

Finding Home (Belgium), Christopher Daley.
Port of Ghent Audience Award: **Young@Heart** (UK), Stephen Walker.
Audience Award: **Hunger** (UK), Steve McQueen.

Report 2008

At the 35th Anniversary edition of the Ghent Film Festival 130 features were presented from all over the world to an audience of 115,000 people. The festival was attended by Woody Harrelson, Richard Jenkins, Laurie MacDonald, Walter F. Parkes, Emmanuelle Béart, Samira Makhmalbaf, Guillermo Arriaga and Walter Salles. The festival celebrated film music with five concerts: John Williams (over 3,000 spectators), Gabriel Yared's tribute to Anthony Minghella, Clint Mansell and The Sonus Quartet, That's All Folks! (celebration of folk music in film with Belgian band Kadril) and the World Soundtrack Awards Ceremony (Angelo Badalamenti & Dario Marianelli performed). – **Wim De Witte**, Programmer.

Giffoni International Film Festival
July 2009

Located in Giffoni Valle Piana, a small town about forty minutes from Naples, the Giffoni

International Film Festival for Children and Young People was founded in 1971 by Claudio Gubitosi to promote films for youthful audiences and families. Now includes five competitive sections: Kidz (animated and fiction feature-length films and short films that tell fantastic stories, juried by 250 children aged six to nine); First Screens (fiction features and animated shorts, mainly fantasy and adventure, juried by 500 children aged 9 to 12); Free 2 Fly sees 400 teenagers (aged 12 to 14) assessing features and shorts about the pre-adolescent world; Y GEN has 350 jurors (aged 15 to 19) and takes a curious look at cinema for young people. Troubled Gaze has 100 jurors (from 19 years old) and is the section which explores the relationship between children and parents. *Inquiries to:* Giffoni Film Festival, Cittadella del Cinema, Via Aldo Moro 4, 84095 Giffoni Valle Piana, Salerno, Italy. Tel: (39 089) 802 3001. Fax: 802 3210. e: info@giffoniff.it. Web: www.giffoniff.it.

Gijón International Film Festival
November 19–28, 2009

One of Spain's oldest festivals (47th edition in 2009), Gijón is now at the peak of its popularity. Having firmly established itself as a barometer of new film trends worldwide, it draws a large and enthusiastic public. Gijón has built on its niche as a festival for young people, programming innovative and independent films made by and for the young, including retrospectives, panoramas, exhibitions and concerts. Alongside the lively Official Section, sidebars celebrate directors who have forged new paths in filmmaking. *Inquiries to:* Gijón International Film Festival, PO Box 76, 33201 Gijon, Spain. Tel: (34 98) 518 2940. Fax: 518 2944. e: info@gijonfilmfestival.com. Web: www.gijonfilmfestival.com.

goEast Festival of Central and Eastern European Film in Wiesbaden
April 22–28, 2009

Founded in 2001 by the Deutsches Filminstitut-DIF with the goal of acquainting a wider audience with the films and cultural landscape of Central and Eastern Europe. From the outset, goEast viewed itself as a forum for East-West dialogue, meaning the festival provides guests with ample opportunity to learn more about each other, to discuss and reflect upon topical issues. The fast-moving process of transformation underway in Central and Eastern Europe, along with the question of a common European identity, are important and much-discussed themes. goEast provides a high-quality festival programme, with a mix of current productions and historical series, a competition for feature and documentary films with attractive awards, an extensive students' programme and related events. The festival hosts FIPRESCI Jury. Deadline: end Dec. *Inquiries to:* Deutsches Filminstitut - DIF, goEast Film Festival, Schaumainkai 41, D-60596 Frankfurt AM, Germany. Tel: (49 69) 9612 20650. Fax: 9612 20669. e:info@filmfestival-goeast.de. Web: www.filmfestival-goeast.de.

AWARDS 2008
The Škoda Award for the Best Film and FIPRESCI Prize: **Magnus** (Estonia/UK), Kadri Kõusaar.
Documentary Award - 'Remembrance and Future': **The Flower Bridge** (Romania), Thomas Ciulei.
Award of the City of Wiesbaden for Best Director: Stefan Arsenijević for **Love and Other Crimes**, (Austria/Germany/Serbia/Slovenia).
Award of the Federal Foreign Office: **At the River** (Ukraine), Eva Nejman.

Report 2008
goEast welcomed 300 invited guests from the world of film to Wiesbaden, and anticipated a lively cinematic week in which directors, producers and actors presented their films in the Caligari FilmBühne. Altogether, goEast

Award winners and jury of the Robert Bosch Stiftung's Co-Production Prize for Young German and Eastern/South Eastern European Filmmakers at goEast Film Festival 2008 (photo: Michael Loewa)

counted more than 9,500 visitors in the course of the festival and accompanying programme. Alongside the competition, with ten current fiction films and six documentaries, the eight festival sections span an interesting range of cinematic highpoints and fascinating cultural discoveries. There was an impressive response to the homage to Armenian director and artist Sergei Paradzhanov and the Portrait of young Hungarian filmmaker Benedek Fliegauf. The separate sections brought together a total of 150 full-length and short films, which were supplemented by a range of film discussions, public debates and panel discussions, as well as the rich programme of accompanying cultural events. An international jury chaired by Eberhard Junkersdorf awarded four prizes worth €29,500 in total. Important goals of goEast are to promote up-and-coming filmmakers and enhance their networking. Annually, young filmmakers from East and West present their work in the Student Film Competition. Additionally, the Robert Bosch Stiftung supported in 2008 with its Co-Production Prize for the second time young talents from East and West with up to €210,000 in total. **– Tanja Bischoff**.

Göteborg International Film Festival
January 23-February 2, 2009

Now in its 32nd year, Göteborg International Film Festival is one of Europe's key film events. With a large international programme and a special focus on Nordic films, including the Nordic Competition, GIFF is Scandinavia's most important film festival. International seminars, masterclasses and the market place Nordic Film Market attract buyers and festival programmers to the newest Scandinavian films. The 30th jubilee, in 2007, introduced a new international competition – the Ingmar Bergman International Debut Award (TIBIDA). Some 1,800 professionals attend and more than 124,000 tickets are sold to 450 films from around 70 countries. *Inquiries to:* Göteborg International Film Festival, Olof Palmes Plats, S- 413 04 Göteborg, Sweden. Tel: (46 31) 339 3000. Fax: 410 063. e: goteborg@filmfestival. org. Web: www.filmfestival.org.

AWARDS 2008
Winner of TIBIDA: **Solitary Fragments** (Spain), Jaime Rosales.
Best Nordic Film: **Let the Right One In** (Sweden), Tomas Alfredson.
The Kodak Nordic Vision Award: Hoyte van Hoytema for the cinematography in **Let the Right One In** (Sweden).
The Church of Sweden Film Award: **Go With Peace Jamil** (Denmark), Omar Shargawi.
The Fipresci Award: **Go With Peace Jamil** (Denmark), Omar Shargawi.
Best Swedish Short: **Instead of Abrakadabra** (Sweden), Patrik Eklund.
Viewers Choice Award, Feature: **Three Miles North of Molkom** (UK), Robert Cannan and Corinna Villari-McFarlane.
Viewers Choice Award, Short: **Instead of Abrakadabra** (Sweden), Patrik Eklund.

Report 2008
The 2008 focus was on the exciting film country Mexico, with the section New Mexico, which was a great success. Actor and first-time director, Gael García Bernal gathered crowds to his seminars – and to his DJ set at the grand Opening Party! Other highlights were the opening film, Swedish Jens Jonsson's feature debut and Sundance winner *The King of Ping Pong* and the popular guests Zoe Cassavetes and indie queen Parker Posey, who presented their charming film *Broken English*. The vast seminar programme included masterclasses with Julie Taymor, Gael García Bernal, Nik Powell and Hou

Hsiao-hsien. Other guests were Ulrich Seidl and Jiri Menzel. The festival celebrated the Swedish premiere of Todd Haynes' *I'm Not There* with a big Bob Dylan party and closed the ten-day long film fest with a Closing Gala Evening, celebrating the award winners first with a dinner indoors, followed by a night of mingling outdoors(!) and at different bars on a nearby street.
– Camilla Larsson, Chief of Communications.

Haugesund – Norwegian International Film Festival
August 20–27, 2009

Honorary President Liv Ullmann with Programme Director Håkon Skogrand, left, and Festival Director Gunnar Johan Løvvik, right, at the 2008 Norwegian International Film Festival (photo: Helge Hansen)

Located in Haugesund, on the West Coast of Norway, the festival is Norway's major event for film and cinema. The Norwegian and Scandinavian film industry is represented by over 1,500 participants, as well as several hundred international buyers, producers and directors. The festival starts with the New Nordic Films market from 20–23 August, the Amanda Award ceremony (the Norwegian 'Oscar') on Friday 21 August and officially opens on Sunday 23 August. Festival Director: Gunnar Johan Løvvik. Programme Director: Håkon Skogrand. Honorary President: Liv Ullmann. *Inquiries to:* PO Box 145, N-5501 I laugesund, Norway. Tel: (47 52) 743 370. e: info@filmfestivalen.no. Web: www.filmfestivalen.no.

AWARDS 2008
Film Critics Award: **The Class** (France), Laurent Cantet.
The Ray of Sunshine: **Happy-Go-Lucky** (UK), Mike Leigh.
Audience Award: **A Man Comes Home** (Denmark/Sweden), Thomas Vinterberg.

Andreas Award: **Troubled Water** (Norway), Erik Poppe.

Helsinki International Film Festival – Love & Anarchy
September 17–27, 2009

The largest film festival in Finland with over 48,000 admissions during the festival's eleven days. Organised yearly since 1988, the festival has found its place as the top venue for the new and the alternative in cinema and in popular culture. The festival has a memorable subtitle, 'Love & Anarchy', adopted from a Lina Wertmüller film from the 1970s. The subtitle Love & Anarchy has turned into a trademark of cutting-edge films over the years: films with a spark of something different, fearlessly plunging into unexplored frontiers. The festival inaugurated a competition in 2008: the Finnkino Prize. The winner of the audience vote gets distribution by the leading operator of multiplex theatres Finnkino. The first prize winner was *Captain Abu Raed* by Amin

Matalqa from Jordan. *Inquiries to:* Helsinki Film Festival, Mannerheimintie 22-24, PO Box 889, FI-00101 Helsinki, Finland. Tel: (358 9) 6843 5230. Fax: 6843 5232. e:office@hiff.fi. Web: www.hiff.fi.

Hof International Film Festival/ Internationale Hofer Filmtage
October 27–November 1, 2009

The Hof International Film Festival – often nicknamed 'The German Telluride' – was founded in the northern Bavarian town of Hof in 1968 by current festival director Heinz Badewitz and several up-and-coming filmmakers of the day (Wim Wenders, Volker Schloendorff, Werner Herzog and Rainer Werner Fassbinder among them) and has since gone on to become one of the most important film festivals in Germany, concentrating both on German films by the new filmmaking generation and on independent movies from abroad. Another kingpin is the retrospective that so far has been dedicated to directors as varied as Monte Hellman, Mike Leigh, Lee Grant, John Sayles, Brian de

Festival director Heinz Badewitz (right) welcomed the Academy Award winner Caroline Link for the opening of the 42nd Hof IFF 2008 with **A Year Ago in Winter** *(photo: Hermann Kauper)*

Palma, Peter Jackson, Roger Corman, John Cassavetes, Costa-Gavras, and Wayne Wang. It's a festival that attracts not only cinemagoers and critics, but also producers, distributors and the media - not to forget the filmmakers

themselves. *Inquiries to:* Hof International Film Festival, Altstadt 8, D-95028 Hof, Germany. Fax: (49) 9281 18816 e: info@hofer-filmtage.de. Web: www.hofer-filmtage.de.

Hong Kong International Film Festival
March 23–April 13, 2009

The Hong Kong International Film Festival Society is a non-profit, non-governmental organisation which develops, promotes and encourages creativity in the art and culture of film through the presentation of the annual Hong Kong International Film Festival (HKIFF). The Society is also committed to organising regular programmes and other film-related activities throughout the year in order to promote the art and creativity of cinema, with an international dimension and outlook. In 2007, the Society further demonstrated its commitment to the development of a vibrant film culture by organising three flagship events: the Hong Kong International Film Festival (HKIFF), the Hong Kong/Asia Film Financing Forum (HAF) and the Asian Film Awards (AFA). *Inquiries to:* Hong Kong International Film Festival Society Office, 7/F United Chinese Bank Building, 31-37 Des Voeux Road Central, Hong Kong. Tel: (852) 2970 3300. Fax: 2970 3011. e: info@hkiff.org. hk. Web: www.hkiff.org.hk.

AWARDS 2008
Golden Digital Award: **What the Heart Craves** (Japan), Takahashi Izumi.
Silver Digital Award: **Little Moth** (China), Peng Tao.
Humanitarian Award for Best Documentary: **Yasukuni** (China/Japan), Li Ying.
Humanitarian Award for Outstanding Documentary: **Bingai** (China), Feng Yan.
Grand Prize, Fresh Wave Short Film Competition: **The Monk** (Hong Kong), Chan Siu-hei.
FIPRESCI Prize: **Wonderful Town** (Thailand), Aditya Assarat.
SIGNIS Award: **Empties** (Czech Republic/UK), Jan Svěrák.

Report 2008
Highlights of the 32nd edition were a complete retrospective of Edward Yang, the world-renowned Taiwanese auteur who passed away in 2007, as well as special sections on Young Taiwanese Cinema, Israeli Cinema and Czech Cinema. Chinese Renaissance, a stage for new films and filmmakers from the Chinese Mainland, once again premiered important new works from directors such as Wang Xiaoshuai, Gu Changwei, and Ning Hao. This year's guests of honour were Yamada Yoji, who recently received a Lifetime Achievement Award from HKIFF's sister event, the Asian Film Awards (AFA), and whose latest film, *Kabei – Our Mother,* was an Opening Film of the 32nd HKIFF, as well as Peter Greenaway and Bela Tarr. Also present were Filmmaker in Focus, Eric Tsang, who contributed two World Premieres along with eight earlier works to this year's film festival, and Ishii Yuya, recipient of the Edward Yang New Talent Award at the 2nd AFA. **– Li Cheuk To**, Artistic Director.

Huelva Latin American Film Festival
November 14–21, 2009

The Latin American Film Festival in Huelva, which reached its 34th edition in 2008, is one of the most important cinematographic contests of its kind. The most outstanding films from both shores of the Atlantic get together in the third week of November in Huelva, in one of the main Latin American cultural events. Due to its international vocation, the Latin American Film Festival in Huelva aims to open the European film market to upcoming talented young people from the Latin American sector, also hosting the Latin American Co-Production Forum where outstanding producers, directors and distributors meet. The best film is awarded a prize known as the Golden Colombus. *Inquiries to:* Casa Colon, Plaza del Punto s/n, 21003 Huelva, Spain. Tel: (34 95) 921 0170/0299. Fax: 921 0173. e: prensa@festicinehuelva.com. Web: www.festicinehuelva.com.

AWARDS 2008
Best Long Feature-Golden Colombus: **The Good Life** (Argentina/Chile/France/Spain/UK), Andrés Wood.

Best Opera Prima: **Parque Vía** (Mexico),
Enrique Rivero.
Special Jury Award: **Rain** (Argentina), Paula
Hernández.
Best Director: Alan Jonsson for **Morenita**,
(Mexico).
Best Actor: Juan Luis Galiardo for
Esperpentos, (Spain).
Best Actress: Valeria Bertuccelli for **Rain**,
(Argentina).
Best Screenplay: Carlos Moreno and Alonso
Torres for **Dog Eats Dog**, (Colombia).
Best Cinematography: Jose Luis Alcaine and
Javier Salmones for **Esperpentos** (Spain).
Audience Award: **Paraíso Travel** (Colombia),
Simón Brand.

Report 2008

After 34 years, Huelva Latin American Film
Festival continues to be the meeting point for
the best Latin American film productions. In
2008, the festival was a great success showing
the quality of films which choose Huelva as the
place to be premiered worldwide. *La Buena*

*Golden Columbus award-winner Andrés Wood, director of La buena
vida (The Good Life) with Eduardo Trías, film director, left at the closing
ceremony of Huelva Latin American Film Festival (photo: Iván Quintero)*

Vida (*The Good Life*) by Chilean film director
Andrés Wood, Spanish actor Juan Luis Galiardo
and the producer and distributor Enrique
González Macho, as well as film masters like
Rafael Azcona and Humberto Solás were some
of the outstanding characters of this past
edition. **– Inmaculada Villaécija**, Head of Press.

Independent Film Week
September 13–18, 2009

Formerly known as the IFP Market, Independent Film Week is the oldest and largest forum
in the US for the discovery of new projects in
development and new voices on the independent film scene. It is qualitatively and quantita-
tively the best and biggest opportunity in the
nation for an independent filmmaker to find a
funder or producer. Annually IFP invites approximately 150 new works-in-development. Projects are accepted into one of three sections:
Emerging Narrative, No Borders International
Co-Production Market, and Spotlight on Documentaries. A wide range of industry decision-
makers make Independent Film Week their annual meeting point in New York to discover new
documentaries and narrative feature projects.
Strategically positioned between the Toronto
and New York Film Festivals, it is an efficient
week for meetings, screenings and re-connect-
ing with colleagues. *Inquiries to:* Independent
Film Week, 104 West 29th St, 12th Floor, New
York, NY 10001, USA. Tel: (1 212) 465 8200. Fax:
465 8525. e: jhe@ifp.org. Web: www.ifp.org and
www.independentfilmweek.com.

International Film Festival and Forum on Human Rights
March 6–15, 2009

The inspiration and impetus behind the International Film Festival and Forum on Human Rights (FIFDH) came from human rights defenders, filmmakers, representatives from the media and the University of Geneva. The FIFDH coincides with the UN Human Rights Council and is a platform for all public and private actors defending human dignity. The festival is an International Forum on Human Rights that informs and denounces violations wherever they take place. Situated in the heart of Geneva, the International Capital for Human Rights, the festival also serves as a go-between for all human rights activists. For one week, it offers debates, original film screenings and solidarity initiatives. With its concept 'a film, a subject, a debate', the aim of the FIFDH is to denounce attacks on human dignity and to raise public awareness through films and debates in the presence of filmmakers, defenders of human rights and recognised specialists. *Inquiries to:* Leo Kaneman and Yaël Reinharz Hazan, Directors, FIFDH Maison des Arts du Grütli, 16 rue Général Dufour, CP 5730 CH 1211 Geneva 11, Switzerland. Tel: (41 22) 800 1554. Fax: 329 3747. e: contact@fifdh.ch. Web: www.fifdh.ch.

AWARDS 2008
Grand Prix FIFDH: **In Prison My Whole Life** (UK), Marc Evans and ex aequo **Suffering and Smiling** (Nigeria), Dan Ollman.
Special Award of the Jury: **Faces** (France/The Netherlands), Gmax.
OMCT Award: **Calle Sante Fe** (Belgium/Chile/France), Carmen Castillo.
Youth Jury Award: **Suffering and Smiling** (Nigeria), Dan Ollman.

Report 2008
The 6th edition of the International Film Festival and Forum on Human Rights (FIFDH), dedicated to Aung San Suu Kyi, confirmed the festival's political and cultural vocation as well as the relevance of its concept: '*a*

film, a subject, a debate'. The formula was applied this year to Darfur, Burma, Mauritania, Russia, Populism, China, International Justice, Environmental Threats, International Women's Day and Europe. For ten days, human rights defenders, decision makers, journalists and artists, refusing political compromises, expressed their views and denounced the abuses to human dignity within a free Tribune, off the 7th edition of the UN Human Rights Council. Over 16,000 festival participants watched the films and the Face2Face performance, participated in the debates, and exchanged ideas. With over twenty quality documentary films in competition and high-level debates, the festival managed what it had set out to do: trigger a real dialogue between the public and specialists. The 2008 International Jury was composed of Ousmane Sow (Artist, Sculptor and President of the Jury), Nancy Huston (French-Canadian writer), Adam Michnik (Co-founder of the *Solidarnosc*), Freddy Buache (Founder of the Swiss Cinemathèque) and Philippine Leroy-Beaulieu (Actress). Among guests attending were: Luis Moreno-Ocampo (Prosecutor of the International Criminal Court), Philippe Vall (Editor-in-Chief of Charlie Hebdo), Betty Bigombe (Ancient Minister of Uganda), Reed Brody (Counsel and Spokesperson, Human Rights Watch), Helen Mack (Alternate Nobel Prize for Peace - Guatemala), Dick Marty (Legal Affairs and Human Rights Committee Raporteur, Council of Europe), Ely Ould Mohamed Vall (Former President of Mauritania), Georges Wolinski (Cartoonist), Xinran Xue (Chinese writer). **– Jeffrey Hodgson**.

FIFDH – 2009 official poster (photo JR, design Lelgo)

International Film Festival of India
Late November 2009

Annual, government-funded event recognised by FIAPF and held in Goa under the aegis of India's Ministry of Information and Broadcasting. Comprehensive 'Cinema of the World' section, foreign and Indian retrospectives and a film market, plus a valuable panorama of the year's best Indian films, subtitled in English. *Inquiries to:* The Director, International Film Festival of India, Sirifort Auditoriums, August Kranti Marg, New Delhi 110049, India. Tel: (91 11) 2649 9356. Fax: 2649 9357. e: ddiffi.dff@nic.in. Web: www.iffi.nic.in.

Istanbul
April 5–20, 2009

The only film festival that takes place in a city where two continents meet, the Istanbul International Film Festival boasts the largest attendance in Turkey with 170,000. In its 28th year, the Festival will hold the fourth of its industry events, Meetings on the Bridge, with the second edition of the feature-film development workshop in its framework. The Festival programme focuses on features dealing with the arts and the artist, or literary adaptations in its main competition, the Golden Tulip; selections from world festivals, with other thematic sections such as 'The World of Animation', 'Mined Zone', 'Women's Films', 'Documentary Time', 'Human Rights in Cinema' with the Council of Europe Film Award - FACE, 'Young Masters' and a comprehensive showcase of Turkish cinema. The deadline for submissions is December 31, 2008. *Inquiries to:* Ms Azize Tan, Istanbul Foundation for Culture and Arts, Istiklal Caddesi 146, Beyoglu 34435, Istanbul, Turkey. Tel: (90 212) 334 0700 exts. 720 & 721. Fax: 334 0702. e: film.fest@iksv.org. Web: www.iksv.org/film/english.

AWARDS 2008
International Competition
Golden Tulip: **Egg** (Turkey), Semih Kaplanoglu.
Special Prize of the Jury International Competition: **The Wave** (Germany), Dennis Gansel.
Special Prize of the Jury National Competition: **Ara**, Umit Unal.
FIPRESCI Prize International Competition: **Ben X** (Belgium), Nic Balthazar.
FIPRESCI Prize National Competition: **Summer Book**, Seyfi Teoman.
FACE Award: **Blind Mountain** (China), Li Yang.
Best Turkish Film of the Year: **Summer Book**, Seyfi Teoman.
Best Turkish Director of the Year: Dervis Zaim, **Dot**.
People's Choice Awards International Competition: **Egg** (Turkey), Semih Kaplanoglu.
People's Choice Awards National Competition: **The Messenger**, Cagan Irmak.
Meetings On The Bridge Feature Film Project Development Workshop Award: **Zephyr**, Belma Bas.

Report 2008
The 27th edition of the Istanbul Film Festival saw another record number of attendees thanks to 478 screenings of a total of 200 films

Alexander Sokurov receiving the Cinema Honorary Award of the 2008 Istanbul FF from CEO Sakir Eczacibasi, right (photo: Pelin Erdogan)

in the programme, which included thematic sections including 'American Independents', 'From the Caucasus to the Mediterranean', retrospectives on Milos Forman and Alexander Petrov, and a special section commemorating the groundbreaking events of 1968. For the first time this year, the Festival restored the classic *On Fertile Lands* by Erden Kiral, a task that it will continue to take on with other lost classics in its future editions. Highlights included masterclasses and panel discussions by Michael Ballhaus, also the head juror of the international Golden Tulip Competition, Marc Caro, Tony Gatlif, Abderrahmane Sissako, Kim Aubry, and Alexander Sokurov, who received the Honorary Cinema Award. Guests included Claudia Cardinale who received the Lifetime Achievement Award, William Klein, Bent Hamer, Pawel Pawlikowski, Brad Anderson, Alain Corneau, Amos Gitai, Lech Majewski, Kiumars Pourahmad, Tommy O'Haver and Nadine Labaki, amongst many others, who presented their films. **– Yusuf Pinhas**, Festival Editor.

Jerusalem International Film Festival
July 9–18, 2009

Celebrating its 26th Anniversary this year, the Jerusalem International Film Festival, Israel's most prestigious cinematic event, offers an alternative Middle East headline – that those of all faiths, ethnicities, and political positions have the opportunity to sit side by side in the shadow of the silver screen – to be moved, to share discourse and, yes, to hope. Our Opening Gala event attracts over 7,000 spectators, under the stars, in the shadow of the ancient Jerusalem Walls. During the festival over 70,000 people increase their awareness of contemporary world cinema. The festival's programme will present 150 films on a wide spectrum of themes and in categories focusing on the Best of International Cinema; Best of New Israeli Cinema; Human Rights and Social Justice. Other categories include: Documentaries; Animation; Jewish Themes; Retrospectives; Avant Garde; Restorations; Television; Special Tributes and Classics. The festival has become the largest local market for international films where distributors from all over the world have the opportunity to bring the finest of World Cinema to the growing and increasingly influential Israeli Audience. Israeli filmmakers set the World Premiere of their films at the Festival knowing that a strong local reaction is tantamount to a new Israeli film's success throughout Europe and the world. International distributors increasingly look to the Festival as a guide to new Israeli film – knowing that a success in Jerusalem means a success worldwide. The festival offers dozens of professional events and seminars designed

Opening Screening Gala below the Ancient Walls of Jerusalem, 2008 (photo: Vera Etzion, © Jerusalem Cinematheque/Israel Film Archive)

to promote and assist local filmmakers and to connect Israel to the European and international industry. The festival has become not only the harbinger and launching point for new and cutting-edge Israeli cinema, but also an active and proud promoter. Past examples include *The Jerusalem Pitch Point*: for the third year consecutively, the festival has functioned as a meeting place for Israeli filmmakers and producers with key members of the European and international film industry whose aim is to encourage and promote co-productions with Europe, and beyond, of Israeli full-length feature films. *Sundance in Jerusalem*: in cooperation with the Jerusalem International Film Festival, Sundance's Feature Film Programme presents 'Sundance in Jerusalem' - an opportunity to meet and hear from distinctive screenwriters and filmmakers whose work has been developed at the Institute. The programme is also an opportunity to have an informal conversation about the 'Labs' with Alesia Weston, Associate Director of the Feature Film Programme, International. Submission deadline: April 1, 2009. *Inquiries to:* Jerusalem Film Festival, Hebron Road 11, Jerusalem 91083, Israel. Tel: (972 2) 565 4333. Fax: 565 4334. e: daniel@jff.org.il. Web: www.jff.org.il.

AWARDS 2008

Wolgin Awards for Israeli Cinema given by Jack Wolgin, patron and long-time supporter of the art of cinema in Israel
Best Feature Film: **Seven Days**, Ronit Elbabetz and Shlomi Elkabetz.

Best Documentary Film: **The Tale of Nicolai & the Law of Return**, David Ofek.
Best Documentary Film Special Mention: **Nuran**, Amikam Shossberger.
Best Short Film: **Around Trip**, Gur Bentwich.
Best Short Film Special Mentions: **The Repentance of Rachamim Hanuka**, Ariel Benbaji and Bait, Michal Vinik.
Best Performances in an Israeli Feature
Best Actress: Hana Azulay Hasfary for **7 Days**.
Best Actor: Alon Aboutboul and Moshe Ivgy for **Out of the Blue**.
Drama Awards in Memory of Anat Pirchi
Best Single Drama: **And Thou Shalt Love**, Chaim Elbaum.
Best Single Drama Special Mention: **Anthem**, Elad Keidan.
Best Television Series: **Arab Labor**, Daniel Paran, Sayed Kashua and Roni Ninio.
Best Television Series Special Mention: **A Taste of Conflict**, Uri Barbash and Ronit Weiss-Berkowitz.
'In the Spirit of Freedom' Awards in Memory of Wim van Leer: **Hunger** (UK), Steve McQueen.

John Malkovich with Lia van Leer, Founder and President of the Jerusalem Cinematheque (photo: Vera Etzion, © Jerusalem Cinematheque/Israel Film Archive)

'In the Spirit of Freedom' Awards in Memory of Wim van Leer: **Little Moth** (China), Peng Tao. *'In the Spirit of Freedom' Awards in Memory of Wim van Leer Special Mention:* **Under the Bombs**, Philippe Aractingi.
FIPRESCI International Critics' Award: **My Marlon and Brando** (The Netherlands/Turkey), Hüseyin Karabey.
Lia Award: **Outside Love** (Denmark), Daniel Espinosa.
Avner Shalev Yad Vashem Chairman's Award: **The Green Dumpster Mystery** (Israel), Tal Haim Yoffe.
Shavim (Equals) Production Grant: **Lod Bypass** (Israel), Orna Raviv.
Wim van Leer Young Filmmaker's Award Fiction Film: **On top of the Water**, Efrat Raz. *Documentary Film:* **Nadine**, Nadine Abu Lashin.

Karlovy Vary International Film Festival
July 3–11, 2009

Founded in 1946, Karlovy Vary is one of the most important film events in Central and Eastern Europe. It includes Official Selection - Competition, Documentary Films in Competition, East of the West - Films in Competition and other programme sections which give the unique chance to see new film production from all around the world. Film Entry deadline: April 17, 2009. *Inquiries to:* Film Servis Festival Karlovy Vary, Panská 1, CZ 110 00 Prague 1, Czech Republic. Tel: (420 2) 2141 1011. Fax: 2141 1033. e: programme@kviff.com. Web: www.kviff.com.

AWARDS 2008
Grand Prix- Crystal Globe: **Terribly Happy** (Denmark), Henrik Ruben Genz.
Special Jury Prize: **The Photograph** (France/Indonesia/Netherlands/Sweden/Switzerland), Nan T. Achnas.
Best Director: Alexey Uchitel, **Captive** (Bulgaria/Russia).
Best Actress: Martha Issová, **Night Owls** (Czech Republic).
Best Actor: Jiøí Mádl, **Night Owls** (Czech Republic).

Special Jury Mention: **The Karamazovs** (Czech Republic), Petr Zelenka and **The Investigator** (Hungary/Ireland/Sweden), Attila Gigor.
Best Documentary Film Under 30 Minutes: **Lost World** (Russia), Sergey Loznitsa.
Best Documentary Film Over 30 Minutes: **Man on Wire** (UK), James Marsh.
Special Mention: **Bigger, Stronger, Faster** (USA), Christopher Bell.
East of the West: **Tulpan** (Germany/Kazakhstan/Poland/Russia/Switzerland), Sergey Dvortsevoy.
Special Mention: **Seamstresses** (Bulgaria), Lyudmil Todorov.
Audience Award: **12** (Russia), Nikita Mikhalkov.
Special Crystal Globe for Outstanding Artistic Contribution to World Cinema: Robert De Niro (USA), Du'an Hanák (Slovakia), Juraj Jakubisko (Slovakia) and Ivan Passer (Czech Republic/USA).
Festival President's Award: Danny Glover (USA) and Christopher Lee (UK).
The Town of Karlovy Vary Award: Armin Mueller-Stahl (Germany).

Krakow Film Festival
May 29–June 4, 2009

The Krakow Film Festival is among Europe's oldest events dedicated to documentary, animation and short films. Screening more than 350 films every year, the diverse programme includes retrospectives, thematic cycles and masters' screenings. However, the core of the festival remains competition screenings divided into three sections: National Competition, International Competition and the newest Feature-Length Documentary Competition. Every year the

festival hosts over 500 accredited guests - filmmakers, journalists and film festivals representatives as well as around 16,000 spectators. Since 2005, the festival has been accompanied by Krakow Film Market and Dragon Forum (pitching), which has become an important event in the film professionals' calendar. *Inquiries to:* Krakow Film Festival, Ul Morawskiego 5/434, 30-102 Krakow, Poland. Tel: (48 12) 294 6945. e: info@kff.com.pl. Web: www.kff.com.pl.

AWARDS 2008
Feature-Length Documentary Competition – The Golden Horn: **Revue** (Germany/Russia/Ukraine), Sergei Loznitsa.
International Competition – The Golden Dragon: **Lightborne** (Spain), Eduardo Chapero-Jackson.
National Competition – The Golden Hobby-Horse: **Gugara** (Poland), Jacek Nagłowski and Andrzej Dybczak.
The Prix UIP Cracow: **Time Is Running Out** (United Kingdom), Marc Reisbig.
Dragon of Dragons Special Prize for Lifetime Achievement: Allan King.

Report 2008
The 48th edition of Krakow Film Festival took place from 30th May to 5th June 2008. Over seven days, 325 films were presented in 110 showings in five screening rooms. Forty-two films took part in the national competition, with 57 films and twelve feature-length documentaries screened in the international section. Spectators also had the opportunity to see a variety of non-competitive screenings, ranging from documentaries to short films and animation. Thematic sections focused on music documentaries, the films of chosen countries (Bulgaria, Italy, Romania, Cuba and Germany this year) and the latest documentary premieres. A special retrospective of Allan King's films, this year's winner of the Dragon of Dragons Special Award for Lifetime Achievement, was held. For the third time, the Festival was accompanied by the Krakow Film Market, featuring twenty digitalised booths with over 550 films available to watch. Among

Krakow Film Festival awards

young filmmakers, the biggest attraction was workshops concerned with the most efficient strategies for promoting documentaries.
– Barbara Orlicz-Szczypula, Head of Programme Office.

La Rochelle International Film Festival
June 26–July 6, 2009

Our world-renowned Festival is non-competitive and screens more than 200 original and new releases from all over the world to a large audience (73,882 in 2008) of very enthusiastic film buffs. The festival includes tributes to contemporary directors or actors, often in their presence (last year: Danielle Arbid [France/Lebanon], Raymond Depardon [France], Werner Herzog [Germany], Mike Leigh [UK], la Tribu Stévenin [France]); retrospectives devoted to the work of past filmmakers (last year: Nicholas Ray, Erich von Stroheim and Josef von Sternberg); 'Here and There', a selection of unreleased films from all over the world; 'From Yesterday till Today', premieres of rare films re-stored and re-edited; 'Carpets, Cushions and Video', video works projected on the ceiling above supine spectators; Films for Children. The festival ends with an all-night programme of five films, followed by breakfast in cafés overlooking the old port. *Inquiries to:* La Rochelle International Film Festival, 16 rue Saint Sabin, 75011 Paris, France. Tel: (33 1) 4806 1666. Fax: 4806 1540. e: info@festival-larochelle.org. Web: www.festival-larochelle.org. Director: Mrs Prune Engler; Artistic Director: Mrs Sylvie Pras.

Las Palmas de Gran Canaria International Film Festival
March 6–14, 2009

The 2009 edition will mark the tenth anniversary of a festival that reflects the growth in Asian film production, the increase in digital possibilities, the renaissance of independent film production in the USA and the overlap of fiction with documentary and experimental cinema. *Inquiries to:* León y Castillo, 322, 4ª Planta, 35007 Las Palmas de Gran Canaria. Tel: (34 928) 446 833/644. Fax: 446 651. e: laspalmascine@hotmail.com. Web: www. festivalcinelaspalmas.com.

Leeds International Film Festival
November 11–22, 2009

Presented by Leeds City Council, the Leeds International Film Festival is the largest regional Film Festival in the United Kingdom. The Official Selection will feature Cinema Versa, Fanomenon, Thought Bubble, Short Film City and KiNETIKA!. In addition, Leeds Film organises year-round exhibition with partner organisations in the city, education programmes and delivers the Leeds Young People's Film Festival. *Inquiries to:* Leeds International Film Festival, The Town Hall, The Headrow, Leeds, LS1 3AD, UK. Tel: (44 113) 247 8398. Fax: 247 8494. e: filmfestival@leeds. gov.uk. Web: www.leedsfilm.com.

Locarno International Film Festival
August 5–15, 2009

The Locarno International Film Festival, one of the world's top cinematic all-feature events, traditionally aims to promote personal filmmaking of artistic merit, to provide a showcase for major new films of the year from around the world and to take stock, in its competitive section, of the new perspectives of filmmaking expression, concentrating especially on such new film directors and industries as command international attention. In fact, the Festival, with its ongoing process of cultural inquiry, has contributed to revealing or confirming directors who are currently enjoying a very wide recognition. Moreover, the Locarno Festival has established itself in recent years as an important industry showcase for auteur filmmaking, a perfect networking opportunity for distributors, buyers and producers from around the world with over 3,300 film professionals and 1,000 journalists attending – together with 180,000 cinemagoers. *Inquiries to:* Festival Internazionale del Film Locarno, Via Ciseri 23, CH-6601 Locarno, Switzerland. Artistic Director: Frédéric Maire. Tel: (41 91) 756 2121. Fax: 756 2149. e: info@pardo.ch. Web: www. pardo.ch.

AWARDS 2008
International Competition
Golden Leopard: **Parque Via** (Mexico), Enrique Rivero.
Special Jury Prize: **33 Scenes from Life** (Germany/Poland), Malgoska Szumowska.
Best Director: Denis Côté for **Elle Veut Le Chaos** (Canada).
Actress Leopard: Ilaria Occhini, **Mar Nero** (France/Italy/Romania).
Actor Leopard: Tayanç Ayaydin, **The Market - A Tale of Trade** (Germany/Kazakhstan/Turkey/UK).
Special Mention: **Feast of Villains** (China), Pan Jianlin and **Daytime Drinking** (South Korea), Noh Young-seok.
Filmmakers of the Present Competition
CP Company Golden Leopard: **La Forteresse** (Switzerland), Fernand Melgar.
Ciné Cinéma Special Jury Prize: **Alicia en el Pais** (Chile), Esteban Larraín.

Golden Leopard winner Enrique Rivero

Michel Houellebecq, whose directorial debut premiered at Locarno

Special Mention: **Prince of Broadway** (USA), Sean Baker.
Leopard for the Best First Feature (International Competition): **März** (Austria), Händl Klaus.
Prix du Public UBS (Audience Award): **Son of Rambow** (France/Germany/UK), Garth Jennings.
Variety Piazza Grande Award: **Back Soon** (France/Iceland), Sólveig Anspach.

Report 2008
Among the highlights of the 61st edition were the complete Nanni Moretti retrospective; the award of the Honorary Leopard to Israeli filmmaker Amos Gitai; the Raimondo Rezzonico Prize for Best Independent Producer to American Christine Vachon; the attendance of celebrated writers Chuck Palahniuk, Alessandro Baricco and Michel Houellebecq, the latter two having chosen Locarno for the world premiere of their directorial debuts. The Piazza Grande has once again offered the audience some unforgettable moments. Following the screening of *Berlin Calling*, the famous German DJ Paul Kalkbrenner transformed the Piazza into a massive dance floor with a live electro mix, while French actor Fabrice Luchini introduced the world premiere of *La fille de Monaco* with all his usual brio.
– Alessia Botani.

BFI London Film Festival
Late October 2009

The UK's largest and most prestigious public film festival presented at the BFI Southbank,
West End venues, and at cinemas throughout the capital. The programme comprises around 200 features and documentaries as well as showcasing over 100 short films. There is a British section and a very strong international selection from Asia, Africa, Europe, Latin America, US independents and experimental and avant-garde work. More than 1,600 UK and international press and industry representatives attend and there is a buyers/ sellers liaison office. *Inquiries to:* Sarah Lutton, London Film Festival, BFI Southbank, South Bank, London SE1 8XT, UK. Tel: (44 20) 7815 1322. Fax: 7633 0786. e: sarah.lutton@ bfi.org.uk. Web: www.bfi.org.uk.

AWARDS 2008
The Sutherland Trophy Winner: **Tulpan** (Kazakhstan), Sergey Dvortsevoy.
11th FIPRESCI International Critics Award Winner: **Three Blind Mice** (Australia), Matthew Newton.
The Times BFI London Film Festival Grierson Award: **Victoire Terminus** (Democratic Republic of Congo), Renaud Barret and Florent De La Tullaye.
The 13th Annual Satyajit Ray Award Winner: **Mid-August Lunch** (Italy), Gianni di Gregorio.
TCM Short Film Award Winner: **Leaving** (UK),Richard Penfold and Sam Hearn.

Report 2008
The London Film Festival rounded off its most successful year to date with the European premiere of Danny Boyle's *Slumdog Millionaire*. The 2008 festival hosted 191 feature films and 109 short films from 43 countries including a record 15 world premieres. There were 398 screenings and 537 visiting international filmmakers, a record 1,096 industry professionals, and the highest ever audience attendance. High-profile international filmmakers and actors attended their film's screenings over the sixteen days. British filmmaking and acting talent was also out in force with a record number of UK films world premiering at the Festival. Benicio Del Toro, Danny Boyle, Michael Sheen and Robert Carlyle were welcomed on stage for Tiscali

Screen Talks while Charlie Kaufman and Peter Morgan discussed their craft at the Script Factory/NFTS Masterclasses. Several new American directors were present for panel discussion 'Indiewood is Dead...Long Live the New, True Indies' including Barry Jenkins (*Medicine For Melancholy*) and Azazel Jacobs (*Momma's Man*), and a host of British directors and producers debated the current state of the UK film industry at the British Film Boom! event. 'Close Up with Time Out' once again sparked debate across the Festival with discussion topics ranging from 'The Ethical Problem of Violence on Film' to 'Cinema Under George W. Bush' and the *Variety* UK Achievement in Film Award was presented to Ralph Fiennes. Two nights of free outdoor screenings on Trafalgar Square brought classic films to the public and were greeted with outstanding attendance figures with over 9,000 film lovers present over the two evenings. In addition to welcoming more members of the public than ever before, the Festival also played host to a record number of industry delegates from 22 countries who participated in a range of events. Over 5,000 people participated in education screenings and events at the Festival with all workshops fully booked. The annual series of Filmmakers' Breakfasts saw over 50 directors complete a total of 238 interviews with international journalists (with 1,260 accredited press delegates from 53 countries). **– Claire Gascoyne**, Public Relations.

Los Angeles Film Festival
June 18–28, 2009

The Los Angeles Film Festival, held annually for ten days in June, showcases the best of American and international independent cinema. With an expected attendance of over 100,000, the festival screens over 175 narrative features, documentaries, shorts, and music videos. Now in its fourteenth year, the festival has grown into a world-class event, uniting new filmmakers with critics, scholars, film masters, and the movie-loving public. *Inquiries to:* Los Angeles Film Festival, 9911 W Pico Blvd, Los Angeles, CA 90035, USA. Tel: (1 310) 432 1240. e: lafilmfest@filmindependent.org. Web: www.lafilmfest.com.

Málaga Film Festival
April 17–25, 2009

Over the past eleven years, the Málaga Film Festival, together with the Goya prizes, have become the two essential appointments for the whole audiovisual sector of Spanish Cinema. It is a festival that brings together all the industry professionals to present their films and to debate questions affecting the audiovisual sector. Some 180,000 visitors attended the Festival in its 11th edition. There were 1,000 accredited journalists (10% more than in the last edition). Four exhibitions were organised: *Nostalgias en blanco y negro (1915-1975: 60 años de cine español a través de la Agencia EFE)*; *Hollywood en España. 101 carteles de la época dorada*; *Historia del cine en Málaga (1898–2008)*; and *Las entrañas del cine.* The President of the Jury in the 11th edition was Guy Braucourt and the winner of the 'Biznaga de Oro' (maximum prize) was F. Javier Gutiérrez's *3 días.* There were 22 feature-film premieres: Official Section and ZonaZine, 28 documentary premieres, 35 short films, 27 video clips, ten Latin American films and 86 feature films between the different cycles. In addition, the Festival has created three audiovisual markets, Malaga Markets: Malaga Screenings (Spanish Film Market); TV Market (Market for Spanish Fiction and Animation Productions for Television); and MercaDoc (European and Latin-American Documentary Market), MercaDoc was represented by 420 accredited people and 310 buyers of 26 countries. 444 documentary programmes were presented in the Video Library. For its 12th edition Málaga Film Festival has a new director in Carmelo Romero. *Inquiries to:* Málaga Film Festival, Carcer 6, 29012 Malaga, Spain. Tel: (34 95) 222 8242. Fax: 222 7760. e: info@festivaldemalaga.com. Web: www. festivalmalaga.com.

International Filmfestival Mannheim-Heidelberg
November 2009

The festival of independent new film artists presents around forty international new features in two main sections, International Competition and International Discoveries. The International Buyers Service: reserved for international buyers and distributors. The Mannheim Meetings: an international co-financing and distribution market for art-house films which runs in parallel to the main event. The international Co-production market is one of only four worldwide co-production meetings (alongside Rotterdam, New York and Pusan). The Sales & Distribution market is dedicated to distributors and sales agents. More than 60,000 filmgoers and 1,000 film professionals attend. *Inquiries to:* Dr Michael Koetz, International Filmfestival Mannheim-Heidelberg, Collini-Center, Galerie, D-68161 Mannheim, Germany. Tel: (49 621) 102 943. Fax: 291 564. e: info@iffmh.de. Web: www.iffmh.de.

Mar del Plata International Film Festival
November 2009

The festival was first held in 1954, but because of a 26-year hiatus is only celebrating its 24th edition in 2009. Held annually since 1996. the festival's President is acclaimed filmmaker José Martínez Suárez. It is the only A-grade film festival in Latin America with an Official Competition, usually comprising around 15 movies, generally two from Argentina. Other sections include Latin American Films, Out of Competition, Point of View, Near Darkness, Soundsystem, Heterodoxy, Documentary Frame, Argentine Showcase, Memory in Motion and The Inner Look. *Inquiries to:* Mar del Plata International Film Festival, Hipólito Yrigoyen 1225 (C1085ABO), Buenos Aires, Argentina. Tel: (54 11) 4383 5115. e: info@ mardelplatafilmfest. com. Web: www.mardelplatafilmfest.com.

Melbourne International Film Festival
July 24-August 9, 2009

MIFF is regarded unequivocally as the most significant film event in Australia. It has the largest and most diverse programme of screenings and special events in the country, in addition to the largest audience. There is also growing international regard for MIFF as a film market place, with a steady increase in sales agents attending. The longest-running festival in the southern hemisphere showing more than 400 features, shorts, documentaries and new media works, presented in five venues. *Inquiries to:* PO Box 4982, Melbourne 3001, Victoria, Australia. Tel: (61 3) 8660 4888. e: miff@ melbournefilmfestival.com.au. Web: www. melbournefilmfestival.com.au.

Miami International Film Festival
March 6–15, 2009

The Miami International Film Festival attracts the best of international cinema and offers participating filmmakers and industry professionals the distinct advantage of showcasing their films in a multi-cultural metropolis within the United States, the world's largest film market. The festival has hosted a diverse offering of films throughout its 25 years. In 2008, more than 450 filmmakers, producers, directors, writers, actors, and industry representatives from around the world were present for screenings as well as for business, educational and social functions. More than 1,300 regional, national and international press organisations have active relationships with the festival. Filmmakers including Luc Besson, Pedro Almodovar, Spike Lee and Wim Wenders have screened their films at MIFF. Distributors such as HBO, Fox Searchlight and Miramax have participated in the Festival's business programmes. *Inquiries to:* Miami Dade College, 300 NE 2nd St, Room 5521, Miami, Florida 33132, USA. Tel: (1 305) 237 3456. e: info@miamifilmfestival.com. Web: www.miamifilmfestival.com.

AWARDS 2008
Dramatic Features: World Cinema Competition Knight Grand Jury Prize: **Tricks** (Poland), Andrzej Jakimowski.

Dramatic Features: Ibero-American Competition
Knight Grand Jury Prize: **Cochochi** (Mexico),
Israel Cárdenas and Laura Amelia Guzmán.
Knight Grand Jury Prize: **Eat, For This Is My
Body** (France), Michelange Quay.
*Documentary Features: World and Ibero-
American Competition*
Knight Grand Jury Prize: **Santiago** (Chile), João
Moreira Salles.
Shorts Competition
Knight Grand Jury Prize: **Homecoming**
(Canada), Connie Diletti.
MIFF Audience Awards
Dramatic Features: World Cinema Competition:
Bliss (Turkey), Abdullah Oguz.
*Dramatic Features: Ibero-American Cinema
Competition:* **La Zona** (Mexico), Rodrigo Plá.
*Documentary Features: World & Ibero-
American Competition:* **Stranded: I've
Come From A Plane That Crashed In The
Mountains** (France), Gonzalo Arijón.
FIPRESCI International Critics Award: **Foul
Gesture** (Israel), Itshak Gradi.

Report 2008

The 25th Miami International Film Festival
presented over 150 unique films and
25 film-related seminars to 80,000-plus
attendees. Premiere and Red Carpet films
included David Schwimmer's *Run Fat Boy
Run*, Michael Radford's *Flawless* with Demi
Moore, Helen Hunt's directorial debut, Danny
Glover's *Africa Unite* and Patricia Riggen's *La
Misma Luna*. Jurors included such notables
as Michael J. Werner, Fred Siebert, Robert
Koehler and Charley Walters. Seminars
included masterclasses for Producers and
Cinematographers, panel discussions on
US Acquisitions, How to Sell Your Story and
Independent Film Financing and hands-on
classes on film techniques, resume writing and
breaking in to the business. **– Betsey Greene
Freeman**, Grants & Partnerships Manager.

Middle East International Film Festival
October 2009

MEIFF is a cultural event dedicated to bringing
a diverse slate of international films and
programmes to the community and introducing
filmmakers from around the world to the
resources of the region. Presented by the
Abu Dhabi Authority for Culture and Heritage
(ADACH), MEIFF is committed to nurturing
relationships and providing opportunities to
those looking to invest in the future of film.
Abu Dhabi is a city unprecedented in its ability
to develop and grow in response to the global
marketplace. MEIFF showcases films in a
number of categories, including films from
the Middle East, Bollywood and beyond in
addition to having the prestigious Black Pearl
Awards where filmmakers compete for Jury
prizes in Fiction, Documentary, Short Film and
Student categories. *Inquiries to:* MEIFF, PO
Box 127662, Abu Dhabi, UAE. Tel: (971 2) 633
0334. Fax: 633 0600. e:contact@meiff.com.
Web: www.meiff.com.

AWARDS 2008

Black Pearl for Best Narrative Film: **Disgrace**
(Australia/South Africa), Steve Jacobs.
Black Pearl for Best Documentary: **Stranded**
(France/Germany), Gonzalo Arijon.
Black Pearl Special Jury Prize: **I Bring What I
Love** (Senegal/USA), Elisabeth Chai Vasarhelyi.
Black Pearl for Best Actress: Ilham Shahoon for
Fawzia: A Special Blend, (Egypt).
Black Pearl for Best Actor: Luca Zingaretti for
Wild Blood, (France/Italy).
Black Pearl for Best Artistic Contribution:
Laila's Birthday (The Netherlands/Palestine/
Tunisia), Rashid Masharawi.
Black Pearl Audience Choice Award: **Saving
Luna** (Canada), Suzanne Chisholm and Michael
Parfit.
Black Pearl for Best Narrative – Short Film: **The
View** (Jordan), Hazim Bitar and Rifqi Assaf.
Black Pearl for Best Documentary – Short Film:
Breadmakers (UK), Yasmin Fedda.
Black Pearl for Best Animation – Short Film:
Jacinta (Mexico), Karla Casteneda.
Best Advertisement – Cultural Category: **Anti
Slavery** (UK), Eric Lynne.
Best Advertisement – Consumer Category:
Battle (UK), Traktor.
Best Advertisement – Artistic Contribution:
Great Pretender (UK), Patrick Bergh.

Black Pearl for Best Narrative – Student Film:
Illusion (Germany), Burhan Qurbani.
Black Pearl for Best Emerging Filmmaker –
Student Film: **Lullaby** (Lebanon), Serena Abi Aad.
Black Pearl for Best Animation – Student Film:
Adherent (Norway), Julian Nazario Vargas.

Mill Valley Film Festival
October 2009

Known as a filmmakers' festival, the festival
offers a high-profile, prestigious, non-
competitive and welcoming environment
perfect for celebrating the best in independent
and world cinema. MVFF presents over 200
films from 50 countries featuring a wide variety
of high-calibre international programming, in
beautiful Marin County just across the Golden
Gate Bridge. Celebrating its 32nd year in 2009,
the festival includes the innovative Vfest,
Children's Film Fest, celebrity tributes, seminars
and special events. *Inquiries to:* Mill Valley Film
Festival/California Film Institute, 1001 Lootens
Place, Suite 220, San Rafael, CA 94901, USA.
Tel: (1 415) 383 5256. Fax: 383 8606. e: mvff@
cafilm.org. Web: www.mvff.com.

Montreal World Film Festival
August 27–September 7, 2009

The goal of the festival is to encourage
cultural diversity and understanding between
nations, to foster the cinema of all continents
by stimulating the development of quality
cinema, to promote filmmakers and innovative
works, to discover and encourage new talents,
and to promote meetings between cinema
professionals from around the world. Apart
from the 'Official Competition' and the 'First
Films Competition', the festival presents 'Hors
Concours' (World Greats), a 'Focus on World
Cinema' and 'Documentaries of the World',
plus tributes to established filmmakers and a
section dedicated to Canadian student films.
Inquiries to: Montreal World Film Festival, 1432
de Bleury St, Montreal, Quebec, Canada H3A
2J1. Tel: (1 514) 848 3883 Fax: 848 3886. e:
commandites@ffm-montreal.org. Web: www.
ffm-montreal.org.

Moscow International Film Festival
June 2009

The large competition remains international in
scope and genres, covering Europe and the
CIS, South East Asia, Latin and North America.
The Media-Forum (panorama and competition)
is devoted to experimental films and video art.
Inquiries to: Moscow International Film Festival, 10/1 Khokhlovsky Per, Moscow 109028,
Russia. Tel: (7 095) 917 2486. Fax: 916 0107. e:
info@miff.ru. Web: www.moscowfilmfestival.ru.

Napa Sonoma Wine Country Film Festival
September 17–27, 2009

World cinema, culture and conscience gather
in the heart of California's premium wine
region, Napa and Sonoma Valleys, just fifty
miles from the Golden Gate Bridge. Films are
screened during the day in select theatres
and at night under the stars in spectacular
vineyard settings. The festival is gently paced,
mainly non-competitive and accepts features,
documentaries, shorts, and animation. All
genres are welcome. Programme categories
are: World Cinema, US Cinema, EcoCinema
(environment), Arts in Film and Cinema of
Conscience (social issues). *Inquiries to:* PO
Box 303, Glen Ellen, CA 95442, USA. Tel: (1
707) 935 3456. e: wcfilmfest@aol.com. Web:
www.wcff.us.

AWARDS 2008
Best of the Festival: **Bliss** (Turkey), Abdullah Oguz.

Actor and screenwriter Molly Bryant with director Bob White, NSWCFF
2008 Best First Feature for **Other People's Parties** *(photo: Stephen Ashton)*

Best World Cinema: **The Maiden and the Wolves** (France), Gilles Legrand.
Best US Cinema: **Crazy** (USA), Rick Bieber.
Best Eco Cinema: **Delta - Oil's Dirty Business** (Greece), Yorgos Avgeropoulos.
Best International Short: **The Letter** (Canada/Russia), Matvel Zhivov.
Best Documentary: **All in This Tea** (USA), Les Blank.
Best Arts in Film: **Caravaggio** (Italy), Angelo Longoni.
Best Cinema of Conscience: **Jump! The Philippe Halsman Story** (Austria), Joshua Sinclair.

Report 2008

More than 4,500 people attended Wine Country's most prestigious cinematic event. The festival showcased 105 films from 31 countries. Highlights included a fascinating masterclass with Chuck Workman who received a Career Achievement Award. Les Blank (*All in This Tea*) received the Bay Area Legendary Filmmaker Award followed by a tea ceremony. A wealth of new talent was discovered including Best Director Branko Schmidt, *The Melon Route* (Croatia), and Chris Warner for his award-winning short, *Lunatic Farmer* (USA). The festival's popular Paseo de Espana featured a dozen films from Spain, including *Lucio* by Aitor Arregi, which won Best International Documentary. **– Justine Warner**, Public Relations.

Netherlands Film Festival, Utrecht
September 23–October 2, 2009

Since 1981, The Netherlands Film Festival presents the latest crop of Dutch feature films, documentaries, short films and television films to the Dutch public as well as an audience of international and Dutch-based professionals. Many of these productions are world premieres, with some competing for the Grand Prize of Dutch Film, the Golden Calf. During the festival, each film genre is allotted its own special day, and retrospectives and special programmes offer a chance to review films from previous years. Furthermore the festival features films made by talented young filmmakers from Dutch

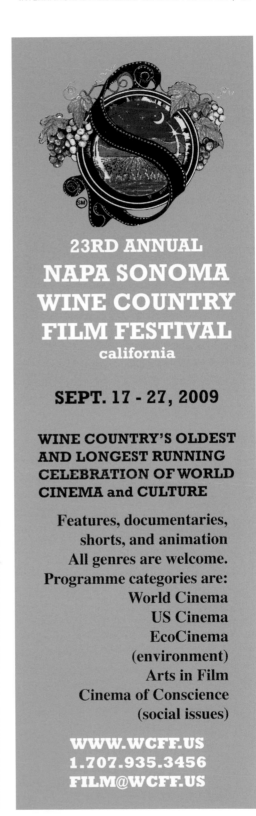

23RD ANNUAL
NAPA SONOMA WINE COUNTRY FILM FESTIVAL
california

SEPT. 17 - 27, 2009

WINE COUNTRY'S OLDEST AND LONGEST RUNNING CELEBRATION OF WORLD CINEMA and CULTURE

Features, documentaries, shorts, and animation
All genres are welcome.
Programme categories are:
World Cinema
US Cinema
EcoCinema
(environment)
Arts in Film
Cinema of Conscience
(social issues)

WWW.WCFF.US
1.707.935.3456
FILM@WCFF.US

NETHERLANDS FILM FESTIVAL 23 SEP- 02 OCT 2009 UTRECHT

22ND HOLLAND FILM MEETING, SEP 24 – SEP 28, 2009
THE ANNUAL GET-TOGETHER OF DUTCH AND FOREIGN FILM PROFESSIONALS

FOR MORE INFORMATION: **WWW.FILMFESTIVAL.NL**

audio-visual institutes and short and long films from Flanders. Talkshows, workshops, parties and exhibitions complete the festival; a unique platform that highlights the very best of Dutch cinema. The Holland Film Meeting (HFM) is a sidebar of the Netherlands Film Festival that provides a series of business-oriented events for the international professionals in attendance. The HFM consists of the Benelux Screenings, the Netherlands Production Platform (NPP), professional workshops and panels, the Variety Cinema Militants Programme and the Binger-Screen International Interview. *Inquiries to:* Netherlands Film Festival, PO Box 1581, 3500 BN Utrecht, Netherlands. Tel: (31 30) 230 3800. Fax: 230 3801. e: info@filmfestival.nl. Web: www.filmfestival.nl.

AWARDS 2008
Best Short Film: **Reef** (The Netherlands), Eric Steegstra.
Best Short Documentary: **Landscapes Unknown (II)** (The Netherlands), Melle van Essen and Riekje Ziengs.
Best Long Documentary: **Bloody Mondays & Strawberry Pies** (The Netherlands), Coco Schrijber.
Best TV Film: **Den Helder** (The Netherlands), Jorien van Nes.
Best Production Design: **Nothing to Lose** (The Netherlands), Elsje de Bruijn.
Best Photography: **In Real Life** (The Netherlands), Menno Westendorp.
Best Sound Design: **Winter Silence** (The Netherlands), Huibert Boon, Alex Booy and Robil Rahantoeknam.
Best Editing: **In Real Life** (The Netherlands), Robert Jan Westdijk.
Best Score: **Tiramisu** (The Netherlands), Michiel Borstlap.
Best Male Supporting Role: Ton Kas for **Vox Populi** (The Netherlands).

Best Female Supporting Role: Olga Louzgina for **Katia's Sister** (The Netherlands).
Best Actor: Robert de Hoog for **Skin** (The Netherlands).
Best Actress: Anneke Blok for **Tiramisu** (The Netherlands).
Best Screenplay: **Katia's Sister** (The Netherlands), Jan Eilander and Jolein Laarman.
Best Director: Joram Lürsen for **Love is All** (The Netherlands).
Best Long Feature Film: **Love is All** (The Netherlands), Jeroen Beker and Frans van Gestel (Motel Films/IDTV Film), San Fu Maltha (Fu Works), Job Gosschalk (Kemna & Zonen).
SPECIAL JURY AWARD: The stunt team Willem de Beukelaer: Willem de Beukelaer, Marco Maas, Ronald Schuurbiers.
Film 1 Audience Award: **Surprise** (The Netherlands), Paul Ruven.
Dutch Film Critics Award: **Calimucho** (The Netherlands), Eugenie Jansen.
Report 2008
At this year's event there was a great

Golden Calf winners: Coco Schrijber, left, with Elsje de Bruin, right, and Robert de Hoog, front at the 28th Netherlands Film Festival 2008 (photo: Felix Kalkman)

emphasis placed on the development of talent. During the ten days of the festival, a short film was written, produced and shot by the cream of young Dutch filmmakers and screened on the last day of the festival. The Golden Calves were awarded during the Dutch Film Gala, which concluded the Festival. This year there were a record number of 145,000 visitors. The NOFF and Festival TV attracted 1.5 million visitors. **– Lotte Niks**, Publicity Department.

Visions du Réel, International Film Festival – Nyon
April 23–29, 2009

Visions du Réel, the International Film Festival in Nyon (a few miles from Geneva) celebrates its 40th anniversary this year and the 15th anniversary of Visions du Réel. Visions du Réel, set in a charming little town on the shores of Lake Léman, is the international capital of the best in cinéma du réel. It offers a tremendous diversity of genres and viewpoints in the presence of an ever larger audience (up 20% last year). It is an exemplary synthesis between a festival and a market: Visions du Réel & Doc Outlook-International Market, featuring a culture of debate, films for all and a way to experience local and international films. Entry deadlines: Festival: 5 January 2009, Market: 15 March 2009. *Inquiries to:* Visions du Réel, 18 rue Juste Olivier, CH-1260 Nyon 1, Switzerland. Tel: (41 22) 365 4455. Fax: 365 4450. e: docnyon@visionsdureel.ch. Web: www.visionsdureel.ch.

AWARDS 2008
International Competition
Grand Prix La Poste Suisse Visions du Réel:
The Lie of the Land (UK), Molly Dineen.
Prix SRG SSR Idée Suisse: **Nuit de Chine** (China/France/Italy), Ju An-Qi.
Audience Prize: **Entre Ours et Loup (24H dans la Ville de N)** (France/Russia), Denis Sneguirev.
Inter-religious Jury Prize: **The Existence** (Poland), Marcin Koszalka.
Young Audience Prize
Prize of the Société des Hôteliers de la Côte:

Closing ceremony of the Festival, with Molly Dineen (Grand Prize winner) and Jean Perret (Visions du Réel director)

Existence (Poland), Marcin Koszalka.
Prize of the DDC: **D'un Mur l'Autre, de Berlin à Ceuta** (Belgium/France), Patric Jean.
Regards Neufs
Prix de l'Etat de Vaud: **Les Hommes de la Forêt 21** (France), Julien Samani and **No London Today** (France), Delphine Deloget.
Cinéma Suisse
Prix George Foundation Meilleur Film Newcomer: **La Mère** (France/Russia/ Switzerland), Antoine Cattin and Pavel Kostomarov.
Prix Suissimage/Société Suisse des Auteurs SSA: **Témoin Indésirable** (Switzerland), Juan Lozano.
From All Sections
Prix 'Regards Sur le Crime': **La Petite Boîteuse** (Switzerland), Robin Harsch.

Report 2008
That makes fourteen. In brief: seven days, 1,600 films received, 160 selected, 39 countries of origin, 41 world premieres, four screening rooms, 220 screenings, 28,000 filmgoers, 1,400 accredited, 700 professionals, 113 filmmakers, 486 media reports, 170 journalists. 2008 was a very good year, so we are told and we are inclined to agree, for four reasons. Firstly, the festival once again convincingly presented a diversity of genres, styles, points of view and narrative approaches. Secondly, spectators came en masse to discover new things. Thirdly, the full participation of professionals within Doc Outlook-International Market has made

it an essential platform. Finally, the spirit of Nyon: its taste, its tone and its voice is composed of a thousand different accents; its culture brings people together in the name of independent creative cinema. Visions du Réel 2008: the lake as a sea. **– Jean Perret**, Festival Director.

International Short Film Festival Oberhausen
April 30–May 5, 2009

The International Short Film Festival Oberhausen is known for its open attitude towards short formats, always looking for unusual, surprising, experimental works. The traditional competitions of the 54th edition – International, German, Children's Shorts and Music Video – provided an extensive overview of current international short film and video production. The 2008 thematic programmes, Border-Crossers and Trouble-Makers and Whose History? looked at aesthetic strategies of political films past and present. Oberhausen also continued its Podium series of lively and very well-attended discussions. Retrospectives of artists Andrew Kötting, Lis Rhodes, Patrice Kirchhofer and Akram Zaatari rounded off the programmes. Deadline for entries: 2 February 2009, entry forms and regulations can be downloaded at www.kurzfilmtage.de from October 2008. Festival Director: Dr Lars Henrik Gass. *Inquiries to:* Oberhausen International Short Film Festival, Grillostrasse 34, D-46045 Oberhausen, Germany. Tel: (49 208) 825 2652. Fax: 825 5413. e: info@kurzfilmtage.de. Web: www.kurzfilmtage.de.

AWARDS 2008
International Competition
Grand Prize of the City of Oberhausen:
Chainsaw, (Australia), Dennis Tupicoff.
Two Principal Prizes: **Jude** (Romania), **Alexandra**, **Radu** and **Vixen Academy** (Russia), Alina Rudnitskaya.
ARTE Prize for a European Short Film:
Kempinski (France), Neil Beloufa.
German Competition
Prize for the Best Contribution: **The Tragedians of the City** (Germany), Eva Könnemann.

Odense international Film Festival
August 2009

Denmark's only international short film festival invites the best international short films with original and imaginative content. Besides screenings of more than 200 National and International short films and Danish documentaries, Odense Film Festival offers a number of exciting retrospective programmes and viewing of all competition films in the Video Bar. The festival hosts a range of seminars for the film professionals, librarians and teachers, educates children and youth in the field of forceful, alternative film experiences and is a meeting place for international film directors and other film professionals in the field of short films and documentaries. Odense Film Festival invites all directors with a film in competition to participate in the festival. *Inquiries to:* Odense Film Festival, Odense Slot, Nørregade 36-38, DK-5100 Odense C, Denmark. Tel: (45) 6551 2823. Fax: 6591 0144. e: filmfestival@odense. dk. Web: www.filmfestival.dk.

Oulu International Children's Film Festival
November 16–22, 2009

Annual festival with competition for full-length feature films for children, it screens recent titles and retrospectives. Oulu is set in northern Finland, on the coast of the Gulf of Bothnia. *Inquiries to:* Oulu International Children's Film Festival, Hallituskatu 7, FI-90100 Oulu, Finland. Tel: (358 8) 881 1293. Fax: 881 1290. e: oek@oufilmcenter.inet.fi. Web: www. ouka.fi/lef.

AWARDS 2008
Kaleva Award: **SOS - The Summer of Suspense** (Norway), Arne Lindtner Naess.

Oulu festival mascot, Vilma

CIFEJ-Prize: **Fighter** (Denmark), Natasha Arthy. *The Little Bear Award:* Outi Rousu.

Palm Springs International Film Festival
January 7–18, 2010

Palm Springs, celebrating its 21st edition in 2010, is one of the largest film festivals in the US, hosting 120,000 attendees for a line-up of over 230 films at the 2009 event. Special sections of the festival include Cine Latino, New Voices/New Visions, Gala Screenings, Awards Buzz (Best Foreign Language Oscar Submissions), World Cinema Now, Modern Masters and the True Stories documentary section. The festival includes a Black Tie Awards Gala – 2009 honorees included Clint Eastwood, Leonardo DiCaprio, Kate Winslet, Ron Howard, Anne Hathaway, and Alexandre Desplat. *Inquiries to:* Darryl MacDonald, 1700 E Tahquitz Canyon Way, Suite 3, Palm Springs, CA 92262, USA. Tel: (1 760) 322 2930. Fax: 322 4087. e: info@psfilmfest.org. Web: www. psfilmfest.org.

Pesaro Film Festival
June 20–29, 2009

The Mostra Internazionale del Nuovo Cinema or Pesaro Film Festival was founded in Pesaro in 1965 by Bruno Torri and Lino Miccichè. Since 2000 Giovanni Spagnoletti has directed the Festival. The Pesaro Film Festival, in addition to being known for the dynamic and original documentation it offers, is synonymous with discoveries, with showcasing emerging cinematographers, with re-readings, with 'Special Events'. *Inquiries to:* Mostra Internazionale del Nuovo Cinema (Pesaro Film Festival), Via Villafranca 20, 00185 Rome, Italy. Tel: (39 06) 445 6643/491 156. Fax: 491 163. e: pesarofilmfest@mclink.it. Web: www. pesarofilmfest.it.

Pordenone Silent Film Festival
October 3–10, 2009

The world's first and largest festival dedicated to silent cinema, now in its 28th year, with its original venue, the Teatro Verdi, Pordenone, entirely rebuilt. Year by year the festival consistently succeeds in rediscovering lost masterpieces from the silent years, all accompanied by original live music. The Film Fair features books, CD-ROMs and DVDs, and provides a valued meeting place for authors and publishers. Festival Director: David Robinson. *Inquiries to:* Le Giornate del Cinema Muto, c/o La Cineteca del Friuli, Palazzo Gurisatti, via Bini 50, 33013 Gemona (UD), Italy. Tel: (39 04) 3298 0458. Fax: 3297 0542. e: info.gcm@cinetecadelfriuli.org. Web: www.giornatedelcinemamuto.it.

Report 2008
The outstanding features of the festival

included the discovery of Alexander Shiryaev, dancer and pioneer genius of animation, whose films had remained unknown for almost a century; French comedies of the 1920s, with the premiere of a new orchestral score by Antonio Coppola for Jacques Feyder's *Les Nouveaux Messieurs*; the silent comedies of the inimitable W. C. Fields; 'Hollywood on the Hudson', highlighting silent feature films made in New York rather than in Hollywood; and Mary Pickford in William Beaudine's *Sparrows* (1926), with a new score by Jeffrey Silverman. Among this year's special guests were Michael York, Michael Nyman, Academy Award-winning animator Richard Williams and the child star of silent films, Jean Darling. **- David Robinson**, Festival Director.

Portland International Film Festival
February 5–22, 2009

Portland International Film Festival will be an invitational event presenting more than 100 films from 30-plus countries to 35,000 people from throughout the Northwest. Along with new international features, documentaries and shorts, the festival will feature showcases surveying Hispanic film and literature, Pacific Rim cinema and many of the year's foreign-

27th Pordenone Silent Film Festival: Michael York and his wife Pat, photo Paolo Jacob

The 31st Portland International Film Festival Opening Night Party at the Portland Art Museum, photo Jason E. Kaplan

32ND PORTLAND INTERNATIONAL FILM FESTIVAL

At the 16th Raindance Film Festival: (left to right) Elliot Grove (founder of Raindance), Faye Dunaway, David Howard (director of **Flick***) (photo: Andreas Tovan)*

language Oscar submissions. *Inquiries to:* Northwest Film Center, 1219 SW Park Ave, Portland, OR 97205, USA. Tel: (1 503) 221 1156. Fax: 294 0874. e: info@nwfilm.org. Web: www.nwfilm.org.

Pusan International Film Festival
October 2009

Established in 1996 in Busan, Korea, PIFF is known as the most energetic film festival in the world and has become the largest film festival in Asia. This world-class event has been promoting Asian and Korean cinema worldwide in particular and screens over 300 films from over sixty countries, many of which are premieres. Also, retrospectives, special programmes in focus, seminars and other related events are presented annually. In addition, its project market – Pusan Promotion Plan (PPP) – has been a platform for moving Asian film projects forward in the international marketplace, along with its own talent campus, Asian Film Academy (AFA), offering various filmmaking programmes for young talent from all over Asia. *Inquiries to:* 1st Floor, 6 Tongui-dong, Jongno-gu, Seoul 110-062, Korea. Tel: (82 2) 3675 5097. e: publicity@piff.org. Web: www.piff.org.

Raindance Film Festival
September 30–October 11, 2009

Raindance is the largest independent film festival in the UK and aims to reflect the cultural, visual and narrative diversity of international independent filmmaking, specialising in first-time filmmakers. The festival screens around a hundred feature films and two hundred shorts as well as hosting a broad range of masterclasses and workshops. *Inquiries to:* Festival Producer, Raindance Film Festival, 81 Berwick St, London, W1F 8TW, UK. Tel: (44 20) 7287 3833. Fax: 7439 2243. e: festival@raindance.co.uk. Web: www.raindance.co.uk/festival.

Report 2008
This year's 16th Raindance Film Festival played host to an electrifying line-up of films, music and events, drawing notable attendees like Bill Nighy, Alfonso Cuaron, Faye Dunaway, Adam Yauch and the Arctic Monkeys. Audience attendance, too, was bigger than ever before, showing a substantial leap over last year's record-setting numbers. Opening and closing galas for Clark Gregg's *Choke* and Mark Tonderai's unnerving thriller *Hush* illuminated London's West End, while festival awards once again honoured the finest in burgeoning and underrepresented film talent from the UK and abroad. Top prizes went to *The Blue Tower* (UK Feature), *Estomago* (International Feature), and *Production Office* (Debut Feature).
– Joe Pearshouse.

Reykjavík International Film Festival
September 17–27, 2009

The festival is one of the most exciting film events in Northern Europe as well as Iceland's major annual film event. The main purpose of the festival is to offer a wide selection of alternative, independent cinema. The festival's intention is to provide cultural diversity, to provoke the public's interest in independent cinema and to impart thereby the film's social importance and to provoke discussions. The

**Reykjavík
International
Film
Festival
17 – 27 September 2009**

→ riff.is

festival emphasises the relation between film and other art forms with art exhibitions, concerts etc. The festival's main award, the Discovery of the Year, the Golden Puffin Award, is dedicated to new filmmakers. *Inquiries to:* Reykjavík International Film Festival, Fríkirkjuvegur 1, 101 Reykjavík, Iceland. Tel: (354) 4117055. Web: www.riff.is.

Report 2008

In 2008, *Tulpan* received the main prize of the Golden Puffin Award, from the category New Visions. The jury consisted of Icelandic director Baltasar Kormákur, who was president of the jury, Icelandic actress Margrét Vilhjálmsdóttir, Finnish director Arto Halonen, Faroe director Katrin Ottarsdottir and Canadian-Armenian actress Arsinée Khanjian. The cinemas are in downtown Reykjavík and were packed most of the time as around 7% of the Icelandic population attended the festival! Philippe Claudell's *I've Loved You So Long* was the most popular film. The audience award went to the Icelandic documentary *Electronica Reykjavík* by Arnar Jonasson. In fact, the festival this year screened many Icelandic films that turned out to be very popular. Many came from the Nordic countries, for example, the opening film *O'Horten* by Bent Hamer. For the first time a whole section, New World, was dedicated to films on environmental issues. RIFF had many side events, for example, for the first time, Sound on Sight, a conference and a market dedicated to music and films. In that relation the popular band, Hjaltalin, wrote and performed music for the old Icelandic film, *Sons of the Soil*, and brand-new documentaries about music were screened. The Transatlantic Atlantic Talent Campus was held for the third

time and participants came from all over the world. RIFF welcomed in 2008 many foreigners, international press, filmmakers and tourists. RIFF's most distinguished guests were Shirin Neshat who received the Creative Excellence Award from the foreign ministry and Costa-Gavras who received the Lifetime Achievement Award from Olafur Ragnar Grimsson, the President of Iceland. – **Hrönn Marinósdóttir**, Festival Director.

Rome International Film Festival
October 2009

Rome is not just a great city, but a city of cinema par excellence and provides not just a festival but a real feast for movie lovers and a great event for all those who work for cinema, show cinema and tell us stories through cinema. The fourth edition will be held in Rome Auditorium, along with screenings at movie theatres and events held in spots that symbolise the city, from the Via Veneto to Piazza del Popolo, from Cinecittà to 'Greater Rome'. The festival has now established itself as a truly unique occasion with the people flocking to the events, exhibitions, encounters and screenings being proof of a great passion and curiosity for culture. *Inquiries to:* Rome International Film Festival, Viale Pietro De Coubertin 10, 00196 Rome, Italy. Tel: (39 06) 4040 1900. e: press.international@romacinemafest.org. Web: www.romacinemafest.org.

AWARDS 2008

Alice in the City Prize for Best Film: **Magic!** (Belgium/France), Phillipe Myul.
Alice in the City Over 12 Prize for Best Film: **Summer** (UK), Kenny Glenaan.
Golden Marco Aurelio Award Best Film: **Resolution 819** (France/Italy/Poland), Giacomo Battiato.
Golden Marco Aurelio Critics' Award Best Film: **Opium War** (Afghanistan/France/Japan/South Korea), Siddiq Barmak.
Silver Marco Aurelio Award Best Actress: Donatella Finocchiaro for **Galantuomini** (Italy).
Silver Marco Aurelio Award Best Actor: Bohdan Stupka for **With a Warm Heart** (Poland/Ukraine).

International Film Festival Rotterdam
January 20–31, 2010

With its adventurous, original and distinctive programming, Rotterdam highlights new directors and new directions in contemporary world cinema, exemplified by its Tiger Awards Competition for 1st and 2nd feature films; the annual showcase of films from developing countries that have been supported by the festival's Hubert Bals Fund, supporting innovative and original film projects from developing countries; the CineMart, the international co-production market developed to nurture the financing and production of new cinema. *Inquiries to:* International Film Festival Rotterdam, PO Box 21696, 3001 AR Rotterdam, Netherlands. Tel: (31 10) 890 9090. Fax: 890 9091. e: tiger@filmfestivalrotterdam.com. Web: www.filmfestivalrotterdam.com.

San Francisco International Film Festival
April 23–May 7, 2009

The oldest film festival in the Americas, in its 52nd year, San Francisco continues to grow in importance and popularity. It presents more than 120 international features and shorts and plays host to more than 80,000 film lovers and hundreds of filmmakers, journalists and film industry professionals, throwing sensational parties, launching new digital initiatives like International Online, celebrating Bay Area film culture and showcasing new technologies. Special awards include the Sky Prize ($10,000 cash for an emerging director), The Golden Gate Awards and the FIPRESCI Prize. *Inquiries to:* San Francisco International Film Festival, Programming Dept, San Francisco Film Society, 39 Mesa St, Suite 110, The Presidio, San Francisco, CA 94129, USA. Tel: (1 415) 561 5014. Fax: 561 5099. e: gga@sffs.org. Web: www.sffs.org.

AWARDS 2008
New Directors Award - First Narrative Feature: **Vasermil** (Israel), Mushon Salmona.
FIPRESCI Prize: **Ballast** (USA), Lance Hammer.
Chris Holter Award for Humour in Film: **Time to Die** (Poland), Dorota Kedzierzawska.
Golden Gate Awards
Documentary Feature: **Up the Yangtze** (Canada), Yung Chang.
Bay Area Documentary Feature: **Faubourg Tremé: The Untold Story of Black New Orleans** (USA), Dawn Logsdon.
Documentary Short: **The Ladies** (USA), Christina A. Voros.
Bay Area Short Film, Second Prize: **On the Assassination of the President** (USA), Adam Keker.
Narrative Short: **Thick Skinned** (France), Jean Bernard Marlin and Benoit Rambourg.
Animated Short: **Madame Tutli-Putli** (Canada), Chris Lavis and Maciek Szczerbowski.
New Visions: **Cabinet** (USA), Todd Herman.
Work for Kids and Families: **When I Grow Up** (USA), Michelle R. Meeker.
Youth Works: **Writing History with Lightning: The Triumph & Tragedy of America's First Blockbuster** (USA), Charlotte Burger.

San Sebastián International Film Festival
September 17–26, 2009

Held in an elegant Basque seaside city known for its superb gastronomy and beautiful beaches, the San Sebastián Festival remains the Spanish-speaking world's most important event in terms of glamour, competition, facilities, partying, number of films and attendance (1,171 production and distribution firms, government agencies and festival representatives from 58 countries, and accredited professionals and 1,091 journalists from 41 countries). Events include the Official Competitive section, Zabaltegi, with its 90,000 Euro cash award Altadis-New Directors, Horizontes Latinos with its 35,000 Euro cash award and various retrospectives. In partnership with the Rencontres Cinémas Amérique Latine in Toulouse, the Films in Progress industry platform aims to aid the completion of Latin American projects. Cinema in Motion 3 is a rendezvous at which to discover projects by moviemakers from Magreb and Portuguese-speaking

African countries and developing Arab countries, presented only to professionals in partnership with Amiens Film Festival and Fribourg Film Festival. *Inquiries to:* San Sebastián International Film Festival, Apartado de Correos 397, 20080 Donostia, San Sebastián 20080, Spain. Tel: (34 943) 481 212. Fax: 481 218. e: ssiff@ sansebastianfestival.com. Web: www.sansebastianfestival.com.

AWARDS 2008
Golden Shell for Best Film: **Pandora's Box** (Belgium/France/Germany/Turkey), Yesim Ustaglou.
Special Jury Award: **Two Legged Horse** (France/Iran), Samira Makhmalbaf.
Silver Shell for Best Director: Michael Winterbottom for **Genova** (UK).
Silver Shell for Best Actress: Melissa Leo for **Frozen River** (USA) and Tsilla Chelton for **Pandora's Box** (Belgium/France/Germany/Turkey).
Silver Shell for Best Actor: Oscar Martínez for **El Nido Vacío** (Argentina/France/Spain).
Jury Award for Best Photography: Hugo Colace for **El Nido Vacío** (Argentina/France/Spain).
Jury Award for Best Screenplay: Benoît Délepine and Gustave Kervern for **Louise-Michel** (France).
Altadis New Directors Award: Li Me de Cai Xiang for **The Equation of Love and Death** (China).
Horizontes Award: **Gasolina** (Guatemala), Julio Hernández Cordón.

Sarasota Film Festival
March 27–April 15, 2009

Ten days of independent film, symposiums and events in a beautiful location; hospitable, inquisitive audiences plus a well-organised and publicised programme. *Inquiries to:* Sarasota Film Festival, 332 Cocoanut Avenue, Sarasota, Florida 34236, USA. Tel: (1 941) 364 9514. Fax: 364 8411. e: jessica@sarasotafilmfestival.com. Web: www.sarasotafilmfestival.com.

Seattle International Film Festival
May 21–June 14, 2009

The largest film festival in the US, SIFF presents more than 250 features, 50 documentaries, and 100 shorts annually. There are cash prizes for the internationally juried New Directors Showcase and Documentary Competition and for Short Films in the categories of: Live Action, Documentary and Animation. Festival sections include: Alternate Cinema, Face the Music, FutureWave, Films4Familes, Contemporary World Cinema, Emerging Masters, Documentary Films, Tributes, and Archival Films. *Inquiries to:* Seattle International Film Festival, 400 Ninth Avenue North, Seattle, WA 98109, USA. Tel: (206) 464 5830. Fax: (206) 264 7919. e: info@siff.net. Web: www.siff.net

AWARDS 2008
New Directors Showcase
Grand Jury Prize: **Everything is Fine** (Canada), Yves-Christian Fournier.
Special Jury Prize: **Mermaid** (Russia), Anna Melikyan.
New American Cinema Award
Grand Jury Prize: **Em** (USA), Tony Barbieri.
Special Jury Prize: **The Bluetooth Virgin** (USA), Russell Brown.
Documentary Competition
Grand Jury Prize: **Derek** (UK), Isaac Julien.
Special Jury Prize: **Combalion** (France), Raphaël Mathié and **Accelerating America** (USA), Timothy Hotchner.
Short Awards Grand Jury Prize: **Rewind** (India), Atul Taishete.
Narrative Special Jury Prize: **Walnut** (Australia), Amy Gebhardt **Dog Altogether** (UK), Paddy Considine **A Mate** (Finland), Teemu Nikki and **New Boy** (Ireland), Steph Green.
Documentary Grand Jury Prize: **Self Portrait With Cows Going Home and Other Works: A Portrait of Sylvia Plachy** (USA), Rebecca Dreyfus.
Documentary Special Jury Prize: **The Ladies** (USA), Christina Voros.
Animation Grand Jury Prize: **The Pearce**

Sisters (UK), Luis Cook.
Animation Special Jury Prize: **Home** (USA), Kim Slate.
Golden Space Needle Audience Awards
Best Film: **Cherry Blossoms-Hanami** (Germany), Doris Dörrie.
Best Documentary: **The Wrecking Crew** (USA), Denny Tedesco.
Best Short Film: **Felix** (Germany), Andreas Utta.
Best Director: Amin Matalqa for **Captain Abu Raed** (Jordan).
Best Actor: Alan Rickman for **Bottle Shock** (USA).
Best Actress: Jessica Chastain for **Jolene** (USA).

Seville European Film Festival
November 2009

The Festival is established as one of the best, showcasing the best films in Europe and shows more than 160 of the most prestigious long feature films, documentaries and short films produced, not only in the European Union, but also in other countries such as Turkey, the Balkan countries, Norway, Russia, Switzerland, Israel and Palestine. The festival attracts more than 66,000 spectators and also includes seminars, lectures, exhibitions and public presentations. *Inquiries to:* Seville Film Festival, Pabellón de Portugal, Avenida Cid 1, 41004 Seville, Spain. Tel: (34 955) 115 586. Fax: 115 587. e: prensa@festivaldesevilla.com. Web: www.festivaldesevilla.com.

Shanghai International Film Festival
June 13–21, 2009

Shanghai International Film Festival (SIFF) main sections include such competitions as Jin Jue Award International Film Competition, Asia New Talent Award, International Student Shorts Award, SIFF Mart with Film Market, China Film Pitch and Catch (CFPC), Co-production Film Pitch and Catch (Co-FPC), as well as others like SIFFORUM, International Film Panorama. *Inquiries to:* Shanghai International Film Festival, 11F STV Mansions, 298 Wei Hai Road, Shanghai 200041, China. Tel: (86 21) 6253 71158. Fax: 6255 2000. Web: www.siff.com.

AWARDS 2008
Jin Jue Awards
Best Feature Film: **Mukha** (Russia), Vladimir Kott.
Jury Grand Prix: **Old Fish** (China), Gao Qunshu.
Best Director: Maris Martinsons, **Loss** (Lithuania).
Best Actor: Ma Guowei, **Old Fish** (China).
Best Actress: Emilia Vasaryova, **Vaclav** (Czech Republic).
Best Screenplay: Marek Epstein, **Vaclav** (Czech Republic).
Best Cinematography: Florian Schilling, **My Mother's Tears** (Germany).
Best Music: Andrius Mamontovas, **Loss** (Lithuania).
Asian New Talent Awards
Jury Prize: **Lucky Dog** (China).
Best Director: Hyeon-gi Hong, **Thirsty, Thirsty** (Korea).
Best Feature Film: **Winds of September** (China/Taiwan), Tom Shu-Yu Lin.

Report 2008
Shanghai International Film Festival plays an pivotal role in promoting the world's promising young talents as well as the collaboration between China's film industry and the rest of the world via its China Film Pitch and Catch (CFPC), Co-production Film Pitch and Catch (Co-FPC) and International Student Shorts Award in addition to the established Jin Jue Award international Film Competition, Asia New Talent Award, Film Market, SIFFORUM and International Film Panorama. In CFPC and Co-FPC 2008, 35 projects out of forty selected from nearly 200 entries have found their partners. More opportunities are waiting there every June in Shanghai. **– Royal Chen**, Advertising & Promotion.

Sheffield Doc/Fest
November 4–8, 2009

For five days, Sheffield Doc/Fest brings the international documentary family together to celebrate the art and business of documentary making. Combining a film festival, industry sessions and market activity, the festival offers pitching opportunities, controversial discussion panels and in-depth filmmaker masterclasses, as well as a wealth of inspirational documentary films from across the globe. Approximately 140 documentary films are screened, mainly from a call for entries made in March. Around fifty debates, discussions, case studies, interviews and masterclasses are presented and there are a number of well-attended social and networking events. The MeetMarket takes place over two days of the festival. It is a highly effective initiative; pre-scheduled one-on-one meetings where TV commissioning editors, executive producers, distributors and other financiers meet with independent producers and filmmakers to discuss documentary projects in development that are seeking international financing. The film programme is also open to the public. *Inquiries to:* Sheffield Doc/Fest, The Workstation, 15 Paternoster Row, Sheffield, S1 2BX, UK. Tel: (44 114) 276 5141. e: info@sidf.co.uk. Web: www.sheffdocfest.co.uk.

AWARDS 2008
Audience Award: **The Fallen** (UK), Morgan Mathews.
Grierson:Sheffield Youth Jury Award: **Order of Myths** (United States), Margaret Brown.
Grierson Sheffield Innovation Award: **Seven Sins of England** (UK), Joe Bullman.

Director of **Japan: A Story of Love and Hate**, *Sean McAllister (left) with the films subject Naoki Satoh, at Sheffield Doc/Fest 2008,* © *Pixelwitch*

Grierson Sheffield Green Award: **Age of Stupid** (UK), Franny Armstrong.
Wallflower Press Best International Student Documentary Film: **Cyanosis** (Iran), Roksareh Ghaemmaghami.

Silverdocs: AFI/Discovery Channel Documentary Festival
June 15–22, 2009

Silverdocs is an eight-day international film festival and conference that promotes the art of documentary film. Silverdocs takes place at the AFI Silver Theatre, one of the premier film-exhibition spaces in the country, and the top art-house cinema in the Washington, DC region. Anchored in the US capital, where important global and national issues are the daily business, Silverdocs is marked by its relevance, broad intellectual range, and wide public appeal. Among its numerous special programmes is the Charles Guggenheim Symposium which, in 2008, honoured legendary film director Spike Lee. Past recipients include Martin Scorsese, Barbara Kopple and Jonathan Demme. *Inquiries*

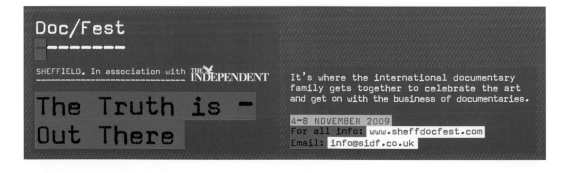

to: AFI Silver Theatre and Cultural Center, 8633 Colesville Road, Silver Spring MD 20910, USA. Tel: (1 301) 495 6720. e: info@silverdocs.com Web: www.silverdocs.com.

AWARDS 2008
Sterling World Feature: **The English Surgeon** (UK), Geoffrey Smith.
Sterling US Feature: **The Garden**, Scott Hamilton Kennedy.

Singapore International Film Festival
April 10–25, 2009

Founded in 1987, SIFF is one of the leading festivals in Southeast Asia. Some 300 films from more than 40 countries are shown to 40,000 viewers through the main, fringe and special programmes and retrospectives. Fringe screenings are free and begin a week before the main programme. The festival's Asian focus and film selection attract programmers from all over the world. The Silver Screen Awards honour the best in Asian cinema, including the NETPAC prize, co-ordinated by the Network for Promotion of Asian Cinema. Since 2003, the festival has begun to highlight the emerging cinema of the Middle East. Selection deadline is January 31, 2008. Festival Director: Yuni Hadi. *Inquiries to:* Singapore International Film Festival, 44B North Canal Rd, Singapore 059300, Singapore. Tel: (65) 738 7567. Fax: (65) 738 7578. e: filmfest@pacific.net.sg. Web: www.filmfest.org.sg.

AWARDS 2008
Best Asian Feature Film Category
Best Film: **Slingshot** by Brillante Mendoza.
Special Jury Award: **Out of Coverage** by Abellatif Abdelhamid.
Best Director: Brillante Mendoza for **Slingshot**.
Best Performance: Inessa Kislova for **Swift**.
NETPAC Award: **Slingshot** by Brillante Mendoza.
Best Singapore Short Film Category
Best Film: **Keluar Baris** by Boo Junfeng.
Special Jury Prize: **Wet Seasons** by Michael Tay.
Best Director: Boo Junfeng for **Keluar Baris**.
Special Achievement Award: **My Home, My Heaven** by Muhammad Eysham Ali.

Best Cinematography: Sharon Loh for **Keluar Baris**.
Best Performance: Magdalene Tan for **Silent Girls**.

Hong Kong actor Winston Chao presented the festival's closing film **Road to Dawn** *directed by Derek Chiu which he starred in*

Report 2008
At the 21st Singapore International Film Festival more than 200 films from 42 countries were shown at seven venues. The winners were judged by a panel of Singapore and international jurors consisting of: Wu Tianming (filmmaker, China), Khadija Al-Salami (filmmaker, Yemen), Dustin Nguyen (Actor, US), Nicholas Saputra (Actor, Indonesia), Low Hwee Ling (Assistant Editor, Infinite Frameworks, Singapore), Anderson Le (Programme Director, Hawaii International Film Festival), Andreas Ungerbock (Editor of *Ray* magazine) and Melanie Oliveiro (Senior Producer/Presenter, Mediacorp Radio, Singapore). **–Yuni Hadi**, Festival Director.

Sitges International Film Festival of Catalonia
October 2009

Sitges focuses on fantasy films and is considered one of Europe's leading specialised festivals and is an essential rendezvous for movie lovers and audiences eager to embrace new tendencies and technologies applied to film and the audiovisual world. *Inquiries to:* Sitges Festival Internacional de Cinema de Catalunya, Calle Davallada 12, 3rd Floor, CP:08870 Sitges, Barcelona, Spain. Tel: (34 93) 894 9990. Fax: 894 8996. e: festival@cinemasitges.com. Web: www.cinemasitges.com

45th Solothurn Film Festival
January 21 – 28, 2010   www.solothurnfilmfestival.ch

Solothurn Film Festival
January 19–25, 2009
January 21–28, 2010

Since 1964, the Solothurn Film Festival has presented an overview of the elapsed year's entire output of Swiss film making. Solothurn is the popular rendezvous for the film media branches and a large public. Beside the main focus on current national film productions of all genres and lengths with many premieres of new Swiss films, the programme includes a retrospective of prominent filmmakers or actors, the music-clip section 'Sound & Stories' and the section 'Invitation' with a selection of films produced in countries bordering Switzerland. Young talents can be discovered in the film school section. The screenings are accompanied by a variety of daily round-table discussions, talk shows, film branch meetings and seminars. *Inquiries to:* Solothurn Film Festival, PO Box 1564, CH-4502 Solothurn, Switzerland. Tel: (41 32) 625 8080. Fax: 623 6410. e: info@solothurnerfilmtage.ch. Web: www.solothurnerfilmtage.ch.

Report 2008
The 43rd Solothurn Film Festival hosted around 1,500 professionals and over 43,000 cinemagoers enjoyed 297 films in different programme sections. The festival opened with one of the rare domestic animated features, Max & Co by the brothers Frédéric and Samuel Guillaume. The main programme proved to be a strong year of documentaries with films such as *Hidden Heart* about the heart surgeon Barnard by Cristina Karrer and Werner Schweizer, *Desert – Who is the Man* by Felix Tissi, *Shake the Devil Off* by Peter Entell or *Bird's Nest – Herzog and de Meuron in China* by Christoph Schaub and Michael Schindhelm, as well as many other views of reality on and

over the world. Controversial discussions about digitization or training in cinematography, showcases and film talks built the frame of the festival. The audience award went to the fiction film *Das Geheimnis von Murk* by Sabine Boss. The award for the best music clip went to Marco Lutz for his music video *Ah, ah, ah, ah.* The retrospective was devoted to the actor Walo Lüönd, who is a popular performer of rather severe and unsophisticated characters in Swiss feature and TV films. **– Ivo Kummer**, Festival Director.

The 43rd Solothurn Film Festival

Slamdance Film Festival
January 15–23, 2009

The festival is organised and programmed exclusively by filmmakers for filmmakers and the sole aim is to nurture, support and showcase truly independent works. In doing so, Slamdance has established a unique reputation for premiering new films by first-time writers and directors working within the creative confines of limited budgets. Slamdance's goal is to strengthen its year-round efforts in support of these artists and to raise the profile and reputation for the further development of other Slamdance media components. As a year-round organisation, Slamdance serves as a showcase for the discovery of new and emerging talent and is dedicated to the nurturing and development of new independent artists and their cinematic vision. *Inquiries to:* Slamdance Inc, 5634 Melrose Ave, Los Angeles, California 90038, USA. Tel: (1 323) 466 1786. Fax: 466 1784. e: mail@slamdance.com. Web: www. slamdance.com.

South by Southwest Film Festival
March 13–21, 2009

The festival explores all aspects of the art and business of independent filmmaking. The Conference hosts a five-day adventure in the latest filmmaking trends and new technology, featuring distinguished speakers and mentors. The internationally acclaimed festival boasts some of the most wide-ranging programming of any US event of its kind, from provocative documentaries to subversive Hollywood comedies, with a special focus on emerging talents. *Inquiries to:* South by Southwest Film Festival, Box 4999, Austin, TX 78765, USA. Tel: (1 512) 467 7979. e: sxsw@sxsw.com. Web: http://sxsw.com.

AWARDS 2008
Jury Awards
Reel Shorts: **Warlord** (USA), David Garrett and **Small Apartment** (USA), Andrew T. Betzer.
Animated Shorts: **Madame Tulti-Putli** (USA), Chris Lavis and Maciek Szczerbowski.
Experimental Shorts: **Safari** (USA), Catherine Chalmers.
SXSW Wholphin Award: **Glory at Sea** (USA), Benjamin Zeitlin.
Music Videos: **TV on the Radio: Me-I** (USA), Mixtape Club & Daniel Garcia.
Texas High School Competition: **Picnic** (USA), Wesley Bronez.
Documentary Feature: **They Killed Sister Dorothy** (USA), Daniel Junge.
Narrative Feature: **Wellness** (USA), Jake Mahaffy.
Audience Awards
24 Beats Per Second: **Throw Down Your Heart** (USA), Sascha Paladino.
Lone Star States: **Cook County** (USA), David Pomes.
Emerging Visions: **In a Dream** (USA), Jeremiah Zagar.
Documentary Feature: **They Killed Sister Dorothy** (USA), Daniel Junge.
Narrative Feature: **Explicit Ills** (USA), Mark Webber.

Report 2008
The SXSW Film Conference has set the stage for some unforgettable moments during the past 15 years. Richard Linklater conversing with Jim Jarmusch, Jeffrey Tambor's Acting Workshops, Robert Rodriguez's HD Panels, and in-depth conversations with the likes of Christine Vachon, Charlize Theron, Bill Paxton, John Carpenter, and Henry Rollins. 2008 Conference highlights include 'Jeffrey Tambor's Acting Workshop', 'Coming Soon: The Making of a Trailer', 'Race, Politics and Drugs: A Harold & Kumar Panel', 16 Joint Film and Interactive panel sessions, and one-on-one conversations with Helen Hunt, Billy Bob Thornton, Harlan Ellison, Stanley Nelson, Michael Eisner and Moby. Last year's festival hosted the premieres of this past summer's most raved about films including Robert Luketic's *21*, *Harold & Kumar Escape from Guantanamo Bay*, *Forgetting Sarah Marshall*, and Michael Blieden's sleeper hit, *Super High Me*. Indie discoveries were plentiful – here's a small sample: *Full Battle Rattle*, *Beautiful Losers*, *Second Skin*, *Humboldt County*, *The Pleasure of Being Robbed*, and *Medicine for Melancholy*. **– Hilary Kerby**, Film Sales/ Marketing Coordinator.

Stockholm International Film Festival
November 19–29, 2009

The Stockholm International Film Festival will this year celebrate its 19th anniversary as one of Europe's leading cinema events. Recognised by FIAPF and hosting a FIPRESCI jury, it is also a member of the European Coordination of Film Festivals. The festival welcomed 125,000 visits during 2007; more than 500 accredited journalists, 420 industry officials and around a hundred directors, actors and producers are present every year. In 2007, some 170 films from forty different countries were presented. Wes Anderson, Jason Schwartzman, Oliver Stone, David Cronenberg, Gena Rowlands, Park Chan-wook, Ang Lee, Quentin Tarantino and Lauren Bacall are some of the distinguished guests. Since 2006 the festival also offers distribution over the Internet through VOD, video on demand. The first titles to be releases are *Hamilton* by Matthew Porterfield, *The Last Communist* by

Amir Muhammad, *Empty* by Veiko Õunpuu, *Your Life in 65 Minutes* by Maria Ripoll and *The Hawk is Dying* by Julian Goldberger. *Inquiries to:* Stockholm International Film Festival, PO Box 3136, S-103 62 Stockholm, Sweden. Tel: (46 8) 677 5000. Fax: 200 590. e: info@stockholmfilmfestival.se. Web: www.stockholmfilmfestival.se

Sundance Film Festival
January 21–31, 2010

Long known as a celebration of the new and unexpected, the Sundance Film Festival puts forward the best in independent film from the US and around the world. For ten days in January audiences in darkened theatres will discover the 125 feature films and eighty shorts that Festival programmers have scoured the world to find. The critically acclaimed Festival presents features and documentaries from the US and around the world, and competition films are combined with nightly premieres of works by veteran film artists for a programme that inspires, challenges, delights, startles and moves Festival goers. Archival gems by early independent filmmakers, animation of every kind, cutting-edge experimental works, midnight cult films, and a jam-packed schedule of panel discussions at Prospector Theatre, Filmmaker Lodge and New Frontier on Main, live shows at the Music Café and a host of spirited parties and events up and down historic Main Street make for a complete film experience that celebrates the art and community of independent filmmaking.

Scene of Park City during 2008 Sundance Film Festival (photo: Brian Ach/WireImage)

Continuing the tradition of sharing the Festival with online audiences, www.sundance.org/festival takes both original content and the nuts and bolts of Festival going beyond the streets of Park City. With short films from the Festival, filmmaker interviews, and breaking news, combined with film listings, box office information and travel tips, Sundance Film Festival Online is a single online source for experiencing the Sundance Film Festival both on the web and on the ground. *Inquiries to:* Geoffrey Gilmore, Director, Festival Programming Department, Sundance Institute, 8530 Wilshire Blvd, 3rd Floor, Beverly Hills, CA 90211-3114, USA. Tel: (1 310) 360 1981. Fax: 360 1969. e: institute@sundance.org. Web: www.sundance.org.

AWARDS 2008
Grand Jury Prize (Documentary): **Trouble the Water** (USA), Tia Lessin and Carl Deal.
Grand Jury Prize (Dramatic): **Frozen River** (USA), Courtney Hunt.
Audience Award (Documentary): **Fields of Fuel** (USA), Josh Tickell.
Audience Award (Dramatic): **The Wackness** (USA), Jonathan Levine.
World Cinema Jury Prize (Documentary): **Man on Wire** (UK), James Marsh.
World Cinema Jury Prize (Dramatic): **King of Ping Pong** (Sweden), Jens Jonsson.
World Cinema Audience Award (Documentary): **Man on Wire** (UK), James Marsh.
World Cinema Audience Award (Dramatic): **Captain Abu Raed** (Jordan), Amin Matalqa.

Tampere Film Festival
March 4–8, 2009

It is a celebration of filmic art during five bright days and late nights. Besides the International, Finnish Short Film and Lab10 competitions, the festival screens a wide variety of films. In 2009 the special themes focus on Vietnam, Switzerland and MoMa. The Canon of Short Film continues to present the best short films of all times. Videotivoli is our event for films made by kids for kids. The festival is also bursting with seminars, exhibitions, concerts and club nights. *Inquiries to:* Tampere Film Festival, PO Box 305, FI-33101 Tampere, Finland. Tel: (358 3) 223 5681. Fax: 223 0121. e: office@tamperefilmfestival.fi. Web: www. tamperefilmfestival.fi.

Telluride Film Festival
September 4–7, 2009

Each Labour Day weekend, more than 3,000 passionate film lovers ascend to the high Colorado mountain village of Telluride for four days of movie heaven. True to long-time Telluride tradition, the programme is kept a secret until opening day when audiences discover the 20 to 25 new narrative and documentary features, with directors, actors and writers in attendance. The festival also showcases rare archival restorations, silent films with live scores, short film programmes, special events and tributes. The 35th festival included Tributes to director David Fincher, who previewed selections from his upcoming film *The Curious Case of Benjamin Button*, British actress and Hollywood studio-era darling Jean Simmons, and Swedish director Jan Troell who unveiled his latest film, *Everlasting Moments*. Each year a Guest Director presents an eclectic series of films. 2008 featured academic superstar, philosopher and cineaste Slavoj Žižek, curating three neglected noirs from different decades and three European rarities. Additionally, the 35th festival spotlighted Romanian director Nae Caranfil, and honoured film critic and director Richard Schickel with the Special Medallion. In partnership with the Italian Silent Film Festival, 'Pordenone Presents' offered Rene Clair's elegant film comedy *The Italian Straw Hat* and a programme of shorts, *Laughing 'Til It Hurts*, both accompanied by Maud Nelissen. The Alloy Orchestra premiered their original score for Josef Von Sternberg's stylised *The Last Command*. Each year there are surprise sneak previews, intimate conversations, seminars in the park and a lively student programme, all book-ended by the Opening Night Feed and the Labour Day Picnic. Screened in nine venues including

Telluride Film Festival (photo: Arun Nevader)

the Abel Gance Outdoor Cinema, the festival presentations meet the highest technical standards using top projectionists. Telluride is a non-competitive festival. Complete past programmes and information about entering features and shorts, programmes for high school and college students can be found on the Festival's website. *Inquiries to:* The Telluride Film Festival, 800 Jones Street, Berkeley, CA 94710 USA. Tel: (1 510) 665 9494. Fax: 665 9589. e: mail@ telluridefilmfestival.org. Web: www. telluridefilmfestival.org.

Thessaloniki International Film Festival
November 13–22, 2009
Thessaloniki Documentary Festival
March 13–22, 2009

In its forty-ninth year, the oldest and the most important film event in South Eastern Europe targeted a new generation of film-makers as well as independent films by established directors. The International Competition (for first or second features) awarded the Golden Alexander (€37,000) to Abdolreza Kahani for his film *Over There* (Iran) and the Silver Alexander (€22,000) to Adrian Sitary for his film *Hooked* (Romania). Other sections include Greek Film Panorama, retrospectives, Balkan Survey, the informative section Independence Days, the thematic section Focus, plus masterclasses, galas and exhibitions. At the same time, distinguished guests including Oliver Stone, Willem Dafoe, Theo Angelopoulos, Takeshi Kitano and Gustavo Santaolalla left their mark on the 49th edition and raised the stakes for the forthcoming 50th Thessaloniki International Film Festival. As always, the festival's Industry Centre acted as an umbrella service for film professionals, who benefited from the services of the Balkan Script Development Fund, Crossroads Coproduction Forum, Agora Film Market and Salonica Studio Student Workshops. The Thessaloniki Documentary Festival – Images of the 21st Century, is Greece's major annual non-fiction film event. Its sections include 'Views of the World' (subjects of social interest), 'Portraits - Human Journeys' (highlighting the human contribution to cultural, social and historical developments) and 'Recording of Memory' (facts and testimony of social and historic origin). The festival also hosts the third largest documentary market in Europe, the Thessaloniki DocMarket. *Inquiries to:* Thessaloniki International Film Festival, 9 Alexandras Ave, 114 73 Athens, Greece. Tel: (30 210) 870 6000. Fax: 644 8143. e: info@filmfestival.gr. Web: www.filmfestival. gr. Director: Despina Mouzaki. Inquiries to: Thessaloniki Documentary Festival (address, website and Tel/Fax numbers as above). Artistic Director: Dimitri Eipides. e: eipides@ filmfestival.gr.

AWARDS 2008

Thessaloniki International Film Festival (49th)
Artistic Achievement Award: **Fövenyóra/ Hourglass** (Hungary/Montenegro/Serbia), Szabolcs Tolnai.
Best Screenplay Award: **Three Blind Mice** (Australia), Matthew Newton.
Best Actress Award: ex aequo to Iona Flora and Maria Dinulescu for **Pescuit Sportiv/ Hooked** (Romania), Andrian Sitaru.
Best Actor Award: ex aequo to Sid Lucero and Emilio Garcia for **Selda/The Inmate** (Philippines), Ellen Ramos and Paolo Villalune
Best Director Award: Celina Murga for **Una Semana Solos/One Week Alone** (Argentina).
Silver Alexander Award: **Pescuit Sportiv/ Hooked** (Romania) Andrian Sitaru.
Golden Alexander Award: **Aan Ja/Over There** (Iran) Abdolreza Kahani.

Thessaloniki Documentary Festival (10th) – Images of the 21st Century
Hellenic Red Cross Audience Award for a Greek film over 45 minutes: **Birds In The Mire** (Greece), Alinda Dimitriou.
Hellenic Red Cross Audience Award for a foreign film over 45 minutes: **As Seen Through These Eyes** (USA), Hilary Helstein.
Hellenic Red Cross Audience Award for a Greek film under 45 minutes: **The Archelon Bubble** (Greece), Eleftherios Fylaktos.
Hellenic Red Cross Audience Award for a foreign film under 45 minutes: **City of Cranes** (UK), Eva Weber.

Tokyo International Film Festival
Late October 2009

Over the nine days of the 21st Tokyo International Film Festival, films from a variety of genres were screened in several intriguing programmes: '*Competition*', which selects the winner of the Tokyo Sakura Grand Prix from a carefully chosen ensemble of premiere films directed by both talented first-timers and recognised directors; '*Special Screenings*', which premieres highly entertaining films prior to their public release in Japan; '*Winds of Asia – Middle East*', which boasts the largest number of films and audience numbers of all the TIFF screenings; '*Japanese Eyes*', which showcases a broad range of Japanese films for the worldwide audience; and a newly launched programme called '*natural TIFF*' to match the

Tokyo International Film Festival 2008, from left Tom Yoda (Chairman of TIFF/TIFFCOM), Yoshino Kimura (Ambassador of TIFF2008), Tony Leung, Anne, Takai Hideyuki (President of UNIJAPAN). © 2008TIFF

ecological theme of the 21st TIFF. TIFFCOM, an entertainment content business market affiliated with TIFF, is expanding every year to establish its position as one of the major business opportunities in Asia. *Inquiries to:* Unijapan/TIFF Office, 5F Tsukiji Yasuda Building, 2-15-14 Tsukiji Chuo-ku, Tokyo 104-0045, Japan. Tel: (81 3) 3524 1081. e: tokyo@tiff.net. Web: www.tiff-jp.net.

Torino Film Festival
November 13–21, 2009

Torino Film Festival is one of Europe's most important cinematographic events and is known for its discoveries as well as for its unique retrospectives. The festival constitutes a meeting point for contemporary international cinema and pays particular attention to emerging cinemas and filmmakers and promotes awareness of new directors whose work is marked by strong formal and stylistic research. Its programme includes competitive sections for international features, Italian documentaries and Italian shorts, as well as spotlights and premieres. *Inquiries to:* Torino Film Festival, Via Montebello 15, 10124 Torino, Italy. Tel: (39 011) 813 8811. Fax: 813 8890. e: info@torinofilm-fest.org. Web: www.torinofilmfest.org.

Toronto International Film Festival
September 10–19, 2009

The Toronto International Film Festival is widely recognised as the largest and most successful public festival in the world. For ten days every September, the Festival becomes a must-attend event for filmmakers, industry professionals, media and the public alike. For over 30 years, the Festival has brought the work of emerging talents and masters of the craft from around the world. As always, the Festival remains committed to supporting Canadian filmmakers and has been a platform for Canada's artists. *Inquiries to:* Toronto International Film Festival, 2 Carlton St, 16th Floor, Toronto, Ontario, M5B 1J3, Canada. Tel: (1 416) 967 7371. Fax: 967 3595. e: customerrelations@torfilm-fest.ca. Web: www.tiffg.ca.

AWARDS 2008
Cadillac People's Choice Award: **Slumdog Millionaire** (UK), Danny Boyle.
Diesel Discovery Award: **Hunger** (UK), Steve McQueen.
Prize of the International Critics (Fipresci Prize): **Discovery Lymelife** (USA), Derick Martini.
City of Toronto Citytv Award for Best Canadian First Feature Film: **Lost Song**, Rodrigue Jean.
CityTV Award for Best Canadian First Feature Film: **Before Tomorrow**, Marie-Hélène Cousineau and Madeline Piujuq.
Award for Best Canadian Short Film: **Block B**, Chris Chong Chan Fui.

Report 2008
The 33rd annual Toronto International Film Festival showcased 312 films from 64 countries on 36 theatre screens across downtown Toronto. The Festival opened with Paul Gross's First World War epic *Passchendaele* and acclaimed Canadian directors Deepa Mehta and Atom Egoyan returned to the Festival with *Heaven on Earth* and *Adoration*, respectively. Yonge and Dundas Square programming brought the festival experience to the general public, with free public performances and presentations by some of the artists and entertainers featured in films at this year's Festival. Performances included Senegalese music sensation Youssou Ndour, and renowned jazz musician and composer Terence Blanchard. This year's programming included the Cadillac People's Choice Award winner *Slumdog Millionaire*, *The Hurt Locker* and *The Wrestler*. Approximately 500 international guests attended the Festival, including Jimmy Page, Isabelle Huppert, Keira Knightley, Lee Byung-hun and Akshay Kumar. – **Press Office**.

Tribeca Film Festival
April 22–May 3, 2009

The Tribeca Film Festival was founded in 2002 by Robert De Niro, Jane Rosenthal and Craig Hatkoff, to spur the economic and cultural revitalisation of Lower Manhattan through an annual celebration of film, music and culture.

The Festival's mission is to help filmmakers reach the broadest possible audience, enable the international film community and general public to experience the power of cinema and promote New York City as a major filmmaking centre. Since its founding, the Festival has attracted more than two million attendees from the US and abroad and has generated close to $500 million in economic activity for New York City. The Festival is anchored in Tribeca with additional venues throughout Manhattan and includes film screenings, special events, concerts, a family street fair, and 'Tribeca Talks' panel discussions. *Inquiries to:* Peter Scarlet, 375 Greenwich St, New York, NY 10013, USA. Tel: (1 212) 941 2400. Fax: 941 3939. e: festival@tribecafilmfestival.org. Web: www.tribecafilmfestival.org.

AWARDS 2008

Best Narrative Feature: **Let the Right One In** (Sweden), Tomas Alfredson.
Best New Narrative Filmmaker: Hüseyin Karabey, **My Marlon and Brando** (Netherlands/Turkey/UK).
Best Documentary Feature: **Pray the Devil Back to Hell** (USA), Gini Reticker.
Best New Documentary Filmmaker: Carlos Carcas (Spain), **Old Man Bebo**.
Best Actress in a Narrative Feature: Eileen Walsh, **Eden** (Ireland).
Best Actor in a Narrative Feature: Thomas Turgoose and Piotr Jagiello, **Somers Town** (UK).
'Made In NY' – Narrative: **The Caller** (UK/USA), Richard Ledes.
'Made In NY' – Documentary: **Zoned In** (UK), Daniela Zanzotto.
Cadillac Audience Award: **War Child** (USA), Karim C. Chrobog.
Best Narrative Short: **New Boy**, Steph Green.
Best Documentary Short: **Mandatory Service**, Jessica Habie.
Student Visionary Award: **Elephant Garden**, Sasie Sealy.
Tribeca All Access Creative Promise Award - Documentary: **She Wants to Be A Matador**, Gemma Cubero and Celeste Carrasco.
Tribeca All Access Creative Promise Award – Narrative: **$Free.99**, Pete Chatmon and co-

Tribeca Film Festival 2009 Attendees wait in line for tickets. Courtesy: Tribeca Film Festival

written by Candice Sanchez McClaren.
Tribeca All Access Creative Promise Award - Emerging Narrative: **The Infinite Life of Stuart Hornsley**, Leigh Dana Jackson.
Tribeca All Access Creative Promise Award - Screenwriting: Bardos, Anslem Richardson.
L'Oréal Paris Women of Worth Vision Award: Alka Raguatham.

Report 2008

The Festival featured 121 features and 79 short films from 41 countries in addition to 14 panel discussions and conversations. Festival organisers estimated a ticketed attendance of over 155,000 to 700 screenings throughout the eleven-day Festival. Notable filmmakers and guests in attendance at the Festival included Madonna (*I Am Because We Are*), Melvin Van Peebles (*Confessions of a Ex-Doofus-Itchy Footed Mutha*), Robert Drew (*A President to Remember*), and Julian Schnabel (*Lou Reed's Berlin*). – **John Kendzierski**.

Tromsø International Film Festival
January 12–17, 2010

Norway's largest film festival, Tromsø International Film Festival is known as an audience festival, presenting the best of current international arthouse cinema and screening more than 150 titles, including a feature competition and several exciting sidebars, among them 'Films from the North', with new shorts and docs from arctic Scandinavia, Canada and Russia. The festival is also an important meeting place for industry professionals. *Inquiries to:* Tromsø International Film Festival, PO Box 285, N-9253 Tromsø, Norway. Tel: (47) 7775 3090. Fax: 7775 3099. e: info @tiff.no. Web: www.tiff.no.

AWARDS 2008
Norwegian Peace Film Award: **Little Moth** (China), Peng Tao.
Aurora Prize: **Water Lilies** (France), Cèline Sciamma.
FIPRESCI Prize: **The Secret of the Grain** (France), Abdellatif Kechicke.
Don Quijote: **Kautokeino-Rebellion** (Norway), Nils Gaup.
Tromsø Palm: **Summerchild** (Finland), Iris Olsson.
Audience Award: **The Orchestra of Piazza Vittorio** (Italy), Agostino Ferrente.

Report 2008
Another record-breaking year for the Tromsø International Film Festival, Norway's largest with nearly 50,000 admissions for the 18th edition. A large snow screen in the main square offered a free peek into the festival

Far North *director Asif Kapaida, left, with actress Michelle Yeoh, at the 2008 Tromsø International Film Festival (photo: Ola Røe)*

programme for all passers-by. Opening film *The Kautokeino Rebellion*, directed by Nils Gaup, had its world premiere at TIFF, and went on to become the biggest box office hit in Norwegian theatres in 2008. Among many international guests, Hong Kong martial arts star and Bond girl Michelle Yeoh was in attendance, starring in British director Asif Kapadia's mythical thriller *Far North*.
– **Anna Klara Måseide**, Marketing and Public Relations Manager.

Valencia International Film Festival – Mediterranean Cinema
October 2009

The Valencia Mostra/Cinema del Mediterrani aims to promote an intercultural dialogue and understanding between the different cultures from the Mediterranean area. The Mostra de Valencia is a specialised film festival organised by the Fundación Municipal de

TROMSØ INTERNATIONAL FILM FESTIVAL
TROMSØ/NORWAY
JANUARY 12TH–17TH 2010
A celebration of art cinema in the polar night – www.tiff.no

Cine. *Inquiries to:* Fundación Municipal de Cine, Plaza de la Almoina 4, Puertas 1,2 and 3, 46003 Valencia, Spain. Tel: (34 96) 392 1506. e: festival@mostravalencia.com. Web: www. mostravalencia.org.

Valladolid International Film Festival
October 23–31, 2009

One of Spain's key events, the festival spotlights the latest work by established directors and newcomers. Competitive for features, shorts and documentaries. Also offers retrospectives, a selection of recent Spanish productions and a congress of new Spanish directors. *Inquiries to:* Valladolid International Film Festival Office, Teatro Calderón, Calle Leopoldo Cano, s/n 4ª Planta, 47003 Valladolid, Spain. Tel: (34 983) 426 460. Fax: 426 461. e:festvalladolid@seminci.com. Web: www.seminci.com.

AWARDS 2008
International Jury Awards
Prix UIP Valladolid: **Tile M For Murder** (Sweden), Magnus Holmgren.
Special Jury Prize: **The One Note Man** (Turkey), Daghan Celayir.
Golden Spike for Short Film: **Careful With That Axe!** (New Zealand), Jason Stutter.
Silver Spike for Short Film: **Hace tiempo pasó un forastero** (Spain), José Carrasco.
Best Director of Photography Award to: Mischa Gavrjusjov & Jan Troell for **Everlasting Moments** (Denmark/Finland/Norway/Sweden).
Music: Kare Bjerko for **Terribly Happy** (Denmark).
Script: Henrik Ruben Genz & Gry Dunja Jensen for **Terribly Happy** (Denmark).

Actress: Maria Heiskanen for **Everlasting Moments** (Denmark/Finland/Norway/Sweden).
Actor jointly: Joao Miguel for **Estômago** (Brazil/Italy) and Unax Ugalde for *La Buena Nueva* (Spain).
Pilar Miró Prize for Best New Director: Marcos Jorge for **Estômago** (Brazil/Italy).
Special Jury Prize: **Retorno a Hansala** (Spain), Chus Gutiérrez.
Silver Spike for Feature Film: **El frasco** (Spain/Argentina), Alberto Lecchi.
Golden Spike for Feature Film: **Estômago** (Brazil/Italy), Marcos Jorge.

Vancouver International Film Festival
October 1–16, 2009

Now in its 28th year, this festival is among the largest in North America in terms of both number of films screened (262 features and 98 shorts) and audience size which totals over 140,000. A wide-ranging international programme with special emphasis on East Asian cinema and nonfiction cinema, VIFF also runs a state-of-the-art year-round Film Centre and hosts an Annual Film & Television Trade Forum. *Inquiries to:* Alan Franey, VIFF, 1181 Seymour St, Vancouver, British Columbia, Canada V6B 3M7. Tel: (1 604) 685 0260. Fax: 688 8221. e: viff@viff.org. Web: www.viff.org.

AWARDS 2008
Audience Awards
Roger's People's Choice for Most Popular International Film: **I've Loved You So Long** (France), Philippe Claudel.
Juried Awards
Citytv Western Canada Feature Film Award:

Fifty Dead Men Walking (Canada), Kari Skogland.
Dragons and Tigers Award for Young Cinema: **Perfect Life** (China/Hong Kong), Emily Tang.
VIFF Nonfiction Feature Award: **Born Without** (Mexico), Eva Norvind.
Most Promising Director of a Canadian Short Film: Drew McCreadie for **The Valet** (Canada).
Women in Film and Television Vancouver's Artistic Merit Award: Tantoo Cardinal for **Mothers & Daughters** (Canada).
International Film Guide Inspiration Award: **Control Alt Delete** (Canada), Cameron Labine.
Documentary Audience Award for Most Popular Documentary Film: **Throw Down Your Heart** (USA), Sascha Paladino.
VIFF Most Popular Canadian Film Award: **Mothers & Daughters**, Carl Bessai.
National Film Board Most Popular Canadian Documentary Award: **Fierce Light: When Spirit Meets Action**, Velcrow Ripper.
VIFF Environmental Film Audience Awards: **Blue Gold: World Water Wars** (Canada/USA), Sam Bozzo.

Report 2008
This year's event was chock full of superb films and the pleasures of discovering them. Visiting filmmakers were in attendance at over 200 of the screenings and the focus on the films themselves was much appreciated by all. Perhaps the festival experience means more than ever when so much time is taken up with economic worries and the 'small screen' experience. A clear majority of the films in the festival were very well attended, substantially voted for and averaged between 'very good' and 'excellent' in public voting. – **Alan Franey**, Festival Director.

Venice International Film Festival
September 2–12, 2009

Under Marco Müller's directorship, the 77-year-old Mostra Internazionale d'Arte Cinematografica is trying to overcome problems such as its old-fashioned facilities on the expensive Lido Island, a vanishing market and heavy political interference.

Mickey Rourke with Darren Aronofsky holding the Golden Lion for **The Wrestler** *(photo: Giorgio Zucchiatti / La Biennale di Venezia)*

Retrospectives, tributes and parties galore, plus exquisite art exhibitions around downtown Venice, make a visit here essential. Wim Wenders was president of the 2008 international jury. Ermanno Olmi received a Golden Lion for Lifetime Achievement award. *Inquiries to:* La Biennale di Venezia, San Marco 2893, Ca' Lolin, 30124 Venice, Italy. Tel (39) 041 521 8711. Fax: 521 8810. e: foreignpress@labiennale.org. Web: www.labiennale.org/en/cinema.

AWARDS 2008
Golden Lion for Best Film: **The Wrestler** (USA), Darren Aronofsky.
Grand Jury Prize: **Teza** (Ethiopia/France/Germany), Haile Gerima.
Best Direction: Aleksey German Junior for **Paper Soldier** (Russia).
Coppa Volpi for Best Actor: Silvio Orlando for **Giovanna's Dad** (Italy), Pupi Avati.
Coppa Volpi for Best Actress: Dominique Blanc for **The Other** (France), Patrick Mario Bernard and Pierre Trividic.

Report 2008
The 66th Venice International Film Festival is organised by the Venice Biennale and the Festival director is Marco Müller, who took up the position in 2004. The aim of the Festival is to raise awareness and promote all the various aspects of international cinema in all its forms: as art, entertainment and as an industry, in a spirit of freedom and tolerance. The Festival will include retrospectives and homages to major figures as a contribution towards raising

awareness of the history of cinema and the line-up will be presented in a press conference in Rome at the end of July 2009. **– Festival Press Office.**

Victoria Independent Film & Video Festival
January 30–February 8, 2009

No matter if it is controversial cinema, Oscar-winning drama, provocative documentary or the list of special guests attending the Victoria Film Festival, this romp through the world of film is the event you don't want to miss! With historic architecture and fabulous vistas, downtown streets are lined with theatres, shops, museums and cafes that provide the perfect backdrop for the home of the boutique schmooze. The Festival screens 150 films at four downtown venues. As Vancouver Island's biggest and longest-running film festival it's the place to see the best of independent cinema in one of the top destinations in the world according to Condé Nast. A great package at the legendary Fairmont Empress is available. The 15th Annual Victoria Film Festival presents the most exclusive industry event of the year. 'Trigger Points Pacific' has only 50 openings for producers who'll have plenty of one-on-one time with 25 top industry acquisition execs in thirty-minute meetings for incomparable access and results. Online registration and information at www.victoriafilmfestival. com. *Inquiries to:* Victoria Film Festival, 1215 Blanshard St, Victoria, British Columbia, V8W 3J4 Canada. Tel: (1 250) 389 0444. Fax: 389 0406. e: festival@victoriafilmfestival.com Web: www.victoriafilmfestival.com.

AWARDS 2008
Star!TV Award for Best Feature: **Adam's**

Apples (Denmark), Anders Thomas Jensen.
Best Canadian Feature: **Amal**, Richie Mehta.
Best Documentary Award: **Saving Luna** (Canada), Michael Parfit and Suzanne Chisholm.
Cineplex Entertainment Award for Best Short Animation: **Madame Tutli-Putli** (Canada), Chris Lavis and Maciek Szczerbowski.
Best Short Award: **Nebraska** (USA), Charles Haine.
Audience Favourite Award: **The Hammer** (USA), Charles Herman-Wurmfeld.
InVision Award for Best Student Film: **Mamitas** (USA) Nick Ozeki.

Report 2008
For the first time the festival took on a home-town feel with opening film, *Motown High*, about a high school R&B band that travels to Motown and ends up singing with Martha Reeves. Director William Fruet's world premiere of *Prodigy* also had a sold-out show of locals who had taken part in the film. Supermodel Irina Pantaeva (*Siberian Dreams*) added sparkle to the festival along with Adam Carolla (*The Hammer*), both of whom had films at the event this year. New emerging director Paul Holahan screened the world premiere of *Hindsight*. A new lounge became the hub of the Festival and featured notable musicians Randy Waldie, Karel Roessingh and Tequila Mockingbird Orchestra. **– Kathy Kay**, Festival Director.

Viennale – Vienna International Film Festival
October 22–November 4, 2009

The Viennale is Austria's most important international film event, as well as being one of the oldest and best-known festivals in the German-speaking world. It takes place every October in beautiful cinemas in Vienna's historic centre, providing a festival with an international orientation and a distinctive urban flair. A high percentage of the approximately 92,100 visitors to the festival are made up of a decidedly young audience. In its main programme, the Viennale shows a carefully picked selection of new films from all over the globe as well as new films from Austria. The choice of films offers a cross section of bold filmmaking that stands apart from the aesthetics of mainstream conventionality and is politically relevant. Aside from its focus on the newest feature films of every genre and structural form imaginable, the festival gives particular attention to documentary films, international short films, as well as experimental works and crossover films. The Viennale receives regular international acclaim for its yearly organisation of a large-scale historic retrospective in collaboration with the Austrian Film Museum, its numerous special programmes, as well as for its tributes and homages dedicated to prominent personalities and institutions in international filmmaking. *Inquiries to:* Siebensterngasse 2, 1070 Vienna, Austria. Tel: (43 1) 526 5947. Fax: 523 4172. e: office@viennale.at. Web: www.viennale.at.

Report 2008

An important feature of Viennale 2008 was the festival trailer *Une catastrophe* by Jean-Luc Godard. In a separate festive screening Werner Schroeter's film adaptation of Bachmann's

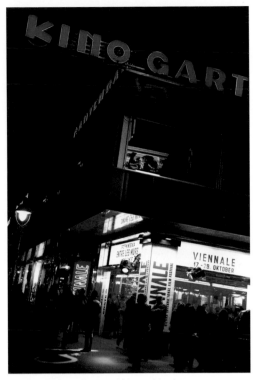

The Gartenbaukino - the Viennale's biggest festival cinema (photo: Ruth Ehrmann)

VIENNALE
VIENNA INTERNATIONAL FILM FESTIVAL

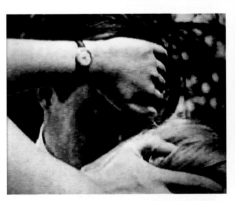

Jean-Luc Godard, «Une Catastrophe», F 2008, Viennale-Trailer 08

OCTOBER 22 TO NOVEMBER 4, 2009

VIENNALE *A-1070 Vienna, Siebensterngasse 2 • Tel +43/1/526 59 47 • Fax +43/1/523 41 72 • office@viennale.at • www.viennale.at*

novel *Malina* was presented in the presence of the film's leading lady, Isabelle Huppert. Well-known musicians such as Garth Hudson and Vic Chesnutt were guests of the Viennale as well as the actresses Jeanne Balibar, Amira Casar and Arta Dobroshi. **– Barbara Heumesser**, Marketing.

Wellington International Film Festival
July 17–August 2, 2009

The Wellington International Film Festival launched its 37th annual programme of over 150 feature films from over thirty countries in 2008 with James Marsh's *Man on Wire*. The festival provides a non-competitive New Zealand premiere showcase and welcomes many international filmmakers and musicians. The festival shares its programme, brimming with animation, art-house, documentaries and retrospective programmes, with its 40-year-old sibling the Auckland International Film Festival. Festival Director: Bill Gosden. *Inquiries to:* New Zealand International Film Festivals, Box 9544, Marion Square, Wellington 6141, New Zealand. Tel: (64 4) 385 0162. Fax: 801 7304. e: festival@nzff.co.nz. Web: www.nzff.co.nz.

Report 2008
The Festival was characterised by a record number of New Zealand feature selections, headed up by premiere screenings of Sima Urale's *Apron Strings* and Vincent Ward's *Rain of the Children*. Popular acclaim flowed for the astonishing fertility of the documentary filmmaking that infiltrated virtually every section of the programme including both opening and closing night (*Waltz with Bashir*) selections. **– Bill Gosden**, Festival Director.

WorldFest–Houston
April 16–25, 2009

The Festival continues to move forward to present the true independent film and its filmmaker, offering a new venue for directors searching for an independent forum for their works. 'Small is Beautiful' for the 42nd Annual WorldFest, where simplicity is the byword,

and a relaxed intimate atmosphere surrounds a special selection of superb new feature and short films. The opportunities for networking and contacts are exceptional. Seminars include Cinematography, Casting, Distribution, Directing/Producing, Writing and more. Deadline: December 15th. *Inquiries to:* WorldFest–Houston, PO Box 56566, Houston, TX 77256-6566, USA. Tel: (1 713) 965 9955. Fax: 965 9960. e: mail@worldfest.org. Web: www.worldfest.org.

Zlín International Film Festival for Children and Youth
May 31–June 7, 2009

The 49th edition of the festival will present a fresh and quality selection of films for children, youth and adults. All parts of the world will be represented in the programme, with Days of Spanish Cinema being the main focus of the 2009 showcase. Film festival Zlín was founded in 1961 and has since established itself over the years as one of world's major events of its kind. The main competition includes: feature films for children and youths, short animated films for children, European debuts and feature films from Visegrad countries. Two specialised sections form integral parts of the festival: Zlín Dog - a festival of student films, Rainbow Marble - a competition of commercials targeted at children. Apart from competition sections, the festival will also present a wide range of feature and animated films, documentaries, thematic showcases and anniversaries, with Spanish cinematography extensively represented throughout the programme. A rich and

Children actors' walk of fame: (left to right) Dana Morávková, Jan Čenský, Lucie Vondráčková, 3 June 2008, Zlín (photo: Pavel Petruška)

entertaining supporting programme for visitors of all ages is, as always, commonplace. *Inquiries to:* FILMFEST s.r.o, Filmova 174, CZ-76179 Zlin, Czech Republic. Tel: (420 5) 7759 2275. Fax: 7759 2442. e: festival@zlinfest.cz. Web: www.zlinfest.cz.

AWARDS 2008

Golden Slipper for Best Feature Film for Children: **Where is Winky's Horse?** (Belgium/The Netherlands), Mischa Kamp.
Golden Slipper for Best Feature Film for Youth: **The Substitute** (Denmark), Ole Bornedal.
The Town of Zlín Award – Special Recognition for a Feature Film for Children: **Gabai Granny** (Japan), Hitoshi Kurauchi.
The Miloš Macourek Award – Special Recognition for a Feature Film for Youth: **Max Minsky and Me** (Germany), Anna Justice.
Golden Slipper for Best Animated Film: **The Bears Stories** (Russia), Marina Karpova.
The Hermína Týrlová Award – Award for Young Artists Aged Under 35: **Our Wonderful Nature** (Germany), Tomer Eshed.
Main Prize of the Children's Jury for Best Feature Film for Children: **Gabai Granny** (Japan), Hitoshi Kurauchi.
Main Prize of the Children's Jury for Best Feature Film for Youth: **St Trinian's** (UK), Oliver Parker and Barnaby Thompson.
The Europe Award: **Just About Love?** (France), Lola Doillon.
International Expert Jury for European Debuts Special Prize: **A Fly** (Russia), Vladimir Kott.
The Czech Minister of Culture Award: Iska's **Journey** (Hungary), Csaba Bollók.
Golden Apple – The Spectator Prize for Most Successful Feature Film: **No Network** (Iceland), Ari Kristinsson.
Golden Apple – The Spectator Prize for Most Successful Animated Film: **Hairy Scary – Two Beautiful Minds** (France), Wolf-Ruediger Bloss.
The Don Quixote Award: **The Substitute** (Denmark), Ole Bornedal.
Ecumenical Jury Award: **The Substitute** (Denmark), Ole Bornedal.
A Commendation of the Ecumenical Jury: **Where is Winky's Horse?** (Belgium/The Netherlands), Mischa Kamp.

Recognition of Creative Contribution in Filmmaking for Children and Youth: Iva Janžurová.

Report 2008

A total of 108,722 visitors, greater public and media attention, new screening venues and programme sections marked the 48th edition of the festival. The film selection comprised a record-breaking 570 films (192 competed in seven sections). With British cinematography being the main focus, the spectators watched 34 British films, accompanied by 24 UK delegations. The Days of British Cinema were organised around three crucial subjects: the 100th anniversary of David Lean's birth, Free Cinema/British New Wave, and the best of 1940s to 1980s. Two other region-focused sections were presented: African Childhood and Israel in Film, Film in Israel. Special guests at the festival included Dakota Blue Richards, Daniel Clark, Randal Kleiser, Christopher Miles and Andrew Schmidt. **– Ondřej Hrudka**, International PR Manager.

Festivals and Markets of Note

AFIA Film Festival, Bøgeskovparken 197, DK-8260 Viby J, Århus, Denmark. Tel: (45) 2826 2399. e: ask@afiafilmfestival.dk. *(International festival for independent filmmakers and video artists, concentrating on artworks that place artistic worth over commercial aspects - March 17-22, 2009).*

ALCINE - Alcalá de Henares/Comunidad de Madrid Film Festival, Plaza del Empecinado 1, 28801 Alcalá de Henares, Madrid, Spain. Tel: (34 91) 879 7380. e: festival@alcine.org. Web: www.alcine.org. *(Competition for Spanish short films, European short films and new Spanish directors' full-length films. Several international sidebars and music sections - Nov.)*

Almería International Short Film Festival, Diputación de Almería, Departamento de Cultura y Juventud, Calle Navarro Rodrigo 17, 04071 Almeria, Spain. Tel: (34 950) 211 100 e: jefadeprensa@almeriaencorto.es. Web: www.almeriaencorto.net. *(Competition for international shorts - Dec.)*

Angelus Awards Student Film Festival, 7201 Sunset Blvd., Hollywood, CA 90046, USA. Tel: (1 323) 874 6635. e: info@angelus.org. Web: www.angelus.org. *(International competition to showcase and award emerging filmmakers, and encourage them to continue creating visionary projects that honour the fundamental dignity of humanity. All genres: drama, comedy, animation, documentary and narrative. Entry forms available online. Screening and awards ceremony held at the Directors' Guild of America, Hollywood - Sept.)*

Anima: Brussels International Animation Film Festival, Folioscope, Avenue de Stalingrad 52, B-1000 Brussels, Belgium. Tel: (32 2) 534 4125. e: info@animafestival.be. Web: www.animatv.be. *(The 100 films in the international competition [short and long films, commercials and music videos], retrospectives, expositions, lessons in cinema, workshops for children, professional days with 'Futuranima' and numerous special events, make this an international event that ought not to be missed - Feb 20-28, 2009.)*

Ann Arbor Film Festival, PO Box 8232, Ann Arbor, MI 48107, USA. Tel: (1 734) 995 5356. e: info@aafilmfest.org. Web: www.aafilmfest.org. *(Cutting-edge, lovingly crafted and artistically inspired films are showcased in the longest-running independent film festival in North America. Featured sections include experimental, animation and narrative, as well as documentary from all over the world - March 24-29, 2009.)*

Annecy/International Animated Film Festival and International Animated Film Market (MIFA), CITA, 18 Avenue du Trésum, BP 399, 74013 Annecy Cedex, France. Tel: (33 4) 5010 0900. e: info@annecy.org. Web: www.annecy.org. *(Annecy has been showcasing the very best in animation for over 45 years, making it one of the industry's leading international competitive festivals, accompanied by a useful sales/distribution market (MIFA) - Festival: June 8-13, 2009; MIFA: June 10-12, 2009.)*

Arab and Arabian Cinema Festival, B-35, Qutab Institutional Area, New Delhi-110016, India. Tel: 91 11 4174 3166. e: supriya@osians.com. Web: www.osians.com. *(The festival enjoys an international reputation for the quality of films screened over nine days complemented by panel discussions, one major seminar each time, an Auction of Popular Culture and Film Memorabilia along with a number of exhibitions and a Talent Campus for budding young filmmakers from South Asia - mid July.)*

Arab Film Festival, 300 Brannan St, Ste 508, San Francisco, CA 94107, USA. Tel (1 415) 564 1100. e: info@aff.org. Web: www.aff.org. *(The festival screens films from and about the Arab World that provide realistic perspectives on Arab people, culture, art, history and politics - late Oct.)*

Aspen Filmfest & Shortsfest, 110 E Hallam, Ste 102, Aspen, CO 81611, USA. Tel: (1 970) 925 6882. e: filmfest@aspenfilm.org. Web: www.aspenfilm. org. *(Shortsfest: Short-subject competition showcasing the great filmmakers of tomorrow and introducing a rich variety of current productions from around the world - April 1-5, 2009; Filmfest: Feature-length invitational that champions independent film at its eclectic, thoughtful and often inspiring best - Sept 23-27, 2009.)*

Atlantic Film Festival, PO Box 36139, Suite 220, 5600 Sackville St, Halifax, NS, B3J 3S9, Canada. Tel: (1 902) 422 3456. e: festival@atlanticfilm. com. Web: www.atlanticfilm.com. *(With a distinctive focus on film and music the festival screens some of the best international, Canadian and Atlantic Canadian films, with opportunities to hear some of the finest artists the region offers - Sept.)*

Auckland International Film Festival, PO Box 9544, Marion Sq, Wellington 6037, New Zealand. Tel: (64 4) 385 0162. e: festival@nzff.co.nz. Web: www.nzff.co.nz. *(The festival provides a non-competitive New Zealand premiere showcase and welcomes many international filmmakers and musicians. Twinned with the Wellington Film Festival - July 10-29, 2009.)*

Augsburg Children's Film Festival, Filmtage Augsburg, Schroeckstrasse 8, 86152 Augsburg, Germany. Tel: (49 821) 153 078. e: filmbuero@t-online.de. Web: www.filmtage-augsburg.de. *(International features for children - March 21-29, 2009.)*

Banff Mountain Film Festival, Mountain Culture at The Banff Centre, Box 1020, 107 Tunnel Moun-tain Drive, Banff, AB, T1L 1H5, Canada. Tel: (1 403) 762 6675.e: banffmountainfilms@banffcen-tre.ca. Web: www.banffmountainfestivals.ca. *(International competition for films and videos related to mountains and the spirit of adventure - Oct 31-Nov 8, 2009.)*

Bangkok International Film Festival, 31/9 2nd Floor Royal City Avenue, New Petchaburi Rd, Bangkapi, Huay Khwang, Bangkok, Thailand. Tel:

(66 2) 203 0624. e: info@bangkokfilm.org. Web: www.bangkokfilm.org. *(The festival showcases more than a hundred feature and short films, representing the works of filmmakers from Thailand, the ASEAN region plus a selection of some of the most exciting and innovative films from around the world - Sept).*

Big Sky Documentary Film Festival, 131 South Higgins Ave, Suite 307, Missoula, Montana 59802, USA. Tel: (1 406) 541 3456. e: programmeming@bigskyfilmfest.org. Web: www. bigskyfilmfest.org. *(The festival will screen 100 films, including world and US premieres, classics, rare and experimental works on Montana's largest screen at the historic Wilma Theater in downtown Missoula, Montana. In addition to ten days of screenings, the event will feature many public and VIP events including panel discussions, galas, receptions and networking round-tables - Feb 13-22, 2009.)*

Bogotá Film Festival, Residencias Tequendama, Centro Internacional Tequendama, Bogotá, Colombia. Tel: (57 1) 341 7562. e: info@bogocine. com. Web: www.bogocine.com. *(International competitive section, National competitive section and side bars - early October.)*

Boston Film Festival, 126 South Street, Rockport, MA 01966, USA. Tel: (1 617) 523 8388. e: info@bostonfilmfestival.org. Web: www. bostonfilmfestival.org. *(Showcasing a selection of feature films, documentaries and shorts. Q&A sessions with directors and actors follow every screening, giving moviegoers first-hand access to the filmmaking process - Sept.)*

Bradford International Film Festival, National Media Museum, Bradford, BD1 1NQ, UK. Artistic Director: Tony Earnshaw. Tel: (44 1274) 203317. e: tony.earnshaw@nationalmediamuseum.org.uk. Web: www.bradfordfilmfestival.org.uk. *(Includes the BIFF Lifetime Achievement Award, the BIFF Fellowship Award, Shine Short Film Award, director showcase, Screentalk interviews and Masterclasses, retrospectives, Film & Music Conference and the Widescreen Weekend - March 13-28, 2009.)*

Brussels International Festival of Fantastic Film, 8 Rue de la Comtesse de Flandre 1020 Brussels, Belgium. Tel: (32 2) 201 1713. e: info@ bifff.org. Web: www.bifff.org. *(Competitive international and European selection for shorts and features - April 9-21, 2009.)*

Camerimage, Rynek Nowomiejski 28, 87-100 Torun, Poland. Tel: (48 56) 621 0019. e: office@ camerimage.pl. Web: www.camerimage.pl. *(Held annually in Lodz, the festival is a forum not only for the presentation, but also for the further development, of international moviemaking. Apart from the Main Competition, the Festival also includes other events such as Student Etudes Competition, Student Panorama, Camerimage Market, Camerimage Forum, Polish Films Competition, special screenings and premieres, various reviews, retrospectives, meetings and also accompanying events such as exhibitions and music performances - late Nov-early Dec.)*

Cape Winelands Film Festival, Films for Africa, 2 Waterkant, 52 Arum Road, Bloubergrandt, Western Cape 8001, South Africa. Tel: (27 21) 5563204. e: films_for_africa@telkomsa.net. Web: http://films-for-africa.co.za. *(The aim of the Cape Winelands Film Festival is to provide a chance to catch up with the rest of the world's cinephiles. The objective is to create a window on world cinemas - March 21-29, 2009.)*

Cartoons on the Bay, Rai Trade, Via Umberto Novaro 18, 00195 Rome, Italy. Tel: (39 06) 3749 8315. e: cartoonsbay@raitrade.it. Web: www. cartoonsbay.com. *(International television and multimedia animation festival - April 2-5, 2009.)*

Chicago International Children's Film Festival, Facets Multimedia Inc, 1517 W Fullerton, Chicago, IL 60614, USA. Tel: (1 773) 281 9075. e: kidsfest@ facets.org. Web: www.cicff.org. *(North America's largest and most celebrated film festival devoted to films for and by children, featuring over 200 of the best films and videos from over 40 countries - late Oct/ early Nov.)*

Chicago Latino Film Festival, International Latino Cultural Center of Chicago, 676 North La Salle Street, Suite 520, Chicago, IL 60654, USA. Tel: (1 312) 431 1330. e: info@latinoculturalcenter. org. Web: www.latinoculturalcenter.org. *(Celebrating our 25th Anniversary in 2009, the festival promotes awareness of Latino culture through a wide variety of art forms and education including film, music, dance, visual arts, comedy and theatre - April 17-29, 2009.)*

Cinanima, Rua 62, 251, Apartado 743, 4500-366 Espinho, Portugal. Tel: (351 2) 2733 1350. e: office@cinanima.pt. Web: www.cinanima.pt. *(International animated films with a National and International competition - Nov.)*

Cinéma du Réel, BPI Centre Georges Pompidou, 25 rue du Renard, 75197 Paris Cedex 04, France. Tel: (33 1) 4478 4516. Web: www.cinereel.org. *(International documentary film festival for the public and professionals to discover the films of experienced authors as well as new talents, the history of documentary cinema as well as contemporary works - March 5-15, 2009.)*

Cinema Jove International Film Festival, La Safor 10-5, 46015 Valencia, Spain. Tel: (34 96) 331 1047. e: info@cinemajove.com. Web: www. cinemajovefilmfest.com. Festival Director: Rafael Maluenda. *(Promotes the work of young film makers and has two competitive sections: feature films screened for the first time in Spain and another for the best, most consolidated shorts on the international scene; these constitute the thrust of a programme which also embraces tributes to veteran filmmakers, young 'cult movie' directors, exhibitions and professional meeting points - June 20-27, 2009.)*

Cinematik International Film Festival Piestany, Bitunkova 23, 900 31 Stupava, Slovakia. Tel: (421 9) 1426 6911. e: info@ cinematik.sk. Web: www.cinematik.sk. *(Focused on young audiences with an emphasis on developing their 'film literacy'. Its core section is a competition named Meeting Point Europe - a selection of the best recent European films voted for by a panel of young European film critics - Sept 10-15, 2009.)*

Cinequest, PO Box 720040, San Jose, CA 95172-0040, USA. Tel: (1 408) 295 3378. e: info@ cinequest.org. Web: www.cinequest.org. *(The festival remains one of the last strongholds for the discovery of new and emerging film artists and presents a dynamic event of 200 international films with over 400 film artists, technologists, and professionals from 34 countries in attendance - Feb 25-March 8, 2009.)*

CineVegas Film Festival, 170 South Green Valley Parkway, Henderson, NV 89012, USA. Tel: (1 702) 952 5555. e: info@cinevegas.com. Web: www.cinevegas.com. *(The festival is a platform for artists and art lovers who are drawn to the edge. Held amidst the unique, unpredictable and intoxicating environment that is Las Vegas, the festival pushes the boundaries of cinema, presenting work by innovative, uninhibited, and renegade artists to an audience of local and national film lovers, journalists, and film industry representatives - June 11-20, 2009.)*

Cleveland International Film Festival, 2510 Market Ave, Cleveland, OH 44113-3434, USA. Tel: (1 216) 623 3456. e: marshall@clevelandfilm. org. Web: www.clevelandfilm.org. *(Ohio's premiere film event features over 240 films originating from close to 60 countries. Visiting filmmakers, panel discussions, and student screenings are all CIFF highlights - March 19-29, 2009.)*

Coca-Cola Cinemagic International Film & Television Festival, 49 Botanic Avenue, Belfast, BT7 1JL, Northern Ireland. Tel: (44 28) 9031 1900. e: info@cinemagic.org.uk. Web: www.cinemagic. org.uk. *(The festival uses the magic of film, television and all forms of the moving image to entertain, educate and inspire. It caters for all young people (aged between 4 and 25) with any range of film and television interest – whether they want to watch and enjoy, create their own work or take things a stage further and find out more about a possible career in the film or television industries - Nov 12-Nov 27, 2009.)*

Cosmic Zoom, Islands Brygge 91, 2300 Copenhagen S, Denmark. e: tea@cosmiczoom. dk. *(Experimental and alternative film - Jan 30-Feb 1, 2009).*

Cottbus Film Festival-Festival of East European Cinema, Werner-Seelenbinder-Ring 44/45, D-03048 Cottbus, Germany. Tel: (49 355) 431 070. e: info@filmfestivalcottbus.de. Web: www.filmfestivalcottbus.de. *(Festival of East European films: features and shorts (competitive), children's and youth film, spectrum, national hits, focus 2009: new cinema from the Black Sea - Nov 10-15, 2009.)*

Crossing Europe Film Festival Linz, Graben 30, 4020 Linz, Austria. Tel: (43 732) 785700. info@ crossingeurope.at. Web: www.crossingeurope. at. *(Celebrating its sixth year in 2009, the anniversary event is organised in cooperation with Upper Austria's capital Linz, the European Capital in 2009. With the European Competition and the European Panorama, the festival offers Austrian premieres of feature films and documentaries that have been highly acclaimed and distinguished with awards at international festivals - but all too rarely find their way into our cinemas. The festival grants a central place to the diversity and richness of the cultural distinctiveness of young European cinema. Apart from the competitions a great choice of festival specials is included in the programme: tributes to outstanding film directors; film evenings centring on music and youth cultures, and more - April 20-26, 2009.)*

Dead by Dawn International Horror Film Festival, 88 Lothian Rd, Edinburgh, EH3 9BZ, UK. Tel: (44) 01383 410281. e: info@deadbydawn. co.uk. Web: www.deadbydawn.co.uk. *(Featuring great cult and classic favourites, new independent and mainstream features and short movies - April 30-May 3, 2009.)*

Deauville Festival of American Film, Le Public Système Cinéma, 40, rue Anatole France, 92594 Levallois-Perret Cedex, France. Tel: (33 1) 4134 2033. e: jlasserre@le-public-systeme.fr. Web: www.festival-deauville.com. *(Sections include: Premieres - non-competitive section dedicated to major American films; Feature Films Competition*

- competitive section of independent feature films aimed at revealing new filmmakers; Panorama - non-competitive section aimed at showcasing the variety of the American film production; Uncle Sam's Docs - non-competitive section dedicated to feature documentary films; Tributes and Retrospectives - Sept.)

Dhaka International Film Festival, 75 Science Laboratory Road, 3rd Floor, Dhaka-1205, Bangladesh. Tel: (88 2) 862 1062. e: amzamal@bdcom. com . Web: www.dhakafilmfest.org . *(The festival will screen approximately 100 films from some 30 countries. There is a competitive section for Asian cinema and categories include: Retrospective, Tributes, Cinema of the World, Children's Film, Focus, Bangladesh Panorama, Women Filmmakers, Independent Films Section and Spiritual Films Section Jan 14-22, 2010.)*

Diagonale, Rauhensteingasse 5/5, A-1010 Vienna, Austria. Tel: (43 1) 595 4556. e: wien@diagonale. at. Web: www.diagonale.at. *(March 17-22, 2009.)*

Divercine, Canelones 2226 Apt 102, Casilla de Correo 5023, 11200 Montevideo, Uruguay. Tel: (59 82) 401 9882. e: ricardocasasb@gmail.com. Web: www.divercine.com.uy. *(Children's festival - July.)*

Durban International Film Festival, Centre for Creative Arts, University of KwaZulu-Natal, Durban 4041, South Africa. Tel: (27 31) 260 1145. e: cca@ukzn.ac.za. Web: www.cca.ukzn. ac.za. *(Featuring over 200 films from more than 95 countries, spread across 300 screenings at 26 venues around the city, the festival will bring together established masters of cinema and innovative new talents from around the world - late July-early August.)*

EU XXL Film Forum & Festival of European Film, Bergsteiggasse 48/4, A-1170 Vienna, Austria. Tel: (43 1) 408 1140. e: office@eu-xxl.at. Web: www.eu-xxl.at. *(Founded in 2003, the festival is an initiative for the advancement of European integration and for cultural exchange. It recognises the special role of audiovisual media and the cultural, social and economic value of audiovisual productions - March 3-8, 2009.)*

Early Melons International Student Film Festival, Radlinského 2803/34, 811 07 Bratislava, Slovakia. Tel: (421 9) 0765 5146. e: info@ earlymelons.com. Web: www.earlymelons.com. *(International student film festival established to propagate European student film production in Slovakia - March 11-14, 2009.)*

EcoVision Festival, Via Francesco Bentivegna 51, 90139 Palermo, Italy. Tel: (39 09) 133 2567. e: info@ecovisionfestival.com. Web: www. ecovisionfestival.com. *(International festival with the aim of promoting cinematographic and documentary production concerning any aspect of environment and nature - June 2009.)*

Edmonton International Film Festival, Edmonton International Film Society, Suite 201, 10816A-82 Avenue, Edmonton, Alberta, T6E 2B3, Canada. Tel: (1 780) 423 0844. e: info@edmontonfilmfest.com. Web: www. edmontonfilmfest.com. *(Independent films from around the globe comprising feature-length dramas, documentaries and shorts - Sept 25-Oct 3, 2009.)*

Emden International Film Festival, An der Berufschule 3, 26721 Emden, Germany. Tel: (49) 4921 9155-0. e: filmfest@vhs-emden.de. Web: www.filmfest-emden.de. *(The main focus is on current film productions from North Western Europe, particularly Germany and the UK. The festival screens over 100 films - June 10-17, 2009.)*

European Independent Film Festival (ÉCU), 108 Rue Damremont, Paris 75018, France. e: info@ ecufilmfestival.com. Web: www.ecufilmfestival. com. *(The festival will showcase filmmakers whose films demonstrate quality, innovation and independence in both form and content. ÉCU 2009's goal is to bring worldwide attention to European independent filmmakers as well as independent filmmakers from the Americas, Africa and Asia. Competitive with sixteen categories - March.)*

FanTasia International Film Festival, 460 Rue St Catherine, Suite 915, Montreal, Quebec, H3B 1V6, Canada. Tel: (1 514) 876 1760. e: info@

fantasiafestival.com. Web: www. fantasiafestival. com. *(Showcases the most exciting, innovative and individualistic examples of contemporary international fantasy/action/horror genres. Submissions deadline May 5 - July 2009.)*

Febiofest - International Film, Television and Video Festival, ASFK, Brnianska 33, 811 04 Bratislava, Slovakia. Tel: (421 2) 5465 2018. e: asfk@asfk.sk. Web: www.febiofestsk.sk. *(International Film, TV & Video Festival focusing mainly on the presentation of new Czech titles - March 30-April 30, 2009.)*

Festival Dei Popoli, Borgo Pinti 82 Rosso, 50121 Firenze, Italy. Tel: (39 055) 244 778. e: festivaldeipopoli@festivaldeipopoli.191.it. Web: www.festivaldeipopoli.org. *(Partly competitive and open to documentaries on social, anthropological, historical and political issues - late Nov.)*

Festival du Cinema International en Abitibi-Temiscamingue, 215 Mercier Avenue, Rouyn-Noranda, Quebec J9X 5WB, Canada. Tel: (1 819) 762 6212. e: info@festivalcinema.ca. Web: www. festivalcinema.ca. *(International shorts, medium and full-length features; animation, documentary and fiction from more than 20 countries - Oct.)*

Festival Internacional de Cine Expresión en Corto Film Festival, Calle Nuñez 20, Centro San Miguel de Allende, San Miguel de Allende Guanajuato 37700, Mexico. Tel: (52 415) 152 7264. e: Web: www.expresionencorto.com. *(The festival is a state-sponsored cultural event that does not charge admission to its viewing audience, which totals over 77,000 people. It receives over 1,300 entries from more than 70 countries in its international competition and screens around 400 films. The festival hosts an International Pitching Market that brings together international producers, distributors and diverse film-financing institutions from around the world, who are interested in participating in co-productions with the top Mexican feature and documentary projects currently in development, as well as presenting a variety of films, conferences, workshops, tributes and activities - July 24-Aug 2, 2009).*

Festival International du Film Francophone de Namur, 175, Rue des Brasseurs, 5000 Namur, Belgium Tel: (32 81) 241 236. e: info@fiff.be. Web: www.fiff.be. *(Since 1986, the festival has promoted French-language film and diffuses French-speaking feature-length and documentary films and tries, for this purpose, to gather in Namur all the directors, producers, screenwriters, actors, distributors involved in French-speaking cinematographic creation. It is really a place of thinking and appointment by the means of conferences and professional meetings. The Festival also contributes to the education and the training of the young people, offering teaching activities and personal spaces. Competitions are held for feature films, short films and first works - Sept 26-Oct 3, 2009.)*

Festival Prix Danube, Mlynska dolina, 845 45 Bratislava, Slovakia. Tel: (421 2) 6061 2491. e: prixdanube@stv.sk. Web: www.prixdanube.stv.sk. *(Competition festival of television programmes for children and youths. Takes place biennially in the following categories: animated, documentary, feature film and educational programmes - Sept 24-Oct 2, 2009.)*

Festroia International Film Festival, Avenida Luisa Dodi 61-65, 2900-461 Setúbal, Portugal. Tel: (351 265) 525 908. e: info@festroia.pt. Web: www.festroia.pt. *(Held in Setúbal, near Lisbon. Official section for countries producing fewer than 30 features per year - June.)*

Filmfest Dresden, Alaunstrasse 62, D-01099, Dresden, Germany. Tel: (49 351) 829 470. e: info@filmfest-dresden.de. Web: www.filmfest-dresden.de. *(Filmfest Dresden is an international short film festival that features short animated and fiction as well as documentary and experimental films. Founded in 1989, it has developed into one of the major short film festivals in Germany and hosts the best-funded short film competitions across Europe. The festival also organises workshops and seminars for young filmmakers. The main sections of the festival are the International and the National Competitions. These are accompanied by various other thematic events. Visitors, the press and film producers also use the festival* *as a meeting place and to exchange opinions and discuss new ideas, with more than 21,000 people attending in 2008 - April 14-19, 2009.)*

Filmfest München, Sonnenstr 21, D-80331, Munich, Germany. Tel: (49 89) 381 9040. e: info@filmfest-muenchen.de. Web: www. filmfest-muenchen.de. *(Germany's largest summer festival screening over 230 films from more than 40 countries - June 26-July 4, 2009.)*

Florida Film Festival, Enzian Theatre, 1300 South Orlando Ave, Maitland, Florida 32751, USA. Tel: (1 407) 644 5625 x 326. Web: www. floridafilmfestival.com. *(Showcases cutting-edge American independent and international film plus educational forums, glamorous parties and other special events - March 27-April 5, 2009.)*

Focus on Asia Fukuoka International Film Festival, 1-8-1 Tenzin, Chuo-ku, Fukuoka 810-8620, Japan. Tel: (81 92) 733 5170. e: info@focus-on-asia.com. Web: www.focus-on-asia.com. *(Dedicated to promoting Asian films which are shown with English subtitles. Non-competitive - Sept.)*

Fredrikstad Animation Festival, PO Box 1405, N-1602 Fredrikstad, Norway. Tel: (47) 4024 9364. e: mail@animationfestival.no. Web: www. animationfestival.no. *(Competitive festival showcasing Nordic, Baltic and international animation including retrospectives, workshop - Oct.)*

Full Frame Documentary Film Festival, 324 Blackwell Street, Suite 500, Washington Bldg, Bay 5, Durham, NC 27701, USA. Tel: (1 919) 687 4100. e: info@fullframefest.org. Web: www. fullframefest.org. *(Showcases over 100 documentaries from around the world - April 2-5, 2009.)*

Future Film Festival, Via del Pratello 21/2, 40122 Bologna, Italy. Tel: (39 051) 296 0672. e: info@futurefilmfestival.org. Web: www. futurefilmfestival.org. *(The festival hosts meetings, special events and workshops about the digital world and animation - Jan 27-Feb 1, 2009.)*

Galway Film Fleadh, Cluain Mhuire, Monivea Road, Galway, Ireland. Tel: (353 91) 751 655. Fax: 735 831. e: info@galwayfilmfleadh.com. Web: www.galwayfilmfleadh.com. *('The Galway Film Fleadh is a wonderful event. Might Rain. Doesn't matter'! Anthony Minghella. The Galway Film Fleadh screens the best of New Irish Films, Feature Documentaries and World Cinema. It also platforms excellence in filmmaking with retrospectives, public interviews, tributes and masterclasses (Peter O' Toole, Jessica Lange, Kathy Bates, Robert Towne, Paul Schrader, Mira Nair, Patricia Clarkson, Abbas Kiarostami, Paolo Taviani and many more). In addition, the Galway Film Fair, a transatlantic bridge for the European Film and Television Industry, hosts 600 one-on-one meetings for producers with projects and invited film financiers, seminars, networking breakfasts and other industry events - July 7-12, 2009.)*

Gerardmer International Fantasy Film Festival, Le Public Système Cinéma, 40, rue Anatole France, 92594 Levallois-Perret Cedex, France. Tel: (33 1) 4134 2109. e: info@gerardmer-fantasticart.com. Web: www.festival-gerardmer. com. *(International fantasy, science fiction, supernatural, psychological thriller and horror films, with competition for features and French-language shorts - Jan 28- Feb 1, 2009.)*

Glasgow Film Festival, 12 Rose Street, Glasgow G3 6RB, UK. Tel: (44 141) 352 8613. e: marketing@gft.org.uk. Web: www.glasgowfilmfestival. org.uk. *(The festival is now the third-largest film festival in the UK. The festival is eleven days of great films, guests, events and parties catering to an audience of more than 25,000 people across twelve key city-centre venues. GFF covers* *all genres from Hollywood blockbusters, screen classics, foreign-language cinema and new media installations - Feb 18-28, 2010.)*

Golden Apricot International Film Festival, 5 Byron St, 0009 Yerevan, Armenia. Tel: (374 2) 1053 3924. e: aafccj@arminco.com. Web: www.gaiff. am. *(The theme of the festival is 'Crossroads of Cultures and Civilizations' and the aim is to build cultural bridges and foster dialogue. It features a multitude of films representing various nations, ethnicities, and religions which collectively depict the full richness of the human experience - July).*

Atom Egoyan, Wim Wenders and Harutyun Khachatryan at the closing ceremony of the 2008 Golden Apricot International Film Festival

Guadalajara International Film Festival, Nebulosa 2916, Colonia Jardines del Bosque, Guadalajara, Jalisco, Mexico. Tel: (52 33) 3121 7461. e: info@festivalcinedgl.udg.mx. Web: www.guadalajaracinemafest.com. *(Mexican and Ibero-American recent quality film productions, increasing the awareness of the world film industry by screening the work of noteworthy Ibero-American film directors and presenting other remarkable and innovative films by upcoming filmmakers - March 19-27, 2009.)*

Haifa International Film Festival, 142 Hanassi Ave, Haifa 34 633, Israel. Tel: (972 4) 8353 515. e: film@haifaff.co.il. Web: www.haifaff.co.il. *(The festival attracts an audience of over 60,000 spectators along with hundreds of Israeli and foreign professionals from the film and television industries. Some 180,000 people take part in the festival activities, including the outdoor events, screenings, workshops, and dozens of journalists from both the print and broadcast media, from Israel and abroad, cover the event. During the festival around 150 new films from the best and most*

recent international productions are premiered with some 220 screenings in seven theatres: feature films, documentaries, animation, short films, retrospectives and tributes - Oct 3-10, 2009.)

Hawaii International Film Festival, 680 Iwilei Rd, Suite 100, Honolulu, Hawaii 96813, USA. Tel: (1 808) 528 3456. e: info@hiff.org. Web: www. hiff.org. *(Established in 1981, the festival seeks to promote cultural understanding between the peoples of Asia, the Pacific and North America through the medium of film - Oct.)*

Heartland Film Festival, 200 S Meridian, Suite 220, Indianapolis, Indiana 46225-1076, USA. Tel: (1 317) 464 9405. e: info@heartlandfilmfestival. org. Web: www.heartlandfilmfestival.org. *(Established in 1991 to honour filmmakers whose work celebrates the positive aspects of life. The festival comprises student and professional films, a variety of special events and a one-of-a-kind experience in one of the Midwest's most inviting cities - Oct 15-23, 2009.)*

Holland Animation Film Festival, Hoogt 4, 3512 GW Utrecht, Netherlands. Tel: (31 30) 233 1733. e: info@haff.nl. Web: www.haff.awn. nl. *(International competitions for independent and applied animation; special programmes, retrospectives, student films, exhibitions - Nov 4-8, 2009.)*

Hot Docs Canadian International Documentary Festival, 110 Spadina Avenue, Suite 333, Toronto, Ontario, M5V 2K4, Canada. Tel: (1 416) 203 2155. e: info@hotdocs.ca. Web: www.hotdocs.ca.

(North America's largest documentary festival, conference and market which presents a selection of more than 150 cutting-edge documentaries from Canada and around the globe. Through its industry programmes, Hot Docs also provides a full range of professional development, market and networking opportunities for documentary professionals - April 30-May 10, 2009.)

Huesca Film Festival, Avenida del Parque 1,2, 22002 Huesca, Spain. Tel: (34 974) 212 582. e: info@huesca-filmfestival.com. Web: www.huesca-filmfestival.com. *(Well-established shorts festival with official competitive sections composed of the Iberoamerican, International and European Documentary contests. The winners of the Award Danzante in the Iberoamerican and International contest automatically qualify to enter the Short Films category of the Academy of Motion Picture Arts and Sciences in Hollywood for the concurrent season - June.)*

Hull International Short Film Festival, Suite 12 Danish Buildings, 44-46 High St, Hull, HU1 1PS, UK. Tel: (44) 01482 381512. e:office@hullfilm. co.uk. Web: www.hullfilm.co.uk. *(Dedicated to showcasing the very best short films from across the world of any genre that run up to a maximum of 45 minutes. The wide and diverse selection of films includes dramas, documentaries, artists' film, video and animation with over 200 films screened. Attended by special guests from the film world and with a host of great events for everyone to enjoy. Numerous competitions, masterclasses, and special programmes - April 21-26, 2009.)*

Hungarian Film Week, Magyar Filmunió, Városligeti, Fasor 38, 1068 Budapest, Hungary. Tel: (36 1) 351 7760. e: filmhu@forum.film.hu. Web: www.hungarianfilm.com. *(Well-established regular showcase presenting the previous year's Hungarian film production to local and foreign professionals as well as to the Hungarian public. The event attracts internationally acclaimed journalists and critics, festival directors and programmers, producers and distributors. Competitive with Hungarian features, documentaries and short films - Jan 30-Feb 6, 2009.)*

Il Cinema Ritrovato, Cineteca del Comune di Bologna, Via Riva di Reno 72, 40122 Bologna, Italy. Tel: (39 051) 552 541. Web: www.immag-ineritrovata.it. *(International festival providing a selection of unknown, little known, rediscovered, and restored films dedicated to cinema history. Selection made among the best film restorations from all over the world - Late June/early July.)*

Imago - International Young Film Festival, Apartado 324 Avenida Eugénio de Andrade, Bloco D, 6230-909 Fundão, Portugal. Tel: (351) 275 771 607. e: info@imagofilmfest.com. Web: www.ima-gofilmfest.com. *(The festival focuses its programming on the short films of young directors from all over the world, which enables them to reach audiences with films that have no commercial distribution in Portugal. The festival is also a meeting point for professionals and students from the audiovisual field via workshops and masterclasses, special screenings for schools within the region and individual meetings - Oct.)*

International Cinematographers Film Festival 'Manaki Brothers', 8 Mart 4, 1000 Skopje, Republic of Macedonia. Tel: (389 2) 3224 334. e: info@manaki.com.mk. Web: www.manaki.com. mk. *(Held in remembrance of Yanaki and Milton Manaki, the first cameramen of the Balkans. The festival is held in Bitola by the Macedonian Film Professionals Association in order to assist in the professional development and growth of film creativity in the Republic of Macedonia and is supported by the Ministry of Culture of the Republic of Macedonia. The main part of the festival programme is Camera 300, the official competition for feature-length films drawn from the most recent European and world production. There is also a short film programme which is non-competitive and presents outstanding films from the latest production year. In addition, 'Manaki Brothers' is dedicated to young, talented filmmakers and workshops, seminars and roundtables are held throughout - late Oct/early Nov.)*

International Documentary Festival of Marseille (FID Marseille), 14 Allée Léon Gambetta, 13001 Marseille, France. Tel: (33 4) 9504 4490 e: welcome@fidmarseille.org. Web:

www.fidmarseille.org. *(The festival presents some 150 of the best international documentaries and features international, national and first-film competitions - early July.)*

International Documentary Film Festival Munich, Landwehrstrasse 79, D 80336 Munich, Germany. Tel: (49 89) 5139 9788. e: info@dokfest-muenchen.de. Web: www.dokfest-muenchen.de. *(Feature-length creative documentaries produced for cinema release plus the most interesting examples of new talent from all over the world; competitive - May 6-13, 2009.)*

International Film Festival Artfilm, Bajkalska 25, 827 18 Bratislava, Slovakia. Tel: (421 2) 5341 4111. e: artfilm@artfilm.sk. Web: www.artfilm.sk. *(Competitive sections for International and Shorts - June 20-27, 2009.)*

International Film Festival Bratislava, Partners Production, Lovinského 18, 811 04 Bratislava, Slovakia. Tel: (421 2) 5441 0673. e: iffbratislava@ba.sunnet.sk. Web: www.iffbratislava.sk. *(International competition of First and Second Feature Films; other sections include Made in Europe, Off the Mainstream, Profile of the Filmmaker - Dec.)*

International Film Festival Innsbruck, Museumstrasse 31, A-6020 Innsbruck, Austria. Tel: (43 512) 5785 0014. e: info@iffi.at. Web: www.iffi.at. Director: Helmut Groschup. *(Films about Africa, Latin America and Asia. International competition, Public Award, Francophone Award and Doc Award - June 9-14, 2009.)*

International Film Festival of Uruguay, Lorenzo Carnelli 1311, 11200 Montevideo, Uruguay. Tel: (59 82) 419 5795. e: cinemuy@chasque.net. Web: www.cinemateca.org.uy. *(Presents independent and documentary films - April 4-18, 2009.)*

International Leipzig Festival for Documentary and Animated Film, Grosse Fleischergasse 11, 04109 Leipzig, Germany. Tel: (49 341) 308 640. e: info@dok-leipzig.de. Web: www.dok-leipzig. de. *(The largest German and second-largest European documentary film festival screens the best, most exciting, moving and artistically outstanding animated and documentary films from more than 50 countries. Competitive - Oct 26- Nov 1, 2009.)*

International Week of Fantastic Film (Fancine), University of Malaga, Vicerrectorado de Cultura y Relaciones Institucionales, Pabellón de Gobierno, 3A Planta, 29071 Malaga, Spain. Tel: (34 9) 5213 2933. e: fantastico@uma.es. Web: www.fantastico.uma.es. *(The festival aims to promote and increase the film culture in and around Andalucía and screens a selection of films produced worldwide, including features and shorts, in the fantastic, horror and thriller genres - Nov.)*

Israel Film Festival, Israfest Foundation, 6404 Wilshire Blvd, Suite 1240, Los Angeles, CA 90048, USA. Tel: (1 323) 966 4166. e: info@israelfilmfestival.org. Web: www.israelfilmfestival.com. *(The festival's aim is to showcase Israel's thriving film and television industry, providing an intercultural exchange that advances tolerance and understanding and enriches America's vision of Israel's impressive social and cultural diversity. The festival has shown more than 800 feature films, documentaries, television dramas and short films to roughly 900,000 film enthusiasts. Since debuting in 1981 with just half a dozen movies, the festival has become one of the nation's leading foreign-film festivals and the largest showcase for Israeli films in the United States as well as a launching pad for several notable US premiere dramas - 2009 dates: May in LA; Nov in NY; Dec in Miami.)*

Jameson Dublin International Film Festival, 50 Upper Mount St, Dublin 2, Ireland. Tel: (353 1) 662 4260. e: info@jdiff.com. Web: www.jdiff.com. *(Founded in 2002 and aimed squarely at the cinema-going public. Non-competitive, largely composed of new international feature films [130 in 2008], including 10 Irish productions or co-productions. Daily Talking Pictures events offer lunchtime panel discussions on a variety of filmmaking topics - Feb 12-22, 2009.)*

Jedensvet - One World International Documentary Film Festival, Clovek v ohrozeni,

Svatoplukova 1, 821 09 Bratislava, Slovakia. Tel: (421 2) 5542 2254. e: info@clovekvohrozeni.sk. Web: www.jedensvet.sk. *(Documentaries on respecting and violating of human rights - Nov.)*

Jihlava International Documentary Film Festival, Jana Masaryka 16, PO Box 33, 58601 Jihlava, Czech Republic. Tel: (420 7) 7410 1656. e: office@dokument-festival.cz. Web: www. dokument-festival.cz. *(The biggest festival of creative documentary in Central and Eastern Europe, showing work from around the world. Screenings are followed by after-film talks and programmes feature accompanying workshops, panel discussions, theatre performances, authors' readings, concerts, and exhibitions. The festival is accompanied by one of the leading events of the year for film professionals from Eastern Europe: the Institute of Documentary Film organises the East European Forum, an encounter of Eastern European documentarists with producers from prominent European TV stations. In collaboration with the IDF we also organise the market of documentary film from Central and Eastern Europe: East Silver - Oct.)*

JumpCuts, 1215 Blanshard St, Victoria, BC, Canada, V8W 3J4. Tel: (1 250) 389 0444. e: communications@victoriafilmfestival.com. Web: www.victoriafilmfestival.com. *(JumpCuts is a youth-oriented festival which celebrates the originality and diversity of young voices and the exciting and always popular programme is sure to delight, move and amaze you. This is an opportunity to witness the talent and enrich the creativity of young people ages 7-15. Free film screenings, free demonstrations, many different workshops. Romp through the world of Animation, Acting, SFX Make-up, Composing, Screenwriting, Camera Techniques and much more! - June.)*

Kidfilm/USA Film Festival, 6116 N Central Expressway, Suite 105, Dallas, Texas 75206, USA. Tel: (1 214) 821 6300. e: usafilmfestival@ aol.com. Web: www.usafilmfestival.com. *(Non-competitive; oldest and largest family film festival in the US. Accepts US and international shorts and features - Jan 12-25, 2009.)*

Leeds Young People's Film Festival, Leeds Film, Town Hall, The Headrow, Leeds LS1 3AD, UK. Tel: (44 113) 247 8389. e: Web: www.leedsfilm.com. *(April 2-10, 2009.)*

Lisbon International Documentary Film Festival, Rua dos Bacalhoeiros, 125, 4°, 1100-068 Lisbon, Portugal. Tel: (351 21) 887 1639. e: doclisboa@doclisboa.org. Web: www.doclisboa. org. *(The only festival in Portugal exclusively dedicated to featuring national and international documentaries - Late Oct.)*

Lucas International Children's Film Festival, c/o Deutsches Filmmuseum, Schaumainkai 41, 60596 Frankfurt/Main, Germany. Tel: (49 69) 9612 20670. e: lucas@deutsches-filmmuseum. de. Web: www.lucasfilmfestival.de. *(Germany's oldest children's film festival which is dedicated to showing independent films from all over the world for children aged from five to twelve - Sept 6-13, 2009.)*

Margaret Mead Film & Video Festival, American Museum of Natural History, Central Park, West & 79th St, New York, NY 10024-5192, USA. Tel: (1 212) 769 5000. e: meadfest@ amnh.org. Web: www.amnh.org/mead. *(The longest-running premiere showcase for international documentaries in the United States, encompassing a broad spectrum of work, from indigenous community media to experimental non-fiction - Mid Nov.)*

Marrakech International Film Festival, BP 14212 Riad Larrouss, Marrakech, Morocco. Tel: (212 4) 324 93/94. e: ffifm@lafondation.ma. Web: www.festivalmarrakech.info. *(Showcase for international feature films - Dec.)*

Mediterranean Film Festival Split, Mihovilova Sirina 1/IV, 21000 Split, Croatia. Tel/Fax: (385 21) 332 449. e: splitmedfilmfest@splitmedfilmfest. com. Web: www.splitmedfilmfest.com. *(The festival will be held for only the second time in the city of Split, the 1,700-year-old Mediterranean town. The festival will screen 15 films from the Mediterranean region. The screenings will be held both outdoors and indoors; in the open-air cinema*

Bacvice and in a cinema Zlatna Vrata, in the centre of the Diocletian's palace. The festival team is an experienced one; young people that have worked on many film festivals in the past. Our aim is to present Mediterranean culture and film production the best way we can, as this is the only festival of Mediterranean films in this part of Europe. Films are not all the festival has to offer. Concerts, exhibitions and roundtable discussions will also programmed. This festival will hopefully become an important centre for presenting films in this part of the world - May 25-30, 2009.)

Mediterranean Film Festival Split

Message to Man Film Festival, Karavannaya 12, 191023, St Petersburg, Russia. Tel: (7 812) 326 8218. e: info@message-to-man.spb.ru. Web: www.message-to-man.spb.ru. (International documentary, short and animated films - June.)

Midnight Sun Film Festival, Kansanopistontie 5, 99600 Sodankylä, Finland. Tel: (358 16) 614 522. e: office@msfilmfestival.fi. Web: www. msfilmfestival.fi. (International and silent films, plus award winners from Cannes, Berlin, Locarno and Stockholm - June 10-14, 2009.)

Minneapolis/St Paul International Film Festival, Minnesota Film Arts, 309 Oak St Ave SE, Minneapolis, MN 55414, USA. Tel: (1 612) 331 7563. e: jim@mnfilmarts.org. Web: www.

mspfilmfest.org. (Presents over 150 films from more than 50 countries - April 17-May 3, 2009.)

Mipdoc, 11 rue du Colonel Pierre Avia, BP 572, 75726 Paris Cedex 15, France. Tel: (33 1) 4190 4580. e: info.miptv@reedmidem.com. Web: www.miptv.com. (Specialist international screening marketplace and conference for documentaries - March 28-29, 2009.)

Montpellier International Festival of Mediterranean Film, 78 Avenue du Pirée, 34000 Montpellier, France. Tel: (33 4) 9913 7373. e:info@cinemed. tm.fr. Web: www.cinemed.tm.fr. (The best recent Mediterranean productions showing what is happening in Mediterranean film before public releases in the fourth quarter of 2009 and the first quarter of 2010. Comprising features, shorts, documentaries and experimental films - Oct.)

Montreal International Festival of New Cinema, 3805 Boulevard St-Laurent, Montreal, Quebec, Canada H2W 1X9. Tel: (1 514) 282 0004. e: info@ nouveaucinema.ca. Web: www.nouveaucinema. ca. (Highlights the development of new trends, in cinema and new media providing a showcase for new, original works, particularly in the fields of independent cinema and digital creation. The festival welcomes Quebec, Canadian and international artists in a convivial atmosphere that prizes public and professional exchange - Oct.)

Mumbai International Film Festival, Rajkamal Studio, SS Rao Road, Parel, Mumbai 400 012, India. Tel: (91 22) 2413 6571. e: info@iff-mumbai. org. Web: www.iff-mumbai.org. (The only independent film festival in India, organised by the Mumbai Academy of the Moving Image (MAMI), whose chairman is renowned filmmaker Shyam Benegal. Full-length feature films only. Sections: Global Vision, with a FIPRESCI award, Retro, Tribute, Focus on Filmmaker, Focus on One Country, Film India Worldwide & Competition for Indian Films, judged by an international jury - postponed: see website for new dates.)

New Directors/New Films, Film Society of Lincoln Center, 70 Lincoln Center Plaza, New York, NY 10023, USA. Tel: (1 212) 875 5610. e:

festival@filmlinc.com. Web: www.filmlinc.com. *(One of the premiere international showcases for the work of emerging filmmakers. It is a non-competitive festival with no separate categories and no prizes awarded. Feature films and shorts are chosen according to quality from all categories: animated, experimental, documentary and dramatic etc. - March 25-April 5, 2009.)*

New York Film Festival, Film Society of Lincoln Center, 70 Lincoln Center Plaza, New York, NY 10023-6595, USA. Tel: (1 212) 875 5610. e: festival@filmlinc.com. Web: www.filmlinc.com. *(The festival shows the newest and cinematic works by directors from around the world, featuring inspiring and provocative cinema by emerging talents and first-rank international artists whose films are often recognised as contemporary classics. The festival is highly competitive with an average of 30 feature films and 15 short films selected each year. There are no categories and no prizes awarded - late Sept-early Oct.)*

Nordic Film Festival, 75 rue General Leclerc, 76000 Rouen, France. Tel: (33 232) 767 322. e: festival.cinema.nordique@wanadoo.fr. Web: www.festival-cinema-nordique.asso.fr. *(Competitive festival of Nordic cinema, including retrospectives - March 18-29, 2009.)*

Nordic Film Forum Scanorama, Ozostrasse 4, Vilnius 08200, Lithuania. Tel: (370 5) 276 0367. e: info@kino.lt . Web: www.scanorama.lt. *(The festival screens a variety of genres including features, documentaries, shorts and experimental films from new and emerging talents that represent contemporary European film. From its beginning as a Nordic Film Forum crossing Lithuania from its capital to the coast, Scanorama has become a successful film festival embracing cinematographic achievements not only of the Nordic countries, but from the whole of Europe - Nov.)*

Nordic Film Days Lubeck, Nordische Filmtage Lubeck, Schildstrasse 12, D-23539 Lubeck, Germany. Tel: (49 451) 122 1742. e: info@filmtage. luebeck.de. Web: www.filmtage.luebeck.de. *(The festival spotlights Scandinavian and Baltic cinema, enabling members of the trade, critics and other*

filmgoers to see the best new productions. Also features a large documentary section. Attendance exceeds 20,000 for more than 130 screenings - late Oct/early Nov.)

Open Air Filmfest Weiterstadt, PO Box 1164, D-64320 Weiterstadt, Germany. Tel: (49 61) 501 2185. e: filmfest@weiterstadt.de. Web: www. filmfest-weiterstadt.de. *(Mainly short films of all genres, formats and lengths although the programme has been extended to include feature films and documentaries. Attending filmmakers may camp in the forest, next to the festival area - Aug 13-17, 2009.)*

Palm Beach International Film Festival, 289 Via Naranjas, Royal Palm Plaza, Suite 48, Boca Raton, Florida 33432, USA. Tel: (1 561) 362 0003. e: info@pbifilmfest.org. Web: www.pbifilmfest. org. *(American and international independent features, shorts, documentaries and large format. Competitive - April 23-30, 2009.)*

Palm Springs International Festival of Short Films & Film Market, 1700 E Tahquitz Canyon Way, Suite 3, Palm Springs, CA 92262, USA. Tel: (1 760) 322 2930. e: info@psfilmfest.org. Web: www.psfilmfest.org. *(Competitive shorts festival and market. Student, animation, documentary, live action and international competition with Audience and Juried Awards. Seminars and workshops - Aug.)*

Philadelphia Film Festival, Philadelphia Film Society, 4th Floor, 234 Market St, Philadelphia, PA 19106, USA. Tel: (1 267) 765 9700. e: info@ phillyfests.com. Web: www.phillyfests.com. *(The festival screens nearly 300 international and USA features, documentaries, shorts and animation from fifty countries to an audience of over 60,000 - March 26-April 6, 2009.)*

Prix Italia, Via Monte Santo 52, 00195 Rome, Italy. Tel: (39 06) 372 8708. e: prixitalia@rai. it. Web: www.prixitalia.rai.it. *(Prix Italia is the oldest and most prestigious International Radio, Television and Web competition. It awards prizes for quality productions in the fields of drama, documentaries, the performing arts (television)* and music (radio); open only to 90 member organisations - Mid Sept.)

RAI Trade Screenings, Via Umberto Novaro 18, 00195 Rome, Italy. Tel: (39 06) 374981. e: info@ raitrade.it. Web: www.raitrade.rai.it. *(International programmeming buyers view RAI productions for broadcast, video and other rights - April.)*

Ravenna Nightmare Film Festival, Via Mura di Porta Serrata 13, 48100 Ravenna, Italy. Tel: (39 05) 4468 4242. e: ravenna@melies.org. Web: www. ravennanightmare.it. *(The festival was founded in 2003 and its dates coincide with the Halloween weekend. The destination for horror in Italy. The main event is the International Competition for features, which usually admits around 10–12 feature films, all of which are national premieres; while the European Competition for short films screens around 15 films. Added to this is a number of Special Events out of competition; various retrospectives from year to year – and, last but not least, parties, music, and literature events featuring important writers of the horror genre. Among our previous guests: Dario Argento, Brian Yuzna, Marco Muller, and our special supporter Valerio Evangelisti - Late Oct.)*

St Louis International Film Festival, 3547 Olive St, St Louis, MO 63103-1014, USA. Tel: (1 314) 289 4150. e: mailroom@cinemastlouis.org. Web: www.cinemastlouis.org. *(Showcases US and international independent films, documentaries and shorts with the 2008 festival screening 250 films from more than 38 countries. Competitive - Nov.)*

St Petersburg Festival of Festivals, 10 Kamennostrovsky Ave, St Petersburg 197101, Russia. Tel: (7 812) 237 0072. e: info@filmfest.ru. Web: www. filmfest.ru. *(Non-competitive, showcasing the best films from around the world - June.)*

San Fernando Valley International Film Festival, 5504 Cleon Ave, North Hollywood, CA 91601, USA. Tel: (1 818) 623 9122. e: festival@viffi.org. Web: www.viffi.org. *(Competition for films and screenplays; showcase for filmmakers and writers who believe in entertainment that should not contain gratuitous violence or profanity - June.)*

San Sebastian Horror and Fantasy Film Festival, Donostia Kultura, Plaza de la Constitucion 1, 20003 Donostia-San Sebastian, Spain. Tel: (34 943) 481 197. e: cinema_cinema@donostia.org. Web: www.sansebastianhorrorfestival.com. *(Cult, cutting-edge horror fantasy festival; short film and feature competition - Late Oct/early Nov.)*

San Sebastian Human Rights Film Festival, Donostia Kultura, Plaza de la Constitucion 1, 20003 Donostia-San Sebastian, Spain. Tel: (34 943) 481 471. e: cinederechoshumanos@ donostia.org. Web: www.cineyderechoshumanos. com. *(Short films and features about human rights - April 23-30, 2009.)*

Santa Barbara International Film Festival, 1528 Chapala Street 203, Santa Barbara, CA 93101, USA. Tel: (1 805) 963 0023. Fax. 962 2524. e:info@sbfilmfestival.org. Web: www. sbfilmfestival.org. *(Given its knack for predicting Academy Award® winners, a proximal distance to Los Angeles and timing close to the big event, the 24th Annual Santa Barbara International Film Festival (SBIFF) in 2009 will once again establish itself as the preeminent Oscar® film festival. In 2008, SBIFF welcomed 18 Academy Award nominees, including Best Actress winner Marion Cotillard (La Vie en Rose), Best Supporting Actor winner Javier Bardem (No Country for Old Men), Best Director winner Julian Schnabel (The Diving Bell and the Butterfly). The 23rd SBIFF hosted numerous other film stars (Angelina Jolie, Cate Blanchett, Clint Eastwood, James McAvoy and Ellen Page, to name a few), held several panels by filmmakers (including Juno director Jason Reitman), screened over 250 international films, and celebrated a plethora of parties during an eleven day spectacular entertainment experience. - Jan 22-Feb 1, 2009.)*

Sao Paulo International Film Festival, Rua Antonio Carlos 288, 01309-010 São Paulo, Brazil. Tel: (55 11) 3141 0413. e: info@mostra.org. Web: www.mostra.org. *(Competitive event for new filmmakers and international panorama - Oct.)*

Sarajevo Film Festival, Zelenih beretki 12/1, 71000 Sarajevo, Bosnia and Herzegovina. Tel: (387

33) 209 411. e: programmes@sff.ba. Web: www. sff.ba. *(The festival presents a wide selection of both competitive and non-competitive films with a focus on Southeast Europe and it's filmmakers who compete in Feature, Short and Documentary film sections - Aug 12-20, 2009.)*

Scienceplusfiction, Via Economo 12/9, 34123 Trieste, Italy. Tel: (39 04) 0322 0551. e: info@scienceplusfiction.org. Web: www. scienceplusfiction.org. *(Focus on sci-fi, fantasy and fantastic cinema - Nov.)*

Short Shorts Film Festival & Asia, 2F Hirakawacho Urban Bldg, 2-4-8 Hirakawacho, Chiyoda-ku, Tokyo 102-0093, Japan. Tel: (81 3) 5214 3005. e: look@shortshorts.org. Web: www. shortshorts.org. *(SSFF & ASIA has been an Academy Awards® accredited short film festival since 2004 and its Grand Prix winner will be eligible to receive an Academy Award nomination. Supporting the Japanese and international film community, the festival presents over 90 short films and invites filmmakers from all over the world, creating a great opportunity for cultural exchange - June.)*

Siberian International Festival - Spirit of Fire, Festival Committee, 1 Mosfilmovskaya St, Moscow, 119992 Russia. Tel: (7 095) 143 9484. e: info@spiritoffire.ru. Web: www.spiritoffire.ru. *(Showcases 15 films directed by young talents; all formats eligible - Feb 20-26, 2009.)*

Silent Film Days in Tromsø, PO Box 285, N-9253 Tromsø, Norway. Tel: (47) 7775 3090. e: info @ tiff.no. Web: www.tiff.no. *(The programme*

The Silent Film Days in Tromsø's venue: Verdensteatret

encompasses not only the great classics of silent film, but also many hidden treasures recovered from national and international archives - and here presented to a new audience. All films are screened with live music composed and performed by international artists. The style of music ranges from the classical piano or organ accompaniment of the silent film tradition to modern arrangements. The performers of last year's festival included Neil Brand (UK), Ben Model (USA) and Matti Bye (Sweden). The venue for the festival is Tromsø's original cinema, Verdensteatret, which opened in 1916 and was built expressly for the screening of silent films - Sept 3-6, 2009.)

Sofia International Film Festival, 1 Bulgaria Sq, Sofia 1463, Bulgaria. Tel: (359 2) 9166 029. e: office@sofiaiff.com. Web: www.sofiaiff.com. *(Showcases new Bulgarian and Balkan films to international audiences - March 5-15, 2009.)*

Stuttgart Festival of Animated Film, Film-und Medienfestival GmbH, Schlosstrasse 84, 70176 Stuttgart, Germany. Tel: (49 711) 925 460. e: itfs@ festival-gmbh.de. Web: www.itfs.de. *(One of the*

largest events for animated film worldwide. The festival showcases a diverse range of animated film starting with artistic short films, through TV series and children's films and rounded off with feature-length animation. The festival focuses particularly on supporting talented young filmmakers with a special sponsorship award and the Young Animation competition - May 5-10, 2009.)

Sunny Side of the Doc, Résidence le Gabut Bâtiment E, 16 rue de l'Aimable Nanette, 17000 La Rochelle, France. Tel: (33 1) 7735 5300. e: info@sunnysideofthedoc.com. Web: www.sunnysideofthedoc.com. *(International documentary market - June 23-26, 2009.)*

Sydney Film Festival, PO Box 96, Strawberry Hills, NSW 2012, Australia. Tel: (61 2) 9318 0999. e: info@sydneyfilmfestival.org. Web: www. sydneyfilmfestival.org. *(Broad-based event screening new Australian and international features and shorts. The Festival has Australia's only FIAPF-accredited Official Competition in which twelve films from around the world will be selected to compete for a cash prize - June.)*

Tallinn Black Nights Film Festival (PÖFF), Gonsiori 21, 10147 Tallinn, Estonia. Tel: (372) 631 4640. e: poff@poff.ee. Web: www.poff.ee. *(In 2009, the Tallinn Black Nights Film Festival [founded in 1997] will celebrate its 13th edition. The festival had around 57,000 admissions in 2008 and together with the Baltic Event it hosted approximately 350 international guests. The 12th edition of the festival screened 500 films, of which 254 were full-length features, at 580 screenings in 8 cities and 15 cinemas. PÖFF, recognised by FIAPF, is a unique event that combines a feature-film festival with sub-festivals and a film industry gathering called the Baltic Event. The PÖFF main programme has two international competitions – EurAsia and Tridens Baltic feature film competition – along with Panorama, Forum and several special programmes. All competing films are judged by international and local juries, with the newest addition of FIPRESCI jury in 2008 that awarded the best Baltic films. The Student and Short Film Festival Sleepwalkers includes*

an international competition for student films - fiction, documentary or animation films; national competition of Estonian short films, and various special programmes. Animation Film Festival Animated Dreams holds an international competition of short animation. Its additional non-competitive programmes include a retrospective of a filmmaker and focus on a country. Children and Youth Film Festival Just Film includes competition of children's films and youth films, and non-competitive special programmes. Nokia Mobile Film Festival MOFF organises a competition of short films made with mobile

Closing Ceremony of the 2008 Tallinn Black Nights Film Festival (PÖFF), Olga and Priit Pärn, directors of the animation film **Life Without Gabriella Ferri** (photo: Rivo Sarapik)

phones. *The Baltic Event film and co-production market screens the newest feature films from the Baltic countries along with a co-production market open for projects from the Baltic countries, Central and Eastern Europe, Russia and Scandinavia – PÖFF main programme Dec 4-13, Children and Youth Film Festival Just Film Nov 28-Dec 5, Animation Film Festival Animated Dreams Nov 25-29, Student and Short Film Festival Sleepwalkers Nov 19-22, 2009.)*

Taormina International Film Festival, Corso Umberto 19, 98039 Taormina Messina, Italy. Tel: (39 094) 221 142. e: press@taorminafilmfest. it or info@taorminafilmfest.it. Web: www. taorminafilmfest.it. *(The festival will celebrate its 55th anniversary in 2009. Films by English-language directors. Restorations. Silver Ribbons awarded by Italian film critics - June.)*

Third Eye Asian Film Festival, Asian Film Foundation, Rajkamal Studio, Parel, Mumbai 400012, India. Tel: (91 22) 2413 7791. Fax: 2412 5268. e: info@affmumbai.com. Web: www. affmumbai.com. *(Cinema arrived in Mumbai, formerly Bombay on the western coast of India, in December 1896 with the package of first ever films made by the Lumiere brothers. By 2000, the Mumbai Film Industry had truly acquired the dimensions of an Entertainment Industry, catering to the entertainment needs of a nation of one billion. Although Asian Cinema has been winning accolades on the international film festival circuit, none of the SAARC countries screen Asian cinema commercially. The Asian Film Festival promotes Asian Cinema worldwide and aims to establish interaction amongst the Asian Film fraternity, as well as creating a dialogue with the West. Extending from Turkey to Japan and divided culturally in the Middle East, West Asia, South Asia, Central Asia and the Far East, Asian Cinema is as diverse and rich as its topography. The Asian countries share cultural similarities and a common socio-economic scenario, facing the problems of poverty, illiteracy, population and the lowly status of women. The Third Eye Asian Film Festival was established to create awareness between each other, amongst Asian countries, with Cinema*

Asian Film Festival
Mumbai   Oct. 8-15, 2009

Read about competitions
www.affmumbai.com

as the common bond bringing people together and fostering understanding between varied cultures. Chairman: Kiran Shantaram. Director: Sudhir Nandgaonkar - Oct 8-15, 2009.)

Tribeca Film Festival Doha Tel: (1 974) 428 3128. Web: www.tffdoha.com. *(The Festival will include a wide range of programmeming and include approximately forty films at Doha's celebrated new Museum of Islamic Art and in cinemas across Doha, from outdoor screenings to movies for children, from documentaries to new Hollywood releases and from independent films to showcases of the very best works by Arab filmmakers. The festival will launch 'The Doha Conversations', thought-provoking and insightful dialogues between icons of world culture set in intimate environments, with the goal of fostering discussion in Qatar and around the globe - Nov 10-14, 2009.)*

Trieste Film Festival, Via Donota 1, 34121 Trieste, Italy. Tel: (39 040) 347 6076. e: info@ alpeadriacinema.it. Web: www.alpeadriacinema.it. *(Central and Eastern European Cinema - Jan.)*

True/False Film Festival, PO Box 1102, Columbia, Missouri 65205-1102, USA. Tel: (1 573) 442 8783. e: info@truefalse.org. Web: www.truefalse.org. *(International documentary festival held at six venues which highlights innovative work with a cinematic scope, creative takes on contemporary currents, and, most of all, work that provokes dialogue about its subject and the documentary form itself - Feb 26-March 1, 2009.)*

Uppsala International Short Film Festival, PO Box 1746, SE-751 47 Uppsala, Sweden. Tel: (46 18) 120 025. e: info@shortfilmfestival.com. Web: www.shortfilmfestival.com. *(Sweden's only international shorts festival. Competitive - Oct 19-25, 2009.)*

USA Film Festival, 6116 N Central Expressway, Suite 105, Dallas, Texas 75206, USA. Tel: (1 214) 821 6300. e: usafilmfestival@aol.com. Web: www.usafilmfestival.com. *(The festival features the best new American and foreign films, the Academy-qualifying National Short Film and Video Competition and special tributes. Accomplished directors and actors appear with their new films [50-plus visiting filmmakers in attendance with more than 75 films] in a setting designed to bring artists together with audiences - April 27-May 3, 2009.)*

Utopiales - Festival International de Science-Fiction de Nantes, 10 Bis, Blvd de Stalingrad, 44000 Nantes, France. Tel: (33 2) 4035 3082. e: marie.masson@congres-nantes.fr. Web: www.utopiales.org. *(Multimedia science fiction festival - Nov.)*

Valdivia International Film Festival, Dirección Vicente Perez Rosales 787E, Valdivia, Chile. Tel: (56 63) 249 073. e: info@ficv.cl. Web: www.ficv.cl/f14. *(International feature contest, plus Chilean and international shorts, documentaries and animation - early Oct.)*

Viewfinders International Film Festival for Youth, PO Box 36139, Halifax, NS, B3J 3S9, Canada. Tel: (1 902) 422 3456. e: viewfinders@ atlanticfilm.com. Web: www.atlanticfilm.com. *(Genres are fiction, documentary, animation or experimental and must be engaging to a family audience - April 21-29, 2009.)*

Vila do Conde, Auditório Municipal, Praça da República, 4480-715 Vila do Conde, Portugal. Tel: (351 252) 638 025. e: submissions@curtas.pt. Web: www.curtasmetragens.pt. *(National and International shorts competitions. Special pro-gramme and retrospectives - July 4-12, 2009.)*

Warsaw International Film Festival, PO Box 816, 00-950 Warsaw 1, Poland. Tel: (48 22) 621 4647. e: wff@wff.pl. Web: www.wff.pl. *(Key event in Poland. Fiction and documentary features. New Films' and New Directors' competition - Oct.)*

Washington, DC International Film Festival (Filmfest DC), PO Box 21396, Washington, DC 20009, USA. Tel: (1 202) 628 3456. e: filmfestdc@ filmfestdc.org. Web: www.filmfestdc.org. *(Celebrates the best in world cinema from over 30 countries - Late April/early May.)*

ZabrebDox, Factum Centre for Drama Art, Nova Ves 18/3, 10 000 Zagreb, Croatia. Tel: (385 1) 485 4821. e: info@zagrebdox.net. Web: www.zagrebdox.net. *(International and competitive documentary film festival - Feb 23-March 1, 2009.)*

Zurich Film Festival, Spoundation Motion Picture GmbH, Bederstrasse 51, 8002 Zurich, Switzerland. Tel: (41 44) 286 6000. e: info@zurichfilmfestival.org. Web: www.zurichfilmfestival.org. *(Over the course of eleven days, in the city with Europe's highest concentration of cinemas, the festival presents film premieres from all over the world, offers cinematic treats to a fascinated national and international audience, and facilitates direct on-the-spot exchange with the filmmakers. With numerous events and parties complementing the cinema programme, the festival offers an ideal platform for networking and exchanging ideas - Sept 24-Oct 4, 2009.)*

Index to Advertisers

62nd
Film Festival Locarno
5–15 | 8 | 2009
Festival internazionale del film Locarno
Via Ciseri 23, CH-6601 Locarno
t +41 (0)91 756 21 21, f +41 (0)91 756 21 49
info@pardo.ch, www.pardo.ch
Main sponsors:
UBS aet MANOR swisscom